Introduction to Philosophy

AVRUM STROLL

University of California, San Diego

RICHARD H. POPKIN

Washington University

Introduction to Philosophy

third edition

HOLT, RINEHART AND WINSTON

*New York   Chicago   San Francisco   Dallas
Montreal   Toronto   London   Sydney*

Senior Acquisitions Editor *David P. Boynton*
Managing Editor *Jeanette Ninas Johnson*
Project Editor *Robin Moses*
Production Manager *Victor Calderon*

Library of Congress Cataloging in Publication Data

Stroll, Avrum, 1921–
  Introduction to philosophy.

  Includes bibliographies and indexes.
    1. Philosophy—Introductions.   I.   Popkin,
Richard Henry, 1923–   , joint author.   II.   Title.
BD21.S78   1979   100   78–15458
ISBN 0-03-021761-X

Photo Credits

THE BETTMANN ARCHIVE—pages 96 (center row), 258 (top row right, center row left, and bottom row), 336 (top row left and right, and center row left), and 408 (top row left and center row left)

THE GRANGER COLLECTION—pages 2, 20 (center row right, and bottom row), 96 (top row right), 188 (center row and bottom row left), 258 (center row right), 336 (top row center and bottom row), and 408 (top row right, center row right, and bottom row right)

HRW PHOTO LIBRARY—pages 20 (top row and center row left), 96 (top row left and center, and bottom row), 188 (top row), 258 (top row left), 336 (center row right), and 408 (center row center and bottom row left)

DR. RICHARD H. POPKIN—page 188 (bottom row right)

Preface TO THE SECOND EDITION

This book has been carefully designed by its authors for use as a text in any of the standard introductory philosophy courses now given on this continent. It approaches the subject via its main branches: epistemology, metaphysics, political philosophy, ethics, and the philosophy of religion. Within each of these domains, the subject matter is treated in a historical or roughly chronological fashion; for instance, the discussion of ethics commences with the moral views of Socrates and then deals, in turn, with the doctrines of Plato, Aristotle, Aristippus, Epicurus, Diogenes of Sinope, Epictetus, Spinoza, Bentham, Mill, Kant, G. E. Moore, A. J. Ayer, and C. L. Stevenson. At the same time, each of these historical surveys is organized around a traditional philosophical problem, or a set of such problems. The discussion of political philosophy, for example, focuses on the question, "Where should the source of political authority lie, and why?"

This book has many features not ordinarily found in introductory texts. Not only does it encompass such unlikely bedfellows as epistemology, political philosophy, and the philosophy of religion; it also includes extensive references to unduly neglected figures in the history of the subject, among them Malebranche, Plotinus, and Gassendi. The authors have also devoted an entire chapter to the contemporary scene, where three important movements, pragmatism, existentialism, and analytical philosophy, are examined. To give the reader some idea of the scope of this chapter, we might mention that the section devoted to analytical philosophy is approximately 18,000 words in length. It includes discussions of logical atomism and logical positivism, and traces the development of the ordinary-language movement through the work of G. E. Moore, the later Wittgenstein, Gilbert Ryle, and John Austin. The sections on pragmatism and existentialism, which form the remaining parts of this chapter, are of a similarly comprehensive nature.

The authors have attempted to organize this material so that the book can be used in introductory courses whose length varies from one full academic year to any portion thereof. Each of the chapters is a self-contained unit and can be studied independently of the others, although the work as a whole is designed to carry the student from a discussion of how we come to know the world (epistemology and metaphysics), and then, finally, to a discussion of the various appraisals we make of it (political philosophy, ethics, and philosophy of religion).

Perhaps one of its most unusual features is that, although it is a collaboration in the full sense, no attempt has been made to suppress or minimize differences in the philosophical outlooks of the authors. For those readers who may wish to take note of such differences, we might mention that Professor Stroll has written the introduction and the material on political philosophy, ethics, and philosophical analysis, while Professor Popkin is the author of the chapters on epistemology, metaphysics, philosophy of religion, and the sections on pragmatism and existentialism.

This revised edition has resulted from many suggestions that we expand the material, as well as update it in terms of current interests. To accomplish this we have eliminated the chapter on logic, which is usually treated in a separate course, and have added much new material. This includes a broader discussion of metaphysical theories; sections on such influential thinkers as Schopenhauer, Bergson, and Whitehead; an enlarged chapter on philosophy of religion to deal with Bible criticism and its import for philosophy; and an expanded chapter on contemporary philosophy, covering, among other matters, developments in existentialism up to its major twentieth-century thinker Martin Heidegger and the relation of his thought to phenomenology. There is also, in this chapter, fresh material on the work of J. L. Austin; and we have revised and added to our original discussions of the writings of Ryle and Wittgenstein. In the chapter on political theory, we have included a discussion of two important contemporary theorists, Sir Karl Popper and Herbert Marcuse. And, finally, there is a new introduction to the book. The reader should further note that relevant selections on the major philosophers discussed in each chapter appear in our volume, *Introductory Readings in Philosophy* (Holt, Rinehart and Winston, New York, 1972).

Our intent in composing this work has thus been to present a synoptic picture of philosophy, written in a simple, nontechnical fashion, and yet, within these limits, to achieve a high degree of accuracy in exposition. But, of course, it will finally rest with the reader himself to decide whether we have achieved these aims.

A. S.
R. H. P.

January 1972

Preface TO THE THIRD EDITION

Even though the second edition of this book was extensively revised in 1972 (see *Preface to the Second Edition* for details), we felt that its continuing widespread use justified another major revision after six years. After a year's planning and writing, and a summer's work together in La Jolla, California, to edit a final draft, we have emerged with a book whose format and contents are substantially altered over the previous edition. We have added about 100 manuscript pages to the text, extensively rewritten various sections of it, updated nearly every chapter (including the bibliographical materials), and added outlines at the head of each chapter.

Though the book continues to have the same emphasis as previously, tying together a problems approach and an historical approach, we have added materials dealing with the applications of philosophical principles. In the Introduction, for instance, we attempt to show how the problem of abortion raises philosophical issues about the nature of a person and about the attempt to provide a systematic and coherent justification for, or against, the practice of abortion. The chapter on ethics presents the application of the principles developed by philosophers of past and present in the domains of medicine, professional activities, and business, and explains the import these principles have for serious matters of public policy. Similar comments apply to the chapters on metaphysics and political philosophy, where current issues are shown to be related to basic philosophical problems.

Among the new materials added are lengthy discussions of the work of Rawls, Bradley, Buber, Bultmann, Bonhoeffer, and the "new philosophers" of France. Our previous treatment of a number of important writers has been greatly expanded, including new information on Nietzsche, Schopenhauer, Heidegger, Husserl, and Marcuse, among others. The result of these endeavors, we believe, is a book which not only gives a broad and (we hope) accurate picture of the major philosophers of the Western tradition, but which also has a contemporary and even an applied focus as well. Much of our commentary is based upon the original textual materials that can be found in our *Introductory Readings in Philosophy* (Holt, Rinehart and Winston), and the two books can be used fruitfully together. Finally, it should be added that the book is designed in units which make it suitable for introductory courses ranging from one quarter in length to an entire year.

Avrum Stroll
University of California, San Diego

Richard H. Popkin
Washington University, St. Louis

Spring 1978

Contents

Introduction to Philosophy

Marketplace of Athens

INTRODUCTION

To the measured view, the world situation today gives little cause for optimism. As one wit put it, "I have the feeling that the world's warranty is running out." There are the obvious perils of nuclear proliferation and an expanding arms race, and extremely tense and dangerous situations in the Middle East and in various parts of Africa. Our energy resources are in danger of running out, the world population continues to explode, racism still haunts a large number of countries, and even in the most advanced industrial nations unemployment remains a persistent and aggravating problem. In all these situations, the picture is one of individuals, groups, nations, even whole races, taking adversary positions toward one another. What accounts for this phenomenon—for the bitterness and hatred which seem to be the order of the day?

No doubt explanations will differ depending on the particular case, and none is likely to be simple. But whatever the explanation, there is one feature which most of these cases share and which cannot be ignored: something that might be called a difference in "philosophical outlook." The eastern socialist countries, for instance, find their "philosophy" in the works of Marx, Engels, and Lenin; yet this common philosophy divides them. Part of their antagonism toward one another arises from their differing interpretations of what that philosophy is, and their assessment of the degree of fidelity toward it which the nations in question exhibit or ought to exhibit. Part of their antagonism toward the western capitalist nations—and vice-versa, of course—can also be traced to differences about the importance and value of the individual person, the purpose and function of the state and the degree to which it is justified in controlling individual behavior. These are differences that run deep and are not easily reconcilable with one another. In nearly all the cases we have mentioned—racism, energy, nuclear power, the population explosion—conflicting sets of strongly held principles seem to be at the core of these disputes, and nearly all of them represent different attitudes and convictions of a philosophical kind. Though it is sometimes asserted that philosophy as a subject is *passé* and of no particular interest to the modern, technologically-oriented man, the facts we have mentioned above and others belie such a claim. It is plain that to the degree that differences in fundamental life style and belief separate people from one another, there is no more important subject for study in the world today than philosophy. It seems equally plain, therefore, that if one is to acquire some measure of understanding of the forces that motivate human beings, it is essential that one acquire some understanding of the nature of philosophy and its influence upon human conduct.

This book attempts to make such understanding possible, or at least to provide some of the groundwork for such understanding. But this, as we shall see, is not an easy task. In the West alone, the history of philosophy runs back some 2500 years. What the study of this history teaches us is hard to compress into a simple general account that covers the full gamut of activities which might plausibly be called "philosophy." We see, for example, that philosophy has changed greatly from its earliest beginnings; yet we also see that in certain respects, which may be fundamental, it hasn't changed at all. Philosophy thus seems at once to deal with new problems and with the same old problems. Which of these captures the nature of the subject if they are different from one another? We also see, as we study the history of philosophy, that its practitioners have offered many definitions, descriptions, or characterizations of the subject—some of them incompatible with one another. Some, for instance, have said that philosophy is Queen of the Sciences, that is, the most general and universal science (as distinct from particular sciences such as physics and chemistry), while others have denied that it is a science at all. Some have said that philosophy tells us about the ultimate constituents of the world, while others have rejected this claim, and indeed the view that philosophy tells us anything about the world at all, ultimate or otherwise. Some have said that philosophy is essentially a rational activity, based upon argument and the adducing of evidence, while others have denied that the use of reason is crucial in philosophy, and still others have denied that there are any convincing arguments in philosophy. The attempt to provide a simple, encompassing and accurate account of the subject thus seems to be an attempt to embrace within a definition a host of apparently inconsistent practices, activities, theories, outlooks, and developments. How can we possibly impose some kind of order on this blooming, buzzing confusion?

Our method of proceeding, in the face of such difficulties, is prompted by a remark of Tacitus, the Roman historian. In his *Germania* he points out that the Germans debated every question twice—once while drunk and once while sober. When it comes to discussing the question, "What is philosophy?"—a natural starting point—it may be desirable to emulate the Germans by discussing the question at least twice, though preferably while sober on both occasions. For, as we have seen, the question is difficult and once around may not be enough. Our intention in this book, then, is to discuss it first in a general way in these introductory pages—working toward a definition—and then to consider it again in the opening parts of the chapters that follow.

By considering its main branches a clear view of the nature of the subject will be achieved. We shall thus be asking, "What is metaphysics?", "What is ethics?", "What is political philosophy?" and so on, but since we shall be covering virtually all of the major branches of the subject, we shall be traversing virtually all of philosophy—only distributively, not collectively. By these two methods—one of them direct, the other somewhat more oblique—the reader will gain a feel for the subject, its history, its main problems, its treatment by eminent thinkers of the past and present, and its contemporary concerns. Through these devices, we hope to show that it is a discipline which has dealt, and continues to deal, with issues of fundamental concern to human beings.

WHAT IS PHILOSOPHY?

Since we are, in effect, looking for a definition of the word "philosophy," let us begin by looking in that place where definitions of words are commonly found: a dictionary. As we shall see, this will turn out to be a very helpful procedure. In the end, it may not be sufficient to give us a full *characterization* of the subject, but it will carry us a considerable way toward the achievement of this goal. Later on, we shall have to supplement this procedure by examining in detail a specific philosophical problem. On the basis of this examination, we may be able to discover additional features that belong to philosophy, and thus flesh out the picture which the dictionary sketches starkly.

Our dictionary, for example, lists seven entries for the word "philosophy," and in addition gives its etymology or origin. The entries are:

1. The study or science of the truths or principles underlying all knowledge, and being (or reality).
2. Any one of the three branches (natural philosophy, moral philosophy, and metaphysical philosophy) accepted as composing this science.
3. A system of philosophical doctrine: *the philosophy of Spinoza.*

4. Metaphysical science; metaphysi
5. The study or science of the principles of a particular branch or subject of knowledge: *the philosophy of history.*
6. A system of principles for guidance in practical affairs.
7. Philosophical spirit or attitude; wise composure throughout the vicissitudes of life.

If we study these entries carefully, we see that they fall naturally into two groups: entries one through six speak about philosophy as a *science* or a *system of principles.* The seventh entry, on the other hand, refers to philosophy as embodying an *attitude* toward life, a "wise composure throughout the vicissitudes of life." This difference between the two categories is significant, and worthy of further exploration. But in doing so, we should avoid drawing two types of conclusions: first, as we pointed out earlier, some philosophers have denied that philosophy is a *science* at all; it would thus be dangerous to put too much stress on this aspect of these definitions. A more hopeful phrase instead is "system of principles" and we shall come to this momentarily. Second, the first six entries deal with philosophy as an organized set of principles, which underlie knowledge and reality, and which are expressed in such branches of human *intellectual* endeavor as metaphysics and history. The seventh entry, on the other hand, seems to conceive of philosophy not so much as an intellectual activity, but as a way of responding to the vagaries of life. But as the occurrence of the word "wise" in the seventh entry indicates, it would be a mistake to infer from this that the mere possession of an attitude, such as composure, constitutes philosophy; for it is only possible to characterize a response to life as "wise" if it is based upon a system of justifiable principles. The distinction between these entries is thus not between principled as opposed to unprincipled life, but rather between inquiries directed toward knowledge and those directed toward the guidance of life. What the dictionary is telling us is that to *know* is one thing, to *respond* is another, but what makes both types of activities "philosophical" is that they are intimately bound up with systems of principles.

We may see this more clearly if we move on from these entries, and look into the etymology of the word "philosophy." Our dictionary tells us that this word comes from two Greek words, "philos" and "sophos," which mean "love" and "wisdom," respectively. On this etymological account, "philosophy" means the same as "love of wisdom." Now there are dangers in courting that "goddess fair, divinest Etymology," for though this is what the Greek words originally meant, none of the entries in the dictionary specifies that this is what they now mean. Nevertheless, let us pursue the etymological clues to see where they lead. If we do so, we find that the entries for "love" and "wisdom" mean the following:

love. n. 1. a strong or passionate affection for a person of the opposite sex. 2. sexual passion or desire, or its gratification. 3. an object of love or affection; a sweetheart. 4. a personification of sexual affection, as Eros or Cupid. 5. a feeling of warm personal attachment or deep affection, as for a friend (or between friends), parent, child, etc. 6. strong predilection or liking for anything: *love of books*. 7. the benevolent affection of God for His creatures, or the reverent affection due from them to God. 8. Tennis, etc. nothing; no score.

wisdom. n. 1. the quality or state of being wise; knowledge of what is true or right coupled with just judgment as to action; sagacity, prudence, or common sense. 2. scholarly knowledge, or learning: *the wisdom of the schools*. 3. wise sayings or teachings. 4. a wise act or saying.

If we look at the various entries in these two columns, we can see that many of them can be excluded as being helpful to our question. Philosophy as the love of wisdom surely does not mean sexual affection for wise sayings, for instance. But there are in this complex of definitions two that seem more plausible. If we interpret "love" to mean the same as "strong predilection or liking for anything," and "wisdom" to mean "knowledge of what is true or right, coupled with just judgment as to action," we get the following composite definition: "Philosophy is the strong liking for the knowledge of what is true or right, coupled with just judgment as to action."

This definition has the immediate advantage of managing to bypass many of the disputed cases, while it captures those that are clearly philosophical. For example, it leaves open the question whether philosophy is a science or not (it replaces phrases like "the science of" by the phrase "a strong liking or predilection for"), or even the question whether it is a rational activity or not. It thus enables us to include within the scope of "philosophy" such "antirational" or perhaps "nonrational" doctrines as skepticism, fideism, existentialism, and even oriental types of quietism. The proponents of such "doctrines" might deny that they are putting forth any scientific or rational account of the world, but all such views either come within the scope of the term "knowledge of what is true or right," or the term "coupled with just judgment as to action." Skepticism, by which Sextus Empiricus, for instance, doubts that knowledge can be acquired, nonetheless provides a theory about how men should act, namely, that they should cultivate an attitude of *epôché* or suspension of judgment toward what is possibly true or false. This doctrine thus falls under that part of the definition which speaks about the cultivation of just judgment as to action. Similar remarks apply to existentialism, quietism, and fideism. The definition also picks up such entries as the seventh, since an attitude of "wise composure" toward life's difficulties involves not just the possession of a psychological disposition to respond, but the additional element that this is a reasonable or justifiable kind of response to such vicissitudes. Our definition shows that philosophy, whether directed toward knowledge of the world, or toward the guidance of conduct, rests upon principles which are organized, can be made explicit, and are ultimately subject to justification in the form of argument and debate. Nothing can be called philosophical which does not exhibit these characteristics. Since the above definition thus has much to say for it, let us adopt it as our working definition in this book. But at the same time, this definition tells us very little about the nature of these principles. Therefore, in order to flesh out the definition and bring it alive, let us look now at a specific philosophical problem to see what additional features can be inferred about philosophical activity from such a problem.

AN EXAMPLE: THE
PROBLEM OF ABORTION

This is a good example of a philosophical problem, raising fundamental questions for parents, legislators, legal theorists, sociologists, physicians, and, of course, for philosophers. Beyond the legal, scientific and medical issues, there is a network of questions which philosophers have addressed and which bear upon this problem: "What is the nature of a person?" "Is the unborn individual a person?" "Is society justified in inflicting death upon the innocent if this can be demonstrably shown to benefit society in general?" "Do the unborn have rights, and if so, what are they?" "When the life of a mother and the life of a fetus are both endangered but only one can be saved, which ought it to be?"

All these questions arise in the attempt to justify abortion. Like many philosophical issues that quickly become exceedingly complex, the problem can be stated in a simple way: "Is abortion—that is, the taking of an innocent pre-natal life—ever justified?" What may be called the Extreme Right to Life Position (hereafter abbreviated to ERLP) answers this question, and offers the following argument in support of its position. First, it claims, a human fetus is a human being (a person). Second, it states, such human beings are innocent of any crime; they have committed no offense against society or against the person bearing them. Third, it argues, it is necessary to find a consistent set of principles (a reasonable philosophy) which would justify our destroying them. Fourth, it contends, since similar cases must be treated in similar ways, such principles would justify the abortion of a pre-natal child only if they would also justify the killing of an innocent post-natal child. Fifth, it holds, no considerations can be found that would justify the latter course of action, and accordingly, it concludes, no principles can be found that would justify the former.

This argument has a number of variations, but something like it is held by the Catholic Church, by many Jews and other religious persons, and by many persons without religious affiliation who are opposed on secular moral grounds to the taking of innocent lives. The basic thrust of the argument is to maintain that there is continuity from the moment of conception to the end of life, and that there is no difference in principle between the way the unborn should be treated and the way the post-natal child (or adult) should be treated. The argument thus challenges those who favor abortion to find some "relevant differences" between the status of pre-natal and post-natal beings that would justify the termination of life for the former but not for the latter, concluding that no such difference can be discovered. This argument, of course, presupposes that human life is intrinsically valuable, that it represents a good in itself and is not merely a means to some higher good. Echoes of this principle are indeed to be found in the writings of many philosophers—for example, in Hobbes, who states that the right to the preservation of one's own life is absolutely basic (*Leviathan*, Ch. XIV) and is antecedent to any rights derived from the rules or provisions of society.

What we wish to stress here is that this statement of the ERLP is a *reasoned* position, appealing to sets of moral principles which taken together, represent a consistent philosophy. Each of the elements in the argument depends upon such a philosophical principle. Any challenge to it must thus be justified in the light of a consistent and persuasive set of principles which arrive at a different conclusion. Before examining such a counter-position, let us begin with some terminological comments that will help clarify the issues involved. Though even "mere" terminological remarks can be used to beg the question, or to introduce tendentious considerations, when properly presented they can be neutral. Let us attempt to state them in as neutral a fashion as possible and thus to provide a terminology which will provide a common ground for discussion which both sides can accept.

After the female germ cell, known as the "ovum," is fertilized by the male germ cell, called the "spermatozoon," it possesses a full complement of twenty-three pairs of chromosomes, one in each pair from each parent. At that stage, the ovum is called a "single-cell zygote." Within twenty-four hours, the single-cell zygote begins to divide, reaching sixteen cells by the third day, and continuing to grow as it moves through the Fallopian tube into the uterus. During the first week, it gradually implants itself in the uterine wall, and at this stage it is commonly called a "conceptus." By the end of the second week, it is usually firmly embedded in the wall of the uterus and from this point until the eighth week of life it is termed an "embryo." Certain human features begin to appear by the fourth week; the embryo acquires a face and incipient limbs, and by the eighth week brain waves can be detected. From this latter period until birth at nine months, it is called a "fetus." Legal abortion is normally permitted before the twelfth week, but in some states (New York, for example) it is permitted by law as late as the twenty-fourth week. A normal fetus will come to full-term in nine months. From the perspective of those who oppose abortion, the process from the moment when the ovum is fertilized to the completion of term is a continuous process of natural growth; and if the process is interrupted by an abortion, the result, according to proponents of the ERLP, amounts to the killing of an innocent human being.

We mention these terminological facts because they allow us to distinguish between forms of the pro-abortion position (PA). There are many such positions, usually distinguished by the particular premise in the ERLP argument that they attack or reject. The first of these concentrates upon the first premise of ERLP, namely that the unborn is from the outset a human being. This view itself is often divided between those who maintain that the zygote is human, but not a person, and those who maintain that the zygote is not human at all. An even more extreme position here would attack the notion that the fetus is a person. But let us concentrate upon the most moderate of these positions. According to this view, abortion of the zygote is justified because the zygote is not a human being at all, though it has the potentiality of becoming one. The contention is that the zygote is simply a mass of living tissue, analogous to a cyst or tumor, and is not yet human, having no human features or characteristics. It can thus justifiably be excised and abortion can be thought of as analogous to a surgical procedure which eliminates an unwanted growth. Variants of this view sometimes argue that the conceptus, though a human being, is not yet a person—a person being something with a mind, with feelings, desires, and so on—and that abortion of a conceptus is justified since it does not involve the killing of innocent *persons*. Both of these positions press home an analogy: they claim that the zygote and/or conceptus stand to a full-fledged human being (or person) in much the same way as an acorn stands to an oak. To prevent an acorn from becoming an oak tree is not identical with killing or cutting down a tree, and that it amounts to a categorical mistake to think that the two cases are identical. It should be noted that all versions of this first position do agree with the proposition that the killing of an innocent human being (or person) is unjustified. They disagree only with the premise in the ERLP argument that the zygote or conceptus qualifies as a human being (or person). One writer who defends this view has stated "At this place, however, it should be remembered that we have only been pretending throughout that the fetus is a human being from the moment of conception. A very early abortion is surely not the killing of a person . . ."

The foregoing line of argumentation is often buttressed by an appeal to the law. In the case of *Roe vs. Wade* in 1973, the United States Supreme

Court held that fetuses are not "full legal persons," and that a woman has the right to an abortion, which is derived from the more general constitutional right to privacy. This decision stated, however, that the latter right is not absolute, being limited by the state's right to regulate medical practice to protect maternal health. Justice Blackman specifically denied that a woman's right was absolute since "a state may properly assert important interests in safeguarding health, in maintaining medical standards, and in protecting potential life."

According to the Supreme Court, the state may also intervene after three months to protect the health of the woman, and the state can proscribe an abortion in the last ten weeks, except to preserve the mother's life. To some, this decision appears to support the view that at certain stages of its development the fetus is not a person, and hence that no killing of the innocent takes place through an abortive procedure.

A still different version of the pro-abortion position attacks the premise that the unborn are indeed innocent. Such an attack might begin by arguing that the notion of "innocence" only applies to *agents*—that is, to beings that have the capacity to choose and/or to refrain from evil actions. The unborn have neither the capacity to choose nor to act, and hence are neither innocent nor not innocent. In effect, this view challenges the contention that the unborn are persons; but in arguing that abortion does not involve the killing of the innocent, it also attacks the second premise of the ERLP argument. This view itself has numerous variants. One of them, for example, holds that if the unborn is conceived through an act of rape, the mother becomes an innocent victim, destined against her will to carry a child to term and to nurture it to maturity. The suggestion here is that in such a case the fetus is party to, or is the result of, a felonious assault against the mother, and that accordingly the mother or society is justified in terminating its existence as part of an effort to redress a wrong. An extension of this argument holds that the mother has rights as a person which are infringed by having to carry a child to term against her will, whether or not the act of conception results from a crime, and that her right must prevail against that of the zygote, conceptus or fetus. In countries suffering from severe overpopulation, this position is defended on the ground that society has a right to limit its population— that a child born into a situation of severely limited resources does in fact inflict injury upon the society and accordingly that abortion is justified upon demand.

Other defenses of the pro-abortion position attack the third and fourth premises of the ERLP argument. It will be recalled that the third premise states that one cannot find a set of principles which would justify the killing of the unborn. In rebuttal of this view, it is sometimes argued that a variety of circumstances would justify the termination of its existence. To bring a child into a world where it will soon starve to death, where it cannot properly be reared, and where its life will be one of pain and travail, is to condemn it in advance to a horrible existence. Some would argue that it is more desirable to spare it such pain and impoverishment than to allow it to suffer, and therefore that when these circumstances obtain, abortion is justifiable on moral grounds. Similar considerations are urged to establish that there is a relevant difference between the unborn and the post-natal infant, and these thus attack the fourth premise of the ERLP argument.

Whether the ERLP position, or any of these opposing views, is correct is not an issue we shall attempt to decide here. Our point is rather to show that the issues raised are not only legal, sociological, medical, or practical, but to a great extent are concerns of a different type or order— namely philosophical. This can be shown by asking the question: "How can one establish on medical or scientific grounds that a zygote is not a person?" The answer to this question clearly involves conceptual issues— issues requiring for their resolution some definition or characterization of what personhood consists of. As such they fall squarely into the domain of philosophy. In the next section, we shall try to bring out, in terms of this example, what is meant by describing a problem as "philosophical," and in so doing will try to explain how such problems transcend or differ from scientific, legal, medical, or practical problems.

Generally speaking, the issues we have mentioned—abortion, racism, the proper uses of energy, unemployment, the population explosion— involve considerations of principle that have been discussed by philosophers of the past and present. From these kinds of problems important and influential theories have developed, such as those of Plato, Aristotle, Hobbes, and others. In the course of this book we hope to show how seemingly simple and ordinary features of our experience can give rise to conceptual difficulties that have led to the development of philosophical theories that attempt to deal with these difficulties.

SOME CHARACTERISTICS OF
A PHILOSOPHICAL PROBLEM

1. *A philosophical problem is not in a straightforward way a problem arising from a lack of factual information.*

The italicized sentence conveys the first of the features characteristic of philosophical problems. One can see this by noting that the question of whether a zygote or a conceptus is a person does not arise because specific pieces of factual information are lacking. Nobody is in doubt about the scientific issues involved—how the ovum is fertilized, how it grows, the role which DNA codes play in this development, and so forth. So in some straightforward sense the issue as to whether the zygote is a person is not resolvable by an appeal to the facts. It is clear that considerations other than scientific considerations are involved in this question.

2. A corollary to the italicized proposition above provides us with a second feature of philosophy: *a philosophical problem is not solvable solely by an appeal to the facts*. This statement seems true if the first proposition is true; for if the problem does not arise through a lack of factual information, it is difficult to see how the possession of such information would be decisive in its solution. (Note: we are not asserting that factual information may not play a role in the solution or resolution of philosophical problems; our claim is that such problems cannot be resolved *merely* by an appeal to the facts.) In the issue about the justification of abortion, what bits or pieces of information would one require in order to dispose of the problem?

3. This gives rise, in turn, to a third aspect of philosophy, namely that *it is primarily a conceptual activity*. This is a somewhat complicated assertion which may be explained by contrasting conceptual with factual problems. Suppose the question is: "How far is it from Los Angeles to San Diego?" Before answering this question, we obviously have to know what the words in it mean; but assuming that there is no difficulty about this—that we are speaking of distance by road, rather than about travel time via automobile or air, and so on—then the answer to the question will be straightforwardly factual. It will consist of statements such as: "It is 110 miles," or "According to my map it is 115 miles," or "By air it will take 22 minutes," and so on. The information contained in such answers may be collected in a variety of ways—by driving the distance personally and seeing what one's odometer reads after the trip, or by checking the distance in an atlas, or by measuring it off an equal-area map. But the important thing to see here is that the facts provide a solution to the problem; there is no special conceptual residue left when such answers are provided.

Philosophical problems are not straightforwardly factual in this way. The free-will problem provides a good example of what we mean in this connection. It is a problem that arises through an incompatibility between certain sets of beliefs one may hold. One may believe (a) that most men are free to choose alternative courses of action from those they in fact choose, and also that (b) every event, including one's choices, has initiating causes, and therefore that (c) everybody's actions are, in principle, wholly predictable. But if (c) is true, then it follows that no man can choose differently from the way he does choose, or act differently from the way he does act and therefore that (d) no man is really free. Our conclusion (d) is thus inconsistent with our assumption in (a) that most men are free. Now what is striking about such a problem is that the facts of human behavior seem indecisive with regard to its solution. We know that some men are now in chains, some are in jail, some appear to be doing what they want to do. But does such a canvass of the factual situation *decide* the issue? The answer is clearly "no," for the problem arises only after all the facts are in. After we ascertain that some men are in chains while others are not, we still cannot decide whether those who are not in chains are free or not.

If the facts cannot be decisive in such cases, then how are they to be dealt with? The answer is primarily by the use of reason. In the free-will problem this involves the considerations of the merits of arguments and what their import is. The problem is thus a conceptual problem, requiring for its resolution some procedures which go beyond a mere gathering or observation of the facts.

4. A fourth important feature of philosophical activity is that *it generally involves an explanation of something*. In the case of the problem about abortion, there is a puzzle about the relationship between bits or pieces of tissue and persons. When do such bits and pieces of tissue become persons, and how does this happen? How can a mere piece of tissue be a person? If a person is not merely a piece of tissue, then what is it? Is it some extramaterial kind of entity? If so, how are we to identify it? Philosophers are thus typically concerned with the removal of puzzles and other signs of conceptual unease. Let us say, then, that philosophy is an activity whose practitioners concern themselves with explaining those features of the world, or our conduct in it, that are puzzling, baffling, unclear, or in some other way not wholly understood. As Aristotle said, "Philosophy begins in wonder." There must be something about the world, or some aspect of it, which demands clarification, understanding, resolution, or explanation. Without such a background of conceptual obscurity, philosophical reflection would not be necessary; indeed, it would not arise at all.

5. A fifth characteristic of philosophy thus arises from the demand for explanation. Accordingly, *any philosophical explanation must involve an appeal to a system of principles*. We may expand on this point as follows. In terms of our example, it is clear that not every explanation for the justification of abortion will do. A philosopher is not simply a person who comes up with an answer to something which he finds bewildering or difficult to comprehend; instead, his answer is designed to be consistent with, and to be followed from, sets of principles which are regarded as true and as applying to the issue in question. To put this more directly, we may say that a philosopher gives answers to questions which assume, presuppose, or explicitly involve sets of principles in the light of which the position to be taken can be accounted for. In the case of abortion, such principles might include a theory about the nature of personhood,

about the rights which persons have, about the conditions under which some rights override others, and so on. The explanation ultimately to be given—whether abortion is justifiable or no—is thus pushed back to a level of higher generality. Broadly speaking, this condition identifies the use of reason in philosophizing with the activity of "theorizing."

6. Additional features of philosophical activity are thus to be found in the concepts of *depth* and *generality*. Depth arises from the need to penetrate what may only be surface phenomena to reach their underlying principles. Just as a scientist, seeing diverse phenomena (such as liquid, solid, and gaseous states) will explain all of them in terms of simpler principles that depict these as various states of some underlying structure, so a philosophical account will attempt to probe beneath the surface phenomena to the underlying causes. This investigation comprises some of the techniques we defined and discussed earlier. *Generality*, on the other hand, arises from the need to see the particular case under discussion as *typical* of a class of cases. Thus Thomas Hobbes, a seventeenth-century English philosopher who sees the world as a machine operating under strict laws of nature, and a human being as a lesser machine ("What is the heart but a spring—and the nerves so many strings?"), draws radically diverse types of phenomena together by means of a mechanical model which explains them all.

The above list of features is not, of course, exhaustive; but these are among the more important characteristics of philosophical activity. Summarizing them, let us see how they fit our earlier definition, namely that "Philosophy is the strong liking for the knowledge of what is true or right, coupled with just judgment as to action." We have said that philosophy is a discipline which (1) involves reflection about the world and its ingredients; (2) is a conceptual, rather than a straightforwardly empirical discipline; (3) involves rational activity, demanding the use of argument, in an effort to make clear some point, position, or doctrine; (4) attempts to provide clarifications of matters that are not clearly understood, that may be mysterious, puzzling, or in some other way peculiar and thus require explanation; (5) involves searching for a "deeper" explanation to cut beneath what is superficial and multifarious. This last requirement involves, in turn, (6) an appeal to principles which underlie such phenomena, and this appeal amounts to (7) theorizing with a resulting systematization and generality. The problem of abortion illustrates many of these points, raising questions about what is true, or right, and just judgment as to action. We conclude, therefore, that the above definition will do for our subsequent purposes, especially as amplified by the considerations we have just discussed.

PHILOSOPHY AND THE
ORDINARY MAN

In selecting the problem of abortion as a way of illustrating the nature of philosophical activity, we have perhaps created the impression that all philosophical problems have social or political or practical implications. Many of the most important philosophical issues indeed have just such implications, but some do not, or at least do not have them to the same degree—the famous Problem of Universals being an example to the contrary. Some philosophical problems of the latter sort—problems about the nature of names, meaning, and reference, for instance—raise puzzles of a more "academic sort." But leaving these aside for the moment, we should ask, "What is the difference between the approach which a professional philosopher takes on the problem of abortion and the approach which a reflective ordinary man takes in dealing with such an issue?" Do the approaches differ in method or kind, or do they differ in degree? Our view is that the difference is a matter of degree rather than a matter of kind. Both the ordinary man and the professional philosopher govern their lives in the light of principles—in this sense, nearly everybody has a "philosophy of life," a set of rules or precepts which he holds more or less explicitly and which he regards as giving coherence, meaning, and significance to his everyday activities. If there is a difference between the professional philosopher and the ordinary man, it is to be found in the degree of explicitness with which they hold such principles. The philosopher is interested in articulating such a set of principles in order to see whether they do cohere as a group and are not inconsistent, and then to see what their implications for living in and for understanding the world are. But insofar as anyone is reflective, he will find philosophical problems arising from such reflection. For as he subjects his principles to scrutiny and analysis, he is likely to find that they seem less sure than they appeared originally, less universal in their application, less defensible, and perhaps less wise. The effort to produce a justifiable, rational, and cogent set of such maxims and principles is thus the initiating factor which leads to philosophical activity, and is found both in the ordinary man and in the great philosophers of the past and present. What happens, for example, when one teaches one's children that they must *always* tell the truth? Is this a defensible proposition? Are there no circumstances in which a lie is justified? Or are there such? But if so, what principles support such exceptions? The answers to these queries are not easy; yet it is just such considerations that are the flesh and blood of philosophy, whether entertained by the ordinary person or by the professional philosopher. Our book will touch on some of these issues. Among the famous problems that puzzle both ordinary men and philosophers are these: Is man merely an animal, destined to live only for a short time upon the earth and then become dust, to disappear forever? Or is there more to a man than that—does he possess a "soul" for example, as Plato argued in the *Phaedo*? And is this something that survives death? Is life merely an accidental thing, or does it have some overriding purpose, and if so, what is it? If everything must have a cause, then how can there be a first cause for all things (such as God)? But if there is no first cause, then where did the world come from? Is there an ultimate, smallest constituent from which a complex world is built up? Clearly it seems that there must be some such thing, since complex things are made of simpler elements. But if there were ultimate simples, what would they look like? Can one imagine something that has no shape, no parts, no other side, and from which the world as we know it is constructed? Or to move away from metaphysics a branch of philosophy which will be discussed in Chapter 2, consider the question whether the end of life is pleasure alone? If it is, then wouldn't it be perfectly appropriate to use drugs in order to expand one's pleasure to the maximum? But if pleasure is not the end of life, then what is? And what role should pleasure play in such a life? As one's consideration of such problems becomes more intense, as reflection on the underlying principles deepens, one moves more and more into the traditional domain of philosophy—into the kinds of famous philosophical doctrines with which this book is concerned. The distinction between the ordinary man and the professional philosopher is thus to be drawn primarily in terms of depth of involvement, rather than in terms of the subject matter with which each is concerned.

PHILOSOPHY AND THE HISTORY
OF PHILOSOPHY

As we explained at the beginning of this introduction, no definition—no matter how lucid—can give the reader a real feel for such a complex subject as philosophy. Definitions in this domain are the beginning, not the end, of wisdom. To go beyond them, for a deeper understanding, one must steep oneself in the traditions, the political, social, and historical circumstances that give rise to real problems for real people. In this book, our orientation stresses that the particular historical setting in which a problem arises is crucial for a full appreciation of the real issues that were under debate. Though something like the problem of universals arises in the classical period, and again in the Middle Ages, and again in the early modern period, the form it takes in each of these periods, and among individual writers, differs. Thus, no one can hope to acquire an understanding of an epoch, and the impact of philosophical speculation upon it, without grasping the historical circumstances that gave rise to the specific issues under debate. For this kind of understanding, we feel there is no better procedure than a study of the history of philosophy. Such a study, if properly pursued, will recreate the intellectual climate in which the great problems of human life arose, will indicate how they were seen both by their contemporaries and by later thinkers, and what attempts were made to deal with them. In our book, we attempt to recreate some of these circumstances, thus adding flesh to the bare bones we have uncovered in this introduction. By this kind of deeper exposure to the subject, the reader will add a major dimension to his appreciation of the subject and its impact on human history. We shall begin with epistemology, or the theory of knowledge, as it is also called, and then proceed to metaphysics, political philosophy, ethics, philosophy of religion and the contemporary scene in philosophy. We hope the reader will find that some of the basic issues of the present world can be better understood when seen in terms of the philosophical issues and theories involved.

chapter 1

The Death of Socrates by Jacques Louis David (1787) (above)

René Descartes (1596–1650); birthplace—France (left)

John Locke (1632–1704); birthplace—England (right)

George Berkeley (1685–1753); birthplace—Ireland (left)

David Hume (1711–1776); birthplace—Scotland (right)

THE THEORY OF KNOWLEDGE

One of the fundamental branches of philosophy is that which deals with the theory of knowledge, or epistemology, a name which comes from the Greek word *episteme*, or "knowledge." The epistemologist attempts to answer such questions as "What can be known?" and "How do we determine whether our beliefs about the world are true or reliable?"

When one first considers these questions, it may seem that to answer them satisfactorily is quite simple. What can be known? Each of us can supply a partial answer by compiling a list of what we ourselves know. For example, we each know such things as our names, our addresses, and our ages. Information of this sort seems to provide a means for beginning to answer the question, "What can be known?" After we have stated the personal information that each of us possesses, we can easily proceed to consult experts in order to find out what else is known. Scientists, historians, geographers, and other learned persons can supply us with a great deal more information. Any encyclopedia tells us still more. These sources may not tell us everything that is known, but they seem, at first glance, to provide the *sort* of answer which our question demands.

When we examine our store of information, we find that some of it is regarded as certain, whereas other parts of it may be open to correction, revision, or even replacement. We feel quite certain about information based on, or derived from, what we personally have experienced. We are fairly sure of information that we have gained from respected authorities. We are less sure of information gained from other sources.

As new information comes to light, we often find that we have to revise our views about what we think we know. We make mistakes. We discover, as the result of new experiences, that we have sometimes come to wrong conclusions, or that we have accepted beliefs which turn out to be false or dubious. Experts whom we trusted are challenged by other experts, so that information that we accept at one time has to be discarded or modified.

Throughout our lives we are continually revising our store of information, the knowledge that we believe we possess. The information we accepted when we were children has had to be corrected in many ways. Our beliefs about Santa Claus, about the superhuman abilities of western frontier heroes, and about animals with human characteristics have had to be discarded. As we mature, what we have learned has led us to accept different views about the nature of the world around us, and about the past. Not too infrequently we have found that even information about which we felt most certain—the dates of our births or the spelling of our names, for example—has to be corrected.

Often views based on our own personal experience turn out to be open to question. We thought that we heard something, or saw something, but when challenged, we can no longer be certain. My wife and I cannot agree about what time in the evening we arranged to meet. I *know* that we arranged to meet at six. When she arrives at seven, she *knows* that we agreed to meet at seven. The argument that ensues never seems to settle the question, though each of us is certain that he is right.

When we realize how often our beliefs change, how much our store of information is revised, and how uncertain we may become about our views when challenged, we may not be so confident that we can give a precise and exact answer to the question, "What can be known?" When we consider that even the most competent and careful experts are sometimes wrong, we may begin to wonder whether there is any information of which we can *really* be sure. The following incident from recent history is of the type that may still further shake our confidence.

Shortly before the outbreak of World War II, a painting was discovered in a château in France. It was immediately identified by art experts as a work of the great seventeenth-century Dutch painter Jan Vermeer. The authorities who examined the painting were sure that it was the only known work from Vermeer's religious period, when he was influenced by the Italian artist Caravaggio. On the basis of the experts' conclusions, the painting was purchased for an immense sum by a Dutch museum, where it was hung as the masterpiece of the collection. Any reasonable man at the time would have had no reason for doubting the authenticity of the work. The best authorities said it was by Vermeer. All the physical evidence seemed to confirm the dating: the canvas was a seventeenth-century one; the paint was about three hundred years old; the painting showed all the expected signs of aging in the form of cracks, dust, and so on. According to our usual criteria, the work appeared to be genuine "beyond any reasonable doubt." Hence, in terms of the degree of certitude usually desired, people were sufficiently sure that the painting was a hitherto unknown work of Vermeer.

Shortly after World War II, Van Meergeren, a Dutch painter, was arrested and charged with the crime of having sold some Dutch art treasures to the Nazis. His defense was that the so-called art treasures in question were not treasures, but paintings that he himself had painted, including the great Vermeer picture of Christ, then hanging in a Dutch museum. In jail, he proved that he was capable of committing such forgeries by doing another one. He explained his method of forgery, which involved employing genuine seventeenth-century canvasses, from which he scraped the paint for reuse. Then he baked the paintings in an oven to get the proper kind of cracking, afterward rubbing them with dust so that they would look sufficiently old and dirty.

At first, Van Meergeren was unable to convince people that he was merely a good forger. They insisted he was making up this story in order to save himself from the charge at issue. After very careful examination of the data, practically all of the experts now agree that Van Meergeren painted the Vermeer Christ (though the argument is still carried on by a few people). They also now insist that it is not even a very good forgery. But they also maintain that at the time that the painting was discovered, there was no reason to doubt its authenticity, and it was reasonable to accept it as genuine. When the painting first came to light, they insist, it would have been most unreasonable to raise doubts, for there were, *at that time*, with the evidence then available, ample grounds for accepting the conclusions of the experts.

This episode in recent art history has been embarrassing for many experts, and for the directors of the museum which paid a fortune for the forged painting (and which is now unwilling to exhibit it). But this sad tale indicates that it is possible that the most reasonable certitude based on the highest standards may, and sometimes does, turn out to be inaccurate.

The initial assurance of the experts was based primarily on their sense information, what the paint looked like, what the canvas looked like, and the type of cracks present. The outcome of the case indicated that things are not always what they seem to be. The painting, which looked as if it were three hundred years old, was actually of very recent vintage. Even in more ordinary cases, we find that our sense information can mislead us. We think that we see a certain object, from a distance, but when we move closer we discover that we actually are seeing something else. When we consider some of the doubts that can be raised about the reliability of our sense information, we may become more shaken about our usual beliefs.

For example, if, when we are rowing, we look at an oar when it is partially immersed in water, it appears to be bent. When we remove the oar completely from the water, it looks straight. In this case, the information we gain from the two situations seems to conflict. How do we tell which impression is the correct one? If we admit that in one of these instances, our senses have misled us, can we ascertain that our senses have not misled us in the other case as well? In actual practice, we accept certain of our sense experiences as accurate, but can we really be sure that they are accurate, or that they will not have to be corrected or revised later on? If we believe that the oar was bent, and then changed our opinion when we removed it from the water, how can we know that we will not have to change our opinion again when more data become available? How do we determine what circumstances are the right ones for viewing an object? Is it possible that the information gained from seeing the object in water is correct, and that the other information gained from viewing the object out of water is wrong?

The apparent conflict of information gained from sense experiences may disturb us, and may even make us skeptical about whether we do, in fact, know anything. These doubts, added to those that may result from considering the variations in our own and others' opinions, the unreliability of experts, and the uncertainty of many of our ordinary beliefs, may lead us to re-examine the question, "What can we know?" When we begin to question our initial assurances we move toward a consideration of the problems dealt with in the theory of knowledge.

Philosophers have been concerned to probe more deeply than we ordinarily do into the nature of the information that we accept. They have inquired into the very source of our information and have questioned the reliability of the information and beliefs that we normally rely on. Philosophers have sought to discover how much knowledge, in the sense of completely certain information, we do in fact possess. (The term "knowledge" is used in many different ways. In this chapter, we shall use the term to designate information or beliefs that are unquestionably true, or that are certain. This, of course, is only one of many possible usages, and many philosophers, including some of those to be discussed, would no doubt define the term either more precisely or narrowly.)

Let us now consider some of the answers that philosophers have offered to the question, "What can be known?" We shall begin by examining the views of some of the thinkers who maintained that human beings are capable of discovering some information that is absolutely certain, and that is beyond all possible doubt.

**EARLY GREEK PHILOSOPHY
AND THE SOPHISTS**

The earliest serious and articulate discussions of philosophical issues that we know of are those of various Greek thinkers of the seventh and sixth centuries B.C.

As a result of these initial philosophical considerations, a great many different theories about the nature of the world were developed by the early Greek thinkers. By the fifth century B.C., many conflicting views were being advocated by different philosophers. Partly as a result of these conflicts, and partly because the center of the intellectual world shifted to Athens, where practical concerns were more important than theoretical and abstract ones, a type of skepticism about what men could actually know arose. Doubts were raised by a group of teachers called the *Sophists*.

Athens became an important city in the Greek world in the course of the fifth century B.C. At that time most of the cities of Greece were separate city-states, some of which had colonies all over the known world, from Asia Minor and the Black Sea area to Italy, southern France, and Spain. Because of commercial rivalries there were many wars among the various city-states and between them and other countries. In the course of these struggles, Athens and some of the other city-states, such as Sparta, became more and more important. In the middle of the fifth century B.C., Athens and Sparta succeeded in defeating the enormous army and navy of the Persians (estimated by Greek writers at more than a million men, as opposed to a few thousand Greeks). After the great land victory at Thermopylae, a pass in eastern Greece, where a handful of Spartans held back the whole Persian army, and after the great naval victory at Salamis, where the Athenian navy destroyed the Persian fleet (both battles occurred in 480 B.C.), Athens emerged as one of the great powers and the cultural center of the ancient world. In the course of the fifth century, Athens produced many famous writers, including the great historians Herodotus and Thucydides, and the world-renowned dramatists Aeschylus, Sophocles, Euripides, and Aristophanes. It became a center for mathematical, scientific, and philosophical study. This glorious period of Athenian history, during which so much of the world's most important art, literature, and thought was produced, continued down through the long wars with Sparta for control of Greece at the end of the fifth century, and through the conquest of Greece in the middle of the fourth century by Philip of Macedon and his famous son, Alexander the Great. But even after Athens had been captured and had lost its power, it still remained one of the important centers of culture and a vital area for philosophical inquiry. As we shall see, much of ancient philosophy took place in Athens,

and the city remained a center for the various early schools of philosophy
for almost a thousand years.

In the period that is of concern here, the fifth century B.C., Athens
was the scene of a most exciting cultural flowering as well as of a great
political development. At this time, Athens became the first important
democratic state in the history of the world. All citizens of the society
(only about 10 percent of the actual residents of Athens) took part in managing the affairs of the city-state through voting on various issues, and
through holding public office. Ordinary citizens, rather than the older noble
families, took over the governing of the society and emerged as an important new class. To answer the need for educating the new rulers of the
Athenian world, a group of teachers appeared called the *Sophists* (originally meaning "wise men").

The Sophists were prepared to teach people what they would need to
know in order to get along in the world, and to teach them how to be
successful. They usually did not teach theoretical subjects like mathematics,
which did not appear to be relevant to functioning in normal human
situations. They seemed to have been teachers of what is now called "life
adjustment" by some of our educators. The Sophists centered their teaching on practical subjects, such as public speaking and the art of winning
arguments. Some of their opponents make it appear that what was taught
was what the English writer Stephen Potter calls "Lifemanship" or
"Gamesmanship"—or how to win games without actually cheating. The
Sophists were not necessarily dishonest, but they gave this impression to
their opponents. To their successful students they seemed extremely helpful in teaching how to get along in the practical world. The Sophists were
the first paid teachers in antiquity, which is another reason their opponents
objected to them. The Sophists scorned theoretical and abstract subjects
because they were useless for getting ahead in the world. They rejected the
type of inquiries of the earlier Greek philosophers who had speculated
about the nature of the universe; according to the Sophists, these inquiries
never got anywhere, and the philosophers could never agree as to what
was true and what was false. Even if they did agree, it would be of no use
to ordinary people.

A story that has come down to us may illustrate what the Sophists
did. The greatest of the Sophists, Protagoras, guaranteed to teach a student how to win law cases in court. Before the course began, Protagoras
told the student that he would have to pay for his lessons only after he had
won his first law case. Once they had agreed on when the payment would
be made, Protagoras gave the student his first and final lesson. He sued the
student for payment. The Sophist argued that if the student won the case,
then, according to their agreement, he had to pay, and if the student lost
the case, then he also had to pay, because that was what the suit was

about. The student had learned his lesson faster than Protagoras expected. He answered that if he lost the case, he should not have to pay according to their agreement. If he won, he should not have to pay, since the court would be judging, in awarding him the victory, that Protagoras was not entitled to his money. The Athenian court decided that the student's reasoning was more convincing, since no matter what Protagoras proved, the student could show that he himself should not have to pay for his law lesson. Thus the student quickly mastered the Sophist technique of reasoning: the construction of arguments to prove whatever one wished, even if the conclusions were paradoxical.

In order to justify their concentration on practical matters, and their rejection of abstract or theoretical speculation, some of the Sophists developed a very negative and skeptical theory of knowledge. This theory is summed up in Protagoras' remark that "man is the measure of all things," and the statement of his fellow Sophist, Gorgias, that "nothing exists, and if it did, nobody could know it, and if they knew it, they could not communicate this knowledge." Protagoras and Gorgias were interpreted as saying that men are not capable of knowing what is *really* going on in the world, and that all that they can know is what *appears* to each of them to be the case. Each man is the measure of what seems to him to be true. Therefore, the Sophists argued, men should not seek absolute knowledge for they will not find it. They should concern themselves only with their own opinions. Each man should learn to live as best he can, by measuring what seems to be the case, according to his own needs and desires. Presumably, any person who had mastered the sophistical techniques would get along better, since, by means of clever methods of arguing and influencing other people, he could make his own opinions, or individual measure of the world, prevail. The Sophists insisted that one should ignore such subjects as mathematics and physics, because one could never tell if the conclusions reached in those areas were actually true. Instead, they taught that a man ought to concern himself only with the way things appear to him, and his own opinions about them. Each opinion is "true" for the man who holds it, and each man can know and care only about his own personal, subjective way of looking at the universe. In sum, according to the Sophists, no absolute knowledge can be attained, and to seek for it is not worthwhile. Opinions or beliefs are relative to the person who holds them. There are none that are absolutely true, true for everyone at all times. All views are subjective and do not have any objective truth value.

Socrates' Attack on the Sophists

In opposition to what some of their contemporaries regarded as the negative, skeptical, subjective, and relativistic theory of knowledge of the

Sophists, the great philosopher Socrates tried to show that there must be some positive, objective, and absolute knowledge that human beings can possess. After him, his student Plato offered an important and elaborate theory to answer the question, "What can be known?"

Socrates (469–399 B.C.) is one of the most memorable figures in the ancient world. We know him chiefly through the picture of him given by Plato. Most of our information about Socrates comes either from Plato's writings, from those of another student of Socrates, the Greek historian and general Xenophon (whose picture of Socrates differs quite radically from that of Plato), and from the famous satire of Aristophanes, *The Clouds*, which attacks Socrates. As will be pointed out in Chapter 4, "Ethics," some people have doubted the accuracy of any of our information about Socrates and have even suggested that he is a mythological or legendary personage, rather than a real individual. For the purposes of this chapter, we shall assume that the information given us by Plato is accurate. Even if some of what Plato says is fictitious, it is his picture of Socrates that has had the greatest influence on the history of thought.

Socrates was a brilliant man who was concerned with finding out how people *ought* to live. He went around Athens accosting the leaders of the society and asking them questions about human affairs. No matter what they answered, he would question their replies until they became completely bewildered. (One of his opponents said, after being trounced in a discussion, "When I talk with you, Socrates, the words seem to get up and walk away.") Socrates discovered, after discussing questions with political leaders, military leaders, Sophists, poets, and others, that everyone had opinions. Each was willing to act upon his own opinions. But no one had actually thought about the questions seriously, and no one knew, or cared, whether his opinions were actually true. Socrates became the "gadfly" of Athens, badgering everyone, and causing them to examine their own views.

Socrates employed what is called "the Socratic method," which consists in asking questions, and examining the answers given, without suggesting any definite solution to the problems raised. By doing this, Socrates brought to light the fact that the people who were considered "wise men" by their society had never examined what they believed or why they believed it, or whether they ought to believe it. As a result of his campaign of questioning his fellow Athenians, Socrates came to the conclusion that he, Socrates, must be wiser than they were, for he knew that he knew nothing. They also knew nothing, but they were not even aware of their own ignorance.

This crusade to awaken the Athenians to a realization of their actual plight, and to make them examine their own lives, led to Socrates' destruction. Either because he had insulted someone, or because of his friendship with certain antidemocratic leaders, or for some other reason, Socrates was finally arrested at the age of seventy. He was charged with corrupting the youth of Athens, and with teaching and advocating un-Athenian ideas, especially in religious matters. The trial, which is described in Plato's *Apology*, provides us with one of the heroic moments in human history. Instead of defending himself, Socrates continued his campaign. He exposed his accusers, and showed that though they thought they knew something, actually, they were not sure that what they said was true, nor were they sure that what they were doing was right. In spite of this "philosophical" defense, Socrates was convicted. Since he refused to apologize, or to promise to reform (that is, to stop asking everybody questions), he was sentenced to death. In 399 B.C., he was executed by being forced to drink a cup of hemlock; thus he became one of the first and greatest martyrs in mankind's search for truth.

Socrates tried to show, through questioning others, that human beings could be justified in carrying on their activities only if they had genuine knowledge. If they were as ignorant as Socrates suspected, then it was actually dangerous for them to act, since they could not be sure that they were doing the right thing. This view of Socrates is presented in some of Plato's *Dialogues*, in which conversations between Socrates and the principal Sophists are presented, especially in the dialogues *Protagoras* and *Gorgias*. (Most of Plato's writings consist of dialogues, which are conversations between Socrates and other people. Platonic scholars are in fairly general agreement that the early dialogues probably represent actual conversations that Plato had witnessed or heard about. In the middle and later dialogues, Plato appears to be using the form of the dialogue as a means of developing and presenting his own philosophy, and using Socrates as a mouthpiece for his own ideas.)

Socrates tried to show, by his method of cross-examination, that both the theory and the practice of the Sophists were extremely dangerous. Teachers like Protagoras and Gorgias insist that knowledge cannot be obtained. Yet, in spite of this, they go about Athens, teaching people how to live, how to behave, and how to get along in the world. When Socrates asked Protagoras what a student would learn from him, the great Sophist answered that each day the student would return home a better man than when he came. Then Socrates demanded to know in what way the student would be better, and what, exactly, he would learn. Protagoras replied, "If he comes to me, he will learn that which he comes to learn. And this is prudence in affairs private as well as public; he will be able to speak and act for the best in the affairs of the state."

But, Socrates insisted, if Protagoras did not actually possess any knowledge, how could he possibly teach anybody what was best? For all that Protagoras could tell, he might actually be teaching the student to do the wrong thing. If one does not know what *is* true, can one be sure that "success" is desirable? Or, it is possible that the students of the Sophists are succeeding in a totally wrong way. If they become good public speakers, and are able to convince other people, they may convince them of the wrong views if they themselves do not have genuine knowledge. Hence, Socrates pointed out, the mere acquisition of skills can be quite dangerous, unless one possesses certain knowledge about how to use the skills, and about what goals ought to be achieved by means of them.

Thus, Socrates maintained, the teachings of the Sophists could cause great harm, since neither the teachers nor the students possessed knowledge. The Sophists and their students might succeed, and might lead others, but could they ever be sure they were not leading themselves and everyone else astray? Those who admitted that they were blind were leading others who did not realize that they were in the same state. The only way that one could be secure in acting and believing was first to discover what knowledge there might be. Until then, Socrates argued it would be unsafe to rush off and do something.

If we assume that Socrates held only the views presented in the early Platonic *Dialogues*, then he apparently never answered the questions that he raised. His task was to nettle people, to force them to examine their lives, because "the unexamined life is not worth living." The solution to the problems that he raised would depend on working out a theory of knowledge, an answer to the question, "What can be known?" Socrates' student Plato attempted to supply the answer.

Plato's Theory of Knowledge

Plato (427?–347 B.C.) came from an aristocratic Athenian family, which hoped to train him to become one of the leaders of society if the nobles should succeed in destroying the democratic government of Athens. Plato was quite young, in his late teens, when he met Socrates. As a result, Plato gave up plans for an active political career. Instead, he followed Socrates around Athens, listening to his debates, and occasionally taking a minor part in them. Plato was much impressed by Socrates' method, by the way he exposed the sham and the hypocrisy of the Athenians, and most of all, by the need, which Socrates had revealed, to engage in a serious search for true knowledge as the basis for all human beliefs and actions. When Socrates was put to death, Plato, along with several of his other disciples, fled from Athens lest they, too, might be punished. For several years, he traveled around the ancient world seeking wisdom. He began to write his famous *Dialogues*, possibly first as a tribute to his teacher, and then later as a way of presenting the solution he thought he had found for the questions raised by Socrates. It is likely that when he was in his early forties and after developing the theory of the perfect commonwealth which appears in *The Republic*, he went to Sicily to try to put his theory into practice. After a series of disasters (including capture by pirates), Plato returned to Athens, where he set up a school for the consideration of philosophical questions. The school, the Academy (so called because it was located in the deme of Aca in Athens), was the first and foremost institution of higher learning in the ancient world. It was to continue as a center for philosophical discussion until A.D. 529, when it was closed by the Christian rulers because it was one of the last remaining strongholds of paganism.

In its simplest form, Plato's answer to the question, "What can be known?" is that what can and must be known are those features of the universe that do not change at all. If knowledge is to be attained, and eventually communicated, there must be something fixed and unchangeable in the world. Plato called these unalterable features of the world "Ideas" or "Forms." In order to clarify this fundamental concept of Plato's theory of knowledge, we shall begin by examining some examples that illustrate, in a simple way, one aspect of Plato's contention that genuine knowledge consists only in apprehension of the Ideas or Forms.

We use the same words or terms to speak about many different and distinct objects. We say "Smith is a man" and "Jones is a man." If Smith and Jones are two separate and distinct individuals, why do we use the same term *man* to refer to both of them? We do this because each has something in common with the other, so that we are able to classify them together. The common element is designated by the general term *man*. Each of the different individuals possesses, or exhibits, a common feature, *manhood*. Hence, no matter what differences there may be between them (Smith may be young and bushy-haired, whereas Jones is old and bald), what they have in common is expressed by the general term *man*.

Such general terms as *man, horse, brown* form a crucial part of our vocabulary. If we did not use such terms, it would be almost impossible to communicate, or express, any beliefs that we possess. Almost anything that we might wish to say, and almost anything that we might think we know, can be expressed only by employing one or more of these general terms. This is related to the problem raised in our introduction concerning the nature of names and what they refer to. The puzzles raised by the problem of universals, especially with reference to general terms and what they name, is fundamental to Plato's thought.

But what do these terms refer to, and what do they mean? How do we come to know their meanings? The particular terms that we use, the proper names, can usually be explained by pointing to, or describing, the objects they name. If we are asked who or what "Smith" refers to, we can answer this by pointing to Smith, or by describing some unique characteristic that he possesses. "Smith is the man who is presently staying in

Room 1014 in the Fairmount Hotel in San Francisco," or "Smith is the man who is married to Barbara Jones." But what do terms such as *man* or *house* designate or refer to? Here a different kind of problem seems to arise, since we cannot point to particular individuals to show what the terms mean or what they name. The particular individuals are, at best, examples of what we mean. "Man" does not *mean*, or *name* "Smith." He is only one of many instances of "manhood," but he, himself, is not "manhood." If "man" designates what Smith, Jones, and three billion other individuals have in common, then pointing to, or describing some or all of the individuals in question is not the same as pointing to, or describing, the feature common to all the individuals, or the classification to which they belong.

Plato contended not only that there is a difference between particular concepts, and general ones, but that one cannot be clear as to what one is saying, or what one knows, about particular things, *unless* one has clear knowledge of the general concepts. A famous illustration of Plato's point appears in his dialogue *Euthyphro*, which presents a conversation between Socrates and the priest Euthyphro. The priest tells Socrates that he is going to the courthouse to accuse his own father of murder. The details of the case make it seem somewhat doubtful that Euthyphro's father is guilty. When Socrates asks him why he is bringing the case to court, Euthyphro replies that it is the holy thing to do. If that is so, Socrates then asks, then what is holiness? Holiness, Euthyphro answers, is doing what I am doing. Socrates points out that this is not a very helpful definition, since, at best, it only points out an example or illustration of holiness. But to know if a particular act is or is not holy, one would first have to know the meaning of the general concept "holiness." Without such knowledge, how could one safely or justly decide if a particularly example of human behavior was or was not holy?

We use general terms all the time. We use them to talk about our experiences, and to report facts such as "This is a cow"; "Waggles is a black-and-white dog." We use general terms to make such judgments as "That was a bad act," and so on. Plato insisted that statements of this sort can be meaningful only if we actually know what the general terms refer to or designate. If we do not, in fact, possess such knowledge, then we actually cannot say anything significant about any subject whatsoever. If the assertion "Smith is a man" is meaningful, one first has to know what being a man means, what constitutes "manhood." If such knowledge cannot be obtained, or if each person merely has a personal opinion as to what the general terms refer to, then genuine communication could not take place. We would not know what we were talking about when we used general terms, or we would each be talking about something different, namely, our private opinions as to what dogs or men were. The fact that human beings are able to communicate with one another led Plato to assume that knowledge of the meaning of general terms must be possible.

If such knowledge is possible, what is it knowledge of, and how do we acquire it? Plato first approached this problem negatively, showing what means could not bring us to such knowledge. Sense experience does not, and cannot, supply us with any knowledge of general concepts. What we see, taste, touch, hear, or smell are particular things, and not general ones. By means of our senses, we may find out what Smith looks like, but we will not find out what man in general is like. Plato insisted that if we did not know by some other means what a man is, we could not tell on the basis of our sense information that Smith is a man. We might be able to enumerate what characteristics he possesses, but simply from looking at Smith we could not determine that these characteristics constitute those of the general concept "manhood" or exemplify it.

Further, Plato pointed out, if we had to depend upon our sense information to find out about general concepts, we would be in a hopeless state. The particular individuals that we perceive keep changing. Smith grows. He gets older. His hair changes color. He gets fatter. He moves from one place to another. If all of the features which we perceive keep changing from time to time, how can we ascertain which, if any, of these characteristics constitute the reason for classifying Smith as a man. Unless we already know, somehow, what a man is, all the data we might accumulate about the ever-changing Mr. Smith would not teach us this concept.

In order to make his point more strongly, Plato presents in the *Meno*, a dialogue involving a none-too-bright disciple of the Sophist Gorgias, an argument to prove that no knowledge can be gained through the learning process, since this would mean that one had found a truth one did not know previously. For, then, Plato asks, if one did not know a proposition up to the very moment of learning it, how could one recognize that it was true? Either everything that we learn we knew before we learned it, or we can learn something that we did not know beforehand. In the first case, no new knowledge is being gained, and hence learning is not actually taking place. In the second case, Plato argued, one cannot learn, because if one acquired new information one would have no way of ascertaining that the new information was true. Presumably, any new information that we could acquire would tell us something about some general concept. Either we understand this concept or we do not. If we do not, then we cannot tell if the information is true. If we understand the concept, then the information is already known, and we are not actually learning anything new. For example, if I am taught that the area of a triangle is equal to half the base of the triangle times its height, and if I can tell that this is true, then I have learned nothing new. If I cannot tell whether this is true, I am not acquiring any knowledge. If I can tell that it is true, it is because I *already* know what a triangle is, and what is true about triangles. In that case, what I am being taught is in fact something that I must already know.

This odd contention that education is impossible, and that anyone who possesses any knowledge must have always possessed it, is called the "Recollection Theory." Plato's explanation of what occurs when we *seem* to learn something is that we are not actually learning (since learning is impossible), but we are actually remembering or recollecting something that we already know. Knowledge consists in awareness of, or understanding, general concepts, which concepts, according to Plato, exist as genuine, independent entities called "Platonic Ideas" or "Forms." If we can ever know anything, we must be aware of these Ideas. Sometimes, certain sense experiences, such as conversing with Socrates, may have the effect of making us remember what we already know. Anyone who is capable of knowing anything already knows it, but, unfortunately, he is not always aware of this. Hence it is necessary, sometimes, to jog people's memories.

To support this theory, Plato presented a discussion in the *Meno* between Socrates and a slave boy. The slave had never been taught mathematics. Socrates asks him how long the side of a square is which has twice the area of a given square? In the discussion, Socrates never tells the slave what the answer is, but only shows him what is wrong with the answers he offers. Finally, after this illustration of the Socratic method in action, the slave boy states the correct answer. It is then pointed out that, first of all, he was never taught the correct answer, and second, that when he discovered the right answer, he could recognize it as true. Therefore, according to Plato's theory, he must have already known the answer, but he must have forgotten it. The conversation with Socrates, in which he was never told the answer, merely served as the occasion for him to remember what he already knew.

Further, according to Plato's Recollection Theory, there can be *no* time at which one could acquire knowledge of Platonic Ideas. Any time that one might designate as the moment of learning would lead to the same difficulty. Thus, in order to acquire knowledge, one must already possess it to be able to recognize it. Since knowledge cannot be gained either through education or through sense experience, it must have *always* been in one's mind. But when could it have gotten there? Since this could not have occurred at any time during a person's life without giving rise to the same difficulties, the knowledge must have been in one's mind before birth. On the basis of this reasoning, Plato asserted that our souls must have existed prior to our birth, and must have always contained all the knowledge they could ever possess. To account for the fact that no one seems to know very much when he is born, Plato suggested that in the process of being born one forgets all that one knows. Later on, if one comes to know anything, it is because one has recalled what was in the soul before birth, and is still there but was only temporarily forgotten. Such knowledge is *a priori*, that is, prior to and independent of any experience.

How does one manage to recall all that can be known? How does one bring oneself to remember the Platonic Ideas? Plato's most detailed answer to these questions appears in the important dialogue, *The Republic*, Books V–VII. The dialogue as a whole deals with a basic problem of political philosophy: what is justice, and, growing out of this, what is the ideal society? In the course of presenting his answer, Plato had someone ask Socrates how this "brave new world" (which will be discussed in Chapter 3, "Political Philosophy," and Chapter 4, "Ethics") might be brought into existence. Socrates answers, "Not until philosophers become kings, and kings, philosophers." How does one become a philosopher? In explaining how the potential philosopher-kings will come to be aware of the knowledge necessary to govern the ideal state, Plato stated his theory of knowledge in detail, and pointed out what he believed can actually be known.

In order to make clear what constitutes knowledge, the various kinds of information that one can acquire about the world are distinguished. The two principal classifications are visible information and intelligible information. Visible information consists of two kinds, the lowest being only vague shadows, the highest being opinions about what is experienced. The most elementary sort of information that we possess is the blurred confusion of colors, sounds, shapes, smells, and so on. Above this there is an organized form of visible information, when experience has been sorted out into groups of colors, sounds, and so on, constituting various patterns. We believe that some of these patterns constitute a dog; others, a person. No matter how much more clear and organized our beliefs and opinions may be than the vague shadows, neither type of visible information can constitute genuine knowledge. Visible information is always subject to change and correction. We can never be completely sure that any particular pattern or organization that we have discovered really constitutes a particular object. We can only have a belief or opinion that this or that is the case. For, on the basis of visible information, one does not know the general concepts, or Platonic Ideas, and hence one does not know what things are really like. We are only aware, on the basis of visible information, how things *seem* to us. Since the appearances of things change constantly, we can never be certain of the truth of the judgments that we make on the basis of our fluctuating and limited experience. Therefore, Plato contended, we cannot obtain knowledge through visible information alone.

Intelligible information can constitute knowledge, since this deals with Platonic Ideas and involves direct acquaintance with them. In ex-

plaining intelligible information, Plato again introduced a twofold classification. The lower type involves the *use* of Platonic Ideas without really
comprehending their natures. In mathematics, for example, one may employ such general concepts as "circle" and "triangle," and merely assume
that they have certain properties. The type of knowledge attained in this
manner is only hypothetical, since it depends upon the assumptions that
are made. If circles have certain characteristics, then the theorems of
Euclidean geometry are true. Starting from certain definitions and axioms
(assumed truths), then, in a strictly logical manner, it is possible to demonstrate that certain propositions about lines, triangles, circles, squares,
rectangles, and so on, are the case. In contrast to this type of conditional
knowledge, the highest and purest form of intelligible information is that
based on direct acquaintance with Platonic Ideas, rather than on assumptions about them. When one knows the nature of a circle, or when one is
directly aware of the concept of a circle, then one has reached the summit
of human knowledge and understanding.

In order to indicate the nature of this ultimate knowledge, and to
suggest what would be involved in attaining it, Plato had Socrates relate
the famous "Allegory of the Cave." In this allegorical tale, the normal
human condition is likened to that of living all the time in a cave, where
one is only able to see shadows cast on a wall by objects and a light source
that is not visible. If one were chained in such a cave, looking only at the
shadows, one's experience would be something like watching a continuous
movie. If we were in this condition from the moment of our birth, we
would assume that the world of shadows, or of the movie screen, was the
real world (as some people who watch TV all the time seem to do). Since
all that we would see in this state would be images on a wall or a screen,
we would not realize that there were any other objects in the world, or
that the ones that we saw depended on some others. If this is approximately what ordinary human life is like, we are only directly acquainted
with visible information, and we have no way of realizing that there is
another and higher type of information which constitutes genuine knowledge.

But suppose, according to the Allegory of the Cave, somebody in this
state was somehow released from his fixed position, and was able to turn
and move around. Suppose, finally, that he could even escape from the
cave. What would happen? At first he would be blinded by the light, and
he would be unable to see the "real" objects as clearly as he had previously seen the shadows. The Platonic Ideas would dazzle him. His first
reaction would be to try to escape back into his former state. Unless he
were forced to contemplate the "real" objects, and unless he were forced
to look at the source of light itself until he became accustomed to it, he
would never gain any knowledge. He would simply retreat again into the

misleading world of shadows and opinions. But if the man were kept in his liberated state long enough, he would be able to know the "real" objects, and finally, perhaps, he would even be able to look at the sun itself. This is the kind of transition and transformation that each human being must go through, Plato tells us, if each of us is to attain knowledge. We must each be liberated from the ordinary world of shadows and beliefs, and we must be held long enough in the pure intellectual world so that we can become used to knowing the Platonic Ideas. Then, finally, we may be able to look upon the brilliant light of Truth itself.

But how can anybody escape from his personal cave, so that he can see the general concepts which are already within him, and how can he be brought to contemplate them so that he will finally reach the state of complete comprehension? To accomplish this, Plato proposed a training system for the potential philosopher-kings to make them conscious of what, in fact, they already know. Although the system is explained in *The Republic* as part of an educational process, it is actually a method for achieving complete recollection. According to Plato's theory, nothing can be learned. Hence teaching can only really be a form of memory training.

The training commences by making the students realize that there is something peculiar about visible information, and that such information is not adequate to provide genuine knowledge about the world. The student is made to see that the objects of sense experience appear to change all the time. These objects seem to have different properties at different times. One of Plato's favorite illustrations is to point out that if one looks at one's fourth finger, and then compares this finger with the fifth and with the third one, a strange situation seems to result. The fourth finger is bigger than the fifth one, and it is smaller than the third. But is the fourth finger big, or is it little? How can the same object be both big and little? Problems of this sort are supposed to puzzle and bewilder the student, and make him question the sort of information that he receives from his senses. When he tries to explain the paradox of the finger that is both big and little, he will find himself seeking for the meanings of the terms, seeking to discover the real nature of "bigness" and "littleness." Thus, the apparent inconsistencies in the sense world will lead the student toward the intelligible world, and will lead him to seek for the Platonic Ideas.

Once this journey has begun, the student is employing his reason rather than his senses as his guide in the search for knowledge and understanding. When this has happened, the second stage in the training process can start. In this stage, the student learns to live in the world of ideas and concepts that he has just entered. To accustom him to this world, he is given years of mathematical training.

The potential philosopher-king first learns arithmetic. This will accustom him to work with ideas alone, and not with the shadows he has experienced in his visible cave. As he becomes proficient in understanding through concepts and meanings and through his employment of general terms, the student will gradually give up his reliance upon what he sees, feels, hears, tastes, and smells. When he becomes able to do computations "in his head," he will be liberated from the world of sense experience. (As a result of this theory, Plato was very much opposed to the employment of audio-visual aids in the study of mathematics. If such devices were used, one's grasp of mathematics would still be limited by one's sensory experience, and one would not arrive at an awareness of the concepts involved. Thus, for example, the person who does sums by counting on his fingers has to rely on his senses instead of his understanding.)

The student proceeds from arithmetic to geometry. In the latter subject, he not only deals exclusively with concepts, but also discovers, or remembers, necessary truths about the ideas of circles, rectangles, and lines. These "remembered" necessary truths will differ radically from the opinions or beliefs he formerly held about the sense world. The necessary truths are about something that does not change—the pure concepts—and these truths can be demonstrated. Thus all the pictures that one might draw of circles and triangles may differ and change, but the necessary truths about circles and triangles will be eternal and unchanging. After a lengthy training in geometry, the student becomes capable of recollecting an entire system of necessary, unchangeable truths. When this has been accomplished, the student has reached the first level of genuine knowledge.

At this point, after the student has become an excellent geometer, he is finally ready for the crucial and final step that will completely free him from the cave of the sense world. This liberation is achieved through the study of "Dialectic." In this area, not only does one become capable of dealing with concepts in reasoning; one also knows and understands the Platonic Ideas. If this stage is ever achieved, the student should then be able to recollect completely all the knowledge that is already within his mind and which he has temporarily forgotten.

Dialectic is, unfortunately, very difficult to describe. Socrates pointed out that one can state precisely what it is only *after* one has reached this final stage on the road to knowledge and understanding. For those who have not arrived at the end of the quest, the best that can be done is to point out how Dialectic differs from mathematics.

According to Plato, each branch of mathematics rests upon certain hypotheses or assumptions. The mathematicians accept these without seeking to discover why they are true. They employ various concepts but do not explain them. They reason about the concept of a circle, but they do not ask, "What is a circle? Why is a circle what it is?" The mathematicians assume that a circle has certain characteristics, and on the basis of this assumption, they proceed. In the dialogue *Theaetetus*, Plato illustrated his point through a discussion between Socrates and one of the greatest Greek mathematicians, Theodorus. Socrates attempts to find out the meanings of the "key" terms used in geometry, and he discovers that the mathematicians do not actually know their meanings. When pressed, the mathematicians become quite vague. They have never examined the basic assumptions from which mathematics has been developed. As far as the mathematicians can ascertain, their subject matter consists only of "dreams about reality."

If one went beyond these "dreams," examined the concepts involved and the assumptions employed, and finally achieved a complete understanding of them, one would then be studying Dialectic. Mathematical studies prepare the way by training the student to use concepts and to discover some of the truths about them. Dialectic begins when one goes beyond mathematics and comprehends the Platonic Ideas. At this point the student has reached the heart of the matter, for he has arrived at pure knowledge that rests on no assumptions or hypotheses, but rather on complete and absolute certainty, gained through direct acquaintance with, and understanding of, the Ideas. He does not have a mere belief or opinion about what might be the case. He does not have a hypothesis that if such and such were true, then something else would have to be true. The student now *knows* because he has directly apprehended the unchangeable Platonic Ideas, and he has grasped why they are what they are. By using his reason, and not his senses, the student has succeeded in knowing the world of Ideas, and, finally, the highest Idea, that of the Good. The potential philosopher-king, at this point, as Socrates said, "at last finds himself at the end of the intellectual world."

To summarize the entire process by which genuine knowledge is attained, one starts out in the cave of visible information. If one rejects the sense world and begins looking at the intelligible world by means of one's reasoning capacities, then the journey has commenced. One then finds some concepts in one's own mind. By mastering various branches of mathematics, one becomes accustomed to dealing with the world of ideas. At this stage, one uses concepts on the basis of certain assumptions and hypotheses. If one then goes on to examine these assumptions and hypotheses, one arrives at the highest level of knowledge. This ultimate knowledge consists of knowing the Platonic Ideas, and knowing why they have the characteristics they do. Such knowledge is absolutely certain, and is made up of truths that have always been in one's mind. The long training process has the effect of making one remember them.

According to Plato's theory of knowledge, then, what can be known? We can know the real world, the world of Platonic Ideas, but not the visible world of shadows and opinions. Plato insisted that these Ideas are not merely features of our minds, but that they are, instead, real objects existing separately from the visible world, and existing as eternal and unchanging entities. Plato, as we have seen, regarded sense information as unreliable, and considered it as constituting only an opinion about what seems to be taking place. Similarly, he regarded the objects of sense experience as merely shadows and illusions. As such, they cannot be part of the real world, since the real world consists of those objects which we are aware of when we possess genuine knowledge. Our senses acquaint us only with the world of appearance, but our reason can lead us to knowledge of reality. The highest information we can attain about the world of appearance is belief or opinion. We can, on the other hand, attain certain and indubitable knowledge, through recollection, about the real world of Platonic Ideas.

Thus, according to Plato, the only knowledge we can have, in the sense of information which cannot possibly be false or dubious, is knowledge of Platonic Ideas. This can be achieved only through the difficult and lengthy process of recollecting, assisted by the study of mathematics and finally of Dialectic. When one finally becomes aware of the nature of a Platonic Idea, the very experience of directly apprehending it suffices to guarantee the knowledge involved. When one has had the experience, one is also aware that it is not possible that this information could ever turn out to be false.

However, with regard to the objects of ordinary life and everyday experience, we are not able to attain any knowledge. Every bit of information that we might acquire about the visible world could turn out to be false. Therefore, strictly speaking, we cannot know the sense world, nor can we have any certain information about the objects we see, hear, touch, taste, or smell. We can have only beliefs or opinions. Hence sciences like physics and chemistry can never provide us with knowledge, and, as Plato said, the scientists can talk only in the language of probability. They can study only the shadows which partake of the Platonic Ideas, and these shadows are never clear enough to provide knowledge. The shadows are, at best, pale and misleading copies or reflections of reality.

According to Plato's theory of knowledge, then, we can only *know* the intelligible world, in the form of mathematical knowledge and knowledge of the pure concepts, or Platonic Ideas. But, for better or worse, we can never gain any knowledge of the visible, physical world around us.

DESCARTES' THEORY
OF KNOWLEDGE

About two thousand years after Plato's death, a somewhat similar answer to the question, "What can we know?" was offered by the famous French philosopher, scientist, and mathematician, René Descartes (1596–

1650). He, too, contended that human beings are capable of attaining indubitable knowledge about reality. But before reaching such knowledge, one first has to become aware of how dubious our accepted beliefs actually are.

René Descartes lived in a rapidly changing world. Much of what people thought was true was being challenged. Both France, where Descartes was born, and The Netherlands, where he lived most of his adult life, were in the grip of religious struggles between the Catholics and the Protestants over the question of what was true in religion, and what means ought to be employed to discover religious truth. The scientific world was also in turmoil, and the entire picture of the physical world was being rapidly changed. The new theories in astronomy of Copernicus (1473–1543) and Kepler (1571–1630); the new biological discoveries made by men like William Harvey (1578–1657); and the new geographical discoveries resulting from exploration in the Americas, Africa, and the Orient were all bringing to light new information and were forcing men to abandon older beliefs. There was intense, and often violent, controversy between the advocates of the formerly accepted theories about the nature of the universe and the partisans of the new views. Almost every belief that had been accepted by previous generations was now under attack.

Young Descartes studied at the Jesuit school at La Flèche, in western France, where he was probably taught the theories of Aristotle. Discouraged by what the school had to offer, Descartes went out into the world to discover for himself what was true. He left his native France and joined the Dutch army as an officer, a common occupation for a gentleman of the period. He travelled with the troops in Holland and Germany during the early stages of the Thirty Years War. The indications are that he did little, if any, fighting, but spent his time talking to intellectuals and pursuing his interests in mathematics. In 1619 in Bavaria he is supposed to have climbed into a large oven to keep warm, and there made a fundamental discovery, which led to the development of the branch of mathematics called "analytic geometry."

As a result of his travels and his own discoveries in mathematics and physics, Descartes began to suspect that the theories he had been taught in school were doubtful or false; in fact, he also began to suspect that almost all the views that were generally accepted at this time were uncertain. He started to question and doubt all the theories that were believed solely because they had been accepted for generations and generations. When he returned to Paris in 1628, Descartes found that many of the bright young men of the time had similar doubts about previous theories, and that they were torn between continuing to accept the old ideas and taking the radical step of believing new ones. Many of these people simply became doubtful about all theories, and hence became complete skeptics. They expressed the view that it is doubtful whether one can ever discover adequate or sufficient evidence about any subject so as to justifiably assert that one possesses knowledge.

A letter of Descartes' describes a meeting he attended during this period at the home of the Pope's representative at Paris. On this occasion, an alchemist (who was later executed for making counterfeit money) was delivering a speech denouncing the traditional theories about the nature of the physical world, and stating the common doubts about whether one could find any way to attain incontrovertible information. The audience, which included several Church leaders and several of the leading scientists of the period, applauded the discourse. Only Descartes rose to challenge the skeptical attitude that had been presented, and to insist that there must be some way to discover information about the world that is completely certain. His own mathematical and physical researches had convinced him that he did *know* something. Descartes had an almost fanatical desire to be certain that no argument, and no future discovery, could ever shake his confidence in what he knew.

Descartes returned to Holland determined to overcome the skepticism that was infecting his age and to find out what portion of our common store of information was *really* certain. To do this, he began an investigation of everything that he thought he knew in order to see if any of it could be considered as absolutely reliable. After several years of intensive examination, he published his results in his famous *Discourse on Method* (1637) and, four years later, in his *Meditations on First Philosophy*. For the remaining years of his life, he developed his theory, fought with his critics, and presented a series of views that were to have an enormous influence in the history of modern thought.

Descartes died in Sweden in 1650, where he had gone to teach philosophy to one of his admirers, Queen Christina. (The story is that the only time she had for her philosophy class was six in the morning. Because of the strain of arising so early, he caught pneumonia and died. In his army days, he claimed, he rarely got up before noon.) Even before his death, Descartes' theories were producing a storm of controversy that was to last throughout the century. Various portions of his views provided the basis for philosophical discussions for the next three hundred years.

In his *Meditations* Descartes presented his answer to the question, "What can be known?" He began by questioning the beliefs that are usually accepted, and by rejecting any that might be doubtful. By testing the views that are held, Descartes felt that those that are uncertain could be cast aside. Then those beliefs that are certain would remain, and they could be employed to provide "a firm and permanent foundation for the sciences," thereby serving as the basis for all of our other knowledge about the world.

In order to find this foundation, Descartes decided that he would reject any opinion that he thought was false or doubtful, *and* also any that could conceivably turn out to be false or doubtful. The test he proposed was that any view should be rejected if any reason could be stated that would make it dubious. In this test it is not required that one actually be in doubt. If there is a possibility, no matter how remote, that a belief is either false or doubtful, then it should be rejected. Unless one is willing to test one's beliefs in this severe fashion, one can never be certain, Descartes insisted, that what one believes is absolutely true and cannot possibly be false.

Since it would be an "endless undertaking" if this test were actually applied to each of our beliefs individually, Descartes proposed instead that the general types of beliefs we possess be tested. We should examine whether beliefs which are based on sense information can possibly be false or doubtful, whether beliefs based on reasonings can possibly be false or doubtful, and so on. If the general type of belief can possibly be rejected, then all the individual beliefs of the same category are to be considered as open to question.

The Cartesian "Method of Doubt" is first applied to one of the major sources of our information, the senses. Is it possible that what we learn through seeing, smelling, tasting, hearing, or touching can possibly be false? When we investigate this question, Descartes pointed out, we find that *sometimes* we are deceived by our senses. An object seen from a distance looks different when we are near it. An object viewed at twilight often looks different when seen in daylight. An object in water frequently appears to be different when it is seen out of water. When one has a cold or a fever a food often tastes different than it does when one is healthy. Since, Descartes argued, information received by the senses is sometimes deceptive, or sometimes has to be corrected or changed, are we *ever* in a position to be completely sure of anything we claim to know? If our senses sometimes mislead us, perhaps they do so all the time. Perhaps even under optimal conditions we are being deceived, but we are not aware of this. If some of our sense information is unreliable, can we ever be completely sure that all of it is not unreliable? Perhaps what we call normal vision, normal hearing, and so on, is illusory, and we are simply used to it. Hence we accept certain experiences as reliable, even though these experiences may in fact be misleading or deceptive. (Perhaps when the optometrist gives us eyeglasses that correct our vision to 20-20, he is only making us have the same illusions that the majority of people have.)

This initial application of the Method of Doubt indicates that our senses are sometimes deceptive, or unreliable. However, this usually happens under special circumstances. The rest of the time we are quite certain about our sense information. We are sure that we have hands and feet. We are sure that we are looking at a page in a book. We feel so certain about these matters that it does not seem possible we could be wrong. However, Descartes pointed out, we may actually be in error, no matter how positive we may feel. When we consider that we have met, or have read about, people suffering from delusions who are completely sure of information that we seriously doubt, then can we be so certain that we are not also deluded? There are people who are sure that they are kings, who are sure that they are wearing valuable jewels, who are sure that they see pink mice, and so on. If deluded people are so positive about what they believe they see or feel, though they are in error, can we be certain that we are not deluded when we feel positive that we see or feel certain things?

One might dismiss Descartes' testing of our sense information by saying that his examination only shows that some people are crazy. Since sane people do not suffer from the same delusions as do people who are mad, why should we cast doubt on our normal experiences just because other people have abnormal experiences?

However, Descartes contended, there are some reasons which can lead us to admit the possibility that even our normal experiences may be unreliable (and hence, by the test he proposed, information or beliefs based on these experiences should be rejected because they are less than completely certain). It is possible that *all* experience is illusory. All of it may be like the experiences that we have in dreams. When we dream, we have the experience of seeing things, tasting foods, hearing sounds, and so on. While we are dreaming, we feel certain that our experience is reliable. Then how can we be certain that our so-called waking experiences are not as illusory as our dream experiences? In fact, how can we be sure that what we consider a waking experience is not actually part of a dream? We may admit that while we are dreaming we cannot be sure, but that as soon as we wake up we are able to tell the difference; we are able to decide what actually happened, and what we merely dreamed. We may have dreamed that we were rowing across the Atlantic Ocean, but when we awaken and find ourselves in our bedroom, we are now sure that the experience of rowing was illusory and was only part of a dream. When we awaken we can perform various tests to ascertain what has actually happened, and hence what portion of our sense "knowledge" is reliable. But, Descartes pointed out, the tests that we perform may also be part of a dream; our experience of awakening may itself be such a phenomenon. We may dream that we have tried to ascertain that the events we are experiencing are actually taking place. We dream that we have pinched ourselves, that we have looked around, asked other people, and so on. Since this has happened to us, or could happen to us, how can we be sure at any given moment that any effort that we made to tell if we are now awake or asleep was not part of a dream? Any evidence we might offer *might* be dream evidence. If we produced witnesses to testify that we were really awake, we might merely be dreaming that these witnesses existed and were so testifying. Hence, Descartes contended, we actually do not have any absolute guarantee that any of our sense experience, past or present, is not part of a continuous dream. (Pascal, in commenting on this section in Descartes, pointed out that we cannot even be sure that what we consider waking up is not actually falling asleep, and vice versa, or that we cannot be sure that we are not living in a continuous dream with two alternating cycles, one of which we call "being awake" and the other "being asleep.")

Descartes' reason for casting doubt on our sense information can be posed in terms of modern science fiction. In a well-known story, *Donovan's Brain*,[1] a brain is kept alive in a jar in the laboratory of a scientist. By means of various electrical devices, and chemical contraptions, the brain is nourished and given various stimuli so that it *thinks* that different events are taking place. In such a circumstance, the brain might receive the stimuli that would produce the effect of eating a juicy steak, or listening to a symphonic concert, when, in fact, nothing like that was taking place. If the scientific techniques were perfect, it might be possible to give the brain the necessary stimuli so that it "experienced" every event that occurs in a given day in the life of any one of us. If we are willing to assume that this could be done, then could any of us be completely certain that it is not, in fact, happening to us right now? Perhaps, for all that we actually know, we are residing in jars in some mad scientist's laboratory, and we are so controlled that we *think* we are complete, active human beings, who walk and talk, and eat and drink! Somewhat similar situations were depicted in TV series such as "Mission Impossible," "The Man from U.N.C.L.E," and "Switch" where completely illusory worlds were created for the villains, who were made to believe they were in submarines about to sink, or in bunkers with World War III going on above them. The villains became so disturbed by these fake worlds that they surrendered or reformed.

Descartes, in applying his test, simply wanted to show that the possibility exists, and cannot be disproved, that all our sense experience is illusory. Whether one thinks the dream hypothesis, or that raised by *Donovan's Brain*, is probable does not matter. What is of concern is that it is possible, no matter how unlikely the possibility may be, that all our information about the outside world and about ourselves may actually be only part of a dream sequence, and may have nothing to do with events in the real world, if there is such a world. If this is possible, then, no matter how certain we may feel about our sense information, it is nonetheless open to doubt.

Descartes then proceeded to carry his investigation of our beliefs one step further. One might be willing to admit that our sense information is, in some slight measure, dubious. But at the same time there seem to be

---

[1] K. Siodimak, *Donovan's Brain* (Knopf, New York, 1943).

fixed and reliable aspects to our information of which we feel certain. Even if we cannot be absolutely certain that our experience is about a real world, and not simply part of a dream, can we not, nonetheless, be sure about various facts about the content of our experience? Whether we are asleep or awake, we seem to be certain that snow is white, that grass is green, that lobsters don't fly, and that bodies don't fall upward. We find that exact sciences can be developed about the materials of our experience, and that these exact sciences provide us with laws about how different objects behave. In view of this, can't we be sure that our scientific information derived from experience is about something, and that the sciences teach us the fixed properties of the world that we live in?

Descartes, continuing to apply his Method of Doubt, pointed out that even our alleged scientific knowledge may be false or doubtful. In our imaginations, we can create objects like unicorns and mermaids which do not actually exist. Our experience may be like our imagination, if the dream hypothesis is a serious possibility. If it is possible that we are always dreaming, we have no way of telling whether the things we experience are patterned after something that really exists. All of what we think we know about the world may be illusory or imaginary; it may be no more than something we "dream up." If this is possible, then both the objects that we may be dreaming of or imagining and the sciences that we work out about them may have no relation to what is actually going on in the world. Objects, such as trees and dogs, might be figments of our imagination, and the sciences concerning them may be just as fictitious as the objects. Physics, chemistry, and biology may be as scientific as the study of unicorns and mermaids. Such sciences could be exact and precise, and still be only about illusory or fictitious objects that do not in fact exist.

Even if one is willing to carry doubt this far, there still seems to be something that we can be certain of. Even if life is nothing but a dream, there is still an order of events, and some fixed relationships within the events. Even if everything that we experience is just a figment of our vivid imaginations, or our wild dreams, every triangle that we can think of has three sides, and every sum of 3 and 4 comes out 7. No matter how illusory that world may be, the geometrical and arithmetical relationships that we discover within it seem to be fixed, reliable, and beyond any serious doubt. Descartes, after pushing us to the brink of complete skeptical despair, appeared ready to give us a straw to clutch when he announced, "For whether I am awake or asleep, two and three together always make five, and the square can never have more than four sides, and it does not seem possible that truths so clear and apparent can be suspected of any falsity or uncertainty."

But, just when we seem about to be rescued from the sea of doubts let loose by Descartes' test, he raised the last, and, perhaps, most far-reaching reason for doubting, a reason which suggests that even the information that we feel most certain about may actually be false, or at least open to question. This climax to his Method of Doubt is Descartes' famous Demon Hypothesis. Suppose, Descartes suggested, there is a deity or a demonic force that has sufficient power to mislead us all without our ever knowing it. If there were such a force, it could lead us astray all the time, and it could systematically deceive us, so that any test we made could also be deceptive. If $2 + 2 = 78\frac{1}{4}$, but we are all forced to think that $2 + 2 = 4$, could we ever find out the truth? No, Descartes insisted, since if we are being deceived by a being powerful enough to affect our thoughts and beliefs, he could also affect any efforts we put forth to discover if we were being deceived. Hence, if such a demonic possibility is actually occurring, the fact that we are absolutely certain that $2 + 2 = 4$, and that a triangle has three sides, would only show how successful the demon has been in influencing us. If there were a demon loose in the world who wished to deceive us, then it would always be possible that *anything* that we thought we knew, and *anything* that we were completely certain of, might actually be false. Therefore, even our most assured beliefs are open to doubt.

In the mid-twentieth century it is, unfortunately, no longer necessary to concoct so remote a possibility as Descartes' Demon Hypothesis in order to indicate this final and ultimate reason for doubting what we accept as most certain. Instead of positing the possibility of some super-natural agency that wants to play tricks on us, we have only to imagine what might happen if we were dominated and controlled by some sinister human agency that wanted to "brain-wash" us. Such an organization, like the one described by Aldous Huxley in *Brave New World*, or by George Orwell in *1984*, might force us to believe all sorts of things that were not true, and might be able to accomplish this without our even being aware that we were being brain-washed. Huxley described a world of people raised from test tubes, in which by proper chemical mixtures they would have intellectual outlooks and beliefs desired by the society. If some mistake were made in the chemical formulae, the misfits who thereby developed would be cast out of the society. Recent work in biochemistry has led to discussions of worlds like Huxley's becoming a reality through genetic engineering, in which duplicates of existing people could be created, or people could be altered by changing their genes.

In Orwell's description of the totalitarian state, the Ministry of Truth brain-washed people all day long, and constantly watched them to make sure they did not have deviant thoughts. Recalcitrant cases were given special treatment until they thoroughly accepted the official views of the society. The processes Orwell described bear an all too uncomfortable resemblance to propaganda and police practices that we now know exist in the present world. In Orwell's society, people are trained to believe that "War is peace," "Freedom is slavery," and even that "2 + 2 = 5." In view of what we now know of propaganda techniques, brain-washing, and so on, can we be sure that we are not, right now, the products of such a world? Can we be certain that we are not being deluded all the time by human or superhuman forces? (Any certainty we may have about this could also be the effect of our brain-washing.)

If we consider an example, such as adding two and two, we may be completely certain that the answer is four, and we may feel that nothing whatsoever could succeed in making us doubt the result. But Descartes' Demon Hypothesis, in its supernatural or its human form, indicates that the result still *might* be wrong. If we tried to check our addition by counting very carefully, by enlisting the aid of many careful and trust-worthy assistants, would we be able to eliminate all doubt? No! Our check might also be the result of some kind of deception, as might also be the check made by our assistants. If we are being systematically deceived, all attempts at checking, and all our methods of reasoning, might be nothing but ways of confirming us in our errors. The demon or the Ministry of Truth might have taught us all sorts of false or illusory processes for seeking the truth, so that each time we employ these methods, instead of getting closer to the truth, we in fact get further away from it. If, in addition, we have been trained to be completely satisfied with the results of these procedures, and to call them "logical," "rational," and so on, we might proceed all through our lives coming to one false conclusion after another, and we might never be aware of it. In such a world, no matter how carefully and logically we reasoned, and no matter what degree of certainty we reached, we could still be in error. In such a world, would there be *anything* left that we could be sure that we knew?

The doubts raised by Descartes' test make us aware that there is an enormous difference between what we originally thought we knew, and what, if anything, we can still be sure that we know. The possibility of (1) sense illusions, (2) the possibility that all our experience is part of a dream, and (3) the possibility that we are being systematically deceived all the time—all these raise serious doubts about the reliability of what we think we know. Do we possess any information at all that can withstand the doubts raised by this test? Descartes' *First Meditation* seems to have eroded all his (and our) confidence in his claims to knowledge: "At the end I feel constrained to confess that there is nothing at all that I formerly believed to be true, of which I cannot in some measure doubt." Everything that he previously thought he knew from ordinary sense experience, every-thing that he thought he knew through scientific study, and everything that he thought he knew through the most careful and exact reasonings—all of this *might* be false. At least, and at the very least, Descartes had offered a reason for doubting each of these types of knowledge.

Descartes' purpose in applying his Method of Doubt to all accepted information, beliefs, and opinions was not to transform everyone into a complete skeptic. Instead, he insisted that by the proper use of doubt, and only by the use of it, can men finally achieve complete certainty about anything. The application of the Method of Doubt makes us see that the foundation upon which our beliefs and assurances rest is extremely shaky indeed. When this had been pointed out, then Descartes proceeded to seek for a basis for our knowledge that would be so certain "that all of the most extravagant suppositions brought forward by the skeptics would be incapable of shaking it." But, Descartes insisted, unless we were willing, at least once in our lives, to test all of our beliefs, we would never be able to find such a secure foundation for our knowledge. Until we had performed such a test, and until we had found some knowledge that could survive such a test, we could never actually be certain that what we believed most strongly would not turn out to be false, or doubtful.

Descartes' *First Meditation* appears to end in a completely catastrophic manner, having eliminated the possibility of any certainty whatsoever. But, Descartes contended, one is obliged to continue on this path of doubting everything until one becomes sure of something; at the very least we can be certain that everything is uncertain. If we can find one truth so certain that it cannot possibly be false, we may then have a starting point for constructing a firm foundation for all human knowledge.

Descartes' *Second Meditation* reveals this starting point. It is discovered by attempting to carry one's doubts to the farthest possible limits. After considering the kinds of doubts offered, we suddenly discover that something must be true. Even if there really is no physical world, even if I am really asleep all the time, and even if I am deceived all the time, I must, at least, exist. No matter what I doubt, or why I doubt it, I must exist to do the doubting.

If we apply Descartes' Method of Doubt, and try to conceive of some conditions under which we might not actually exist, even though we think we do, we discover that there is something very peculiar in this case. Any time that we attempt to pose our doubts we find that we have to exist in order to have the doubts. If, perchance, there really is a very powerful demon who is at work deceiving me, and making me believe things that are not true, can he make me believe I exist when actually I do not? To be deceived by the demon I must exist, and so, at least I can be sure of my existence.

To put the matter in another way, let me try my utmost to doubt that I exist. Suppose that I exist, but that I am mistaken in this. But, if I think I

exist, I have to be here to do the thinking. If I doubt that I exist, doubting
is a form of thinking. So, once again, I must exist to engage in doubting.
Any time that I consider the proposition "I exist," and ponder whether it
is true or false, I must obviously be present in order to contemplate the
matter.

Thus the statement, "I think, therefore I am," (better known in its
Latin version, "Cogito, ergo sum"), has the peculiar property that whenever it is entertained by anyone it *must* be true. Every time that I attempt
to conceive of some way in which it could possibly be false or doubtful, I
find I only succeed in confirming its truth. For each time I must engage in
thinking, and if I think, I have to exist to do the thinking. Every argument
against the proposition turns out to be one more proof of its truth.

The following anecdote may help to illustrate this. An American
philosopher, Morris Raphael Cohen, who taught at City College in New
York during his lifetime, was once giving a course in which he explained
Descartes' views, and the reasons Descartes gave for doubting everything.
He then told the students to read the *Meditations*. After the next meeting
of the class, one of the students came up to Professor Cohen. The student
looked terrible, desperately in need of sleep and a shave. He told Professor
Cohen that he was extremely disturbed, and was unable to get any rest
after reading Descartes, because he was no longer sure that he existed.
"Please, Professor Cohen," he is supposed to have asked, "tell me. Do I
exist?" And Professor Cohen is reported to have stared at him, and to
have asked in return, "Who wants to know?"

Descartes was sure that because of the peculiar character of the
proposition "I think, therefore I am," he had finally found a truth so
certain that no skeptical argument could cast doubt on it. If every doubt
served to reveal once more that this proposition was certain, then here,
perhaps, was the point at which to begin the construction of an indubitable foundation for human knowledge. If one examined this truth, and
discovered why it was true, or what features of it showed that it was true,
then one might be able to set up a standard or criterion for judging all
other propositions, and for determining whether they really are true.

At the beginning of the *Third Meditation*, Descartes scrutinized the
proposition, "I am a thing that thinks," to discover what it is that convinced him of its truth. The only thing that he could find is what he called
"the clear and distinct perception" of what is asserted. This would not be
sufficient to convince him were it possible that something could be clearly
and distinctly perceived, and yet could also turn out to be false. Therefore,
the features of clarity and distinctness are the marks or characteristics of a
true proposition.

If we review this reasoning more carefully, Descartes' contention
may become more apparent. By the Method of Doubt, a proposition has

been discovered that is absolutely certain, that cannot possibly be false. When we look at this proposition, why are we so convinced that it is true, and cannot possibly be false? Only because we see "clearly and distinctly" what it asserts. This, and this alone, according to Descartes, is the basis for our certitude. Now, if it were at all possible that something could be both "clear and distinct" and also false, then clarity and distinctness would not be enough to convince us beyond all possible doubt. Since we are so convinced, we are then justified in concluding that whatever is clearly and distinctly conceived of or perceived must be true. The one case of which we are certain provides us with a general rule, because the one case could not be certain (that is, it could be doubted) unless the general rule were also certain. Thus, by inspecting one truth, we discover a measuring stick to apply to all propositions to determine whether they are true or not. If the measuring stick were not accurate, then we could not have found the initial starting point, the one truth of which we cannot avoid being certain.

The meanings of Descartes' key terms *clear* and *distinct*, are not, at first sight, particularly clear and distinct. In *The Principles of Philosophy*, he offered the following explanation: "What a clear and distinct perception is. There are even some people who, in their entire life, perceive nothing so accurately as to be able to judge it properly. For the knowledge on which a certain and uncontestable judgment can be formed, ought not only to be clear, but distinct as well. I call that clear which is present and apparent to an attentive mind, just as we say that we see objects clearly when, being present to the perceiving eye, they operate on it with sufficient strength. But the distinct is that which is so precise and different from everything else that it contains nothing within itself but what is clear."

This passage may seem to make matters more baffling. What Descartes appears to mean is that an experience or an idea is called "clear" whenever it is sufficiently forceful so that we cannot avoid being aware of it. He usually offered two kinds of examples, the first consisting of vivid sense experiences, such as toothaches, and the other of thoughts or ideas, such as mathematical concepts or mental activities, say, wishing and thinking. In all these examples, we are presumably forced to be aware that something is taking place, either in our sense experiences or in our minds.

In a subsequent passage in the *Principles*, Descartes stated that an idea can be clear without being distinct, but that it cannot be distinct without at the same time being clear. Thus "clarity" and "distinctness" are two separate characteristics. An experience or an idea is clear but not distinct, Descartes said, when we are aware of, but at the same time are not sure of, its exact or precise nature. To illustrate this, Descartes offered the case of a toothache. Anyone who has a toothache knows that he has it. And if he cannot avoid being aware of it, then the experience of the toothache is "clear." But, when we have this sort of experience, we are not really certain what a toothache is, or where it is located. We cannot tell if it is an event in our mind, or an event in the physical tooth, or both. It is often very difficult for us to tell the dentist which tooth is bothering us. (This type of problem becomes more evident with headaches, which, when we have them, make themselves known clearly enough. But when we try to describe and locate them, we often find that we become extremely vague.)

The difficulty Descartes was pointing to is that we can have experiences which are sufficiently forceful so that they rank as "clear," but at the same time we are not able to know them, or describe them, so that they can be definitely distinguished from everything else. When we can describe or define an item so that there is no possibility of confusing it with anything else, then it is "distinct" as well as "clear." Any idea that we could define precisely enough so that it would be "distinct" would also have to be clear, since we would be able to make the distinctions involved in defining the idea only if it were sufficiently forceful. The idea of a circle, for example, is "distinct," since a definition of a "circle" can be given such that one can distinguish a circle from everything else there is. We are able to give a definition of a circle only because we have a clear idea of it. With regard to the toothache, even though the experience is clear, we unfortunately are not able to give an adequate definition of it that avoids all possibility of vagueness and confusion.

In terms of these notions of clarity and distinctness, we can now proceed to examine Descartes' theory of knowledge. If, for the reasons offered earlier, we can be sure "that whatever is clearly and distinctly conceived is true," we can now go on from our first truth, and our standard for measuring truths, to discovering additional truths. We can now examine our ideas to see which of them can be classed as "clear and distinct."

In the course of the *Third Meditation*, Descartes indicated that the ideas we receive from our sense experience or our imagination are not both clear and distinct. Some are neither, and others are only clear. But, in addition to all of our sensory experiences of things like trees and houses, and of our imaginings of items like mermaids and unicorns, there is still another kind of idea, which will prove to be the source of all of our further knowledge. This type is called an "innate idea," because it cannot be the result of either our sense experience or our imagination.

The kind of ideas that Descartes found to be innate are the mathematical ones, and the idea of God. The ideas of circles, of numbers, and of God have features which cannot come from our experience or imagination. For example, neither the circles that we see nor the ones that we can draw are perfectly round. They do not meet the definition of a circle as "the locus of all points equidistant from a given point." Thus we could not acquire this idea of a circle from our experience, since nothing in experience conforms exactly to the definition. We could not acquire the idea from our imagination, because, Descartes insisted, our imagination is based on our experience. Descartes' point becomes more evident with regard to the idea of God, or the idea of a Perfect Being. God is defined as "a substance that is infinite, eternal, immutable, independent, all-knowing, all-powerful, and by which I myself, and everything else, if anything else does exist, have been created." No object in my experience is infinite, eternal, and so on. Therefore, I could not derive this idea from my experience. Also, I do not have the properties within me; hence I could not invent the idea. Thus, ideas like those of circles and of God must have another source, and must have come to us by some other means than experience or imagination. They are, therefore, called "innate." They are *a priori*, that is prior to and independent of all experience. (Recently the noted theoretician of linguistics, Noam Chomsky, in his book *Cartesian Linguistics*, has offered a new version of the theory of innate ideas, contending that our ability to use language must be innate and cannot be gained from experience.)

If we examine the idea of God or a Perfect Being further, we are forced to the conclusion that there must be a Being with at least the properties included in the definition. I have a clear and distinct idea of God. (The fact that a precise definition of the term *God* can be given indicates this.) Now, where does this idea come from? Not from my experience, since there is nothing infinite, eternal, immutable, and so on, in my experience. Not from myself, since I cannot find these perfections in myself. I am aware of all sorts of defects in myself. So, I am not a Perfect Being. Next, Descartes contended, the cause of an idea must have in itself at least the properties of the idea. (He maintained that this thesis was clear and distinct, and hence true.) I am imperfect; hence I cannot be the cause of my idea of God. In fact, if the cause of an idea must have at least the properties of the idea, then the idea of God could come only from a Being who was at least "infinite, eternal, immutable, etc." Therefore, since I possess such a clear and distinct idea, there must be a Perfect Being, a Being who has created me and has given me this idea.

Thus, from the fact that I have clear and distinct ideas, I am able to establish a further truth: that there must be a God who has given me these ideas. At the beginning of the *Fourth Meditation*, Descartes announced on the basis of this discovery that he had found a means to proceed from the contemplation of God to knowledge of many other truths about the world. This is accomplished by showing that the God who must exist cannot be a deceiver, and hence that whatever He makes us believe must be true.

Descartes' argument is that our clear and distinct idea of God shows that He cannot be a deceiver. Our idea of God is that of a Perfect Being. Committing fraud or deception is an imperfection. Therefore, according to our idea of God, He cannot defraud or deceive. (Some of Descartes' critics were most skeptical at this point, and insisted that a finite, limited being like Descartes could not be so sure that a Perfect and Omniscient Being might not have very good reasons for deceiving humans. They pointed out that if Descartes accepted the Bible as an accurate account of God's behavior, then there are some passages which indicate that God has already engaged in deceptions.)

If God is not and cannot be a deceiver, then we can also be sure that God is not and cannot be the evil demon introduced in the *First Meditation*. Then the knowledge that God gives us, and forces us to believe, cannot be rendered suspect any more by the hypothesis that the world might be run by a Cosmic Deceiver. The *Fourth Meditation* eliminates the possibility that we might be the victims of some kind of demonic menace. Freed from this danger, we can now proceed to find out what it is that God wishes and forces us to believe. With the Demon Hypothesis set aside, we can now put complete trust in whatever knowledge God gives to us.

When we examine our rational faculties, we find that we are forced to believe things about only clear and distinct ideas. Any time that we are confronted with a clear and distinct idea, we are compelled to assent to it, that is to accept whatever we conceive of clearly and distinctly as true. Since God, who is Omnipotent, makes us believe this, and since He cannot be a deceiver, we can then be sure that we have not erred when we assent to something that is clear and distinct. We also find that we are not compelled to believe anything that is not clear and distinct, and that we can suspend our judgment on these matters. If we do make a decision about matters that are unclear or indistinct, it is on our own responsibility and not God's. Hence, regarding unclear and indistinct ideas, we have no assurance based on our idea of God that what we may decide or wish to believe is true. Our judgment is guaranteed only with regard to the small area of clear and distinct innate ideas that we receive from God.

Descartes contended that falsity and error are due to a basic human defect. Unfortunately, we want to decide questions even when we do not have clear and distinct ideas. Our will to judge goes beyond the guaranteed limits of our judgment, and we come to conclusions about ideas when we no longer have God's assurance that we are doing the right thing. Any time that we make a judgment about any ideas that are not clear and distinct, we are taking a chance, and we are liable to err. If we make a mistake, it is then always our fault and not God's. If we were able to restrict ourselves so that we judged only when we had to, then we would never be wrong. Thus in mathematics we can attain certain knowledge because our ideas are clear and distinct. But with regard to judgments based on sense experience, there is always the danger of error because our ideas may be clear without being distinct.

Since we have a guarantee from God, who is no deceiver, about our clear and distinct ideas, what can we actually know? We can know with certainty that we exist, that God exists, and that, because God cannot deceive, whatever is clearly and distinctly conceived is true. Since we have clear and distinct ideas in mathematics, we can be sure of our mathematical knowledge as long as it involves only these ideas. But beyond this, can we be certain that mathematics applies to anything? Can we be certain that there is a physical world? Our mathematical knowledge that is guaranteed by the fact that God would not deceive us, is knowledge only about ideas in our minds. Is it possible to gain knowledge about anything outside our minds other than God?

When we examine our clear and distinct ideas, we find the only ones that we have of physical objects are ideas of their mathematical properties. Thus when we think of a body, if we are clear and distinct about it, we think of it as having a certain size, shape, position, and so on. We can have clear and distinct ideas regarding these matters, since what we can know are the mathematical relationships. But this still does not allow us to establish that bodies exist apart from us. We know only that, if the dimensions of a body are 4 by 3 feet, it has a certain volume if it exists. But the question still remains, "Does it exist?"

In the *Fifth* and *Sixth Meditations*, Descartes admitted that we cannot answer this important question by examining our clear and distinct ideas of bodies. Such ideas do not tell us whether there are bodies or not. Our only way to establish that there are bodies is by indirect means, such as the very elaborate and intricate proof offered at the beginning of the *Sixth Meditation*. We find that we have a natural tendency to believe that there is a physical world, and to believe that our sense experience consists of ideas relating to such a world. When I see a tree I have a natural tendency to believe that there is a physical tree outside me, and that the one I see is related to and produced by the physical one. But does this prove that there is actually a tree outside me?

According to Descartes, there are three possibilities. First, that I myself am the cause of my ideas of physical objects, that there really are no physical objects, and that it is simply an error that I attribute my experience to a physical world outside me. Second, that God produces my ideas of physical objects, that there really are no physical objects, and that it is simply an error that I attribute my experience to physical objects. Third, that there are physical objects, corresponding to some extent to my experience, from which I get my ideas, and that I do not err in following my natural tendency to attribute my experience to a physical world outside me.

The first possibility is ruled out by the fact that I have no awareness of creating my own experience, and that I cannot make myself experience what I want to. The second possibility could be true. God has the power to give me the sense experience I have even if there are no physical objects corresponding to such experience. However, He has also created me with a natural tendency to believe that there are physical objects. If there actually are none, then God would be deceiving me in giving me the ideas, and making me think that they had another source. Since God is no deceiver, the second possibility is ruled out. All that remains is the third one. Hence we can also be sure that there is a physical world, corresponding to some extent to our experience.

What can we know about this physical world? Only what is clear and distinct. This means that we can know only the mathematical properties of physical objects. We cannot be sure that they have colors, smells, or tastes, since we do not have clear and distinct ideas of these properties. Hence our scientific knowledge amounts only to mathematical physics, treated in terms of our clear and distinct ideas, a knowledge of the physical world in terms of its properties of extension and motion. The mathematical properties, Descartes believed, sufficed to explain all natural objects, whether animate or inanimate.

Descartes, then, started with grave doubts as to whether we could know anything, and ended with the contention that we could have a very extensive amount of indubitable knowledge. We can know with absolute certitude that we exist, that God exists, that God is no deceiver, that whatever we clearly and distinctly conceive of is true, that mathematics is true because we conceive it clearly and distinctly, that a physical world exists since God makes us believe that one does, and that insofar as we have clear and distinct ideas about the physical world, we can have a certain and indubitable science of it (that is, insofar as our ideas of physical objects include geometrical and arithmetical relationships, we can be certain about these aspects of the physical world). What we cannot know with certainty is whether the indistinct features of our sense experience are true, whether the colors, sounds, smells, tastes, and feelings that we have correspond to any objective state of affairs. As long as we judge only about the clear and distinct ideas that God has implanted in us, we cannot err. When we go beyond this, we no longer have any way of freeing ourselves from doubt.

MALEBRANCHE'S THEORY OF KNOWLEDGE

An interesting development of Descartes' theory of knowledge occurs in the writings of Father Nicolas Malebranche (1638–1715), a French priest. Malebranche was dissatisfied with all the theories about the universe that he had studied, but one day by chance he found a work of Descartes' in a bookstore in Paris. He meditated upon Descartes' views for several years, and finally, in 1674, published the first volume of his great work, *The Search after Truth*, in which he presented a modified form of Descartes' philosophy. Malebranche spent the rest of his life fighting against a great many opponents and trying to prove that his views, as well as those of Descartes, were not unorthodox from a Christian standpoint. Nevertheless, the Jesuits succeeded in having the teachings of both philosophers forbidden in France. (Actually, the principal issue on which Descartes was attacked does not involve anything that we have discussed. He was challenged primarily for his explanation of transubstantiation. Malebranche was attacked principally for his views on grace and on the problem of whether God is responsible for evil.)

To a large extent, Malebranche's theory of knowledge is similar to that of Descartes. However, Malebranche disagreed with Descartes' view about the basis of our knowledge of the existence of the physical world. Malebranche argued that there cannot be any demonstration that God *had* to create a physical world. If God is all-powerful, then He can do what He wishes, and He is not required to create anything that He does not wish to. From examining the idea of God that we have, all we can tell is that there is no necessary relationship between God's Nature and the existence of anything. Hence, Malebranche insisted, we cannot tell from the clear and distinct idea of God whether there is or is not a physical world. If there is one, God has arbitrarily decided to create it.

Further, when we analyze our idea of God as an All-Powerful Being, we see that He must be the cause of everything. If He were not, then there would be some power that God does not possess. Thus God must be the cause of our ideas and of everything that takes place. The knowledge that we can obtain consists of the illuminations that God decides to give us. This comprises our clear and distinct ideas. (Malebranche disdainfully classified sense experience as "feelings.") We have only clear and distinct ideas of mathematical objects and of God. When we try to think about physical things, the only ideas that we can have, as distinct from feelings, are mathematical ones. (There is a passage in Malebranche's *Dialogues on Metaphysics* where a student is asked to discuss music. The student begins to sing, and Malebranche informs him that this is no time for amusement. The student next describes the structure of musical instruments, but Malebranche insists that he is not interested in carpentry. They finally discuss mathematical relationships, the only clear and distinct ideas that we can have about music.)

Mathematical information gives us knowledge about what Malebranche called "intelligible extension," which exists in God and not in the outside world. When we know anything, we are knowing ideas in the Mind of God. Malebranche summed this up in his slogan, "We see all things in God." It is God who allows us to know anything by illuminating us, and letting us see something concerning the intelligible extension in Him. We can have indubitable knowledge about intelligible extension, and this is our knowledge of mathematics and mathematical physics. But we cannot know anything about the physical world, even that it exists, since this is not included in what we "see in God." We cannot prove, as Descartes tried to, that because of the Nature of God, there must be a physical world. According to Malebranche, it does not follow that God *must* have created a world. By means of our rational capacities, we can compile a vast sum of knowledge about mathematics and about the physics of intelligible extension. But we can know nothing whatsoever about the physical objects that may or may not exist outside us. As we shall see later on, in Chapter 2, "Metaphysics," Malebranche consistently followed out the consequences of this view, and even contended that we can have no contact with a physical world, if there is one. All our ideas and feelings are caused by God, and they would be the same whether a physical world exists or not.

Thus in Malebranche's version of the Cartesian theory, we can know with complete certainty only about God, and about mathematical ideas, the intelligible extension that we are allowed to see in God by His Illumination. If anyone is seriously worried about whether there is something else in the universe, such as physical objects, it is fortunate that we have another source of information, Revelation. In the first chapter of Genesis we are told that, in fact, God has created a physical world. It is only by faith, and not by any rational means, that we are able to gain any information about this aspect of the universe.

CRITICISMS OF RATIONALIST
THEORIES OF KNOWLEDGE

The theories of knowledge of such philosophers as Plato, Descartes, and Malebranche are classified as "rationalist theories" because they maintain that we can acquire information that cannot possibly be false by the use of our reason alone. Many rationalist theories, including the three discussed above, insist that we cannot attain any certainty by means of our senses, nor can we attain certainty about the objects of sense experience. What we can know are mental objects, and these are known by reason and not by the senses. It is often asserted by the rationalists that the objects that we can know with complete certainty are the real and important ones of the world, and that the others are either illusory, unreal, or trivial.

Ever since the time of Plato there have been many philosophers who have criticized the assertions of the rationalists, especially their contention that they have actually discovered some information that cannot possibly be false. The opposition has expressed doubts that any human being has achieved—or could achieve—such a high degree of certitude. They have also attacked the view that there actually are such objects of genuine knowledge as Platonic Ideas, or Descartes' innate ideas, or Malebranche's intelligible extension. Even the most certain propositions offered by the rationalists, such as "I think, therefore I am," have been subjected to a searching scrutiny, and, according to the critics, have been found less than absolutely certain.

If we turn to particular criticisms, and start with some of those directed against Plato's views, the critics have attacked Plato's basic contention that we have to be aware of Platonic Ideas in order to communicate information, and in order to recognize what is occurring in our experience. The fact that we all use general terms, such as "dog" and "square," may not prove that these general terms mean the same thing for each of us or that there exist real Platonic Ideas, such as "dogness" and "squareness." Plato had insisted that we could not know what we were talking about unless we were aware of what general terms meant, through apprehending the independently existing Platonic Ideas. But many philosophers, including some whom we shall consider in the next section, have said that in a sense we do not have general knowledge. They contend that when we talk about "dog" and "square," we are only referring to a group of particular cases we have experienced. Hence it is quite possible that our experience has been misleading, or that we use the words differently from the way other people use them. The critics are suggesting that the mere fact that general terms occur in languages, and are necessary to discuss our experience, is not sufficient proof that these terms have a special kind of meaning, or that they refer to objects different from the particular ones found in ordinary experience.

Some of Plato's opponents have argued that he never actually showed that the skepticism and relativism of the Sophists was unjustified. Instead, Plato only assumed that we *can* have knowledge. Plato pointed out that if the Sophists were right, then each man could only state his own opinion, and no one would have a guaranteed basis for asserting anything. *If* our lives are based on more than mere opinion, Plato argued, we must be able to obtain knowledge. The critics contend that this does not show that we possess more than mere opinions. Plato's argument is based on pointing out what would be the case if the Sophists were correct. The sad results he indicated do not actually disprove the Sophist theory, nor do they show that a totally different theory must be accepted instead.

Many of the critics have also expressed doubts that there are any such objects as Platonic Ideas, or if there are, that any human being is acquainted with them. Platonic Ideas, unlike other kinds of objects that we are acquainted with, cannot be sensed. Plato's descriptions of what they are like are often very baffling, being either metaphorical or vague. The method that he offered us for "recalling" the Ideas seems too time-consuming, with no guarantee that it will work. The Platonist can reply, of course, that the critic has not tried hard enough to "recall" the Ideas. When and if he does, all his doubts will disappear as soon as he is confronted with a Platonic Idea. All that the critic can do is keep repeating that he has never become acquainted with a Platonic Idea and doubts that he ever will.

Both Plato's Recollection Theory and Descartes' theory of innate ideas have been criticized because there does not seem to be any evidence of the prior existence of knowledge in our minds. The theories appear to run counter to our ordinary experience, in that babies and, in fact, most people exhibit no signs of possessing Platonic or innate ideas. The rationalist can reply, however, that the theory is not incompatible with our experience. Neither Plato nor Descartes contended that anybody was aware of having the ideas *until* the moment of recollection, or until he had applied the Method of Doubt. The theories are offered, primarily, as explanations of the knowledge that we find we have. The rationalists insist that their opponents can give no plausible explanation of how we are able to possess any absolutely certain information. (As a result, many of the opponents deny that we actually do have any such information.)

When we turn to specific criticisms of Descartes, we find that much of the philosophical work done in the last three centuries has involved developing criticisms of the Cartesian theory. When the *Meditations* was first published, appended to it was a series of criticisms by leading philosophers, scientists, and theologians of the time, plus Descartes' replies to his critics. These initial attacks contain most of the important objections that have ever been made to Descartes' theory. We shall here consider one basic point raised by two of the important scientists of the time, Fathers Mersenne and Gassendi, and by Descartes' first Jesuit opponent, Father Bourdin.

They all contended that Descartes' Method of Doubt is too destructive. If one took seriously the doubts raised in the *First Meditation*, the critics maintained, it would never actually be possible to achieve the degree of certitude Descartes said he discovered later on. Once one accepted the possibility that an evil demon exists who could systematically deceive everybody, then could one ever find anything that was completely certain? If the demon could deceive us about even our most evident reasonings, then could we be sure that he did not deceive us about our own existence, or about any of the certainties that came after that? Any arguments that Descartes might offer to show that we cannot doubt our own existence might be the result of the demon's efforts. Even the argument proving that God cannot be a deceiver may actually be another one of the demon's clever deceptions. If one accepted all the doubts of the *First Meditation*, each step one took afterward could always be challenged and cast in doubt because the evil demon might be at work. Descartes answered that he had not intended the initial doubts as serious ones, but only as hypothetical ones. But if this were the case, then he had admitted that he never had, in fact, applied the Method of Doubt to its fullest extent, and thus he could not be sure that the truths he discovered were absolutely certain.

His critics pointed out that when all was said and done, Descartes had introduced a possibility of doubt that could never actually be eradicated, no matter what certitudes he produced. We could never be sure that the truths we are forced to accept are the absolute truths known to God. For all that we can ever tell, we have to believe these truths, but, from God's point of view, our truths might actually be false. We might possess this wonderful system of innate ideas in our minds, but could we ever be really sure that these truths in our minds also constituted truths about something *outside* our minds? The wonderful system of Descartes might only consist of a group of beliefs which we had to accept, but which we could never check against the real world. All that we ever know are our own ideas. Every demonstration offered by Descartes to show that our clear and distinct ideas must be true is itself only one more idea in our minds. Thus, no matter how hard Descartes might try, he could never show that our innate ideas did not constitute merely a delusion or illusion *in our minds*.

This objection, which he called "the objection of objections," Descartes admitted, shows that ultimately we could never go beyond discovering what was indubitable to a human being, and that what was indubitable to a human being might still be false in some absolute sense. But, then, Descartes insisted, this did not matter since we could not know what went on beyond man's world. If we were not willing to accept mere human certitudes, we would have to "shut the door on reason." This might be the case, but it revealed that Descartes now had to admit that he could not eliminate all possible doubts, and that he could not achieve a degree of certitude that no skeptic could challenge.

These criticisms indicate that Descartes either doubted too much or too little. If he had ever really accepted the doubts of the *First Meditation*, could he overcome them in order to discover the knowledge that followed in the later *Meditations*? If he never actually had the doubts, then could he ever be sure that the truths he proclaimed were not open to question? Thus, either he was too much a skeptic to discover rational knowledge, or too little a skeptic to be certain of the knowledge he believed he had discovered. (Perhaps somewhat in despair after arguing for many years with his critics, Descartes wrote that he believed that once in one's lifetime one should raise every possible doubt, and should inspect all of one's beliefs to see if they were really certain. But one should do it *only once!*)

Malebranche had sought to avoid one of the pitfalls that he saw in Descartes' theory of knowledge: trying to ascertain whether the ideas that we have in our minds apply to a reality outside our minds. Malebranche insisted that our ideas *are* reality. When we have an idea, we are "seeing God," thereby knowing something directly about the intelligible extension in the Mind of God. This might eliminate the difficulty involved in establishing that our truths are the same as God's truths, since any truth that we know is really God's idea, and not our own. However, some of Malebranche's critics pointed out that this theory appears to raise even greater difficulties than the problems it is intended to solve. Since we all make mistakes sometimes, how can we ever tell when we are "seeing God," and when we merely think that we do? Can we tell the difference between being illuminated by God, and thinking that we are illuminated when we are not? If we have to judge by the ideas that we possess, we are once more involved in Descartes' basic difficulty: attempting to establish what is true outside our minds by what is inside our minds. If we judge by what is in God's Mind, then we have to have some way of distinguishing a true vision of the Divine Mind from an illusion. Either everything that we know is one of God's ideas, in which case it seems difficult, if not impossible, to explain how we sometimes have false information, or else only some of our ideas are God's ideas. If the latter is the case, then we would need some guaranteed means for distinguishing our human fancies from the Divine Truths among our ideas. And we can always ask, regarding any proposed means for distinguishing the two, "Is the means itself a Divine Truth, or is it merely another human delusion?"

Besides the difficulties involved in each of the particular rationalist theories that we have considered, there is a general type of objection to any theory of knowledge that maintains that human beings are capable of discovering or have discovered information about the world that cannot possibly be false. The great changes that have occurred in what we think we know about the world from Plato's time, or even from the time of Descartes and Malebranche, down to the present have made many philosophers exceedingly skeptical of pretensions to absolute knowledge. The picture of the universe accepted by scientists nowadays is radically different from that of the past. Can we be sure, in view of the revolutionary changes in scientific information that have occurred, and continue to occur, that what is regarded as absolutely certain at any given time will not be rejected or revised at a later date?

The rationalist philosophers might reply that the advances in science should not cast any doubts on their assertions, since science deals only with the world of sense experience, and not with the unchangeable realm of

Ideas. The rationalists have not stated that any information about objects in the visible world was indubitable. Instead, they said that there was another and more important world, concerning which we could achieve absolute certainty. The rationalists might contend that our knowledge about this "real" world has not changed at all, no matter what new information may have been gained about the sense world.

The opponents, in turn, can point out that the rationalists have never agreed among themselves as to what is true about this so-called real world. From Plato onward, different and competing theories have been offered. The proponents of each have contended that their theory is completely certain, and is a description of the genuine knowledge that we can have about the real world. Many incompatible propositions have been presented to us with complete assurances that they are "self-evident," "indubitable," and so on. Some of these do not appear to us to be "self-evident," but, rather, seem to be highly questionable. (If one looks at the list of axioms and postulates that Descartes presented in his answer to Mersenne, which he said are clear and distinct and evident, one is likely to be quite dubious about the whole matter.)

One extremely skeptical critic, Pierre Bayle (1647–1706), went so far as to question whether the fact that a given proposition was self-evident was sufficient evidence that it was also true. Bayle, who was raised as a Protestant, then briefly was a convert to Catholicism, and then returned to his original faith, claimed he was a Protestant in the true sense of the term—he was against everything that was said and everything that was done. His most famous work, *The Historical and Critical Dictionary* (1697–1702), attacked practically all the theories in philosophy, theology and science, past and present. In it he shocked his rationalist contemporaries by maintaining that a proposition could be self-evident and yet false. He tried to offer many examples of self-evident truths that are known to be false. Perhaps what the rationalist philosophers accept as self-evident is only a human measure of what we find that we cannot doubt. But this would only indicate our psychological limitations, and would tell us nothing about the truth of the propositions in question.

When one looks at that branch of human knowledge that the rationalists have usually considered as the best example of unquestionable and certain information—mathematics—one finds that even here there may be some grounds for doubting the rationalists' contentions. There have been some changes in our mathematical knowledge, and some of the views of earlier mathematicians have been either rejected or revised. There are even some disputes among present-day mathematicians over which theorems, and which branches of mathematics, can be considered as *really* certain and indubitable. Even though there have usually been fewer disagreements among mathematicians than among experts in any other field, the fact that there have been, and still are, some disagreements and changes in the subject indicates that mathematics may not be as certain as the rationalists would have us believe. The late philosopher of mathematics, Imre Lakatos, in his brilliant "Proofs and Refutations" (1964), has shown, by examining the history of a supposedly certain mathematical theorem set forth in the eighteenth century, how doubts creep into alleged mathematical certainties, and that the efforts to dispel these doubts do not completely succeed.

One particular development in geometry has raised some serious doubts as to whether this branch of mathematics provides indubitable knowledge about the world we live in. In the nineteenth century it was found that one could develop what are called non-Euclidean geometries. These are geometrical systems whose axioms differ from those of the standard Euclidean geometry. In each of these different geometries, theorems can be demonstrated which are not true in Euclidean geometry. Also, each of the non-Euclidean geometrical systems is perfectly consistent logically. Then which of these geometries provides us with true knowledge about the world? Each one of the systems is as logical, as evident, as clear and distinct as the others. To select one as the absolutely true one seems to be an entirely arbitrary and unjustified procedure. The fact that there can be alternative systems in geometry suggests, perhaps, that a given system does not contain one unique group of certain truths about the real world. Rather, it may present a series of sets of possible truths about various worlds which may or may not actually exist.

Some of the critics, in addition to casting doubts upon the rationalists' contention that we possess any indubitable and absolutely certain knowledge, have argued that we do not even need such knowledge to get along in this world. We seem to get along adequately, in our ordinary affairs, employing information that well might turn out to be false or doubtful. We manage to solve many of our problems by using scientific information which is not absolutely certain. Plato and Descartes maintained that there were grave dangers in living one's life on the basis of "mere" probabilities. But this may be all the information that we are ever actually able to find, that we ever want to find, and that we ever seem to need.

THE EMPIRICAL THEORY
OF KNOWLEDGE

Another view developed in opposition to the rationalist approach is called "the empirical theory of knowledge." Empiricists have felt that it is futile to search for absolute truths about the so-called real world, since we do not seem capable of finding any. They have therefore suggested that it would be more fruitful to start with the actual situation of human life, and to examine what information we have, where we get it from, and what degree of reliability it may have. Hence the empiricists insist that we should begin by examining our sense information, even though it may not be completely certain, since these data seem to be the source and foundation of most of what we think we know.

The modern empirical theory of knowledge is mainly the achievement of various English philosophers of the last three hundred years. In recent years, the empirical approach has become more and more popular in the United States as well, so that it is now probably *the* dominant philosophy in the English-speaking world.

It has been argued that empiricism developed principally in countries where there was a strong concern with practical and worldly problems. This has been offered as an explanation of the pervasive influence of empiricism in England, and more recently in North America. However, if this theory is correct, it seems somewhat odd that there has not been a corresponding interest in empirical thought in other countries where practical concerns have been of great importance—The Netherlands, Belgium and Switzerland, for example. In these societies, practical concerns have played a great role, but possibly because of their religious traditions or because of other factors, the philosophers have, by and large, continued to be concerned with the major modern rationalist theories of the French and German schools.

Whatever may be the reason, the modern empirical movement began early in the seventeenth century in England. That country was achieving world importance battling with Spain, France, and The Netherlands for control of the New World and for trade with the Orient. English commerce was expanding greatly, in large measure because of the practical achievements of the many great English scientists of the seventeenth century. While such famous English adventurers as Sir Francis Drake and Sir Walter Raleigh were laying the foundations of a great geographical empire, such scientific adventurers as Robert Boyle, Robert Hooke, and Sir Isaac Newton were making astounding discoveries and advancing new theories that were to provide the foundation for the modern empire of science and technology.

During a period of rapid physical and intellectual expansion that was beset with wars against their Continental rivals and interrupted by political and religious strife at home, many English thinkers began to sound the new note that was to dominate English thought thereafter. Writings by some of the scientists, the theologians, and the political theorists (often one individual appearing in all three guises) suggested that we should abandon the quest for a certainty which seems unattainable. Instead, these writers proposed that we settle for what we can find, the practical and useful information that is available to us. The theologian and scientist Joseph Glanvill announced, *"While men fondly doat on their private ap-*

*prehensions, and every conceited Opinionist sets up an infallible Chair in
his own brain, nothing can be expected but tumult and disorder.*" The
theologians, the scientists, and the political writers advocated that, instead
of seeking absolute truth, we should seek what we are capable of finding
—probable hypotheses that can be checked and tested by the course of
our sense experience. The theologian William Chillingworth proclaimed
that one cannot find any absolute truths about religion. Therefore one
ought to follow the practical methods of ordinary men to discover the
most reasonable or probable hypotheses about man's relations to God.
The scientists of the Royal Society insisted that it is impossible to find the
true nature of things. However, by a careful examination of our sense
experience, we can discover extremely important hypotheses about what is
taking place in the world. These hypotheses have enormous practical importance in terms of solving many human problems and improving
human life. The astounding achievements of the scientists of the Royal
Society, especially those of Hooke, Boyle, and Newton, were among the
fruits of this new outlook, and made even the most rationalistic philosophers on the Continent sit up and take notice. A reflection of this empirical approach can be seen in the many important developments in English
society in the seventeenth century: its achievement of religious peace and
toleration, its political democracy, and its Anglo-Saxon legal system.

The spokesmen for this new outlook regarding human knowledge
were not primarily professional philosophers, but, rather, were practical
men engaged in such worldly tasks as running the affairs of their country.
They were not really concerned with the traditional problems of the
philosophers, but instead with developing a new approach to knowledge
that would aid mankind in getting along in this world. Knowledge was no
longer to be considered as contemplation of eternal truths about "reality."
Instead, according to the famous phrase of Sir Francis Bacon, "knowledge
is power," the power to control nature for man's benefit.

Bacon (1561–1626), the Lord Chancellor under James I, was the
first important proponent of the empirical point of view in the seventeenth
century and was, perhaps, its greatest propagandist. In his *Novum
Organum* (*The New Instrument*), Bacon denounced the traditional philosophers, and ridiculed the futility of their search for Truth. Instead he
insisted that it was only by means of the examination of nature that
mankind could gain any useful information. Through the careful sifting of
our sense experience, we would gain knowledge and also power to control
the natural world.

John Locke's Theory of Knowledge

The most important statement of the empirical theory of knowledge
in the seventeenth century was made by John Locke (1632–1704). Locke
had been trained at Oxford as a medical doctor, but instead of practicing

medicine he became the private secretary to the Earl of Shaftesbury, and the tutor of his son. Locke and his patron had to flee from England because of their political involvements during the period of the Restoration. Until William of Orange became the King of England, after the Glorious Revolution of 1688, Locke lived in exile in The Netherlands. He then returned to his native land, and became one of the chief spokesmen for the new form of government, the constitutional monarchy. His writings on political theory (which we will consider in Chapter 3, "Political Philosophy"), on religion, and on the theory of knowledge were very popular and successful. Soon Locke was regarded as the greatest philosophical exponent of the new spirit in England.

The most extended statement of his empirical theory of knowledge appears in his *Essay Concerning Human Understanding*, an extremely lengthy work. In it Locke attempted to answer the question, "What can we know?" by discovering the nature and source of our knowledge, and the degrees of certitude that can be attained. By employing what he called "the plain historical method," Locke hoped to make both a positive and a negative contribution. He wished to show what can be known and how sure we can be about it as well as to show what cannot be known with the capacities that we possess, so that we might stop seeking for what cannot be found. This would serve to make us appreciate the merits of the information that we are able to acquire, while freeing us from further futile searches for information that we have no way of gaining.

Locke began his *Essay* by trying to justify the empirical theory about the origins of our knowledge, the thesis that our knowledge derives from our sense experience. To do this, Locke first attacked the opposite thesis, that of the rationalists: that we possess innate ideas that are the foundation of whatever knowledge we have. He insisted that there is not the slightest shred of evidence that there are any ideas or principles in our minds which have been there prior to our sense experiences, or that there are any ideas or principles in our minds which exist independently of all sense experience. When one examines the examples of innate knowledge that the earlier rationalist philosophers had said were implanted in our minds by God, one finds that many human beings are, in fact, unaware that they possess such knowledge. For instance, neither children nor idiots seem to know anything about the so-called innate truths of mathematics or philosophy. (The earlier English rationalist philosopher whom Locke was attacking, Herbert of Cherbury [1583–1648], had asserted that one could discover the innate truths by taking a poll of all mankind. But then if one found that children or idiots did not have any of the same ideas as the rest of mankind, this would indicate that there are no universally held truths, and, hence, no innate ideas. Herbert of Cherbury had tried to guard against just such an attack as Locke's by insisting that one did not have to count "persons who are out of their minds or mentally incapable."

But how is one to tell who falls into this classification? For Herbert, it seems that anyone who does not know the innate ideas is either out of his mind or mentally incapable. Thus one first has to use the innate ideas as a standard to tell whom to poll, which begs the whole question.)

Locke dismissed as silly or nonsensical the rationalist view, which both Plato and Descartes held, that one can possess the innate truths without being aware of them. What can be the significance of the innate ideas if they can be implanted in our minds without affecting our awareness at all? The innate ideas seem to make no difference in our mental lives. Hence the rationalist theory appears to be of no importance. An empirical inspection of human beings indicates that most of them know nothing about the alleged innate truths. If people actually have these truths in their minds, they apparently are not influenced at all by them.

Therefore, if we are going to try to understand what human beings know, we would do better, according to Locke, to start with the actual state of affairs. If we merely look at what occurs in our own lives, and reflect on our own experience, we will realize that our minds, at the outset, are no more than "white paper, void of all characters, without any ideas" (Locke's famous *tabula rasa*, that is, blank tablet). All that we know or think about are ideas that have come from experience. Locke contended that if we carefully examine the contents of our minds, we will see that everything that we are aware of comes either from our sense experience or from reflecting on the operations of the mind. Self-analysis will convince us that there are only two sources of our ideas and what we know about them—sensation and reflection.

To make his basic empirical thesis more convincing, Locke tried in the second book of the *Essay* to trace all of our ideas back to experiences of sensation or reflection. He called the units from which we build our knowledge "simple ideas." These ideas or experiences are completely uncompounded, that is, they are not composed of any other elements. (An "idea" for Locke is anything that is present to the mind.) Examples of these basic ideas are the yellow of a tulip, the taste of sugar, the smell of a rose, and the desire for a juicy steak. We learn the simple ideas from either sensation or reflection. Our minds have the ability to store up these experiences as memories, to repeat them when we wish, and to combine them into "complex ideas" after we have once experienced them. In the course of the second book of the *Essay* Locke attempted to show which of our ideas are the simple ones, and to show how the rest of what we are aware of is built up from these basic units which are derived from sensation and reflection. If it can be shown that we acquire all of the simple ideas from experience, and that everything that we think about is either a simple idea or a compound of simples, then Locke's theory of the origin of our knowledge has been established.

If all of our ideas come from experience, either as simple ideas, or as compounds of them, can we also tell which of our ideas are those of "real objects" and which are not? The fact that we have an idea is no guarantee that it is the idea of some object which exists outside our minds. Since we are able to reproduce and combine the simple ideas, it is possible that some of our ideas are made up by ourselves out of the basic ingredients. For example, the fact that we have an idea of a three-headed monster, composed of simple ideas that we have experienced of color, shape, and so on, does not show that a three-headed monster really exists in the world. If we inspect the ideas that we possess, how do we tell which "have a conformity with the real being and existence of things"? The problem occurs not only with regard to objects of our imagination, but also with regard to those which appear to be objects of immediate sensation. Can we ascertain that the objects of the actual world have all the features of which we are conscious in our experience? Locke, in seeking some stand-ard by which it can be determined which of our ideas informs us about "reality," was trying to establish what we can actually know about the world outside our minds by means of "the way of ideas."

We are able to distinguish two types of ideas among our experiences, Locke said. One of these consists of the ideas of primary qualities, the other of the ideas of secondary qualities. The former are features of our experience that must belong to the experienced object. The latter, the secondary qualities, are not in the objects themselves, but are the result of powers in the objects which can produce certain sensations in us by means of their primary qualities. Locke believed, for example, that when we see an apple, some of the qualities, the primary ones, that we perceive, belong to the real apple. These are its size, shape, solidity, and motion—qualities which a scientist might treat in analyzing the object. The other qualities—color, taste, smell, warmth, or coldness—are the secondary ones, which exist in our minds and not in the object itself. However, these secondary qualities are, in Locke's theory, produced by powers in the real apple. These powers are able to act upon us, so that when we look at an object of a certain size, shape, and so on, we also see yellow.

The distinction between primary and secondary qualities may ap-pear, at first, to be odd or arbitrary. However, if we consider what we are told about the objects of our ordinary experience by present-day physicists and chemists, we may see that Locke's point is often taken for granted in scientific analyses. We are told that ordinary objects, such as chairs, ta-bles, and people, are composed of collections of atoms moving rapidly in space, and that the atoms are further composed of groups of electrically charged particles moving rapidly in the space within the atoms. Most of the qualities that we usually perceive, the color, the warmth, and so on, are not "in the objects," but result from the action of certain features of the atomic groups upon our sense organs. Only certain features that we can perceive belong to the "real" table, which is composed of atomic constituents and their motions. In addition to its actual properties, the perceived one has those features which result from stimuli affecting our sense organs. Many of the perceived qualities would not be seen in the real object. If we could see the world as it actually is, according to Locke's theory, all that would be there would be the primary qualities.

If one is willing to accept this view, one can ask further, "How do we acquire ideas of objects from our experience?" We experience conglomerations of simple ideas, some of which are of primary qualities, and some of secondary ones. How do we put these collections together into ideas of objects? Why should we come to the conclusion that a certain color, smell, size, and shape all belong together to something called a "rose"? Locke asserted that as a result of experiencing a group of simple ideas together, and of always experiencing them together, we decide that they must belong to *one* object. We are not able to conceive of these simple ideas without assuming that there must be something that holds them together, or that there must be something to which they are attached. We are led to the conclusion that these groups of ideas must belong to something called a "substance," or a "substratum," on the basis of the constant grouping of sensations in our experience. This substance holds together the primary qualities and produces the secondary ones. When we see a pink color, smell a delightful fragrance, see a certain shape, and so on, we cannot but believe that this group of ideas belongs to one thing because the ideas are always experienced together. The one thing is the substance that we call a rose. It holds together the primary qualities of size, shape, and solidity and produces the secondary ones of color and smell.

What is a "substance"? Is it something that we experience? No. It is something that we are led to suppose, or to believe in, on the basis of our experience. It "stands under" the ideas of sensation that we have. If we are asked for a precise description of a substance, we find that we have to believe that it exists, but we cannot give any clear statement as to what it is. In Locke's famous phrase, it is "a something, I know not what." To explain the matter further, Locke related the tale about the Indian who asserted that the world was supported by a huge elephant, who was in turn standing on the back of a huge tortoise. When the Indian was asked what the tortoise was standing on, he answered like Locke, "something, I know not what." He knew that there must be something, but what it was he could not say. Thus no matter how vague our idea of substance may be, we still believe that it must be something, and must be that which the primary qualities belong to, and that which the secondary qualities are produced by.

With this much of Locke's theory in mind, we can now proceed to consider his answer to our question, "What can we know?" and to the question, "How reliable is our knowledge?" Knowledge, Locke declared in the fourth book of the *Essay*, consists of the discovery of the respect in which various ideas agree or disagree. There are four kinds of agreements or disagreements of ideas. (1) Any two ideas can agree or disagree in being either the same or different. For example, the idea of a circle is different from that of a square. (2) Two or more ideas can agree or disagree in terms of some relationship to each other, as the ideas of father and son do. (3) Ideas may agree or disagree in terms of coexistence, or belonging together. Thus the ideas that are part of one substance agree in coexistence. (4) Ideas can agree or disagree in terms of "real existence," that is, in being about something that actually exists outside the mind.

These are the four kinds of agreements of ideas that we can know about. Next, we have to ascertain how much knowledge of each type we can have, and how certain we can be about each. The highest degree of certainty that we can attain, Locke declared, is that of intuitive knowledge, where we simply "look" at two or more ideas and see immediately that something is true about them. Such knowledge is irresistible. As soon as the ideas of "square" and "circle" are present to the mind, we are forced to see that "a square is not a circle." This truth is indubitable. Similarly, when we examine the ideas of white and black, we see immediately that "white is not black." Hence when we possess such intuitive information about our ideas, we have attained complete certitude in much the same way as Descartes said we would with regard to clear and distinct ideas.

Unfortunately, not all agreements or disagreements among ideas can be known intuitively. Often, when we "look at" our ideas, we cannot determine immediately whether or not they agree in some respect. In order to find out, we must connect the ideas with other ones. The relating of each of the ideas to others until we are able to decide whether they agree or disagree is called a "demonstration." The type of knowledge gained thereby is demonstrative knowledge, which is less direct than the intuitive kind, but almost as certain. Each step in a demonstration consists of an intuitive "look" at two or more ideas. Locke gave the example of the geometrical theorem that the sum of the three angles of a triangle equals two right angles. "Looking at" the ideas of the three angles of a triangle and of two right angles is not enough to tell us immediately if they agree or not. However, by introducing other ideas which we can see are the same as the sum of the three angles of a triangle, and the same as the sum of two right angles, the mind finds that the ideas do in fact agree. A demonstration is thus a series of intuitions. Hence it ought to yield completely certain knowledge. However, in carrying out the demonstrative process, we may omit some connecting idea or fail to notice the absence of intuitive certainty at some point in the series. If the chain is long, Locke said, there is more likelihood of error than if there are only a few connections. Since errors are always possible, demonstrative knowledge can never be as certain as intuitive knowledge.

Strictly speaking, only intuitions and demonstrations provide us with genuine certainty. However, there is a lesser type of assurance that we all rely on and that Locke felt should also be counted as a kind of knowledge. This is "sensitive knowledge," the assurance we have that any particular thing exists. We feel quite certain that some of our experiences deal with "real events," in spite of the doubts raised by Descartes to the effect that we may be dreaming, that we may be deceived, and so on. In practice, Locke insisted, people have no doubts that they can distinguish looking at something, and remembering or thinking about it. The taste of an orange is quite different from the recollection of it. Being burned by a fire or hitting a wall is different from thinking of these events happening. Because of this, Locke argued, we do actually have enough assurance to tell when there is something occurring outside our minds and when there is not, although we may not be able to eliminate theoretical reasons for doubt in these cases. This assurance may be groundless, and hence it is less certain than a demonstration or an intuition. Just the same, this kind of certainty suffices for our usual purposes.

In terms of these three types of certainty, Locke considered the question, "What can we know?" He showed that what we can know is severely limited if we accept his empirical theory. We can know about only those things of which we possess ideas. This restricts our knowledge to that with which we have been acquainted through sensation and reflection. And we are further limited in terms of what we can know about the ideas that we acquire in our lifetimes. Intuition and demonstration inform us of only a few of the ways in which ideas can agree or disagree, and our sensitive knowledge only assures us that some of our ideas relate to things existing outside our minds. When we total up what we can know of the various kinds of agreements and differences of ideas, the limitations on our knowledge become evident.

We can always tell intuitively that two ideas are the same or different if the ideas are sufficiently clear. We can thus acquire a good deal of certain but unexciting knowledge in the form of "An elephant is not an oyster," or "A male sibling is a brother." We can obtain a good deal of information about the relations of ideas by demonstration. The fields in which such knowledge can be gained, according to Locke, include only mathematics and, to some extent, ethics and political science. In other areas, it is not possible to demonstrate the connection between ideas.

The difficulties and limitations involved in acquiring knowledge become more acute with regard to the last two kinds of agreements or disagreements of ideas. We cannot tell, in advance of experience, by either intuition or demonstration, what ideas have to, or ought to, coexist. We learn only from the sequence of actual conjunctions that occur in our experience that water and wetness coexist, and that gold and yellowness coexist. The amount of information we can have about the coexistence of ideas depends upon the extent and variety of our experience. But, Locke insisted, "There is no discoverable connection between any secondary quality and those primary qualities which it depends on." From the size and shape of an object, we cannot tell that it has any particular color or smell. All our knowledge about the relation of primary and secondary qualities is restricted to what we can experience.

What we can know about the real existence of ideas is even more limited. By intuition we can be certain only of our own existence. By demonstration we can establish only the real existence of God. Our only evidence of the real existence of anything else is our none-too-certain sensitive knowledge, which only gives us assurance about the ideas immediately present to our senses. Beyond this, Locke said, we have to recognize our limitations and remain in ignorance about what we cannot know.

Locke declared that, because of the limitations on our knowledge about coexistence and real existence, we cannot establish an absolutely true science of physical or spiritual things. Our empirical information is restricted to the ideas we experience, and to our strong feelings, when experiencing some of them, that something exists outside of us. But why these ideas occur in the combinations they do, or whether they really exist, cannot be discovered. Thus any sciences that human beings can develop about physical or spiritual things will be limited to empirical information and will always be less than completely certain. Neither the world of spirits nor that of bodies will ever be fully understood.

Is it possible, in view of these restrictions, that each person knows only his own private world? Locke insists that his empirical theory did not have to lead to such skeptical conclusions. Some of our knowledge is objective and conforms to the real nature of things. Simple ideas must relate to something outside us, since the mind is incapable of inventing ideas. All it can do is combine them. But simples, by their very nature, cannot be combinations of any other ideas. "From whence it follows, that simple ideas are no fictions of our fancies, but the natural and regular productions of things without us, really operating upon us." Secondary qualities must be the results of the actions of some powers in external things. Hence we can be sure that our ideas of primary and secondary qualities conform in whole or in part to the real nature of things.

The intuitive and demonstrative knowledge that we possess about mathematics and morality is certain, though not necessarily objective. The relationship of ideas in these realms is unquestionable, but we cannot be certain that these ideas relate to real occurrences. Hence our mathematical and moral knowledge is conditional. *If* the ideas in these areas "agree with the reality of things," *then* we possess certain real knowledge. The problem of ascertaining whether the condition has been met remains.

To summarize, Locke attempted to develop an empirical theory of knowledge that would show where our knowledge comes from, how extended it is, and how certain it is. Locke claimed that our knowledge came from experience, and that it extended as far as the limits of our experiences. Its certitude is less than could be desired. We can be sure that two ideas agree or disagree when this is obvious by intuition. We can also be sure of the agreement or disagreement of ideas when this is demonstrable. But the major portion of our knowledge, sensitive knowledge, we can only be sure of when we are having the experience. Yet, Locke felt that this type of knowledge is enough to guide us through life.

Criticisms of Locke's
Theory of Knowledge

Locke attempted to show that all our knowledge comes from sense experience. Critics have contended that the development of Locke's theory exhibits many of the basic strengths and weaknesses involved in the empirical approach. Locke's answer to the question, "What can we know?" seems to restrict our possible knowledge on the one hand to what we can experience, and then on the other hand, to extend our possible knowledge far beyond the limits of experience in order to avoid the apparent skeptical consequences of his theory.

In ruling out Platonic Ideas or innate ideas, has Locke unduly limited what can be known? Locke appealed to the common sense of mankind, and to the usual developmental process of human beings in order to discard the crucial foundations of the rationalist's knowledge. He considered nonempirical ideas to be fictitious or illusory. Rationalist critics have questioned whether he was justified in this. Most people might be unaware of these crucial ideas, but that does not prove that they do not exist, and are not known in some person's mind. And the fact that perhaps 99.99 percent of our ideas can be traced back to experience does not prove that there is not another .01 percent which is innate.

Further, these critics could argue that the skeptical conclusions of Locke's theory indicate the dangerous consequences of ignoring or denying the existence of nonempirical ideas. Locke, by the end of the *Essay*, concluded that most of the propositions that we accept are not known with complete certainty to be true. This conclusion appears to follow logically from an examination of the ingredients that are admitted into Locke's theory. But, the critics might contend, this conclusion may suggest that Locke's theory is defective in that it ignores or rejects a class of ideas (nonempirical ones) that would provide a more certain basis for our information. The limited certitude achieved by Locke's approach might be the effect of the author's "unjustified" rejection of the theory of innate ideas, rather than the effect of the nature of ideas themselves.

On the other side, critics have pointed out that if Locke consistently held to his empiricism, he would have had no basis for contending that any of our knowledge is objective or about the real nature of things. The substances, which are the objects of our knowledge, are not known as ideas. Hence can we know anything about them if knowledge is the perception of agreement or disagreement among *ideas*? Further, can we actually tell that our ideas of primary qualities are characteristics of objects outside us? Primary qualities, as we know them, are merely ideas. Secondary qualities are also known as ideas, and not as the effects of unperceived powers. If all of our knowledge is restricted to ideas, then how can we determine that our ideas must have an objective cause or source, and how can we determine that our ideas conform in some degree to the real nature of things? Thus, the critics contended, Locke's empiricism seems to lead to a skepticism about the reality of our knowledge, and not to any genuine assurances that we can know something about the world outside our minds. Thus, perhaps, if Locke's account is true, the consequence is that nothing can be known of reality.

Bishop Berkeley's Theory of Knowledge

The empirical theory of knowledge was further developed in the eighteenth century by George Berkeley and David Hume. Berkeley (1685–1753) was born and brought up in Ireland. He attended Trinity College, Dublin, where the views of Malebranche and Locke were popular. From considering these theories, Berkeley worked out his own philosophy when he was quite a young man, in his early twenties, and in 1710 published his work, *The Principles of Human Knowledge*. Three years later a more popular version of his theories appeared in the *Three Dialogues between Hylas and Philonous*. These works, which have become classics of British philosophy, were regarded as ridiculous in their time. Berkeley's philosophy was regarded as the strangest and silliest ever presented.

Berkeley gradually rose in importance as a personage at Court, and as a prelate of the Church of Ireland. For several years he worked on a plan to establish a college in Bermuda. In 1728 he sailed to the New World, and lived in Rhode Island until 1731. Though his project failed, Berkeley had considerable influence on the development of higher education in America. His gift of books and money greatly assisted young Yale

College. The first president of King's College, now Columbia, was Berkeley's first American disciple. In the nineteenth century, when the westernmost university was founded in California, its location was named after the Irish philosopher, who in a poem about America had written, "Westward the course of empire takes its way." After his return from the New World, he was appointed Bishop of Cloyne in Ireland. Besides attending to his clerical duties, Berkeley spent the latter years of his life trying to convince people of the virtues of an American Indian cure-all—tar water —for many of mankind's ills.

Berkeley's avowed aim, in presenting his philosophy, was to combat atheism and skepticism by demonstrating the "reality and perfection of human knowledge." Philosophers like Locke, Berkeley charged, had cast doubts on the reliability of some of our ideas, especially upon some of those derived from our sense information. These doubts lead to paradoxes, inconsistencies, and difficulties until we end up in "a forlorn skepticism." The basic cause of this disaster, Berkeley insisted, was that the philosophers refused to believe what everyone else accepts: that the things we perceive with our senses are the real things of the world. The philosophers, from time immemorial, have persisted in distinguishing things from ideas. Locke, with his distinction between primary qualities, which are in objects, and secondary qualities, which are in objects only as potentialities, is the latest offender. Once this sort of distinction has been made, Berkeley said, then the philosophers would be led to doubt what other men know, and to believe things that are preposterous. The answer of philosophers such as Locke to the question, "What can be known?" is so strange that it leads ordinary men to doubt the merits of other truths propounded by philosophers and theologians. Hence philosophy leads men eventually to doubt religious truths by confusing them and baffling them with its paradoxical theories.

In his *Three Dialogues*, Berkeley tried, in striking fashion, to present his indictment of philosophy, especially Locke's, and to vindicate commonsense beliefs about what can be known. The characters in the dialogues are Philonous ("lover of mind," who is Berkeley's spokesman) and Hylas (which means "matter"). Hylas begins the discussion by reporting that he has heard that Philonous is an extreme skeptic who does not believe that material substance exists. Philonous announces that he will show that this opinion is neither skeptical nor in opposition to common sense. The alternative view, that matter exists, will be seen as the real cause of skepticism.

First, a few basic terms have to be defined before Berkeley can argue his case. A skeptic is one who doubts everything, or who denies "the reality and truth of things." Hylas then accuses Philonous of being a skeptic because, in denying the existence of matter, he will be led either to deny the real existence of sensible things or to deny that one can gain any knowledge of them. (A sensible thing is something immediately perceived by the senses, such as a sound or a smell.) Berkeley's thesis, however, is that Hylas (or John Locke) is the real skeptic, since it is he who actually denies that sensible things really exist, or that we can know anything about them. Philonous and Berkeley, on the other hand, by denying the existence of matter will vindicate our knowledge of sensible things.

The discussion starts by examining the nature of sensible things. What we perceive immediately by the senses are colors, shapes, sounds, tastes, odors, feelings, and so on. Are the sensible things just perceptions whose reality consists in their being perceived, or do they have some existence apart from our experience of them? Hylas, the materialist, insists that sensible things exist independently and distinctly from their being perceived.

To undermine this view, Philonous starts with our experience of heat. Does what we experience exist independently, apart from our experience, in material objects? When we experience extreme heat, what we actually feel is a severe pain. No one believes that material objects contain pains. Hylas answers that the pain is in the mind, *but* the heat is in a material object. But which is the sensible thing? Philonous points out that if one puts one's hand near a fire, one feels only one thing, pain, which Hylas has already admitted exists only in the mind. The same is true about other degrees of heat, which are felt as pleasant or painful sensations. Since no one believes that pleasures or pains are in material objects, the sensible thing—heat—cannot have an existence outside the mind. Philonous offers one further point, in case one is not fully convinced. If a warm hand and a cold hand are placed in a bowl of water which is at room temperature, the water will feel warm to one hand and cold to the other. Is the water, then, simultaneously warm and cold? This conclusion can be avoided by maintaining "that heat and cold are only sensations existing in our minds."

The same type of reasoning can be applied to other sensible qualities. Tastes are experienced as various kinds of pleasures and pains. Is the pleasant taste of candy in the candy or in the mind? How could a pleasure be in a material object? Hylas contends that one of Locke's distinctions will explain the matter. There is a difference between the way we perceive certain qualities and the way in which they exist in objects. A taste is experienced as a pleasure or a pain, but exists objectively in a different way. Philonous dismisses this point by showing that they are discussing *only* sensible things, our immediate sensations, not some "insensible qualities" that may or may not be in external objects. The immediately perceived qualities have been admitted to exist "in the mind." For the purposes of the argument, it does not matter where unperceived qualities may be.

Philonous extends the discussion to other kinds of experience. He shows that odors are merely pleasant or painful sensations that vary from person to person. These variable pleasures and pains must also be "in the mind." The same is true about sounds. The noises we hear are sensations that cannot exist apart from the mind. Is there a noise if no one hears it? If "noise" means what we experience, then if no one experiences it, of course, there is no noise. What about colors? They are experiences that we have that vary depending on the lighting conditions, the state of our eyes, the kind of optical instruments we use, and so on. Does any given object have all the colors that we can perceive at different times of the day and night, and with different kinds of glasses? If not, then these experiences, too, must exist in the mind, and not independently in the objects.

Hylas tries to fight back by introducing the distinction between sounds and colors that we immediately perceive, and sound waves and light waves which exist in the outside world. Real sounds and colors are the waves, while the experienced sounds and colors are only subjective, and exist only in us. Philonous immediately points out that this would lead to the conclusion that real sound and real color are never perceived, since we do not perceive the waves. We hear noises and see colors. Since the discussion is about the reality of *sensible* things, the existence of unsensed sound and light waves is irrelevant. The fact that Hylas has admitted that sensed sound and color exist only in the mind suffices to advance Berkeley's thesis.

At this point, Hylas introduces Locke's theory of primary and secondary qualities as a way of avoiding accepting Berkeley's conclusion that sensible things are only ideas in the mind, and do not exist independently. The secondary qualities—the colors, tastes, and smells—exist only in the mind. The primary qualities of extension, motion, and solidity really exist in physical objects. Hence some ideas of sensation are of actual qualities of external objects and some are not.

Berkeley attacked this theory by presenting an argument that had been advanced earlier by some of the French skeptics. The distinction between primary and secondary qualities is untenable on the basis of the empirical theory of knowledge. All the qualities are immediately perceived by the senses in the same way. If we admit that some of them are in the mind, how can we avoid concluding that *all* of them are in the mind? The reasoning that shows that secondary qualities are subjective applies as well to primary ones. All the qualities are known as ideas. What we experience varies according to where we are and how we feel. Our experiences of the size, shape, and motion of objects are as variable and dependent on our state and conditions as are our experiences of color, sound, and taste. On the basis of the empirical theory, we can tell only that all the qualities are experienced as sensations. Hence we have no justification for treating some of the qualities as objective and others as subjective.

Philonous puts the case in another way. All our experience consists of sensations. Only sentient beings, that is, beings who are capable of feelings, can have sensations. Therefore, inanimate, material objects cannot have sensations. Hence the sensible things, those immediately perceived by the senses, the sensations, cannot be "in" unthinking, unfeeling material objects.

Hylas, like anyone else who has been exposed to Berkeley's argument for the first time, is still unwilling to concede. He admits that what we know are sensations, and that sensations cannot exist in something that does not perceive. However, as Locke had argued before him, Hylas insists that it is necessary to suppose that there is some material substance or substratum that our sensations belong to, or come from. Philonous points out that we do not learn about this alleged material substratum from our experience, since it contains only sensations. We cannot conceive of it because our ideas are all of sensible things. Hence we cannot conceive of anything different from our sensations that is supposed to exist outside our minds, and supposed to be the basis for our sensations.

To make his case as striking as possible, Berkeley issues his famous challenge. If the opponents can conceive of any groups of qualities or sensible things existing outside the mind, then Berkeley will grant that this is the way things are. Hylas accepts the challenge and announces that nothing is easier than "to conceive of a tree or a house existing by itself, independent of, and unperceived by, any mind whatsoever." Hylas insists that at the very moment he is thinking of such a tree or house. But, Philonous points out, the tree or house is being conceived of by Hylas, and hence is in his mind. Anything that one might think of would be a thought, and thus would be in a mind. Any time that one tried to think of something existing outside all minds, the thought would, of course, be in some mind.

Hylas still persists in trying to defend his Lockean outlook. Whatever we may perceive immediately is an idea, and ideas can exist only in minds. But, then, why can't there still be something called "real objects" that exist independently and externally from minds? These "real things" could be known through our ideas, without being our ideas. For example, we can know about Julius Caesar (the real object) from looking at a picture of him (the idea).

Philonous responds by pointing out that we have no way of learning about these supposed real objects. If all our knowledge comes from the senses, and it consists entirely of ideas, then how could we know anything about something that is not an idea? The example of the picture is misleading, since we learn both about the picture of a person and about the person from sense experience. The picture and the person are both sensible things, not real objects known to be existing apart from all sensations.

The contention that ideas can represent real objects, Philonous asserts, is a strange theory indeed. Ideas are fleeting, changing, and ephemeral. Real objects are supposed to possess a fixed, immutable, real nature. Ideas can be perceived, whereas real objects cannot. Then ideas are not like the objects they are supposed to represent. How can anything be like an idea but an idea? Therefore, there can be no resemblance between the supposed real objects and the sensible things of our experience.

When one sees that the theory of the existence of real, material objects makes no sense, one can then see also that Hylas' views lead to complete skepticism. Originally Hylas had insisted that the reality of sensible things consists in their existence outside the mind. But now he has been forced to admit that they could not exist outside the mind and hence, by his own definition, that they could not be real. And, according to his own definition of "skeptic" (someone who denies the reality of sensible things), he is now shown to be one.

Hylas is reduced to the point where his belief in the real, external existence of material objects has been destroyed. He now denies that there are any real objects. Instead, he declares, everything is just a dream. This conclusion, Berkeley insists, was the unfortunate result of the Lockean position. If one believes that there must be a real, material substance existing outside the mind, then one is forced to realize that none of our sense experiences can belong to it. The qualities that we know by the senses can only be "in the mind." Had Hylas and Locke been complete empiricists, they would not have been disturbed by this conclusion. However, they had the nonempirical view that our sensations, in order to be real, had to belong to independent material objects. When they are shown that there cannot be any such objects, they lapse into skepticism, because they then feel that there cannot be *any* objects in the universe, and that whatever is perceived is only an illusion since it cannot exist outside the mind.

Philonous and Berkeley declared that the way to avoid skepticism was to realize that sensible things are real and that their reality consists in their being perceived. Berkeley's famous dictum is "to be is to be perceived," *esse est percipi*. Sensible things, like chairs and tables, are real because we perceive them, and not because they have some kind of independent existence outside the mind. The mistake of previous philosophy was that of distinguishing things and ideas, and counting only the former as real. Once the mistake had been made, it would soon follow that things could not be known, since all that we are ever acquainted with are ideas. Hence skepticism would result, unless one adopted Berkeley's cure.

If things exist because they are perceived, does this mean that things exist only when perceived, and that they disappear when not perceived? Does this mean that we cannot be sure of the existence of anything but what is immediately perceived? Berkeley at this point revealed his positive theory, a completely different one from Hylas' or Locke's and which he contended would not lead to skeptical conclusions. Sensible things exist because they are perceived. Since they are ideas, they must exist in the mind. But since their existence does not depend on *my* mind, and since I am convinced that they exist distinct from being perceived by me, there must be another mind in which they exist. "As sure, therefore, as the sensible world really exists, so sure is there an infinite omnipresent spirit, who contains and supports it."

Berkeley's positive theory, called immaterialism, stressed the points that ideas can exist only in minds, and that they must have an existence independent of *my* mind, or that of any other finite being. My inability to create ideas at will, and my inability to experience whatever ideas I wish, is taken as a sufficient indication that the ideas must be in, and be controlled by, another Mind. To this extent Berkeley's theory is quite similar to that of Malebranche's view that "we see all things in God." The items of the world do not jump in and out of existence when I perceive them. Instead, all sensible things have a continuous existence in the Mind of God, and are perceived occasionally by various human beings.

A famous limerick by Ronald Knox sums up Berkeley's case:

> There was a young man who said, "God
> Must think it exceedingly odd,
> If he finds that this tree
> Continues to be
> When there's no one about in the Quad."
> Reply
> "Dear Sir:
> Your astonishment's odd:
> *I* am always about in the Quad.
> And that's why the tree
> Will continue to be
> Since observed by
> Yours faithfully,
> GOD"

Berkeley insisted that his unusual theory was the only one that united both the true contentions of empirical philosophy and the beliefs of ordinary common sense. Any other theory, he said, denied what everyone was sure of, and led, ultimately to skepticism. The philosophers recognized that *"the things immediately perceived are ideas which exist only in the mind."* Ordinary people believe that *"Those things they immediately perceive are the real things."* Berkeley contended that his theory united these two views instead of putting them in opposition.

Previous theories of knowledge had distinguished ideas and things. Then they had admitted that what we perceive are ideas. After this a problem arose of gaining knowledge of things from our ideas. When skeptical critics of Descartes and Locke showed that it is not possible to know anything but our ideas, the philosophers, like Hylas, "sat down in a forlorn scepticism," despairing of obtaining knowledge about the real things of the world, while scoffing at the ordinary man who took what he perceived for the real things.

The immaterialist theory identifies the ideas and the things. Hence the quest for some mysterious underlying substances is ended, since there is nothing "behind" the ideas to be known. Immaterialism is a consistent empiricism, plus a metaphysical theory about the nature of reality. Our ideas all come from experience. Hence what can be known by our ideas is what we immediately perceive. Instead of treating this as subjective or illusory, all we have to recognize is that what we immediately perceive are both ideas and real things, since they are one and the same. A real tree is the collection of ideas that we perceive. The way we know that there is a real tree is that we perceive it. The ordinary man always knew this. The philosophers had forgotten it because they persisted in seeking for a real object other than their ideas, a "real" object that could never be known or described. The immaterialist regains the simple and obvious truth of common sense by realizing that things and ideas are the same. Hence, neither the immaterialist nor the man of ordinary common sense will be a skeptic, because they both know sensible things with complete certainty.

Since the reality of sensible things depends not on *my* perceiving them, but on the fact that they are also perceived by God, the world of ideas has a permanence and stability and order. What I know about are ideas in the Mind of God, ideas which I know about sometimes, but which exist all the time. Each of these ideas is a real thing, and what I know about it is true. My knowledge can be systematized by studying the sequence of ideas and their relations. Such knowledge constitutes genuine science. Berkeley maintained that what, in effect, we are doing when we try to understand the world, is a form of Divine mind-reading. The whole order of ideas is a sequence of signs which we are given. By enlarging our comprehension of them, we are learning more and more about what God's Mind is like.

Since God plays a crucial role in Berkeley's theory, in accounting for the objective character of our knowledge, Berkeley realized that he could not hold that all our knowledge comes from the senses. We do not know about God from sense experience. He is not just one more idea in our minds. Hence there must be another source of information, which is that of "notions." Ideas are passive. We perceive them directly and "see" their content. In contrast to ideas, notions are our intuitive awareness of activities. The basic notion is our awareness of ourselves. We become aware of ourselves whenever we engage in any activity, such as thinking, willing, moving, perceiving. What we are aware of is not a collection of colors, sounds, shapes, and so on, but of an agent who acts. From our notion of ourselves we construct a notion of God as the Omnipresent Spirit. By analogy we assume that there must also be other finite spirits like ourselves, such as other people. The world known by notions is that of spirits, finite and infinite.

After Philonous had outlined Berkeley's spiritology and had shown how this explained the basic structure of the universe, Hylas suggested that one might also intuit a notion of matter, and then Berkeley's theory of knowledge would become almost the same as Locke's. Philonous strenuously rejected this addition to his theory. He pointed out that one can only have a notion of an active agent. Matter, according to both Locke and Descartes, is inert and passive, since it consists of only extended, solid parts in motion. Since matter is not, by itself, active, we cannot have a notion of it. (In his notebooks, Berkeley had pointed out that if matter could initiate its own activity, it would be God.)

Berkeley showed that a consistent development of Locke's empiricism would lead to a doubt that one knows anything except the ideas in one's mind. Berkeley showed how a consistent theory could be developed out of his claim, "To be is to be perceived." The universe does not shift every time our ideas change, because God is the Universal Perceiver.

Criticisms of Berkeley's Theory of Knowledge

During the last two hundred years a great many philosophers have tried to refute Berkeley's arguments. Berkeley felt that he had successfully resolved all of the difficulties that existed in earlier theories of knowledge. He was also convinced that his theory, unlike those of his predecessors, vindicated common sense. However, his readers, then and since, have usually felt that his theory is fantastic. Even if, as Hume said, "it admits no answer," it also "produces no conviction."

Many critics have challenged Berkeley's theory of notions, and have insisted that all that we actually know, we know by our senses. If this is so, then we have no way of knowing about spirits, or about God. The Berkeleian theory would then have to be drastically emasculated, so that all that could be known would be merely a sequence of ideas whose real existence would be unknowable (a theory much like that of Hume, which we will examine next).

Berkeley had contended that his answer to "What can be known?" is that at least all our common-sense information that has been carefully examined is true. Many critics have challenged this thesis, either by pointing out that common sense is not as reliable as Berkeley thought or by arguing that Berkeley's theory is not actually as much in agreement with common sense as he would have us think.

Since ancient times philosophers have pointed out that the occurrence of errors in our ordinary information raises grave doubts about common sense. The progress of the sciences also seems to indicate that the world of genuine knowledge is unlike that of ordinary experience. The empiricist has a difficult task (though not an impossible one, as many contemporary philosophers have tried to show) in connecting the items of everyday experience with the results of modern science.

The problem of sense errors appears to pose a more serious difficulty for Berkeley. He asserted that everything that we see is real. Then what about optical illusions, strange perspectives, and so on? Berkeley insisted each one of them is real. The error occurs only when one judges that the bent oar one sees in water will be followed by a bent oar seen out of water. Each and every experience is equally real and is an experience of a real thing. Then which oar is real, the bent one, the straight one, or both? Berkeley has to hold the last alternative unless he would be willing to concede that ideas are not necessarily the same as things. If both are real, then is this the same as the belief of ordinary common sense?

Many other criticisms have been raised against Berkeley's theory of knowledge. Some of them will appear in our later discussions. But in spite of the fact that there have been very few adherents of immaterialism, Berkeley's arguments have remained most important for all later considerations of the nature of our knowledge. His negative evidence that we actually do not know anything about the material world has had great influence on many modern theories of knowledge as well as theories of the nature of the real world.

David Hume's Theory of Knowledge

David Hume (1711–1776) followed the empirical theory of knowledge perhaps further than either Locke or Berkeley wished, and developed a view which has become one of the most important for contemporary thought. Hume's views arose from considering Berkeley's arguments and from following out the arguments of French skeptics, such as Bayle, and Scottish moralists, such as Hutcheson. He presented a position which has remained fundamental in philosophical discussions ever since.

Hume belonged to a minor Scottish noble family. He attended the University of Edinburgh until he was thirteen or fourteen. After some unsuccessful attempts at finding a career, and apparently after a nervous breakdown, young Hume left for France in 1734 to write his views about the "new scene of thought" he had discovered. In 1739–1740, his first work, *A Treatise of Human Nature*, was published, and according to the author it "fell dead-born from the presses." In the next decades, Hume began to gain fame as a diplomat, a critic, and an essayist on political and religious themes. His *History of England* became the best seller of its day.

By the end of his life, Hume was perhaps the best-known English writer, notorious for his unorthodox views in religion and politics (so that his contemporaries called him "the great infidel" and "the gentle skeptic"). His final work, the *Dialogues concerning Natural Religion*, which will be discussed in Chapter 5, "Philosophy of Religion," develops his critical views in this area.

Hume's theory of knowledge, as presented in his *Treatise* and its more popular version, the *Enquiry concerning Human Understanding*, attempts to answer the question, "What can be known?" by examining the processes by which men gain their knowledge and beliefs. Hume proposed developing a "science of man," by applying the experimental method of Newton to the area of human mental events. Since it is men who discover knowledge about mathematics, physics, history, and so on, if we can understand the thinker, perhaps we can discover what he can actually know. The materials for this study, Hume insisted, can come only "from a cautious observation of human life." We may not be able to find "the ultimate qualities of human nature," but at least we may be able to reach some general hypotheses about the origins and nature of what we can know. (Hence Hume, at the outset, seems to be carrying on the same sort of inquiry as Locke had done before him.)

The basic ingredients of all our information are impressions and ideas. These differ only in the "degree of force and liveliness, with which they strike upon the mind," the impressions being the more forceful and lively. There are simple and complex impressions and ideas, the simples being those that "admit of no distinction or separation," while the complexes can be divided into parts. On examination, we find, according to Hume, that there is a great resemblance between impressions and ideas. Our simple ideas are all just like our simple impressions, except with respect to force and vivacity, and the simple impressions have always preceded the ideas. (With regard to complexes, the laws of resemblance and precedence apply only to the simple parts.) This shows, Hume contended, that all our ideas come from experience, and that we possess no innate ideas.

We retain and deal with the ideas by means of two faculties, memory and imagination. Memory preserves the ideas and the order in which they occurred, whereas the imagination is free and allows for the arrangement of the ideas in any order that we wish. However, we find that we tend to think in patterns. When one idea comes to mind, others follow automatically by the association of ideas, "a kind of ATTRACTION, which in the mental world will be found to have as extraordinary effects as in the natural."

The extraordinary effects appear when Hume presented his views about what can be known, especially about what can be known about the causal connections of events. Knowledge, for Hume, consists of intuitive and certain information gained by inspecting two or more ideas, and by finding that they stand in some relation to one another, as for example, that they are different, that one is more blue than another, and the like. Such knowledge cannot be false, since it depends only on what one "sees" when one looks at the ideas in the imagination. This leads to a limited amount of indubitable information about the obvious qualities or relations of ideas. By connecting a series of such intuitions, we can gain demonstrative knowledge, which Hume believed could actually occur only in a subject like arithmetic.

However, we also discover that our information about which ideas are causally related *does not* come from a mere intuitive inspection of our ideas. Most of our information about what is occurring outside our immediate experience depends on causal connection. But how do we tell what ideas are so connected? If we examine either two ideas or two impressions that we think are causally related, what do we actually perceive? We see, Hume insisted, that they are contiguous and successive, but we do not see that they are necessarily connected. We feel that there is more to the sequence of events than just one happening next to and after another. We feel that one *must* make the other happen. But how do we gain any knowledge about this crucial aspect of our information about the world?

Hume contended that since the necessary connection was not immediately evident, we ought to ask ourselves two questions: (1) Why do we think that every event must have a cause? (2) Why do we think that particular causes must necessarily have certain effects, how do we reach such conclusions, and why do we believe them?

An examination of the first question reveals something quite surprising. Although everyone believes that every event must have a cause, it is neither intuitively obvious nor demonstrable that this must be the case. Our impressions and ideas do not come with signs that they must be caused. Since we can separate them from one another, and consider each one individually, we do not have to think of them in terms of their causes. And, since each idea or impression can be conceived of as uncaused, that is, having no necessary antecedent, it is possible that they also exist that way. Hence no demonstration can prove the impossibility of uncaused events. In fact, Hume showed, the demonstrations that have been offered all beg the question. In order to prove this they actually assume that every event must have a cause. The causal principle, though neither obvious nor demonstrable, seems so fundamental that we all accept it. Why? And where does the principle come from?

In order to answer these questions, Hume turned to his second problem: why do we believe that particular causes have particular effects, and why do we infer from one to the other? Our causal reasoning consists of an impression of sense or memory, an idea of a related event, and a mysterious connection or inference between them. A noise is heard. The idea of someone playing the piano comes to mind. The problem is how do we infer from the sound to its alleged cause? All sorts of other ideas might have come to mind. In hearing the sound, we do not also experience the piano-playing; yet we believe it must be occurring to cause the effect we perceive. The process involved cannot be logical reasoning, since there is no necessity for us to think of the idea of a piano player rather than of a lady skier.

If it is not reason that leads us to connect events causally, then it must be experience. The repetition and constant conjunction of events lead us to associate them together. When one of them occurs, we automatically think of the other, and we call one the cause and the other the effect. But why should this happen? Why should the fact that two items have been conjoined in past experience result in our thinking of them as causally related? If this were a rational inference, it would have to be based on the principle of the uniformity of nature, "that instances, of which we have had no experience, must resemble those of which we have had experience, and that the course of nature continues always uniformly the same."

But is there any evidence that the principle of the uniformity of nature is true, and has to be true? We can easily conceive of the world's changing its character in the future. Therefore we cannot demonstrate that nature *has* to be uniform. Further, our experience up to now provides us with no evidence about what the future will be, or must be. The sun has risen every day up to today. Does this show that it must rise tomorrow? We can only be sure if nature is uniform. But can we tell that nature is uniform, or only that it has been uniform *up to today*? Thus the principle of the uniformity of nature, upon which so much of our reasoning about the world around us depends, can never be demonstrated or established by experience. No matter how many times we check, we can still discover only that nature continues to be uniform up to this moment, but not that it will be a moment later. Scientific laws tell us what will happen if nature continues to be uniform, but they do not, and cannot, show that it will be uniform.

In view of all this, why do we believe in the principle? We cannot prove it, and we cannot find adequate evidence for it. Hume insisted that there must be a basic feature of human nature, which he called a habit or custom, that accounts for our belief and the way it operates upon us. We experience the same sequence of events, or we find that the same events are constantly conjoined. After this sort of experience has been repeated several times, it then happens that when one of the conjuncts occurs, we automatically think of the other, and we think of it in a forceful and lively manner. Theoretically, our imagination being free, we could bring any idea to mind. Actually, because of our psychological nature, one particular idea comes to mind, and has some of the force and vivacity of immediate experience. The strength of the conception of the idea constitutes my belief in the occurrence of the conjoined event. Thus, when I hear a certain sound, I automatically think of a piano being played by a player, and this thought is almost as lively and forceful as the experience. This happens because the events of sound and piano player have been conjoined over and over again in the past, and because I have a habit or custom of associating ideas according to past sequences, and of transferring some of the force and vivacity of present experience to associated ideas, and hence believing in them. Thus, the principle of the uniformity of nature is, as far as we can determine, a principle about how we think and feel rather than about how the world behaves.

In discovering the psychological roots of our belief in the uniformity of nature, Hume found that he had also uncovered the basis for our belief in the necessary connection between events. We do not perceive any necessary connection, no matter how many times the sequence is repeated. But, after experiencing the constant conjunction of events several times, we *feel* that one event causes or produces another. Why? Nothing that we know about events constitutes evidence for this conclusion. Hence it must be something in our psychological attitude toward the events. We have, in fact, Hume contended, a propensity to think about events in a certain way, and this propensity is a determination of the mind to think of one idea after an impression, or another idea after having experienced the constant conjunction of events. This determination, or strong feeling, is the necessary connection that we talk of. We never perceive the piano player producing the sounds we hear. Instead, we see him making certain movements, and we hear the sounds. After experiencing this phenomenon over and over again, our natural propensity leads us to think of the piano player when we hear the sounds, and to think of him in a strong and lively manner. The necessary connection between the events is found, then, not in the observable sequence, but in the way we think about it. Thus, a cause can be defined as "an object precedent and contiguous to another, and so united with it in the imagination, that the idea of the one determines the mind to form the idea of the other, and the impression of the one to form a more lively idea of the other."

According to Hume's theory, our "knowledge" of what is going on outside immediate experience consists in discovering the constant conjunctions that have occurred and are occurring; and expecting, because of our psychological habits and customs, that these will continue to occur. The scientists, like the rest of the human race, are seeking for laws of constant conjunction upon which to base their expectations. The sciences provide us with the most careful bases for belief for thinking about the world, but they never tell us what *must* occur. Each scientific law describes some constant conjunction in observable experience with great precision, but it never shows that these events have to be conjoined. Because of our habits, scientific discoveries are one of our best sources for gaining probable information about the further course of nature, in terms of how we think about it.

Thus Hume's investigation into how we think led him to conclude that we cannot actually know anything about what the universe is like, but only about how we think and feel about it. The ingredients of our mental world are only a series of impressions and ideas. We can discover no necessary connections between them. We associate them together, and have strong beliefs about them on the basis of our psychological propensities, habits, and customs. We have no way of telling whether these impressions and ideas correspond to any actual external objects, or whether our beliefs about their relationships correspond to actual relationships. All that we are ever acquainted with is the sequence of impressions and ideas that constitute our experience. Our psychological factors "people the universe." But we can discover neither an external nor an internal substance to which our experience and our beliefs relate. We have no impression, and hence no idea, of an external object, nor of something called "ourselves." Hence all our "knowledge," as far as we can tell, is only about our streams of consciousness.

If this were not enough to make us skeptics about what we can know, Hume further pointed out that our beliefs and opinions are the result of a complicated and sometimes conflicting set of propensities, habits, and customs. One habit leads us to organize our experience "causally," according to the constantly conjoined sequences of events. Others lead us to believe that bodies exist outside us, that there is some sort of continuous self inside us, and that there is probably some sort of intelligent force that is responsible for the order in our experience. These various habits create order and coherence among our impressions and ideas. Some of the habits create one type of order; others, another. Sometimes the habits can create conflicting orders, so that what we believe according to one set of habits disagrees with what we believe on the basis of another.

In terms of all this, what *should* we believe? Which set of habits leads us to true knowledge? Ultimately, Hume asserted, we cannot answer these questions. We cannot justify what we believe. All that we can do is point out why we believe it, what habits and propensities operate upon us. Fundamentally, our beliefs are irrational. They result not from rational thoughts or processes, but from psychological causes. We can point out that certain sets of beliefs are what we call "normal" or "reasonable," and others are not, but we cannot show that the former are the true ones. The "reasonable" man believes fire will burn, the sun will rise tomorrow, the external world exists, and so on. He believes all this because he has the normal set of psychological habits. The madman may believe the exact opposite because his habits are different or deformed. But we cannot show that the beliefs of the "reasonable" man conform to the nature of things, while those of the madman do not.

When, as the result of this analysis, one tries to lapse into complete skepticism, one finds that our habits will not even permit this. Philosophy, Hume said, would render us completely skeptical were not Nature too strong for it. "Nature, by an absolute and uncontrollable necessity has determined us to judge as well as to breathe and feel." Hence even the skeptic has to be a believer because of his propensities and habits. The philosopher may realize that there are no adequate reasons for believing anything, and that we have no way of ascertaining whether any of what we believe is true; but when he emerges from his study, he believes that the world exists, that he exists, and that the world will continue in the future as it has in the past, and so on. Because of inexplicable, basic qualities of human nature, he will believe all of this, for it strikes so forcefully upon him. Hence we may not be able to know anything except the contents of immediate experience, and possibly some demonstrations in arithmetic (although Hume raised some doubts even about this), but we can and must believe all sorts of matters, even though we cannot tell if our beliefs are true or false.

Criticisms of Hume's
Theory of Knowledge

Hume's examination of the question "What can we know?" seems to have led to an extremely negative and skeptical conclusion. We are not able to achieve certainty, according to Hume, with regard to matters of fact. We can be sure only of information about those relations of ideas that can be intuited or demonstrated. This may tell us something about ideas and impressions that we are immediately aware of, and about certain arithmetical relations of ideas. However, we cannot, unfortunately, gain any information that is completely certain about events that are not immediately perceived, nor about any necessary connection between what we perceive and any "hidden springs and principles of nature."

Critics have maintained that this skeptical result is the natural outcome of the empirical theory of knowledge.

One of Hume's Scottish contemporaries, Thomas Reid, 1710–1796, contended that Hume's conclusions were the logical development of the way the problem of knowledge had been posed in modern thought, first by Descartes and Malebranche and then by Locke and Berkeley. They had all conceived of knowing reality by means of ideas. The empiricists had restricted this process to ideas gained by sensation. Hume had justly shown, in these terms, that nothing could be known about any world beyond that of ideas. However, Reid insisted, since Hume's results are unacceptable in that they conflict with the common sense of mankind, one must reject the assumptions on which they are based, that is, that the problem of knowledge is to be analyzed in terms of ideas. Instead, Reid proposed examining what can be known in terms of the common principles that everyone believes and has to believe, and in terms of a realistic theory of perception—a theory in which it is maintained that we directly perceive real things and not ideas.

Reid's criticism of Hume is not actually a refutation of Hume's skeptical arguments, but rather a way of avoiding them by making common sense the arbiter of what we claim we know. Reid and his disciples, who created a school of Common Sense Philosophy that was popular in England and America for several decades, did not offer any genuine justification for our knowledge claims about the external world, but insisted that we do and must believe them. By analyzing what common principles we all have, what assumptions about the world run through our linguistic discussions about it, and what is involved in the perceptual process, they showed that we can and do make knowledge claims that all sane people accept, including even Hume. This is the common sense of mankind, and Reid contended that when a philosophy, no matter how consistent, runs counter to this, we must reject that philosophy and stick with common sense. Reid's insistence on the priority of common sense to philosophical argument, and on the analysis of the assumptions we all accept in terms of our language behavior, has been revived in the twentieth century, in the views of G. E. Moore and some of the Ordinary Language philosophers, who will be discussed in the chapter on Contemporary Philosophy.

Other more rationalistic critics contended that Hume had only shown that if one restricts our source of knowledge to sense information, then the senses cannot provide us with necessary and certain knowledge about the world. Rationalists from Plato onwards had already pointed this out.

Immanuel Kant (1724–1804), the great German philosopher, felt that Reid had really missed Hume's point. Hume's work required a reinvestigation of the problem of knowledge to discover where our knowledge comes from and what justifies it as necessary and certain. Granting the empiricist's claim that all of our knowledge begins with sense experience does not mean that it comes from this experience. Kant assumed that we have knowledge that is certain. He then proceeded to develop a theory of an *a priori* source, in addition to experience, that could account for this knowledge, and that enables us to recognize and judge the content of experience. (His theory will be discussed in the next chapter.)

Others have insisted that Hume had shown that neither the senses nor reason were adequate to account for absolutely certain knowledge. Therefore we must seek beyond these faculties into the realm of faith for the basis of our knowledge.

Still other critics have contended that there is a fault in Hume's analysis of the problem of knowledge that leads to his conclusion. Some have said that Hume, in effect, atomizes our experience, and thereby loses the very connections which provide us with knowledge. On Hume's account, each experience is a separate and distinct impression, with no necessary connection with any other. But, these critics have asked, is this the way experience actually occurs? Or does it occur with the connections imbedded in it? If the latter, then we ought to be able to gain knowledge from examining experience, and not have to relegate all of the causal ingredients to the realm of habits and feelings.

In reaction to some of these criticisms, many contemporary empiricists, especially the logical positivists, have defended some of Hume's negative conclusions. They have pointed out that the limited and probable information gained by our senses, and organized by our habits and propensities, seems to be all that we actually "know," and all that we need to "know." In spite of the assertions of various rationalist philosophers from Plato onward, there is still doubt as to whether any necessary and certain information about the world has been, or can be, gained by the use of the capacities human beings possess. However, in spite of this, men have, especially in the last four hundred years, greatly extended their information about the world. This extension, the achievement of modern science, seems to have grown out of sense information, no matter how unreliable and uncertain it may be. Hume has shown, in keeping with the modern scientific tradition, that discoveries about the world that depend on our sense information are always tentative. He has also shown that our discoveries depend as much on what human nature is like as on what our experience is like. As we increase our understanding of ourselves and increase our realms of experience, our information about the world grows too. This information may always be open to doubt and correction, but the modern empiricists insist that it is adequate for our needs in predicting and controlling our world. And no other type of information, regardless of the assertions of various philosophers, appears to be as useful in human affairs.

Hence Hume's skepticism may not have led to any fatal or disastrous consequences in pointing out how uncertain is our alleged "knowledge." Instead, Hume may have simply clarified our human situation, so that we may learn to live with probabilities and uncertainties instead of seeking for unattainable absolute truths by means of our senses and our reason.

SUMMARY

In this chapter we have examined the question "What can we know?" We have seen that the question is far more complicated than it appears at first sight. Our ordinary, everyday assurances are not as well founded as we might wish. When we seek for guarantees that certain of our beliefs about the world are absolutely true, and cannot possibly be false, we enter into the problems that are involved in epistemology, or the theory of knowledge.

Two major traditions, that of the rationalists and that of the empiricists, have attempted to discover what we can know, how we gain this information, and how certain we can be of it. The rationalists have argued that it is possible to achieve certainty by means of some sort of rational process. They have usually supported their case by referring to the kinds of truths discovered through mathematical reasoning, and then they have sought to show what must be the case if we do possess information that cannot possibly be false.

The empiricists, from Locke onward, have scoffed at such rationalistic theories and have insisted that one has to begin with the very ingredients of ordinary sense experience if one is to discover any information about the world. As the theory developed from Locke to Berkeley to Hume, it was found that there was less and less that we could be certain of if all of our "knowledge" comes from sense experience and is based upon it. But, the empiricists have maintained, that is all we can, or need, "know."

Philosophers since Hume have tried either to accept and develop his views, or to find some way of avoiding his skeptical conclusions by rejecting his empirical premises, or by modifying some part of his theory. Many theories of knowledge have been offered. But it is still a matter in dispute as to whether any have succeeded in resolving problems raised by Hume.

Hence the seemingly simple task of accounting for, and justifying, the assurance that ordinary people have of what they think they know turns out to be extremely difficult, indeed. The attempt to construct a theory of knowledge that is both credible and consistent involves some of the most difficult problems men have had to deal with.

BIBLIOGRAPHY

Berkeley, George. *Three Dialogues between Hylas and Philonous*, edited by C. Turbayne (Bobbs-Merrill, Indianapolis, 1965).

Chappell, Vere C., ed. *Hume: A Collection of Critical Essays* (University of Notre Dame Press, South Bend, Ind., 1974).

Collins, James. *The Continental Rationalists: Descartes, Spinoza, Leibniz* (Glencoe Press, Beverly Hills, Calif., 1967).

Collins, James. *The British Empiricists: Locke, Berkeley, Hume* (Glencoe Press, Beverly Hills, Calif., 1967).

Copleston, Frederick. *A History of Philosophy*, 8 vols. (Image Books, Garden City, N.Y., 1963–1967). A multivolume history of philosophy beginning with the Greek thinkers.

Cornford, F. M. *Plato's Theory of Knowledge* (Routledge and Kegan Paul, London, 1935).

Descartes, René. *The Philosophical Works of Descartes*, edited by E. S. Haldane and G. R. Ross (Dover, New York, 1967). Contains Descartes' *Meditations*, as well as the original objections and replies to the work.

Hume, David. *An Enquiry concerning Human Understanding*, edited by L. Selby-Bigge (Oxford, New York, 1966.)

———. *A Treatise of Human Nature* (Oxford, New York, 1958).

Joad, C. E. M. *Guide to Philosophy* (Random House, New York, 1939). An elementary exposition and examination of many problems and views in epistemology.

Livingston, Donald W., and King, James T., eds. *Hume: A Re-evaluation.* (Fordham University Press, New York, 1976). New studies on Hume in honor of the 200th anniversary of his death.

Locke, John. *An Essay concerning Human Understanding*, 2 vols. edited by John W. Yolton (Everyman, New York, 1965).

Malebranche, Nicolas. *Dialogues on Metaphysics*, translated and edited by M. Ginsberg (Macmillan, New York, 1923).

Montague, William P. *The Ways of Knowing* (Macmillan, New York, 1928). A survey of some epistemological problems and of the solutions that have been offered.

Moore, G. E. *Philosophical Studies* (Humanities Press, New York, 1959). A series of essays by a major twentieth-century philosopher about problems in the theory of knowledge.

Plato. *Great Dialogues of Plato*, translated by W. H. D. Rouse (New American Library, New York, 1960). Contains the complete text of *The Republic, Meno*, and other writings.

Popkin, Richard H. *The History of Skepticism from Erasmus to Descartes* (Harper & Row, New York, 1968).

Russell, Bertrand. *A History of Western Philosophy* (Simon and Schuster, New York, 1945). A witty presentation and criticism of some of the major philosophers by one of the most important living thinkers.

———. *Human Knowledge: Its Scope and Limitations* (Simon and Schuster, New York, 1948).

———. *The Problems of Philosophy* (Oxford University Press, New York, 1959). An excellent introductory presentation of the problems of epistemology.

Stroll, Avrum, ed. *Epistemology: New Essays in the Theory of Knowledge* (Harper & Row, New York, 1968). A collection of discussions by contemporaries on the problem of knowledge.

Turbayne, C. M. *A Treatise Concerning the Principles of Human Knowledge by George Berkeley with Critical Essays,* (Bobbs-Merrill, Indianapolis, 1970).

chapter 2

Plato (427?–347 B.C.); birthplace—Greece (top left)

Aristotle (384–322 B.C.); birthplace—Greece (top center)

Epicurus (341–270 B.C.); birthplace—Greece (top right)

Critik
der
reinen Vernunft

von

Immanuel Kant,
Professor in Königsberg,
der Königl. Academie der Wissenschaften in Berlin
Mitglied.

Dritte verbesserte Auflage.

Riga,
bey Johann Friedrich Hartknoch.

Above, clockwise from top left: Baruch Spinoza (1623–1677); birthplace —the Netherlands; Gottfried Wilhelm Leibniz (1646–1716); birthplace —Germany; Immanuel Kant (1724–1804); birthplace—Germany; title page of Kant's *Critique of Pure Reason* (1790)

METAPHYSICS

WHAT IS METAPHYSICS?

To the uninitiated, metaphysics seems, at the outset, the most forbidding branch of philosophy. The name itself evokes images of doctrines so abstruse or so abstract that no ordinary human being can be expected to understand them. In everyday parlance such an adjective as "metaphysical" may be used synonymously with "fanciful" or "imaginary," thus lending support to the idea that metaphysical theories are pure speculations, having little to do with the practical world in which we live. Whether these suggestions are well founded or not is a matter we shall inquire into later in this chapter.

Despite such suspicions about the field, metaphysics received its name in a simple and prosaic way. In Greek, the term literally means "after physics." Andronicus of Rhodes introduced it in the first century B.C., as a designation for those unnamed books which appeared after a work called the *Physics* in the original manuscript collection of Aristotle's writings. The subject matter of metaphysics, to a large extent, has been concerned with the sort of problems Aristotle considered in the works which appeared after the *Physics*.

The appropriateness of the original Greek term is indicated by the fact that the earliest Greek philosophers, in the two centuries before Plato, wrote treatises which were often entitled *Concerning Nature*. The Greek word for nature is "physis," and these writings, as one might have expected, dealt with problems of natural science. But they also contained speculations about the nature of reality which transcended the bounds of what we would now regard as legitimate scientific inquiry. They offered theories about what the ultimate objective constituents of the world were, what accounted for or caused the world as we know it. The Greeks often failed to distinguish between these differing sorts of enterprises, whereas today we tend to restrict the term "metaphysics" to those speculative hypotheses which attempt to go beyond scientific accounts in explaining the nature of reality.

The impetus to engage in metaphysical speculation is not confined to philosophers. Although the kind of questions which philosophers eventually formulate may look very abstract, in everyday life we often come up against situations which suggest metaphysical issues and theories. We are quite accustomed to classifying some of our experiences as real and some as unreal, or illusory. For example, is the image we see in a mirror real? Where does it exist? In the mirror or behind it? Or does it exist anywhere at all? Most of us unreflectingly relegate the mirror image to some kind of metaphysical limbo, and are amused by the child or the dog who is confused and who mistakes the image for the reality. Where does the image we see with the naked eye exist in comparison to the image seen with eyeglasses? Which reflects reality? We may not have a clear conception of "reality," or what *really* exists, or has being, but in distinguishing between the image and the reality it reflects, are we not tacitly accepting some sort of metaphysical distinction between appearance and reality? Are we not distinguishing between certain of our experiences, calling them "real" in contrast to other experiences which we term "unreal" or "illusory"? In such cases, we seem to have an unconscious or instinctive basis for separating those items in our experience which we believe to be real from those which we designate as seeming to be so, or as merely appearing to be so.

The metaphysician, like the ordinary man, finds the distinction between appearance and reality, what actually does exist, of overwhelming importance. But unlike the ordinary man, he attempts to provide a systematic answer to the questions "What is the ultimate nature of reality?" and "What are the actual components of the world we live in?" Like all philosophers, he is interested in discovering, and making explicit, those principles which lie behind our uncritical judgments of the world. For example "What principles dictate our calling certain experiences 'real' and certain other experiences 'illusory'?" "Can these principles be justified?" "Is it possible to discover the true nature of reality—and if so, what is it like?" Such questions as these provide the impetus to traditional metaphysical theorizing.

In attempting to answer these questions, metaphysicians have tried to work out complete systems about the nature of reality. In terms of their systems, these metaphysicians have believed that we can gain a more complete, more coherent picture of how the various facets of the universe fit together than even science can give us. Indeed, in terms of such systems, it is argued, we can then appreciate how the structure of the world revealed by the sciences relates to other aspects of the cosmos.

In order to illustrate the nature of metaphysical speculation, let us consider how the attempt to explain the nature of change led certain Greek philosophers into profound theories about the nature of reality. Although we are all aware of the fact of change, of the fact that things seem to alter, it is difficult to give a satisfactory account of this phenomenon. As we shall see, each theory which the Greeks advanced in order to explain this commonplace fact led to difficulties and perplexities as great as, or greater than, the problems with which they had begun.

THE PROBLEM OF PERMANENCE
AND CHANGE

Beginning with Thales (636?–546? B.C.), who came from the Greek city of Miletus in Asia Minor (now southwestern Turkey), the earliest Greek metaphysicians stressed two factors in their answers to the question "What is reality?" One was that change seemed to be a basic feature of Nature, and the other was that there appeared to be certain permanent features of reality. At every moment, things change all around us. But, in spite of such changes, there seems to be some underlying permanent, unchanging stuff or structure in the universe. The problem for the first metaphysicians was to account for these two radically different aspects of reality.

The school of Thales and his followers, Anaximander and Anaximenes, attempted to work out explanations of reality by asserting that underlying all the apparent changes, there is a real, unchangeable element. The changes are only apparent. Fundamentally, reality is one thing, which, however, appears in different guises at different times. For Thales, reality was water or wetness; for Anaximander, it was the "boundless" or the Infinite; and for Anaximenes, it was air. But each insisted that no matter how much the apparent world might change, the real world remained the same.

Difficulties soon arose with regard to these theories. If everything changed all the time, could there actually be any permanent, real, unchanging feature of the universe? And, if reality were actually unchanging and unchangeable, how could it have anything to do with the apparent world of change, and how could it explain the world of change? As early philosophers explored these problems, it seemed to them that change and permanence were incompatible, and that reality had to be one or the other, either ever changing, or completely permanent.

Heraclitus' Theory

Heraclitus (540?–475 B.C.) developed a metaphysical theory which maintained that change was the only reality. Everything is in constant flux, so that, according to his famous saying, "You cannot step twice into the same river." The river, and everything else, changes constantly, so that it is never the same again. Every aspect of the world that we ever experience comes into being and passes away. No objects or properties of the world remain constant. There is constant strife between the different elements in the universe, and the only thing that does not alter is a cosmic balance maintained by the continuous change of everything. The only permanent feature of the universe is the ever-true principle that everything changes. There is no underlying, fixed "stuff," like water or air, that stays the same.

A later follower of the theory of change, Cratylus, showed that if one took Heraclitus seriously, one would be led to the conclusion that a changing world is an unintelligible one. If everything changes all of the time, then reality does not stand still long enough to be described. Objects change, and so do the words we might use to talk about them. By the time that we tried to say something about reality, we would have changed, the words and their meanings would have changed, and our listener would have changed. Hence, Cratylus concluded, one cannot even step once into the same river, since it is not the same by the time one gets one's foot into it. All that one can do is to wiggle one's finger when one hears something, since it is futile to try to communicate. Our language and our selves are in constant flux. Hence, if reality is forever changing, there would be no permanent feature of it to describe, nor any permanent means of describing it, nor any permanent describer.

Parmenides' Theory

If the theory that everything changes had its difficulties, so did the opposite theory, that there is something permanent which constitutes reality. This latter view was developed by the fifth-century B.C. philosopher Parmenides. He argued that if there is a permanent, unchanging structure to reality, this cannot come into being, pass away, move, separate, have parts, and so on. If this structure is what is, what exists, Being, what could it have come from? From something different, which would have to be Non-Being (and hence, would have to be something that did not exist); or from itself (that is, from Being)? The former case is impossible, since as Parmenides insisted, "Non-Being is not"; it does not exist. The latter case means that Being has not been created, but is preceded and, by the same reasoning, is followed by, itself.

Similarly, if Reality, or Being, had parts, what could they be? Either the parts are real, and hence are Being, or they are not. If not, then they do not exist. If the former, then the parts are the same as the whole, and they are not actually different from Being. By the same kind of argument, one can show that Being cannot move. Where could it move to? To what is, or to what is not? The latter does not exist, and hence cannot be a place. The former is Being, and hence, no motion would take place, since what is, Reality, can have no place other than where it is to move to.

The conclusion of all this, according to Parmenides, is that the one thing that can be said about Being is that it is. It cannot move, change, have parts, and so on, without becoming what it is not, and hence, without becoming nonexistent. If Being or Reality had any other properties than existence, then it would not be real, since what is not existent is nonexistent. Being must remain forever the same, since any difference would involve Non-Being, or what does not exist. The only truth that can be stated is Parmenides' unexciting summary of his theory, "Being is, Non-Being is not."

If this theory of permanence leads to the view that reality cannot have any changing, growing, or particular features, then what is the status of the fluctuating world that we live in, and see all around us? Parmenides insisted that the world of ordinary life and experience is not Being or Reality, and if not, then it must be unreal. It must be an illusion, since it cannot actually exist (that is, be part of the world of Being). The world *appears* to have parts, to move, and to change. But, in reality, it cannot have any of these features. Hence we should ignore the illusory world of appearance and contemplate the Real World of Being. The logic of Parmenides' argument then raises a fundamental problem—whether we should accept the conclusions of apparently valid logical reasoning, or should give preference to the apparent evidence of experience, even if we cannot explain it consistently.

Parmenides' disciple, the famous mathematician Zeno of Elea, a Greek city on the Italian coast, carried the argument even further. He contended that, although our everyday experience seemed to indicate that things move, change, and have parts, in fact, motion, change, and division are impossible on the basis of the kind of logic Parmenides employed. If one tried to explain the obvious movements, changes, and divisions of experience, one would be led to paradoxical, that is, contradictory or counterintuitive results, or impossible conclusions. Hence these apparent facts of experience must be unreal. The only theory that avoids the difficulties is that of Parmenides: that the world consists only of one unchanging Being.

Zeno's Paradoxes

To prove his point, Zeno developed a series of arguments to show that our ordinary conceptions of motion, change, and division are paradoxical. These arguments, which have played a continuing role in the history of mathematics and metaphysics, attempt to show that if one examines simple situations in which something seems to move, one is led, by inexorable logic, to contradictory or impossible conclusions. Hence, what appears to be the case cannot actually be the case. We may see things moving and changing, but they cannot *really* move or change.

One illustration of his thesis that Zeno offered is the well-known problem about Achilles and the tortoise. Suppose Achilles runs ten times faster than the tortoise, and the tortoise has a ten-yard lead when the race begins. Will Achilles ever pass the tortoise? Apparently, yes. If one could set up such a race, Achilles would seem to pass the tortoise between the eleventh and twelfth yards of the course. But, Zeno argued, this cannot actually happen. First, Achilles must run ten yards to catch up to the tortoise. By the time he has run that distance, the tortoise has moved ahead one yard. When Achilles runs up to where the tortoise was, he is no longer there, for he has moved on one tenth of a yard. In fact, each time Achilles reaches the previous position of the tortoise, the tortoise has reached another position farther on. No matter how long the race goes on, Achilles will have to move through every point where the tortoise has been located before he can pass him. Each time Achilles reaches such a point, the tortoise is at another point. Hence Achilles will have to pass through an infinite number of points in order to catch up with the tortoise. If it takes him some time to pass through each one of these points, it will take him forever to catch up. The ordinary conception of motion, then, cannot be accepted, since to pass through a finite distance would seem to require an infinite time.

Zeno offered another argument to establish that motion cannot really take place at all. In order for an object to move from one place to another, it will first have to move half the distance between the places. In order to move half the distance, the object will first have to move half of the half, and half of the half of the half, and so on, ad infinitum. If each of these partial motions requires some time to be completed, no matter how short, then it will take an object an infinite time to move any distance, since it will have to move through an infinite number of positions.

A version of this argument shows that a similar difficulty applies to any object having parts. If an object has two parts, then it must have at least three parts since some part must separate or distinguish the two parts; otherwise, the two parts are not different, and there are no parts. So if there are two parts, there must be three; and if three, four; and so on, ad infinitum. If these parts are of any size at all, no matter how small, then the whole object, composed of an infinite number of them, must be of infinite size, and composed of an infinite number of parts. It must be infinite in both number of parts and size.

Another argument presented by Zeno to show that an object cannot *really* move maintains that if an object is to move from one place to another, it must move either where it is or where it is not. If it moves where it is, it is not actually moving, but is standing still. It cannot move where it is not, because it cannot be where it is not, but only where it is. Hence, in spite of appearances to the contrary, an object cannot move.

This type of argument was later used to show that Socrates could not have died. He either died when he was alive, or he died when he was dead. If the former, he was dead and alive at the same time, an obvious impossibility. If the latter, then he must have died twice, also a patent impossibility. Hence Socrates never could have died. A story is told that once in Athens a follower of Zeno was expounding these arguments. He waved his arm wildly to emphasize his point and managed to dislocate his shoulder. A doctor who had been in the audience came up to examine the problem. He told the patient that his condition was impossible since the shoulder was either dislocated where it was, or dislocated where it was not. If the former, then it was not dislocated. If the latter, it could not be there to be dislocated. Hence the patient could not *really* have a dislocated shoulder. We are told that at this point the speaker gave up his Zenonian theory, and requested that his dislocated shoulder be repaired, no matter how it got that way.

The paradoxes of Zeno were offered as support for Parmenides' metaphysical theory. Zeno had sought to show that what *appeared* to be the case—that objects move, change, and have parts—cannot really be the case. The fact of movement may be undeniable. But it is only an apparent fact. In *reality*, if Zeno's arguments are conclusive, things cannot move and have parts. Hence, Reality must be one, unchangeable and immobile.

The theory of permanence, developed by Parmenides and Zeno, seemed to lead to the conclusion that Reality could not be like the world of experience, that the world of experience is unintelligible, and any attempt to understand it would only lead to paradoxical and contradictory views. But when we turn to the real world, there is nothing to be said or to be known about it other than that it *is*.

The two metaphysical views dealing with problems of change and permanence—that reality is change, and that reality is permanence—led to unsatisfactory results. Heraclitus and Cratylus seem to have shown that if change is the fundamental feature of reality, then nothing can be permanent enough to enable us to comprehend or describe it. Parmenides and Zeno, on the other hand, seem to have shown that if the fundamental characteristic of reality is permanence, then everything that we see and know around us must be illusory, and the real world must be so permanent that nothing can be said of it except that it exists. Each theory appeared to be logical but, at the same time, to involve a conclusion that was undesirable, if one wished to account for the various aspects that seemed to be real.

Pluralistic Solutions

In the generation after Zeno, attempts were made to offer metaphysical theories that could encompass both change and permanence as basic features of reality. Empedocles, Anaxagoras, and Democritus each developed a theory that reality was permanent and immutable, but that it was composed of moving parts. Democritus, for example, contended that reality was composed of uncreated, indestructible, and unalterable units called atoms. These atoms form the totality of what exists. They are separate, different entities, all in motion. The multiplicity of atoms and their movements account for the apparent changes in the world, although in reality, the world is always the same (since it is always made up of the same unlimited collection of atomic units).

The pluralistic metaphysical systems of Empedocles, Anaxagoras, and Democritus were all directed toward showing that there must be some truth in both the theories of change and of permanence. But none of these theories appeared to overcome the difficulties raised by the earlier arguments of Heraclitus, Cratylus, Parmenides, and Zeno. Plato and Aristotle, in the fourth century, offered more extensive metaphysical systems which attempted to explain the fundamental nature of reality in such a way as to do justice both to the permanent and changing features of the world. Plato's views tended more to stress that reality must be permanent and unchanging, while Aristotle's laid more emphasis upon the reality of change.

PLATO'S METAPHYSICAL THEORY

We have already discussed some of the features of Plato's metaphysics in dealing with his theory of knowledge. Plato agreed with Parmenides and Zeno that the real world must be permanent and immutable. However, Plato also maintained that the real world is composed of many things, the various Platonic Ideas or Forms, rather than just one entity, Being.

Plato's answer to the basic metaphysical question, What is reality? is that fundamentally it is the Forms of things that are real, and not matter or "stuff." Things, as we perceive them, are forever changing and altering. They seem to have, as Parmenides and Zeno had previously shown, impossible properties. The same thing, at different times, has different properties. It appears large in some circumstances, and small in others. It seems to be dark at one time, and light at another. When we examine the sense world in terms of what we perceive, we find that it possesses no permanence, stability, or coherence. Such a world cannot be *real*, but can only consist of illusory appearances.

However, in the sense world, we discover the first glimmerings of what reality actually is. The forms of things, unlike the things themselves, are unchanging and intelligible. The former are apprehended by reason, the latter by the senses. Individual dogs may be in a continual state of alteration, and may, ultimately, be illusory entities. But, the form of a dog, "dogness," is immutable. The meaning of the term "dog" is always the same, even though each particular dog passes through an ever-changing life cycle. Hence, Plato contended, what is real is the totality of Forms or Platonic Ideas, and these real objects account for whatever stability and intelligibility the world of illusory sense experience may possess.

Reality is, then, solely to be identified with Platonic Ideas. These, in Plato's account, are meanings. Since they are unaffected by the changes that take place in the sense world, they must have an existence distinct from the world of appearance. The Ideas exist in their own realm, which we become acquainted with, not through sense experience, but through thought and comprehension. When we understand, what we are doing is apprehending a Form or Idea.

If it was asked, "Why do the Ideas have the characteristics they do?" Plato offered a somewhat mysterious and mystical answer. All of the Ideas share in common the features of permanence, stability, and intelligibility. To account for this, Plato proposed that there must be an Idea of Ideas, the Idea of the Good, which is the ultimate reality and the source of the reality of everything else. In his metaphorical pictures, Plato likened the Idea of the Good to the sun, which illuminates everything including itself. When one has the climactic experience of knowing the Idea of the Good, suddenly "everything is clear." The awareness of this Idea is like a mystical experience. It is beyond understanding. It is ineffable. And yet it explains all else. When one has had this experience, one then comprehends why all the other Ideas are what they are, because they partake of, or participate in, the Idea of the Good.

If the realm of Ideas is the real world, is there any connection or relationship between this world and the world of appearance or illusion that we see all around us? There are some real or permanent features to the sense world. Though its various elements may change all the time, the forms in it remain fixed. Thus, though a box may change its shape in the course of time, the characteristics of "squareness" and "cubeness" which the box exhibits stay the same. In Plato's terminology, things participate in, or partake of, the Ideas or Forms, and this accounts for the real or permanent features in an otherwise unreal world.

Two further features of Plato's metaphysical theory are set forth in his various attempts to explain this relationship between the real world and the world of appearance. Participation, or partaking, Plato insisted in the dialogue entitled *Parmenides*, is not like possessing a piece of an Idea. An Idea is not like a pie that is sliced up, so that each thing that partakes of it has one of the pieces. If this were the case, each thing would actually partake of a different Idea, since each piece would be separate and distinct. Also, such an interpretation would mean that Ideas were actually parts of things, and were located in the unreal world. Instead, Plato insisted, the relationship between Ideas and things was to be understood in terms of one of his favorite analogies, that of the sun and what it shines on. Things receive whatever degree of reality they have from the Ideas. The forms that things have exemplify the Ideas without actually being the Ideas. It is analogous to the fact that in daylight things are illuminated by and exemplify the sun's light, without containing the sun. Thus, although things, in possessing various forms, participate in or partake of the Ideas, the Ideas still remain independent of and unaffected by things.

In Plato's picture of the nature of reality, the real world has the characteristics of Parmenides' realm of Being, except for the fact that Plato's real world contains multiplicity as well as permanence. The world of change is seen in both theories as an essentially unreal world, though Plato allowed a faint glimmer of reality to enter into the sense world, through the relationship of participation between things and Ideas. Parmenides, as well as Zeno, was unable (and was probably not interested in doing it) to present any explanation of the apparent features of the apparent world. Plato's participation theory attempts to show that the "real" characteristics of the sense world can be accounted for. He further proposed a hypothesis about how these characteristics got into the sense world, and why the sense world has the history that it does.

In the dialogue *Timaeus*, a theory is offered to explain how the real world acts on, or causes, the activities in the sense world. The real world, if it is unchanging, cannot do anything, and hence cannot initiate any changes or motions in the apparent world. Therefore, there must be an active force or agent who is able to bring certain features of the world of Ideas into the world of things. And this agent must be different from an unchanging Idea.

The agent, called the "Demiurge" or "Demiurgos," a subordinate deity, exists on the border line between the unchanging world of pure form and the chaotic world of matter. The latter realm, in itself, is completely formless (otherwise, some of the Ideas would already be in it). It is indescribable. But it has the capacity to receive or contain some degree of form. The Demiurge tries to introduce form and order into the chaotic material world by trying to impose the characteristics of the real world on the material one. This results in images or copies of the Ideas appearing in the sense world. Circularity, rectangularity, greenness, heaviness, and so on, are introduced into the material world, giving it some recognizable order, such as we find in the visible world. Because the Demiurge places forms in the material world, we are able to describe and identify objects at various times and places.

Unfortunately, however, the material world is too unstable to maintain the forms given to it. It can only participate in them, or partake of them, for limited periods of time. Therefore, the apparent order or form keeps changing, and the visible world is always in flux as it receives forms and loses them. The world of time, then, is "the moving image of eternity," receiving its eternal aspects through the work of the Demiurge, and losing them in endless chaotic motions. The study of the visible world, such as the science of physics, can only "speak the language of probabilities," since there is nothing permanent in the apparent world that can be described.

Plato's metaphysical theory emphasizes the Ideal intelligible reality as the important and significant realm of the universe, while, at the same time, it tries to give some account of the world of appearance. The theory, besides proposing an answer to the question "What is reality?" also leads to some conclusions about man's relations to the real world.

Human beings belong to both the real and the apparent worlds. Our bodies are physical, and hence part of the material, visible world. Our sense information consists of the images we receive of the apparent, illusory world. On the other hand, our minds are immaterial and are capable of knowing the real world of Platonic Ideas. In addition to possessing bodies and minds, Plato maintained that we also had souls which directed our activities and interests. Our bodies want to "descend" into the material world of appearance, while our minds want to soar upward in order to contemplate the real world. The soul is portrayed as being like the driver of a chariot, directing two horses pulling in opposite directions. The human soul is attempting to steer while it is trapped in its prison, the body.

If the soul is able to direct a harmonious life in these circumstances, it can eventually lead a human being to liberation from the sense world, and to the goal of contemplation of the real world. This will be accomplished by eliminating one's dependence on the physical world. Though one lives in physical circumstances, and has physical needs, these do not have to dominate one's life. A life directed in terms of the ultimate goal of contemplating reality, while lived in a physical context, should, after the death of the body, enable the soul to soar upward to the perfect world of Ideas.

This conclusion to Plato's metaphysical theory led to an otherworldly view, which is usually called "Platonism." Many of Plato's followers, in the centuries since he propounded his philosophy, have emphasized the importance of the world of Ideas, while derogating the sense world. These followers, who are called "Platonists," have insisted that what is worthwhile in the world can be found only in the real world. Hence, the physical world should be neglected or ignored, while men should pursue the goal of contemplation of the world of Ideas to obtain some kind of mystical insight into the nature of ultimate reality. Because of the development of Platonism, some scholars have questioned whether Plato himself was actually a Platonist, since Plato was so interested in certain worldly matters, such as political society, as we shall discuss in the next chapter.

NEO-PLATONISM

One of the most influential forms of Platonism in the history of Western thought is Neo-Platonism. This theory was first developed by Plotinus (A.D. 205?–270), a philosopher who studied at Alexandria in Egypt. He is also supposed to have traveled to India and Persia and learned about Oriental philosophy. He set up a school in Rome and there taught his doctrines and wrote his *Enneads*, a group of treatises on philosophy.

Plotinus's Neo-Platonic theory is a metaphysical view stressing the dynamic relationship between the real world and the apparent one, through which a human being could achieve salvation. The world of Ideas was seen not only as the real world, but also as the creative power which emanated down to the sense world and issued forth whatever reality that world possessed. The universe was conceived of as a "great chain of Being," starting with the completely real being, the One, or God, or the Idea of the Good, whose very nature overflowed into lesser realms of being, such as the world of Ideas, human beings, animals, inanimate objects, down to matter, "the last faint shadow of reality." Reality was conceived in terms of unity. The more unity anything possessed, the more real it was. Matter was almost totally diffuse, hence the least real. The One was total unity, hence the most real. From it the world of Ideas and the World-Soul emanated and had almost as much reality. The concepts of Plato's world of Ideas were hypostasized, that is, conceived of, as real active beings. Each level of reality, according to Plotinus, emanated from its own nature the being and reality of lesser entities. The universe was portrayed as an eternally overflowing fountain, in which the One overflowed, thus producing the next lower level of reality, which overflowed, producing the next, and so on. The process continued down the "great chain of Being" until the stream of reality petered out in the material world.

In this theory, the aim of human existence was seen as an attempt to move up the ladder of existence, to become more real. To accomplish this, men were to direct all their interests and attention to what was above them on the "great chain of Being." By philosophizing they could liberate themselves from the sense world, and become more and more part of the intelligible world. The more one could understand, the more one would become like what one understood. Ultimately, if successful, one would reach the culmination of the "journey of the mind to God," by a mystical union with the One. Thus the final end of seeking to understand the nature of reality would be to become absorbed by what is most real, and to lose all of one's individuality which merely represents lesser degrees of reality. Through philosophizing, through art, and through mystic experience of unity with the One, Plotinus saw the path to human salvation, and of liberation from the lesser reality of sensory and material worlds.

Neo-Platonic metaphysics has been extraordinarily influential in Western thought because of its religious implications. Philosophers in the Judaeo-Christian tradition have seen this form of Platonism as a metaphysical interpretation of their religious views. By transforming Plato's Idea of Good into the God of Scripture, by emphasizing the Divine Creativity of the real world, and portraying man's quest for God as a liberation from the sensible world, theologians produced a Platonic metaphysics which they believed explained their own religious views.

After Plotinus, St. Augustine (A.D. 354–430) developed Neo-Platonism into a Christian philosophy, in which the One of Plotinus's theory became the Divine Power Himself, who created the material world out of nothing and organized it according to the Divine pattern of the world of Ideas. When Jewish and Christian theologians came in contact with Greek philosophy, some of them sought to express their religious convictions in terms of metaphysical conceptions. At first they found Platonism, and later Neo-Platonism, most congenial, since it seemed to them to mirror their religious views in philosophical terms. Probably part of their motivation was to make their religious beliefs intelligible to and respectable to an audience raised on Greek philosophy.

Two centuries before Plotinus, the Jewish philosopher Philo, a contemporary of Jesus who lived in the cosmopolitan Greek city of Alexandria, portrayed Platonism as a philosophical account of the same message that God had revealed to Moses in historical terms. Plato, who had stated the Divine Revelation in metaphysical terms, was seen as only a slightly less important figure than Moses. Early Greek Christian Church Fathers from Alexandria, such as Clement and Origen, followed in the same vein at the end of the second century, using Platonism to express their Christian views.

Neo-Platonism remained a basic religio-philosophical way of understanding the nature of reality. Its metaphysics was adapted by Moslem and Jewish thinkers, as well as Christian ones, to explain the nature of reality according to their respective religions. For centuries the philosophy of Plotinus and his followers has remained important, influencing, among others, the metaphysical views of the Renaissance Platonists and the German Idealists.

The metaphysical movement initiated by Plato attempted to answer the question "What is reality?" by starting with the Parmenidean contention that reality is what is permanent and unchanging. The real world, however, in Plato's theory, is not just one thing, but has many components, the various Forms or Ideas, which explain the multiplicity of things in the world. Further, the Demiurge accounts for the dynamic features of the world, explaining how the permanent world comes in contact with the changing, apparent world, and how the former gives meaning and a degree of reality to the latter. This theory about the nature of reality gave rise to certain other-worldly and religious attitudes and views. It suggests that the real world is the important one, and hence that we should concentrate our interests and efforts upon it. The studies that are worthwhile according to this view are those that deal with reality, like mathematics (which deals only with pure Forms), and not those that deal with appearances and illusions, like the sciences of the visible world. Finally, it contended that our lives should be lived in terms of our relations with the real world, and not in terms of the unreal and unimportant features of the visible world.

ARISTOTLE'S METAPHYSICAL THEORY

One of Plato's students, Aristotle (384–322 B.C.), rejected his teacher's views, and developed a metaphysical theory which found the basic features of reality in the natural world and in the process of change. Aristotle had studied in Plato's Academy for about twenty years before he left to follow out his interests in natural science, especially biology. For several years he collected and analyzed specimens of natural organisms. He then returned to his native Macedonia, where his father had been the court physician, in order to become the teacher of young Alexander the Great. When the Macedonians had conquered Athens, Aristotle returned to establish his own school, the Lyceum. Because of the fact that courses were taught while the teacher and the students were walking around the gardens, Aristotle is known as the "Peripatetic" (one who walks about), and his followers, the "Peripatetics." Aristotle's theories of metaphysics, ethics, political philosophy, and so on, were presented as lecture courses in the school. The writings that have come down to us are probably either the students' notes, or some of Aristotle's that he used in his courses. They were preserved in a trunk, and discovered hundreds of years later.

Aristotle's metaphysical views are rather complex, and, like the theories of most philosophers, are subject to varying interpretations. We shall consider one interpretation of his theory here. At the end of the chapter, the student will find suggested additional readings, some of which contain divergent explanations and evaluations of Aristotle's and other philosophers' theories.

In his works, *The Physics* (or On Nature) and *The Metaphysics*, Aristotle began with a rejection of Plato's theory that the real world must be a different one from that with which we are immediately acquainted in our ordinary experience. Instead, Aristotle insisted that what we experience must be what is real, and that the changing nature of the visible world must be a fundamental characteristic of reality. The changing natural world is intelligible if we can discover what its actual constituents are, and how they operate.

Every natural object is always undergoing change. But in this process there is not only something that changes, there is also something that stays the same. Instead of dismissing the changing object because it is not completely permanent, and therefore unreal, one should, Aristotle maintained, try to understand what change involves in order to ascertain what reality consists of. To do this, one must understand the "four causes" involved in any change.

The four causes are actually four answers to questions one might ask about anything that changes: What is it that changes (the material cause)? What does it change to, what form does it acquire (the formal cause)? What makes it change, what produces the alteration (the efficient cause)? And for what reason or purpose does it change, what goal is being achieved by the change (the final cause)? One of Aristotle's favorite examples may make the differences between these causes clearer. When a block of marble is changed into a statue, the material cause is the matter that changes, the marble. The formal cause is the shape or form that it changes to, the form of the statue. The change is brought about by an agent, the efficient cause, in this case the sculptor. Finally, and possibly most important for Aristotle, there must be a reason why the marble is changed into a statue. The final cause in this case is the purpose to be achieved by the change, perhaps the creation of a beautiful object that the sculptor wishes to make.

In every change, then, there is something that remains the same, the matter, and there is something that changes, the form. The original object has the potentiality to become something else. And change is thus a process of actualizing potentialities, by altering matter in one form so that it becomes matter in another form. The constant underlying matter can remain the same, though it acquires another form. Thus when the acorn grows into an oak, in a material sense there is a real, permanent element, while in a formal sense there has been a real change.

Some changes, Aristotle observed, are induced by outside agents, while most changes seem to require no external director. The former type, which he labeled "violent" or "unnatural," occurs when something interferes with the ordinary course of nature. For example, a tree can be transformed into a desk, but this is not the natural, normal development. This process occurs only when a human being comes on the scene and alters the normal course of events.

Natural change, which Aristotle saw exhibited everywhere and especially in the biological kingdom, involves no outside interference. The object, left by itself, naturally changes and acquires new forms. Seeds grow into plants and trees, puppies grow into dogs, kittens into cats, and planets move around in their appointed orbits. Normal, natural changes all appear to be purposeful. The objects naturally alter, actualizing one set of potentialities rather than another. A tree has the potentiality to be a bed, but it never naturally changes into one. Puppies never grow up to be cats, and planets do not change their courses. Why? Because, Aristotle insisted, each object has a final form that it is trying to acquire, and has an innate tendency to actualize that form if nothing interferes with its natural development.

The goal or purpose is, then, the all-important cause of natural change. It, rather than anything external to the object, directs the way each object develops. Every object in nature acts in a purposeful or teleological manner, striving to attain some end. Stones try to fall downward toward the center of the earth; acorns try to grow into oak trees; and so on. The final form or goal in each case leads the object to exercise its natural tendencies and abilities so that it can become actually what it has the potentiality to be.

Since the type of changes that occur naturally are regular, each kind of object must have a goal or final cause that is proper to it. By inspecting what the objects do naturally, and what they have the capacity to do, it is possible to ascertain what purpose each species is trying to achieve. Some species, such as inanimate objects like stones, only change position, and do not seem to have the capacity for any other type of change, like growth. Therefore, the goal of stones must be to reach a certain place. Further, since they all move naturally downward, and only move in other directions when kicked or thrown, the purpose of the natural movement in stones, then, must be to reach a definite downward position, namely, the center of the earth.

On the basis of this type of analysis, Aristotle concluded that all natural objects, with the exception of God, are composed of matter and form. The matter of each species has the potentiality for receiving various forms, or for being "informed." Pure or prime matter has the potentiality for receiving all possible forms. It is, in Aristotle's terminology, pure potentiality, that is, it can become anything. All natural objects, however, are composed of some type of informed matter, thereby limiting their potentialities. Stones cannot acquire legs; horses cannot become philosophers or musicians. Within the limitations of each object's potentialities, it strives to acquire that form proper to its species. And, hence, all natural change can be understood as the attempt by each natural object to realize or actualize the final form of its kind. Each natural object begins its career composed of a type of matter with potentialities, and in a certain form. It goes through a series of inner-directed changes seeking to acquire its proper form or goal.

The natural changes which occur indicate that each species has a goal relative to it, and an ultimate goal common to all things. The relative goals enable one to define and distinguish species, since each has its own proper final form. Stones are trying to reach the center of the earth, acorns are trying to become oaks, puppies are trying to become dogs, and people are trying to become rational and social beings. But why? Why does each species go through this endlessly repetitive process in which each individual member of the species tries in his own way to achieve the goal of the species?

Aristotle found the answer in a common feature of all change. Every change is an attempt to achieve another state or form. Change continues as long as the object still has the potentiality to receive another form. Hence change will continue until objects reach a state in which no further acquisition of forms is possible. The ultimate goal, then, of every object is to achieve a state of immutability and immobility, a state of complete rest. Movement and change are attempts to reach a different state. The completely different state is that in which no further alteration of any kind is possible.

Every object that is composed of matter and form can still change, since, as long as it is material, it still has the potentiality to receive other forms. Each object, on achieving its relative form, can still acquire other forms, because of its material cause. Thus, after the acorn becomes an oak, it can and does proceed to change by degenerating. The only type of object that could reach a complete state of immutability would be one that had no more potentialities, and hence no more matter. Thus, the only objects that could achieve the ultimate final form of all things, complete rest and unchangeability, would be those that are composed only of pure form.

When we survey the many kinds of objects in the universe, we find that they approach or approximate their ultimate goal of permanence—complete rest or immutability—in varying degrees. Observable objects can be graded in a scale from the highest approximation to the lowest. On the top of the scale, according to Aristotle, are heavenly bodies. They have reached a state of complete rest in all respects except one. They do not grow or decay. They do not change color or shape. They do not undergo any irregular motions. The only type of change that happens to them is change of position, in what Aristotle thought were regular circular orbits (then regarded as the most perfect type of movement). This would indicate that the heavenly bodies do not possess any potentiality for any other kind of change. Their ceaseless regular movement indicates that they are forever seeking complete and final rest, by changing their positions. Like everything else that is material, they fail to achieve this ultimate goal, since they are forever actualizing their continually existing potentiality for change of position. But the heavenly bodies come closer to the ultimate goal in that they change in only one way, and this change is constant and of the most perfect kind.

Objects on the surface of the earth are not able to approach as close to the achievement of the ultimate goal as celestial objects can and do. All terrestrial objects change in many respects. They change in position, in qualities, in state of growth and decomposition. The living objects all die, and hence never reach any permanence and complete rest and unchangeability as individuals. The inanimate ones are subject to decomposition and destruction.

Living objects are able to attain a degree of permanence and stability only as species rather than as individuals. Each separate organism perishes, but the species is perpetuated. Hence each living species achieves an approximation to the ultimate goal of all things through reproduction of the species. Its relative goal is to develop in its own way so that it can reproduce the species. The acorns grow into oaks so that more acorns can be produced to grow into other oaks, and puppies grow up to be dogs so that they can produce more canine progeny.

Human beings differ from other living beings in that they can approximate the ultimate goal not only by reproducing their species and thereby, according to Aristotle, "participating in the eternal and the divine," but also by being able to achieve another sort of permanence, that of thinking of unchanging forms. When we are able to think of pure forms, our minds reach a state of completeness and permanence. Our minds achieve a state of pure form in contemplating an unchanging object.

In view of the fact that every object in the universe is trying to achieve a state of pure form in which it cannot change any more, there must be, Aristotle argued, an actual entity which has the properties of the ultimate goal. This entity, called the "Unmoved Mover," is the goal, or final cause, of all change. As such, it must consist of pure form, with no matter whatsoever; otherwise, it would still have some potentiality, and thus be able to change in some respect. It is unmoved because movement is toward some unrealized potentiality. Since it is immaterial, it is incapable of any type of motion. But, at the same time, by being what everything else wants to become, it is the final cause of the motion of all other objects. Everything in the cosmos, from stones, animals, and people up to heavenly bodies, goes through its natural process of change and development in order to approach the perfection, the immutability, of the Unmoved Mover. Everything loves the perfect state of pure form and wants to attain it. Hence, it is love that makes the world go on, in its endless, ceaseless series of changes, movements and alterations. The Perfect Being, the Unmoved Mover, does nothing to bring this about. But, just by existing, it motivates and activates everything else to pursue the sort of perfection and immutability that each object and each species desires to achieve for itself.

Unfortunately, this unending, changing Aristotelian cosmos has a frustrating aspect for everything in it except the Unmoved Mover. Everything actualizes its potentialities in a purposeful, or teleological way, striving toward its goal. The series of processes which each species undergoes in order to achieve its relative end, and to pursue its final cause, or ultimate goal, is bound to end in failure. Every natural object, except the Unmoved Mover, remains, in spite of all of its changes, a material object. Hence, all material things are still capable of change and can never become pure form. Even the celestial objects, which are the closest to achieving the goal, never do, and never will. They will go on forever traveling in their perfect, circular orbits, without ever completely losing their potentiality for further movement. The world, then, according to Aristotle, comprises an unending series of changes, all aimed at achieving the same goal, but none of them actually succeeding in doing so.

While all this is going on, the Unmoved Mover remains serene, perfect, and uninvolved and unaffected by all the changes. The Unmoved Mover, often identified with the God of various religious traditions, is, in Aristotle's metaphysics, totally inactive. If He could act on the world, or in response to desires and needs of various entities in the world, then He could change and move, contrary to His nature. Thus, for Aristotle, the Unmoved Mover cannot be a creative or providential deity. He can only be pure form, thinking about Himself. If He could think about the changing things in the universe, He could change in one aspect, that of the ideas He was aware of. Therefore, the Unmoved Mover must remain unchangeable in all respects, but, at the same time, He is the final cause of all change.

Aristotle's metaphysical system attempts to describe reality in such a way that it can be both permanent and changing. The real world is not the invisible world of Ideas that Plato spoke of (the existence of which Aristotle doubted very much). Rather, the real world is the natural one, which, when properly understood, can be seen to contain both matter capable of change as well as form, the permanent state matter is trying to achieve. Each object both really is what it now is and really has the potentiality to become what it will be. The final cause, or purpose, is the crucial feature of reality that makes it possible to explain and describe the features of the world.

Aristotle contended that his metaphysical theory could account for what everybody knew, that there is a real natural world which is always changing, without having to deny either the permanent or the changing aspect of the universe, and without having to introduce a hypothetical other world to explain the characteristics of reality. He could accept Heraclitus' view that everything changes, without accepting the conclusion that change is the only reality. Besides the fact of change, there is also the matter which changes, the form it changes into, and there are the final causes, relative and ultimate, that remain constant and enable us to understand and describe the universe.

EUDOXUS' AND ARISTOTLE'S
ANSWER TO ZENO

Since change was taken by Aristotle as a basic feature of reality, he had to reject the arguments and conclusions presented by Parmenides and Zeno. Not only is change an actual, real occurrence; it is also explicable. Employing a mathematical theory developed by a fellow student in Plato's Academy, Eudoxus of Cnidos, Aristotle offered an answer to the paradoxes of Zeno in his *Physics*. The arguments of Zeno presuppose that a series of discrete and distinguishable changes must take place when something changes or moves from state A to state B. Zeno then argued that in order for the complete change or motion to take place, a part of it had to occur first. The parts could be divided to infinity, and hence an infinite number of changes or motions would have to occur in a finite time before any motion could take place. According to Eudoxus and Aristotle, the paradoxes result from the assumption that space and time can be infinitely divided. Since, in fact, no space, and no object, can be or ever is divided into an infinite number of parts, the particular problems Zeno developed do not actually occur. The process of change is a transition from state A to state B, not state A first, and then state B. Achilles during the race is not located at successive points A and B at successive times, but he is in transition from A to B. Similarly, the arrow is not first at its starting place, and then at the end of its course. Instead, it is in the process of moving from the beginning to the end. Achilles, or the arrow, can be located, approximately, by dividing the distance they are traversing into intervals, and making the intervals more and more precise. In so doing, an infinite number of intervals is never actually constructed. Instead, a finite approximation is worked out, which can still be further corrected. This indicates that distances, alterations, and so on, can *potentially* be divided ad infinitum, according to Aristotle's and Eudoxus' theory, but they cannot *actually* be divided into an infinite number of places, times, and so on. The motion of any object can be explained in terms of the intervals it traverses during its process of change or motion. The intervals can be made as small as one likes. But there never are and never will be an infinite number of intervals, and, hence, Zeno's arguments will never apply.

To illustrate this, if one asks at what point Achilles will actually catch up with the tortoise, the question becomes, "In what interval is he in the process of moving through the interval in which the tortoise is moving?" Given the original situation—that Achilles runs ten times faster than the tortoise, and the tortoise begins with a ten-yard lead—then the answer is that Achilles passes the tortoise between the eleventh and twelfth yard markers. If one desires a more exact answer, the passing occurs in the interval between 11.1111111111 and 11.1111111112 yards. More and more precise formulations of the size of the interval can be made by calculating smaller and smaller intervals, but, at no time in the calculation will it be necessary that Achilles has to traverse an infinite number of places before he catches up to the tortoise. Hence, the reasoning of Zeno, argued Eudoxus and Aristotle, does not apply.

What, in fact, this answer amounts to is that Eudoxus managed to develop a mathematical system which includes a method for locating and describing objects in terms of intervals instead of in terms of points. Such a system avoids the sorts of situations which lead to the Zeno paradoxes. Eudoxus' mathematical system, especially his "method of exhaustion," proved invaluable in Greek mathematics by enabling mathematicians to compute the areas of nonrectilinear figures, such as circles or ellipses, without requiring them to complete a calculation of an infinite number of steps.

Aristotle also answered the arguments of Parmenides. These, he insisted, resulted from a failure to distinguish an object from its properties. According to Parmenides, if an object changed, it had to change from what it was, an existing thing, to what it was not, a nonexisting thing. Since it could not be what it was not, it could not change. But, Aristotle replied, an object is not identical with its properties. The properties are forms that it has at a given time, plus the potentiality for having other forms. The object, in the sense of its material cause, remains the same through change. It is an existing being at the beginning of the process and at the end of it. It changes only in respect to its formal cause because of its final cause (presuming it is a natural change). Hence the object has not become nonexistent through change; it has only become different.

Aristotle's answer to the question "What is reality?" insisted on the genuine, real nature of both change and permanence, and sought to show that both aspects of reality could be understood if seen in terms of the fundamental teleological character of the universe. The real world consists of all natural objects, which are informed material objects striving toward a final cause relative to their species, and an ultimate goal, the state of pure form. Each object is real, but achieves a different degree of perfection because of its four causes. In addition, in view of the purposeful character of all change, there must be a real being who is the ultimate goal of all change, the Unmoved Mover. His very existence as the pure form that everything wants to become leads all natural objects to actualize their potentialities.

The Later History
of Aristotelianism

The Aristotelian system of metaphysics played only a slight role in the history of ancient thought, but a very vital one in more recent times. Through a series of accidents, the writings of Aristotle were lost for several centuries. By the time they were rediscovered and made known, philosophical interest had shifted more to religious and ethical concerns. Platonism and Neo-Platonism predominated. In the Middle Ages, Aristotle became very influential and was known as "The Philosopher," and, in Dante's famous phrase, as "the master of them that know."

In the world of the Moslem empire that extended from Spain in the west to India in the east, the views of Aristotle were revived in the early Middle Ages. Moslem and Jewish philosophers, especially in the eleventh and twelfth centuries, found in Aristotelianism an extraordinary metaphysical system for explaining the natural world. Aristotle had examined every type of changing object he could find, and had provided the medieval thinkers with the rudiments of practically every science. He had developed theories of change about inanimate and animate objects, and composed all his finds and theories into one vast system. The Arabic philosopher Averroës (1126–1198), and the Jewish philosopher Maimonides (1135–1204), developed versions of Aristotle's system to fit with the tenets of their religions. (They did it by mixing in Neo-Platonic elements which they thought were from works of Aristotle, but were actually from writings of Plotinus and his followers.) The works of Averroës, Maimonides, and other Arabic and Jewish philosophers, as well as those of Aristotle, were translated into Latin in Spain, where the cultures of Islam, Judaism and Christianity were intermingled. The Latin versions entered Christian Europe, where they caused a great stir. Some of Aristotle's theories (as well as some of Averroës') were soon found to be in conflict with official Christian doctrines. Aristotle's views of the nature of God, of the eternality of the world, and of the possibilities of the immortality of the human soul, all seemed to lead to heretical conclusions. The great Christian philosopher St. Thomas Aquinas (1225–1274), an Italian who taught at the University of Paris, developed a synthesis reconciling Aristotelian and Christian views, somewhat similar to Maimonides' treatment of Judaism. St. Thomas's philosophy, called "Thomism," became the official philosophy of the Catholic Church, and dominated Christian Europe up to the Renaissance (though at the time of St. Thomas, the teaching of Aristotle's philosophy had at first been forbidden, because Church authorities thought it was too dangerous and in conflict with accepted Christian dogmas).

Aristotle's metaphysical system began to be rejected when modern science came on the scene. The notion of the universe as entirely purposeful, to be understood in terms of final causes, conflicted with the development of a purely mechanical view of the action of natural objects. Materialistic theories, like that of Epicurus, which we shall consider next, were preferred, since they seemed to be more in keeping with the picture of reality worked out by the scientists.

EPICURUS' METAPHYSICAL THEORY

Before turning to more modern metaphysical theories and problems, we shall consider one other ancient view that tried to explain how reality could be in a constant state of change and yet be permanent as well. The metaphysical system of Epicurus is not actually original with him. Most of his views were taken over from the atomist Democritus, mentioned earlier in this chapter. However, the system as we know it has come down to us in three letters of Epicurus, and in the famous poem "On the Nature of Things" by the Roman Epicurean, Lucretius. (The ethical theory of Epicurus, hedonism, will be discussed separately in Chapter 5, "Ethics.")

Epicurus (341–270 B.C.) came from the Athenian colony of Samos. According to one account, he became a philosopher when as a youth a teacher in school taught him that in the beginning of the world there was chaos. Epicurus is supposed to have asked, "And whence came the chaos?" When the teacher could not answer, he went off to find the answer. He apparently quarreled with several people who claimed to have the answer, but he finally adopted Democritus' philosophy, which he modified slightly. He began his own school, establishing it in Athens at the end of the fourth century in a garden that became known as "The Garden of Epicurus," where his disciples lived and tried to follow his teachings.

The Epicurean answer to the question "What is reality?" is that the real world is composed of nothing but atoms of different sizes and shapes, and empty space. The indivisible atomic units have no properties except their configurations (and possibly their weight). They comprise all of reality, and their actions and interactions can account for all of the features of the universe. The atoms are completely permanent. They can be neither created nor destroyed. And, unlike Aristotle's conception of natural objects, the Epicurean atoms were conceived of as absolutely purposeless.

The original Greek meaning of "atom" is "that which cannot be cut or divided." Hence, according to Epicurus, no more fundamental unit could exist, nor could atoms have parts. Since atoms are the fundamental constituents of reality, every object larger than an atom is composed of a collection of atoms. The atoms have an infinite variety of sizes and shapes. Some are cubic, some spherical, some cylindrical, some pyramidal, some hooked, and so on. All of the objects that we ever perceive are nothing but collections of various atoms, plus empty space. Not only are physical objects, such as stones, mere atomic collections; so also are animals and people.

The atomic level of the universe stays the same all the time. No matter what happens, the world is still composed of nothing but atoms and empty space. The atoms never change. No new ones come into being. No old ones ever disappear. What changes in the real world is only the arrangement of atoms. And when the arrangements and aggregations of atoms change, the various apparent objects in the world alter. The real world remains always constant in composition, but not in position. The apparent world of objects, being simply the effect of a given state of the atomic universe, is in constant flux, as one arrangement of atoms is followed by another.

The movement of atoms, as well as their size and shape, is a basic feature of the real universe. The atoms have always moved, and always will move, in a downward direction. In the original theory of Democritus, the atoms were thought of as always falling straight down, but at varying rates of speed, possibly because of a difference in their weights. Because of their different velocities, collisions occur. The collisions then lead to an effect like that of colliding billiard balls. The atoms bounce off in different directions, striking other atoms in turn, causing them to alter their paths, and so on. Each collision leads to a rearrangement of the atomic universe, and, hence, to a change in the composition of the apparent universe. The changes we perceive—from trees growing to rocks falling to people moving around—are all caused by atomic collisions and the chain reactions that follow therefrom.

In Democritus' version of the theory, the real universe was conceived of as being completely determined. This means that one state of the universe followed necessarily from the one before it. If a person knew the present position of all the atoms, the directions in which they were moving, and their rates of speed, he could calculate exactly (with an infinite number of electronic computers) what every future event must be, and what every past event must have been. Every event in the whole history of the universe is entirely determined by the positions of atoms and their movements. (Unfortunately, in the context of Greek science of ancient times, this completely deterministic theory proved quite useless, since the atomists had no way of locating any atoms, or of measuring their movements. They could only hypothesize that if certain atoms were in a particular place, and moving in certain ways, then a particular event would have to occur.)

Epicurus insisted instead that atoms not only move downward, but also, occasionally, swerve out of line for no reason whatsoever. Whenever this "gentle swerve" of an atom takes place, the whole arrangement of atoms is changed, since each swerve will cause a chain reaction of motions. Because there is no reason for the swerve, it is not possible to predict the future course of atomic movements, and, hence, the future course of events. No matter how much one studies the present position and movement of all the atoms, one will never be able to determine exactly what will happen next, since any of the atoms may suddenly swerve, and thereby alter all the data.

Though Democritus and Epicurus disagreed over whether or not the universe was completely deterministic, they did agree that the universe was completely materialistic. The only real objects are material ones, and everything can be explained or understood in terms of the motions of the units of matter, the atoms. Their materialism extended to everything, including the mind and its functioning, and even, in Epicurus' theory, to the nature of God.

Minds as well as bodies were considered material objects. Minds differed from bodies in that they were composed of a special type of atom, called the soul atom. The soul atoms were finer, and were perfectly spherical. Mental events, like thoughts, were explained as the effect of collisions of soul atoms. When something stimulated a sense organ by an atomic collision, this in turn moved the soul atoms, and the result was, let us say, the idea of a beautiful blonde. Epicurus tried to explain all our ideas and feelings as the effects of atomic collisions on our sense organs or on our internal ones, which then caused the soul atoms to move. The occasional swerve, when it occurred among soul atoms, explained our apparent freedom to will or think something different from what would be expected by the atomic collisions.

The difference between a living being and an inanimate one was, in the metaphysical system of Epicurus, that living beings contained soul atoms, whereas inanimate ones did not. When a person or an animal died, all that happened was that his soul atoms departed from the arrangement or collection that constituted the living being, leaving only the regular atoms. The soul atoms would then be gathered up into another collection, and hence another living creature would come into being. The soul atoms, like any others, could be neither created nor destroyed. But combinations that contained them could be changed, giving rise to the apparent phenomenon of the life and death cycle among living things.

Since everything that exists is a material object, this was true of the gods as well. Epicurus was willing to accept the fact that there are gods, since people report that they see them, speak with them, and so on. The experiences people have must be caused by some contacts with external atomic collections that correspond to the ideas we have. The gods must be atomic collections, composed of the finest and most perfect atoms. Also, Epicurus theorized, the gods must be located very far away, in the interstices between universes. The gods cannot act or interfere in the world's affairs, since all events are due to the collisions of atoms. Epicurus' materialistic theology was intended to keep people from worrying about Divine retribution. If one accepted his materialistic metaphysics, one would realize that the gods, though they really exist, can do nothing in this universe, and hence cannot affect the lives of men.

Unlike Aristotle's picture of the world, nothing in Epicurus' world happens for a purpose. All events, both on the inanimate and the animate level, occur solely because of the positions and movements of atoms, and not because of any goals that might be achieved. Epicurus sternly condemned the all-too-human attitude that the world was made for man, and that the events occurring in it do so because of human interests and purposes. This view, called "anthropocentricism," is, according to the Epicureans, at complete variance with the real nature of things. The sequence of events is due solely to "the fortuitous concourse of atoms," and not to any human or cosmic wishes or goals.

Man's wishes, thoughts, and ideals are not real features of, or factors in, the world except as effects of atomic motions. Our mental world results from the movements of body atoms and soul atoms, and, hence, provides no clue or guide to what the future course of the universe ought to be. If we take our ideas seriously, we will worry about things that are almost illusory, rather than recognizing the real state of affairs: that events occur only for material reasons, and are not influenced by anyone's thoughts. The only reality our mental world has, including our sense experience, is that it, like anything else, is produced by the collisions of atoms.

The metaphysical theory of Epicurus and Democritus attempted to explain the nature of reality by accepting, in part, both the theories of Parmenides and of Heraclitus. The real world is permanent and unchanging in terms of its content. The atoms are always the same, and they are the only form of being. But the atoms are multiple and different from each other, and are forever changing positions. Their movement is a Heraclitean feature of the real world, leading to a constantly changing apparent world of perceivable objects. These objects are in a constant state of flux since they are only temporary arrangements of atoms or the effects of them, subject to alteration every time an atomic collision takes place.

Democritus tried to show that atomic metaphysics was not refuted by the Zeno paradoxes. To do this he offered a theory of motion in which objects were conceived of as moving from one point to another by jumps, rather than by continuous movements. When an object moved from A to B, according to Democritus, it did not move half the distance, and half of the half, and so on, until it moved through an infinite number of positions between A and B. Instead, he said, the real object moved by a series of jumps of atomic size. It was at one position for a moment, and next it was located at the next position. But it was never in between these two. It simply leaped the distance. Hence, since the object did not move continuously across a distance, the problems raised by Zeno did not apply. Similarly, Democritus argued, the Zeno paradoxes that were based upon the infinite division of an object were inapplicable. Objects could be divided only into atomic unit parts. The so-called axiom of Archimedes—that for every size there is a smaller one—did not apply to real physical objects, since, in fact, atoms were the smallest possible units. This theory contended that in the real world a type of change occurred that was radically different from apparent change. The latter was perceived as continuous. When one tried to explain it, the paradoxes of Zeno seemed to raise insoluble problems. Since the real world changed discontinuously, by jumps, the same sort of problems did not arise.

Hence reality could be conceived of as being comprised of the atomic units which were permanent, changing their positions discontinuously. The perceived world, consisting of ever-changing objects, was experienced as changing continuously. Such a world could not, as Zeno and Parmenides had pointed out, be understood in itself. It could actually be understood only as an illusion resulting from the real events in the atomic world.

The Epicurean and Democritean vision of the world as completely materialistic and purposeless is one of the great metaphysical systems which philosophers have developed. It offers one of the major answers to the question "What is reality?", for it portrays the real world as one composed only of material particles and their positional changes. Everything else is understood in terms of the way it is produced by the changes in the positions of real atoms. This all-encompassing theory purports to reduce to an absolute minimum the ingredients needed to describe and explain reality: atoms, their motions, and empty space. Other ingredients employed in other metaphysical theories, such as ideas, minds, and purposes, are seen either as the effects of atoms, or as illusions having no reality except as thoughts caused by the motions of soul atoms and body atoms.

The Epicurean metaphysics failed to gain many adherents in ancient times, partly because there was no science that could provide a means of describing the actual nature of the alleged material reality. Epicurean physics was almost entirely guesswork. It was presumed that rough things must be composed of rough atoms, smooth things of smooth atoms. Foods like honey, presumably, were composed of round atoms that glided over the tongue, whereas sharp tastes were due to jagged atoms striking on the tongue atoms. But who could tell? There was no way of putting the atomic theory into scientific practice.

In addition to the difficulties involved in employing it, the Epicurean theory was developed at a time when philosophical interests were moving in the direction of ethical and religious concerns. Over the following centuries, dominated by various religious movements, especially those of the Judaeo-Christian tradition, Epicureanism was pushed aside as contrary to the religious picture of the world. It was not until the period of the development of modern science, in the sixteenth and seventeenth centuries, that there was a revival of interest in Epicureanism. Such thinkers as Gassendi and Francis Bacon saw in it an achievement of ancient times that could lead modern men to a better comprehension of the world in which they lived.

MODERN METAPHYSICAL THEORIES

Modern metaphysical systems, beginning with those of the seventeenth century, were based, in part, on the earlier theories. But the basic concern was no longer so much the problem of permanence and change as it was to distinguish appearance from reality, and to describe and explain the relationships of the various aspects of reality, especially the relationship between mind and body.

In the course of the sixteenth and seventeenth centuries, there was a growing realization that the metaphysical system accepted and taught in the schools—that of Aristotle—was no longer adequate or acceptable. The rich body of metaphysical speculations and theories developed during the Middle Ages and the Renaissance in Christian Europe and in Islam did not appear to fit in with the new conceptions about the universe (though many of these earlier theories, both Aristotelian and anti-Aristotelian, were to provide important insights and arguments for the "new philosophers"). The new findings and theories of astronomers, physicists, physicians, explorers, and others seemed to indicate that the real world was radically different from that portrayed by Aristotle and by many medieval thinkers. Planets did not go in circular orbits. It was found that they were other than perfectly spherical bodies, and that they moved in a way no different from the movement of terrestrial objects. In fact, the findings of Galileo, Descartes, and others indicated that the same set of laws described the changes of both celestial and terrestrial objects. These laws contained no reference whatsoever to the final cause or purpose of change. Instead, all motion appeared to be describable and explicable exclusively in mathematical terms and in accordance with mechanical laws. The findings of some of the medical theorists, such as Michael Servetus and Sir William Harvey, indicated that living beings operate by mechanical principles and not by teleological ones. The discoveries of the explorers indicated that many of Aristotle's views about the types of organisms in the world, as well as the structure of the world, were not true. In sum, the tremendous amount of new information which came to light in the sixteenth and seventeenth centuries required a new way of looking at and understanding the world, a new metaphysics to answer the age-old question, "What is reality?"

Scientists had made astounding progress by describing reality in geometrical terms. They had found that when objects were analyzed into their geometrical features—their size, position, and motion—it was possible to discover a system of laws which governed the movements and changes of things, and which allowed for predicting the future course of events. The success of the "new science" seemed to indicate a new basis for distinguishing appearance from reality, one which would justify the use of certain branches of mathematics as the way of analyzing Nature. Basically, the new metaphysics, suggested by several of the early seventeenth-century thinkers, Galileo, Gassendi, Mersenne, Hobbes, and Descartes, among others, saw reality as a "mechanism," analogous to a clock or other machine. The geometrical relationship of the parts, and the way in which they were moving, determined the course of events. Kepler and Galileo had insisted that the Book of Nature is written in mathematical characters, because God is the Great Geometer. His creation, the world mechanism, operates entirely according to the principles of moving geometrical objects. Final causes are not in nature, and are of no help in understanding nature. The nongeometrical features of experience, such as colors, sound, tastes and smells, are not aspects of reality, but are illusions which exist only "in the mind." The mechanistic conception of the world, shared by almost all the "new scientists" and "new philosophers" of the seventeenth century, saw nature as real, and as comprised only of mathematically measurable parts. All other features of nature found in our experience were relegated to the status of appearance or illusions.

DESCARTES' METAPHYSICAL THEORY

René Descartes took it upon himself to work out a full-fledged metaphysical system to provide the foundation and justification for the mechanical picture of Nature. He wished not only to describe the "real" features of the natural world, but also to show how the real physical world was related to other aspects of reality—mind, and God. The Cartesian system, which contains ingredients from previous metaphysical systems, especially Plato's and St. Augustine's, is the first major metaphysical theory of modern times. It has provided the basis for most of the later metaphysical systems that have been developed. Many of these have attempted to overcome the difficulties and problems arising in Descartes' philosophy.

In considering Descartes' theory of knowledge, in Chapter 2, "The Theory of Knowledge," we have seen the general structure of Descartes' picture of the nature of the real world. Reality, for him, is made up of three basic entities, or substances—God, Mind, and Matter. Everything else that exists is a modification or a particular example of one of these. Each thought is a modification of mind, and each physical object a modification of matter.

In one sense, God is the only substance. In the *Principles of Philosophy*, Descartes defined a substance as "a thing which exists in such a way as to stand in need of nothing beyond itself in order to exist." The only entity which is absolutely independent of all others is God, and "all other things can exist only by the help of the concourse of God." God is the only creative substance. His Will is the cause of everything that happens in the mental or physical realm. Somewhat inconsistently Descartes states that mind and body are substances, "for these are things which, in order to exist, stand in need of nothing but the concourse of God." No other cause or explanation is needed to account for the existence of mind and body beyond God's creative activity. Mind and body are the two most general classifications to which every real thing belongs. Everything that we can think of, or know about, with the exception of God, is a form or modification of either the mental substance or the physical one.

Each created substance possesses an essential property which makes it what it is, and accounts for the general characteristics of any modification of it. The essential property of mind is that it thinks. All the ways in which the mental substance exists in this world can be classified as various forms of thought. Since mind is different from body (otherwise they would not be two distinct substances), its essential characteristics must be different from those of body. Specifically, for Descartes, this means that minds cannot take up space or be extended. If they were, they would be forms of body. Since, in his theory of knowledge, he maintained that we possess clear and distinct ideas of each, and since each is a substance, they cannot have common properties.

Body, in contrast to mind, is that which is extended. Every form in which a material object can exist can be defined or described in terms of its extensional features—its size, shape, position, and movement. The physical world, then, is conceived of as a vast extended machine. Each part can be described in terms of its geometrical properties. The parts move according to laws that God enacts. Since the machine is basically only extended parts, its activities must be due to an active force outside the material world. In view of what we know of the properties of the three substances, only God is a creative and active substance. Hence He is the cause of all movements of bodies. Not only did God create matter; He also conserves and controls it at all moments in history. Since, up to the present moment, God acts regularly on the natural world, the entire world-machine operates as a harmonious physical order that modern science can describe in terms of mathematical laws.

Descartes applied his theory of the nature of matter to everything that is extended. The whole extended order is mechanical, and so are its parts. Thus not only are the movements of stars and stones to be understood in terms of their extensional properties; so also are living beings. Animals, according to Descartes, are really automatic, small, self-propelling machines. Discoveries like that of the circulation of the blood indicated the purely mechanical principles that governed animate beings.

Further, since all parts of the physical world are extended, and whatever is extended is material, the natural world is a vast continuum of material parts, lying adjacent to one another. Movement takes place solely by impact and contact, since there can be no empty space for things to move in. (Were there empty space, it would be measurable. Were it measurable in terms of its extension, it would then, by definition, be material.) The whole world-system is pictured as an endless series of standing dominoes; one is pushed, and pushes the next, which pushes the next, and so on. God, as the only active agent, supplies the initial push, plus all the others, supplies the source of power for the whole system, and keeps the whole system in existence and in operation. The scientists, through their study of the clear and distinct ideas of the material world that God gives them, can describe the whole material world exactly and precisely, as long as God so wills.

There is only one entity in the entire created world that is not a part of the mechanical world-system. This is mind, which thinks, wills, and so on. The Cartesian conception of mind, which has been described as that of "the ghost in the machine," is that of a substance which takes up no space whatsoever. As a result, the theory suggests that there is, and can be, no connection between the mental world and the physical one. The material world operates by one portion pushing on the next one. But, if a thought has no extension, can a material object push on it, or can it come in contact with a physical entity?

This raises one of the most difficult problems in Cartesian metaphysics, that of the relationship between mind and body. Descartes, like anyone else, was impressed by the evidence that the mind does influence the body, and vice versa. Judging from our common-sense experience, this seems to happen all the time. A sharp object, such as a knife or a pin, jabs a part of our body, and we immediately have the idea of a pain. We decide that it is time to leave the house, and our body responds by getting up and moving toward the door. In these sorts of cases, the unextended mind and the extended body seem to influence each other. But how is this possible in view of the entirely different characteristics of each kind of substance?

Descartes scrutinized the medical evidence available in his day and came to the conclusion that there must be some sort of contact between the mind and the body in the nervous system. He found that physical events did not seem to influence thoughts unless the nervous system was stimulated. And he was much impressed by the fact that artificial stimulation of the nervous system could produce illusory thoughts and experiences. For example, a man who had lost a leg could have the experience of stubbing his toe if his nervous system were properly stimulated. Hence what happened in the nervous system certainly did appear to affect what happened in the mind.

To explain this, Descartes offered the theory that interaction between mind and body took place in the pineal gland, which is located at the base of the brain. (One hypothesis as to why he chose the pineal gland for this role is that it had recently been discovered by anatomists, and no one at the time knew what function it had in human life.) Presumably, the pineal gland was some sort of in-between entity, through which the extended body could exert some type of push on the unextended mind, and through which thoughts could direct bodily motions.

To his contemporaries, the pineal-gland theory seemed to cause more difficulties than it resolved. It still did not explain how that which is extended can move or push that which is not, and vice versa. And it raised the problem of what type of entity the pineal gland might be. Was it material or immaterial? Whichever it might be, the question arose, "How could the pineal gland come in contact with modifications of a substance with which it had nothing in common?" In the course of discussions with his critics on the question, Descartes admitted that the details of how the influence of mind on body and body on mind took place were not known; nevertheless, the occurrence of interaction had to be accepted. Writing to Arnauld in 1648, Descartes stated, "Accordingly, though we are not in a position to comprehend either by reasoning, or by any comparison with other things, how the incorporeal mind can move the body, nevertheless, we are not able to doubt that it can in view of the most certain and evident experiences that make us immediately aware of its so doing." Earlier Descartes had told the Princess Elizabeth that "those who never philosophize, and who only employ their senses, have no doubts that the soul moves the body, and that the body acts on the soul." The process of interaction might be inexplicable, but the fact that it takes place cannot be denied.

Descartes' critics were not satisfied. His picture of reality as composed of three separate and distinct substances might provide a metaphysics in keeping with the findings of early seventeenth-century science about the nature of the physical world, but it seemed to leave too many difficulties with regard to the relationships between the substances. The sharp and complete distinction between material and mental substance seemed to make their interaction a genuine impossibility, no matter where the point of contact might be located, or how obvious the experience of interaction might be.

Also, the overpowering and overwhelming position of God in Cartesian metaphysics appeared to destroy the usefulness and importance of the two created substances, mind and body, in explaining anything about the nature of reality. If God was the only creative, active agent in the real world, then neither mind nor matter could actually possess any causal power. The ultimate explanation of why anything happened was that God so willed. Instead of explaining the natural world in terms of the nature of matter, the final explanation in Descartes' system of metaphysics was in religious and mystical terms. The universe, when completely understood, would be seen as entirely theocentric. God is the only agent and is the constant source of whatever exists and of whatever happens. The physical and mental realms are only partial ways of describing created aspects of the Divine Universe. In this sense, the Cartesian answer to the question "What is reality?" finally becomes the theological view that reality is God and what He wills.

HOBBES' METAPHYSICAL THEORY

Immediately following the publication of Descartes' metaphysical views in his *Discourse on Method* and his *Meditations*, other philosophers advanced criticisms against this new theory, and attempted to show that a more consistent and plausible view could be offered to explain the nature of the real world, and that such a view could give a more satisfactory solution to the mind-body problem. One of the first to attack Descartes was the bellicose English philosopher Thomas Hobbes (1588–1679). He was one of those whose objections to Descartes' theories were published as an appendix to the *Meditations*, along with Descartes' answers. Later, especially in *De Corpore* (*Concerning Bodies*), and in the early sections of *Leviathan*, Hobbes presented his own metaphysical views.

Basically, Hobbes' theory is more materialistic than Descartes'. He agreed with his opponent that the physical world was real, and was to be understood as a vast mechanism. However, he insisted that the mental world was actually part of the material world, and not a separate substance, and that the mental world could be understood as an effect of the physical motions taking place inside and outside the human body. In this respect, Hobbes' views about the nature of the human mind represent an early version of the theory of some of the twentieth-century behavioristic psychologists.

The real world, according to Hobbes, is composed of bodies. A body is defined as *"that, which having no dependence upon our thought, is coincident or coextended with some part of space."* The crucial features of bodies, by which we understand them, are their positions, their magnitudes (sizes and shapes), and their motions. All other features—colors, hardness, and so on—are classified as accidents, that is, qualities that are not part of the essential nature of the object, that are not common to all bodies and that appear and disappear without changing or destroying bodies. The essential features enable us to construct a science of the natural world consisting of mathematical laws about the movements of bodies.

Up to this point, Hobbes was in agreement, more or less, with all the other mechanists of his time. The novelty in his theory occurs when mental events are conceived of as just the effects of the actions of bodies, and not as modifications of another substance called mind. Hobbes regarded the very notion of an "incorporeal substance" as nonsensical. It is like a square-circle in that the terms mean incompatible things. "Incorporeal" means "without body," and "substance," "that which stands under." In order to stand under something, a substance has to be corporeal. Hence there cannot be a separate mental substance, different from bodies.

Not only is the notion of a mental substance meaningless; it is also unnecessary, since it is possible to describe all mental events in terms of physical ones. All mental events either are sensations or are derivative from our sensations. The sensations are all the result of motions impinging on the sense organs.

> The cause of sense, is the external body, or object, which presseth the organ proper to each sense . . . ; which pressure, by the mediation of the nerves, and other strings and membranes of the body, continued inwards to the brain and heart, causeth there a resistance, or counter-

> pressure, or endeavour of the heart to deliver itself, which endeavour, because *outward*, seemeth to be some matter without. And this *seeming*, or *fancy*, is that which men call *sense*. . . .

The qualities that we sense—sounds, colors, smells, and the like—"are in the object, that causeth them, but so many motions of the matter, by which it presseth our organs diversely. Neither in us that are pressed, are they any thing else, but divers motions; for motion produceth nothing but motion." Hence, Hobbes concluded, "sense, in all cases, is nothing else but original fancy, caused . . . by the pressure, that is, by the motion, of external things upon our eyes, ears, and other organs thereunto ordained." Thus, sensations are the effects of the motions of external bodies, affecting our sense organs, which in turn affect the parts of our nervous system, which result in our having the experiences we do. The external object does not have all the qualities that we experience, but it causes them. It is only extended and moving, but its actions upon us result in our seeing green, feeling warm, and having other such reactions.

After explaining how sensations derive from physical events, Hobbes then argued that our imagination and memory ideas were those of "decaying sense." After the original impact, motions continued in our nervous system and in our brains, so that we could think of events *after* they had occurred, until the effect totally dissipated. Reasoning was conceived of as a process, called "ratiocination," in which sensations and the lingering aftereffects are given names, and then the names are ordered according to similarities and differences. The reasoning process, according to Hobbes, is like the sorting and arrangement of cards or counters by a modern IBM machine.

This explanation of mental events appears to eliminate the difficulties caused by the mind-body problem in Cartesian philosophy. If there is no separate mental substance, then there is no problem of explaining how mind and matter can relate. Mind and mental events are simply subclasses of physical events and can be explained by the sequence of physical events. Hence, if reality consists of nothing but matter (and God, in Hobbes' theory), there appears to be no difficulty in explaining the connection between what we think about and what is happening outside us.

Hobbes' metaphysical system, and some of those that have been proposed as further developments in the materialistic tradition, have tried to explain all the features of reality in terms of the sole "real components," matter and motion. The crucial problem in such views is that of showing how mental events can be explained without admitting that they belong to a different category (and hence that reality is made up of more than matter and motion). Hobbes started a tradition of resolving the mind-body problem by explaining all mental events in terms of material ones. This has proved very fruitful in inspiring research to establish laws relating the sequence of physical events to that of mental events. But the question still remains whether a system like Hobbes' actually obviates the need to allow an independent status, in some respect, to mental events. If it does not, then his metaphysics will prove inadequate to encompass the actual constituents of the world, and to explain them.

Hobbes' actual metaphysical theory admitted two types of substance, one material, the other Divine. Although Hobbes, in his many writings, did not seem to question that "God hath made and governs the world," many of his contemporaries considered him an atheist. They pointed out that the Hobbesian system reduced the role of God to a minor function. God accounted for the existence of the physical world and the laws by which it operated. But, in its present state, the actions of the material world were alleged by Hobbes to be sufficient to explain any and all events that now occur, or that will occur in the future history of the universe. Thus, God's actions may have been necessary to get the system started, but they do not appear to be required now. The present world can be conceived of as a perpetual-motion machine, operating entirely by its own laws and producing all the occurrences in the world. Thus, though Hobbes may have insisted that reality contained two substances, God and body, only the category of body is actually requisite in order to formulate a complete materialistic metaphysics about the world in its present form and state.

Some materialists have presented this theory in a more extreme form than Hobbes did. Some American behavioristic psychologists in this century, including the founder of the movement, John Watson, have insisted that there are no mental events in the sense of conscious items called "thoughts" or "sensations." Instead, they have contended that what we call mental events are just forms of behavioral activity. Such activities may be movements of various parts of the body, sounds uttered by the vocal cords, tensions in certain muscles, facial expressions, and so on. These events can be analyzed in terms of the kinds of stimuli to the sense organs and of the kinds of responses that the organism makes. This theory, in spite of its success in discovering laws about stimuli and responses, has been considered inadequate by many thinkers because it seems to deny an obvious fact—that mental events occur—and seems to lead to a metaphysical view that fails to allow any reality for mental events.

Because of this, some schools of contemporary psychology, including segments of the behavioristic movement, have adopted the less extreme Hobbesian view, which is nowadays called "epiphenomenalism." This theory admits that mental events are real occurrences, but says they are by-products of the real material causal process, playing no genuine part in the sequence of events. Thoughts, sensations, and feelings are seen as analogous to the smoke that rises from a fire. The real world consists of a chain of material events that can be explained entirely in terms of the motions of various portions of the material world. While these motions are taking place, an offshoot or a by-product occurs—the mental events. These result from the causal sequence, but themselves produce nothing further. The reason why we think or feel anything at any given time can always be explained in terms of the motions of bodies, and requires no appeal to the contents of our consciousness.

CRITICISM OF A MATERIALISTIC THEORY OF MIND

Although the materialistic view about the nature of mind and mental events may be accepted by many present-day psychologists, either in its Hobbesian-epiphenomenalistic form or in the more radical version of Watson and his followers, some philosophers have insisted that this view contains many difficulties that make it inadequate as an explanation of the mental world. These critics point out that a mental event is strikingly different from its supposed cause. As Hobbes had suggested, the cause is nothing but a body in motion acting on a sense organ. The mental event has the richness of color, taste, smell, and the like. Hence, even if mental events are caused by bodily events, the effect seems to be of a different type and a different order from its cause, and the cause does not seem to explain why we experience what we do, instead of the actual course of events. Why should we experience color just because bodies move? Why don't we merely experience what is happening and nothing more? The qualities of experience, feeling, and thought do not appear to have their roots in the alleged real world, since it does not possess these qualities. According to the critics, what, in fact, the psychologists discover is that whenever certain physical events occur, certain mental events follow. When our knowledge of psychological laws reaches a more complete state, it may even be possible to predict what we think, perceive, or feel from what is happening physically inside and outside us. But none of this indicates that our mental experience is nothing but the physical events taking place. To reduce the mental events to the physical events is to lose and ignore the unique characteristics of mental experience. The chemical constituents of a steak and their actions upon our taste buds may be followed by our tasting it, but there is a world of difference between the chemistry of the meat and what we experience in eating it. We would be very unhappy if we ordered steak and then experienced only the chemical reactions and not the taste. But, we are quite happy to experience the taste without the slightest awareness of the "real" physical events that may also be happening.

A further example may illustrate this criticism more sharply. If the state of our knowledge ever reached the point where one could determine what someone was experiencing and thinking from changes in his blood pressure, electrical impulses in his brain, and so on, scientists doing the measuring and the subject being measured would each be aware of totally different things. The scientists would see a collection of instruments, and from these could predict what the subject thought and felt. But the subject would actually have the thoughts and feelings and would not have to infer them. If the subject were reading a book, the scientists might be able to ascertain the plot of the volume from the effect—the various physiological conditions in the subject. The subject, knowing nothing about his physiological state, would have the direct experience of reading the book. To determine that somebody is sad and being sad oneself are obviously two different things. No amount of scientific knowledge, the critics insist, will ever change one into the other. Hence the cause of an event and the experience of the event will always be different.

A recent scientific development has posed this point in another form. In the last twenty-five years or so, computing machines have been developed which seem to be able to perform the same type of physical action which we do when we think. The machines are able to solve complicated mathematical problems, some more complicated than any human being can handle. The question whether these machines think has been discussed. As soon as the issue was joined, and arguments were offered to show that the answer was "yes," and others that it was "no," the standard philosophical gambit was introduced: the contention that it depends upon what is meant by "think." If thinking means the series of physical events taking place in the nervous system, then the series of events taking place in such digital computing machines seems to be close enough to what goes on in us to say that machines, in this sense, think. If thinking means a series of behavioral activities culminating in oral or written responses, then machines think, in this sense, since they can answer questions put to them about the materials stored in them. One machine theorist has maintained that the day is fast approaching when a thinking machine can be constructed in the form of a robot that will be indistinguishable from a human being in *all* its responses. It will give an acceptable human answer to any question that it is asked; hence, if thinking is judged by its behavioral effects, such a machine will be said to think. However, to reach the heart of the matter, if thinking means having conscious mental experience each of us is directly aware of, then does a machine think? At this point, we cannot tell. In fact, in this sense we cannot tell if any entity but ourselves thinks. But we can tell that we do. The machine may say that it is sad. Another person may report that he is sad. In neither case can we ascertain that accompanying this remark is a certain immediate feeling. But when we are sad, we know it immediately and indubitably.

The critics of complete materialism and epiphenomenalism insist not only that we must admit that mental events are different from physical ones and cannot really be explained by them (though laws may be discoverable showing that when a certain physical event occurs, a certain mental event will follow), but also that we have to take mental events seriously in their own right, no matter why they occur. In our daily lives, it is what we think, feel, and perceive that affects us, and not why these events take place. The actual course of mental events is of paramount importance to us. No matter why mental events occur, we take them seriously in terms of their contents, and not in terms of their origins. For example, I am terrified by a nightmare when it occurs, even if it is only the effect of having eaten pickles and ice cream before I went to bed. Thus, the critics contend, an explanation of mental events is required that is of a different order from one that accounts for physical processes.

SPINOZA'S METAPHYSICAL THEORY

If Hobbes' "tough-minded" materialism appeared too extreme to his contemporaries, the theory of Baruch Spinoza was considered even more extreme and dangerous. Spinoza's life and career will be discussed in greater detail in Chapter 4, "Ethics." He grew up in the Spanish-Portuguese Jewish community in Amsterdam, where his initial intellectual training was in theological studies, centered around explanations and justifications of Judaism. Young Spinoza rejected the authority of the synagogue and of the Jewish tradition. He argued against the revealed status of the Bible, and the reasons given by the orthodox community for following the traditional laws of Judaism. After his excommunication from the synagogue, Spinoza turned to the study of modern philosophy, especially that of Descartes. He wrote an exposition of Cartesian philosophy, probably as a textbook for one of his students, which contained some of his criticisms of this system. His own system appeared in his famous work, the *Ethics*, published in 1677, the year of his death. The work, which was already known to many through manuscript copies that circulated among the learned in Europe, was immediately denounced, and the author was accused of "having reduced atheism to a system," and of being the most "vile atheist" there ever was. These accusations may seem strange at first when it is seen that the fundamental substance of his metaphysical system is God, the sole explanation and cause of all events. After we have presented his system, we will examine the basis for the accusations.

Spinoza's answer to the basic question of metaphysics, "What is reality?" is that it is composed of substance and the modifications or forms that substance takes. He attempted to demonstrate that there can be only ONE substance, called "God" or "Nature," which has an infinite number of attributes or ways of being characterized. We, however, can know only two of these ways: thought and extension. All the things that we can know about, including ourselves, are modes of these two of God's attributes, ways in which these attributes appear. Reality is basically one thing, seen by us in two different ways. Hence his system is usually called a form of "metaphysical monism."

Spinoza's system is expounded in his *Ethics* in the form of geometrical demonstrations, based on a series of definitions of key terms, and axioms. Substance, one of his fundamental notions, is defined in a similar way to that employed by Descartes when he explained the sense in which God, and God alone, is a substance. For Spinoza, a substance is self-explanatory. Its very nature provides the reason why it exists, and why it has the characteristics it does. Further, a substance is the cause of itself, since it is self-explanatory. And something that is the cause of itself cannot be conceived except as an existing entity. The other key terms defined by Spinoza at the outset are "attribute," "mode," and "God." An attribute is what we discover as a defining property for understanding the nature of a substance. A mode, on the other hand, is the way a substance appears at a particular time. It is a condition or state of a thing which is not essential or unalterable. And a mode, by definition, is understood in terms of the substance of which it is a mode. God is defined as "Being absolutely infinite, that is to say, substance consisting of infinite attributes, each one of which expresses eternal and infinite essence."

Spinoza contended that his definitions are not simply arbitrary ways of using terms. Besides the fact that his contemporaries would recognize that much of his usage derives from medieval theology, Spinoza also maintained that if one had a "true and adequate" conception of what he was talking about (his equivalent of Descartes' clear and distinct ideas), one would recognize his definitions as correct ones for the entities in question. Further, he introduced an axiom stating, "A true idea must agree with that of which it is the idea." Hence, if the definitions are true ideas, which presumably a rational mind can determine, they then correspond with the objective entities being defined.

The axioms of Spinoza's system, like those of Euclidean geometry, set forth certain basic relationships between things. From the axioms it will be possible to demonstrate the fundamental truths about substances, attributes, and modes. The axioms relevant to the part of Spinoza's system that we shall consider are that (a) "everything which is, is either in itself or in another thing"; (b) "that which cannot be conceived through another must be conceived through itself"; and (c) "those things which have nothing mutually in common with one another cannot be mutually understood through one another, that is to say, the conception of one does not involve the conception of the other." The first of these indicates that everything that exists must fall into the classification of a "substance" or a "mode," since these are the only two possibilities. A thing is understood or explained either in terms of itself or in terms of something else of which it is a form or a feature. The second of the axioms indicates that if something is not a mode, then it has to be a substance, the only other possibility. The last of the quoted axioms states that if two things have nothing in common, then they cannot stand in the relation of substance and mode, since one cannot explain the other, nor can one be understood in terms of the other.

With these definitions and axioms, Spinoza then proceeded to show the nature of substance in order to establish that (1) by definition a substance must exist, (2) God exists, (3) there cannot be two or more substances, (4) hence only God exists, and finite things are modes of God to be understood in terms of one of His two knowable attributes, thought and extension. The first few propositions prove the complete independence of one substance from another, if two or more exist. If two substances have different attributes, they can have nothing in common since each substance is understood through itself in terms of its attributes. If they do not have the same attributes, then there is no common basis through which they can be mutually conceived.

Then, Spinoza pointed out that "in nature there cannot be two or more substances of the same attribute or nature." If they were different substances, they would have to be distinguishable. Since substances are conceived of in terms of themselves, they would have to be distinguishable in terms of their attributes. If, therefore, they had the same attributes, they could not be distinguished, and hence could not be different.

If substances cannot have a common attribute, they also cannot produce or cause each other. If one caused the other, then one could be understood or explained in terms of the other. But, by definition, substances are understood only in terms of themselves. Further, since different substances can have nothing in common, an axiom has already established that things having nothing in common cannot be understood in terms of each other. Therefore, each substance must be the cause of itself, and cannot be produced or caused by anything else.

Having shown that it follows from the definitions and axioms that whatever substances exist must be completely independent and isolated worlds, Spinoza next pointed out that "it pertains to the nature of substance to exist." Since a substance has to exist, and must be the cause of itself, this means, by his definition, that its essence necessarily involves existence, and that by its very nature a substance cannot be conceived of except as existing.

If whatever substances that can be conceived of have to exist, God, by definition, must exist. The concept of God introduced at the outset is that of a substance consisting of infinite attributes. Since a substance must be the cause of itself, and hence its essence involves existence, it is then impossible to conceive of God (that is, understand what the term means) without realizing that He must exist.

Now, since it follows from the definitions of the terms "substance," "cause of itself," and "God," that the substance, God, must exist, Spinoza then went on to show that, from the other information established about the nature of substance, "besides God, no substance can be nor can be conceived." Since God is a substance consisting of infinite attributes, each one of which expresses eternal and infinite essence, if there were some attribute that God did not possess, His nature would be limited in some respect, and hence not be infinite. If one could conceive of another substance, one would have to conceive of it as existing (it pertains to the nature of substance to exist), and as having some attribute or attributes. Whatever attributes it had, these would have to be attributes that God also possessed. But, as has already been established, there cannot be two or more substances with a common attribute. Hence God can be the only substance, since there can be no attributes for other substances to possess in view of God's infinite nature, and the fact that He must exist.

Since God is the only possible and actual substance, "Whatever is, is in God, and nothing can either be or be conceived without God."

Thus, if everything must be conceived of through God, everything must be a mode of God. The only way we are able to conceive of the underlying structure of the universe is in terms of the attributes of thought and extension. Hence although God possesses an infinite number of attributes, each expressing His nature, we know only two of them, and we have to conceive of the nature of reality in terms of them alone.

The series of demonstrations that leads to Spinoza's metaphysical conclusion that reality consists of one substance, God or Nature, and that everything else is just a mode of one of two of God's knowable attributes, thought and extension, may appear to be forced. If one grants that the arguments are sound, one may question their basis, the definitions and axioms. Certain conclusions may follow from these, but, perhaps, the definitions and axioms are merely arbitrary ones invented by Spinoza. Why does one have to accept his starting point?

Spinoza's answers given in his letters, his comments on Descartes, his explanations on the nature of definitions, and his discussions of the propositions which are interspersed in the text of the *Ethics*, point out that the basic terms he employed are those he believed to be uniquely adequate to explain the nature of reality. To understand the nature of reality one has to know why it is what it is. This involves explaining it in terms of something. If there were something that could explain reality, it would be more real than what it explained. Hence ultimately reality must be self-explanatory. Underlying its various features there must be a substance which is both the cause of itself and the explanation of everything else that exists.

To this extent, Spinoza was in agreement with Descartes and with most of the metaphysicians of the seventeenth century. There must be one creative, self-explanatory substance if any of the other features of reality are to be made intelligible. But, then, following the logical consequences of this, Spinoza insisted that there could be only one substance. Descartes had admitted that, in the sense in which God was the cause and explanation of everything, He was the only substance. Accepting this, Spinoza maintained that mind and body, then, could not be substances, since they each had to be conceived of in terms of God. Anything that one could conceive of had to be in terms of that which explained it, and which explained why it existed. Hence everything conceivable was, in fact, conceived of in terms of the one self-explanatory substance, God or Nature. Descartes' attempt to make matter and mind real substances depended upon changing the meanings of the terms involved. With striking logical consistency, Spinoza developed his pantheistic conclusion, namely that everything is God, and that God is the explanation of whatever exists.

If one tried to conceive of something that was not an aspect of God, as soon as one tried to understand it, it would immediately become evident that the conception had to be explained in terms of an attribute or mode of God. Anything that could be described or defined would have to be explained in terms of the only categories we possess, thought and extension. The conception would have to be that of a physical thing or an idea. As soon as this is recognized, it is seen that the conception, no matter how fertile our minds may be, is, in fact, understood in terms of the divine attributes.

Spinoza's metaphysical theory about the nature of reality, then, portrays the real universe as composed, basically, of one entity, God. God is understood by us in two different ways, in terms of thought or extension. The individual things in the world are seen as modes, or ways in which the divine attributes can appear at a given time. Modes are real insofar as they are understood as aspects of reality, and as necessary derivations from the nature of God.

However, the finite modes, the individual entities that exist at a given moment, are not completely real. They are temporary and finite ways in which the nature of God appears to us. The universe seen *sub specie aeternitatis* ("under the aspect of eternity") would be seen strictly in terms of God, and His attributes. The temporary and limited modes would have lost their meaning and their reality, and would be seen as illusory or incomplete views of the nature of God. To this extent, Spinoza's system resembles that of Plotinus. Everything that exists is real insofar as its being and meaning derive from the fundamental substance. But the most complete reality, the one substance seen in itself, does not involve the limited and finite individual modes that appear and disappear in the course of history. In a sense, the historical world is illusory, since the real, divine world is timeless and unchanging, and is one and only one thing. The degree to which the world of history, and the individuals who exist in history, are real is the degree to which they are explained by the one substance.

In Spinoza's metaphysics, a new type of answer is introduced to the mind-body problem. The mind and the body are not separate substances with nothing in common, as they are for Descartes. And they are not simply the same substance, as in Hobbes' theory. Instead, for Spinoza, they are two different ways of looking at, or understanding, the Divine Nature. The mental world and the physical world are actually the same thing, God or Nature, described from two different points of view. It is something like describing the same state of affairs in two different languages. The mental world and the physical world are parallel sequences of events, both describing the same series of finite modes of God in alternate ways. Mind and body do not interact, since they are really just two sides of the *same* coin. And one way of looking at it cannot be reduced to the other.

This theory, called "psycho-physical parallelism," maintains that physical events, such as pushing a pin into someone's flesh, do not cause thoughts of pain, nor do decisions or desires cause sequences of physical actions. Instead, the movement of the pin is one way of describing a mode of God, and the thought of pain another. For every mental event, there is a corresponding physical event, and vice versa. Spinoza declared that "the logical order of the mind is identical with the physical order of nature." One can study reality either as a necessary, determined sequence of physical events, or as a logical system of thoughts. In either case one is studying the same thing. One sequence does not cause, produce, or influence the other. Both are parallel ways of describing God or Nature. Hence, there is no mind-body problem of the type that existed for Descartes: the attempt to bridge the gap between two totally different realms. Nor is the problem the same as that which Hobbes tried to resolve: reducing mental events to physical ones, or explaining their occurrence in terms of physical actions and movements.

In view of the fact that Spinoza's metaphysical theory maintains that God is reality, it may seem strange that this "God-intoxicated man" was seen by his contemporaries as the most extreme type of atheist. However, Spinoza made clear in his presentation in the *Ethics* that the God who was the fundamental reality in his system could not have the characteristics of the God of traditional Judaeo-Christian theology. Spinoza's God could not be a supernatural being, but is a natural being, the natural world. He has no personality, He plays no role as a dramatic actor in the world's history, and He can perform no miracles. The picture of God accepted by the Judaeo-Christian tradition was rejected completely by Spinoza. He regarded it as a superstition grown out of human fears and ignorance, and due to the tendency for human finite modes to see the universe in terms of their own interests and concerns.

Since Spinoza's metaphysical theory pictured reality as solely an impersonal God, to be known and loved more through the study of physics and mathematics than through any traditional observances, it was, from the point of view of the Judaeo-Christian tradition, a form of atheism. Spinoza denied that any personal God existed, that there could be such a Being, or that the picture of the world given in Scripture could be true of the real world.

Spinoza's philosophy may have been more consistent than Descartes', and may have resolved some of the difficulties in Cartesianism, but it was totally unacceptable to the thinkers of his day, mainly because it was in complete opposition to the accepted religious views. It was not until the late eighteenth and early nineteenth centuries that Spinoza's views were taken seriously, especially by the German metaphysicians.

MALEBRANCHE'S
METAPHYSICAL THEORY

At the same time that Spinoza's views appeared in Holland, Father Nicolas Malebranche in France presented his novel version of Cartesianism, which attempted to avoid some of the major difficulties in Descartes' system. Malebranche (1638–1715), a priest trained in traditional Catholic theology, saw in the metaphysical system of Descartes a new version of the Neo-Platonic theory of St. Augustine. God was the source of all truth and being. Reality consists of God and the ideas in His Mind, plus the beings He has created.

The ideas in the Divine Mind comprise what Malebranche calls "intelligible extension." Intelligible extension takes up no space. It is the ideas of extended things, the mathematical relationships, through which we understand any object that we know of. Since the relationships involved are eternal and are unaffected by whether they are known by any particular individuals, Malebranche argued that the world of intelligible extension must exist apart from, and be independent of, temporal individuals, such as human beings, who sometimes know about the mathematical relationships. Since the formulas of intelligible extension are eternal, immutable, and so on ($2 + 2$ always has equaled and always will equal 4), the world of intelligible extension must be located in something that is also eternal and immutable, namely the Divine Mind.

Intelligible extension neither *is* the Divine Mind nor the creation of the Divine Mind. If intelligible extension were God's Mind, Malebranche believed his theory would become something like the "vile atheism" of Spinoza, identifying God with the logical order of the universe. If intelligible extension had been created by God and was subject to God's will, then, Malebranche felt, it would lose some aspects of its complete reality, since its existence and its characteristics would always be contingent on God's decisions. It could be changed if God so willed, and hence the mathematical relationships would not necessarily be either immutable or eternal. (Descartes had contended, in one of his discussions, that God could alter mathematical truths if He so willed, and hence that it is possible that $2 + 3$ will equal 6 tomorrow. This side of Descartes' theory, called "voluntarism," was rejected by Malebranche.)

Intelligible extension, as an eternal, immutable system of relationships of mathematical ideas comprising intelligible reality, is coeternal with God. It has not been created, nor can it be in any way changed. It exists eternally and immutably in the eternal, immutable, infinite Mind of God.

The real world of God and the ideas of intelligible extension in His Mind constitute an unchanging universe, something like Plato's world of Ideas. In addition, there is a created universe, which we actually cannot know, but of which we can be made aware. We cannot know it because it is not comprised of intelligible parts (otherwise it would merely be more of the system of relationships of intelligible extension).

The created world contains minds and their feelings (including all of the sense experiences that we have) plus the world of physical extension, or bodies. As indicated in Chapter 2, "The Theory of Knowledge," Malebranche was at great pains to argue that there is no demonstrative evidence that bodies or even a physical world exists. We have a natural tendency to believe that bodies exist, but at the same time we are acquainted only with ideas of bodies, their shapes, sizes, and motions, which are really parts of the world of intelligible extension; and with feelings about bodies, their colors, smells, tastes, and so on, which are really sentiments in us, in our minds. Hence, what we usually consider to be physical bodies are actually ideas in the Mind of God, and feelings in ourselves. Our conceptions and perceptions of bodies are not those of independently existing physical things.

The total real world could be, Malebranche pointed out, simply God, the intelligible extension in His Mind, and the sequence of feelings in us.

If this was what reality consisted of, we could account for everything that we know about reality through mathematics and mathematical physics, and everything that we experience through our senses and our feelings. We would find that there is a sequential order to our experience, and that it seems to be correlated with the intelligible aspects of the world. Every time a certain configuration and motion was present, one would also have certain feelings of color or taste. God could establish such laws, and could give us a regular world of thoughts and experiences without there being any material reality as well. In such a case, we would have an unfortunate, inaccurate tendency to attribute or relate ideas and feelings to a nonexistent world of bodies.

The decisive evidence for Malebranche that there is a physical world consists not in any facts or any reasonings, but, instead, simply the statements in the beginning of the Book of Genesis. Our revelatory information assures us that God has created a physical world. Hence, on the basis of what Scripture tells us and what we know by reasoning and experience, we know that reality contains God, the world of intelligible extension, our feelings, *plus* an independent material world. The physical world presumably is patterned or formed according to the structure of the intelligible world. Hence the relationships of extension that we know by reasoning apply to physical things as well.

Our knowledge about the nature of bodies, gained from studying the world of intelligible extension, can be stated entirely in terms of mathematical relationships. The essence of bodies does not involve *any* creative power. This means that bodies, by themselves, cannot *do* anything or *cause* anything. Their natures, known to us through the intelligible world, contain no concept of causal agency, efficacy, or power. In fact, Malebranche argued, if bodies could somehow act by themselves, this would deny what we know about God, that He is All-Powerful, because it would mean that a body could do something whether God wanted it to or not. The omnipotence of God, according to Malebranche, prevents anything else in the entire universe from possessing any independent creative force or power. If God is All-Powerful, every other entity in the world must be genuinely powerless.

If this is so, what makes anything happen? Why does one body *seem* to move another, as appears to happen when one billiard ball strikes another? Why do vibrating musical strings *seem* to produce music, and not smells? And why do physical actions *seem* to produce mental effects, such as pains or feelings? Why do mental events, such as decisions and desires, *seem* to influence physical occurrences?

In Malebranche's version of the Cartesian metaphysical system, all causal relations appear to be completely mysterious. The natures of bodies, minds, and intelligible extension seem to preclude any explanation about why events or changes happen. Minds are things which think and feel. Bodies are things which are extended. Intelligible extension is the eternal, immutable system of mathematical relationships. None of these realms seems to have any basis for interacting or interconnecting with another, and none of them has within itself any causal force or power.

The mystery is entirely explained by God, the only active, causal agent in the universe. Strictly speaking, He is the cause of each and every event in the world. Malebranche makes his theory clearest in his analysis of how and why anything happens in the physical world, and how and why the physical and the mental world seem to interrelate, and operate according to some sort of harmonious system.

Starting with a simple case such as a billiard ball moving toward another one, Malebranche pointed out that the motion of one physical body implies nothing about the motion of another. If we analyze the mathematical properties of the moving ball, we will not be able to determine what will happen when it strikes the other ball. We will find no causal properties in the moving ball. Hence, for all that we can tell from the nature of the moving ball itself or that of the stationary ball, the result of their collision is completely indeterminate. Anything might happen. The balls might go up in smoke. They might change color. They might move.

It is God who determines what will happen, and who makes it happen. Anything that God wishes is possible, so that He can create any order that He cares to. Since He is the only Being with causal power, He can make anything take place. However, Malebranche insisted, God operates by the simplest and most economical system of general laws. Thus the first time that two billiard balls collide, God decides what will happen in keeping with the general system of laws that He has already decreed. Accordingly, though each and every action is directly caused by God, all the actions are produced as part of a general, economical system. When we discover the laws of moving bodies, we can then predict with accuracy what will happen next, not because of any inherent properties in bodies, but because of God's uniform action according to the general laws that He has already decreed.

The analysis that Malebranche offered about the occurrence of bodily events applies as well to the sequences of bodily and mental events. A body cannot, by itself, cause another body to move, and it cannot cause a feeling or thought to occur either. (To make his point as startling as possible, Malebranche insisted that all the angels and devils, acting in unison, could not move a piece of straw unless God so willed.) When we bite into a pear, why do we experience a taste, rather than hear music, see colors, and so on? Nothing in the nature of ourselves or in the nature of the physical object, the pear, requires the result. The explanation, according to Malebranche's theory, is that when God makes one series of events occur in the physical world, He makes a corresponding set of events occur in the mental world, according to general laws. Having decreed a set of general laws, God then makes people experience tastes whenever certain physical events occur, and so with our other sense experiences. (This becomes, for Malebranche, the explanation of why God permits evil and pain. God always acts according to general laws, so that when people have certain desires, murders occur. When certain physical actions occur, we experience pains, and so on. It is more in keeping with the perfection of God that He operate by general laws than that He constantly alter the system simply to make people happy.)

Malebranche's metaphysical theory provides an explanation for the relationship between the mind and the body, an explanation called "occasionalism." In fact, if he is right, there is no connection whatsoever between a mental event and a physical event. A pin pushed into my finger cannot and does not *cause* me to experience pain. The absence of physical food in my physical stomach does not *cause* me to experience hunger. No mental event could influence a physical event, or vice versa. But because of God's constant and continuous causal action, the occurrence of an event in one realm is the occasion for the occurrence of a corresponding event in the other realm. God is the sole cause of all events. Since He operates by general laws, the unrelated events occur in patterns. There is no necessary connection between any two events, but one is the occasion of the other in view of God's causal actions, and in view of His uniform laws. Thus when God causes the physical pin to enter my physical finger, He at the same time causes me to feel pain. The mental event is not caused by the physical one, but the occurrence of one is the occasion of God's action to cause the other in view of the uniform way in which He runs the world.

Though we may feel convinced that there is more connection between events than the occasionalist thesis would admit, Malebranche pointed out that his theory accounted for all the events that occur, and that there is no evidence counter to his theory. Any experiment to determine if physical events can produce mental events or vice versa would show that a sequence occurs. But it could not show that the sequence was not due to God's control of *all* events. Implausible as the occasionalist theory may be, its advocates stressed the fact that it could not be disproved by examining any of the events that occur in this world.

Malebranche's metaphysical theory stressed the view that what is real is God's world. God and the ideas in His Mind, intelligible extension, constitute the eternal, immutable reality. God's creative power and activities account for the various forms of temporal reality, ourselves, the physical world, and the developments in both the mental and the physical world. We know only those ideas and feelings that God causes us to be aware of. According to Malebranche's favorite line from the Bible, "In Him we live, and move, and have our being."

Malebranche's theory, and especially his occasionalist thesis about the lack of any real connection between mind and body, were to have far-reaching influences on subsequent theories, especially those of Berkeley and Hume. As we shall see, to some extent Malebranche's attempt to work out a thoroughly consistent version of Cartesianism was to be the occasion, if not the cause, of an antimetaphysical movement.

LEIBNIZ'S METAPHYSICAL THEORY

Before turning to some of the more critical developments in the history of modern metaphysics, we will consider the last of the brilliant Continental theories of the seventeenth century, that of Gottfried Wilhelm Leibniz (1646–1716). Leibniz was born in Germany and studied at the Universities of Leipzig, Jena, and Altdorf. He then entered the diplomatic service, first of the Elector of Mainz, then of the House of Hanover, and finally of the Queen of Prussia. All his life he was concerned with problems in mathematics, physics, philosophy, philology and linguistics, jurisprudence, history, and many other subjects. He carried on an immense correspondence with scholars all over the world about questions in all these fields, and made many important contributions of his own toward solving various problems. He is probably best known for his work in mathematics, where he and Isaac Newton, apparently independently, discovered the principles of the calculus at about the same time. (They and their followers argued for many years about which of them plagiarized from the other. The evidence finally indicated that neither of them had, but that, both being mathematical geniuses, they had come to the same theory quite independently.)

Leibniz's concern with philosophy began during his university studies. In the period 1672–1676, he was on a diplomatic mission in Paris, and there came in contact with many of the important philosophers. He also briefly visited England and Holland, and met Spinoza. In France, he began disputing with some of the leading Cartesian philosophers, especially Malebranche and Antoine Arnauld, and with some of the leading French skeptics. As a result of his opposition to Cartesianism, to the pantheism of Spinoza, and to the negative views of the skeptics, Leibniz began to formulate his own theory in a series of articles in the learned journals of the time. These views engendered a series of controversies in which Leibniz was able to develop his metaphysical system. During his own lifetime, it was best presented by him in some of his articles and in his vast correspondence. He published a few books against Locke's theories, against Pierre Bayle's, and against others, but his shorter statements of his case were the most effective. In recent years, a great many more presentations of his views have been found among the quantity of papers that he left. A man of great erudition, fantastic memory, and brilliant intellect, he loved to argue for his theories against all opponents.

Leibniz was dissatisfied with the metaphysical views of Descartes, Spinoza, and Malebranche, especially with regard to the relationship between the mind and the body. He felt that a more consistent and more plausible theory could be developed if one examined the nature of reality in terms of the sort of truths that we can know about it. Our true knowledge, and the reasons why it is true, will indicate certain characteristics about the real world.

Every true proposition, according to Leibniz, is one in which the predicate of the statement is contained in the subject. Thus, for example, in the true proposition "A red rose is red," the predicate, "red," is contained in the subject, "red rose," and the predicate is, to some extent, identical with the subject. The way in which we discover whether a proposition is true is, in fact, in Leibniz's logical theory, by reducing it, if possible, to a statement of an identity either of the form "A is A" or "AB is A." For example, the proposition "A square is a rectangular figure whose sides are equal" is found to be true by analyzing the subject to discover what it means. When the term "square" is defined in mathematics, its definition becomes "a rectangular figure whose sides are equal." Therefore the proposition is actually of the form "A (a square) is A (a rectangular figure whose sides are equal = a square)." The proposition states an identity, and hence is true.

Any proposition that is true must be a statement of an identity. Some statements can easily be reduced to identities, whereas others cannot. If they are all true, some propositions must be explicitly identical, and others only implicitly. This means that in some cases, notably in mathematics, the true propositions can be shown by a series of logical steps to be statements of the form "A is A" or "AB is A." In other areas, the true propositions cannot be so reduced to identical form (principally because we cannot know the full and complete definitions of the terms). But, since there is only one condition that makes a true proposition true, these statements must be identities, too, though this cannot be demonstrated in all cases by a series of logical steps.

The propositions that can be logically shown to be identities are primarily those of logic and mathematics. These propositions are called "necessary" ones, since, Leibniz held, they had to be true for all possible worlds. The terms involved no special conditions that limited when and where the propositions were true. Hence, a statement like "$2 + 2 = 4$"

must be true no matter what else occurs in the world, or what world exists or may exist.

Other true propositions which cannot be reduced to obvious identities are called "contingent," since their truth is dependent on the actual conditions that prevail. If they were true in all possible worlds, then they could be shown to be evident identities. Thus the proposition "A dog is a four-legged creature" is true, but true only for a world in which dogs have certain characteristics, and not true otherwise. The proposition "The sun is shining today" is true by virtue of the special conditions that prevail in this world at a certain time and place. If we knew and understood all of the conditions that prevail in this world, and that have to prevail, we could reduce contingent true propositions to identities. But this would require infinite knowledge and ability which we do not possess. Only God is capable of seeing why all the contingent propositions have to be true, and, hence, of seeing them all as identities.

Although we are not capable of reducing all contingent truths to identities, we can see that the very conditions of truth tell us something important about the nature of the subjects of true propositions. There must be a necessary and sufficient reason why true propositions are true (Leibniz's famous principle of sufficient reason): "nothing is without a reason, or no effect is without a cause. Otherwise there might be a truth which could not be proved *a priori* (independent of experience), or which could not be resolved into identical truths; but that is contrary to the nature of truth, which is always, either expressly or implicitly, identical." The sufficient reason, according to the nature of truth, must be that the predicate of a contingent proposition has to be contained in its subject. The subject of every true contingent proposition must contain and account for every predicate that can be applied to it. Thus, for example, every true statement that can be made about my dog—that she is black and white, that she was born in 1963, that she hates dog food, that she barked at the postman on March 12, 1970—must be true because the subject, "my dog," contains in her essence or nature all the things that can be predicated of her.

This analysis of the nature of contingent truths led Leibniz to the formulation of his metaphysical theory. What are the subjects of contingent true propositions? They are any individual things or substances that we can speak about. These substances must have the characteristic that they contain within themselves all the predicates or properties they can ever have; otherwise, true statements about their properties would not be true by virtue of the subject containing the predicate. Thus, the reason why I can assert true propositions about my dog must be that my dog, as a substance and not simply a term in a proposition, contains within herself all the properties that she can possess. The reason why she can or does possess these properties must be due to her nature; otherwise, the properties would not actually be contained in her. All the properties that she can have, past, present, and future, must be contained in herself. She is black and white because that is part of her nature. She is lying down at this very moment because that is part of her nature. She was barking three minutes ago because that is part of her nature. She will be chasing a rabbit at 6:48 P.M. tomorrow because that is part of her nature.

The substances which comprise the real world are called "monads." Anything that can be the subject of a true proposition is a monad. These include people, animals, places, things, parts of these, and so on. Unlike atoms, monads do not have to have any particular size or shape. Instead, what characterizes them is that they are capable of activity, and, hence, of having properties predicated of them. Monads are centers of activity, each containing all the properties that can ever be predicated of it. Each monad must be "windowless," that is, it must contain all its properties within itself, and cannot receive them from outside itself; otherwise, its predicates would not be contained in the subject. Thus, though it may appear that the monad, "a nail," is being struck by another monad, "a hammer," and that the nail's properties, such as its position and shape, are being changed by the hammer, this cannot be the case. The nail must contain all its properties, possible and actual, within itself; otherwise, the true propositions asserted about the nail would not be true.

Thus each monad is actually a self-contained universe. But it is also a universe which "contains" every other universe, since a true proposition can be asserted about any given monad stating its relation to another monad, for example, "My dog is not the Empire State Building," "My dog is not a planetary body," "My dog did not bark at Julius Caesar," and so on. Every monad is related to every other one, but related intrinsically, not extrinsically. This means that the relationship of one monad to another one is due to the internal nature of the first, and not to any external fact about either one of them. The nature of my dog must contain her relationships to everything else; otherwise, again, the true propositions about her relationships would not be true. Hence her monad and every other one must contain the whole universe in terms of its relationships to everything in the universe. Each monad is then said to "mirror the universe," each in its own way. Each is an expression of the same universe, "but the expressions vary in perfection like different representations or drawings in perspective of the same town seen from different points."

If each monad is self-contained, and each mirrors or pictures the rest of the universe in its own way, what accounts for the similarity and coherence of the pictures? No monad can influence or affect another, since they are all self-contained. Yet my dog barks at a rabbit when the rabbit is running by, and not at a different time. Presumably, since my dog's monad is self-contained, she could bark at the rabbit whenever her own nature made her do it, regardless of where the rabbit was. However, she only does bark at the rabbit when the rabbit is nearby. The harmonious interaction of monads cannot, by their natures, be due to any action of one upon another, or of some outside agency upon them all. The explanation, Leibniz insisted, was that there must be a pre-established harmony among all the monads. Their natures are such that they are all, throughout eternity, in harmony. Thus, because all the monads are perfect of their kind, it does not happen that, for example, I meet Jones (according to my monad's nature) when he is a thousand miles away (according to his monad's nature). Although our monads never influence or affect one another, they always operate harmoniously, according to pre-established patterns. And so what is true according to my monad reflects and harmonizes with what is true according to all the other monads in the universe.

The theory of the pre-established harmony, Leibniz asserted, allows for a more satisfactory theory of the relationship of the mind and the body than that of either Descartes or Malebranche. The mind and the body are each different monads and hence do not interact. But the events in one are in a pre-established harmony with the events in the other. Hence when an event in my body takes place, as, for example, sitting on a thumbtack, an event takes place in my mind, that of experiencing a pain. The bodily event neither caused nor occasioned the mental event. But since the two monads are in a pre-established harmony, the events in one realm do, in fact, correspond with the events in the other, without requiring some mysterious point of contact (Descartes' theory of the pineal gland), or some Divine intervention (Malebranche's theory).

To explain his view, Leibniz offered the illustration of the mind-body relationship in terms of two clocks which agree perfectly, that is, they keep exactly the same time. This might be due to three different reasons. First, the clocks might be connected in some way so that the actions of one influenced the actions of the other (Descartes' theory of interaction). Second, there might be some outside agent who constantly acted upon the clocks so that they constantly agree (Malebranche's theory of occasionalism). Last, it is possible that the clocks are so well made to begin with that they will always keep the same time (the pre-established harmony). In terms of the mind and the body as the clocks, Leibniz argued that Descartes' theory of mutual influence has to be abandoned because "we cannot conceive of material particles or properties, or immaterial qualities, which can pass from one of these substances to the other," since each substance is totally different from the other. Malebranche's theory is implausible in view of its conception of God as constantly intervening in each and every event that takes place.

Thus, there remains only my hypothesis; that is, the way of harmony pre-established by an antecedent Divine contrivance, which from the beginning has formed each of these substances [mind and body] in a way so perfect and regulated with so much accuracy that merely by following laws of its own, received with its being, it nevertheless agrees with the other, just as if there were mutual influence, or as if God, in addition to his general cooperation, constantly put his hand thereto.[1]

Leibniz's answer to the question "What is reality?" is that reality is made up of independent monads, each constituting a center of activity, and each acting in a pre-established harmony with all the others because of the laws of each one's nature. The whole system must have a necessary and sufficient reason; hence there must be a Being, God, who is the cause, or reason, of the existing world of monads.

God, from all eternity, knew all the possible monads, plus all the necessary conditions of any possible world. From all the possibilities, He chose and established in harmony the actual or real world that exists in this universe. This is the best of all possible worlds, principally because God chose it out of all the possibilities. If there were a better possibility, God as the perfect, all-knowing Being, would have chosen it. This best of all possible worlds is the world with "the greatest variety together with the greatest order." Any other world, presumably, would have been worse, in the sense that it would have contained fewer monads or that it would have less than a perfect harmony. If, for example, it contained a monad "George Washington" who was the seventeenth President of the United States, this monad would not have been harmonious with all the ones in this world. If God had chosen a world that contained all the monads contained in this one, minus one, that of a notorious murderer, such a world would have had less variety and harmony than the one that exists. Hence the best of all possible worlds is the one that exists, and is the one that contains the greatest number of mutually possible monads in a pre-established harmony.

Leibniz' metaphysical system portrays reality as a harmonious collection of active centers, monads, each operating independently according to the laws of its own nature. The ultimate reason for the system is that God chose it. God chose it because it is the best of all possible worlds in terms of variety and harmony. This system, Leibniz contended, answers all the

---

[1] Leibniz's "A Letter of Leibniz on His Philosophical Hypothesis and the Curious Problem Proposed by His Friends to the Mathematicians" (1696), which appears in *The Philosophical Works of Leibnitz*, translated by George Martin Duncan (Tuttle Morehouse & Taylor, New Haven, 1890), Vol. XV, pp. 92–93. This passage also appears in Smith & Grene *From Descartes to Locke* (Phoenix, Chicago, 1960) p. 304 n.

questions that philosophers have asked about the nature of reality. It explains what it is and why it is that way. It offers an explanation in keeping with all the facts that we know about the world. And it avoids the inconsistencies and the dangerous irreligious views of previous metaphysical systems.

One might object that the theory is at variance with everybody's ordinary experience of interaction between substances. But, Leibniz could reply, the ordinary belief in the matter is inconsistent. No matter what may *appear* to be the case, different substances cannot interact. The theory propounded by Leibniz may seem implausible, but he could point out that it is no more implausible than that of any other metaphysician. We may not see monads, and we may find it hard to believe that they can be completely self-contained, and be the cause of all their properties. But, Leibniz insisted, his theory did offer a consistent explanation of all the truths we can know about reality. It also allowed for the reality of all the properties that we ever experience, instead of just the mathematical ones, since all the properties, sensed or not, would follow from the nature of each individual monad. And, finally, as Spinoza and Malebranche could also have argued about their own theories, no evidence can be offered from our experience that is incompatible with this metaphysical theory. Hence, no matter how incredible a metaphysical system like Leibniz' might seem to be from the point of view of common sense, its author could and did argue that it presented a completely consistent explanation of the nature of reality and one which could not be disproved.

Leibniz' theory had a great influence on philosophers, especially in Germany, where it became almost the official theory of the German universities throughout the eighteenth century. It remained in vogue until ridiculed by Voltaire in *Candide* (where he showed that the view that this is the best of all possible worlds cannot actually be accepted by a reasonable person in the light of all the evil that occurs), and until criticized by Kant in his attack on all metaphysical systems.

LOCKE'S METAPHYSICAL THEORY

John Locke (1632–1704), whose empirical theory of knowledge was examined in Chapter 1, "The Theory of Knowledge," tried to advance a somewhat tentative metaphysical theory on the basis of his empirical views about what we could know. His theory of knowledge seemed to lead to the conclusion that we could not actually know anything about the real nature of things. All that we could know about were the ideas present to our minds. However, on the other hand, we are almost compelled to believe both that there is a reality behind our ideas and that it has some of the characteristics of our ideas.

When Locke considered the possibility that reality was nothing but a collection of ideas in our minds, he rejected this because we cannot make up or create the simple ideas out of which all of our knowledge is built. We may know nothing except our ideas, but there must be something which is the source or cause of our ideas, which constitutes reality. We can only discover something about this reality in terms of our ideas, whenever we can establish that "there is a conformity between our ideas and the reality of things."

But when can we tell that there is such a conformity? First, when we are confronted with the simple ideas which we are incapable of creating. These ideas, we can be sure, either represent features of real things or are caused or produced by features of real things. But, then, what are these real things that can possess the properties of our simple ideas, or can produce them in us?

Any attempt to find the answer leads into epistemological difficulties. The only real existences that we can know with any certainty are ourselves, whom we each know intuitively, and God, whose existence can be demonstrated (see Chapter 1, pages 73–74). When we try to know those beings which have the properties of our simple ideas, or which produce them, we find we are unable to gain any information at all about the nature of such beings. But we are also unable to doubt their existence, since we cannot conceive of the qualities we experience not belonging to, or inhering in, something: "not imagining how these simple ideas can subsist by themselves, we accustom ourselves to suppose some *substratum* wherein they do subsist, and from which they do result, which therefore we call *substance*."

When we try to discover what the nature of this substance is, we find that we do not know what it is except that it is a supposition of "something we know not what" that supports qualities which are capable of producing simple ideas in us. We are unable to discover anything more about the nature of this something. We can describe the group of qualities that we suppose exist together and in one thing. But we cannot, unfortunately, know what the thing is, or why and how it binds together the qualities that we experience.

If the substances that constitute reality cannot actually be known, but have to be supposed as the foundation or location of the simple ideas that we are aware of, then what general kinds of substances must there be? Though we cannot be too sure, we suppose that there are, in general, two kinds of substances, physical or material ones and nonphysical entities or mental ones. The material ones are those that we suppose underlie groups of qualities such as size, shape, solidity, color. The spiritual ones are those that we suppose underlie "the operations of the mind, viz. thinking, reasoning, fearing, and so on, which we, concluding not to subsist of themselves, nor apprehending how they can belong to body, or be produced by it, are apt to think these the actions of some other substance, which we call spirit." In the case of both bodies and spirits, Locke insisted, we do not and cannot have any clear and distinct ideas as to what they are. We suppose that experiences of mental qualities inhere in, or belong to, something called spirit, or mind, and experiences of physical qualities belong to or inhere in something called body. In both cases, we will always remain ignorant as to what the substance is, but at the same time it would not be rational or even psychologically possible to deny that there is a something holding the different groups of experienced qualities together.

If our information about these fundamental constituents of reality, the substances, is so vague and indefinite, can we really be sure that there actually are two totally different types of substances, minds and bodies? Locke admitted that strictly speaking we cannot be positive that matter does not think, nor that minds are not extended and solid, since we do not know the real nature of any substance. But, at the same time, we are unable to conceive how the same something that underlies material qualities can have mental qualities, or how the something that underlies mental qualities can be extended or solid. So we "reasonably" suppose that there are two different sorts of substances, bodies, which are material, and spirits, which are immaterial, though we can never, of course, be sure that this is the case.

Locke's metaphysical theory is thus a limited and tentative view as to what reality may be, and what we seem to be forced to believe about reality. Since we are unable to accept the possibility that only our ideas exist, and that they do not exist, or subsist, in anything, we accept, instead, the view that there must be substances in which our ideas inhere, or to which they belong, or by which they are produced. Though we can never know anything about these substances, we suppose that they exist, that they are the constituents of reality, and that they fall into two general classifications, bodies and spirits. To our certain knowledge, we can only be sure of the existence of ourselves and of God, and we cannot be too definite as to what we are, or what God actually is like. Hence our picture of reality will always be extremely indefinite, both as to the true nature of reality and as to the means by which its various parts are related. We believe that something real must exist. Beyond this, we can actually do little more than pile one supposition on top of another. In spite of this limitation on our knowledge, Locke was unwilling to come to any skeptical conclusions about the vague general features of his metaphysical view. No matter how little we could know about reality, and no matter how dubious this knowledge might be, Locke still felt that because of our psychological make-up, we had to accept a belief in the existence of a physical world composed of unknown material substances, and of an immaterial world composed of unknown spiritual or mental substances.

BERKELEY'S METAPHYSICAL THEORY

Bishop George Berkeley (1685–1753) was convinced that Locke's philosophy led to a "forlorn skepticism." Locke's epistemology separated ideas and things, and ultimately made things unknowable. This fundamental defect was illustrated by his metaphysics, in which he was forced to confess that we really did not know any substances, but were compelled to suppose that they existed. Also, Berkeley contended that since Locke had a false metaphysics (in that he believed that matter, or material substance, existed), he could never hope to comprehend reality. Instead, Berkeley proposed that what was needed was a new conception about the nature of reality and how we come to recognize it.

Basically, Berkeley's metaphysical contention is that the only things which are real are ideas and spirits. Ideas, or sensible things (those things which are immediately perceived by the senses), are real because they are perceived. They are not qualities which belong to mysterious physical or material things. Instead, Berkeley insisted, ideas are things whose being or reality consists in their being perceived. Sensible reality understood in this way requires no unknown something in which it inheres. All the perplexities that resulted from trying to find this mysterious something are due to the unfortunate mistake of not realizing that ideas are things. Philosophers had mistakenly supposed that ideas were copies of, or the effects of, things. Then they had sought for the real things, and could not find them. They found only the ideas, and concluded that the ideas were unreal, and that reality could not actually be known. By adopting Berkeley's key to the puzzle—that things are exactly what they appear to be, that is, things are the ideas that we experience—we immediately realize that sensible reality is known. The world of appearance is then a real world. It is a world of ideas which exists because it is perceived, and exists exactly as it is perceived.

The real sensible world exists as a sequence of ideas in minds. Since the ideas are not produced by any particular human mind, and since they do not depend for their existence on any particular human mind, there must then be an Infinite Mind in which they exist, and in which their order is produced. Hence reality must have another dimension, that of active substances which can produce or affect ideas. The substances are characterized by their creative activity, their ability to cause events. Intuitively, we know ourselves as finite active centers capable of perceiving, thinking, willing, and so on. By inference, we realize that God must be an Infinite Spirit capable of producing all the ideas and causing us to perceive them. The foregoing theory accounts for the location of the world of sensible reality as ideas existing fully in the Divine Mind, and partially in individual minds. This, in turn, accounts for the changes in the sensible world as the result of God's causal agency and the activities of finite spirits.

Berkeley's metaphysical theory is to a large extent just a development of Malebranche's. (Berkeley was known in his day as the Irish Malebranche, and as the "sincere Malebranchist.") Malebranche had said that reality consists of God, the ideas in His Mind (the world of intelligible extension), and the effects of God's will—the created world. The material world in Malebranche's theory exists as a creation of God, but it is unknown to us and it has no effect on us. God causes events to occur in the material world on the occasion of the occurrence of events in the mental and spiritual world. Berkeley's metaphysics eliminates the material world which Malebranche had said was known only through Revelation. (Berkeley argued that the passage of Scripture which Malebranche appealed to, the opening lines of Genesis, does not say that God has created a *material* world, but only that He has created a world, which may well be the world of sensible things.) Further, Berkeley converted the world of intelligible extension into the world of sensible things, the perceived and perceivable ideas in the Mind of God. The created world becomes that of finite spirits, like ourselves, and the sets of ideas that God makes us know. In this form, Berkeley had transformed the Cartesian metaphysics of God, mind, and matter as the components of reality into a metaphysical system involving only God and mind. (And since there are no bodies in Berkeley's system, the mind-body problem in its seventeenth-century form no longer recurs.)

IDEALISM

Berkeley's theory, which he called "immaterialism," the world conceived of without matter, is one of the first major modern *idealistic* theories. Idealism in metaphysics is the theory that the fundamental reality from which everything can be explained is mental rather than material. (It is often the case, though it does not necessarily have to be so, that someone who is an idealist in metaphysics also has an "idealistic" outlook about human moral problems. To avoid confusion between the metaphysical theory and the moral outlook, the former should preferably be called "ideaism," which is, unfortunately, difficult to pronounce.)

Solipsism

There are many different forms of the idealist theory of metaphysics that have played and continue to play a role in philosophical inquiry. Berkeley's version and the corresponding revision of Malebranche's theory (eliminating the category of the material world) have had few adherents, but have nevertheless inspired extreme forms of idealism which other philosophers have tried to refute. One such view is "egoism" or "solipsism," which maintains that reality consists of nothing but the individual and the ideas that he is aware of. For example, since I do not directly perceive anything but myself and my ideas, can I be sure that any other thing or any other mind exists, or that reality has any other components besides myself and my ideas? The solipsist declares that the answer is "no." Berkeley had avoided solipsism in his own theory by stressing the contention that his ideas had to be independent of himself since he could not control them or create them, and that it simply was not plausible to believe that ideas existed only when he perceived them. But the solipsist can point out that no one actually possesses any evidence whatsoever that ideas exist when not perceived by oneself, and that one cannot tell that one's ideas are not controlled and created by oneself unconsciously. Thus, nothing in my experience assures me that my ideas must have a source other than myself, and must be controlled by some other being. Hence, the solipsist can argue that, from what anyone knows directly, he can never find any evidence that solipsism is not true. All the events that take place in my life, all of my relations with other people and other things, are experienced as ideas in my mind. Therefore, the entire world may, for all that I can ever tell, be nothing but a series of ideas in my mind.

Solipsism has functioned more as a threat to various theories than as a theory itself. Opponents have tried to show that views like those of Descartes, Malebranche, Leibniz, Locke and Berkeley, if consistently followed out will end in a type of solipsism. Proponents of these metaphysical theories have then tried to show that there is, or must be, some way that we can establish that reality consists of more than one person and his ideas.

Fichte's Subjective Idealism

At the end of the eighteenth century the German metaphysician Johann Gottlieb Fichte (1762–1814) developed a new metaphysical theory, subjective idealism, from the solipsistic outlook. Solipsism seems implausible to almost everyone because of the character and content of ordinary experience, for each of us seems to be in contact with other people and other things all the time. Even if we cannot find any evidence to disprove solipsism, we are still unwilling to accept it. One of the main reasons for our antipathy to this view is the one that Berkeley stressed: our ideas must have a source or cause which does not seem to be ourselves. Fichte worked out a metaphysical theory to account for the origin of our ideas in terms of a creative, ever-developing mind whose efforts to realize his potentialities generated the various features of the world that we are aware of.

At the outset, Fichte stated, two major metaphysical theories are possible: idealism, explaining reality in terms of mental causes; and materialism, explaining reality in terms of material or physical causes. It is not possible to prove or disprove either of these theories, though each one can point out difficulties in the other. Before he can proceed to comprehend the universe, the metaphysician first has to take his stand and decide whether he is an idealist or a materialist, not on the basis of evidence but on the basis of faith or preference.

If one has decided to look at the world in terms of mind and mental causes as fundamental, one will then, according to Fichte, see and understand everything as the result of the generative activities of the real mental substance, called the Ego. The world as we experience it has two basic aspects, the self that we are immediately aware of, and that which is other than self, the Non-Ego. When we are conscious and able to comprehend the nature of our experience, we see it in terms of two factors, the object, or outside world, and the subject, ourselves. Both of these can be understood, from the idealist point of view, only in terms of an underlying creative mental or spiritual agent who has produced the two-sided, objective and subjective world. In the quest for an understanding of reality, the subjective idealist sees that the world of consciousness, that of the self and the Non-Ego, can only be understood as the effect of something. By the idealistic decision, that something must be immaterial. By its effects, it must be seen as creative and developing.

The Ego, the ultimate reality and source of consciousness in Fichte's theory is not a mind in the solipsistic sense. It is that which can produce mind, as well as the content of mind, the world of ideas. Hence it must be more than any individual mind. It is an impersonal, universal creative force which gives rise to, or accounts for, each individual mind, and that which each individual mind is conscious of. The Ego, in striving for its own development and self-realization, appears in the form of individual selves and in the form of the objective Non-Ego. The universal Ego creates by willing to achieve its self-realization and self-development. Reality, seen in its most general aspects (instead of from the finite, limited perspective of individual selves), is nothing but the development of the Ego. Each of us can "strike through" the curtains of individuality that envelop our consciousnesses to a vision and comprehension of the world as it really is. When we accomplish this, we see and understand everything in terms of the Ego developing. The developmental process provides the metaphysical key in that each stage and each form of the universe can be understood as a part of the creative process of the Ego, seeking its own complete expression and realization.

Hegelian Metaphysics:
Objective or Absolute Idealism

The most famous modern metaphysician is Georg Wilhelm Friedrich Hegel (1770–1831), who developed Fichte's subjective idealism into the all-encompassing theory of objective or absolute idealism. Hegel, born at Stuttgart, Germany, studied theology at Tubingen, as well as natural science, philosophy, and classics. He began teaching at Jena, where he started publishing his views. His first important work, *The Phenomenology of Mind*, was completed in 1806, but its publication was delayed a year due to Napoleon's conquest of Jena. After several other teaching posts, Hegel was appointed to Fichte's professorship at the University of Berlin in 1818, where he became a famous and influential figure. He died of cholera in an epidemic in 1831. His writings and his lectures (many of which were only published after his death) developed his system. For a period, Hegel's views dominated the philosophical scene in his native Germany as well as influencing thinkers throughout the rest of Europe and in the United States. Some of the German refugee intellectuals who fled Germany during the Revolution of 1848 started the first philosophical movement in the United States, the St. Louis Hegelians, and the first American philosophical journal, the *Journal of Speculative Philosophy*. The antimetaphysical movements of the twentieth century are, in large measure, directed against the Hegelian system, while many of the nonidealistic metaphysical theories of recent times derive from various aspects of Hegel's thought. Hegel's philosophy is one of the most abstruse and complex that has ever been developed. We shall attempt here to deal with only a few of his major themes.

One of Hegel's principal contentions is that the whole of reality, including everything in the known universe, can be understood only in terms of an Absolute or Objective Mind which is in the process of evolution throughout the history of the world. The Absolute Mind is striving to become a transcendent, self-contained, self-conscious, completely free Being. Each stage in the history of the world is an expression of the Absolute's inner struggle to attain complete self-realization. The evolutionary process is an attempt by the Absolute to become completely rational and intelligible.

The earlier stages of the development of the Absolute could neither explain nor account for natural and historical events. The attempts by philosophers to construct theories that would give complete explanations of the nature, source, and meaning of the universe were all incomplete, unsatisfactory, and contradictory. This was due to the fact that the Absolute was still in an incomplete and contradictory form, but it was constantly striving to overcome this situation by making itself more intelligible and consistent, and by making its expression, the World, also intelligible and consistent. The world, as it has appeared in history, represents a series of successive approximations by the Absolute in its quest toward completeness, rationality, and comprehensiveness. This occurs by both cancelling out and taking over more limited and primitive forms of existence into more developed and advanced ones. This process is both an intellectual one, which can be comprehended through the process of logical development to more and more complete truths, and a natural one, through temporal development, as the world reaches greater and greater coherence. Thought and being are identical and the way they each develop reveals the ultimate features of reality, the Absolute.

According to Hegel, one can see the Absolute's developmental process in the history of the natural and human world. The universe began as nothing but discrete and separate particles. Nothing in the universe, at this initial stage, explained why these particles existed and how they were related. Any theory that attempted to describe or explain the universe in its initial, almost chaotic stage, would run into difficulties and contradictions, since the elements then present in the world would be inadequate and insufficient to account for the entire universe. The Absolute, in its attempt to make itself more rational and intelligible, then synthesized or organized the elements into a pattern, that of the physical order of the world.

The physical system was more intelligible than what preceded it, but it was still inadequate to explain why events occur. Any theory of the world in purely physical terms contained conflicting and contradictory elements, as the early Greek natural philosophers discovered. Hence a completely rational and intelligible explanation of the world could not be worked out on the physical level. The Absolute, therefore, developed to a higher stage, the chemical one. When this stage, in turn, proved to be incomplete and to involve inconsistencies and contradictions, a further stage emerged, the biological one, followed by the human one. The evolution of the world through the different stages represented, for Hegel, "the march of reason through the world." Each stage represented a more complete expression of the Absolute or Objective Mind, and each successive expression could be described in terms of a more consistent explanation of everything in the universe.

According to Hegel, the process by which the Absolute develops is a logical one, which appears to us in experience as a historical one. This process is called "the dialectic." In its intellectual and logical form it consists of a process by which contradictory views of the universe are reconciled through a synthesis. A theory of the world (the thesis) is contradicted by another theory (the antithesis). The conflict between the theories is overcome by synthesizing them in another theory (the synthesis) that contains the partial truth of the two antithetical views. Their contradictory elements are eliminated, and the partial truths they each contain are brought together in the synthesis. The process that carries through this transformation is untranslatable by a single term in English. The German verb that Hegel uses for it is *aufheben*. It means, among other things, (1) to annul or cancel out; (2) to preserve; and (3) to elevate. All of this is supposed to happen when contradictories, the thesis and antithesis, are cancelled out. They are also preserved and raised up (elevated) in the synthesis. Each of the antithetical theories is an incomplete account of the nature of reality containing some element of the truth about reality. The synthesis is more complete, and retains the element of truth that is in each thesis and antithesis. But it, the synthesis, in turn, can be opposed by its antithesis; it then has to be reconciled into a new synthesis, and so on, until a complete, rational formulation of reality can be stated which admits of no contradiction or antithesis and which encompasses all truth.

The Absolute is constantly striving to make itself completely rational by overcoming the dialectic of thesis and antithesis through more and more complete syntheses. The achievement of complete self-realization will involve an all-encompassing synthesis that will reconcile all the partial truths into one total truth about reality. When the Absolute is able to reach this level of complete intelligibility, its inner logical struggle will have ended. When this occurs, so will the expression of this developing process, world history, come to an end. Each stage of the dialectical process is expressed externally as a stage in the developing history of the world. When the Absolute achieves completion, so does its expression, the cosmos. Both will be completely coherent, intelligible, and rational.

Our understanding of the universe develops in the course of the dialectical struggle, just as the universe does. Until the world reaches a stage of complete intelligibility, we can only have as complete an understanding of it as its own development admits of. Each philosopher can see the world only as coherently as the world then is. The history of philosophy reflects the dialectical process and growth of the Absolute. The final metaphysical system, that of Hegel, is only possible because the Absolute has reached, or is about to reach, its final culmination. When the Absolute has become completely rational, a system of thought that expresses its nature will be identical with what it is. Complete Thought and complete Being will be one and the same thing.

As Hegel saw his own philosophy as the extension of completed reason, fully comprehending the totality of Being, so he also saw the society around him as the historical fulfillment of the dialectical process on the human level. Man began his journey in history on an animal level, dominated by passion and egoistic attitudes. Then he began to recognize others as equal, as also possessing some freedom, and thereby limiting his own. The conflicting situation was synthesized into various social forms like marriage, legal systems, social units, property relationships, etc. These social forms contained conflicts between the individual and society, and were reconciled and synthesized into moral societies, into states. The best form of the State is one which contains no conflicts and acts solely for the realization of everyone, that is, the realization of Objective Mind. Hegel saw the national state that was emerging in Europe as the fulfilment on the human level of the metaphysical process involved in the development of reality. It unifies its members in terms of language, customs, religion, ideals, and eliminates internal conflicts. The stronger the State, the more it accomplishes this, and the closer people are brought to self-realization and to the Absolute. The Prussian State, Hegel felt, was the best example of this. In 1806, during the height of Napoleon's conquests in Europe, Hegel looked upon the French Emperor as the incarnation of the World Spirit or Objective Mind. Napoleon, whether he realized his role or not, was bringing the human race together, creating a strong national state, and so on. Hegel originally intended to present his *Phenomenology of Mind* to the World Conqueror when he returned to Paris, so that Napoleon could understand the role he was fulfilling. This adulation of Napoleon disappeared as the effects of his conquest of Germany became apparent. Then, Hegel came to the conclusion that the Prussian state was the best example of the development of the Absolute in history, nearing its full completion.

Hegel's metaphysical system portrays reality as essentially Mind in the process of development toward complete rationality and intelligibility. Earlier idealistic theories had stated that only mind is real, and that only mental actions and causes could explain the world of experience. Berkeley's form of idealism had seen the real universe as essentially static, consisting of the set of ideas in the Mind of God. All that changed was the sub-set of ideas that we were aware of at any particular moment. Fichte added a dynamic element to the idealistic thesis, contending that the Ego was creative, and that it causally generated the subjective and objective features of our experience. Hegel objectified thought, mind, and its process of development, and conceived of them as features of an independent object having no personal or subjective characteristics. The Hegelian Absolute or Objective Mind is reality. It manifests itself outwardly as the developing process of world history, with each stage necessarily occurring to overcome the defects of the preceding one. Inwardly, the Absolute is a system of ideas developing by the dialectical process into a totally unified and coherent truth. The final and complete metaphysical system which states and explains what reality is will be the Absolute itself, expressed in intellectual terms.

Hegel's system also was open to political interpretations and played a role in the social and political struggles of the mid-nineteenth century. The conservative Hegelians saw the Prussian state in its actual form as the fulfillment of Hegel's dialectic of history. No further changes or development were needed, and the perfection of the Prussian state should be guarded against opposition. On the other hand, the so-called left Hegelians called for changing, alienating, and overcoming the contradictions embedded in the Prussian state through revolutionary change if necessary. Karl Marx's theory of dialectical materialism, which we will turn to next, was heavily influenced by the leftist Hegelians.

Dialectical Materialism

Hegel's idealistic metaphysical theory represents the most complete attempt to explain the whole nature of the world, including its history, in terms of mind and mental processes. Shortly after Hegel's death, another German thinker, Karl Marx (1818–1883), presented a metaphysical theory which built upon one element of Hegelian metaphysics, the dialectical process, while denying the other, that mind is the fundamental reality. Marx's most famous theories are those of his political philosophy, which form the basis for present-day Communism. These will be treated in detail in Chapter 3, "Political Philosophy." Here we will only indicate the way in which he "stood Hegel on his head," and transformed Hegelian idealism into a materialistic theory about the nature of reality.

Marx insisted that reality is nothing but a collection of physical or material forces in operation. The natural world is not, as earlier materialists had asserted, simply a series of material parts in motion from one spatial position to another. The natural, material world is also a developing one, evolving according to a dialectical process. Each stage of the material world contains certain physical contradictions which it overcomes in syntheses. The movement, in nature, of thesis, antithesis, and synthesis constitutes the process of natural development of evolution, moving toward a final goal of a completely coherent and organized nature.

In the present stage of the world, the process of dialectical materialism is best seen in human history. Human beings are material entities. All the features of their lives are determined by the material processes in which they are involved. Human institutions, attitudes, ways of life, and beliefs are all the products of physical man's relationships to physical nature. Those features which are peculiar to the human situation are the ones involved in man's attempts to produce the material goods necessary for his continued existence. The way in which man is related to nature in the productive process determines all the other facets of his life. It is in terms of the development of economic processes and systems that we can see the dialectical process in operation in human history.

Every economic system that has developed in the course of history contains contradictory or conflicting features, the theses and the antitheses. The conflicts between the contradictory elements have beeń resolved by syntheses, new economic systems, which in turn "contain the seeds of their own destruction" in their antithetical elements, and so on. The conflicts in the medieval economic system between the roles in the economic system of the serfs, the lords, the burgers, and so forth, have been resolved dialectically in the present economic system, capitalism. This system contains conflicts in that the employer owns the means of production, whereas the worker produces. Because of the conflicts in the system, certain material contradictions occur, and are expressed in the form of wars, depressions, and so on. The necessary, determined movement of nature to overcome contradictions will finally result in a new synthesis, an economy in which there is no longer any conflict between the producer and the owner of the means of production, because the producer will become the owner. At this point, the final Hegelian synthesis will occur in the complete self-realization of Nature. All contradictions will have been overcome, and a totally rational natural and social order will have been achieved.

Marx's metaphysical system denied the idealistic elements in Hegel's theory, but made the developmental ones fundamental. Reality, conceived of as entirely material, could be understood only in terms of the dialectical process of its evolutionary change. But Marx was not alone in considering the developmental aspect as crucial. Other metaphysicians in the nineteenth and twentieth centuries also stressed the changing, evolving character of reality. In terms of the discoveries in nineteenth-century biology that culminated in Darwin's theory of evolution, many metaphysicians saw reality as being like a biological organism. The changes that take place are part of an evolving process of growth. The processes do not necessarily aim at one, final culmination, as they do for Marx. Nor are they about to produce the final and complete stage of Reality. However, in such a biological conception of reality these philosophers have found a way of explaining the many aspects of the natural and human world as part of a cosmic developmental scheme.

OTHER METAPHYSICAL THEORIES

We will briefly consider four of these theories, those of Schopenhauer, Bradley, Bergson, and Whitehead.

Arthur Schopenhauer (1788–1860) was a late German contemporary of Hegel's who despised the metaphysicians of his day (especially Hegel, whom he regarded as a charlatan). He developed a very pessimistic and antirational view of reality. Early in his life, he wrote his most famous works, *On the Fourfold Root of the Principle of Sufficient Reason* (1813), and *The World as Will and Idea* (1818), which earned him the post of lecturer at the University of Berlin. He felt that all of the successors of Kant, and especially Hegel, tried to establish some kind of transcendent knowledge that would explain everything. But Kant (as we'll see later in the chapter) had ruled out all such attempts.

Instead, according to Schopenhauer, the key to understanding the world was the recognition that will was the fundamental factor in the universe. Everyone is aware of himself both as a spatial and temporal object, and as a willing, active agent. Schopenhauer claimed, in examining self-consciousness, that the latter, which would seem to go beyond Kant's categories, was realized. We also can see that our observable behavior is nothing other than the objectification of our will, our desires, our impulses. The body is not a separate and distinct entity from the will, but is just the way our volitional nature appears in experience. The mind, which the idealists made the central feature of reality, not only is an independent rational entity, but also is an expression of our unconscious volitions. Our intellectual views are the ways the will makes us see the world in terms of our inner drives.

What is the case about human individuals is also the case about nature in general. Schopenhauer's main work is entitled *The World as Will and Idea*. The world appears as a series of phenomena, or ideas. It is in reality the expression of a cosmic will, which, unlike Hegel's Absolute, is not rational, has no goal or purpose, but is just endless blind striving. It is the force or power that makes everything happen, but it is not trying to achieve anything. As a result, human life and world events are purposeless and hopeless. Schopenhauer grimly portrayed the suffering involved in all existence, and insisted it served no purpose and was getting nowhere. If one could see behind the scenes of reality, one would see only blind force, and nothing more.

In view of this extremely pessimistic picture of reality and the human situation, Schopenhauer could only recommend trying to quiet one's own will through aesthetic and somewhat mystical activities. The appreciation of art, a sort of "will-less perception," could give one some relief from the strivings of one's will. Similarly, he saw in Oriental thought, which he greatly appreciated, ways of achieving some peace. Art is outside of the willful activities of the human intellect, and thus can be appreciated for its own sake. The art object is like a Platonic Idea proving knowledge far superior to particular empirical or rational data. Because of the character of art, it alone can provide one with a kind of peace.

Schopenhauer's stress on the unconscious and volitional character of life played a significant role in the development of more recent theories about human nature, such as Freud's. In the generation after Schopenhauer, Nietzsche turned his theory into an optimistic one, stressing the possibilities of the full unleashing of the will. Instead of trying to hide or escape from one's unconscious strivings, Nietzsche advocated that each person should try to express his will honestly and completely. Nietzsche regarded Schopenhauer as too weak-kneed to follow out, the implications of his own theory. In Nietzsche's book, *Human, All Too Human*, he took Schopenhauer to task.

Francis Herbert Bradley (1846–1924) was an English Hegelian metaphysician. He went to Oxford, where interest in German idealistic metaphysics was very strong. His major metaphysical work was *Appearance and Reality* (1893). In it he tried to show that (1) the world of appearance cannot be described without contradictions, and (2) the world of reality, of the Absolute, resolves all of the contradictions and explains everything.

In the section on appearance, Bradley neatly laid out all of the classical paradoxes that result from trying to describe the world in terms of space and time, in terms of causal relations, in terms of primary and secondary qualities, and in terms of things in themselves (see subsequent section on Kant). The Zeno paradoxes, Humean skepticism, and all sorts of puzzles generated by previous philosophers result. For example, as Bradley began his account, the Zeno paradoxes would prevent any account of experiential activity from being consistent if it involves describing events in terms of spatial or temporal terms. Other similar paradoxes would prevent logically consistent description in relational terms, causal terms, or any aspect of appearances.

Bradley's development of the paradoxical characteristics of the world of appearances is done very deftly. When he turned from the morass of the world of appearance to the world of reality, the first characteristic of this latter world is and must be its logical consistency. It is second to its harmoniousness.

In exploring what reality would have to be like if it had none of the contradictory aspects of appearance, Bradley saw that it would have to be beyond thought. Thought makes or creates the very distinctions that lead to the self-contradictory paradoxes.

Reality would have to be like the Hegelian Absolute, transcending thought. It is the mind that makes us aware of the self-contradictoriness of appearance, and which leads to look beyond. But in so doing, the mind must be surpassed, since the categories it thinks generate the inconsistencies in our descriptions of experience.

Bradley, in trying to give characteristics to the Absolute, quickly found himself torn between the inconsistencies of his analysis of appearance, and the denial of the reality of what seem to be fundamental features of the world, such as that it exists in space and time. This led Bradley at times to hold a theory of degrees of reality. The most real had no contradictory elements, the less real was full of contradictions. Hence the Absolute would be most real, and then there would be a claim of lesser being, all of which existed in some sense.

Bradley's form of Hegelianism dominated Oxford philosophy until after World War I. Some of the English views we will consider in the chapter on "Contemporary Philosophy" are reactions to the influence of Bradley and his followers.

The French philosopher Henri Bergson (1859–1941) who became professor of philosophy at the College de France in 1900, and received the Nobel Prize for Literature in 1927, presented a different metaphysical view, based first of all on the recognition of the distinction between real, experienced time or duration, and scientific time. The latter is measured mathematically by instruments like clocks. The former is what we are aware of as active and ongoing. Considering the world and ourselves in terms of scientific time allows for the development of a mechanistic picture of things, and for their description in materialistic scientific conceptions. But since this kind of time does not correspond to the actual experience of life, the world described in terms of it is an abstraction that is illusory if taken as reality. Real duration, that which is biologically felt, justifies free will. Mechanical time is fixed and deterministic, whereas real duration is open and indeterminate (hence, free).

To appreciate what is actually taking place, one has to distinguish what is grasped by the intellect and what is known by intuition. Man, in his biological development, became a rational intellectual creature in order to cope with his situation and with other persons around him. His intellectual activities have been predominantly of a practical nature. To achieve control of his situation, man has portrayed everything around him in scientific terms. This has led to great practical accomplishments, but not necessarily to knowledge of reality. Mechanical models have been constructed or "carved out" of experience, but they have not gotten to the real core of things.

Besides having intellectual capacities, man also has an instinctive intuitive ability, that does enable him to see directly what is going on. Intuition is not linked to practical concerns and social needs. It is able to give us a disinterested genuine grasp of real duration and development. Intuition, unlike intellect, does not require symbols, concepts or abstraction and is able to give us absolute knowledge.

Genuine metaphysics, for Bergson, results from intuition, not from intellectual activity. The latter at best yields scientific knowledge which never actually encompasses reality. Traditional metaphysics has been intellectual, and hence unsuccessful. Intuitive knowledge can supplement intellectual knowledge and thus yield genuine understanding of what is going on.

This understanding is set forth in Bergson's best-known work, *Creative Evolution*. Intuitively we find we are in a world of evolving biological creatures. What is true of ourselves as living beings is generally the case for all beings. We find we are not the result of some kind of mechanical evolutionary process, but rather that we exist and develop in real time through a creative and vital impetus. This *élan vital* is an all-pervading feature of the biological world, and drives it forward in a constantly creative evolutionary pattern. It is the cause of the different kinds of beings that emerge historically.

Bergson saw the development of things from physical-chemical entities to man as the result of this vital impulse or impetus. Unlike Hegel, he did not see the progression as the result of some predetermined plan, or as achieving some ultimate purpose. And, unlike Schopenhauer, he did not see it is as the result of some blind, purposeless will. The development that has occurred and is occurring has significance. Other developments could have occurred. The creative force led to what we are now. It can be described in religious terms, the vital force can be considered as God (though in a quite different sense from that employed in traditional religion). The divine purpose of what has happened and is happening can only be grasped intuitively, not intellectually. A kind of intuition, namely mystical experience, which only few experience, provides the clearest knowledge of reality.

Bergson's metaphysics attempted to provide knowledge of reality beyond what could be known scientifically. In stressing intuition over intellect, his theory is somewhat antirational. In finding the key to understanding in creative evolution, Bergson used the nineteenth century emphasis on biological evolution to provide a basis for a suprarational or mystical comprehension of reality. His theory enjoyed great popularity in the first half of the twentieth century.

Another metaphysical view stressing biological processes as the way to understand reality was that of the English philosopher and mathematician Alfred North Whitehead (1861–1947). Whitehead began his career as a mathematician. He collaborated with Bertrand Russell at Cambridge University on their all-important study, *Principia Mathematica* (1900–1911), a three-volume attempt to show that all of mathematics can be derived rigorously from the basic principles of formal logic. This work became fundamental for the development of modern mathematical logic. Whitehead then went on to write about modern developments in physics, especially in connection with Albert Einstein's theory. Finally in the 1920s, when Whitehead had been appointed professor of philosophy at Harvard, he started writing on metaphysics. He made an outstanding effort to create an all-embracing metaphysical system that would include modern scientific cosmology. Whitehead's major metaphysical works are *Science in the Modern World* (1927), *Process and Reality* (1929), *Adventures in Ideas* (1933), and *Modes of Thought* (1938).

Whitehead contended that the universe could not be understood in terms of substances and mechanical models, but only in terms of organisms—dynamic, creative, interdependent entities in the process of development. If we try to describe what is going on in experience, we will find not static structures, but dynamic processes. We do not find separate, independent entities, but interrelated ones, interacting. In elucidating immediate experience, by giving an adequate generalized description of it, we should remain true to its concrete character, and not abstract only elements of it. Philosophies which have done the latter have presented pictures of the world which replace the concrete entities of actual experience with useless abstractions. In so doing they commit what Whitehead called "the fallacy of misplaced concreteness," in which the abstractions are made part of a metaphysical system instead of the items of genuine experience. A system like Descartes' does this by "bifurcating nature," seeing it in terms of two separate, distinct abstractions: mind and body. This is no longer true to the concrete experience, and hence is inadequate as a description of the world. Such a system also generates all sorts of philosophical problems in trying to give a coherent explanation of experience. Whitehead saw the weakness in modern philosophy from Descartes to Hume in terms of misplaced concreteness and useless abstractions. The sort of divisions that the early modern philosopher made between body and soul, between the different items in experience, the atomizing of experience (in Hume), all led to making concrete what wasn't *really* in nature. It also led to dividing or bifurcating nature so that its actual unity was described in terms of two or more unrelated or unrelatable entities. To recapture the physical world as a part of man's world, and vice-versa, one has to see it all as processes. As long as one does not, one will just generate false or useless theories about nature and the cosmos.

When, instead, a generalized description of concrete experience is given, one finds certain fundamental features of it. The most basic feature of every thing and every event is creativity, and this accounts for novelty in the world. In addition, one finds that there are actual entities, and relations among them. Concrete experience does not consist of isolated individual things, but rather of things, plus what Whitehead called "prehensions," the relatedness of things to other things in terms of emotions, feelings, purposes, values, and causal connections. Hume's point that we do not perceive causal connections is avoided in Whitehead's theory, since

Whitehead claims that we prehend rather than perceive the causal connections. If there is some process that Whitehead's viewpoint is pointing to, then Hume's point would no longer be decisive.

These actual concrete entities and their relationships are developing organically, dynamically. They are perpetually persisting, but in so doing become part of a creative advance, involving their relations to other entities. Everything, with the exception of God, in Whitehead's view, is occasioned by something else, is related to what else has happened, is happening, and what else will happen. The developmental process that is going on can be described in terms of an on-going creative advance in which experienced feelings, and physical and conceptual events are being brought into harmony. Things are moving and growing towards a state of satisfaction. God is seen in this view as both the unlimited potentialities of development and as that which processes are drawn to for their final satisfaction. He is also an entity in the world Who shares in its organic development, and through His love preserves everything, and gives everything some significance or purpose.

Whitehead's biologically oriented metaphysics attempted to show how reality could be understood in terms of employing organisms rather than mechanisms as the fundamental way of characterizing the universe. Others, like Charles Sanders Peirce, John Dewey and the Jesuit thinker, Teilhard de Chardin, have also offered metaphysical theories stressing the organically developing character of reality.

CRITICISMS OF METAPHYSICS: HUME AND KANT

While metaphysicians have been working out their theories about the nature of reality, and showing what is wrong with other metaphysical views, some philosophers have contended that there is something wrong with the whole enterprise of metaphysical speculation, and that metaphysical questions are basically unanswerable. The history of metaphysics gives some initial plausibility to this view, since for the last two and a half millennia there has been a succession of metaphysical theories, each pointing out defects in the preceding views, and each maintaining that it contains the final and true answer to the question "What is reality?" But the disagreement among metaphysicians still goes on. This, some critics have suggested, indicates that there is some basic difficulty in determining what constitutes a true answer in the field of metaphysics. And this in turn suggests that there is something peculiar about the field itself, or about the questions that it seeks to answer.

Indeed, at least two major theories have been developed in order to show why there are basic difficulties and limitations in the metaphysical enterprise which prevent it from ever coming to a successful or satisfactory result. These theories, suggested by David Hume (1711–1776) and Immanuel Kant (1724–1804), have analyzed the nature of metaphysical reasoning. Both Hume and Kant contend that they have found why metaphysicians have not discovered and will never discover the true nature of reality.

Hume's Criticisms

Hume's critique of metaphysics developed out of his empirical theory of knowledge and out of his skepticism. His attitude was forcefully expressed in the conclusion of his *Enquiry concerning Human Understanding*, where he said, "When we run over libraries, persuaded of these principles [those of Hume's philosophy] what havoc must we make? If we take in hand any volume of divinity or school metaphysics, for instance; let us ask, does it contain any abstract reasoning concerning quantity or number? No. Does it contain any experimental reasoning concerning matter of fact or existence? No. Commit it then to the flames: for it can contain nothing but sophistry and illusion."

Hume's reason for this sweeping conclusion stems from his view that the only meaningful conceptions are those based either on sense impressions or mathematical ideas (which are ultimately derived from sense experience, too). The basic concepts of the metaphysicians—"substance," "reality," "matter," and "mind"—are meaningless in terms of this empirical criterion, since none of these notions derives from sense experience or is a mathematical concept. If we attempt to understand what the metaphysicians are saying, we find, in fact, that they are not making significant statements, and therefore, that their views are actually unintelligible.

If what we can know about the world is based upon what we experience, plus the inferences we make from the constant conjunctions of various aspects of experience on the assumption that future experiences will resemble past ones, then how can we determine whether or not there is a reality beyond experience, or whether our experiences belong to some unexperienced real objects? Experience tells us only about experienced objects. If metaphysicians are seeking knowledge of the unexperienced objects that are supposed to constitute reality, we cannot tell what they are talking about, or whether their assertions are true or false.

To show this, Hume examined the central concept of most metaphysical systems, that of "substance." Most metaphysical disputes centered about the number and the nature of the substances that comprise the real universe. In order to determine whose theory of substance is true, one first has to ascertain what we know about substance. To do this, we have to start with the idea of substance. But where could such an idea come from and what could such an idea be?

If it be convey'd to us by our senses, I ask, which of them, and after what manner? If it be perceiv'd by the eyes, it must be a colour; if by the ears, a sound; if by the palate, a taste, and so of the other senses. But I believe none will assert, that substance is either a colour, or sound, or a taste. The idea of a substance must therefore be deriv'd from an impression of reflexion, if it really exists. But the impressions of reflexion resolve themselves into our passions and emotions; none of which can possibly represent a substance. We have therefore no idea of substance, distinct from that of a collection of particular qualities, nor have we any other meaning when we either talk or reason concerning it.[2]

Our empirical meaning of substance is just the particular group of qualities that we experience together. But substance as something that underlies or accounts for experience is a meaningless concept.

The unintelligibility of the metaphysical notion of substance becomes more obvious when we examine what metaphysicians such as Descartes, Spinoza, Malebranche, or Leibniz say about the characteristics of substance. They say that a substance is that which can exist by itself, that it requires nothing other than itself through which it must be conceived, that it requires nothing other than itself in order to explain itself, or to account for its existence. These characteristics, if they are intelligible, apply, Hume contended, to each and every perception. Every idea that we have can be thought about by itself, apart from every other. When we think of an idea we do not have to think of any other to explain or account for the one that is present to the mind. Hence each individual idea seems to be a substance.

The metaphysicians would object, and insist that Hume has misunderstood what a substance is. It is entirely different from a perception. It is that which explains or accounts for the characteristics of a perception, and it is that which the qualities perceived belong to, or inhere in. But, Hume replied, we know only about perceptions. We have no ideas of anything different from a perception that might explain them, nor have any idea of that entity which perceptions might belong to. According to the metaphysicians, "A substance is entirely different from a perception. We have, therefore, no idea of a substance."

We know only our perceptions. In examining them, Hume insisted, we find no need for an explanation of their existence or their characteristics. Nothing that we know about perceptions requires that they belong to something else, or that they inhere in anything else. The perceptions or ideas occur. They are, and they are what they are. Some are green. Some are round. They are experienced as separate and distinct entities. In examining them, we cannot tell where they come from, nor what they belong

²David Hume, *A Treatise of Human Nature*, Selby-Bigge ed. (Clarendon Press, 1951), Oxford, Bk. I, Pt. I, sec. vi, p. 16.

to. Our experience does not seem to require that we find answers to these questions. (Since the answers would involve knowing about matters beyond our experience, we could not discover any meaningful answers anyway.) "What possibility then of answering that question, Whether perceptions inhere in a material or immaterial substance, when we do not so much as understand the meaning of the question?"

Neither the materialist nor the idealist theory about the nature of reality makes any sense, Hume contended. The concepts that are crucial in these theories, matter and mind, are both unknowable and unintelligible. Starting with matter, Hume argued, as Berkeley had earlier, that we could not actually conceive of any solid, extended stuff in motion, which was supposed to comprise the real world, and supposed to cause or produce our perceptions. If, as all the modern metaphysicians seem to agree, the secondary qualities found in immediate experience, the colors, sounds, tastes, smells, and so on, cannot be features of a supposedly independently existing material world, then what can such a world be like? The secondary qualities, the metaphysicians say, are subjective and are only "in the mind." But the very same reasons that are offered to prove this will also prove that extension, solidity, and motion are subjective experiences, "in the mind," as Bayle and Berkeley had shown. Once we conclude that the sensible qualities of color, sound, taste and smell have no "continu'd and independent existence . . . there remains nothing in the universe which has such an existence."

If we cannot conceive of matter as an independently existing substance, neither can we conceive of mind as a substance. If the mind or self is supposed to be that entity which our ideas belong to, can we ever form an idea of it? "For my part, when I enter most intimately into what I call *myself,* I always stumble on some particular perception or other, of heat or cold, light or shade, love or hatred, pain or pleasure. I never can catch myself at any time without a perception, and never can observe any thing but the perception." We are not acquainted with something different from our ideas that all our ideas belong to. All that we know about is the succession of ideas. We can neither conceive of nor imagine a something that underlies the ideas; neither can we conceive of how the ideas could belong to something that is not an idea. Hence Hume denied that it made sense to conceive of mind as a substance. He did not, however, deny the existence of mind. He challenged only the way in which metaphysicians insisted upon analyzing and accounting for mental events.

The metaphysicians' view that the substances, mind and matter, are what our ideas belong to, and are what cause our ideas, Hume found meaningless. Since we cannot conceive of the substances, we cannot conceive of the ideas belonging to or inhering in them. Since our knowledge about causal relations consists solely of what we know about conjunctions of items *in* our experience, and how we feel about them, we have no way of knowing about conjunctions which involve items *outside* our experience. The concept of "cause" has meaning only with regard to perceptions or ideas. Hence assertions about substances causing or producing ideas are actually meaningless, since we know nothing about whether substantial events are constantly conjoined with experienced events, and we have no way of gaining such information.

In terms of Hume's empirical critique of metaphysical concepts, certain major metaphysical problems simply disappear. The mind-body problem which had been so important from Descartes onward is not a problem if one rejects the metaphysicians' notions of mind, matter, and necessary connection. The problem arises from supposing that mind and matter are two entirely different substances. Then a grave difficulty arises in explaining how there can be any connection or relation between them. If the unintelligible concepts of the two substances, and of necessary connection, are omitted, is there any mind-body problem left? What remains is only the problem of whether mental events, such as tastes and sounds, can be constantly conjoined with physical events, such as movements of extended objects? Hume insisted that the answer was, obviously, "yes," since we experience such constant conjunctions all the time. A certain taste is regularly conjoined with the physical configuration of an orange. Certain sounds are regularly conjoined with the movements of strings in certain musical instruments. So it is evident that mental events are, in fact, conjoined with physical ones.

The metaphysician might object, and say that Hume has again missed the whole point. No one has disputed the obvious fact of conjunction of mental events with physical ones. But what the metaphysicians were trying to do was to explain why this should take place, since mind and body are so completely different. But in answer to this, Hume's point is that the problem of why constant conjunctions take place is unanswerable, since we never have, nor can have, any information about this. We do not know why any events occur, nor why they occur in the sequences in which they do. It does not matter whether we are investigating a sequence of mental and physical events, or merely mental events, or only physical ones. When a rock breaks a window we do not ask what it is in the rock that produces the change in the window. The problem of how events are produced is just as mysterious in one realm as in the combinations of two realms. Hence the mind-body situation contains no essentially new or different difficulty. If we restrict ourselves to what we can know, the actual conjunctions of events that do occur, we will find that laws are discoverable about the relations of mental and physical events, and, hence, that there is no special mind-body problem.

In general, Hume found that the analysis of metaphysical problems showed that they were meaningless and unanswerable. The concepts involved could not be given any significance in terms of the items known in our experience. Instead of worrying about the bogus issues, Hume felt that one should first make clear why the problems are meaningless, and then go on to examine why it is that supposedly intelligent people worry about them. The study of metaphysics, in these terms, became the study of metaphysicians, the attempt to find an explanation for the strange kind of mental aberration that had developed in so many profound minds from Greek times to the present era. A pathological study of the metaphysical mind at work might indicate the cause of this peculiar mental illness.

There are psychological reasons, Hume found, why certain types of people are trapped into seeking for answers to metaphysical questions. In his *Treatise*, Hume offered a case study of the Aristotelian philosopher. He attempted to show the sequence of mental operations by which such a philosopher manages to create, in his imagination, the fictitious entities that he reasons about. When such behavior is compared with normal thinking, it indicates that there is a metaphysical idiosyncrasy which leads certain philosophers astray into a never-never land of their own making.

The problem begins when the metaphysician notices, as any competent philosopher would, that there is something strange about the beliefs ordinary people accept. For instance, almost everybody believes that he "sees" a connection between those objects that are constantly conjoined in experience. The metaphysicians realize that this is not true. Every experienced object is separate and distinct. One comes to the conclusion that there is a connection between conjoined objects only because of the human habit of associating events, and expecting the future to be like the past. Since nobody perceives any necessary connection between events, or the power that produces events, the metaphysician then dedicates himself to chasing a bluebird—seeking for the "real" causal agency that operates behind the scenes. The metaphysician is smart enough to free himself from the error of the common man: believing that he sees the connections between events. But the metaphysician is not wise enough to prevent himself from searching for the causes of events in an unseen world. The metaphysician's error lies in his belief that since the ordinary person's view about causality is mistaken, some other view must be true. He searches endlessly for the true reason why events happen. And, "what can be imagin'd more tormenting than to seek with eagerness, what for ever flies us; and seek for it in a place, where 'tis impossible it can ever exist?"

However, according to Hume's diagnosis of the case, nature gives the sorry metaphysician some consolation. After he has created terms and used them for a while, he naturally suspects that he is talking about something. Originally, the terms "are wholly insignificant and unintelligible." But they satisfy the metaphysician's needs because, by constant reiteration, he thinks he is saying something significant. Although the words remain meaningless, the metaphysician comes to believe that they have a secret meaning which could be found by serious reflection. Thus the metaphysicians talk to themselves and each other about "substance," "cause," and so on, and not only think that they are saying something, but that they have found the answer to their quest for an ultimate explanation of why things happen. "By this means these philosophers set themselves at ease, and arrive at last, by an illusion, at the same indifference, which the people attain by their stupidity, and true philosophers by their moderate scepticism. They need only say, that any phenomenon, which puzzles them, arises from a faculty or an occult quality, and there is an end of all dispute and enquiry upon the matter."

The metaphysicians, in inventing their fictitious objects and then believing in them, exhibit, according to Hume, behavior similar to that of children and poets. "We must pardon children, because of their age; poets, because they profess to follow implicitly the suggestions of their fancy: But what excuse shall we find to justify our philosophers in so signal a weakness?" The mental disorders of the metaphysician, he concluded, can be explained, but not excused.

Immanuel Kant's Criticisms

Kant (1724–1804) presented an analysis of the metaphysical enterprise that is more complex than Hume's critique of metaphysics but is similar to it in several respects. Kant sought to show that the attempt to gain knowledge about the nature of reality was bound to fail for philosophical rather than psychological reasons. When we find out what necessary and universal knowledge we are capable of attaining, we shall see, Kant contended, that because of the limitations on our knowledge we shall never be able to gain any in the area of metaphysics.

Kant was born and brought up in Königsberg in East Prussia. There he studied at the university, at which he later became a professor. He was originally a follower of the metaphysical theories of the German Leibnizians. Then, as Kant himself said, reading Hume's works awoke him from his dogmatic slumbers. The skeptical criticisms offered by Hume made Kant question the views he had previously accepted, and led him to investigate the bases of all human knowledge. After many years of reflection, he published his theory in his famous *Critique of Pure Reason* (1781), and in more simplified form in the *Prolegomena to Any Future Metaphysics* (1783).

At the outset of his examination of what we can know, Kant made clear that he accepted the empirical view that all knowledge begins with experience, *but* also argued that "it does not follow that it arises from experience." Without experience, we would have no knowledge. But, Kant maintained, what we know is not only what we are presented with in experience. Experience is organized and classified by us in the very process of knowing, so that what we know is the product of experience and of the functions of our own thinking faculties.

In his analysis of human knowledge, Kant was principally interested in examining the nature of the *a priori* information we could gain about the world, that is, information which is universal and necessary. In both mathematics and physics, he insisted, propositions could be arrived at that were true, and had to be true, of all possible experience. The theorems of arithmetic, for instance, apply to any experience that we have ever had, or could ever have. Could there also be, he asked, any such universal and necessary information about the nature of reality?

When we examine what *a priori* knowledge we possess, we find that it falls into two classifications, analytic and synthetic knowledge. The former is like Leibniz's necessary truths. Analytic judgments are those whose truth can be ascertained without reference to any experience, or any facts, whatsoever. An inspection of the terms involved suffices to determine if the proposition is true. The predicate of a true analytic judgment is contained in the subject. "Analytic" derives from the term "analysis" which means the separation of something into its component parts. Thus, for example, "All bodies are extended" is true because the definition of "body" is "that which is extended." "A triangle has three sides" is similarly analytic, since "triangle" means "a three-sided figure." No appeal to the facts is needed to determine that such a proposition must be true.

In contrast, synthetic judgments are those whose truth cannot be determined solely from an analysis or breaking down of the terms involved. "Synthetic" derives from "synthesis," or putting together. The predicates of these judgments contain some information not included in the subjects. The ordinary kind of synthetic judgment (called a "synthetic *a posteriori* judgment" by Kant) is a statement of empirical fact, such as "My dog has black and white spots" or "California has more inhabitants than New York," or "The New York Mets won the World Series." Such propositions do not state universal or necessary truths and hence are not *a priori*. The propositions do not have to be true, and they certainly do not have to be true at all times and places. There was a time, not long ago, when New York had more inhabitants than California. A synthetic *a priori* judgment, however, is one that would be necessarily true. It cannot, therefore, be a simple empirical judgment, since, as Hume had earlier shown, no empirical proposition is necessarily true. Hence a synthetic *a priori* judgment would have to be such that its predicate contained information not already contained in the subject, and yet not be a simple empirical proposition. And, of course, such a judgment would have to be universally and necessarily true.

Kant contended that there were synthetic *a priori* judgments in both mathematics and physics. The proposition "7 + 5 = 12" is not true because of the definitions of the terms. An analysis of the terms "7" and "5" would not reveal that they could be combined, and that their sum would be 12. Something more is involved in the predicate than the mere content of the subject.

> That 5 should be added to 7 was no doubt implied in my concept of a sum 7 + 5, but not that that sum should be equal to 12. An arithmetical proposition is, therefore, always synthetical, which is seen more easily still by taking larger numbers, where we clearly perceive that, turn and twist our conceptions as we may, we could never, by means of the mere analysis of our concepts and without the help of intuition, arrive at the sum wanted.

In geometry, a similar synthetic factor is involved. If we examined the concept of "a straight line," we could never determine that "a straight line is the shortest distance between two points," because the notion of "straight" does not contain that of "shortest" when it is broken down into its component meanings. Hence, since the proposition in question is necessarily and universally true, it must be a synthetic *a priori* truth rather than an analytic one. In physics also, Kant maintained, there are propositions which must be true, but which are not true by definition, such as "Every event has a cause."

The problem of knowledge becomes for Kant one of explaining how synthetic *a priori* knowledge is possible, since the answer to this question will account for our capacity to gain knowledge about the world which is not merely definitional but is also universal and necessary. The character of the truths we know in arithmetic, geometry, and, to some extent, physics, indicates that we *do* possess synthetic information that is necessary. But how does this happen? Kant's answer to this question delineates what, according to his theory, we can know and what we cannot.

To begin with, he contended, the "form" or "order" of our experience is necessary and universal. Every experience that we have had, and every one that we can conceive of, has a spatial and temporal character. We always perceive or imagine things spread out in space, and happening in a time sequence. We cannot think of an object without its having a place, or without its occurrence being part of some successive series of events. If we think of a ball, we think of it being somewhere at some time. It is not possible for us to think of an experience not occurring in space and time. We could not even recognize or describe an experience without these characteristics. If the spatial and temporal characteristics are then forms of all possible experience, how do we come to know about them? Not from experience itself, Kant argued, because they would not then be either universal or necessary. As examination of everything that we have experienced would only show that, up to now, every experience we know of has been spatial and temporal. But this would not prove that every one has to be of this form. Others, not yet experienced, might be different. But since these forms are universal and necessary conditions of all possible experience, Kant insisted, it must be a precondition of experiencing that experience be spatial and temporal. These conditions, called the "forms of intuition," must be imposed by us on anything that we are aware of, since we are always aware of things spatially and temporally. Because we impose these forms on experience, not only does every experience come in temporal and spatial patterns; it must do so. Then, because of the characteristics of every possible experience, we can be certain that mathematical truths about the forms of intuition will apply to the world of experience. The truths of arithmetic and geometry, as truths about temporal succession and spatial distance, have to be universally and necessarily true.

In order to make judgments about experience, there must be further conditions we impose on it. If we forced our experience to be only temporal and spatial, we would perceive it but be unable to describe it. We would be spectators, but no more than that. However, we can, in fact, make true judgments about experience. Hence there must be intellectual preconditions that we impose on all the information we receive, so that such judgments are possible. These preconditions are called "the logical functions of judgment," and the "pure concepts, or categories, of the understanding." The complex details of Kant's theory cannot be developed here. In brief, his contention is that every judgment that we can make about experience has a certain logical form and deals with certain types of relationships between items in our experience. All judgments are either positive or negative. They are either about all, or some, or none of a subject. They are about either possibilities, actualities, or necessities. They deal with either substances and their properties, causes and their effects, or coexistents. And so on. A list can be made of the logical forms of all possible judgments, and about the general categories of concepts and their relationships that can occur in any possible judgment. The logical conditions as well as the categorial ones determine, prior to any particular experience, what sorts of judgments we can make about it. These preconditions are, therefore, universal and necessary, since they have to apply to any judgment whatsoever, at any time and place. These preconditions cannot be derived from experience; otherwise, they would be neither universal nor necessary.

Kant's thesis is that the world of experience, the phenomenal world, is the result of something outside the mind, plus the *a priori* conditions imposed upon it by the mind. Our mental structure determines the way in which we will perceive experience, and what sorts of things we will be able to say about it. But what, specifically, is experienced can be ascertained only from experience. The forms of experience and of judgment are thus *a priori*, but the contents are not. The forms of intuition, the logical functions of judgment, and the categories comprise the conditions imposed by us on all possible experience, but they do not and cannot create the content of experience.

The situation portrayed by Kant is analogous to wearing tinted glasses which cannot be taken off. Anything that we see will be affected by the glasses. If we know the nature of the glasses we can determine apart from any experience that all experience will have certain characteristics imposed on it by our employing them to see. These characteristics will then be universal and necessary. But the contents we experience still cannot be determined by the characteristics that all experience must possess because of our wearing the glasses. It is the task of what Kant called "Critical Philosophy" to study the glasses, that is, the conditions of all possible experience and all possible judgments about experience. It is the task of the particular sciences to study the content of actual experiences.

Although Kant disagreed with Hume and contended that we could attain synthetic *a priori* knowledge about the world, he did, however, agree with Hume that metaphysical knowledge about the nature of reality was unattainable. For we cannot know, Kant maintained, what sort of reality lies behind our mental apparatus, or behind the phenomenal world. We can find neither the mental substance, the I-in-itself, nor the physical substance, the thing-in-itself, which may be responsible for what we know.

The reason why we are unable to discover any metaphysical knowledge is that we have no means of ascertaining if the forms of intuition, the logical functions of judgment, and the categories apply to anything that is not part of the phenomenal world or the realm of possible experience. We do not know if mental or material substances exist in a spatial or temporal world, since our forms of intuition are only ways in which we must experience phenomenal entities. We simply do not know what the forms of unexperienced and unexperienceable objects may be. Similarly, we do not and cannot know if the *a priori* conditions of all possible judgments about experience, or the *a priori* categories employed in all possible judgments about experience, apply to items beyond all possible experience. The necessary conditions which enable us to gain knowledge about the forms of all possible experience may or may not apply to the self and the things-in-themselves. But since we can find no means of ascertaining if they apply, we cannot ascertain that we possess any way of thinking about objects outside all possible experience, and hence that we possess any means for thinking about metaphysical objects.

The metaphysicians who attempt to move from the necessary knowledge we possess about the phenomenal world to necessary knowledge about the noumenal (nonempirical) world, will always, Kant insisted, get into hopeless difficulties. There is simply no way of reasoning from either the form or the content of experience to any metaphysical truths whatsoever. The metaphysicians who have tried to develop theories about the nature of reality from what we know about the necessary conditions of all possible experience, or the content of actual experience, either have committed simple logical fallacies or have ended up with contradictory conclusions. The arguments employed by philosophers to establish the nature of mental substance turn out to contain logical errors. When philosophers have attempted to establish some truths about the nature of things-in-themselves, they have, instead, produced only antinomies—conclusions which can be both proved and disproved. The arguments offered to show that the world is finite, and that it has had a beginning in time, can be countered by equally good arguments to prove the opposite. In view of the limitations on our knowledge, we have no way of ascertaining which of two contradictory metaphysical propositions is true, or even more probable than the other. The arguments offered by metaphysicians, Kant maintained, to show that there must be some Being, God, whose nature explains the way the universe is, turn out to be, when carefully examined, inconclusive arguments, proving nothing. Hence when the metaphysician attempts to reason beyond all possible experience, and beyond our mental schema for judging possible experience, he finds that he can be certain of nothing, and can only flounder in bad or inconclusive or contradictory arguments.

The traditional metaphysical quest, then, according to Kant, cannot succeed. The most that we are capable of discovering are those conditions that regulate what we can know about the world of experience. These regulative principles cannot be used as a means of discovering the constituents of the real world, since, as far as we can ever tell, they are valid only for the phenomenal world. Whenever we try to transcend the world of all possible experience, we are stopped by the limitations of our own rational equipment, as revealed by the fallacies, antinomies, and illusions of traditional metaphysics. The metaphysician who tries to use the forms of intuition and the conditions of pure reason to discuss the Self, the thing-in-itself, and God, is courting intellectual disaster. He can only wander in a maze of errors, contradictions, and inconclusive results. If he restricts himself to the realm where genuine, necessary, and universal knowledge is possible, he will, in effect, abandon the hopeless search of traditional metaphysics for knowledge about the nature of reality.

CONCLUSION

Metaphysicians from Thales down to the present day have tried to answer the question "What is reality?" The attempt to answer the question has revealed certain basic and perennial problems that metaphysicians have tried to resolve. Over the two and a half millennia of metaphysical inquiry, a great number of answers have been offered to the basic question of metaphysics, but no definitive conclusion seems to have been reached.

Because of the criticisms of the entire metaphysical enterprise raised by Hume and Kant in the eighteenth century, and by thinkers in the present century, many philosophers have concluded that metaphysical questions cannot be answered and that metaphysical systems are really meaningless conjectures. Many contemporary philosophers, especially those of a positivistic or analytic persuasion, contend that metaphysics is not dissimilar to an intellectual illness which deserves to be treated by therapeutic philosophical methods. Other twentieth-century movements have followed Kant's analysis of the subject, and have insisted that the traditional quest of the metaphysician ought to be abandoned, and should be replaced by the study of "categorial analysis," the examination of the necessary conditions involved in our knowledge.

Others, in spite of the criticisms of the Humeans and the Kantians, have insisted that metaphysical research is both a valid and a most important endeavor. They contend that human beings demand to know what *is* real, and why the world has the characteristics it does. The contemporary metaphysician finds that his classical predecessors have contributed important insights to discovering the nature of reality, but that in terms of what we now know, and now think about the world, new theories still remain to be developed, their implications explored. And when these theories are propounded, metaphysicians will probably continue to debate their age-old problems, while other philosophers try to convince them that the problems are either meaningless or unsolvable.

SOME MODERN
APPLICATIONS

Some of the recent developments in the scientific and political worlds suggest that new forms of old metaphysical problems are still with us, or that they are appearing in contexts quite different from the old ones. For example, having seen earlier in this chapter the ancient criticisms of atomism, we have also lived through a very rapid change in physical theories about the basic units of matter. Until the late 1930s the atom was the fundamental unit. Then the experiments of Lisa Meitner and the work on the atomic bomb showed that the modern chemical atom (not the Epicurean one) could be split. Under proper conditions one could divide it into its component parts, the neutron, the proton, and the electron. Further work with more and more elaborate research equipment uncovered other still more minute parts, such as the neutrino and the meson. After that, it was theorized by Professor Gell-Mann of Cal Tech that there must be a still more fundamental particle, the quark. By now (1977) there have been five kinds of quarks discovered and a sixth is predicted. We are told that these are the ultimate building blocks of matter. But then, what would happen if a quark were divided in half, or demolished into bits? What are the bits? Can there be ultimate units of nature? A consistent scientific theory would have to meet the age-old objections to atomism.

Another kind of "metaphysical" problem that has reared its head is that which is arising from the development of computers—namely, is it possible to create artificial intelligence? Is intelligence actually just a mechanical function in our brain that can be duplicated outside of the brain? Computers can perform far more complex mental tasks, like arithmetical computations, than almost any person can. Computers can play chess; they can scan whole books in a couple of minutes and pick out certain words.

With all of this ability, can we say that computers think, or does thinking require some sort of nonmechanical entity to initiate the thinking? Some of those who insist that there must be some nonmechanical force or substance behind thinking activity point to the need to have a human being to program the computer. Without the human input the computer would do nothing.

But those who believe mental events can be reduced to physical ones point out that the study of the brain, which has advanced greatly in the last twenty-five years, shows how the various so-called mental capacities of the brain can be reduced to electrical impulses and chemical reactions. Maybe the human mind is nothing but a physical organ in operation.

Recently, one of the leading brain physiologists, Sir John Eccles, and a leading contemporary philosopher, Sir Karl Popper, have combined forces to oppose the reduction of intelligence to mechanical processes. Eccles, who won the Nobel Prize for his work on brain physiology, and Popper argue that one cannot explain mental behavior by reducing it to physical actions. The physical events that are measurable do not contain the elements that constitute a perception or a thought—sound, color, or feeling. Where do these elements (which are the core of what we are aware of) come from, and what accounts for the changes in them? Eccles and Popper have gone back to a version of Descartes' mind–body interaction theory to give their explanation of what is going on. In fact, Eccles claims there is experimental evidence that mental events can influence physical ones.

Another old metaphysical argument which is recurring is the explanation of origin of life. Biological research has made enormous progress in finding out the character of the basic elements of living things. The critical biochemical unit, DNA, seems to determine what each organism

will be like. Does this indicate that living beings are really just very complex material ones, or does it indicate that there is a special element of
life, a vital something, that differentiates living beings from inert ones?
Professors Harold Urey and Stanley Miller of the University of California,
San Diego, have devised a theory, and have tried to show experimentally,
that a very large electric charge shot through inert chemicals can cause
some kind of organic reaction. Perhaps the first life arose this way with no
special vital force. If biologists manage to grow DNA in test tubes without
starting with any living elements, this should indicate that vitalism as a
theory is not necessary. The vitalist insists that there will always have to
be some life-force element to explain the biological world we live in.

A quite different sort of metaphysical problem arises from some
aspects of TV entertainment and from some modern political events that
deal with distinguishing illusion from reality. (For a review of these discussions, see pages 84 and 47—48.)   In case one does not believe that
the brain-washing techniques described by Orwell will work, one only has
to read the accounts in American newspapers for 1975–1977 of how the
CIA and other United States governmental agencies experimented in trying
to achieve behavior modification through the use of drugs, sensory dep-
rivation, and many other means. If one considers the facts that governments (including our own) have used such tactics, and that the techniques
used on the TV programs could only too easily be adapted by such powerful political groups to keep the citizenry in a world of illusion, one realizes
that the possibility of being unable to tell actuality from deception is a very
real one.

Hence, as we can see, the age-old metaphysical problem of determining
the distinction between appearance and reality remains a live issue. And it
may well be one of the most important issues that we have to face, since
there are forces that want to cast illusory views of the world upon us. The
Cartesian problem has changed from a speculative metaphysical one to a
pressing political one.

BIBLIOGRAPHY

Allen, Reginald E. *Greek Philosophy: Thales to Aristotle* (Free Press, New
    York, 1966). Selections of the major texts in Greek philosophy.
Aristotle. *Selections*, edited by P. Wheelwright (Odyssey Press, New York,
    1951).
Beardsley, Monroe C. *The European Philosophers from Descartes to Nietzsche*
    (Modern Library, New York, 1960). Selections from the major European
    philosophers of the seventeenth, eighteenth, and nineteenth centuries.
Bergson, Henri. *Creative Evolution* (Greenwood Press, Westport, Conn., 1975).

Berkeley, George. *Three Dialogues*, edited by C. Turbayne (Bobbs-Merrill, Indianapolis, 1965). Contains full text of the work, plus an excellent introduction.

Blanshard, Brand. *The Nature of Thought*, 2 vols. (Allen & Unwin, London, 1964). A modern presentation of idealism.

Burtt, Edwin A. *The English Philosophers from Bacon to Mill* (Modern Library, New York, 1939). Contains selections from Hobbes, Locke, Berkeley, and Hume.

———. *The Metaphysical Foundations of Modern Physical Science* (Routledge and Kegan Paul, London, 1959).

Descartes, René. *Philosophical Works*, edited by E. S. Haldane and G. R. Ross (Dover, New York, 1967).

Drake, Durant. *Invitation to Philosophy* (Greenwood Press, Westport, Conn., 1969). An elementary presentation of some of the major metaphysical theories.

Ewing, A. C. *A Short Commentary on Kant's Critique of Pure Reason* (University of Chicago Press, Chicago, 1967).

Gardiner, Patrick. *19th-Century Philosophy* (Free Press, New York, 1969). Selections from leading metaphysicians of the period.

Hume, David. *An Enquiry concerning Human Understanding* (Oxford, New York, 1951).

———. *A Treatise of Human Nature* (Oxford, New York, 1951).

Kant, Immanuel. *Prolegomena to Any Future Metaphysics* (Open Court, Chicago, 1949).

———. *Selections*, edited by T. M. Greene (Scribner's, New York, 1929).

Kemp Smith, Norman. *New Studies in the Philosophy of Descartes* (Russell & Russell, New York, 1963).

Kirk, G. S., and Raven, J. E. *The Pre-Socratic Philosophers* (Cambridge University Press, London, 1957).

Luce, Arthur A. *Berkeley's Immaterialism* (Russell & Russell, New York, 1968).

Malebranche, Nicolas. *Dialogues on Metaphysics*, edited by M. Ginsberg (Macmillan, New York, 1923).

Montague, William P. *The Ways of Things* (AMS, New York, 1976). A survey of many metaphysical problems and theories.

Plato. *Timaeus* (Bobbs-Merrill, Indianapolis, 1954).

Popkin, Richard H. *The Philosophy of the 16th and 17th Centuries* (Free Press, New York, 1966). Contains selections from the major thinkers of the period.

Rand, Benjamin. *Modern Classical Philosophers* (Houghton Mifflin, Boston, 1936). Contains selections from original writings of philosophers from the sixteenth century onward, including texts of the nineteenth-century German metaphysicians.

Ross, Sir W. D. *Aristotle* (Oxford, New York, 1942). A survey of Aristotle's philosophy.

Schopenhauer, Arthur. *The World as Will and Idea*, translated by R. B. Haldane and J. Kemp (AMS, New York, 1976).

Smith, T. V., and Grene, Marjorie. *From Descartes to Kant* (University of Chicago Press, Chicago, 1957). Contains selections plus illuminating introductions.

Strawson, P. A. *Individuals: An Essay in Descriptive Metaphysics* (Methuen, London, 1959). A contemporary presentation of metaphysical issues.

Taylor, A. E. *Plato: The Man and his Work* (Barnes & Noble, New York, 1961).

Whitehead, Alfred North. *Science and the Modern World* (Free Press, New York, 1967). A discussion of certain metaphysical themes and how they developed over the last few centuries, by one of the great twentieth-century metaphysicians.

chapter 3

Thomas Hobbes (1588–1679); birthplace—England (left)

Jean Jacques Rousseau (1712–1778); birthplace—Switzerland (French) (below)

Karl Popper (1902–   ); birthplace—Austria (British) (above)

Karl Marx (1818–1883); birthplace—G e r m a n y (above)

Title page of Marx's *Communist Manifesto* (1848) (right)

Herbert Marcuse (1898–   ); birthplace—Germany (American) (right)

POLITICAL PHILOSOPHY

WHAT IS POLITICAL PHILOSOPHY?

At some time or other, almost everyone who is reflective has been dissatisfied with some of the conditions of his life. His dissatisfaction may be concentrated upon a narrow range of conditions—upon the relations with the members of his family, for example. But it may have a wider focus as well. A person may come to feel that the present state of the world is not what it should be. He may be distressed by the growing incidence of crime in the streets and violence, by the increasing pressures toward political conformity, by the mounting tension between powerful nations. Perturbation about these things may lead him into deliberations which transcend his personal concerns and which are directed toward society at large. When this happens, he may be well on the way toward formulating a political philosophy.

Generally speaking, deliberations about society fall into one or the other of two distinct but closely related classes. Those comprising the first group are concerned with understanding why society is as it is: why, for instance, there is juvenile delinquency, violence, war, poverty, and so on. If pursued long enough and carefully enough, such reflections may result in the discovery of causal (scientific) laws explaining these matters. The other type of speculation is quite different. It does not seek to discover factual truths, although it may (or may not) make use of them. Instead, it is concerned with the goals at which society ought to aim and with the appraisal of those it already has.

These two types of inquiry are logically independent of each other; a person may engage in the former without engaging in the latter, or he may emphasize one at the expense of the other if he wishes to do both. Insofar as he tends to pursue inquiries of the first kind, his investigations will lead him toward, and eventually into, the domains of psychology, anthropology, political science, and economics. Insofar as he stresses the latter, he moves toward the area dominated by ethical theory.

Traditionally, what is called "political philosophy" encompasses both types of speculation. The typical political philosopher is concerned, on the one hand, with finding out why society presents the kind of picture it does, and, on the other hand (if the picture does not please him), with suggesting recommendations that will improve it. The former sort of inquiry may involve him in theories about human nature, the effects of institutions upon human conduct, and the origin of specific social practices. The latter sort of inquiry may lead to proposals that are highly ideal and drastically removed from the conditions under which we now live, or even might live; at other times, they may require only a slight modification in society.

Because political philosophy has such intimate connections with the social sciences and with ethics, it is difficult to draw the line that separates it from these other disciplines. Yet that it is a unique discipline, dealing in its own way with problems not treated in these other branches of intellectual endeavor, seems beyond dispute. Such queries as "Who should rule society?" "Is there a special kind of obligation called 'political obligation' and if so, what is its source, and how can its existence be justified?" "Is there a defensible distinction between freedom of opinion and freedom of action?" "Is freedom compatible with organization?" "What ought to be the function of the state in a properly run community?" and so forth, doubtless in part involve an appeal to the findings of the social sciences and to those of ethics, but they unquestionably pose difficulties of their own as well, which traditionally have been the special concern of the political philosopher.

Perhaps the most effective way of illustrating the nature of the discipline is to show, with reference to an actual example, how certain of its characteristic questions arise and how a typical political theorist deals with them. For this purpose, we shall select some of the views expressed in the early writings of Jean Jacques Rousseau (1712–1778), touching on them lightly here. Later in the chapter, we shall deal in more detail with his celebrated mature work, the *Social Contract* of 1762.

It was customary for philosophers of the seventeenth century to make a distinction between the presocial life of man and his life in civil society. Since no hard anthropological data were in fact available about presocial man—or man "in the state of nature," as these writers termed it—the distinction they made was based upon a hypothetical historical account of what life in such conditions must have been like. The point of the distinction was to get at "natural man"—as man must have been before being subject to social constraints, conventions and laws. Writing a century later, Rousseau picked up this distinction from such thinkers as Hobbes, Spinoza and Locke. In his *Discourse on the Origins of Inequality* (1755), he produces such an historical account, which is probably not intended to be taken literally. Nonetheless, his language suggests that he is describing some primitive period in human history and speaking about the conditions of life which prevailed at that time. The result is a picture of natural man. As Rousseau depicts him, natural man is free from external restraints and pressures, and is thus able to act in accordance with his natural impulses and inclinations. Leading an isolated existence in the wilderness, but able to satisfy his basic desires for food, shelter, and sex without difficulty, man is seen by Rousseau as benevolent, conciliatory and as not disposed to inflict suffering upon his fellow creatures. The instinct for self-preservation which every member of the animal kingdom possesses is tempered in man by compassion, and does not in general lead to aggressive and egoistic behavior, but to cooperation; presocial life is thus seen as peaceful in the main.

The disposition for cooperation gradually leads to the development of rudimentary or primitive communities, based mainly on family ties. This historical period thus lies halfway between presocial and fully civil social life, and Rousseau thinks of it as a golden age where human happiness flourishes. In such conditions, man's basic nature is thus fulfilled. But primitive social life brings with it technological advance, and the development of agriculture and metallurgy. With them emerges the distinction between what is "mine" and what is "thine." From such advances and social distinctions, the notion of property develops. But with the establishment of property, primitive society disappears and is replaced by a more complex social order. And in this new order, class divisions arise between rich and poor, between the powerful and the weak. Primitive society, with its absence of constraint and domination of one individual over another, thus gives way to complex, modern society with institutionalized class divisions. Through such institutions as the church, law courts, banks, and government itself, the inequality of the system deriving from property rights is made permanent.

For Rousseau, this represents the ultimate in irony. Such institutions are originally developed to make human life more pleasant and presumably freer. But, according to Rousseau, they turn out to have the opposite effect. Civil society becomes more and more dominated by them, and as it does, it produces inconveniences in living that far exceed anything man could have experienced in the state of nature or in primitive communal life. Through the establishment of private property, for example, the master-slave relation arises and with it such vices as servility, envy, cruelty and hatred. In the end, then, civil society fails to fulfill its proper function of improving the quality of human life, and instead only serves to increase human misery. In a stirring remark, Rousseau summarizes the existing state of affairs when he writes: "Man is naturally good and only by institutions is he made bad."

What, then, can be done to alter this situation? Rousseau demands a radical reform of most existing societies, with the aim of making them more simple and hence less liable to block the efforts of human beings to express their fundamental natures. His proposed model of an ideal social organization is based upon the Swiss city-states of the eighteenth century which, like their ancient Greek counterparts, permitted every male citizen to participate directly in government. Such participation allowed citizens to develop their capacities and to function as equals sharing responsibility within the social milieu. All this, for Rousseau, is in sharp contrast to the (then) existing commercial societies which, he felt, served mainly to pervert man's natural goodness rather than to preserve or improve it.

From this brief summary, it can be seen that Rousseau's outlook involves psychological and biological elements in its account of human nature, ethical elements in holding that a free, simple, and natural life for man is a good one, a sociological theory about the repressive function of institutions in modern society, and perhaps a historical or an anthropological account of presocial living conditions. These ingredients provided a base for his proposals that society be made more elemental and less artificial, in the belief that if this were done, the evils of modern society would be eliminated or at least minimized. These proposals for a new society form the core of his political doctrine. It is this core which succeeds in tying these diverse elements into a *philosophy*—a unified view about the nature and purpose of society. Traditional political philosophies represent complex views of this sort.

Like ethics and epistemology, political philosophy has been influenced by recent developments within philosophy itself. Because of this influence, contemporary treatises on political theory often differ so radically in their subject matter from such traditional works as Plato's *Republic* or Mill's *On Liberty* that it may be fruitful in further illuminating the nature of political philosophy to subdivide it into *meta-political* and *hortatory political* theories. Hortatory political theories may be defined as those which are mainly concerned with recommending the adoption of certain ideal or improved societies, whereas meta-political theories are those mainly devoted to analyzing the key terms which may appear in such recommendations. Meta-political theory is thus a branch of contemporary philosophical analysis and what we have said about this discipline elsewhere (see page 260) will apply to it, with the additional proviso, of course, that the notions being analyzed are those belonging to the domain of hortatory political theory. These include such concepts as "rights," "sovereignty," "the state," and "law." In the remainder of this chapter, it should be added, our attention will be focused entirely upon hortatory political theories.

These introductory remarks do not pretend, of course, to give the reader a full and accurate description of the nature of political theory. But in order to provide a more complete account, we shall have to adopt some other mode of procedure. And in this situation, no better scheme can be devised than to expound the views of some of the major political thinkers in detail. Let us turn to this task now.

PLATO'S POLITICAL DOCTRINES

As we have indicated, political philosophy can be distinguished from the other areas of philosophy by the kind of problems it grapples with. Almost all of these problems, in one way or another, are concerned with attempts to outline a better world. Perhaps the most remarkable of all such efforts is to be found in Plato's *Republic*, which brings to this task a veritable treasure house of economic, psychological, epistemological, metaphysical, and even esthetic insights. If we examine the structure of *The Republic* carefully we can see that it is built around three major questions: (1) What characteristics should an ideal society have? (2) Is such a society desirable? (3) Is it possible to bring such a society into existence? It is clear from information we have about Plato's life that these questions were not merely the results of idle speculation but were posed from a sense of urgency.

Plato lived in a country which was made up of small, autonomous city-states. These city-states not only frequently engaged in warfare with one another, as in the bloody twenty-seven-year-long conflict between Athens and Sparta, but they also fought against such major powers as Persia. And even within the city-states themselves, especially within Plato's native city of Athens, civil strife was not uncommon. When, under Pericles, the democrats ruled Athens, they initiated harsh measures against their opponents, most of whom, like Plato, came from the aristocracy. When the democrats were toppled from their positions of authority, their aristocratic enemies exacted retribution from them in savage reprisals. Plato's teacher and friend, Socrates, was put to death by the democrats while they were in power, an event which Plato never forgot and which he immortalized in such dialogues as *The Apology* and *The Phaedo*. To Plato life must have indeed seemed precarious and uncertain.

It was more than clear that society must be remade. But how? To begin with, what characteristics should an ideal society have?

Mainly, he argued, it should minimize class conflict. From his own experience, Plato saw that the greatest barrier to human happiness lay in the constant struggles between rival factions within the corpus of society. No one could feel at ease or be content within a community which might explode at any moment. Domestic instability put pressures on the individual which were even more severe than those applied by external foes, and they had to be relieved if men were to achieve equanimity. But how could such harmonious relations be developed? His answer to this question is complex; like Rousseau's philosophy, it involves a psychological theory.

Plato assumed that society resembles an individual human being. Of course, it is larger, more complex, and more intricate; but at the same time, like a human being, it grows and decays, flourishes and falls ill; it sometimes operates rationally and sometimes not. This doctrine has been called the *biological analogy,* and in the subsequent history of political thought it has had immense influence. For Plato, in effect, society is nothing but "the individual writ large," as he put it in a memorable phrase. The implication of this doctrine is that through the study of the smaller entity, the individual human being, rules can be discovered which can be applied to the larger thing, society, and which, if applied, will assuage its troubles. It seemed natural to Plato, then, to begin his investigation of society by investigating the nature of the individual.

The psychology of the time analyzed every human being into two different, but basic, ingredients—a physical body and a "soul." The soul, it was held, is not a simple, indivisible entity but is composed of three parts—a rational part, which deliberates, thinks, remembers, or believes; a spirited part, which makes a man courageous, cowardly, or rash; and finally a part containing the passions or the appetites, such as the desires for sexual satisfaction, food, and drink. Each of these elements has a particular role to play in a normal human being. If the rational element were lacking, for example, a person would be mentally defective; if he had no desires, he would be a thing without emotions and feelings.

Moreover, if any element dominates the others, the person in question will not be psychologically healthy; if he is controlled by his passions, for instance, he will be neurotic and anxious. It is only when these elements function in mutual concord that man can be described as being psychologically perfect. In such a case, each element will play its proper role and none will dominate the others. To a remarkable extent this theory is in accord with contemporary psychological opinion, which holds that a man is psychologically fit when he is well adjusted, when he is not unbalanced, frustrated, and given to extremes of behavior.

Plato felt that this same analysis can be applied to the state. Like the individual soul, the ideal state would require a hierarchical class structure. It must have (1) leadership, (2) soldiers to defend it, and (3) workers to provide the necessities of life. Each of these needs can be met by developing a class of individuals to perform the corresponding functions. So Plato's ideal society has a tripartite class structure; the ruling class, which is analogous to the rational element in the soul; the soldiers who resemble the spirited element, and the workers who correspond to the appetitive element. For Plato, then, an ideal society would be one in which each class performs its duties without attempting to invade the areas dominated by the others. Such a society would provide the stability requisite to domestic tranquillity.

In order to guarantee that each class would stay within its legitimate bounds, Plato provided a number of safeguards designed to achieve this purpose. The first of these consisted of tests to select individuals who would fit most naturally into each group. These tests were intellectual, moral, and physical. Up to the age of twenty, all children were to be raised in common; at the end of that time, those who passed the intellectual, moral, and physical tests were to form the class of prospective rulers; those who failed were to become workers. The class of rulers later was to be divided into those who were to become warriors and those who were to enact future legislation for the society, that is, the rulers proper. Behind this system of tests lies another psychological assumption of Plato's—that by nature some men are more fitted for certain kinds of jobs than others. The function of the tests was to discover who was best equipped for which job. Plato felt that a society in which people did that for which they were best fitted would be less likely to be disturbed by intramural hostilities than one which distributed human talent arbitrarily, as did the existing societies of his day.

Second, Plato advocated a system of censorship to be applied to the youth of his ideal community. Plato defended the necessity of censorship, mainly on moral grounds but also by an appeal to certain psychological facts. He pointed out that children learn through imitation; if they are exposed to a wide variety of influences indiscriminately, they will imitate what is bad as well as what is good. By restricting their range of experiences, especially in the areas of literature, music, and poetry, it would be possible to inculcate only virtuous habits in them; and in this way, potential sources of delinquency, neurosis, and crime (all of which tend to unsettle society) could either be eliminated or at least reduced.

Third, the warrior class was to be used not only to combat external aggression but also to act as a police force for the purpose of maintaining order within the society. As a final precaution, Plato also insisted that the ruling class not be allowed to own property or even to have families. They

196 Introduction to Philosophy

were required to live in communal dwellings, with their necessities supplied by the state. Their children were to be taken away at birth and raised
in special nurseries with other children. Plato realized that the struggle to
acquire property and the love of one's family are among the most powerful of human motivations. Even the most dedicated men when faced with
the choice of placing their family interests above the interests of the state
might be swayed to do the former. It was thus necessary to eliminate such
possibilities.

Plato's answer to his initial question—"What characteristics should
an ideal society have?"—may be summarized, then, as follows: (1) It
should have a tripartite class structure; (2) the classes should be chosen
according to the capacity of their members to perform various types of
duties (this, for Plato, suggested the equality of women, by the way); (3)
censorship should be instituted in order to develop virtuous habits in the
young; (4) the warriors should function as a police force to quell potential class strife; (5) the rulers should not be allowed to own private
property or have private families.

Plato's answer to his second question—"Is such a society desirable?"
—has for him an obviously affirmative answer. He thinks it unmistakably
better to have a society which operates harmoniously than to have one
riddled by unrest and dissension. Like individuals, societies may be neurotic, frustrated, and unhappy. From a psychological point of view, then,
the choice for Plato between a harmonious and a disharmonious social
order is reducible to the choice between health and disease. But if this is
the situation, the alternative to be preferred is clear.

Nevertheless, even assuming that this is so, Plato must still overcome
one further obstacle before his theory can be regarded as complete;
namely, can such a society be brought into existence? Is such a plan
merely philosophical conjecture, or is it a practical possibility? His answer to this question is cautiously affirmative. Roughly, it consists in
arguing that his ideal commonwealth will be feasible if two conditions can
be met: (1) It must be ruled by people who have knowledge and (2) it
must be ruled by people who have absolute authority. As Plato points out,
this is a paradoxical suggestion, one which runs counter to prevailing
opinion. For in existing corporate bodies, those who are given power are
not wise and those who are wise are not given power. Before a perfect
society could be put into operation, these conditions would have to be
reversed. And is this possible? Again, Plato's answer is in the affirmative.
It consists in outlining a procedure which, if followed, would lead to a
confluence of power and knowledge in the ruling class. This procedure has
been explained in more detail in Chapter 1, pages 36–39.

In effect, Plato's plan amounts to a state-supported program for
training the most intelligent members of society to become rulers. Those

who complete the program will automatically assume power and, because of the nature of their training, will have acquired the requisite information for proper leadership. The program is an extension of Plato's earlier suggestion that all children be raised in common from birth until the age of twenty or so. Those who pass tests given at this time will be separated from those who fail and then provided with further training. This more advanced program has various stages, at any one of which some candidates may be dropped.

The main emphasis in it is upon the study of subjects (such as mathematics, psychology, economics, and philosophy) that will provide the ruler with the kind of knowledge directly relevant to the problems of leadership. But besides this, the need for practical experience in administration is recognized, and the candidates are to be given opportunities to govern in minor administrative posts. The entire program would last for thirty years; those who complete it would become full-fledged rulers of the state. In this way, the blend of authority and knowledge would be achieved, and accordingly the ideal society would pass from the blueprint stage into fact.

It is important to point out that no one from the warrior or artisan classes is to be allowed to participate in the administration of the government. This is what Plato means by saying that his rulers are to have absolute authority. For him, ruling, like medicine, is a skill. In order to rule one must have an innate talent for it (discovered by testing methods) to begin with and then be given intensive training to develop the original capacities. To allow an uninstructed and by nature ill-equipped person to make political decisions seemed to Plato as ridiculous as permitting the man on the street to direct the conduct of a surgical operation. The untrained man would inevitably blunder and the result would be the kind of social distress which Plato's system was devised to counter.

Put into practice, this conception would lead to an antidemocratic, authoritarian society. It would be one which operated *for* the people, but it would not be operated *by* them, since they are not capable, either by heredity or by training, to decide what laws and policies will be in the best interests of all.

If we look at this summary of Plato's political views, it can be seen that the question which Plato finds of crucial importance is "Who should rule society?" His efforts to reconstruct existing society and to eliminate its evils depend upon his solution to this difficulty. But the difficulty is not peculiar to Plato; it occurs again and again in the history of political thought, and almost all the major thinkers have struggled with it. The basic issue between democratic and antidemocratic political philosophies centers about it. In general, democratic thinkers, like Locke and Mill, have responded that the people should rule; while nondemocratic expo-

nents, like Plato, Machiavelli, Hobbes, and Hegel, have rejected this answer either in favor of single individuals or in favor of small groups. What
makes Plato's *Republic* so valuable today as an object of study is that we
find in it one of the clearest and most powerful arguments against democratic government, an argument which must be countered if democratic
societies are to be given a theoretical justification.

Let us make the steps in this argument explicit, showing how each is
supported by evidence and why, taken in conjunction, they seem to entail
a nondemocratic conclusion. Later we shall see if the argument can be
met from a democratic point of view. It runs as follows:

1. Ruling is a kind of skill, or science.
2. Men vary inherently in their abilities to acquire any skill and hence
   vary in their natural capacities for ruling.
3. Those who naturally have the greatest capacity for ruling should be
   trained in this skill in order to develop their innate powers.
4. On the assumption that we want the best possible laws for society,
   they ought to be made rulers of it.

Therefore, In order to guarantee that their edicts will be put into effect,
they must be given absolute authority to implement them.

What evidence supports the steps in this argument? The evidence for
the truth of the first premise (that ruling is a science) is based on the
common knowledge that rulers sometimes make mistakes. But to say that
one is, or can be, mistaken seems to imply that ruling involves the mastery
of a body of information and is thus a science just as mathematics or
physics or gardening is a science. Plato sees little difference between the
inept ruler and the inept gardener; both make mistakes that stem from
lack of knowledge. Secondly, it is a factual truth that men differ from each
other innately; and hence it is plausible to believe that just as some men
by nature can run faster than others, so some men are naturally more
gifted to be rulers than others. If these two premises are admitted to be
true, they make the inference to the third attractive indeed; for who would
want to deny that those who have the greatest capacity for ruling should
be trained to do so? Moreover, since all but the eccentric will grant that
the purpose of ruling is to provide the best laws for society, then it is
similarly plausible to argue that those who are most fitted should be made
rulers of it. From these premises, it is difficult to resist drawing Plato's
conclusion—namely, that the rulers should be given 'absolute power. For
if they are not given unlimited authority, is this not tantamount to saying
that someone other than those best fitted to do so should make the final
decisions? Surely this is unacceptable to a rational mind.

The power of this argument seems irresistible, especially when summarized in the form of a dilemma. Either the trained must rule, in which

case one will have authoritarian government, or the untrained must rule, in which case one will have improper government. To Plato, the choice between these options seemed simple; he accepted the former in order to avoid the latter. But for one who favors democracy, this cannot be his choice. Is there, then, any escape for him from these undesirable alternatives?

Criticism of Plato

There are a number of ways, from a democratic standpoint, of countering Plato's argument. The first is to deny that ruling is a science, even a practical science like medicine. Scientific activity has two different aspects, a theoretical one and a practical one. The theoretical aspect is primarily concerned with the discovery and accurate statement of a body of principles termed "laws." Such laws give us very general information about the world, such as the information that all freely falling bodies fall at a specified rate of speed. A good scientist is one who is familiar with this body of information and who can utilize it to discover further information of a similar kind. A second aspect of science is concerned with the use of such information in order to alter or change the world. This aspect is called "applied science." Engineering may be labeled an applied science which uses, to a great extent, the body of laws developed in theoretical science.

It is clear that Plato thinks of his ideal rulers as being both theoretical and applied scientists. They are to be trained with the aim of discovering a body of principles for ruling which they will then apply in order to change society for the better. But democratic theorists point out that this analogy is misleading. There may be practical maxims which a ruler can follow on occasion, although even here he must exercise caution in their application. But so far as anyone knows, there is no body of principles for ruling, at least in the sense in which there are laws of physics which an engineer can apply when faced with a practical problem. But if not, then ruling is not analogous to physics—or indeed to any other science; and by a parity of reasoning, rulers are not applied scientists. Instead, ruling seems more like an art which some people have a talent for and which some do not. There is no particular reason to believe that this talent can be learned or that the most intelligent members of society will possess it to the highest degree. It thus appears that Plato's program for training future leaders rests upon an untenable assumption.

But second, even if ruling were a science, it can be maintained that Plato has drawn the wrong conclusion from this fact. The conclusion which Plato draws is that the ruler must be given absolute authority in order to enact legislation that is designed to further the real (as distinct from the apparent) interests of the people. He is to do this for their own good, even if in some cases this means *forcing* them to act in ways which they do not like or approve of.

But in giving the ruler such powers, Plato distorts the analogy between the ruler and the scientist. For the scientist is not concerned with values or with what ought to be the case, but only with facts (with what is or will be the case). For instance, it falls within the purview of science to predict the physical effects that will attend the explosion of a nuclear weapon. But if a scientist who has this information also insists that such a weapon be employed against an enemy nation, he goes beyond his functions as a pure scientist and engages in moral and political activity. Plato's mistake, in effect, consists in arguing both that the ruler is a kind of scientist, and also that because this is so, he ought to be empowered to make value decisions for the people.

A third and even more devastating criticism can be directed at Plato's scheme from the standpoint of ethics. As we shall point out in greater detail when we come to discuss his moral theory (pp. 263 ff.), he assumes that those who possess knowledge will always act virtuously or, what is equivalent, that immoral behavior stems from ignorance. This is why he wishes to form the ruling class out of the most intelligent members of society. Since they have the best chance of acquiring knowledge, they will also—in his opinion—have the best chance of acting virtuously or justly.

But many democratic theorists reject the assumption that "knowledge is virtue" as Plato puts it. They point out that, on the contrary, our everyday experience runs counter to this point of view. Intelligent men are often moral lepers; they may be cruel, untrustworthy, disloyal, or dishonest. When put into positions of public trust, they may work for their own interests rather than for the public good. In the face of this sort of evidence, these theorists insist that there is no reason to believe that Plato's plan would furnish society with just leaders, dedicated to working in the public interest.

Finally, in rejecting the Platonic view that the ruler ought to have absolute authority to enforce his decisions, democratic theorists point to the woeful experiences which people have suffered at the hands of rulers when they have granted absolute power to them. As Lord Acton once remarked, "Power corrupts, but absolute power corrupts absolutely." It is true that the ruler must have some authority to make decisions, especially when he must mediate between conflicts of interests among the citizenry. But such authority does not have to be absolute. In the end, the rulers must be responsible to the people. If rulers abuse their power and work for their own ends, as too many have done, it is imperative that they be replaced. By granting them absolute power, we have no assurance that they will not strive to achieve their own ends. In spite of the many controls which Plato suggests upon the use of power, a clever ruler can always find ways of turning authority to his own advantage. For this reason, it has always seemed to democratic theorists that the only safe way of making sure that power is not abused is to give those who exercise authority as little of it as possible.

Apart from the four objections we have just considered, some democratic theorists reject Platonism for another, and perhaps even deeper, reason. As they see it, Plato considers the relation between the ruler and the citizen to be a dependency relation, like that between a parent and his child. The ruler who makes important decisions for the citizens is like a solicitous parent acting in the interest of his offspring. But there are grave dangers for the child in such a relation. If his decisions are always made for him by someone else, then he will always remain an adolescent. And so it is with the citizen, too. If he is never given the opportunity to act upon his own initiative, he will never become mature. He must be allowed to make his own decisions, even if these should sometimes be misguided; for in so doing, he will begin to assume responsibility for his actions and will in the process begin to realize his fundamental capacities for living. In brief, this objection contends that self-government is essential to the development of an independent, mature, and self-reliant citizenry and that any social plan which takes away this right will in the end be stultifying.

THE POLITICAL PHILOSOPHY
OF THOMAS HOBBES

There are striking similarities not only between the political views but also between the lives of Plato and Thomas Hobbes (1588–1679). Both men lived in periods of great social unrest and suffered personal misfortunes as a result. Both utilized the knowledge derived from their experiences as a springboard for the theoretical reconstruction of existing societies. In the process, both were led to a defense of absolute authority. Like Plato's *Republic*, Hobbes' *Leviathan* is more than a political treatise, although this is its main theme. It is also a compendium of epistemological, ethical, metaphysical, and psychological doctrines, all of which are brought to bear with great power and subtlety upon the problems of society. The result is a philosophical masterpiece, whose main teachings are still of immediate relevance to any consideration of the political issues which face the contemporary world.

Born in 1588 (supposedly prematurely when his mother was frightened by a report of the Spanish Armada), Hobbes lived through some of the most unsettled years in English history. Today we think of England as enjoying one of the most stable governments in the world; but in the seventeenth century, the opposite was the case. During this century, England was in turmoil. One monarch was decapitated, and internal and external wars were fought. Hobbes was caught up in those vicissitudes and buffeted about by them. Even though he switched allegiance from one party to another, he always managed to do so inopportunely. The result was that when Charles I was beheaded, Hobbes, who supported the royalist cause, was forced to flee for safety to France, where he lived in exile for eleven years, until 1651. When the people's champion, Oliver Cromwell, assumed power, Hobbes made successful overtures to him, acts which nearly cost him his life. Assassins in the pay of royalists tried to kill him, but Hobbes evaded them and made his way back to England. When Charles II regained the throne, Hobbes' life again hung in the balance. He was able to save it only at the cost of agreeing, in 1662, to publish no more on political matters. From these events, he quickly learned two lessons which he constantly stresses in his political writings: (1) Where there is no government, chaos will prevail in the relations of men with each other and (2) such chaos can only be prevented if the government possesses enough strength to quell any dispute between its citizens. Taken in conjunction, these points lead him to the conclusion that the sovereign must be given absolute authority, and that this is the only alternative to life in a state of social upheaval.

These observations were based upon a theory about human nature which is fundamental to his political doctrines. It is this theory which explains why society, without a governing authority, will necessarily be chaotic. According to Hobbes, man is by nature a selfish and egoistic creature. He is motivated by internal and private desires which require satisfaction if he is to be happy. His conduct is explainable, in the final analysis, by uncovering his motives, and these in turn are always found to be directed toward the satisfaction of private wants, such as the desire for food, sex, fame, money, and power.

In order to focus attention on this point, Hobbes begins *Leviathan* by describing what life must have been like before societies came into existence. His portrait reveals a host of asocial, savage, aggressive, and competing individuals, each attempting to gratify his basic desires. This state of affairs gradually becomes more and more intolerable; for in the effort to satisfy their desires, men begin to injure each other; squabbles over desirable objects arise and some individuals are harmed in attempting to acquire them. The result is that life becomes a veritable "war of each against all," as Hobbes puts it, in which no man, not even the strongest, is really safe. In a penetrating phrase, Hobbes characterizes life in what he calls "the state of nature," as being "solitary, poor, nasty, brutish, and short."

Obviously, this state of affairs cannot continue if men are to survive. Recognizing this, they agree among themselves to erect and abide by a set of rules which serve to govern their conduct. In effect, they agree to abandon the attempt to satisfy their desires *ad libitum* in order to avoid the harmful consequences of attempting to do so. This agreement, or "covenant" as Hobbes terms it, explains the origin of society. Society thus develops from the recognized need for peace. But, at the same time, this covenant creates government, for men cannot be trusted to abide by the rules they have created. If they suspect they can violate them with impunity in order to gratify their desires, they will do so. The only way, therefore, to secure domestic tranquillity is to ensure that the rules will always be capable of enforcement. This implies that the power of enforcement be vested in an agent, who is himself not part of the social fabric but outside it. Moreover, if he is to be effective in maintaining social order, his authority must be absolute; for if it were not, he could not settle all issues which might arise among the citizenry. Even if certain abuses were to arise from his possession of unrestricted power, the society he controls would nevertheless be a peaceful one. Given the choice, Hobbes prefers the evils of absolute power to the evils of life in a society which does not contain authority. For, at the very least, the existence of such authority will guarantee the survival of those obedient to it.

For Hobbes the question of whether dominance should be given to a single individual or to a group is not essential to his fundamental thesis. But he does regard it as important and gives what must be acknowledged as compelling reasons for holding that the sovereignty be invested in one person—a king. In this respect, he is a monarchist, a view he no doubt in part adopted in order to curry favor with King Charles I. But apart from his personal motives, the arguments he offers in favor of monarchy are strong. To begin with, he points out that the function of the sovereign is to preserve peace. If power were divided among a group, then peace would be endangered whenever disagreement developed within the group; and given his psychological theory, this possibility could not be discounted. In such a case, the power of enforcement would be weakened, resulting perhaps in civil war and the very kind of dissension civil society was developed to avoid.

Further, as every administrator knows, secrecy may be an important element in planning and implementing social policies. If the state wishes to build a superhighway, it is important that the location of the roadway be kept secret until the requisite land is purchased. But if the sovereign power is composed of a group, it is easier for important information to slip out; the greater the number of people involved, the greater the danger. Here the advantages of a monarchy are not to be underestimated.

Finally, a king's decisions are "subject to no other constancy than human nature, but in assemblies there ariseth an inconstancy from the number." What Hobbes means is that the absence or presence of a few men can alter the decision which a government will take in framing laws; in the case of a monarchy, these vicissitudes obviously will be reduced to a minimum.

In developing this authoritarian political doctrine, Hobbes did not try to gloss over its practical implications. He stresses that the contract which initiates society is entered into voluntarily by the citizenry. They are not forced or coerced into making such an agreement. But since the agreement involves their abandoning their rights to the sovereign, and hence of giving up their freedom of action, from then on they are bound by his dictates. For example, no subject can make a new covenant or give his allegiance to any other sovereign, provided that the monarch is capable of protecting him. Such an act would be equivalent to treason; and it should be noticed that the decision as to whether the monarch is capable of protecting the subject always rests with the monarch.

On the other hand, no breach of the contract is possible by the sovereign because he has not entered into any contract with the citizens. They have compacted among themselves to give up their autonomy to him. He is thus in no way obligated to them through any contractual arrangement. What follows from this is that the monarch is outside the law and cannot act either justly or unjustly toward anyone. "Justice" for Hobbes is defined as behavior in accordance with the laws laid down by the sovereign; it thus makes no sense even to say that the sovereign acts in accordance with the law or not in accordance with it; and thus his relations with the citizenry can never be illegal or unfair.

Moreover, any minority group which disagrees with the dictates of the monarch must eventually acquiesce or be suppressed by force. For if such disagreement were allowed to exist, it might lead to internal dissension, or rebellion. To allow opinions to prevail which run counter to his authority is to admit the existence of divided authority, and this is incompatible with the basic premise upon which civil society is constituted. Likewise, the monarch must always have the final say in adjudicating any disagreements among the citizenry. For only in this way can peace be maintained within the social structure.

Hobbes began *Leviathan* in England and completed it in exile in France. To some extent, the declining fortunes of the English royal family are reflected in the latter portions of the book, perhaps in ways that are inconsistent with the main doctrine. In seeking to ingratiate himself with democratic elements in power in England, Hobbes inserted sections into *Leviathan* which give the citizens certain liberties. He defines them as "those things the subject may justly refuse to do even though commanded by the sovereign." In justifying his granting the subject such liberties, Hobbes falls back upon a doctrine of natural rights. These are rights which all men possess in virtue of being human beings and which in some cases they cannot transfer by agreement, even if they want to. The most important of these is the right to self-preservation. For instance, the monarch's order to a subject to kill, wound, or maim himself or not to resist anyone who assaults him can rightly be disregarded by the subject. Further, he is not bound to testify against himself in a criminal action, since this is tantamount to forcing him to injure himself. A command for dangerous military duty may be refused if the intention of the sovereign in issuing it was not to preserve the peace but to wage an aggressive war (although no man can refuse to defend the nation when it is attacked). And finally, the obligation of subjects to the sovereign ceases when the sovereign is no longer able to protect them. As Hobbes puts it, "the end of obedience is protection," and should the monarch fail in providing such protection, obedience should cease. It was this provision, in particular, which angered Charles II, who felt that the ruler has a divine commission which cannot be revoked by his temporary fortunes in war. Today, this point seems mild enough, but to Hobbes' royalist contemporaries it appeared treasonable.

Criticism of Hobbes

Although one may quarrel with the details of the Hobbesian political *Weltanschauung*, there is no doubt that it fixes upon fundamental issues. If we grant that men are autonomous beings with rights of their own and moreover that they are fundamentally selfish, how can we achieve a stable political order without the imposition of absolute force? That this is no mere academic query is abundantly clear. Even in our time the urgency of Hobbes' question strikes us most forcibly, perhaps, in the present international situation. If nations are substituted for individuals, the Hobbesian account of life in the state of nature seems to fit them exactly. International relations appear little different from a war of each against all. Each nation strives in its relation with others to satisfy its own interests, and the result of this activity is only too frequently conflict between them. As Hobbes has lucidly seen, nations are caught in an impossible dilemma. Their efforts to maintain their autonomy are incompatible with their desires to have world peace. And his solution to this dilemma is one which is being urged today. Those who favor world government implicitly assume the diagnosis found in *Leviathan*: they merely extend the range of its application from individual persons to sovereign states. Their conclusion that force must be vested in an agency over and above individual nations if peace is to be guaranteed is, in effect, a rewording of Hobbes' main thesis.

Nonetheless, the account is not above criticism. As we have pointed out, it is a blend of a number of ingredients—a group of (presumably) historical statements about the origin of society, a psychological theory about human nature, and a set of political precepts about who should rule. As we shall see, not all of these elements have been found equally persuasive by philosophers.

David Hume (1711–1766), for example, pointed out in his famous essay, "Of the Original Contract," that there is little evidence in support of Hobbes' account if this is taken as depicting the historical genesis of society. For one thing, such events would have taken place before historical records were kept; what life was like before societies came into existence is a matter of conjecture. There is thus no particular reason to suppose that Hobbes' account is historically correct. Moreover, Hume argues, such a theory explains the *origin* of political obligation by appealing to the drawing up of a contract. But if so, it cannot be used to account for the obligation which men *now* feel toward the societies in which they live. Men today abide by social rules, but they do not contract to do so (where and when did you contract, for instance, and with whom?). Unquestionably political obligation exists, but it can hardly be explained by appealing to a contractual arrangement for the reasons mentioned; but if not, the version of the origin of society that depends upon such a social compact must be rejected.

This objection may be met in several ways. First, there is historical evidence that some *governments* have come into existence by the explicit framing of covenants (for example, the governments of the United States and of the First French Republic). Admittedly, Hobbes is speaking of *societies*, not governments, but the procedure adopted is in principle no different and it could have happened. But this is, in any case, not the main issue. Hobbes is not trying to give an exact anthropological or historical version of the creation of primitive society; instead he is trying to give a philosophical justification for the existence of the body of rules which regulate the conduct of men toward each other (thus whether we call the set of such rules "society" or "government" is immaterial). Whether men ever really gathered in groups and drew up such rules is irrelevant to his purpose. What he is stressing instead is that one's allegiance to society, or to government, is basically voluntary. The obligation to obey the dictates of society arises from the recognition that laws must be instituted and obeyed or chaos will develop. Such obligation cannot be imposed by force or developed by the inculcation of habits. If men were forced to be members of an organization, they would feel no sense of obligation to support it in times of distress; similarly, the appeal to habits may explain why men obey the laws of society but cannot explain why they feel obliged to do so. Obligation is the result of a conviction that obedience to the law is the only alternative to anarchy, and it is this point which Hobbes wishes to drive home.

A more penetrating attack on the theory can be directed against the psychological picture of human nature upon which it rests. This attack

I

has two prongs: the first denies that men are basically motivated by desire and asserts, in contrast, that they often have rational bases for their actions. The second claims that a distinction must be made between various kinds of desires which motivate men; some are selfish and some are not. Thus even if one agrees that men are motivated by desires, it does not follow that all such desires are necessarily egoistic, and that life without rules would accordingly be a war of each against all (this is the position of Hume, among others). Let us take up each of these points in turn.

The former of these positions holds that the wellsprings of human action may be traced to reason as well as to desire or to other nonrational factors. For instance, Hobbes himself seems to admit that men *recognize* or understand that obedience to the rules of society is necessary; and is not such recognition or understanding rational? To this, a Hobbesian will retort as follows: Men are always motivated by the last and strongest of their desires. Obligation is not founded in reason but in the desire to avoid the harmful consequences of the state of nature. This desire is stronger than the desire to satisfy other wants if these can be seen to lead to harmful consequences. Reason, to be sure, plays an important role here. It can show men what the consequences of implementing their desires are likely to be. If these consequences are such that men will not desire them, they will choose some other course of action; but desire or aversion (emotional factors) are the motivating causes in all such cases.

II

The second attack upon the psychological theory is much sharper. It agrees that men are always motivated by desires but points out that not all desires are "egoistic," if this term is taken to mean that each individual always puts his interests ahead of those of others. For instance, men may desire to contribute to the happiness of others, even at the expense of satisfying their own desires. Do we not sacrifice our interests, even our lives in some cases, for those of our family, wives, friends, and country? The point can be put clearly by describing some desires as "altruistic" rather than as "egoistic." Thus even if we grant that men naturally are motivated by desires, this view does not entail that their behavior is always selfish or that it is by nature antisocial.

This point, if accepted, undermines much of Hobbes' argument. For if men by nature are not always selfish, then it does not follow that only the creation of an absolute authority will guarantee their living peaceably with each other. Democratic theorists often subscribe to the thesis that men are motivated by nonrational factors but do not see in this fact the need for submission to an omnipotent sovereign. They point out that men's interests are highly diverse and cover a wide range of activities. A ruler who is given absolute power will generally not reflect this spectrum of interests but will instead constrain it in ways which seem fitting to him. But this is intolerable, since it may serve to block many of the desires which men feel are among the most important to satisfy. What seems to be required for satisfactory living in a society is not that there should be a total absence of conflict within it but only that the degree of conflict should not be so great as to endanger the implementation of the majority of wants which men wish to satisfy.

The real problem that society faces, say these theorists, is to give its executive enough authority to prevent most conflicts, and yet not enough to prevent the satisfaction of the wide range of interests which may occasionally lead to such conflicts. Proper government is to be located somewhere between these extremes, rather than at the authoritarian end of them. For Hobbes, the choices which seem open to a citizen are submission either to the evils of tyranny or to the evils of anarchy. But to democratic thinkers this has always seemed a false dichotomy. A third alternative is feasible. It is possible to have both law and order and the absence of tyranny, and in the writings of John Locke, greatest of all democratic theorists, we find the attempt to justify this position.

THE POLITICAL PHILOSOPHY
OF JOHN LOCKE

Like Hobbes, his older contemporary and fellow countryman, John Locke (1632–1704) lived through the period of unrest which attended the struggles of democratically minded Englishmen to abolish absolute monarchy. "From the time that I knew anything," Locke wrote a friend in 1660, "I found myself in a storm which has continued to this time." In 1675, Locke's patron, the Earl of Shaftesbury, fell from power and, in danger of arrest, sought political asylum in France. Locke accompanied him, returning to England in 1679 after Shaftesbury's position was restored.

But his stay was short. Further plots against Charles II were uncovered in 1681 and Shaftesbury was suspected of complicity in them. Once again in danger, he was forced to flee, this time to Holland. Because of his known liberal views and his close associations with Shaftesbury, Locke also came under surveillance. Fearful of imprisonment, he followed Shaftesbury to Amsterdam. When James II, successor to Charles, was deposed in the Glorious Revolution of 1688, Locke re-entered England. This revolution, it should be mentioned, was essentially a middle-class uprising, and although it culminated in the enthronement of another strong monarch, William of Orange, it also brought with it real concessions to democratic rule. A Bill of Rights was passed by Parliament, which gave that body such important powers as control over finances and the right to regular and frequent meetings.

Locke's *Two Treatises on Civil Government*, published in 1690, contains a justification of these advances. But it goes beyond this, too, in providing a general statement of the aims and purposes of government which has been a cornerstone of democratic theory since his time. The political writings of such men as Jefferson and Paine in America and Montesquieu and Rousseau in France bear witness to Locke's influence. The constitution adopted by the United States government in 1788 is almost point for point in accord with the main proposals for an ideal state suggested by Locke in the *Two Treatises*.

The *First Treatise on Civil Government* is now regarded as an anachronism. It contains an attack upon Sir Robert Filmer, who attempted to defend the doctrine of the divine right of kings. But the *Second Treatise* is still a living document. Almost all the important elements of democratic theory (with certain exceptions we shall mention later) are to be found in it. These are, first of all, the view that law, not force, is the basis of government; secondly, that men have rights derived from nature, which no government can legitimately infringe; thirdly, that government is the servant of the people and not its master, and finally, that the will of the people is to be determined by majority vote.

Locke supports these principles by a lengthy argument which begins in a manner reminiscent of that employed by Hobbes in *Leviathan* but soon diverges from it. Like Hobbes, he seemingly attempts to trace the origins of society to their source, which he also locates in a primordial "state of nature." But his description of the state of nature is a far cry from Hobbes' portrait of a war of each against all. He points out that a state of war involves the attempts by an individual or group to acquire complete dominance over others. In such a case, all rules are abrogated and humanity, in effect, retreats into the jungle to fight it out. Such a situation may arise even in civil society, with the breakdown of government. It is thus not a condition peculiar to the state of nature and should not be confused with it.

For Locke the state of nature is primarily distinguished from civil society by the absence of settled government. It is thus not generally the domain of aggressive and selfish acts. Instead, he believed that men live amicably with each other, although sometimes conflicts break out among them. On the whole, the overriding atmosphere is one of peaceful cooperation. The controversies which develop come about because men have personal possessions, such as land, livestock, and homes, which they have created through their own labor. Sometimes thefts occur or disputes arise over the boundaries of a parcel of land. Even though such problems may frequently be settled fairly, this is not always so. Those who are injured may, in anger, exact undue retribution from those who have transgressed against them; or what is equally bad, they may lack the strength to punish a stronger individual who has committed some offense. For such reasons as these, men come to realize that an explicit code of rules regulating human conduct must be established. In compacting to form such a set of regulations, they create government, and thus pass from the state of nature into civil society. Locke's appeal to an original compact is thus an endeavor to explain how government originates, and given its origin, what its ultimate justification must be. His analysis thus differs from Hobbes'. Unlike Hobbes, who traces both the origin of society and the origin of government to an original compact, Locke's genetic account reveals primitive man as already living in society—but without government.

Locke thus deals with the origin of government in order to point out that civil society is created for the purpose of making human life more convenient. Any government which arises from such a compact is thus under an immediate obligation to work for the general welfare of its citizens. In particular, such a government will have three main tasks: it must contain (1) a legislature to lay down consistent and uniform laws, (2) an executive who will enforce them, and (3) a judiciary which will settle disputes between the citizens impartially and fix the degree of punishment which is to be levied against those convicted of misbehavior.

These provisions serve the further purpose of preventing those who govern from seizing and abusing power. The emphasis upon law is basic in this regard, a point which is not always understood clearly, even by democratic proponents. Laws are often conceived as hindrances to action on the part of the citizenry and as constraints which should be removed, if possible. This was the view of the nineteenth-century anarchist Mikhail Bakunin, for example. But Locke saw that laws also play a positive role. They protect citizens from the unwarranted use of power and in this way provide them with security. They are thus necessary conditions for freedom from anxiety and fear.

What is characteristic of nondemocratic governments is that they employ their power arbitrarily and in a nonlawlike manner. Such governments will issue mandates whenever convenient to circumscribe the activities of individual citizens. What is permissible behavior today may be intolerable tomorrow. The effect of such practices is to keep a citizenry on tenterhooks. Not knowing what conduct is allowable, the people will live in dread of offending those in power. To this situation, government by law is the only alternative. And by "law" Locke had a very specific notion in mind. He meant those rules which are drawn up by freely elected representatives of the majority of the people and which are then openly published so that all men may become familiar with them. This creates the presumption that behavior is permissible which is not explicitly forbidden by codified regulations; and the effect of such a presumption is to give the members of society freedom from anxiety in pursuing their everyday activities.

The second important ingredient in Locke's doctrine is what is called the *theory of natural rights*. The reasons which led Locke to this view are somewhat complex. Primarily, they stem from his belief that God created all things, including men. Thus, in a significant sense, every human being is God's property. When anyone attempts to achieve complete authority over another, he is in effect seizing a possession of God. This is why any form of despotism is unjust. What follows from this theory is that men have certain rights which accrue to them merely because they are God's creatures. They have these rights in the state of nature, and they have them after civil society is formed. These rights include the right to life (hence no man can justly be destroyed by another), to freedom (hence no dictatorship is legitimate), and to property.

This doctrine was influential in the development of such important bulwarks of individual freedom as the American Bill of Rights. In effect, it states that certain domains of human activity are inviolable. No government can infringe upon them legitimately. Some theorists succeeded in extending the list of rights to include freedom of speech, the right to worship freely, the right of peaceful assemblage, and so forth. For Locke one of the most important rights is the right to own property. As he says,

> Though the earth and all inferior creatures be common to all men, yet every man has a property in his own person: this nobody has any right to but himself. The labor of his body and the work of his hands we may say are properly his. Whatsoever then he removes out of the state that nature has provided and left it in, he hath mixed his labor with, and joined to it something that is his own, and thereby makes it his property.[1]

Besides providing protection against tyranny, Locke's theory of natural rights has had two other important consequences in practice. It has led some theorists to identify democracy with capitalism—that is, with the right of individuals to own property. It has also suggested the doctrine of the fundamental equality of all men, a doctrine which implies that the law of a democratic society must never favor one class over another because of such factors as wealth or racial origin. This condition has been written into the American constitution, which grants every man a fair trial if he is indicted for a criminal offense.

The third ingredient of Locke's political philosophy is his attitude toward government. This attitude has had momentous practical implications. From Locke's time on, democratic theorists have stressed that government is an instrument of the people, working in the interests of the people and hence responsible to them. Civil society is created only in

---

[1] John Locke, "A Second Treatise Concerning Civil Government," reprinted in *The English Philosophers from Bacon to Mill*, ed. by E. A. Burtt (Modern Library, New York, 1939), p. 413.

order to overcome irregularities in the state of nature and accordingly to foster the public good. But the point which Locke stresses is that government, being a creation of the people, is a servant of the people. It is given power to do those things which the people find it inconvenient or impossible to do themselves, just as we hire a typist to handle our correspondence if we are busy. But if such a person misuses the power we have delegated to him, he should be dismissed. And this is true of government, too. It is important to see, Locke says, that power is *delegated* by the people, not *surrendered* by them as Hobbes had thought. If any government attempts to usurp such power it should be dismissed. If it refuses to step down, then rebellion against it is justified. The ultimate location of power is in the hands of the people. Government is merely an instrument for carrying out their will.

The fourth ingredient in his theoretical framework for democracy is the idea of majority rule. Locke states that civil society is formed by the consent of individuals making a compact in the state of nature. In creating such a society, they give the community power to act as one body. But this body should always act, as he says, "whither the greater force carries it, which is the consent of the majority." If this were not so, then minority groups would impose their will upon the vast body of the citizenry, and this would be a step toward tyranny. What follows from this is that minority groups must submit to the dictates of the majority wherever there is an issue among them. For otherwise, as Locke says, "this original compact, whereby he with others incorporate into one society, would signify nothing, and be no compact, if he be left free and under no ties than he was in before, in the state of nature."

These elements provide a theoretical outline for democratic government; but Locke spells them out in great detail as well. He envisages a state whose government is divided into three parts, each of which would constrain and supervise the others. Locke terms these the *legislative, executive*, and *federative* branches of government. The duties of the former pair are to initiate and enforce laws, respectively, while the role of the federative branch is to supervise the relations between the government and foreign nations. Locke also insisted that a judiciary be established to assess the guilt or innocence of anyone accused of infringing the law, but he did not explicitly mention it as a separate branch of government. This was suggested later by Montesquieu (1689–1755), writing under the influence of Locke, and then picked up from him by the founding fathers of the American republic.

The main burden of Locke's *Second Treatise* is to curtail the abuse of power by the executive. In every way feasible, he restricted the authority of the executive. To begin with, Locke stressed that the legislature, as the people's representative, is to be strongest in the state. Only it can make laws; the executive is given the reduced status of enforcing them. Moreover the power of punishment is taken away from the executive and placed in the hands of the judiciary. The executive, as in present-day England, is to be an elected representative of the people. He is appointed by the majority party from within its ranks, and his tenure thus depends upon his conformity to the will of the legislature. Should he act contrary to their wishes, he is to be removed immediately.

Because of these constraints, Locke felt that the executive could safely be given certain powers. Locke grants him the power to invoke and dismiss the legislature (although even here the maximum length of adjournment was to be fixed by law). Locke gives him this authority because he feels that it is necessary for the executive always to remain at his post. The law must always be enforced. On the other hand, the legislature should be allowed to adjourn, since the creation of new laws is not continuously required. The greatest power which the executive is given is that of "prerogative." This is the power to "act, according to the discretion of the executive, for the public good with the prescription of the law, and sometimes even against it." The executive requires such authority in the event that a national crisis, such as war, develops when parliament is not in session. This doctrine has also become part of democratic tradition. It was exercised in the United States in 1950 when President Harry Truman, unable to consult with Congress in time, sent troops to support South Korea which was being invaded from North Korea. But such powers are always understood to be merely temporary; if an executive attempts to perpetuate them, he is to be removed from office.

In these views, we find a powerful alternative to the position of Hobbes that men can live peacefully together only if they submit to an absolute monarch. Locke shows how order results from the rule of law, and yet how being based upon law, it does not involve despotic control. Nevertheless, plausible though this view is, it has been criticized in various respects.

Criticism of Locke

As might be expected, antidemocratic theorists have sharply rejected Locke's doctrines. Friedrich Nietzsche (1844–1900) raged against the view that political power be vested in the people on the ground that they are too stupid to use it wisely. Other critics have asserted that a few outstanding individuals are more important than the mediocre mass of humanity and that society should be directed toward satisfying their needs rather than those of the majority. But curiously enough, some of the most telling criticisms of Locke come from philosophers who, on the whole, are democratically minded. Because of space limitations, we shall confine ourselves to an examination of criticisms of this kind.

The first of these is to be found in the writings of some democratic socialists. They point out that Locke's theory contains a contradiction at its base. Locke, they argue, wishes to maintain both that political power ought to protect private property and also that it ought to work for the common good. (Locke defines political power as "a right of making laws . . . for the regulating and preserving of property, and of employing the force of the community in the execution of such laws; and all this only for the public good.")[2] But, these critics say, what about those cases where the possession of property is incompatible with the public good? They cite case after case where the economic well-being of the majority has been sacrificed to the well-being of a few, and then defended on the ground that the possession of property is a right. Looked at more generally, this kind of criticism stresses that Locke's conception of democracy is a narrow one. Locke thinks that the aim of democratic government is to achieve political security for its members against the inroads of an aggressive despot. Insofar as he considers economic security to be a problem at all, he believes that the right to possess property will solve it. Socialists feel that such an outlook is too narrow. They argue that economic security must be extended in a democratic community to all, including those who do not possess property. The achievement of this aim, they insist, must be one of the basic goals of any society designed to work for the public good.

There is little doubt that these remarks fix upon a fundamental weakness in Locke's account. It is clear that, unlike certain of his contemporaries, Locke did not foresee the possible jeopardy to domestic tranquillity which the right to private property entailed. But at the same time, it should be pointed out that he can hardly be blamed for this oversight. The dangers which he failed to anticipate were to become fully apparent only a century after his death, with the flowering of the industrial revolution. In his day, the fundamental threat to freedom came from rulers who were striving to impose their wills upon the people; that he was acutely aware of this peril is obvious from our previous discussion; and that he emphasizes it, at the expense of the need for economic security, is not surprising. Some exoneration from the weight of this objection must thus be allowed.

The most profound criticisms of Locke from a democratic standpoint, though, are to be found in the writings of John Stuart Mill (1806–1873), especially in his essays, *Utilitarianism* and *On Liberty*. Although in agreement with most of the elements in Locke's political doctrines, Mill could not accept, without some qualification, either the doctrine of natural rights or that of majority rule. Let us turn to his analysis of these conceptions now.

2 Locke, *op. cit.*, p. 404.

As we shall indicate in more detail in the chapter on "Ethics," Mill's writings contain one of the classical expositions of *utilitarianism*. The core of this doctrine is to be found in what Mill alternately called the principle of utility or the greatest happiness principle. This principle maintains (1) that the test of the rightness or wrongness of any action is to be found in its consequences, and (2) that if the consequences of an action provide a balance of pleasure over pain for the greatest number of people, the action is right; if not, it is wrong and should not have been done. As Mill saw, this doctrine is incompatible with Locke's theory of natural rights. Locke's view implies that certain types of actions ought to be absolutely immune from governmental interference. But as Mill indicates, sometimes actions which fall within such areas of immunity may be detrimental to the public welfare. For instance, if freedom of speech is regarded as a natural right which cannot justifiably be constrained by the use of governmental power, it follows that a man who incites people to riot, thereby causing injury to someone in the ensuing chaos, should escape punishment. For Mill, such a consequence is intolerable. If a man's actions, whether verbal or otherwise, lead to widespread social harm and little social benefit, they should be circumscribed by the use of public authority. For this reason, he rejects Locke's view.

The disagreement between Mill and Locke is not over whether freedom of speech, say, is a desirable social practice. On this point, they are in complete harmony. Both recognize certain freedoms as essential to any government which can be called "democratic." Rather, Mill's disagreement with Locke is over how the fundamental freedoms are to be justified. Mill does not think a justification in terms of a set of God-given rights is tenable. For him, the doctrine is as unsatisfactory when used to defend freedom of speech as it was for Locke himself when it was employed to justify the right of kings to rule. Mill's alternative proposal is that freedom must be defended by appealing to its utility as a social practice. He tries to show that the indiscriminate suppression of speech, for example, has effects which are more harmful to society than allowing its free exercise.

The main consequence which follows from his view is that none of the traditional freedoms can be regarded as an absolute right, to be exercised at any time or in any set of circumstances. All of them must be curtailed in those cases where they prove inimical to the happiness of the greatest number, since the achievement of this goal is the main aim to which society ought to be directed.

On the whole, democratic theorists have accepted Mill's re-evaluation of the status of rights. They have agreed that the welfare of society must in all cases be the overriding consideration in terms of which social behavior is judged. But nonetheless, they say, even if this be granted, Mill's position is still consistent with adherence to a modified form of the doctrine of "rights." On this interpretation, "rights" are defined as those domains of individual behavior which can justifiably be invaded by society only when it can be established that the public welfare is genuinely menaced. In practice, this means that the onus for interfering in the behavior of individuals is always on the state. It must prove its case by providing evidence in a court of law that the conduct of the individual has been harmful to the social fabric. This more moderate interpretation of "rights" represents a clear retreat from Locke's original doctrine and a corresponding concession to the power of Mill's criticism. But, nonetheless, it still provides considerable protection for the individual against tyrannical rule. It creates the presumption that the citizen is innocent until proven guilty, a presumption which, in practice, has been a formidable obstacle to governmental abuse of power.

Mill's most trenchant criticism of Locke, however, is directed against the concept of majority rule. Like Locke, he accepts majority rule as being essential to democracy but wishes to restrict its scope in certain respects. In particular, Mill thinks that a democratic government ought to be one which not only provides for majority rule but which also protects, wherever possible, minority interests. He points out that the majority itself can be tyrannical; that it can impose a despotism upon nonconforming individuals as fierce as that of an absolute monarch. His defense of the minority as in the issue involving so-called "natural rights" again rests on utilitarian grounds. In effect, he tries to prove that the suppression of minority interests, *in general*, is more injurious to a commonwealth than their toleration.

In taking this stand, Mill may be looked upon as adding a new dimension to democratic theory. It is a dimension which Locke had, for all practical purposes, overlooked. To be sure, in his *Letter of Toleration* Locke had argued that dissenting minorities should be permitted freedom of worship; but he had not generalized this principle. Indeed, he even refused to grant toleration to atheists on the grounds that "promises, covenants and oaths, which are the bonds of human society, can have no hold upon an atheist." It was Mill who first saw clearly that in a free society, nonconforming individuals of all stripes must be tolerated; otherwise, democracy will merely exchange one form of tyranny (that of the absolute ruler) for another (that of the majority). His argument in favor of this principle is a lengthy one. Let us turn now to his famous essay *On Liberty*, where it occurs, and follow his reasoning.

THE POLITICAL PHILOSOPHY
OF J. S. MILL

Mill begins the essay by tracing the historical developments which lead to modern democratic states. This development has had three main stages. In the first, the struggle for liberty emerges as a struggle to curtail the powers of absolute rulers. Those who engage in this struggle have an ambivalent attitude to the ruler: they consider him necessary to society but at the same time dangerous to it. He is regarded as the preserver of the commonwealth against its foreign and domestic enemies and yet as a person who contributes certain abuses of his own (which arise from the use of unrestricted power). The main goal of the early "libertarians," as Mill denotes them, was thus to circumscribe the powers of the ruler in order to minimize or prevent these abuses. This was done in two ways: (1) by invoking a doctrine of natural rights which rendered the citizen safe from the arbitrary use of power by the sovereign and (2) by developing a constitution which restricted the power of the ruler in such important matters as the raising of taxes.

Through the gradual extension of the scope of these devices, the power of absolute monarchs dwindled and finally was eliminated for all practical purposes. A second stage was thus reached in which the people came into control of society. They manifested their will through representative bodies, like the British parliament. In the light of this new situation, democratic theory was modified. Some French thinkers, for example, urged that all restrictions upon the ruling body be removed. In their view, to restrict the power of the delegates of the people was in effect to restrict the power of the people itself, and this was pointless.

But as things developed, theory did not coincide with practice. Even though they were representatives of the people, ruling groups developed their own interests, which in some cases did not coincide with the interests of the majority. Mill describes the situation in a memorable remark. "It was now perceived that such phrases as 'self-government' and 'the power of the people over themselves' do not express the true state of the case." The need for limitations upon any kind of governmental power which makes a distinction between those ruling and those ruled became apparent. In the third stage of democratic development, such limitations were again instituted. In this way, the ruled were again afforded protection against the possible abuse of authority by their own representatives.

The effect of this last development was to insure the enactment of the will of the majority. But this advance brought with it a kind of tyranny which such theorists as Locke had not envisaged. This tyranny manifested itself in two different ways: the first through the passage of laws which hampered minority groups, and the second—even more serious—through the imposition of the tastes of the majority upon nonconforming individuals even where there were no laws to justify such an imposition. Serious as was the former of these two evils, it was not nearly so dangerous to human freedom as was the latter. Constitutional guarantees and the doctrine of natural rights, even on its more moderate interpretation, prevented the majority from invading with impunity some areas which the minority considered sacred. But the greater danger lay in those cases where no law existed and the majority attempted to impose its will upon individuals who refused to conform to its practices. The effect of such pressure upon dissenting individuals was often strong enough to deprive them of the usual benefits of society, such as the right to hold a job or to teach what they believed.

For Mill, the fundamental problem which faces a democratic society can be put in this way. Some conduct which runs counter to prevailing practices cannot be tolerated; for instance, no one ought to be allowed to shoot off a weapon in a public place merely because he feels inclined to do so. On the other hand, if freedom is to be allowed, some idiosyncratic behavior must be tolerated. The question is: where does one draw the line? Or as Mill put it, "What are the legitimate powers which society has over the individual?"

His answer is contained in this famous passage:

> The object of this Essay is to assert one very simple principle as entitled to govern absolutely the dealings of society with the individual in the way of compulsion and control, whether the means used be physical force in the form of legal penalties, or the moral coercion of public opinion. That principle is, that the sole end for which mankind are warranted, individually or collectively, in interfering with the liberty of action of any of their number, is self-protection. That the only purpose for which power can be rightly exercised over any member of a civilized community, against his will, is to prevent harm to others. His own good, either physical or moral, is not a sufficient warrant. He cannot rightfully be compelled to do or forbear because it will be better for him to do so, because it will make him happier, because, in the opinions of others, to do so would be wise or even right. These are good reasons for remonstrating with him or reasoning with him, or persuading him, or entreating him, but not for compelling him, or visiting him with any evil in case he do otherwise. To justify that, the conduct from which it is desired to deter him must be calculated to produce evil to someone else. The only part of the conduct of anyone, for which he is amenable to society, is that which concerns others. In the part which merely concerns himself, his independence is, of right, absolute. Over himself, over his own body and mind, the individual is sovereign.[3]

The principle stated in the above passage is itself justified by Mill on utilitarian grounds. If the conduct of an individual is not harmful to society it must be tolerated, even if it should prove harmful to himself. For whatever unhappiness is produced for the individual in question, it will be less extensive than that which would accrue to society in general if all nonconformist behavior were suppressed.

[3] John Stuart Mill, "On Liberty," reprinted in *The English Philosophers from Bacon to Mill,* p. 955.

Mill attempts to demonstrate this point by using freedom of speech as an example. He indicates that if the free exercise of speech were prohibited, society would be harmed in three ways. To begin with, the opinion which is suppressed may well be true. If the nonconformist is not permitted to voice his views, the majority of men may never be given the opportunity to exchange its false beliefs for those which are true. By abolishing the right to speak freely, society thus may be the loser. Moreover, it is clear, Mill points out, that simply because the majority of people hold a given belief, it does not follow that it is true. For instance, the majority believed that the earth was at the center of the universe; its representatives forced Galileo to recant when he disagreed; but today, we recognize that it was Galileo who was right and not they.

In general, what is wrong with suppressing a dissident opinion, *without giving it an opportunity to be heard first*, is that, by so doing, we assume our own infallibility. But, as Mill remarks, no man is infallible. It is therefore important to check and recheck one's basic beliefs, especially if the evidence seems to run counter to them. The effect of such a practice will be the development of a more mature citizenry, one which bases its political decisions on reason insofar as this is possible. In the long run, there is little doubt that rational political action is likely to prove more beneficial to society than nonrational action.

The second argument which Mill propounds begins by assuming that the suppressed opinion is in fact false. But nonetheless, he argues, it is important to hear it. For one thing, a true opinion may be held as a prejudice, or for the wrong reasons. By hearing the contrary opinion expressed, the individual citizen may be awakened to the need to rethink his own view. By doing so, he will come to understand it better and to hold it on rational grounds, that is, to look for evidence which supports it. As we have already mentioned, this may be of immense practical importance in his further efforts to improve society.

Mill's third reason for requiring that the opposite opinion not be suppressed without giving it a chance to be heard is particularly relevant to the issues which face the Western world today. What is sometimes called the "Western way of life" is opposed by the practices of such nations as Soviet Russia and Communist China. Mill would argue that it is important that the doctrines of the major political thinkers of these nations be taught in American schools so that they can be understood and evaluated. His point is that political issues, like those which separate East from West, are highly complex. Even if we cannot accept *in toto* views which oppose our own, nonetheless such views may contain important insights which we may wish to apply to our own political practices in order to improve them. Put more generally, Mill's position is that most political doctrines which have been widely accepted have much in them that is true and much in them that is false. By not allowing views which run counter to our own to be expressed, we may lose the opportunity to utilize whatever is of value in them. It is Mill's belief that in the long run such a restrictive policy would prove detrimental to our own interests, and thus on utilitarian grounds, it ought to be rejected.

Criticism of Mill

In spite of their fundamentally similar outlooks, the views of Mill and Locke diverge importantly at certain points. Locke's great achievement lay in his construction of the essential framework which he believed any democratic society must possess. This framework rests upon four cornerstones: (1) the belief that government must be based on law, not decree, (2) the doctrine of natural rights, (3) the doctrine that government is the servant of the people, not its master, and (4) the principle of majority rule. For Mill these are neither necessary nor sufficient conditions for achieving a democratic community. As we have seen, he could not accept the doctrine of natural rights or any conception of majority rule which did not make some provision for the protection of minority interests as well. Further, and unlike Locke, Mill inclined more and more toward a form of democratic socialism as he grew older. Even as early as 1848, he developed a number of plans for the more equal distribution of the products of labor, and in this way he proposed to broaden the aims of democracy to include economic equality as well as political equality. Under the influence of his wife, the former Harriet Taylor, whom he married in 1851, he even envisaged a society in which the institution of private property would not exist. He did not work out these conjectures in detail, but nonetheless in moving in such a direction, he may be looked at as adding further strokes to the picture of a good society which Locke had originally painted in 1690.

As might be expected, such forthright views have aroused equally fervent objections. Among these we may distinguish two strains: those which attack Mill's utilitarianism and those which attack his defense of individual liberty.

Critics of utilitarianism point out that if this doctrine were consistently applied, it would have social implications which are paradoxical, that is, which run counter to that intuitive notion of fairness which forms a basic ingredient of democracy. The notion of fairness underlies many of democracy's fundamental tenets, for instance, that all men should be treated equally before the law. This principle states that no individual, or group of individuals, ought to be discriminated against by the law but that the law ought to apply equally and without prejudice to all. Now this tenet implies, among other things, that criminals convicted of the same offense should receive the same punishment. To punish one malefactor more severely even though both are guilty of identical crimes would be to apply the law with bias and thus to violate our sense of what the law is supposed to stand for. But, if all this is conceded, it seems to raise difficulties for a utilitarian. Suppose, for example, that by punishing a given criminal far more severely than anyone else convicted of the same crime, we could deter future crimes of that sort. Admittedly it would be unfair to single him out for excessive punishment—but would we not be justified in doing so on the ground that by abolishing crimes of this kind we were contributing to the greatest happiness of the greatest number?

Undoubtedly, Mill would say no. In answer to the criticism, he would point out that the practice of applying the law fairly in all cases will, *as a matter of fact*, contribute more happiness to society than any departure from it. But this defense hardly seems decisive, since it makes the dispute rest upon a matter of evidence in areas where evidence is hard to come by. Nor does it really meet the objection squarely. The issue is not whether a given act will or will not cause the greatest happiness of the greatest number, but whether the greatest happiness principle itself is compatible with our sense of social justice.

Apart from the question of the adequacy of utilitarianism, there are difficulties in Mill's defense of individual liberty. To begin with, Mill assumes throughout the essay *On Liberty* that human conduct can be divided into two distinct classes: conduct which affects only the individual himself and conduct which affects society. Mill's contention is that society is never justified in interfering with conduct of the former sort. But, critics ask, are there any actions which really only affect one person and no others? It is hard, they say, to imagine any. Consider an individual, having no family ties and living apart from large centers of population, who decides to commit suicide. Does his action only affect himself?

These critics argue that in all probability it will affect others, too. If he does in fact commit suicide, he must still be buried—and this may be at public expense if he leaves no funds. Or his action, should it become known, may set a bad example to those in an equally distressed state of mind. These critics admit, of course, that it is logically possible that there might be an individual whose acts did not impinge upon the social fabric, but they go on to argue that the likelihood that there could be a great number of such individuals is very small indeed. It thus seems that Mill's basic distinction applies at best only to a very limited number of individuals and not to most people in a society. But if not, it is hardly a useful distinction upon which to rest a case for defending individual freedom from governmental interference.

Finally, it has been suggested that Mill's defense of minority groups in a democratic society is either impossible or unnecessary. Minority interests cannot be preserved in those cases where they clash with the interests of the majority. In such circumstances, in accordance with the principle of majority rule, the minority will always have to give way, since the majority, if sufficiently aroused, can always pass laws through its representatives and thus impose its will upon any dissenting group. On the other hand, in those cases where the majority interest is not involved, the minority may do as it pleases. It seems, then, that in either case a defense of the minority is pointless.

There is much in this last criticism which Mill might have agreed with. For one thing, he does not wish to reject majority rule. The laws of a democratic society, he points out, if passed by a majority must be binding upon all. In defending the right of the minority to dissent, he is not advocating their right to flout the law. His claim is somewhat weaker, but nonetheless important. For one thing, he stresses that in those circumstances where there is no explicit law, majority opinion should not be allowed to dictate the behavior of those who object to it. No individual should be dismissed from his job because his conduct invites public criticism and yet violates no law. And secondly in those cases where public opinion against a nonconforming individual or group is so strong that laws are passed against the group, the burden is always on the public to prove that those in disfavor are actually engaging in conduct which is injurious to the public welfare. In practice, Mill's defense rests upon the fact that in any legal issue the onus of proof always rests upon the state. As we have already mentioned, such a presumption in the law has proved a powerful obstacle to indiscriminate interference in individual conduct.

At the beginning of this chapter, we pointed out that political theorists have traditionally been concerned with procedures for improving existing societies. These procedures have been both theoretical and practical. To a great extent, they involve the question of where the source of public power should be located. Plato, Hobbes, Machiavelli, and Nietzsche, for example, argued that power should be given to special groups or individuals, and should be absolute once granted. For Locke and Mill, on the other hand, the ultimate sources of political power are always to be located in "the people." And for both of them, though with profound qualifications in each case, the will of the people is to be expressed through majority vote. Their views, when put into practice, have generally led to an enlargement of human freedom, which both of them regard as a fundamental value. But not all theories which regard human freedom in this light, and which defend the sovereignty of the people, without ultimately identifying it with the will of the majority, have had this result. The political views of Jean Jacques Rousseau (1712–1778) represent a case in point. No writer has protested more vehemently against the inequities of modern society, or stood more vigorously in defense of human freedom. Yet it should be remembered that it was in the name of "liberty, fraternity, and equality"— a slogan derived from Rousseau—that the terrorism of the French Revolution was justified.

There is thus some ambiguity in how to classify Rousseau—is he an exponent of democracy or not? Some commentators have argued that he is. Ronald Grimsley, author of the article on Rousseau in the *Encyclopedia of Philosophy*, defends this interpretation. He writes:

> This conception of political right is essentially democratic insofar as the source of all political authority, and, therefore, of all true sovereignty must always lie with the people as a whole. Moreover, such sovereignty is both inalienable and indivisible, since as the basis of freedom itself, it is something that can never be renounced by the people or shared with others.[4]

Yet, Bertrand Russell, in his *History of Western Philosophy*, offers a different appraisal of Rousseau, saying of him:

> He is the father of the romantic movement, the initiator of systems of thought which infer non-human facts from human emotions, and the inventor of the political philosophy of pseudo-democratic dictatorships as opposed to traditional absolute monarchies. Ever since his time, those who considered themselves reformers have been divided into two groups, those who followed him and those who followed Locke. Sometimes they co-operated, and many individuals saw no incompatibility. But gradually the incompatibility has become increasingly evident. At the present time, Hitler is an outcome of Rousseau; Roosevelt and Churchill of Locke.[5]

THE POLITICAL PHILOSOPHY OF ROUSSEAU

Let us turn now to the political philosophy of Rousseau, as expressed in his major work, the *Social Contract* of 1762, in order to see why it is regarded in such diverse ways by competent critics. We have already seen, in the introductory remarks to this chapter, that the fundamental theme in Rousseau's early monograph, the *Discourse on the Origin of Inequality*, is a critique of modern society, whose institutions, based on the possession of property, give rise to social inequality. In the *Social Contract* the emphasis is shifted; here it is freedom which occupies the central stage— Chapter I of this book opens with the stirring remark, "Man was born free, but is everywhere in bondage." Yet equality plays an important role in this work as well. Indeed, as we shall see, Rousseau's work turns on a tension between the concepts of freedom and equality, and it is this tension that gives rise to the difficulties in classifying him as a defender of democracy or as a defender of autocracy.

---

[4] Ronald Grimsley, "Rousseau, Jean Jacques," *The Encyclopedia of Philosophy*, ed. by Paul Edwards (Macmillan and Free Press, New York, 1967), Vol. VII, p. 223.
[5] Bertrand Russell, *History of Western Philosophy* (Allen and Unwin, London, 1946), p. 711.

There is a second important shift in emphasis between the doctrines of the *Discourse on Inequality* and those of the *Social Contract*. In the former work, life in a "state of nature" is seen as essentially benign, and the drives of men toward self-preservation are seen as tempered by benevolence and compassion. But in the *Social Contract* the emphasis is upon the power and freedom which each man uses as instruments for self-preservation. Accordingly, life in the state of nature is no longer pictured as idyllic. Rousseau states, in fact, that:

> Men have reached a point where the obstacles hindering their preservation in the state of nature are so obstructive as to defy the resources each individual, while in that state, can devote to his preservation. This being the case, that primitive condition cannot continue; humankind would perish if it did not change its way of life.[6]

The solution, of course, is to live in some form of political association, but the problem which each individual faces if he wishes to leave the state of nature is this: "Can I give up my power and freedom without being injured?" As Rousseau puts it—and this is *the* fundamental problem as he sees it:

> Is a method of associating discoverable which will defend and protect, with all the collective might, the person and property of each associate, and in virtue of which each associate, though he becomes a member of the group, nevertheless obeys only himself, and remains as free as before?[7]

The social contract, according to Rousseau, provides a solution to this problem. It does so by allowing men freely and unanimously to form a society which by its very nature treats each equally. This guarantee of equal treatment—the inequality of nature being replaced by the equality of law—will protect each person. Thus, through equality of association and equality of treatment men will remain as "free as before."

Such an association requires that each person be willing to join it freely and without reservations. In joining, he gives up (alienates) all of his rights to the community. The reason he must abandon his rights is that if he did not there would be no public judge able to decide disputes; he would "be his own judge on this or that point, and so would try before long to be his own judge on all points." Thus the state of nature would persist, and the association would necessarily become useless or tyrannical.

In a famous, paradoxical remark, Rousseau explains why each will remain free under such conditions. "Each," he writes, "gives himself to

---

[6] Jean Jacques Rousseau, *The Social Contract*, trans. and ed. by W. Kendall (H. Regnery and Co., Chicago, 1954), p. 13.
   [7] *Ibid.*

everybody; so that . . . he gives himself to nobody; and since every associate acquires over every associate the same power he grants to every associate over himself, each gains an equivalent for all that he loses, together with greater power to protect what he possesses."

The social body which results from this association now becomes a "collective moral body." It is made up of as many members as there are voices in the assembly, and it acquires through such an act of agreement, its unity, its collective self, its life and its will. This body is called "the state" when it is passive, "the sovereign" when it is active, and a "power" when compared with bodies of a similar sort. The compacting individuals are called "the people" when thought of collectively, as "citizens" in terms of their participation in the state, and as "subjects" when subordinated to the laws of the state.

What Rousseau means by the above terms may be put as follows. By saying that the resulting society is a collective moral body he means two things—(a) that it is legitimate, that is, that its basis is agreement, not force, and (b) that it is the source or basis of all social rights. Thus, for him, it makes no sense to speak of presocial man as possessing "property," though he may possess things; or as acting in ways that are either just or unjust, right or wrong, moral or immoral, or as having duties, obligations and rights. All of these things arise or are made possible from the fact that man is a *social* being. As he puts it, "Social order is a right—a sacred right which serves as the basis for all rights."

The fundamental problem of the *Social Contract* is thus seen in relation to this attitude to the state. For given that the state of nature is impossible and that man must live in some sort of social order, the question arises, when is such a social order a legitimate one? His point is that not all societies are legitimate, that is, are genuine moral bodies, and his problem is how to distinguish those that can exercise legitimate authority from those that cannot. His answer is one that vests sovereignty in the people as a whole; namely, that a society is legitimate only when it is created by the unanimous agreement of all who are to be members of it. This makes illegitimate, as we have said, societies based upon heredity, "nature," or force.

In putting forth such a view, Rousseau is speaking about the creation of society, not the creation of government. The social contract between individuals does not create the governing body of that association. For him, government may take many forms—it may be democratic, monarchical or even aristocratic; the best government will depend on the circumstances in which the society finds itself—but the point is that no matter what the form, government is always a servant of the people, never its master. Rousseau's view thus differs from either Hobbes' or Locke's. The former sees both society and government as the creations of covenant, while the latter sees only government as the product of such an agreement. For Rousseau, it is only society—an association—that is created in this way. What he is thus arguing is that only *societies* created by unanimous agreement are legitimate forms of political association.

All this looks radically democratic, since sovereignty is clearly vested in the people *collectively*. But the distinction between their collective powers and their powers as *individuals* is very important in the theory. For in making such an agreement, each individual gives up his power and freedom to the state, and must obey whatever conditions the collective body stipulates. It is for this reason that some commentators have seen in Rousseau a defense of totalitarianism. Rousseau is very explicit on this point. He states:

> To the end, therefore, that the social pact shall not be a meaningless formality, it includes, by implication the following undertaking, in the absence of which the other undertakings it includes would have no binding force: whoever refuses to obey the general will shall be constrained to do so by the entire body politic, which is only another way of saying that his fellows shall force him to be free.[8]

It should be noted that this totalitarian strain—the idea that society can compel a person "to be free"—is connected with what Rousseau calls "the general will." This is a mysterious notion, which is not identical with the will of the majority, or in some cases, not even identical with the unanimous will of the total citizenry. In its most straightforward form, it seems to be identical with the collective interest or good of society. But the difficulty is how to ascertain what this is; according to Rousseau this is a task, not for the executive power of society, but for the legislator. It is not even a task for the people, for though "a people always wills, it does not always see what is good for it." For Rousseau, individual members of society see the good they are rejecting; while taken collectively, they will the good they do not see. The result then is that individuals and public alike need someone to guide them. This person he calls "a legislator." It is the legislator who will always act for the public good, and in the common interest, framing legislation directed toward these ends.

Rousseau's description of the legislator makes one wonder whether any person could actually qualify for such a job. He describes him in the following words:

> The task of discovering the best laws, i.e., those that are most salutary for each nation, calls for a mind of the highest order. This mind would have insight into each and every human passion, and yet be af-

---

[8] Rousseau, *op. cit.*, p. 18.

fected by none. It would be superhuman, and yet understand human nature through and through. It would be willing to concern itself with our happiness, but would seek its own outside us. It would content itself with fame far off in the future, i.e., it would be capable of laboring in one century and reaping its reward in the next . . . *In a word*: Law-giving is a task for gods *not men.*[9]

In short, the theory of the "general will" holds that when a collective body or association is formed, it becomes a moral *person*, and such a moral person will have a will. This will is identical with the common interest or good of society, taken collectively. Thus the suggestion is that independently of the wills of individual persons there is a collective social will which may or may not coincide with the totality of wills of the persons in society, taken individually. It is this idea that leads him to say that "the sovereign needs only to exist in order to be what it ought to be." And it is the legislator, acting in a god-like manner, who expresses the general will of society through appropriate legislation.

Criticism of Rousseau

As we have seen, the fundamental thrust of Rousseau's doctrine in the *Social Contract* is an attempt to construct an ideal political society, one that is legitimate. For him, such a society must treat each of its members as equal to one another, both in terms of receiving his free consent for the formation of such a society, and then in its subsequent treatment of him. This latter point is very important since it provides a theoretical foundation for the notion that law provides equality. Unlike nature, in which men are unequal, depending on their physical strength and the circumstances of their birth, society equalizes men; it does so by providing a set of rules which eliminate discrimination, partisan persuasion, and unfair treatment of its citizens. But along with providing a set of conditions that guarantee equality, it must also allow men to remain free. Society must not create a new bondage if it is to be a moral agent, the source of all rights and privileges. The social contract, seen as a compact between free individuals in the state of nature, guarantees such a society. It counts each individual equally in the formation of the social order, and it treats each equally thereafter in the construction of its laws; moreover, since each person abandons his individual rights, powers, and privileges to the total community, which is just the collection of the citizens itself, no freedom has been lost; it has merely been distributed collectively, rather than individually.

In theory, all of this sounds fine, but at a very abstract level. The problems arise when we attempt to apply the abstract theory in practice;

[9] Rousseau, *op. cit.*, p. 41.

and here a main defect in Rousseau's work appears. This is that the practical applications become either very vague or wholly untenable. They are vague in the sense that one does not know what the general will dictates in terms of practical politics—is it in the general interest of society to build this bridge, or to fight that war?—or if one could determine what the general will was in a given case, then in order to make sure that everybody adhered to it, one would have to force people who disagreed to conform to it. But this would certainly be an abridgement of the freedom of the individuals who disagreed with what the general will dictated.

Unlike Locke and Mill, who specify ways in which something approximating the general will can readily be determined (that is, by a vote in crucial matters, with the majority being empowered to decide), Rousseau leaves such a determination vague. His answer is that it will depend on the legislator; but as we have seen, his description of the "ideal legislator" hardly corresponds to anyone resembling a practical politician. The result is therefore that the theory either justifies the extreme suppression of those who disagree with a strong legislator, speaking in the name of the general will, or it is so vague that one could never apply it in practice. The tension between the pulls of equality and freedom thus fragment the doctrine to a point where it is not applicable, given that it provides no specifiable way of determining what the general will, that is, the common interest, is in given cases.

In the end, then, though the theory purports to give sovereignty to the people, it does not; by giving it to them "as a whole" or "collectively" it fails to show how it can be used by them "individually" or in groups, and thus in the end it fails to give it to them at all. This is a dubious defense of democracy.

Like the views of Rousseau, the doctrines of our next theorist, Karl Marx, raise similar questions. Marx argued against social inequality, especially economic inequality, and thought that men could not be fully free if they were constrained by their economic situation. Like Mill and Locke, Marx thought of himself as an exponent of democracy; but like Rousseau his ideas have led to the establishment of some of the most tyrannical communities in human history. Was Marx mistaken, or have his views been perverted? Let us look at them and see.

THE POLITICAL PHILOSOPHY
OF KARL MARX

Like Locke and Hobbes before him, Karl Marx (1818–1883) lived in a turbulent world. It was one in which several traditions reached climaxes simultaneously, impinged upon each other, and clashed violently. The monarchical tradition was still strong, even if fighting desperately for its life; nationalism was rife everywhere throughout Europe; democratic movements were becoming more powerful than ever; and socialism, for the first time, emerged as a political force. In the cataract which developed out of these converging streams, Marx was buffeted about violently. He was exiled from his native Germany twice, the last time for thirty-four years. He was tried for high treason (but acquitted). Three newspapers which he edited were forced to suspend publication within a period of less than a decade and, jobless, he spent the major portion of his life in extreme poverty. Nonetheless, he continued to write, pouring out an immense quantity of material on economic and political subjects. Today, his influence is greater than ever. For better or for worse, almost half of the contemporary world seems cast in the mold of his ideas.

Marx was born in Treves, Prussia, in 1818, in a typical middle-class German household. His boyhood was uneventful, and he exhibited few signs of the revolutionary ardor which was to characterize his later years. He went to the universities of Bonn and Berlin with the intention of taking a degree in law, but while at Berlin he fell in with a group of radical thinkers, led by the brothers Bruno and Edgar Bauer, who called themselves *Die Freien* (The Free Ones). This was the turning point of his career. He switched from law to philosophy and earned a doctor's degree in that subject in 1841. He then decided to pursue an academic career, but, because of his radical views, found university doors closed to him. Eventually he obtained work on a newspaper, the *Rheinische Zeitung*, and became its editor within a short time. In 1843, after several clashes with the government, the newspaper was suppressed by the censors, and Marx, in order to avoid arrest, fled to Paris. From about this time on, Marx began the long series of political writings which were to continue for the next four decades. The works of this period—"the Early Marx" as they have been called—differ greatly from his more mature products. As recent research, initiated to a considerable extent by Herbert Marcuse, into these neglected works indicates, Marx at this period was humanistically inclined and far less dogmatic than the late proponent of "scientific socialism." This "early Marx" has had a great influence on theoreticians now working in the Soviet Union and other Eastern European countries, such as L. Kolakowski, G. Lukacs, and Adam Schaff.

But in spite of the comparative moderation of these works, and even though he was now living in France, he was not safe. In conjunction with Friedrich Engels (1820–1895), whom he met in Paris and who was to become his lifelong friend, he began contributing articles to the *Vorwarts*, a radical German-language periodical published in Paris and smuggled into Germany. At the request of the German government, French authorities expelled them because of the inflammatory nature of the articles in this publication. From Paris, Marx and Engels went to Brussels, where they joined a secret communist group called "The League of the Just." In 1847, this organization decided to engage in open political action. Marx and Engels wrote a pamphlet for the group entitled *The Manifesto of the Communist Party* which not only expressed the aims of socialism but demanded that they be implemented by force and violence. The effect of the *Manifesto* upon working groups from its opening sentence ("A spectre is haunting Europe, the spectre of Communism!") to its dramatic conclusion ("Working men of all countries, unite!") was electrifying. This pamphlet became the rallying point of various proletarian movements. Within months, it had been circulated all over Europe and its authors had become famous.

In 1848, revolutions broke out in France and Germany. Marx seized the opportunity to return to Cologne, where he founded a new journal in which he openly advocated armed resistance to the king of Prussia, as well as the nonpayment of taxes. For this, he was brought to trial for treason but was unanimously acquitted. Despite his acquittal, though, he was again forced to leave Germany and in 1849, after some hesitation, decided to settle in England. This country became his home for the remainder of his life. In 1864, he helped found the International Workingmen's Association, an organization designed to better the lot of all workers, regardless of their national origin. Marx's functions within this organization were primarily those of theoretician and teacher, roles for which his continuing research into the nature of capitalism singularly fitted him. In 1867, this research culminated in the publication of Volume I of *Das Kapital* (Capital), his greatest work. Because of illness brought on by penury and overwork, Marx was unable to finish more than the first volume. After he died in 1883, two of the remaining three volumes were completed by Engels, working from Marx's manuscripts and notes, and a fourth was later edited by Karl Kautsky (1854–1938).

In explaining Marx's doctrines, it is convenient to break them up into three distinct but nevertheless closely related parts. The first is a metaphysics, mainly derived from the leading German philosopher of the day, G. W. F. Hegel (1770–1831), in which Marx attempts to show that the course of human history, including its socioeconomic development, follows a lawlike pattern, called the "dialectic." Capitalism represents a passing stage in history and, in accordance with the dialectical pattern, is destined to be replaced in the future by a different kind of economic arrangement which Marx calls "socialism." The second important ingredient in Marx's philosophy is an economic theory which is intimately connected with the foregoing metaphysic. In it, he attempts not only to explain in a technical, detailed way how capitalism works but also to diagnose the various factors inherent in it, which will eventually lead to its decay. The final element of his philosophy is again closely related to the metaphysics and to the economic theory. It contains an ethical doctrine which stresses the importance of recovering certain fundamental human values which Marx believes capitalism is systematically destroying. Let us take up each of these divisions in more detail now.

The Dialectic | Although Marx had only contempt for Hegel's form of philosophical idealism and hatred for his reactionary deification of the Prussian state, he nevertheless believed that Hegel had found in the "dialectic" a law which explained the nature of historical change. Since the "dialectic" plays an important role in Marx's analysis of the future of capitalism, we shall digress momentarily to indicate what Hegel meant by the term and then show how Marx's interpretation of it differed from his. But in order to do this, it is convenient to look backward to Ancient Greece, since Hegel derived the concept from his older contemporary, J. G. Fichte (1762–1814), whose original source, in turn, seems to have been Plato.

The dialectical method serves a specific philosophical purpose in Plato's writings, a purpose intimately connected with Plato's conviction that in order to acquire knowledge one must transcend the kind of information acquired through sense experience. The dialectical method is, so to speak, an instrument which can be used for this purpose, since it enables one to grasp those features of the world which are not accessible to the senses. If someone wishes to know what friendship is, what piety is, or what virtue is, there is nothing he can see, nothing he can touch, no experiment he can perform, by way of finding out. In these kinds of cases, the inquiry must be dialectical if he hopes to attain an answer. What then is this method of inquiry?

Superficially it might be described as follows. It involves the asking of questions by an interlocutor (usually Socrates), the giving of answers to these questions by those being interrogated, and the critical analysis of these responses by the interlocutor. The process is repeated until an answer is found which is satisfactory and which thus supplies the information originally being looked for. The process is a logical one, involving the use of reason without employing observations. This is why, according to Plato, it can give us information which the senses cannot.

The opening of *The Republic* contains a classical illustration of the use of the dialectical method. Socrates initiates a conversation among a group of his friends by asking them "What is justice?" One of his companions, Cephalus, proposes as an answer a definition: "Justice is honesty in word and deed." Socrates now critically assesses this answer. He does this by looking for what logicians call a "contrary case" to the definition, a case in which we ordinarily would say that someone was just and yet was not honest. He points out that if an insane person were to come to your home to kill a friend who was there, it would be unjust for you to tell him where your friend is. Justice, in such a circumstance, requires that you ought not to tell the truth, indeed, requires that you lie if necessary. The counter example shows that the term "justice" and the phrase "honesty in word and deed" are not synonymous—and if not, Cephalus' definition is incorrect. A new definition must therefore be sought. Such a definition is suggested by Polemarchus and criticized by Socrates who again finds a contrary case to it. Polemarchus' definition is thus likewise not acceptable. A third definition is then stated, a contrary case proposed, and so on until a definition which is presumably unobjectionable is arrived at. In this way, the true nature of justice is gradually discovered.

Hegel was greatly impressed by this procedure. In studying it, he thought he noted that the play of ideas follows a three-stage, almost stepwise process. He called the first stage, which consists of the original definition, the "thesis"; the second or opposing stage, the "antithesis"; and the proposal of a new definition which attempts to combine what is correct in both thesis and antithesis, the "synthesis." Insofar as Hegel employed the terms "dialectic" to denote a logical process with this stepwise movement of ideas, he was using it in much the same way as Plato.

But except for this similarity, his conception differs radically from Plato's. For Hegel, the dialectical process is more than linguistic. It is an actual process which the world exemplifies and which can be discovered through the study of history. The rise and fall of nations especially reflects this pattern. A nation comes into existence, develops an opposing nation to itself, and conflicts between the two break out. From the struggle, a new nation arises, which in turn develops its opposition—and so on *ad indefinitum*. For Hegel, nations thus occupy positions in the dialectical movement of history which are analogous to the positions occupied by definitions and the objections to them in the Platonic scheme.

Marx accepted much in this view. He thought, like Hegel, that change takes place through the logical opposition of contending forces and that the pattern of such change could be grasped through the study of history. Like Hegel, he viewed the dialectic as a law in a strict sense of the term—that is, as laying down conditions which must of necessity prevail. For both of these thinkers, then, world history follows an inevitable path, and men seem to be merely pawns in a stream which they cannot divert. This is why they each seek to explain historical change by looking to deep-lying forces beyond human control.

Marx's originality, though, lies in those respects in which he differs from Hegel. For Hegel, the forces which cause world change are not so much nations per se as the "spirit" or "soul" of these nations. The soul of a nation develops with the eventual purpose of realizing itself in an all-encompassing mind, or "the absolute" as Hegel terms it. As a materialist (influenced by Feuerbach), Marx could not accept an explanation of change which referred to such dubious entities as the "soul of a nation" or "the absolute." Instead, he felt, an explanation could only be genuinely informative if it appealed to material factors. Impelled by this conviction, he was led to look for other causes to which this dialectical analysis could be applied. The results of his investigation are genuinely startling.

He argues that although nations are subject to dialectical development, as Hegel had claimed, the actual motivating factors are the classes within nations. It is these which develop opposition to themselves and which thus are the sources of conflict and the resulting synthesis. But, Marx stresses, even this account does not go deep enough, for social classes are themselves products of material factors—and it is these which any correct analysis of change must eventually appeal to. Such factors, he claims, are to be found in the means by which society produces goods. For the kind of productive technology a society has invariably develops a corresponding class structure within it. When the prevailing mode of manufacturing goods lay in the use of hand mills, for instance, the class system called "feudalism" came into existence. When steam mills replaced hand mills, capitalism, with its class system, replaced feudalism. And changes in the productive system of capitalism will eventually cause it to be replaced, too. For Marx world history, in effect, follows the dialectical changes which ensue from changes in the means of producing goods. Indeed, no better summary of Marx's position on this matter can be found than that given by Engels who, commenting on the *Manifesto* nearly fifty years after he had collaborated with Marx on it, wrote:

> The *Manifesto* being our joint production, I consider myself bound to state that the fundamental proposition, which forms its nucleus, belongs to Marx. That proposition is: that in every historical epoch, the prevailing mode of economic production and exchange, and the social organization necessarily following from it, form the basis upon which is built up, and from which alone can be explained, the political and intellectual history of that epoch; that consequently, the whole history of mankind (since the dissolution of primitive tribal society holding land in common ownership) has been a history of class struggles, contests between exploiting and exploited, ruling and oppressed classes. . . .[10]

Marx's Economic Theory | As we have already indicated, Marx's economic theory is intimately tied to this analysis of change. It enables him to explain how class warfare will develop within capitalism, and then how this will lead to the collapse of that system. His explanation runs some-

[10] Karl Marx and Friedrich Engels, *The Communist Manifesto* (Appleton-Century-Crofts, New York, 1955), p. 5.

thing like this: capitalists are mainly motivated by the desire to acquire profits as large as possible. In order to achieve this goal, they must continually strive to improve the means of production, either by inventing new techniques or by trying to improve those already in use. On the whole, they are successful in these efforts, and new devices are constantly being developed and old ones improved. The effect of these developments upon society is twofold: (1) They enable a greater volume of goods to be produced than before, so that there is, in capitalism, a constant tendency for the quantity of goods being produced to rise. (2) They sharply reduce the number of people being employed to do similar jobs (the cotton gin, for example, required the employment of fewer workers than were previously needed to sort an equal amount of cotton). Now both of these tendencies work toward the ultimate advantage of the employer and to the ultimate disadvantage of the worker. As productivity rises, the owner's profit increases too, since a greater volume of goods is being produced at a lower cost to him, and as machines replace laborers, his wage costs drop as well. Thus as productivity rises, his production costs become substantially lower and his profits correspondingly higher. At the same time, this increase in profit for him is accompanied by a tendency toward increasing unemployment among the workers.

We thus witness in a developing capitalist economy, according to Marx, two growing and incompatible tendencies, both due to increasing productivity. The first is that the profit of the "entrepreneur" (or owner) tends to increase in the long run; the second is that the rate of employment tends to decrease. And both of these tendencies are magnified through competition. The owner, wishing to sell as large a volume of goods as possible, must undersell his competitors. In order to do this, he must cut his costs. Since the same technological devices are available to all owners, the only place where he can significantly save in production expenses is in the wages he pays for labor. Because of growing unemployment due to the development of more efficient machines, workers will compete for the available jobs and thus will accept work at lower and lower salaries. As the labor costs of the employer drop, his profits rise, and his chance of competing successfully against other entrepreneurs becomes stronger. Those entrepreneurs who cannot compete successfully go out of business (as do their employees), adding to the growing pool of unemployment, which again drives wages down.

Thus, as capitalism develops, there is a tendency for the wealthy to become wealthier and for the poor to become poorer. Intermediate classes will be wiped out and society will eventually be divided into two classes: a small but wealthy group whose members own the means of production and a large but impoverished class of people who are dependent upon the owners for their livelihood. Resentful of this state of affairs (becoming more "class conscious" as Marx puts it), the workers will finally rise and expropriate the wealth of the so-called *bourgeoisie,* or owners. A new society will be created in which the means of production are owned in common and there is no "exploitation" of the proletariat (workers).

In this connection it should be mentioned that, according to Marx, the overthrow of capitalism can be accomplished only by a revolution—by the use of force and violence. The reason why peaceful means cannot be used to achieve a *genuinely* socialist society is explained by Marx's analysis of the role of the state. For him and for most of his important followers (for example, Engels, Lenin, and Trotsky) the state is an instrument owned by those who control the wealth of society, and it is used by them for the purpose of exploiting the masses. All the avenues of the state are designed for maintaining the *status quo,* that is, for maintaining in power those who own the prime sources of wealth. Law courts, the police, even government itself, are agencies which reflect, consciously or unconsciously, the interests of the ruling class. When the ruling class is seriously threatened by a revolt from the dispossessed, these agencies will always act to prevent the ruled from assuming control of society. Accordingly, it is hopeless for the proletariat to attempt a drastic revision of society by peaceful means: in the end force must be employed.

The dialectical pattern is easily traceable in this (primarily) economic analysis. We begin with a thesis, that one ought to work for a profit. If pursued, this leads to the development of a wealthy class of individuals. But necessarily the development of such a class can take place only at the expense of the workers. The concentration of wealth thus implies the emergence of a class whose interests are antithetical to those of the *bourgeoisie,* the so-called "proletariat." As the latter become more conscious of their lot, their resentment against the capitalists grows and finally conflict breaks out between them. Society thus exhibits a contradiction which is synthesized or resolved only when a new social stage is reached. This stage is socialism.

Had Marx's views about the future of capitalism rested only upon his use of the dialectic, they might never have assumed the importance they have today. They might well have disappeared with the decline which accompanied Hegel's philosophical stature in the late nineteenth century. But as we have suggested, not all of Marx's critique of capitalism depends upon his metaphysical outlook. His detailed descriptive account of capitalism is independent of the truth of the dialectic and must be evaluated separately. Since this is so, let us examine this account somewhat more closely.

Like most economists, including such supporters of laissez-faire as Adam Smith and David Ricardo, Marx accepted a labor theory of value. The point of the labor theory is to allow the economist to determine the economic value which an item possesses. The conclusion drawn is that the value of any commodity is identical with the cost of the labor which goes into its production, under specified conditions. This part of Marx's economic analysis was thus not original. But Marx utilized the labor theory of value to invent another theory, the "theory of surplus value." This doctrine explains the origin of profit for the entrepreneur in a capitalist economy. According to Marx, the ordinary worker lacks the capital to buy or invest in an industry. In fact, the only commodity having economic value which he owns is his capacity to do work. This he sells to the capitalist. In return for his labor, the capitalist pays him a wage. But normally the wage paid him is far less than the value of the items he produces for his employer. The difference between the value of the items he produces and the wage he receives is what Marx means by "surplus value." The surplus is taken by the employer and used for various purposes, such as retooling and rent, but some of it he pockets as profit.

The theory of surplus value is crucial in Marx's analysis of capitalism. In it, Marx finds the economic key which accounts for the causes of conflict between the workers and their employers. Such conflict originates in two ways. To begin with, capitalism involves an inequity to the worker and a corresponding resentment on his part. For the workers produce the wealth through their efforts but do not receive a fair proportion of it. A disproportionately large amount is taken by the capitalist in the form of profit.

Secondly, capitalism engenders incompatible interests between the workers and the owners. The capitalist wishes to accumulate as large a surplus value (profit) as possible, which he can do only if he pays the lowest possible wages and sells his commodities for the highest possible price. On the other hand, the worker wishes to receive the highest possible wages for his work and to buy goods as cheaply as possible. These aims are diametrically opposed and in the end will lead to strife between the two groups—strife which will result in the eventual victory of the proletariat and the inauguration of a socialist society.

Marx's Ethics   By now, the connection of Marx's ethical doctrines with the preceding economic and metaphysical theories should be abundantly clear, although before proceeding to illustrate the relation in a detailed way, it might be wise to interject a word of qualification at the outset. In a sense, it may be misleading to describe Marx's writings as even containing an ethical "theory," since he does not have an explicit, highly developed moral system. In fact, he thinks of himself as a neutral, dispassionate scientist, objectively analyzing a certain phase in human history and not as a moralist at all. But in spite of this self-estimate, and even in spite of his intentions to the contrary, there is no doubt that his analysis of capitalism is pervaded by a strong element of moral disapproval. Capitalism, in his eyes, is not only an unworkable economic system, but beyond that it creates relations among men which are essentially immoral. Such relations come about through the incessant striving after profits. In the effort to acquire and preserve wealth, men ignore or push aside their fellows. Competition rules the day, and in the end society takes on the look of the jungle.

This is a tragic picture. For capitalist society has the potential to make life more comfortable than ever before. In its emphasis upon technology, it has developed instruments that can be used for easing and enhancing human existence. But, unfortunately, it misuses these instruments to a great degree. It forces children into labor; it creates a depressed class of workers, dependent for their livelihood upon the largesse of the rich; it produces internal conflict and unhappiness—and all this for profits. As Marx says in a memorable passage:

> In our days everything seems pregnant with its contrary; machinery gifted with the wonderful power of shortening and fructifying human labor, we behold starving and overworking it. The new-fangled sources of wealth, by some strange weird spell, are turned to sources of want. The victories of art seem bought by the loss of character. At the same pace that mankind masters nature, man seems to become enslaved to other men or to his own infamy. Even the pure light of science seems unable to shine but on the dark background of ignorance.[11]

Indeed, he argues, modern capitalist society not only values its technology for productive purposes but begins to worship the objects produced by such a technology, giving them the kind of respect and devotion which should be rendered to human beings. Marx calls this tendency "fetishism," thus bringing out, in a profoundly ironical and touching way, the primitive nature of the social practices which a highly advanced capitalistic society begets. The effect of this modern form of "fetishism" upon society is disastrous. Human beings come to view each other as machines, to be treated as instruments having no intrinsic value or worth, while machines, on the other hand, acquire an inflated value and become the ends which men worship.

A society in which such practices constitute the norm is doomed to what Marx calls "self-alienation." This term, for Marx, denotes the plight of the average man in a modern capitalistic state. Instead of bringing people more closely together, such a society eventually isolates them from each other. Each man becomes an island, cut off from his fellows, unbeloved and unwanted by the industrial machine when he can no longer

---

[11] Karl Marx, *Selected Works* (International Publishers, New York, 1933), Vol. II, 427–428.

serve it. What is particularly tragic in this picture is that it is a thing of man's own making; this is why Marx calls it *self*-alienation. Man has succeeded in making society intolerable for himself.

This situation can only be altered if a system which puts emphasis upon profits is abandoned. Since the profit motive is essential to capitalism, the eventual remedy for man's moral plight is the adoption of a noncapitalist economy. Only in this way, according to Marx, will morality again prevail in human affairs.

Before turning to an appraisal of Marx's philosophical views, it is worth reiterating that he is to be classified with those philosophers, like Locke and Mill, who have defended the rule of the many against the rule of the few. In effect, his criticism of capitalism is that it is a socioeconomic system which gives the control of society to an elite which owns the means of production, and that this elite uses the power deriving from such ownership to advance its own ends and interests at the expense of the public welfare. It is clear that the alternative which he favors is government by and for the people. More specifically, the ideal which he espouses is that of a social system in which the state as an instrument of exploitation has "withered away," and all decisions are to be arrived at by the citizenry cooperatively. This transition to a communist state is to take place via a series of stages, beginning with the destruction of capitalism, moving through a period of "dictatorship by the proletariat," into a socialist, somewhat "mixed" economy—where the principal means of production are to be publicly owned, but where there is still some private enterprise—into a fully communal society, a veritable *gemeinschaft*, or family. Marx's positive comments about this development are not worked out in detail, compared with his extensive, negative critique of capitalism, and accordingly it is difficult to know how much weight to place upon them.

Nevertheless, to the extent that such brief remarks do contain a positive theory, they raise serious questions about whether Marx's interest in the welfare of the people is sufficient to characterize him as an exponent of democracy, where this is interpreted as a society based upon majority rule and upon prescribed procedural rules for voting, for creating and enforcing the law, and so forth. Marx's comments about his ultimate communist community—an association lacking a state with coercive powers over its people—seems closer to the model of a good society espoused by certain anarchists than it does to the check-and-balance views of Locke and Mill. Like Rousseau, Marx is willing to vest power in "the people" without prescribing how such power is to be exercised. Presumably in a communist state "pure democracy," where everyone participates directly in the affairs of government, would be the method to be adopted; but in any large, complex modern and highly industrialized society such an ideal would prove difficult to put into practice. The practical alternatives thus seem to be either that the communist state must be very small, like the city-state ideal espoused by Rousseau—or that anarchy must prevail.

Opponents of Marx have also stressed that he demands the establishment of socialism by the use of force and violence if necessary and that this seems incompatible with the notion of government by law, one of the fundamental tenets of democratic theory. Those who proffer this objection point out that once a society sanctions the use of force and violence, such methods become the prevailing practice. The only alternative to this, these critics argue, is to provide a transition to socialism by peaceful, gradualistic means, in which maximum diversity in human behavior is to be tolerated; but such a development implies that the state will continue to exist and will be used as a force to prevent unlawful behavior, while at the same time attempting to better human life.

Supporters of Marx have replied to such objections by stressing that even Locke and democratic theorists influenced by him, such as Thomas Jefferson, contend that rebellion is justified when governments exercising absolute authority cannot be removed by any other measures. Was it not Jefferson who wrote that the "tree of liberty must be refreshed from time to time by the blood of tyrants"? For Marx, the owners of the means of production are tyrants of this sort. They control the state and use it as an instrument to oppress the people, and since this is so, one cannot employ the usual legal resources of the state (such as the courts, or representative legislative bodies) in order to abolish their control. Rebellion is thus not only necessary but justifiable. To some, this means that force and violence will always be necessary. In fact, in calling attention to the ways in which economic power can be used to subvert democratic political processes, Marx can be thought of as suggesting that genuine political democracy is impossible without economic equality. In stressing this point, he is, as it were, extending the meaning of the word "democracy" and giving it a broader significance than is traditional. But as we have seen, there is implicit in Locke's conception of the "public good" such a doctrine, and Mill was moving in a similar direction, too. The difference between these writers and Marx thus seems to some to be one of degree or emphasis rather than one of principle.

Apart from the question of how Marx is to be classified, Marx's main doctrines have been challenged by philosophers working both within and without the Marxist tradition. Indeed, the volume of criticism which has been directed against Marx is so great that we cannot here hope to list all such objections let alone discuss them. Among the more important which should be mentioned, though, are the following: (1) Marx's reliance upon the dialectic has been objected to on several grounds: (a) that the notion of the dialectic is metaphysical and *a prioristic*, and not subject to empirical verification, (b) that in fact history does not develop in accordance with any such pattern, and (c) that Marx's belief in the *necessity* of the dialectic is inconsistent with his belief in the ultimate disappearance of classes. This set of objections, which involves the rejection of what is called "historicism" is to be found prominently in the work of Karl Popper, a contemporary theorist whom we shall discuss later in this chapter. (2) Marx's moral theory has been objected to on the ground that it refers to an early phase in the development of capitalism which has all but disappeared; in this connection, it is pointed out that the prediction of increasing "self-alienation" in capitalistic societies has not materialized, and that, in fact, capitalism has brought about a state of affluence, prosperity, and well-being among men which surpasses anything known historically. (3) It is also contended that Marx's analysis of capitalism, which depends upon the acceptance of the labor theory of value, is no longer taken seriously by economists. The labor theory of value is now regarded as being neither a true nor even a convenient hypothesis. In general, it is inferred from this that Marx's description of the working of "the market" in capitalism was far too simple, and, accordingly, that his general picture of capitalism is incorrect. (4) It is also pointed out that those nations of the world that have put Marxism into practice have been among the most despotic in history and that it is primarily in capitalist societies that political freedom flourishes. These critics see economic rights as indissolubly linked with political rights and argue that state control over such rights inevitably brings with it the disappearance of political freedom. Such authors as George Orwell, in his books *Animal Farm* and *1984*, and Milovan Djilas, in his work *The New Class*, claim that the formation of power groups, even in a socialist society, is inevitable, and that the abuse of such power can invariably be expected unless the exercise of it is accompanied by the traditional democratic safeguards.[12]

In spite of space limitations, let us look in some detail at one penetrating criticism of Marx's economic theories. According to Marx, it will be remembered, capitalism in inevitable steps will lead to a divided soci-

[12] The late George Orwell, the English novelist and political critic, became disillusioned with the attempt to bring about a better world through the socialistic methods used in the Soviet Union and employed by Communist parties throughout the world. Milovan Djilas, a Communist theoretician, rose to become one of Tito's top assistants in Yugoslavia, but became embittered by the form which socialism took in that country. As a result of the publication of this work, he was stripped of power by Tito and imprisoned. An enormous literature has been developed in the past fifty years, beginning with E. Zamiatin's *We*, through A. Koestler's *Darkness at Noon*, B. Pasternak's *Dr. Zhivago*, to A. Solzhenitsyn's *One Day in the Life of Ivan Denisovich* and his most recent novel *Cancer Ward*, attacking the totalitarian methods of the Soviet Union.

ety: one element of it will control most of the wealth in the community, the other element will be impoverished and forced to work at subsistence levels for members of the first group. This part of Marx's economic doctrine is sometimes called the "law of increasing misery." In meeting this criticism, defenders of capitalism raise two objections. To begin with, they point out that capitalism has been the dominant economic system of the world for several centuries now, and yet the prediction has never been confirmed. The lot of the worker in highly developed countries, instead of growing worse, is steadily getting better. His laboring day has been cut and promises to be shortened even further through additional developments in technology. His wages are higher than ever; he has considerable economic security through the development of pension schemes and other "fringe" benefits. He has a wide variety of jobs from which to choose. No other economic system, it is asserted, has benefited the working class to a similar degree.

Second, these critics claim that although capitalism suffers from periods of inflation and unemployment, these have always been of relatively brief duration. In every such case, they say, the system has been able to solve its difficulties. Using methods of modern finance, which involve governmental monetary control over interest rates, and control over the amount of money in circulation, and such legal means as antitrust laws to inhibit the growth of monopolies, modern governments—often working through international monetary controls—have managed to lessen the impact of periods of recession and retrenchment. Moreover, such devices as labor unions, retirement plans, and social security schemes have all been instrumental in helping the majority of workers to benefit from the system. There is no foreseeable limit to the number of such measures which can be developed, and because this is so, there is no reason to believe that the picture depicted by the law of increasing misery will ever be realized.

Marxists have attempted to counter both of these charges. They point out that although the standard of living in some capitalistic countries (for example, the United States and Canada) is now higher than it used to be, this is not uniformly true (Spain, Portugal, Saudi Arabia and certain South American countries are cited as counter instances). They point out that the favorable position which certain nations occupy in this respect only confirms, on an international level, the Marxist thesis of the law of increasing misery. Those capitalistic nations that enjoy high living standards have achieved them primarily at the expense of those nations that do not. This is particularly true of the "third world" countries—those of Africa and Asia—where the majority of people endure living conditions as grim as anything encountered in England in the early days of the industrial revolution.

Moreover, these defenders of Marx argue, the view that capitalism is able to solve its periodic economic crises is highly misleading. Not only do such "solutions" take an inordinate amount of time, during which many people are thrown out of work, or suffer from inflation, but the measures that are effective are essentially socialistic in spirit and execution. For instance, the growth of labor unions in order to restrict the size of the available labor pool is one such device; social security, as its name implies, is another; deficit spending and monetary controls *by the state* is a third; the restrictions upon the growth of monopolies *by government* is a fourth, and so on. In effect, Marxists regard these as halfway measures toward an ultimately rational system of production and distribution of goods. They argue that insofar as such measures are adopted, the world is now going socialist, in one form or another. This development is taking place somewhat more rapidly in France and Italy, and has already been realized in Yugoslavia, China, Soviet Russia, and Czechoslovakia. History, they assert, is bearing out Marx's predictions that a socialist world is just around the corner.

However one evaluates these claims and counterclaims, it is clear that Marx must be ranked as one of the most influential political theorists of all time. Certainly the contemporary scene, whether at the theoretical or practical level, can hardly be understood without seeing it against the background of Marx's work. Though it has been nearly a century since Marx died, the Marxian tradition has continued in the work of Lenin, Plekhanov, Chairman Mao, Che Guevara, Fidel Castro, George Lukacs in Hungary, Franz Fanon in Algeria, among others. In particular, the work of Karl Popper and of Herbert Marcuse, two of the most distinguished contemporary political philosophers, both show the influence of Marx's thought. In Popper's case, the influence has been negative, and has led to a devastating critique of Marx; but even Popper has said of Marx,

> It is tempting to dwell upon the great similarities between Marxism, the Hegelian left wing, and its Fascist counterpart. Yet it would be utterly unfair to overlook the difference between them. Although their intellectual origin is nearly identical, there can be no doubt of the humanitarian impulse of Marxism. Moreover, in contrast to the Hegelians of the right wing, Marx made an honest attempt to apply rational methods to the most urgent problems of social life. The value of this attempt is unimpaired by the fact that it was, as I shall try to show, largely unsuccessful. Science progresses through trial *and* error. Marx tried, and although he erred in his main doctrines, he did not try in vain. He opened and sharpened our eyes in many ways. A return to pre-Marxian social science is inconceivable. All modern writers are indebted to Marx, even if they do not know it. This is especially true of those who disagree with this doctrine, as I do.[13]

[13] Karl R. Popper, *The Open Society and Its Enemies* (Princeton University Press, Princeton, 1950), p. 274.

In the case of Herbert Marcuse, the situation is different. Though critical of Marx in certain fundamental respects, Marcuse regards himself not as carrying on, but as extending, the Marxist tradition. With Marx's shadow providing the background, let us look at the work of Popper and Marcuse from this perspective.

THE CONTEMPORARY SCENE:
POPPER AND MARCUSE

Karl Popper was born in Vienna in 1902. As a student, his main interests lay in mathematics and physics, and accordingly, he was greatly attracted to the work being done in philosophy of science by members of the Vienna Circle (see chapter on Contemporary Philosophy). Though never a formal member of the Circle, his first book, *The Logic of Scientific Discovery* was published by the Circle in its Journal, in 1935. In 1937, Popper accepted a post at Christchurch University in New Zealand, and it was while there that he wrote his important political treatise, *The Open Society and Its Enemies*, first published in 1945. This work, as we shall see, contains a major attack upon those whom Popper regards as the enemies of democracy (The Open Society), such as Plato, Heraclitus, Hegel, and Marx. In 1945, Popper became Senior Reader at the London School of Economics, and in 1949, Professor of Logic and Scientific Method at that institution. In 1964 he was knighted by Queen Elizabeth II.

Popper is primarily a philosopher of science and a logician, and has made fundamental contributions to those fields. It is important to stress this point because his fundamental criticism of Marx stems from his own investigations into the nature of science. According to Popper in the *Open Society and Its Enemies*, Marx's work rests upon a fundamental misunderstanding of the nature of science. As we have seen, Marx thought of himself as a social *scientist*, that is, as a tough-minded investigator of society, viewing it without presuppositions or bias in order to understand how it works. According to some critics, such as the economist Joan Robinson, Marx's greatest contribution to social science was his discovery that societies are not immutable—that they change, and change in a lawlike manner, which can be understood through scientific inquiry. But such change, because of its slow pace, can only be detected and its patterns elicited, through an historical study. Through the study of history, for example, one can see how feudalism gives way to capitalism; and how capitalism, as a stage in human history, will itself grow, develop and decline. For Marx, therefore, scientific socialism and the historical method converge. But in particular, according to Popper, Marx believes that science discovers immutable and final truth. That the laws of science are necessary and inevitable, Marx takes to be evident. In his attempt to understand the workings of society, in particular of capitalist society, Marx thus attempts to uncover a set of immutable laws, which dictate change, and which, as he predicts, will reveal how capitalism will give way to a new socialist phase in human history.

For Popper, this analysis contains two fallacies. The first is that since the growth of knowledge itself exercises a powerful influence on the course of history, and depends upon the insights of original geniuses—such as Newton and Einstein—neither the growth of knowledge nor its historical consequences in practice can be predicted. Marx thought that the science of society would produce such laws that predictions made in accordance with them would hold universally. But historical change is not straightforward in this way; rather it is an unpredictable set of developments, moving in a more or less haphazard fashion. In his work called *The Poverty of Historicism*, published in 1957, Popper constructs a formal refutation of historicism—and thus of Marxism as a special case of historicism—which runs as follows:

1. The course of human history is strongly influenced by the growth of human knowledge.
2. We cannot predict, by rational or scientific methods, the future growth of our scientific knowledge.
3. We cannot, therefore, predict the future course of human history.
4. This means that we must reject the possibility of a *theoretical* history; that is to say, of an historical social science that would correspond to *theoretical* physics. There can be no scientific theory of historical development serving as a basis for historical prediction.
5. The fundamental aim of historicist methods is therefore misconceived; and historicism collapses.

The first major mistake of Marx, then, was to misconceive the nature of scientific inquiry. Like Marx, Popper maintains that scientific method can be applied to the study of society, but that this method in no way resembles what Marx believed it to be. Science is not identical with historical inquiry, or even with inductive procedures. Rather it involves the creative exercise of imagination in the formation of hypotheses, which are "scientific" only if in principle they are falsifiable. Marx's claims, based upon the discovery of immutable dialectical patterns of historical development, are not falsifiable and hence not scientific. Popper also stresses that science, even when best established, is never certain, but always subject to constant revision in the light of new evidence; there is thus nothing that corresponds to "immutability" in science.

The second major mistake of Marx (and it is true of other "historicists" as well) is to think that science applies to the *whole* of society; that there are laws of the whole system. This Popper calls "holistic" or "Utopian social planning," and opposes it to what he terms "piecemeal social engineering." According to him, the belief in inevitable historical laws, applying to the whole of society, leads to the view that the whole of society should be remodeled in accordance with a definite plan or blue-print. The main difference between these approaches then is that the holistic social reformer decides beforehand that a complete reconstruction of society is possible and necessary. With a vision in mind of a new social order, he radically alters the structure of existing society. But for Popper this attitude has far-reaching negative practical consequences. As he puts it:

> It prejudices the Utopianist against certain sociological hypotheses which state limits to institutional control; for example, the one mentioned above in this section, expressing the uncertainty due to the personal ele-ment, the "human factor." By a rejection *a priori* of such hypotheses, the Utopian approach violates the principles of scientific method. On the other hand, problems connected with the uncertainty of the human factor must force the Utopianist, whether he likes it or not to try to control the human factor by institutional means, and to extend his programme so as to embrace not only the transformation of society, according to plan, but also the transformation of man. . . . It seems to escape the well-mean-ing Utopian that this programme implies an admission of failure, even before he launches it. For it substitutes for his demand that we build a new society, fit for men and women to live in, the demand that we "mould" these men and women to fit into his new society. This, clearly, removes any possibility of testing the success or failure of the new so-ciety. For those who do not like living in it only admit thereby that they are not yet fit to live in it; that their "human impulses" need further "organizing." But without the possibility of tests, any claim that a "sci-entific" method is being employed evaporates. The holistic approach is incompatible with a truly scientific attitude.[14]

This second mistake, the failure to see that science rests upon trial *and* error, upon the advancement of tentative hypotheses and their with-drawal in the light of contrary experience, again can be traced back to a failure in Marx to understand the nature of the scientific method. Holism is thus an untenable interpretation of the nature of science.

Popper's own positive views, in contradistinction to historicists such as Marx, stress the piecemeal, patient, tentative methods of grappling with social issues. These consist in *specific* solutions to specific problems, mainly aimed at minimizing human distress. For Popper, for example, the question which traditional political theorists have regarded as funda-mental, namely, "Who should rule?" should be replaced by the question, "How can institutions be devised that will minimize the risks of bad

[14] Karl R. Popper, *The Poverty of Historicism* (Routledge & Kegan Paul, London, 1957), pp. 69–70.

rulers?" Popper thus stands in the tradition of such writers as Locke and Mill, who wish to enlarge human freedom by restricting the power of rulers to abridge such freedom. The presupposition of all his writing is that dogmatism in any form, whether masking itself as science or as social reform, is dangerous and inimical to liberty. Social advance is thus to be achieved under conditions where the power of the sovereign to initiate wholesale and radical reforms is minimized, and instead is to be the outcome of specific actions devoted to the solution of specific problems and abuses.

Criticism of Popper

Let us mention briefly two criticisms which have been made of Popper's views. The first is that his own view of science is not a conventional one; that it overemphasizes the tentative and piecemeal nature of scientific investigation, and thus produces a picture of science which hardly distinguishes it from philosophy or from any other sort of critical (but nonempirical) inquiry. According to these critics, science is composed of strata, that is, of a spectrum of activities. Some of these activities, at the lowest level of inquiry, have resulted in laws that are so highly established that it is now inconceivable that future discoveries would overturn them, or cause radical revisions in them. Most of the laws of macroscopic bodies in physics are of this order. But at a higher level of theory, science engages in activities whose findings are more dubious and which may in the future require radical revision. Popper's mistake, according to some philosophers of science, is to conflate these various strata, and the laws emanating from them, into a single, overly simple picture of science. It is thus possible, they argue, that the now tentative developments of science might result in the future in well-established, general laws, including those that might apply to society. One cannot, therefore, rule out the possibility of discovering laws which apply to society in something like the sense that Marx had in mind. Such laws would be universal—just as the law of falling bodies is—but might only be *true* of any actual segment of human history given certain historical conditions. The law of falling bodies is universal, yet it does not apply to all bodies at all times and in all conditions, but only to those bodies obeying certain physical conditions. Under those conditions, it does hold of such bodies. The laws which Marx attempted to discover might have much the same general character. Though not always applying, they might apply when the appropriate conditions develop. Thus the law of increasing misery does not always apply; it will hold only when capitalism reaches its final phases, where the possibility of economic expansion is limited or nonexistent, and so forth. Though Marx might have been wrong in thinking that such laws lead to infallible predictions, he was not misguided—as Popper claims—in thinking that universal laws, analogous to physical laws, could be discovered about society.

A second criticism of Popper attacks his concept of piecemeal engineering as too negative. According to this objection, Popper does not see that society is controlled in fact by powerful forces which can only be removed or destroyed by radical procedures—procedures which amount to a total reconstruction of society. Moreover, it is argued, even piecemeal engineering in the end will only make sense if it is directed in the service of a general scheme, whose aim is the total betterment of mankind. It will do no good to treat as a local phenomenon a difficulty—such as pollution —which may stem from deeper underlying causes, such as the profit motive, so characteristic of capitalism. The contention, then, is that Popper's views amount to a defense of the *status quo*, with its existing power structures, and do not provide a guide to a deeper attack upon the underlying causes of human misery, such as those diagnosed by Marx. It is this sort of thrust which we find prominently developed in the work of Herbert Marcuse.

The Political Philosophy
of Herbert Marcuse

Marcuse was born in Berlin in 1898, and studied at the Universities of Berlin and Freiburg, receiving his Ph.D. from the latter institution in 1922. For the next decade he did postgraduate research work at Freiburg, studying for several years with Martin Heidegger, the famous existentialist. In 1932, Marcuse, Theodor Adorno and Max Horkheimer founded the Frankfurt Institute for Social Research which through its application of Marxist theory to practical social problems became a center in Germany for a group of radical sociologists, economists, and philosophers. With the rise of Nazism, Marcuse left Germany, first going to Switzerland and then in 1936 to the United States. During the Second World War he served as an intelligence analyst with the Office of Strategic Services. In the years that followed, he taught at a number of institutions—Columbia, Harvard, and Brandeis, and in 1965, after retiring from Brandeis, he joined the staff at the University of California, San Diego.

Marcuse is the author of five important works which, though showing the strong influence of Freud, Hegel, and Marx, are highly original studies of society. They are *Reason and Revolution* (1941), *Eros and Civilization* (1955), *One-Dimensional Man* (1964), *An Essay on Liberation* (1969) and *Repressive Tolerance* (1965) (which appeared in a volume authored by Marcuse, Robert Wolff and Barrington Moore entitled *A Critique of Pure Tolerance*). It is the last of these which is of special interest to us here, but before turning to it let us briefly describe some of the other works, since their doctrines are intimately connected with those expressed in *Repressive Tolerance*.

Eros and Civilization, subtitled a "Philosophical Inquiry into Freud," attempted to describe a nonrepressive society. Freud had argued (for example in *Civilization and Its Discontents*) that society necessarily frustrates man's basic instincts, which are on the whole aggressive and antisocial, in order to establish and preserve civilization. Thus collective human survival depends upon society acting coercively against the dispositions in human nature for aggressive and egoistic behavior.

But Marcuse points out that the problems of scarcity, which reinforce such antisocial impulses and thus impel people to obtain their own security at the expense of others, have essentially been overcome in materially affluent societies. The need for repression is thus no longer required because the technical possibility of producing all the material goods for society now exist. The conditions thus obtain which would allow culture —seen as the free development of the self (Eros)—to supplant the previous style of Western civilization as culture-bound to Logos, that is, to domination.

But not much later, Marcuse's own views had become less optimistic. In his 1961 preface to *Eros and Civilization*, he commented that though the conditions for such freedom exist, "The very idea of a nonrepressive civilization, conceived as a real possibility of the established civilization at the present stage, appears frivolous." He was now disposed to argue that the transition to a new stage of civilization could only be effected through a subversion of the traditional intellectual and material culture, through the liberation of instinctual needs and satisfactions which up to now had been repressed. But some three years later, in *One-Dimensional Man*, he was even more pessimistic about such an outcome.

This work, as a study of the ideology of advanced industrial society, acknowledges the power of the established social order to arrest and prevent social change. Its basic thrust is to show, in a concrete way, how technology serves to institute novel and more efficient controls over society. In an important sense, it is both an expansion of fundamental insights of Marx and a rejection of one of Marx's most important doctrines—the Law of Increasing Misery. Marx had written (see quote on page 237), "The new-fangled sources of wealth, by some strange weird spell, are turned to sources of want. The victories of art seem bought by the loss of character. At the same pace that mankind masters nature, man seems to become enslaved to other men or to his own infamy. Even the pure light of science seems unable to shine but on the dark background of ignorance."[15] *One-Dimensional Man* expatiates on this theme; in it, Marcuse develops a doctrine in which society, though possessing the technological means for eliminating want, repression, and control, now exercises control in more and more subtle ways. The anti-Marxist element in

15 Karl Marx, *Selected Works* (International Publishers, New York, 1963), Vol. II, pp. 427–428.

this suggestion is that capitalism, with its highly-developed controls over society, will not lead to a situation in which the majority of people are reduced to a subsistence level of existence, but instead will produce affluence, while at the same time exercising those controls over humanity which scarcity no longer requires or justifies. There is a cautious suggestion in this work that reversal of this trend is possible, though remote, given the overwhelming dominance of the established society as expressed in news media, politics, culture, research, science, thought, and even philosophy.

An Essay on Liberation is Marcuse's what a society would be like— if it could be obtained—which lacked such domination. Here Marcuse stresses that the subversion of existing society will arise only if men and women begin to deny the exploitative power of the establishment—this is the needed subversion anticipated in *Eros and Civilization*. In a very cautious and guarded way, he sees the beginning of these developments in the growing struggles in the Third World for national liberation, in the world-wide student movement, and other types of minority developments.

Almost all of these later doctrines can be found expressed in a clear and powerful way in his *Repressive Tolerance* of 1965. Here Marcuse argues that freedom has yet to be created, even for the freest of existing societies. Under certain existing conditions, he argues, the tolerance of some ideas, forms of speech, policies, and behavior turns tolerance into an instrument of servitude. Accordingly, he maintains, the restoration of freedom of thought may necessitate the withdrawal of such civil rights as speech and assembly from groups which demonstrably promote aggression, discrimination, race hatred, and other forms of regressive social policies. To do otherwise is to pervert and frustrate the social function which tolerance was historically conceived to fulfill. The inability of the normal democratic procedures and liberties to forestall the (legal) takeover by the Nazis of Germany is recalled: "If democratic tolerance had been withdrawn," he writes, "when the future leaders started their campaign, mankind would have had a chance of avoiding Auschwitz and a World War."

Criticism of Marcuse

Though other writers have advanced some views not dissimilar to those expressed by Marcuse, his originality lies in providing such views with an explicit theoretical foundation. The sweeping character of his doctrines makes him perhaps the first full-fledged philosophical theorist of modern, affluent, industrial society. In this respect, he differs from the major thinkers of the Marxist tradition, who see dominance by power groups as stemming from lack of economic resources. Where there is scarcity, according to the traditional view, men will act in selfish, egoistic, and antisocial ways in order to secure for themselves an undue proportion of available goods. Social systems are thus conceived as devices for backing those elements in society which wish to obtain a disproportionate amount of the available goods. The power elite—whether kings or elected "representatives" of the people—are viewed in this light.

But Marcuse sees the situation differently. For him, the interesting, and deplorable, condition of contemporary society is that even where such conditions of scarcity do not obtain, the disposition to continue to control human beings persists. But now it persists in much more subtle and profound ways. The sophisticated machinery of modern technology is employed by those who control society to "moronize" the public, and to control it in subtle and effective ways. The result is that it is not the people who in fact rule, but these special groups.

Marcuse thus sees himself as a defender of democracy. As he writes in *Repressive Tolerance*:

> In this case, the discussion can have as a frame of reference only a democratic society, in which the people as individuals and as members of political and other organizations, participate in the making, sustaining and changing of policies. In authoritarian systems, the people do not tolerate— they suffer the established policies.[16]

His work is thus clearly in the tradition of those who defend the right of the people to govern themselves. But this, he argues, is possible only where the majority of the people can make informed and rational decisions about matters of public policy. And it is just these conditions which are absent from democratic societies in the present stage of civilization. For paradoxically enough, those who control the media of information— speaking the language of freedom and tolerance—restrict the sources of information, debate, and argument which make government by the people possible. The people are not given the information to make rational decisions about matters of public policy; instead, they are subtly manipulated, coerced and constrained to hold doctrines which run counter to their real interests. Marcuse's demand for a *restriction* upon such controls stems from a basic desire to make democratic government work. He thus defends a form of censorship in order to make freedom possible—a view which reverses the traditional libertarian position we have seen espoused in Mill's writings, especially *On Liberty*.

Critics have strongly objected to this doctrine. Though many of them agree that modern society exercises just such subtle "co-optive" controls

---

[16] Herbert Marcuse, "Repressive Tolerance," in *A Critique of Pure Tolerance* (with R. P. Wolff and Barrington Moore, Jr.) (Beacon Press, Boston, 1965), p. 92.

as Marcuse depicts, they feel that his recommendations will not bring about a state of self-government as that is ordinarily understood. Instead, they argue, his doctrines would produce a state which would have an official censor. Marcuse, in effect, wishes to censor those who are unofficial censors of society; but his proposals will only produce a state of affairs in which the unofficial censor will be replaced by the official censor. The plausibility of his view, they state, turns upon the fact that Marcuse's censor will inhibit *only* the activities of those he feels to be highly injurious to the realization of self-government. But then how is one to insure that such a censor will restrict himself in these ways? More basically, they claim, the resulting society, whatever its merits, must not be confused with a self-governing society. Its citizens will cast their votes, not based on *all* the information and debate that may be available, but on information that has been sifted through the censorial sieve.

In effect, what is wrong with Marcuse's argument according to some critics is that it presupposes that censorship in a democratic society is a *legitimate* political device. But this assumption is inconsistent with the fundamental principles of self-government which cannot impose any restrictions upon the right to know. If Marcuse's solution could be implemented, these critics say, the resulting "democratic" society would be governed by an elite, exercising benevolent control over others, and this is surely incompatible with the concept of self-government as that has been traditionally understood.

Many of these critics are in agreement with Marcuse that in modern democratic societies the ideal of self-government is not realized in practice. But, they contend, one does not close the gap between ideal and practice by compounding the number of repressive forces—whether they are to be called "objective censors" or "the military-industrial complex" —but by eliminating or neutralizing them. The present society in which we live does not provide guarantees that distortion will always be confronted by truth in an open forum, but it does in general provide for this *possibility* (for example, the extensive left-wing press) and it is a goal worth striving for. It is better, they argue, to take one's chances with the system as it is than to give it up entirely by building an official form of censorship into it. What self-government entails is not only the possibility of, but also the need for, political action by those who wish to change the society in which they live. By instituting a system of censorship, no matter how well intended its aims, one minimizes the possibility of such action, and substitutes for the political struggle, with its contending interests, a system in which doctrinal purity is the highest ideal. Involvement in politics is thus the correct answer to the difficulty diagnosed by Marcuse. As these critics see it, the struggle is endless, but its possibility and necessity are what democracy is all about.

THE NEW PHILOSOPHERS

Marcuse's work was especially influential in Europe during the late 1960s and early 1970s. Though many European intellectuals still believe that his analysis of post-industrial society—and especially its tendency to "moronize" and "coopt" a majority of citizens—is correct, there has been sharp criticism of the theory of repressive tolerance. The leaders of this movement are a group of French writers called "The New Philosophers." Among them are Bernard-Henry Levy, whose book, *Barbarism With a Human Face*, launched the movement; André Glucksmann, whose *The Master Thinkers* sold 65,000 copies in an eight-week period in 1977; Jean-Marie Benoist (*Marx is Dead*); Philippe Nemo (*The Structural Man*); Guy Landreau and Christian Jambet (*The Angel*); and Maurice Clavel. Most of these writers were persons who participated in the outburst of protest that nearly brought France to its knees in 1968; many of them were Communists or Maoists. But in the 1970s, greatly influenced by the revelations of Soviet suppression of civil liberties as described in Solzhenitsyn's *The Gulag Archipelago* (1974), they have united in opposition to Marxism in all of its forms. As Glucksmann writes: "We are a handful of pebbles in the pond. The pond is Marxism and it is our opposition to it that brings us together."

The central insistence of this group is that theory must take account of its political implications, and that the left has not only been guilty of ignorance and cowardice but also of complicity in refusing for so long to admit and challenge the brutalities of the Soviet political system. Emerging from the very heart of Marxism, and speaking with an expertise and immediacy that only those steeped in that tradition can command, they argue that Marxism is monstrous by its very nature, not by any accident of history or by the sorts of personalities (Stalin, Malenkov, Beria, and Brezhnev) that the system has allowed to float to the top. On the other hand, leaders of the French, Italian, and Spanish Communist parties are presenting a modified form of communism which they claim is compatible with democracy.

Their own positive views, though seldom explicitly acknowledged as stemming from such, seen to harken back to Mill's *On Liberty* and to Popper's *Open Society and Its Enemies*. Bernard-Henry Levy, for instance, who is the most pessimistic of the lot, is convinced that the notion of making things better is a total illusion, but moreover that it is the kind of illusion that leads to totalitarianism. He rejects as a kind of "arrogance" the whole idea of "enlightenment," the idea that through reason and education one can gradually produce a better society. Instead, he believes that the intellectual's attempt to force his values upon the people is a form of domination that attempts to mold man to society, rather than developing a kind of society that reflects the differences and divergences in the values men hold. In particular, the socialist ideal of producing a "new man" is singularly abhorrent to him. This "new man" will be a parody of an authentic human being, a veritable robot developed to satisfy the will of society.

Levy is not a nihilist or radical anarchist. His positive view seems to come close to what Popper has called "peacemeal engineering," the notion that instead of the imposition of a holistic blueprint upon society, what is needed is a persistent, detailed, and practical effort to patch things up, to correct in a detailed and limited way inefficiencies, and thus to improve society by dealing pragmatically with specific problems. The aim is thus to improve society by a step-by-step process instead of trying to solve all its problems by an overall, systematic program. The effect is to reassert the importance of the individual against the state, to reduce the power of the "masters of society," and thus to reduce the domination of society over individual persons.

Marcuse's notion that society tends to be a repressive force is captured and elaborated by these writers, but their stress is different. In particular, they reject the concept that any imposition on freedom of expression is ever justified in the name of the overriding importance of the state. Whether the impact these writers will have upon social and political theory in Europe will lead to a resurgence of libertarianism remains questionable given the dominance that various forms of socialism still exercise. But it is clear that their protests are being taken seriously and may well have long-range influence.

In the United States, similar defenses of forms of the liberal tradition have been mounted, notably by John Rawls in his monumental work, *A Theory of Justice* (1971), and by Robert Nozick's *Anarchy, State and Utopia* (1974), works which, to be sure, themselves differ in theoretical stance. (For a discussion of Rawls' work see the chapter on ethics, pp. 324 ff.)

THE CONTEMPORARY SCENE: SOME CURRENT ISSUES

We have stressed in this chapter that the problems of political theory are on the one hand ancient and persistent problems which come down to us in roughly the same form as they were posed by Plato and Aristotle, and are on the other hand problems that arise in new circumstances and therefore demand different treatment. In the latter respect, the applications required of certain principles may lead to different solutions and different analyses. The rise of modern science since the seventeenth century and its resultant spin-offs in technology have created radically different circumstances for applying such political principles. We have seen the effects which science has had upon man's understanding of his place in the universe and the implications which this has had for religion and morality. The technological changes brought about by scientific developments have created that huge upheaval in man's behavior which has lasted for two centuries and is traditionally called the Industrial Revolution. We have hardly seen the last act of this drama as it plays itself out in a variety of ways—its impact upon the environment, upon population, upon the nation–state, upon life styles. All of these developments, as we have already indicated in the preceding chapters, raise serious problems of a political and social sort. They raise problems about man's ability to control such technology—in particular, the horrendous power contained in nuclear weapons, the ceaseless demand for energy, and the ability to work out an economic system which equalizes privilege and at the same time provides a decent level of well-being for all.

From a long-range standpoint, the latest of such scientific developments which has immense implications for mankind is to be found in biology. In the past decade, new understandings of the nature of life at the microbiological level have been achieved, and on the basis of this kind of experimental work it now appears likely that the slow working of nature in creating evolutionary change can be interfered with by man. Scientists are now in the incipient phases of being able to alter the genetic make-up of microbes, changing their DNA components and thus creating new organisms. The potentiality of altering human genetic materials in a radical way now lies on the horizon. Clearly this raises not only scientific questions about the propriety of such research, but, more importantly, political and moral questions. Suppose that disease can be eliminated by selective elimination of those genetic defects that lead to such illnesses as cancer, heart disease, and sickle-cell anemia. Suppose indeed—and this is not an unlikely prospect—that human beings can be made immortal. What are the political consequences of such a development? Does it then mean that the race should be stabilized so that no further new persons will be allowed to be born? Does it entail that everyone suffering from a disabling disease should be required to undergo a genetic transformation? Who is to make such decisions and what kinds of political organizations at the state, national, and international levels would be required to make wise and judicious decisions? If cloning (the reproduction of a certain person to produce exact copies) is ordained in order to select the best and most suitable persons for such a Brave New World, who is to decide who the best are, and what will the political and moral consequences of such decisions be? These are among the great issues that will face the world of the twenty-first century; along with those perennial issues of war, racial problems, economic pressures, and the control of the population, such issues will test the mettle, courage, and intelligence of new generations.

Despite the changing character of such challenges provided by these new scientific and technological breakthroughs, it nonetheless remains clear that the ancient political problems remain the same: "Who is to rule the new society?" "What is the purpose or end that such ruling should try to achieve?" "What ought to be the power of the state versus the right of each individual to realize his or her own capacities?" "How much diversity in behavior can be allowed in society?" The answers to these questions are not easy; if they can be found, they will differ in detail from the answers supplied by Plato, Aristotle, Hobbes, Locke, Rousseau, Kant, and Mill. But some of the answers will make use of some of the principles developed by these philosophers. Accordingly, to read their works, to understand and reflect upon their basic insights, will always be relevant to any assessment of, or decisions about, man's ultimate welfare as a social being.

BIBLIOGRAPHY
Classical Works
Aristotle. *Politics* (Oxford, New York, 1958).

Hegel, G. F. *The Philosophy of History* (Dover, New York, 1956).

Hobbes, Thomas. *The Leviathan* (Bobbs-Merrill Library of Liberal Arts, Indianapolis, 1958). Also reprinted in an abridged version in *The English Philosophers from Bacon to Mill*, edited by E. A. Burtt (Modern Library, New York, 1939).

Locke, John. *Second Treatise on Civil Government* (Bobbs-Merrill Library of Liberal Arts, Indianapolis, 1952). Also reprinted in *The English Philosophers from Bacon to Mill*, edited by E. A. Burtt (Modern Library, New York, 1939).

Machiavelli, Nicolo. *The Prince* (Modern Library, New York, 1950).

Marx, Karl. *Das Kapital*. Selections from this work are to be found in a three-volume edition, published in New York in 1967 by the International Publishing Company.

————. *Early Writings* (Random House, New York, 1975).

————, and Friedrich. Engels, *The Communist Manifesto* (Pelican-Penguin, Baltimore, 1968).

Mill, John Stuart. *On Liberty* (Bobbs-Merrill, Indianapolis, 1956).

More, Sir Thomas. *Utopia* (Norton, New York, 1975).

Plato. *The Republic* (Oxford, New York, 1952).

Rousseau, J. J. *Social Contract* (Pelican-Penguin, Baltimore, 1968).

Modern Works
Marcuse, Herbert. "Repressive Tolerance," in *A Critique of Pure Tolerance*, edited by Robert Paul Wolff, Barrington Moore, and Herbert Marcuse (Beacon Press, Boston, 1969).

————. *One Dimensional Man* (Beacon Press, Boston, 1964).

————. *An Essay on Liberation* (Beacon Press, Boston, 1969).

Popper, Karl. *Conjecture and Refutations: The Growth of Scientific Knowledge* (Harper & Row, New York, 1969).

———. *The Open Society and Its Enemies*, 5th ed. (Princeton University Press, Princeton, N. J., 1966).

———. *Poverty of Historicism* (Harper & Row, New York, 1977).

Rader, Melvin. *Ethics and the Human Community* (Holt, Rinehart and Winston, New York, 1964).

———. *Ethics and Society* (Greenwood, Westport, Conn., 1968).

Sabine, George. *A History of Political Thought*, 3d ed. (Holt, Rinehart and Winston, New York, 1961).

Weldon, T. D. *States and Morals* (Transatlantic Press, Levittown, N.Y., 1973).

chapter 4

Socrates (469–399 B.C.); birthplace—Greece (below left)

Aristotle Contemplating the Bust of Homer by Rembrandt van Rijn (1653) (below)

Jeremy Bentham (1748–1832); birthplace
—England (above)

John Stuart Mill (1806–1873); birthplace
—England (above right)

George Edward Moore (1873–1958); birthplace—England (right)

ETHICS

WHAT IS ETHICS?

Although the philosopher's use of the word "ethics" resembles the ordinary, nontechnical employment of that term in certain respects, it also differs from it sharply in others. When the ordinary man uses this expression, he is almost always referring to a set of principles, or a set of rules, which sanction or forbid certain kinds of conduct. For example, when he speaks of the "ethics of the medical profession," he has in mind that set of principles which determine the conduct of the physician vis-à-vis his patients and other members of the profession. Or again, when he uses the phrase "business ethics," he is generally referring to the code (usually implicit) which regulates, or at least ought to regulate, the conduct of a businessman toward his customers, employees, and competitors.

The philosopher commonly uses the word in this sense, too. In speaking of "Christian ethics," for instance, he will generally be referring to certain principles of conduct accepted by members of that religion—principles such as are found in the Ten Commandments. But the philosopher also uses the word in a somewhat broader sense. More typically, he employs it to denote a branch of philosophy whose subject matter differs on the whole from that (say) of epistemology, or logic, or metaphysics. The problem of explaining the nature of ethics, in this broader sense, is thus tantamount to showing how it differs from the other divisions of philosophy.

We might begin this task by stressing that the difference between the other branches of philosophy and ethics is not that the former are theoretical while the latter is merely practical. Ethics is a theoretical subject. It mainly differs from the other divisions of philosophy in what it theorizes about. Whereas the logician deals with the nature of argument and the epistemologist with the nature of knowledge, the moral philosopher specu-lates about the nature of the good life, about the ultimate worth of the goals men seek, and about the supposed propriety of certain courses of conduct.

As thus conceived, ethics is partly a "normative" or "hortatory" discipline and partly an "analytical" or "meta-ethical" one (for a fuller discussion of these terms see Chapter 3, "Political Philosophy," pages 192–193). Insofar as a moral philosopher engages in normative ethical speculation, his activities will result in theories which recommend, ap-praise, and justify the selection of certain goals and/or certain courses of conduct as being morally worthwhile. Insofar as he is "analytical," he will try to explain the meaning (or meanings) of the key terms which appear in such recommendations, appraisals, and suggestions. He may do this, of course, without committing himself to any hortatory doctrine, or he may do this in the process of, or preliminary to, advocating some such view. But in either case, the result of his inquiries will be formulations that go beyond the merely practical in attempting to give a theoretical account of the matters under consideration.

At the same time, in asserting this we should not be understood as suggesting that ethics has no relevance to the practical difficulties which confront ordinary men. On the contrary, ethical theorizing almost always stems from the efforts of human beings to solve the practical, immediate, and pressing problems which arise in everyday living; in the final analysis, the test of such theorizing will lie in its capacity to help them do so. Consider a situation of the following sort, by way of example: Suppose that a man believes he should not take a human life, and suppose that he also believes he is obligated to defend his country against foreign invaders. What should he do when his country is attacked? If he refuses to fight for it, he violates his obligation to defend it. If, on the other hand, he does fight for it, he may take a human life in the course of doing so. What ought he to do in these circumstances?

Moral philosophy begins from and its results are relevant to situa-tions of this sort. The philosopher puts himself, as it were, in the position of a man caught in a moral dilemma. But unlike the plain man who may be satisfied with finding a personal solution to a problem, the philosopher probes more deeply. He generalizes beyond the immediate case, attempt-ing in the process to develop principles that can be consistently applied not only to the particular matter in question but also to all moral perplexi-ties, and in this way to be of service in resolving them.

What distinguishes the moral philosopher from the ordinary man is thus not the subject matter of his speculations, nor is it the practical implications of such speculations; it is the extent to which they are pushed. In this respect, the philosopher also differs from the psychiatrist, the social worker, the reformer, the minister, or the newspaper columnist who gives advice to the "lovelorn." All of these persons may, in the exercise of their professional duties, utilize theories of one sort or another in dealing with moral matters, but their manner of doing so is not likely, as it is with the philosopher, to issue in further theories, or even to extend the limits of those which are being appealed to. The difference is perhaps merely one of degree, but it is a difference worth noting nonetheless.

Moral theories are not only studied by philosophers because they may have important consequences for everyday living, but also because they are of intellectual interest in their own right. Doctrines which appear sound upon a first examination may, under scrutiny, seem defective and in drastic need of repair if their basic principles are not to be rejected. By way of illustration, consider some of the perplexities involved in Kant's moral theory. Kant argues that everyone ought to behave as if his course of conduct were to become a universal law. On this ground, he maintains, lying is never morally justifiable, since no one could desire that lying become a universal practice. But if this analysis is accepted, then certain difficulties appear elsewhere in the system, especially when it is applied to conflicts of duties. Suppose, for instance, I promise to keep a secret, and then someone else insists that I reveal it under conditions where I am obliged to tell the truth (such as in a court of law when under oath). If I tell the truth, I will break my promise to keep the secret, and if I keep my promise, I will not tell the truth. Yet it seems a consequence of the Kantian position that, as a moral being, I must always tell the truth and always keep my promises. Does this mean that there is a fundamental inconsistency in Kant's doctrine—or can the difficulty somehow be overcome? Part of the motivation for studying ethics lies in the efforts by philosophers to answer such queries—and in so doing, of course, to provide intellectually satisfactory accounts of the principles which ought to govern the behavior of men.

As can be inferred from these remarks, ethics is a discipline in which human conduct, human character, and human aims are studied via the media of theories about them. This being so, let us turn now to a consideration of some notable and important theories of this sort.

THE MORAL VIEWS
OF SOCRATES

There is no doubt that the pre-Socratic philosophers reflected deeply upon moral matters. But the information we have about their speculations is so fragmentary that any attempt to attribute explicit ethical theories to these thinkers is bound to be conjectural at best. Rather than attempting any such reconstruction, therefore, we shall turn to the views of a man about whom we seem to have a store of information. This is Socrates, the protagonist of the Platonic dialogues. But even in this case, there are difficulties. Since Socrates reputedly wrote nothing, the main evidence for his opinions comes to us second hand and primarily from Plato's writings. Are the views he espouses in these works really his own or those of the author? The question is one which has exercised the ingenuity of scholars for nearly two thousand years.

Some authorities have even taken the radical position that Socrates never existed at all—that he was merely a creation of Plato's fertile literary imagination. This supposition is not widely accepted nowadays. Not only does it run counter to the evidence that Socrates was mentioned by writers of his own time, such as Xenophon and Aristophanes, but also to the fact that many of the important moral doctrines of ancient Greece can be traced back to an original Socratic source. Socrates was the informal teacher not only of Plato but also of many others who gathered in the agora at Athens to hear him speak. This group included Phaedo of Elis, Euclid of Megara (not to be confused with Euclid, the famous mathematician), Aristippus of Cyrene, and Antisthenes of Athens.[1] All of these men later developed schools of philosophy which were to compete with Plato's Academy and Aristotle's Lyceum in importance. All of them regarded themselves as pupils of Socrates and attributed to him the fundamental insight on which they built their various systems—the insight which is often stated as "virtue is knowledge." Each of them, to be sure, interpreted these words in radically disparate ways, Aristippus understanding them to mean that pleasure is the sole good, Antisthenes construing them to mean that the only thing worth having is a character immune to the vacillating influences of the material world, and so on.

Given this evidence, it seems probable that somebody named "Socrates" did exist in Athens in the fifth century; that this person had become famous among the philosophically inclined youth of the city; and that he held definite, and strikingly important, views on moral matters. Assuming these things to be so, what were these views and how did they eventually lead to the development of such diverse schools of thought as hedonism, Cynicism, and Platonism? Let us attempt to answer these questions now.

As we shall try to show in this chapter, the history of hortatory ethical speculation, whether ancient or modern, can be interpreted in the

[1] The Roman author, Aulus Gellius, claims that in spite of an edict which was passed forbidding Megarians to enter Athens, Euclid, disguised as a woman, regularly came at night to hear Socrates discourse on philosophy. Euclid and Phaedo were part of the small group in attendance at the death of Socrates (as related in Plato's *Phaedo*).

light of the attempt to answer two questions: (1) What is the good life for man? (2) How ought men, insofar as they are moral beings, to behave? By the time of Immanuel Kant (1724–1804), each of these questions seemed enormously different from the other and each seemed to pose difficulties in its own right. But for Socrates, the answer to the second seemed obvious. Men ought to act in such a way as to achieve the good life. It was the first question which was the more troublesome—namely, what constitutes the good life? In dealing with this problem, the teaching of Socrates can be summarized in a sentence: *The good life can be discovered if and only if men have knowledge.*

In a sense, this remark is an evasion. It does not directly answer the question. Socrates does not purport to tell us what the good life is (here he differs from the Cynics, Stoics, Aristotelians, and hedonists) but only what we must do in order to discover it. Nevertheless it was a remark of great historical significance. It was accepted by almost all the major Greek moralists who followed Socrates (with some qualifications in the case of Aristotle). On this point, they were in agreement. It was from their efforts to specify the nature of the good life that disagreement ensued. The various schools we have mentioned were mainly to arise from such disagreements.

The doctrine we are discussing is sometimes termed "the Socratic paradox." The paradox lies in the fact that although men in fact act immorally, none do so deliberately. For it was Socrates' belief that if a man knows what is good, he will always act in such a way as to try to achieve it. Evil, seen from this standpoint, is thus always the product of ignorance (that is, a case of a man believing something to be good when it is not). Socrates defended this point of view by the following argument: The good, he maintained, is that which is most serviceable to men. Everyone aims at doing that which is most serviceable to himself. It is, accordingly, unthinkable that anyone should not do that which he recognizes as being most serviceable to himself. If anyone should act in a way which is not conducive to his own good, therefore, this action must result from a failure to recognize what is good in those circumstances. It follows from this that immoral action is always due to lack of knowledge. It is this doctrine which is often summarized in the epigram "virtue is knowledge," and perhaps also in the remark "nobody errs wittingly."

PLATO'S ETHICS

As we have indicated, it is difficult to determine where in the Platonic writings, composed as they were over a period of nearly fifty years, the views of Socrates leave off and those of Plato begin. One common interpretation suggests that in the early dialogues, Plato is primarily a reporter, dramatizing the views of his teacher with consummate literary skill but on the whole accurately relating them, whereas the middle and later dialogues reflect his own opinions almost entirely. Scholars who adhere to this interpretation, which is a commonly accepted one, generally distinguish Plato's outlook from that of Socrates on two counts: (1) Socrates is usually interpreted as having refused to commit himself on the question of whether knowledge can be attained at all. His characteristic activities of probing into the grounds for men's beliefs, his role as the "gadfly" of Athens, were designed to show that ordinary men invariably make important moral decisions without having the requisite knowledge to make them properly. This is a portrait of Socrates which emerges from the early dialogues, such as the *Euthyphro* and *Charmides*. In these dialogues, Socrates skeptically says of himself that he is the wisest of all men because, unlike others, he knows that he knows nothing. But in the later dialogues, he is far more dogmatic, arguing that knowledge is possible and even indicating how it can be attained. Scholars who distinguish between the views of Socrates and those of Plato maintain that it is Plato himself who is speaking at these later junctures. (2) Again, it is the Socrates of the early dialogues who argues that if a person does not have knowledge, he will act immorally, whereas a similar, but nevertheless, different position is suggested by the Socrates of the later works, such as *The Republic*. In this treatise, Socrates maintains that it is possible for some men to lead the good life without possessing knowledge. They might do so if they are men having a virtuous character which has been molded through their imitating people who are already virtuous. But in all such cases, they will lead the good life only haphazardly, or accidentally, as it were. It is only if they possess knowledge that they will necessarily act morally. Once again, scholars ascribe the latter doctrine to Plato, the former to Socrates.

Let us accept the interpretation which distinguishes between their views, since it will help us bring out the main features of the moral standpoint which is traditionally associated with Plato's name. This doctrine is intimately connected with Plato's celebrated theory of knowledge, on the one hand, and with his equally famous political theory, on the other. For this reason, no full account of his moral views is possible without treating these other subjects at the same time. Since both have already been discussed in Chapter 1, "The Theory of Knowledge," and in Chapter 3, "Political Philosophy," we shall not discuss them in detail here. We shall touch upon them only insofar as they directly bear upon any accurate account of the moral theory itself.

Like Socrates, Plato never definitely answers the question "What is the good life for man?" But that he regarded the question as fundamental is beyond cavil. Throughout his writings, he suggests one answer after another; but those he arrives at are either held tentatively or rejected elsewhere. In the *Protagoras*, for instance, he entertains the hypothesis that the good life is a life of pleasure; yet in the *Gorgias* and again in the *Phaedo*, he explicitly denies pleasure to be a good at all. The question is returned to repeatedly in such dialogues as *The Republic, Laws, Philebus* and *Timaeus*, without an answer being fixed upon. What motivates this intensive search for the good life is that Plato, like Socrates, believes that if a man knows what is good, he will always act so as to try to attain it. The problem, of course, is to ascertain what goodness consists in.

Plato differs from Socrates not only in believing that knowledge of the good is possible but also in specifying how we can go about achieving it. His contention is that discovering the nature of the good is an intellectual task analogous to that required in order to uncover a deep-lying scientific law. Just as the latter cannot be discovered by untrained people so the former cannot be either. In order to discover the nature of the good life men must be subjected to a long period of intellectual training in such subjects as mathematics, astronomy, music, and philosophy. Through such intensive instruction, they can eventually acquire knowledge—and once having knowledge, they will then be in a position to understand the nature of the good. In this way, the search for the good life is tied to the theory of knowledge.

The reason why men must possess knowledge in order to understand the nature of the good is somewhat complex to explain (for a much fuller treatment of this point, see pages 36–39). But roughly, the explanation is this: For Plato, goodness is a form (or idea or universal). Such forms, being unchanging and eternal, are never apprehended by the senses, which grasp only changing things. Instead, they are apprehended through the use of reason (this remark would have to be qualified in a more detailed explanation in order to accommodate Plato's mysticism in Book VI of *The Republic*, but it will suffice for our purposes here). Insofar as reason dispenses with props derived from sense experience, it moves more and more toward an awareness of such forms. When a person finally apprehends them, he possesses knowledge. The understanding of the nature of the good life is, in this way, equated with the eventual possession of knowledge.

The connection between the moral theory and the political doctrine is less complex to unravel, even though it involves touching upon Plato's psychological analysis of human nature. This analysis begins from the supposed fact that men differ innately or inherently. Thus, by nature some men have the capacity to run faster than others, some to be taller than others, and some to learn better than others. It also seems a fact of nature that not all men have the capacity to acquire knowledge. Plato felt that it would be pointless to subject those having such intellectual limitations to years of academic training whose goal would be the acquisition of knowledge. Nonetheless, unlike Socrates, he believed that such individuals could be trained to lead good lives. Indeed, he argued, it was essential for the development of any harmonious society that the majority of people in it be moral, even if they were not capable of grasping the nature of the good by rational means. For these individuals, a different training program would have to be instituted. The result is that Plato's blueprint for an ideal social organization contains two highly dissimilar proposals for educating people, depending upon whether or not they have the capacity to acquire knowledge.

Those who do not are to be educated under conditions of strict censorship and are to be debarred from ruling society. Their training is designed to produce individuals of commendable character, who will obey the laws passed by the rulers and work harmoniously with their fellows. Individuals having such a character can be produced, though, only if the circumstances in which their habits are formed are carefully supervised in order to eliminate undesirable influences—and hence the need for censorship. Plato's assumption is that once such desirable habits are instilled in the majority of the people they will, on the whole, act virtuously, although deviations from this pattern will undoubtedly take place in those circumstances where habits cannot provide them with a guide to conduct.

It is otherwise with those having the potential ability to acquire knowledge. They are to receive intensive instruction which will not only develop virtuous habits in them but also enable them to acquire knowledge. Once having acquired knowledge, they will come to understand the nature of the good. This will ensure their always acting rightly or morally, and hence will guarantee their being good rulers. The result will, of course, be a just society.

From the standpoint of pure moral theory (as distinct from its applications to politics and religion, for example), Plato's claim that knowledge of the good life is possible has been of the greatest theoretical importance. Platonism constitutes one of the classical bulwarks against a commonly held point of view often termed "moral skepticism." In Plato's own day, the most vigorous exponents of this outlook were the Sophists, but it is an outlook which has never really vanished from the philosophical scene. Even today it is commonly encountered, not only among professional thinkers but also among ordinary men who look at moral matters reflectively. They will often boast that it is their "philosophy of life."

Advocates of this doctrine maintain that moral standards or moral principles, such as "thou shalt not steal," are basically the products of arbitrary human decisions. Such decisions, they argue, merely reflect the attitudes, preferences, tastes, opinions, and likings which people have. But since such attitudes, preferences, tastes, and so forth are, in the last analysis, beyond the control of reason, the decisions which reflect them can have no rational justification or objective validity. Whether an action is to be counted as right or wrong thus ultimately depends upon whether someone approves or disapproves of it. If he approves of it, it is right; if he disapproves, it is wrong—and that is the end of the matter. Indeed, in a sense, the same action may be both right and wrong. Seen from one standpoint, it may be right; seen from another, wrong. What label we choose to apply to it depends upon the point of view from which we see it. It thus makes no sense to ask whether the action is *really* right or *really* wrong—no more than it makes sense to ask whether Smith's liking grapefruit is really right or really wrong. It follows from this principle that anybody's opinion on moral matters is as "good" as anyone else's, whether he be minister or madman, sinner or saint. The oft-quoted remark of Protagoras that "man is the measure of all things" is a succinct expression of this point of view.

In Plato's eyes, such precepts made a mockery of morality. Indeed, his philosophy—whether in ethics, politics, or epistemology—can be regarded as an effort to combat this destructive influence. The idea that goodness is an independently existing entity, to be apprehended by an act of rational intuition, is the key to his attack in ethics upon this form of skepticism. For Plato, whether a given course of action is good or not no more depends upon men's attitudes, opinions, desires, wishes, or beliefs than does the truth of the mathematical statement that one plus one is equal to two. This latter statement is true whether we like it or not, approve or disapprove of it, believe or disbelieve it. Likewise, whether something is good or not is an independently existing fact which remains to be discovered if men can be trained to do so.

What Plato is urging here is that moral standards are just as objective as the principles of physics or the theorems of mathematics. Those who think morality is merely a matter of opinion think so because they lack the knowledge to judge otherwise. On the other hand, for Plato, statements like "Gratitude is due to benefactors" or "It is wrong to steal" are true in the same sense as the statement "The distance from the earth to the moon is 239,000 miles" is true. A man may doubt the latter statement if he lacks the requisite astronomical knowledge; he may doubt the truth of the former statements if he lacks the requisite moral knowledge. But if he possesses such knowledge, he will see what they are as objective as the truths of science or mathematics, and differ from them only in their subject matter.

Criticism of Plato's Ethics

As we have tried to bring out in the preceding account, Plato's ethical outlook rests upon two basic assumptions: (1) If a man knows what is right or good in given circumstances, he will never act immorally in those circumstances. (2) Moral rules have an objective validity which is in no way dependent upon men's tastes, opinions, or preferences. Attractive as both these notions seem, they are not immune from severe, perhaps fatal, criticism. Take the first assumption, for instance.

According to this principle, men always aim at what they think to be good. But if they do, then how can we account for the obvious fact that people often act immorally? As we have pointed out, Plato's answer is that such behavior always stems from a lack of knowledge. Sometimes in believing a thing to be worthwhile, one may be mistaken. Accordingly, such a person may strive to attain something which is evil, although he may not realize that this is so. He may thus act immorally without ever having really intended to.

Now to hold such a view is to maintain, in effect, that evil is never done deliberately or voluntarily. But this raises a difficulty, since the only actions for which a man can be held responsible are actions he intends to do. If I knock over a vase accidentally, it would be silly to blame me for doing so. On Plato's position it would appear that evil conduct falls into the class of such involuntary acts and therefore that no one can properly be held responsible for the evil he does. Does this mean, then, that Plato's moral theory cannot account for the ordinary notion of responsibility, or does it mean that people can be held responsible for acting morally but not for acting immorally? Either alternative seems unacceptable. Little wonder, then, that the assumption which begets this dilemma has been named "the Socratic paradox."

But this is not the only difficulty connected with the assumption. As Plato formulates it, the principle implies that men always behave to further their own real interests whenever they can discover what they are. Since the good, according to Plato, is that which always furthers a person's real interests, it follows that in any given case when the good is known, men will seek it. On this interpretation, the principle seems to state a psychological law about the factors which motivate human actions. But if it does, then the "law" in question is surely incorrect. Although men may sometimes act to further their real interests when they know where these lie, it is simply untrue that they always do so. There are individuals, for example, who know that smoking will be harmful to them and yet who continue to smoke. How can we explain their behavior? One plausible answer is that *knowingly* they are willing to sacrifice their real interests in exchange for pleasure, even for the sort of transient pleasure which ensues from smoking. But if this is so, then Plato's thesis, when interpreted as a psychological account of how men always behave, is plainly false. Yet what other cogent interpretation can we give to the principle?

Of course, there are ways out of the difficulty if one is willing to adopt them. One might still insist that the principle is true, and then defend it by identifying the good with pleasure, as Aristippus and Epicurus were to do. On this interpretation, men always act so as to try to achieve pleasure. Such a defensive ploy neutralizes the counterexample we have mentioned above. But since Plato explicitly rejects such a maneuver, no escape of this kind is open to him.

The second fundamental assumption of Plato's system—that moral laws have an objectivity which is independent of men's tastes and preferences—has been subjected to criticism of equal force. This principle implies that in any given set of circumstances, there is a morally correct way of behaving, and further, that it can be discovered through the exercise of reason. But to maintain this is to maintain, as Plato does, that moral problems are always capable of rational resolution: for through the use of reason one can come closer and closer to seeing which moral rule objectively applies to a given case. It is this thesis which has often been attacked.

Plato's mistake, according to these critics, lay in thinking that moral problems and scientific problems are fundamentally analogous when, in fact, they are radically dissimilar. Scientific problems, these critics agree, are in principle always subject to rational solution; but they deny that this is true of moral perplexities. Consider the difference between the following pair of cases, for instance. Imagine a surgeon deliberating whether to operate on a patient whom he suspects of having appendicitis. Should he operate now, or wait until later in the hope that the patient will recover spontaneously, thus eliminating unnecessary surgical risks? His vacillation in such a case is due to the lack of information he has about the patient's condition. Even the most careful diagnostic procedures and the most sensitive tests may not give him the information he requires for making an ïnerrant decision. But if he did have more information, or perhaps better information, he would have no difficulty in deciding what to do. Moral problems are obviously sometimes like this. We may not be able to decide whether Jones is an honest man or a hypocrite because we may not have the relevant information about his motives. If we had such information, we would have no difficulty in making an accurate assessment of his character. But, our critics go on to say, some moral perplexities are not like this at all. Even where, by hypothesis, we have all the relevant facts, we still may not be able to make an objective, incontestable decision. Suppose, for example, that we are the members of a jury trying a case in which the defendant has been accused of euthanasia (mercy killing). Suppose further that we know all the facts which are relevant to the case. We know that the defendant has killed someone dying of an incurable disease; we know that the patient was in great pain; we know that the act was done from the highest motives; we know that the patient requested it be done—yet we may still not know what judgment to pronounce upon the propriety, rectitude, or legitimacy of the act.

How then do we decide in such a case? In the final analysis (so the objection goes), what judgment we make will depend upon how we *feel* about the matter, not upon what we know. The moral decisions men make, the principles which they invoke in such circumstances, are thus not independent of their feelings, preferences, opinions, and tastes—but instead are often the expressions of them.

No philosopher of antiquity, perhaps no philosopher of any period, has stated this point of view more forcefully or with greater clarity than Aristotle. Even though his ethical outlook is never fully divorced from Platonic influence, it is, in certain basic ways, sharply at variance with that of his teacher, as we shall now see.

ARISTOTLE'S ETHICS

Aristotle's moral theory resembles Plato's in a number of important respects. It is intimately connected with a "realist" metaphysics; it stresses the important role which reason plays in the good life; it puts great emphasis upon the development of virtuous habits; it argues that happiness can only be achieved in a suitable social context. Yet in spite of these close affinities with the earlier doctrine, its fundamental stress is radically different. It is a far more empirical theory, less hostile to pleasure as a component of the good life, and positively opposed to the Platonic conception that moral laws have a validity independent of men's interests, attitudes, desires, and tastes. It is clear that no brief account is likely to do justice to an outlook of such scope and complexity, but nonetheless let us attempt, as best we can, to bring out its salient features.

Without excessive distortion, Aristotle's ethics can be pictured as an attempt to answer two questions: (1) What is the good life for man? (2) How ought men, insofar as they are moral, to act? The metaphysical and political doctrines are deeply involved in his answer to the first question and the celebrated doctrine of the mean[2] in his answer to the second. In order to unravel the complexities of the theory, let us consider each of these answers separately.

The Relevance of the *Metaphysics* and the *Politics* to the *Ethics*

Like the pre-Socratics, Aristotle found the concept of change a puzzling one. His struggle to provide a satisfactory explication of this notion forms one of the dominant themes of his important treatise, the *Meta-*

---

[2] Often erroneously referred to as "the doctrine of the *golden* mean"; the phrase so far as we know, does not occur in Aristotle.

physics. The outcome of this struggle is the famous doctrine of the four causes, which contains his solution to the problem. This doctrine maintains that change always proceeds, as Aristotle puts it, "from potentiality to actuality." In spite of this forbidding terminology, the idea which it represents is not difficult to grasp. According to Aristotle, all change can fruitfully be explained as the gradual development of the innate characteristics which a thing possesses. For instance, an acorn has certain inherent capacities, or tendencies, which slowly manifest themselves as the acorn changes into an oak tree. The tree which results from this process can be thought of as representing the fulfillment (or "actualization") of these innate tendencies (or "potentialities").

Now all such change, Aristotle points out, is invariably regular, orderly, and predictable. Although we may not be able to foresee the exact shape which the resulting tree will have, we can accurately predict that the acorn will not develop into a cedar tree, into a cow, or into a human being. Within limits (fixed by the species to which the thing belongs), the entity which anything will become is determined at the beginning of the developmental process by its innate constitution. As a result, and in an important sense, each thing has some "proper" goal or "proper" limit which it can, and ought to, attain if all goes well. In the case of an acorn, it is to become an oak tree. What is it in the case of a human being?

Here the theory becomes somewhat more complex, since Aristotle's answer depends on an intricately worked-out conception of human nature. Human beings, he argues, are part of the animal kingdom. Like animals, they require food, drink, shelter, and so forth in order to develop their innate capacities. But at the same time, being *human*, they are different from the other members of this "kingdom." Now what distinguishes man from the other animals is that he alone has the innate capacity to become a thinking being, to reflect upon history, to make conjectures about the future, to develop theories about the nature of things, and so forth. The ultimate goal which is proper to a human being will thus be mixed; it will be a goal which man shares with the animals, and it will be a goal which is uniquely his. As Aristotle puts it, it will consist in his becoming a *rational animal*.

The moral implications of this doctrine are immediate and obvious. For Aristotle, no specification of the good life will be adequate which does not take man's unique nature into account. The good life must be one which is good *for man*. And since man is, above all, a rational being, the good life will be one which must be conducted under the governance of reason. As we shall see, Aristotle does not mean that the good life is identical with a life of reason, but he does insist that unless reason is utilized by man, he cannot lead a life which is proper to his nature, and unless a life is proper in this sense, it cannot be a good one for him.

This brief account of the relation between the moral theory and the metaphysics only brings out one aspect of Aristotle's total doctrine, however. In particular, it leaves out the social or political element. Human dispositions, Aristotle argues, cannot be realized in isolation. Man, from birth, depends upon others—not only in order to survive infancy but beyond this to develop those characteristics which distinguish him from the brutes, such as the ability to use language and the ability to feel remorse, gratitude, and friendship. Man is thus essentially a social animal, and it is only within the larger framework of a community that his full development can take place. As Aristotle says in a well-known phrase, "He who is unable to live in society or who has no need, because he is sufficient for himself, must either be a beast or a god."

What, then, is the good life as Aristotle envisages it? In the effort to answer this question, he departs drastically from the tradition of Platonic rationalism. Instead of trying to deduce the nature of the good life by the use of reason alone, Aristotle adopts an empirical approach to the problem. He begins to examine the behavior, practices, and talk of ordinary people, and what he notices is that men of common sense invariably attribute one characteristic to lives that they are willing to describe as "good." The characteristic is happiness. Aristotle's answer to the query "What is the good life for man?" is based upon such empirical findings, and it can be stated in a sentence: *The good life for man is a life of happiness.*

But this answer, so far, is not very helpful. We should still like to know, beyond this, what the common man intends when he says the good life is a "happy" one. Does he mean that it is devoted to sensual gratification, to the acquisition of riches, to becoming famous—or what? Unfortunately, if we were to ask the average person, we might find some difficulty in comprehending the reply. Either what he says will be vague, ambiguous, or inconsistent, or he will be unable to answer articulately at all.[3] Aristotle conceives of his work in ethics as an attempt to remedy this deficiency: he is trying to answer for the common man, to explain more carefully, more lucidly, and more accurately than such a person could what he means when he says that a good life is a life of happiness. The *Nicomachean Ethics*, which is the chief of three treatises on ethics sometimes attributed to Aristotle (but possibly the only one which is genuinely his), can thus be regarded as one of the earliest examples of what is now called *analytical philosophy.*

The definition which Aristotle proposes is this: "Happiness is an activity of the soul in accord with perfect virtue." This is, of course, not what the ordinary man would *say* if he were asked what he meant by

[3] "For it is beyond the power of ordinary people to make distinctions." See Bk. X of the *Nicomachean Ethics.*

"happiness," but according to Aristotle it is what he would mean, even though he would not put his remarks in such a technical vocabulary. And the ideas which are incorporated into this succinct statement are indeed intuitive and not difficult to understand. We might expand what Aristotle has in mind by fixing on the key words "activity," "virtue," and "soul," beginning with the last of these.

In saying that happiness is an activity of the "soul," Aristotle is explicitly rejecting any simple pleasure theory which identifies happiness with bodily sensations or pleasurable feeling tones. If this were all that happiness consisted in, then man would be no different from the brutes. Such pleasures, as we shall see, must be components of any good life for Aristotle; but happiness for a rational being involves more than pleasure. Ingredients fitting to his cognitive faculties must be included as well.

The word "activity" is equally important. In using this term, Aristotle is stressing that happiness is not a fixed or static thing, nor is it a final "goal" or object we arrive at if we behave in certain ways. Those who hold this view tend to think of happiness as if it were a prize for successful living, like the cup one might receive for winning a tennis tournament. This view suggests that happiness is something we approximate to as we play the moral game, so to speak, and that if we play it successfully we will receive an award for doing so.

But this is precisely what Aristotle is denying. Happiness is not a thing of any sort or a final prize which one can attain if he tries hard enough. Instead, it is something which accompanies the ordinary (and extraordinary) activities of daily life. Indeed, happiness can be thought of, on the Aristotelian model, as being something like persistence. A man who follows a certain course of conduct persistently does not arrive at a goal called "persistence." Instead, it is his way of doing things—for instance, of refusing easily to be beaten by circumstances, of returning again and again to a task in order to solve it. Now happiness resembles persistence in being a way of engaging in the various activities of life, such as reading, walking, making love, working, and so forth. If one does these things in a certain way, then we can declare him to be happy. For instance, if he enjoys eating, intellectual conversation, friendship, and so forth and is not frequently downcast, depressed, tense, and insecure—then he is what we call a "happy" man. Happiness is thus a *concomitant* of the things we do, not a position we are trying to reach by doing them. It is this point which Aristotle is attempting to bring out by saying that it is an "activity" of the soul.

The other key word in this definition is "virtue." Like Plato, Aristotle thinks of each thing as having a specific function or role which it ought to play, depending upon the kind of thing it is. The word "virtue" is thus used by him in much the same way as we use the word "function."

For instance, the virtue of a knife is to cut things; the virtue of a hammer to drive home nails, and so on. The virtue of a human being, as we have seen, is to be rational. Accordingly, man is fulfilling his natural function, his virtue, when he lives in accordance with the dictates of reason. He may do this in two ways: either through speculation of a philosophical sort or in conducting the affairs of his daily life. The former use of reason, Aristotle calls "intellectual virtue"; the latter, "moral virtue." It is this latter (or practical) use of reason which mainly interests him, and most of the *Nicomachean Ethics*, in one way or another, is devoted to an examination of it. What Aristotle is attempting to show therein is how the use of practical reason will lead to happiness. In saying that "happiness is an activity of the soul in accord with perfect virtue," Aristotle is again emphasizing that the use of reason is an essential condition for achieving happiness. And with this comment, we come to the second major section of Aristotle's moral theory, the famous doctrine of the mean, in which this point is explicitly developed.

The Doctrine of the Mean

The doctrine of the mean is Aristotle's answer to the question "How ought men, as moral beings, to act?" His answer, in effect, is that men ought to live moderately, in accordance with the dictates of practical reason. If they will do this, he argues, they will be happy. The doctrine of the mean is thus developed by him to explain how men ought to behave in order to achieve happiness. Let us turn to the main elements of this doctrine.

Being happy, according to Aristotle, is something like being properly nourished. The question "What ought a man to do in order to be happy?" is thus like the question "How much food should a man eat in order to be properly fed?" Aristotle's reply is that there is no proper way of answering this question without some empirical investigation—and in saying this, his break with Plato becomes complete. For such an answer implies that ethics is not an *a priori* discipline, with rigid laws and principles which can be discovered independently of experience, as Plato had believed. The answer to the question "How much food should a man eat in order to be properly nourished?" will depend upon all sorts of empirical factors. It will depend on the weight of the person involved, on the work he does, on whether he is sick or healthy, and so forth. A man who is a professional athlete will, in general, require more nourishment than a man who is a clerk in an office. A large man will generally require more food than a small man—but not always. The proper amount of nourishment which any given person will need can therefore only be established by trial and error: if a person eats a certain amount of food and still remains hungry, he should eat more; if another person were to eat the same amount and were to feel satiated, he should eat less. The correct amount of food one should consume is thus a "mean" between the extremes of eating too much and too little; but there is no way of telling *a priori* what this amount ought to be for a given individual.

It is important for a full comprehension of this doctrine that "mean" not be identified with "average." Let us assume that two ounces of food per day is too little and that forty-eight ounces is too much. Does this imply that the average of these quantities (twenty-five ounces) is exactly what every well-nourished person should eat? Aristotle's answer is that this amount might be the correct quantity for some individuals; but it is unlikely that it would be the proper amount for everyone since people differ so greatly. All one can say is that what is proper is an amount somewhere between these limits; and this is what Aristotle intends by the word "mean."

There are at least two important implications for ethics in this doctrine. The first is that there are a number of different, but proper, ways of living for people. What is proper for one individual may not be proper for another, since people differ in so many fundamental ways. And secondly, the correct way of living for any given person cannot be determined through the use of reason alone. It can only be established by the sorts of experimental procedures we have indicated. These points can be summarized, in the technical parlance of philosophy, by saying that Aristotle is both a relativist and an empiricist in ethics.

These same remarks apply to happiness, of course. The proper mode of conduct for any given individual will depend upon the kind of person he is—upon his physical capacities, his temperament, his interests, and his desires. There is thus a multiplicity of good lives: indeed, as many as there are human beings who differ fundamentally from each other. But any attempt to lead *any* good life must follow the dictates of practical reason: it must be conducted in accordance with the doctrine of the mean. One who follows the mean will be "virtuous" and, in being so, will achieve happiness.

For Aristotle, "virtue" thus always denotes a mean which lies between extremes. Courage is a virtue which lies between cowardice and rashness; liberality, between prodigality and frugality; pride, between vanity and humility. In all these cases, virtuous behavior is reasonable behavior. A man who is rash is foolish because he exposes himself unnecessarily to danger; a coward is foolish because he has fears he need not have. To act courageously is to be reasonably cautious, without exhibiting cowardice. It is thus always proper behavior for anyone. But in saying this, Aristotle must be understood to be implying that courageous behavior for one person may not be courageous behavior for another. What would be courageous conduct for a professional boxer facing another would be rashness for the man with no pugilistic experience. Each of these virtues will thus denote different sorts of behavior for different people, depending upon the kind of people they are and upon the circumstances in which they find themselves.

It is obvious that this doctrine is enormously different from Plato's. For Plato, right action is independent of the kind of individual who does it and of the circumstances in which it is done. But Aristotle's outlook is far less austere, far less rigid. This disagreement in their basic philosophies never emerges more clearly than in their differing attitudes toward pleasure. For Plato, at his most austere, pleasure is utterly bad and is to be avoided. But this is not Aristotle's view. As he sees it, pleasure is never entirely bad; indeed, on the whole, it is desirable. But the good life (a life of happiness) is not identical with a life of pleasure. For the good life, as Aristotle says, "is a serious thing," whereas there is something trivial about a life wholly devoted to pleasure. Nonetheless, every happy life must contain some pleasure in it. A happy life must be lived over a period of time ("one swallow does not make a summer"). If there were no pleasant episodes in a lengthy life, it would be barren and unfortunate and not happy. "For no man," Aristotle writes, "can be happy on the rack."

Criticism of Aristotle

If we leave aside the criticisms which have been directed at the teleology implicit in Aristotle's metaphysics, we find two commonly proposed objections to the moral doctrine itself. The first of these maintains that the doctrine of the mean does not provide an accurate analysis of the concept of "virtue." In particular, there seem to be virtues which do not lie between extremes. For example, there is no middle course between keeping a promise and not keeping it. The same applies to telling the truth. Either one tells the truth when asked or one does not. Virtues like these do not seem open to a relativistic analysis of the sort Aristotle is suggesting. In this respect, they seem better analyzable by a theory like Plato's which holds that whether one is virtuous or not does not depend upon the sort of person one is or upon the situation in which one finds oneself. If this criticism is correct, Aristotle's account is too narrow to do justice to the many different kinds of virtues men recognize.

The second criticism is perhaps even more important. As Bertrand Russell states it:

> There is something unduly smug and comfortable about Aristotle's speculations on human affairs; everything that makes men feel a passionate interest in each other seems to be forgotten. Even his account of friendship is tepid. He shows no sign of having had any of those experiences which make it difficult to preserve sanity; all the more profound aspects of the moral life are apparently unknown to him. He leaves out,

one may say, the whole sphere of human experience with which religion is concerned. What he has to say will be useful to comfortable men of weak passions; but he has nothing to say to those who are possessed by a god or a devil, or whom outward misfortune drives to despair.[4]

As Russell points out, the doctrine of moderation is not a creed to which all men can subscribe. A man who is temperamentally passionate and romantic may find that life in accordance with the mean does not bring him happiness. Throughout the *Ethics*, Aristotle assumes that moderation in conduct will provide happiness; but he never offers any evidence for this thesis. For some people, Aristotle's advice would prove irksome, restraining, and confining. To follow it would bring them unhappiness, not happiness. Such individuals require a more dynamic philosophy of life, one which will more adequately reflect the strivings, yearnings, anxieties, and tensions of men driven by their passions and emotions. Hedonism, which we shall consider next, is a philosophy which met some of these needs, although it was not until the nineteenth century, with the rise of romanticism, that this point of view was to be fully expressed.

HEDONISM: THE PHILOSOPHY
OF ARISTIPPUS AND EPICURUS

Aristippus of Cyrene, who was an older contemporary of Plato and like him a onetime student of Socrates, is usually described as the founder of the hedonic school. The philosophy of this school takes its name from the Greek word for pleasure, *hedone*, since it holds that pleasure is the *sole* good. Aristippus interpreted this doctrine in a radical way, which was to be qualified by later hedonists. He maintained not only that the sole thing worth acquiring is pleasure but also that since the past is gone and the future uncertain, the only pleasures worth having are those of the moment. Ironically enough, Aristippus is supposed to have been led to the position through his association with Socrates, to whom the doctrine would obviously have been anathema. But as we pointed out earlier, it is one way of defending the Socratic principle that all men aim at what they believe to be good. For if the good is to be equated with pleasure, as Aristippus claimed, certain objections which can be urged against the Socratic thesis are quickly rendered impotent.

But although Aristippus is reputed to have founded the hedonic school, its most famous representative is unquestionably Epicurus of Samos (341–270 B.C.). That his doctrines have been and still are influential can be judged from the fact that the word "epicure" has become

---

[4] Bertrand Russell, *A History of Western Philosophy* (Simon and Schuster, New York, 1945), p. 184.

common coin in modern European languages. Of course, the present meaning of the term has little connection with any doctrine Epicurus suggested. As it is now used, "epicure" denotes a gourmet, a person whose main delights consist in the enjoyment of fine wines and fastidiously prepared food. Epicurus was anything but an epicure in this sense of the term. He suffered from stomach trouble, ate bland foods, drank only water, and strongly advocated abstemious living. It is possible that the word acquired its modern connotation through a legend which developed later to the effect that a garden which Epicurus had purchased, and in which he did his teaching, was used by him and his disciples for riotous living.[5] But the evidence we have suggests that such reports are apocryphal. Consider this sentence, for example, from a letter which he sent a friend:

> I am thrilled with pleasure in the body when I live on bread and water, and I spit on luxurious pleasures, not for their own sake, but because of the inconveniences that follow them.

This is hardly the sort of remark one is likely to associate with a gluttonous figure, drunkenly cavorting about his garden.

As we have mentioned, Epicurus strongly advocated abstemious, temperate living. Indeed, his moral philosophy mainly consists of advice for living moderately but pleasantly. Like Aristippus, he considered pleasure to be the sole good, but unlike him, he did not identify pleasure with bodily sensation, or even with positive enjoyment of any sort. The good life, as he saw it, is mainly a life which contains as few painful experiences as possible and which is devoted to repose and intellectual pursuits.

In this connection, he made a sharp distinction between those pleasures which have painful concomitants or consequences and those which do not, and he strongly recommended that everyone avoid pleasures of the former sort. Sexual love is to be avoided, he argued, because it is accompanied by fatigue, remorse, and depression; gluttony, because it leads to indigestion; fame, because it is often followed by disappointment; and the drinking of wine, for reasons which are only too well known. Friendship, philosophical contemplation, and the viewing of works of art are pleasures which do not possess such defects. This is why they are to be pursued by anyone who wishes to lead a good life.

---

[5] These rumors were mainly spread by his philosophical opponents, who not only rejected Epicureanism as a philosophy but also resented the inroads it made in their own ranks. Arcesilaus, who headed the Academy in the third century B.C., was especially irritated by the fact that no Epicureans ever abandoned their principles, while the members of other schools often defected to Epicureanism. He explained this fact by saying, "A man can always become a eunuch, but a eunuch can never become a man."

Epicurus modified the hedonic doctrine of Aristippus in a number of respects. He felt it was more important to lead a life which was pleasant in the long run than to acquire momentary pleasures; he thought some pleasures were intrinsically better than others, whereas Aristippus had argued that among present pleasures there is no distinction of kind, but only of intensity. Epicurus also felt that reason served the role of distinguishing worthwhile from inferior pleasures and of distinguishing pleasures not attended by pain from those which were—and hence, he argued, reason must be employed in any effort to lead a good life. He felt, unlike Aristippus, that the avoidance of pain was more important than the acquisition of positive enjoyments; and, in this connection, he argued that in any case in which conduct gave rise to no pain, such conduct would be preferable to conduct which led to much positive enjoyment but some pain.[6] Some, or all, of these qualifications appear in most versions of hedonism expounded since: for example, we find in Epicurus's writings an anticipation of Mill's famous remark that it is "better to be a dissatisfied human being than a satisfied pig."

Some scholars claim to have noticed a further, important difference between the views of Aristippus and Epicurus. In order to explain the point of divergence between them, it is necessary to make a distinction between what is called "psychological hedonism," and "ethical hedonism." Psychological hedonism is the doctrine that men *in fact* pursue pleasure, and only pleasure, in their lives, while ethical hedonism maintains that whether men do so or not, this is what they *ought* to do. A typical formulation of psychological hedonism is to be found in Book X of the *Nicomachean Ethics*, where Aristotle attributes such a doctrine to Eudoxus, the famous Greek mathematician. Aristotle writes:

> Now Eudoxus thought pleasure to be the chief good because he saw all, rational and irrational alike, aiming at it: and he argued that, since in all what was the object of choice must be good and what most so the best, the fact of all being drawn to the same thing proved this thing to be the best for all: "for each," he said, "finds what is good for itself just as it does its proper nourishment, and so that which is good for all, and the object of the aim of all, is their chief good."[7]

Most scholars look upon Epicurus and Aristippus as psychological hedonists. Epicurus, for instance, maintained that the only absolute good is pleasure "after which all things strive," and this was clearly the view of Aristippus as well. It is also clear that Aristippus was an ethical hedonist. He believed that pleasure is the only thing worth having, and therefore

---

[6] A later hedonist, Hegesias, even advocated suicide on the ground that it would guarantee a "state of being" which contained no pain at all.

[7] Aristotle, *Nicomachean Ethics*, Bk. X, Chap. 1, §§ 1172–1173.

men ought to strive to acquire it, even if some degree of pain accompanies their efforts to do so. But Epicurus, as we have seen, did not subscribe to this form of the doctrine. He held that not all pleasures are worth acquiring. Not only is there a distinction between kinds of pleasures, so that the highest are always to be preferred, but those pleasures which are accompanied by, or followed by, pain are bad and are positively to be avoided. In the light of these qualifications, Epicurus is often interpreted as holding a modified form of ethical hedonism, distinct from the stronger version accepted by Aristippus.

It should be mentioned, in concluding this exposition of hedonism, that these two forms of the theory are logically independent of each other. One might hold psychological hedonism without holding ethical hedonism, and conversely. For instance, one might believe that men are motivated to seek pleasure and believe at the same time that they ought not to do so. In a sense, this is Epicurus's position, since he explicitly recommends the avoidance of those pleasures having painful concomitants. But this is not the only variation of the theory which philosophers have commonly adopted. Some thinkers have refused to accept the psychological form of the theory but have espoused the ethical form of it. Those who adhere to such views deny that men are motivated to seek pleasure as the sole end of their activities but go on to urge that since pleasure is the only thing worth having in its own right, everyone should strive to attain it. Henry Sidgwick, the nineteenth-century British moralist, and the late William Savery, of the University of Washington, are modern representatives of this position.

Criticism of Hedonism

Let us begin our critical appraisal of hedonism by examining the psychological version of the theory first. This doctrine, from the time of Aristippus to the present day, has exercised a magnetic attraction for both the plain man and the professional thinker. In the latter category, we may mention (out of a much larger list) such famous names as Lucretius, Hobbes, Spinoza, Gassendi, Voltaire, and Bentham. It seems obvious that a doctrine which has attracted such keen intellects cannot be dismissed lightly. What, then, have thinkers found so compelling about it? There are many answers, of course, but two in particular stand out. To begin with, psychological hedonism attempts to provide a single, encompassing explanation for every type of voluntary action which men undertake: and it is a source of satisfaction for any theorist to discover a principle of this sort. Psychological hedonism, like Newton's law of universal gravitation, fulfills this requirement admirably. Consider any voluntary action: Why do men do it? The answer is always the same and is simple to grasp. Men act as they do because they are seeking pleasure!

Secondly, a powerful argument can be invoked in support of the theory. This argument makes use of a distinction (called the "means-ends" distinction), whose cogency seems beyond dispute. Let us illustrate it here and then show how it can be used in support of psychological hedonism. The point of the distinction is this: some things may not be worth having in their own right but are only worth having because they enable one to acquire things which are worth having in their own right. The former class of things are thus valuable only as *means* to things which are *intrinsically* or *inherently* valuable.

Now in terms of this distinction, the psychological hedonist challenges anyone to show that anything other than pleasure is inherently valuable. Take wealth, for example. What is the point, he asks, of striving to become wealthy? Not just to possess money, because money is a means for acquiring other things, such as a fine house, a new car, or beautiful clothes. But each of these in turn, he maintains, is not an end in itself. Each is worth having only because we ultimately derive pleasure from having it. It is thus pleasure which men *really* strive for, and all other things have value only insofar as they are means to this end.

Interpreted in this way, psychological hedonism has attracted thinkers because it seems to offer a psychologically true account of the conscious behavior of human beings. But if the theory is interpreted as giving such an account, it may be rejected on the ground that it is not in accord with present-day scientific findings on these matters. Psychologists agree that people are sometimes motivated by the search for pleasure, but they also point out that this is not always so. Some individuals may initially attempt to acquire wealth as a means to pleasure, but after a time they may come to look upon money as an end in itself. In psychological language, they become "fixated" on money and eventually disregard the use to which it can be put for acquiring pleasure. Such individuals may be so strongly motivated in this direction as to disregard or even reject the pursuit of pleasure if it interferes with their efforts to hoard wealth. Stories of misers who live in wretched circumstances, while having a fortune hidden beneath the floor boards of their hovels, are commonplace. Money, not pleasure, is the goal which such individuals seek—and for this reason, psychologists deny that psychological hedonism can be accepted as an accurate picture of all conscious human motivation. In a way, this point is similar to a famous argument which Bishop Joseph Butler[8] directed against psychological hedonism. Butler's contention was that we do not seek pleasure but things. For instance, if a man is hungry, he does not seek pleasure but food; if thirsty, water; if cold, warmth, and so on.

---

[8] Joseph Butler (1692–1752) was a famous English clergyman and author of *Fifteen Sermons* (1726) and *The Analogy of Religion* (1736).

Unfortunately, psychological hedonism is not so easily defeated as these examples might suggest, and because this is so, one wonders whether it ought to be interpreted as a scientific account of human behavior at all. This suspicion is reinforced when we consider the kind of answer the votaries of the doctrine will make to the counter-cases we have just proposed. The psychological hedonist will maintain, for instance, that a miser is a person who actually gains pleasure by hoarding money. The miser is merely giving up the usual means for obtaining pleasure, such as living in a decent house, eating well, and so on. All he has done is to limit the means for obtaining pleasure to the acquisition of money. Money has not become an end in itself—rather it has become the *sole means* for achieving pleasure, but pleasure is still the end for which he strives.

When the theory is defended in this way, one wonders how it could be refuted at all. What could possibly count against the truth of the theory, if such cases as we have mentioned do not? If nothing will count against a theory, then it cannot be looked upon as a scientific account of human behavior. For if nothing will count against it, even in principle, then there is no way of deciding whether the theory is true or false. But if not, we may reject it on the ground that it no longer provides an adequate explanation of human conduct. What is characteristic of any theory having explanatory power is that its truth or falsity depends upon facts. But if facts make no difference to the validity of a theory, it can no longer be regarded as being about the facts in the world, including facts of human motivation. Such a theory may well be "true," but if so, it is true by definition and, in being so, has become irrefutable by becoming trivial.

Let us now turn to the ethical version of hedonism. Like most classical moral theories, ethical hedonism can be looked upon as attempting to answer two questions: What is the good life for man? How ought men, as moral beings, to act? The ethical hedonist replies to the former query by saying that the good life for man consists of pleasure alone and to the latter by saying that men ought to act so as to obtain pleasure. What can be said, then, against these views?

As we have already pointed out, most hedonists concede that sometimes the effort to acquire pleasure will also produce pain. For instance, if a man begins to use narcotics in the expectation that such drugs will give him pleasure, he must also recognize, on the basis of empirical information, that in the long run he is likely to suffer a considerable amount of pain as a result of this practice. Epicurus described this situation by saying that some pleasures are bad and are to be shunned. But if this defense is accepted, we cannot say that the good life is simply identical with a life of pleasure; and if not, we should have to abandon the main tenet of hedonism. Epicurus attempted to bypass this difficulty by finding pleasures that do not have painful concomitants or consequences, and argued that such pleasures—being of a higher order—constitute the good life. But this approach will not do, since even friendship, intellectual activity, and repose, which form the class of such pleasures, may sometimes be accompanied by pain. For example, if a friend dies, one may suffer intensely from sadness at his death.

Other hedonists, however, have rejected this solution to the difficulty. They contend that pleasure itself is never bad—even the pleasure one obtains from using narcotics. It is only the painful effects which are evil. If a technique could be devised which would eliminate the dangerous and painful consequences of using narcotics, who would deny that the pleasure one gained by such a practice was good? The present arguments about whether marijuana should be legalized often revolve around this point.

This defense is theoretically unassailable, but it has practical difficulties which make it dubious that ethical hedonism can offer acceptable advice for one's conduct in daily life. For we cannot, as a matter of fact, always separate the painful concomitants and effects of a course of action from the pleasurable ones. To advise one, as ethical hedonists do, to seek pleasure is, in effect, frequently to advise one to seek pain as well, since the two cannot at times be disassociated. Ethical hedonism, consequently, must sometimes advise one to forego the pursuit of pleasure when this will produce pain, and thus its practical advice seems inconsistent with the theory.

Lastly, let us consider the thesis that everyone ought to act so as to obtain pleasure. This doctrine seems plausible at first glance, but further reflection shows that it violates our deepest intuitions about how men—as moral beings—ought to behave. Consider the following case: Suppose that a policeman has been given the duty of protecting a bank; suppose further that it is suspected that an attempt will be made to rob the bank on a certain night. Suppose, finally, that after lying in wait for several hours on that night, the policeman becomes weary of his surveillance and decides to leave his post for a bar where he can have a drink. Most men would say that if he deserted his station for this reason, he would be acting wrongly. If he replies that he acted properly because he was seeking pleasure, this defense would be laughed out of court. The plain man feels that sometimes one ought to act so as to acquire pleasure, but not always. Sometimes one has certain obligations which he must fulfill, even if in doing so he does not acquire pleasure. If ethical hedonism is interpreted as a theory about how men ought to behave in society, the objection we have mentioned shows that it cannot be regarded as giving an adequate account of such behavior.

Hedonism, even though theoretically attractive, can thus be seen to violate our ordinary feelings about what constitutes moral behavior. Do we not object on moral grounds to the "playboy"? The objection is not merely that he seeks superficial pleasures, such as those of the table, the grape, and so on, but more fundamentally that pleasure is not the main object for which men should strive. The plain man is, with regard to pleasure, more an Aristotelian than an Epicurean. He feels that sometimes pleasure is a worthwhile object, and in fact that no life can be happy without some pleasure in it. But he finds the doctrine that pleasure is the *only* worthwhile goal objectionable—and accordingly rejects it on the ground that it contains advice which he ought not to follow.

CYNICISM AND STOICISM

Although Cynicism and Stoicism are generally distinguished from each other and treated separately, we shall not adopt that procedure here, since the difference between these schools is more one of emphasis than doctrine. As Juvenal remarked, the "Cynic differs from the Stoic only by his cloak." Both schools were greatly influenced by the Socratic teaching that virtue, not pleasure, is the goal for which men should strive; both stress that virtue is an internal matter, or a matter of character; both put great emphasis upon the value of the individual; both are practical philosophies, offering consolation to men in time of crisis; in this respect, both can be looked upon as philosophical reactions to the collapse of the Greek city-states and the Alexandrian empire as stable political units.

When social institutions of this magnitude break down, men are naturally led to consider how they may achieve *personal* salvation. The answer which Cynicism offered was that all the fruits of civilization are worthless—government, private property, marriage, religion, slavery, and all artificial pleasures of the senses. Salvation is to be found in a rejection of society and its values. For what is worthwhile is to be found within a man. The good life is a virtuous life, and virtue is a state of mind; or more accurately, virtue consists in having a character which is not affected by the vicissitudes of daily living. The Cynics thus advocated a rejection of the goods of the world, and in this way they tried to show men that by ignoring such externals they could achieve happiness.

Some of the Cynics carried this doctrine to its logical conclusion and lived frugal, even miserable lives. Diogenes of Sinope (412–323 B.C.), who is famous as the philosopher who went about with a lamp looking for an honest man, was an extreme case of this sort. He lived in a wooden tub, "inuring himself to the vicissitudes of the weather," as one commentator has put it. The single wooden bowl he possessed he burned upon seeing a peasant boy drink from cupped hands. He rejected all refinements —of dress, food, and personal cleanliness. Alexander the Great, a man who normally struck terror in the hearts of his subjects, once visited him, and touched by the miserable conditions of his life, offered to grant him any request he might make. Diogenes asked Alexander to step aside so that he might see the sun, at which Alexander is supposed to have cried, "If I were not Alexander, I would be Diogenes!"

As one might guess, a philosophy which demanded such sacrifices from its adherents could hardly be expected to win much popular support. Cynicism[9] gradually gave way to Stoicism, which also stressed the value of developing a character immune to the influences of the material world but without making the same practical demands upon its followers. No Cynic, living as they did, could possibly have become a king. But Stoicism was to have its emperors, among them Marcus Aurelius, greatest of the Antonines.

Indeed, Stoicism was to become the dominant philosophy of the Western world for the five centuries which followed the death of Alexander (323 B.C.). Not only did it sweep over Greece and the Greek cities in Asia Minor, but it became, in practice, the official philosophy of Rome until it was replaced by Christianity. During these five centuries Stoicism underwent some developments, but mainly in its metaphysics. Its ethical doctrines remained relatively unchanged, so that whether we treat Greek Stoicism or Roman Stoicism here is a matter of little importance.

The founder of Stoicism[10] was a certain Zeno of Citium, who was born in 340 and died in 265 B.C. (He is not to be confused with Zeno of Elea, the originator of the logical antinomies.) Zeno of Citium was a pupil of Crates, a Cynic of Athens—and it is via the influence of Crates upon Zeno that a bridge was established which connected Cynicism with Stoicism. But the bridge is even longer than that. For Crates, as a young man, was a disciple of Antisthenes, the founder of the Cynic school, who in turn attributed the source of his views to Socrates, with whom he had studied. This influence was never forgotten by the Stoics, even by the later Stoics like Epictetus. In emphasizing the importance of developing a virtuous character, they always regarded themselves as preserving the teaching of Socrates, especially as this was interpreted by the Cynics. In fact, when Epictetus comes to describe his ideal character, the model before his eyes is a combination of Socrates and Diogenes. The perfect Stoic, he says, has "neither country nor home nor land nor slave; his bed is the ground; he is

[9] The word "cynic" comes from the Greek word *kynos*, which means doglike ("canine" is the English equivalent). The word was supposedly applied to the Cynics because of the animal-like conditions in which they lived. It is also possible that the name of the sect derives from "Cynosarges," which was the name of a building in which Antisthenes, the founder of the school, first taught.

[10] "Stoicism" is a name derived from the Greek word *stoa*, which means porch. Zeno is supposed to have lectured from a building having a brightly painted porch; hence the application of this term to the school of philosophers who used this place for their meetings.

without wife or child; his only mansion is the earth and a shabby cloak; he must not be bound by the common ties of life; he must not be angry with a wrongdoer but pity him," and so forth.

Like Cynicism, Stoicism is a philosophy which offers consolation to men in time of stress. Consolative philosophies invariably arise when the sources of security provided by stable political institutions are swept away and when it is believed the severity of the collapse is too great for any hope of social reconstruction. This was characteristic of the Stoic outlook. Given a crumbling world, the Stoics held that the best any man can hope to attain is some degree of personal salvation. Stoic moral philosophy thus mainly consists of advice to individual men for obtaining happiness in the face of adverse social circumstances. And its basic principle for achieving this end can be stated in a line: Learn to be indifferent to external influences!

This was the invariant theme of Epictetus (b. A.D. 60), who began life as a Roman slave and rose to become a powerful official in the government. In his famous discourse on *Progress or Improvement,* he tells us why a man must learn to cultivate an attitude of indifference:

> Where then is progress? If any of you, withdrawing himself from externals, turns to his own will to exercise it and to improve it by labor, so as to make it comfortable to nature, elevated, free, unrestrained, unimpeded, faithful, modest; and if he has learned that he who desires or avoids the things which are not in his power can neither be faithful nor free, but of necessity he must change with them and be tossed about with them as in a tempest, and of necessity must subject himself to others who have the power to procure or prevent what he desires or would avoid; finally, when he rises in the morning, if he observes and keeps these rules, bathes as a man of fidelity, eats as a modest man; in like manner, if in every matter that occurs he works out his chief principles as the runner does with reference to running, and the trainer of the voice with reference to the voice—this is the man who truly makes progress, and this is the man who has not traveled in vain. But if he has strained his efforts to the practice of reading books, and labors only at this, and has traveled for this, I tell him to return home immediately, and not to neglect his affairs; for this for which he has traveled is nothing. But the other thing is something; to study how a man can rid his life of lamentation and groaning, and saying, Woe to me.[11]

As this passage from Epictetus implies, the Stoics believed that whether something is good or not will depend upon one's attitude toward it. They expressed this belief by saying that "virtue resides in the will—that only the will is good or bad." If a man has a good will (and he can have one by remaining untouched by and indifferent to external influ-

---

[11] Epictetus, *The Discourses and Manual* (Oxford, New York, 1916), I, 55–56.

ences), his essential character cannot be injured by the outward happenings of his life. Other men have control over external matters which impinge upon your life: they can put you in jail, torture you, or make a galley slave of you. But nonetheless, if a man can be indifferent to these events, those who have such power over external matters will not have power over the man himself. For the ability to injure a person lies in the ability to make him suffer, and if a man can rise above suffering, no one will really have authority over him. Such a man will be a free man, since he will be emotionally and intellectually independent of the vicissitudes of the world—and thus, even though the world may be in a state of collapse, this will not prevent him from achieving personal happiness or well-being.

Insofar as the moral philosophy of the Stoics differs from that of the Cynics, it does so in being intimately connected with an elaborate metaphysical system (the Cynics thought all theoretical philosophy was worthless). For example, the Stoics believed in a deterministic world—one in which everything happens in accordance with a predetermined plan. Nothing happens by chance or by accident. Now virtue, as Epictetus pointed out in the passage we have considered, consists in having a will, or character, which is "conformable to" the happenings of nature. That is, if a man can learn to accept what happens, and if he will accept that all that happens is part of a preordained arrangement which he is powerless to change, he will avoid the frustration, anxiety, and despair which comes from trying to alter the course of events. A man who understands this and who acts accordingly is free. It is only the man who struggles to alter things who thereby remains in bondage to them. But it is not only external happenings that can constrain. One must also learn to free oneself from the grip of desire and passion as well. Only by developing indifference to them can one's commitment to the world be fully broken.

As we can see from this brief account, the theoretical differences between Stoicism and Cynicism are negligible. But the practical behavior of the members of the two schools often differed substantially. The Cynics, feeling that they were powerless to rebuild the world in which they lived, renounced it—and all of its goods. But the Stoics maintained that this sort of abnegation was unnecessary. A person does not have to give up the fruits of civilization, they argued, provided that he does not become attached to them. It is only insofar as a man is affected by such things that he will not be free. But if he can remain unaffected, there is no reason why he should not continue to make use of them. Thus, although some of the Stoics, like Epictetus, lived simple, ascetic lives, in the tradition of Socrates and Diogenes, others became sybarites and voluptuaries—in fact, as we have said, even emperors.

The main effect of Stoicism and Cynicism was to place the burden for becoming a good or bad man directly upon the individual himself, rather than upon society, or even upon God. And this was a development whose repercussions have been felt in moral philosophy, in one form or another, to the present day.

Criticism of Cynicism
and Stoicism

Leaving aside the dubious claim that men can utilize the fruits of civilization while at the same time remaining indifferent to them, we might direct three criticisms at the Stoic outlook. The first of these is connected with the doctrine of indifference itself. Although men of common sense believe that moral rectitude is, to a great extent, a matter of character, it is hard to accept the thesis that such rectitude is identical with, or somehow connected with, being indifferent to the affairs of the world. If a child is injured in a traffic accident and is in pain, it would appear callous to most men to suggest that indifference is the proper way to react to the situation.[12]

A second, and more serious, criticism involves the Stoic notions of freedom and determinism. The Stoics held that everything which happens, whether it be the outcome of a football game, the movement of the planets around the sun, or one's trying to decide whether to buy a new car, is destined to happen according to a prearranged schema. But if this is so, then it is obviously impossible to alter any of the circumstances in which we find ourselves. For what will happen must inevitably happen, and there is no way we can prevent it. It thus seems that we are puppets of fate, moved by the strings of destiny. But if this is true, then we are never "free" but are always "constrained" or "compelled" to behave as we do. For to say that we are free implies that we could have acted differently from the way we do act. If the Stoics are right, we could not have acted differently since all our actions are determined for us in advance.

The consequence that we could not have acted differently from the way we did act raises immense difficulties for Stoic moral theory. For one thing, this thesis seems incongruous with the advice that a person should alter his character so as to become indifferent to things which he formerly prized. For in holding to the principle that everyone ought to strive to attain a state of indifference, the Stoics were clearly implying that every person is free to change his character; that he can, if he wishes, alter some of the natural events in the world—namely, those which go into making up his character or will. It thus appears that there is a fundamental inconsistency in Stoic theory: man is capable, and yet not capable, of

---

[12] Sextus Empiricus pointed out that the Stoic position also has the consequence that rape, incest, and cannibalism, if performed indifferently, would become properly moral acts.

revising the master plan of the world. If we accept the latter of these alternatives (that man is not free to rearrange things), then it is pointless to recommend that he attempt to alter his character. For if his character is determined in advance and according to plan, how can he possibly alter it? On the other hand, if a man is free to choose a different character, then the doctrine that all events are determined in accordance with some over-all design must be false.

This puzzle, which beset Stoic moral theory, has come to be known as the free-will problem. It has proved, since the time of the Stoics—indeed, since the time of Socrates—to be one of the most persistent and intractable problems in the history of philosophy, and some thinkers are convinced that no adequate solution to it has yet been proposed. Since limitations of space prevent a full discussion of this issue, we shall not pursue the point further here. But it must be remembered that the problem is one which vexed the Stoics, and try as they might, they were never able to solve it.

The third criticism maintains that Stoicism gives acceptable moral advice for certain special circumstances of life, but that it does not offer an ethic which is suitable for man's everyday needs. If a person knows in advance that he may be interrogated for military secrets if captured by the enemy, it makes sense for him to try to develop an attitude which will enable him to withstand torture. The philosophy of indifference may be helpful in such a situation; by trying not to think about the pain which is being inflicted on him, he may be able to avoid giving way to it. Or even apart from unusual circumstances such as these, we know that men, in the course of their daily activities, often become upset by happenings which are not really important in their lives: a window broken by a child, a book mislaid, and so on. The cultivation of equanimity may be an effective antidote to any tendency to react abnormally to these events. As a philosophy, Stoicism can be thought of as underlining the folly of magnifying trivia beyond their real worth.

But, although the Stoic outlook may be helpful in such circumstances, to practice the doctrine of indifference consistently would be to miss many of the things which make life most worth living: love, friendship, pride in achievement, and so on. For this reason, Stoicism tends to lose its appeal when the conditions in which people live greatly improve. If all's well with the world, it is ridiculous to be indifferent toward it; instead, it should be lived in and enjoyed. Stoicism was born when Hellenic civilization was in a state of decay, and it offered wise counsel for dealing with the exigencies of the time. But as conditions changed, the possibilities for reform no longer appeared so remote as the Stoics had believed. At that point, the Western world required a philosophy containing a dynamic and positive program for helping it reconstruct its social environment. Christianity was to supply such a moral system, and was, as a result, to replace the inward-looking, negative doctrine of the Stoics.

Like Cynicism and Stoicism, Christianity is in part a philosophy of consolation; but it also possesses constructive features which appealed to men in their efforts to overcome the social mire in which they were enmeshed. The result was a new society, the medieval synthesis, as it has been called, which was destined to last for more than 1000 years. But since this is a story too extensive to be examined here, we shall leap this gap of time and turn instead to modern moral speculation.

THE ETHICS OF SPINOZA

The transition from Ancient Greece to Modern Europe does not seem so abrupt when one considers Baruch Spinoza (1632–1677). In his conception of the function of philosophy and in terms of his personal conduct, he could well have been a Cynic or a Stoic sage. Like the Greeks, he felt the role of philosophy was to make the universe intelligible and to exhibit man's place in it. Like some of his predecessors among the Hellenes, he lived a solitary, frugal, studious existence, turning his back on the things men ordinarily pursue in order to engage in philosophical activity. The result of his reflections was a general view about the nature of the universe and a philosophy of life based on it, which has few, if any, peers in modern European thought. This view is presented in its complete form in a treatise called the *Ethics*, the title of which is to some extent misleading. For in that work, Spinoza's vision ranges over the whole gamut of philosophical subjects: metaphysics, epistemology, psychology, theology, politics—and, of course, moral philosophy.

It goes without saying that we cannot hope to deal here with all these topics, even though they bear importantly upon his ethic. For not only is Spinoza's treatment of them extensive, subtle, and profound but it is difficult to explain (at least briefly) in terminology other than his own. The *Ethics* is cast in a quasi-mathematical format, using a vocabulary of axioms, postulates, lemmas, theorems, definitions, and so forth. This unusual (some would even say inappropriate) terminology for a treatise on morals has led to considerable misunderstanding; indeed, no philosopher of genius has been so variously interpreted by his critics. His conception that God and Nature are identical (this "hideous hypothesis" as Hume called it) led the poet Novalis to describe him as a "god-intoxicated man," and Hume, on the other hand, to refer to him as "that famous atheist." Some commentators look upon him as a Cartesian, others as an anti-Cartesian; some see his doctrines as the final working out of presuppositions made by the Greeks, while others regard him as laying the foundations for modern thought. For nearly one hundred years after his death in 1677, his writings were thought to be unimportant and were ignored, until interest in him was revived by Goethe. As these remarks indicate, the difficulties which confront any interpreter of Spinoza are immense; accordingly, we can hope to sketch here only the barest outline of the doctrine for which he is now famous. But before turning to this task, let us look at the details of his life.

Baruch Spinoza was born in the seventeenth century, in "the century of genius," as Alfred North Whitehead called it, and he was to become one of its brightest luminaries. The date was 1632, the place Amsterdam. His grandfather, a Spanish Jew, had fled the Inquisition for Holland, where religious dissenters were tolerated. His father was also a pious man, whose life was bound up with the affairs of the Jewish community in Amsterdam. Young Baruch was reared in the religious schools of the Amsterdam Synagogue, and was a prize student. He studied both traditional Jewish materials, the Talmud (a legalistic-philosophical commentary on the Old Testament), the works of medieval Jewish philosophers and some of the current polemical writings of his teachers and other theologians of the Amsterdam Jewish community. Spinoza's serious interest in philosophy stems from his student days. After leaving the community he went on to study modern philosophy, especially that of a philosopher who was the talk of Europe. This was René Descartes (1596–1650), whose system was to prove the inspiration for Spinoza's own.

Having naturally a critical turn of mind, which was reinforced by his studies, Spinoza gradually became estranged from the tenets of Judaism. Becoming involved with some free-thinkers in the Jewish community, he began to question the bases of the religion. In spite of threats and bribes, he slowly withdrew from participation in the life of the Jewish community, refusing eventually to engage in the traditional ceremonies of that religion or to attend the synagogue. As a result of this apostasy, he was excommunicated at the age of twenty-four by means of a document traditional in its harshness of language. The excommunication paper reads, in part, as follows:

> The heads of the Ecclesiastical Council hereby make known that already well assured of the evil opinions and doings of Baruch, de Espinoza, they have endeavored in sundry ways and by various promises to turn him from his evil courses. But as they have been unable to bring him to any better way of thinking: on the contrary, as they are every day better certified of the horrible heresies entertained and avowed by him, and of the insolence with which these heresies are promulgated and spread abroad, and many persons worthy of credit having borne witness to these in the presence of the said Espinoza, he has been held fully convicted of the same. Review having therefore been made of the whole matter before the Chiefs of the Ecclesiastical Council, it has been re-

solved, the Councillors assenting thereto, to anathematize the said Espinoza and to cut him off from the people of Israel, and from the present hour to place him in Anathema with the following malediction. . . .

Let him be cursed by the mouths of the Seven Angels who preside over the seven days of the week, and by the mouths of the angels who follow them and fight under their banners. Let him be cursed by the Four Angels who preside over the four seasons of the year, and by the mouths of all the angels who follow them and fight under their banners. . . . Let God never forgive him for his sins. Let the wrath and indignation of the Lord surround him and smoke forever on his head: Let all the curses contained in the book of the Law fall upon him. . . . And we warn you, that none may speak with him by word of mouth nor by writing, nor show any favor to him, nor be under one roof with him, nor come within four cubits of him, nor read any paper composed by him.

After being excommunicated, Spinoza lived in Amsterdam for four years until, in 1660, he moved to Rijnsburg, a small village near Leyden. He was in contact with thinkers of a wide range of opinions. In Rijnsburg, he mastered the art of grinding and polishing optical lenses, an occupation which was to provide him with the means for devoting the major portion of his life to the study of philosophy. In 1663, he moved to Voorburg, near The Hague, where he lived for the remainder of his short life. By 1673, his fame had spread beyond the confines of Holland; his correspondence with distinguished persons grew; Leibniz had come to see him; and he had been offered the chair of philosophy at Heidelberg University (which he characteristically refused on the ground that it might prevent him from speaking freely on controversial subjects). In 1677, he died of a lung infection, aggravated, it is said, by the dust from the lenses which he polished.

Spinoza was perhaps the most admirable person among the great philosophers. His life was a model of integrity, unselfishness, and consideration for others. He never gave way to rancor, even when subjected to intense criticism. Those who knew him literally worshiped him. On the day of his death, knowing that he was about to die, he remained calm and unafraid. To the very end of his life, he lived in accordance with the moral principles which he had arrived at through the study of philosophy.

In order to illustrate the attractions which both the thinker and the man have exercised upon subsequent generations, we shall quote here at length from the opening sections of his brilliant, unfinished work, *On the Improvement of the Understanding*. This work aimed to put into simple language the doctrines which had been so abstrusely stated in the *Ethics*. Although incomplete, the material which we have constitutes one of the most moving pieces of philosophical writing in existence. Both the man and the doctrine come through to the reader with a tremendous impact. Here is the way the treatise begins:

After experience had taught me that all the usual surroundings of social life are vain and futile; seeing that none of the objects of my fears contained in themselves anything either good or bad, except insofar as the mind is affected by them, I finally resolved to inquire whether there might be some real good having power to communicate itself, which would affect the mind singly, to the exclusion of all else: whether, in fact, there might be anything of which the discovery and attainment would enable me to enjoy continuous, supreme, and unending happiness. I say "I *finally* resolved," for at first sight it seemed unwise willingly to lose hold on what was sure for the sake of something then uncertain. I could see the benefits which are acquired through fame and riches, and that I should be obliged to abandon the quest of such objects, if I seriously devoted myself to the search for something different and new. I perceived that if true happiness chanced to be placed in the former I should necessarily miss it; while, if, on the other hand, it were not so placed and I gave them my whole attention, I should equally fail.

Therefore I debated whether it would not be possible to arrive at the new principle, or at any rate at a certainty concerning its existence, without changing the conduct and usual plan of my life; with this end in view I made many efforts but in vain. For the ordinary surroundings of life which are esteemed by men (as their actions testify) to be the highest good, may be classed under the three heads—Riches, Fame, and the Pleasures of Sense: with these three the mind is so absorbed that it has little power to reflect on any different good. By sensual pleasure the mind is enthralled to the extent of quiescence, as if the supreme good were actually attained, so that it is quite incapable of thinking of any other object; when such pleasure has been gratified it is followed by extreme melancholy, whereby the mind, though not enthralled, is disturbed and dulled.

The pursuit of honors and riches is likewise very absorbing, especially if such objects be sought simply for their own sake, inasmuch as they are then supposed to constitute the highest good. In the case of fame the mind is still more absorbed, for fame is conceived as always good for its own sake, and as the ultimate end to which all actions are directed. Further, the attainment of riches and fame is not followed as in the case of sensual pleasures by repentance, but, the more we acquire, the greater is our delight, and consequently, the more we are incited to increase both the one and the other; on the other hand, if our hopes happen to be frustrated we are plunged into the deepest sadness. Fame has the further drawback that it compels its votaries to order their lives according to the opinions of their fellow men, shunning what they usually shun, and seeking what they usually seek.

When I saw that all these ordinary objects of desire would be obstacles in the way of a search for something different and new—nay, that they were so opposed thereto that either they or it would have to be abandoned, I was forced to inquire which would prove the most useful to me: for, as I say, I seemed to be willingly losing hold on a sure good, for the sake of something uncertain. However, after I had reflected on the matter, I came in the first place to the conclusion that by abandoning the ordinary objects of pursuit, and betaking myself to a new quest, I should be leaving a good, uncertain by reasons of its own nature, as may be gathered from what has been said, for the sake of a good not uncertain in its nature (for I sought for a fixed good), but only in the possibility of its attainment.

Further reflection convinced me that if I could really get to the root of the matter, I should be leaving certain evils for a certain good. I thus perceived that I was in a state of great peril, and I compelled myself to seek with all my strength for a remedy, however uncertain it might be —as a sick man struggling with a deadly disease, when he sees that death will surely be upon him unless a remedy be found, is compelled to seek such a remedy with all his strength, inasmuch as his whole hope lies therein. All the objects pursued by the multitude not only bring no remedy that tends to preserve our being, but even act as hindrances, causing the death not seldom of those who possess them, and always of those who are possessed by them. There are many examples of men who have suffered persecution even to death for the sake of their riches, and of men who in pursuit of wealth have exposed themselves to so many dangers that they have paid away their life as a penalty for their folly. Examples are no less numerous of men, who have endured the utmost wretchedness for the sake of gaining or preserving their reputation. Lastly, there are innumerable cases of men who have hastened their death through overindulgence in sensual pleasure. All these evils seem to have arisen from the fact that happiness or unhappiness is made wholly to depend on the quality of the object which we love. When a thing is not loved, no quarrels will arise concerning it—no sadness will be felt if it perishes —no envy if it is possessed by another—no fear, no hatred, in short no disturbances of the mind. All these arise from the love of what is perishable, such as the objects already mentioned. But love toward a thing eternal and infinite feeds the mind wholly with joy, and is itself unmingled with any sadness, wherefore it is greatly to be desired and sought for with all our strength. Yet it was not at random that I used the words, "If I could go to the root of the matter," for, though what I have urged was perfectly clear to my mind, I could not forthwith lay aside all love of riches, sensual enjoyment, and fame. One thing was evident, namely that while my mind was employed with these thoughts it turned away from its former objects of desire, and seriously considered the search for a new principle; this state of things was a great comfort to me, for I perceived that the evils were not such as to resist all remedies. Although these intervals were at first rare, and of very short duration, yet afterwards, as the true good became more and more discernible to me, they became more frequent and more lasting; especially after I had recognized that the acquisition of wealth, sensual pleasure or fame, is only a hindrance, so long as they are sought as ends, not as means; if they be sought as means, they will be under restraint, and, far from being hindrances, will further not a little the end for which they are sought, as I will show in due time.

I will here only briefly state what I mean by true good, and also what is the nature of the highest good. In order that this may be rightly understood, we must bear in mind that the terms good and evil are only applied relatively, so that the same thing may be called both good and bad, according to the relations in view, in the same way as it may be called perfect or imperfect. Nothing regarded in its own nature can be called perfect or imperfect; especially when we are aware that all things which come to pass, come to pass according to the eternal order and fixed laws of Nature. However, human weakness cannot attain to this order in its own thought, but meanwhile man conceives a human character much more stable than his own, and sees that there is no reason why he should not himself acquire such a character. Thus he is led to seek for means which will bring him to this pitch of perfection, and calls everything which will serve as such means a true good. The chief good is that he should arrive, together with other individuals if possible, at the possession of the aforesaid character. What that character is we shall show in due time, namely, that it is the knowledge of the union existing between the mind and the whole of Nature. This, then, is the end for which I strive: to attain such a character myself, and to endeavor that many should attain to it with me.[13]

It is surprising how many of the key notions in Spinoza's moral philosophy are compressed into the final paragraph of this quotation. It contains not only brief statements of his relativism and of his determinism, but also, in a very condensed form, a statement of his conception of the good life for man. Let us go over this part of the quotation again in the hope that by unpacking these notions we can elucidate the moral philosophy which rests upon them.

Consider, then, the third sentence of this final paragraph. Spinoza writes: "Nothing regarded in its own nature can be called perfect or imperfect; especially when we are aware that all things which come to pass, come to pass according to the eternal order and fixed laws of Nature." These words indicate that Spinoza, like Descartes and the Stoics before him, was a determinist. But unlike them, he accepted the full implications of the doctrine and denied that freedom exists. No man is free to act differently than he does; all his actions are determined by the "choices" he makes; and all his choices are determined by antecedent events. Consequently, no one could have chosen differently from the way he does choose, and consequently no one could have acted differently from the way he does act. Men are thus the predictably behaving puppets

---

[13] Baruch Spinoza, "On the Improvement of the Understanding," reprinted in *Selections from the Philosophy of Spinoza*, ed. by J. Wild (Scribner's, New York, 1930), pp. 1–5.

of destiny, with no chance to alter the plan according to which things happen as they do.

Another important doctrine is expressed by the second sentence of this paragraph, namely: "In order that this may be rightly understood, we must bear in mind that the terms good and evil are only applied relatively, so that the same thing may be called good and bad, according to the relations in view, the same way that it may be called perfect or imperfect." These words indicate that Spinoza, like Aristotle, is advocating a form of relativism in moral theory. As he sees it, whether a thing is to be counted as good or as evil will depend, in the last analysis, upon the point of view of those affected by it. Nothing is thus inherently good or bad. A thing is always good relative to a given person in given circumstances or bad relative to a given person in given circumstances. Depending on the individuals involved, and on the circumstances, the same thing may be either good or bad.

For instance, if a person is ill and penicillin helps him recover, then in those circumstances one can say that penicillin is good *for that individual*. But if penicillin makes him worse (as it sometimes does), then it is bad *for that individual*. Goodness and badness are not inherent characteristics of penicillin in the way in which its chemical structure is an inherent property of it. In itself, penicillin is neither good nor bad; it only becomes one or the other depending upon the use to which it is put.

These two notions, relativism and determinism, play fundamental roles in the moral theory which follows. On the basis of his relativistic conception of goodness, Spinoza is led to infer that the things men ordinarily strive to attain (for example, riches, fame, and sensual delight) become valuable only in terms of the attitudes we take toward them. Human happiness is thus a matter of attitude, an internal matter as it were, and is not to be located in the things we ordinarily strive to possess. The mistake that men make consists in their attributing value to things which are inherently neutral. By doing this, they make their happiness depend on possessions which are ephemeral, transitory, and fickle. When these things are lost, as they invariably are, men are plunged into despair. The solution to this predicament consists in the recognition that a happy life can be achieved by developing an attitude of *self*-reliance, which will replace an attitude of reliance upon external things. This is what Spinoza means by saying that man's chief good consists in the possession of a certain "kind of character."

But this raises a crucial question, indeed two crucial questions: Is it possible to specify the nature of this attitude, and if it is possible to do so, can men learn to develop it? Spinoza's reply is in the affirmative to both questions and is intimately connected with his belief in determinism.

The attitude of which he speaks is a complex one: it is in part rational, in part emotional. The rational part consists in the recognition of the truth that all events must happen as they do; the emotional part, in an acceptance of this fact. Stated otherwise, Spinoza is contending that a person will achieve happiness when he comes to understand that there are limits to human power. By coming to understand that everything that happens must happen necessarily, one will no longer struggle fruitlessly against the course of events. If a tragic happening occurs, it is pointless to give vent to emotion over it; there is no way it can be recalled, no way we can turn back the clock. Its occurrence is part of a natural pattern which we can learn to understand but not alter. By looking at every event as part of a larger system, by looking at things, in Spinoza's phrase, *sub specie aeternitatis* ("from the standpoint of eternity"), one will no longer be upset, frustrated, and frightened by the occurrences that take place in one's life. In this way, through adjusting one's outlook to accept what happens, one can learn to live a happy life.

Spinoza's moral philosophy can thus be interpreted as offering guidance to men which, if accepted, will enable them to avoid anxiety, fear, and unhappiness. These arise only when we become slaves to our emotions—the man who does not look at life from the standpoint of eternity is a man in "human bondage," as he puts it. Man can liberate himself by understanding that the course of nature is a necessary course and also by understanding that nothing that happens is "good or bad in itself" but is so depending on how we view it. By adjusting our outlook, by learning to accept the world as it is, we can free ourselves from our emotional slavery to its vicissitudes—and when this happens we will have developed that state of mind and that state of character which will make us happy. Such a state of mind, as Spinoza puts it, consists in "the knowledge of the union existing between the mind and the whole of Nature."

This philosophy of life is movingly summarized in the passage which ends the *Ethics*:

> I have finished everything I wished to explain concerning the power of the mind over the emotions and concerning its freedom. From what has been said we see what is the strength of the wise man and how much he surpasses the ignorant who is driven forward by lust alone. For the ignorant man is not only agitated by external causes in many ways and never enjoys true peace of soul, but lives also ignorant, as it were, both of God and of things, and as soon as he ceases to suffer ceases also to be. On the other hand, the wise man, insofar as he is considered as such, is scarcely ever moved in his mind, but, being conscious by a certain external necessity of himself, of God, and of things, never ceases to be and always enjoys true peace of soul. If the way which, as I have shown, leads hither seem very difficult, it can nevertheless be found. It must indeed be difficult, since it is so seldom discovered, for if salvation lay ready to

hand and could be discovered without great labor, how could it be possible that it should be neglected almost by everybody? But all noble things are as difficult as they are rare.[14]

Criticism of Spinoza

Spinoza's moral philosophy answers the question "What is the good life for man?" by arguing that the good life is a life of virtue and that virtue is an internal matter, a matter of character. With some justice, therefore, one might describe Spinoza's position as a sophisticated variant of Cynicism and Stoicism. Since the theory thus raises difficulties analogous to those we have already discussed in considering these earlier philosophies, we shall not attempt a lengthy criticism of Spinozism here. We might, however, touch upon the nature of certain of these difficulties, before passing on to a discussion of utilitarianism.

First of all, it is clear that Spinoza, like the Stoics, did not effectively resolve the conflict between determinism and freedom. His thesis is that if a person can come to realize that "what comes to pass must come to pass," he can also learn to accept this fact, and in this way achieve equanimity. But, it might be objected, if all events in nature are necessitated, a person is really powerless to alter the attitudes he has. Either he will have the sort of character which will allow him to take the long range view of things, or he will not. But if the latter, then there is nothing he can do about re-developing it. On this point, Spinoza's philosophy seems hung on the dilemma that it offers advice which is either unnecessary or impossible.

Second, Spinoza's suggestion that men look at happenings *sub specie aeternitatis* suffers from the same defects as the Stoic suggestion that men ought to view the world with an attitude of indifference. At times this is useful advice to follow; people do become upset by trivial happenings, they do become enslaved by their emotions. But there are times, most of us feel, when one should give way to one's emotions. If a friend dies, grief will not bring him back, to be sure; nonetheless, it may be a measure of one's feeling. A person who never exhibits any emotion would be regarded as shallow and inhuman by most men. There is a certain callowness in too easily giving way to emotion, but there is a certain callousness in not giving way to it at all.

Finally, if people were to accept Spinoza's advice and take the detached, long-range view of things, they might miss some of the most profound of human experiences—experiences in which new levels of character are reached, or even created. It is difficult to imagine Beethoven composing the last quartets in a spirit of Spinozistic repose. For some individuals, like Beethoven, the adoption of such an outlook might be temperamentally impossible; but even if it were possible, it might be in-

[14] Baruch Spinoza, *Ethics*, reprinted in *Selections*, ed. by J. Wild, pp. 399–400.

compatible with their continuing to work as creative artists, since such work is often the expression of emotional and mental turmoil. If obeyed, Spinoza's recommendations might serve to minimize the total misery and unhappiness which people experience, but they might also lead to a world from which the deepest experiences had been expunged.

Like Stoicism, Spinozism is essentially a philosophy of consolation. It is a philosophy designed to achieve personal happiness for those who accept its precepts. On the whole, it stresses a way of life which is introspective and antisocial; those who adopt it are not likely to revise, or try to revise, the social milieu in which they find themselves. In these respects, it differs diametrically from the next moral theory we shall consider, utilitarianism, which is outward looking, interpersonal, and optimistic about removing the causes of unhappiness which spring from defects in the social order.

UTILITARIANISM:
JEREMY BENTHAM AND
JOHN STUART MILL

The basic notions involved in what is now called *utilitarianism* have had a lengthy history, although the doctrine was only given this name, so far as we know, in 1802 by Bentham.[15] At the beginning of Book IV (420) of *The Republic*, for instance, Socrates propounds a thesis which is not unlike modern utilitarianism, and again in the early part of the eighteenth century, embryonic versions of it, some with theological overtones, are to be found in the writings of John Gay, Francis Hutcheson, William Paley, and David Hume. But the two thinkers who are mainly responsible for the present, mature form of the theory are Jeremy Bentham (1748–1832) and John Stuart Mill (1806–1873).

Bentham and Mill stand in an interesting relationship to each other. Bentham's formulation of utilitarianism is rigid, uncompromising, radical, and comparatively crude, while Mill (although nominally a follower of Bentham) considerably modifies, qualifies, and softens the doctrine. The relation between Mill and Bentham, from a theoretical standpoint, is thus similar to the relation between Epicurus and Aristippus in the development of hedonism; in both cases it is the younger man who tempers the original doctrine.

From an intellectual standpoint, both Bentham and Mill led remarkable lives. Bentham's intellectual activities began almost in infancy, and were never to flag during the course of his long life. At the age of three he had read Rapin's *History*; at five he could play simple melodies on the violin; at six, he commenced the study of French; at twelve, he became a

---

[15] In a footnote at the beginning of the second chapter of his famous essay *Utilitarianism*, Mill mistakenly refers to himself as the inventor of the term.

student at Oxford; by the time he was twenty-eight, his writings on English law had attracted considerable attention in Britain; and at forty-one, with the publication of the *Principles of Morals and Legislation* (1789), he had become an international celebrity.

But prodigious as these feats were, they were exceeded by those of Mill; indeed, it is not unfair to describe Mill as the most incredible prodigy in modern philosophical history. Mill's father, James Mill, a distinguished author in his own right and a disciple and friend of Bentham, was greatly influenced by the Benthamite doctrine that a man's character, and even his intellect, can be completely determined by his education. As a result, John Stuart was not allowed to attend a public school but was carefully educated under the stern tutelage of his father. His intellectual achievements as a child were astonishing. By the age of eight, he had mastered several languages, including Latin and Greek; even before this time, he was given the task of tutoring his sister in a number of academic subjects; and by twelve, he had worked through a larger quantity of classical literature than most college students ever read. Like Bentham, Mill's interest in intellectual subjects never diminished; some of his most important publications were composed during the last decade of his life.

Bentham and Mill had another characteristic in common: they are among the great reformers of history. Bentham, who was somewhat sickly and nearly a recluse, nevertheless exercised a tremendous influence on the development of nineteenth-century British institutions. He became the leader of a group of reformers, called "the Philosophical Radicals," who were to a great extent responsible for beneficial social and political changes in a rapidly industrializing England. The British criminal code, for example, was considerably improved through the efforts of this group. When Bentham died, Mill became the leader of the movement and pursued its ends with vigor and skill. Both of these men opposed monarchy and aristocratic privilege; both opposed imperialism; both supported the trade-union movement; both advocated women's suffrage; and both lived to see their efforts crowned with a considerable degree of success.

Both had interesting, fertile, and inventive minds—Bentham, particularly so. He conceived a scheme for a model prison (his "panopticon"); he was perhaps the first person to suggest cutting canals through the Isthmus of Panama and the Isthmus of Suez; and although his later writings are dull, pedantic, and difficult to read, he coined hundreds of words in a never-ending search for accuracy of expression. Many of these terms are still in common use, among them the following:

> minimize, maximize, deterioration, unilateral, self-regarding, dynamic, detachable, cross-examination, international, codification, antipathetic, exhaustive.

Bentham and Mill became utilitarians as a result of their interest in reform. They developed the doctrine through their search for a principle which would enable them to determine, with scientific objectivity and accuracy, whether an act (in particular, a legislative act) was morally justifiable. In attempting to discover such a criterion, they rejected any appeal to authority, intuition, divine guidance, feeling, sentiment, and emotion. The principle which they finally hit on seemed to them to avoid these defects and to provide an objective standard, in terms of which the merit of any course of action could be established with scientific accuracy. They called this principle the *principle of utility*, and it formed the base for what they believed was the first moral system ever erected on scientific principles.

A typical formulation of the principle runs as follows: An action is right if it tends to produce the greatest happiness for the greatest number of people; otherwise it is wrong. But since Bentham and Mill were hedonists, they also produced an alternative formulation in which happiness is equated with pleasure. As so interpreted, the principle maintains that an action is right if it is productive of the greatest amount of *pleasure* for the greatest number; otherwise, it is wrong.

As they conceived it, utilitarianism is a moral philosophy which rests on two main tenets: (1) Pleasure is the only thing worth having in its own right; and hence the good life for man is ultimately a life of pleasure. (2) Insofar as men are moral agents, they should act so as to produce the greatest amount of pleasure for all concerned. By "the greatest amount of pleasure," they did not mean absolutely the greatest amount, irrespective of whether this would be accompanied by a large amount of pain. Rather, they interpreted this phrase to mean that it should be the greatest *balance* of pleasure over pain that should be produced for the greatest number. They thus realized that sometimes efforts to produce the greatest amount of pleasure *per se* could also produce amounts of pain in quantities that were undesirable. Therefore, the principle of utility meant that it should be the largest excess of pleasure over pain for the greatest number that men should try to achieve. Actions which bring out this consequence will be right, and actions which do not will be wrong and ought not to be done.

However, the identification of utilitarianism with hedonism is now considered to be merely an accidental feature of the theory. Some modern thinkers (for example, G. E. Moore) have developed nonhedonistic versions of the doctrine by denying that happiness and pleasure are to be equated. They argue, on the contrary, that the essence of utilitarianism is to be found in the importance which it places upon the effects or consequences of actions. If an action produces an excess of beneficial effects over harmful ones, then it is right; otherwise, it is wrong. When formulated in this way, hedonism can be seen not to be a necessary feature of the doctrine, since "beneficial effect" does not have to be identified with "pleasure."

What is common to all forms of utilitarianism, whether hedonistic or not, is that they make a sharp distinction between the moral worth of an action and the moral worth of the agent who does it. The utilitarian stresses that the effects of actions make them right or wrong, not the motives from which they are done. Men frequently act from the highest motives, yet they may do something which has undesirable consequences. Hitler may well have acted from the desire to improve Germany by purifying the Aryan race, yet his actions led to torture, genocide, war, and the eventual devastation of Germany. A utilitarian would condemn his behavior on the ground that it produced a balance of pain over pleasure. Or again, a doting parent may act in such a way as to spoil his child. As these examples indicate, men may act from morally impeccable motives (from a sense of duty, honor, love, or justice) without necessarily doing acts which are morally commendable.

Bentham and Mill thought the principle of utility provided a criterion in terms of which anybody could decide, in a perfectly objective way, whether an action was right or wrong. For instance, if one adheres to a strict hedonistic form of the theory, as Bentham did, it becomes purely a scientific matter to determine whether an action will, or will not, cause an excess of pleasure over pain for the greatest number. We merely calculate the amount of pleasure the act produced and the amount of pain, and we have our answer as to whether it was right or wrong. Bentham even went so far as to develop a procedure for making such calculations. This "hedonic calculus" contained seven factors, on the basis of which one could measure the amount of pleasure or pain an act produces (these factors referred to the intensity of the pleasure, its duration, its extent, and so forth).

On the whole, Mill accepted the main tenets of utilitarianism as drawn up by Bentham. He agreed that moral problems were, in principle, amenable to scientific treatment and that the principle of utility was the key to any such procedure; he agreed that a distinction must be made between the rightness or wrongness of an action and the moral worth of the agent who performs it; he accepted Bentham's identification of happiness with pleasure. But in spite of this measure of agreement, his theory differs in certain important respects from Bentham's.

Bentham assumed that, in calculating the amount of pleasure an action will produce, each person is to count equally; moreover, he assumed that there were no qualitative differences between pleasures, but only quantitative differences, such as intensity and duration; thus, for Bentham, any calculation of pleasure involved only quantitative factors. Mill disagreed with these assumptions. Like Epicurus, he believed that the pleasures of the intellect are qualitatively different from, and also superior to, those of the body. Accordingly, he distinguished between *kinds* of pleasures, arguing that some were more valuable than others. Further, since "the wise" alone are capable of acquiring these intellectual pleasures, the effects of actions upon wise men must be given a different value than the effects of actions upon the nonwise. Mill thus rejected the thesis that each person is to count equally in any assessment of the rightness or wrongness of an act. As he says in an oft-quoted remark:

> It is better to be a human being dissatisfied than a pig satisfied; better to be Socrates dissatisfied than a fool satisfied. And if the fool, or the pig, are of a different opinion, it is because they only know their own side of the question. The other party to the comparison knows both sides.[16]

These emendations removed certain paradoxical features from Bentham's version of utilitarianism, but, as we shall show, they were to create difficulties of their own as well.

Criticism of Bentham and Mill

Two different types of criticism can be directed against a hedonistic utilitarianism such as that explicitly avowed by Bentham and accepted, but modified, by Mill. The first set of objections applies to any moral doctrine which looks upon the consequences of actions as determining their rightness or wrongness; the second concerns any form of hedonism which holds that some pleasures are more valuable than others. Let us consider objections of the latter type to begin with.

We have seen that both Bentham and Mill regard pleasure as the only thing worth possessing in its own right. All other things have value only insofar as they are *means* to this ultimate goal. The principle of utility is consequently not the ultimate criterion of goodness; this is a role reserved for pleasure. Instead, the principle of utility functions as a secondary standard, to be used for determining the value of things as means for producing pleasure. But pleasure, it should be reiterated, is the ultimate standard in terms of which all such means are to be judged.

If this is a correct description of the doctrine, then Mill's modifications seem inconsistent with it. In holding that some pleasures are intrinsically more valuable than others, he seems to be denying that pleasure is the ultimate standard for measuring values. For if pleasures can be compared in value, there must be some standard beyond pleasure by reference to which the comparison can be made. If this is what his modifications of the theory do imply, then they run counter to the main tenets of utilitarian-

---

[16] J. S. Mill, *Utilitarianism*. Reprinted in *The English Philosophers from Bacon to Mill* (Modern Library, New York, 1939), p. 902.

ism. If, on the other hand, they do not imply that such a standard exists, then how can he justifiably assert that some pleasures are "better" than others?

These difficulties can be put in yet another way. We have seen that the aim of Mill and Bentham is to create a scientific ethics—that is, one in which moral problems become susceptible to objective resolution. The principle of utility is the key notion in such a theory, since it enables anyone to decide whether an action is right or wrong, merely by determining the *amount* of pleasure or pain the action will cause. But Mill's modifications seem inconsistent with the use of the principle of utility; for if some pleasures are intrinsically or qualitatively better than others, how can we measure the *amount* of pleasure an action will produce? Is the pleasure one gets from hearing a Beethoven quartet "greater" or "less than" the pleasure one gets from drinking water when thirsty? If Mill holds that it is possible to measure such pleasures objectively, then he seems driven back into the position that there is an ultimate standard, other than pleasure, which can be appealed to in judging the comparative value of differing pleasures. If, on the other hand, there is no such standard, how can we determine the *amount* of pleasure an action will produce? But if this cannot be determined, then of what use is the principle of utility in helping us to judge whether a given action is right or wrong?

Finally, if pleasure is considered to be a type of sensation one experiences, Mill's contention that there are qualitative differences in pleasures does not seem to accord with the facts of introspection. Introspection reveals differences in the intensity of pleasures, or in their duration, but such differences are differences of degree, not of kind. It is true that pleasant sensations may be generated by a variety of factors which do differ in kind, such as by one's reading a book or eating well-prepared food. In supposing that pleasures differ qualitatively, Mill may well have erroneously identified the sensations produced by such processes as reading and eating with the processes themselves. This mistake, technically known as the "process-product" fallacy, is a subtle one, but easy to make. Nevertheless, even if this does not explain what led Mill to develop his modified form of hedonism, it should be stressed that the position has often been attacked as being incompatible with the facts as they appear to the introspecting subject.

Let us now turn to the second class of difficulties alluded to earlier—those connected with an attempt to assess the rightness or wrongness of an action in terms of its effects or consequences.

Besides the difficulties which Mill's distinction between kinds of pleasures introduces, there are other practical and theoretical problems involved in determining how much happiness (or pleasure) an action will give rise to. It is assumed by Bentham and Mill that it is the *total* number of consequences which must be taken into account in any moral appraisal of an action. For if we merely count the immediate amount of pleasure or pain which an action produces, we may be radically mistaken in deciding that it is right (or wrong); a long-range survey of the effects of the action may give different results from these. Television, for example, may have produced a large quantity of pleasure shortly after its introduction, but its long-range effects may be detrimental to the social and intellectual well-being of mankind.

If we say, therefore, that the total effects of an action must be taken into account in deciding whether it is right or wrong, we immediately come face to face with the objection that we can never really decide whether any action is right or wrong. For every action may have an infinite number of effects, and to wait an infinitely long time before deciding that an action is right (or wrong) is not to decide at all. The principle of utility was developed as a practical test for ascertaining whether actions are right or wrong, but if we cannot apply the principle until all the effects of an action are known, then its practical value seems nil.

Mill was aware of this difficulty and attempted to meet it as follows: He argued that by generalizing from the immediate effects of an action, one could predict its total effects with a high degree of probability. In this way, he argued, decisions about the merit of an action could *in fact* be arrived at with a high degree of accuracy. In accordance with this suggestion, one might therefore reformulate the principle of utility as maintaining that an action is right if it is likely (on the basis of probability theory) to produce the most beneficial results in the long run.

But this defense raises difficulties of its own. In particular, it introduces into the assessment of any action those subjective considerations which Mill and Bentham were so anxious to avoid. For a man who now decides that an action is right, or wrong, will be basing his decision on his *belief* that the action will have beneficial consequences in the long run. And such a belief might be mistaken, even though it rests on the best available evidence. In such a contingency, are we to say that the action is both right and wrong—right because it seemed likely to produce the most beneficial results but wrong because in fact it did not do so? This seems too paradoxical a position to maintain. Or what happens in those cases where later probabilities overwhelm earlier ones? In such circumstances are we to say that an action we previously had decided was right is no longer so—or what?

The difficulty is particularly acute for those individuals who wish not only to *judge* actions to be right or wrong, but beyond this to base their future conduct on the principle of utility. A man who chooses a certain course of conduct in the belief that it will have desirable consequences may, after a time, come to see that he was mistaken. Are we to say in such a case that he acted wrongly in acting on the best probabilities, or are we to say that he acted rightly? Either answer engenders difficulties for the theory. If we maintain that he acted rightly, but was mistaken, we have given up the traditional utilitarian view that a right action is one which *in fact* has the most desirable total consequences. On the other hand, if we adopt the position that he acted wrongly because the long-range effects of his action were undesirable, we seem to be pushed into the position that it is the *total* consequences of any action which must be taken into account in any assessment of it. But in the latter case, as we have mentioned, we seem saddled with a criterion in the principle of utility which cannot be used for practical purposes.

Apart from such technical considerations as these, the theory is often objected to on the ground that any appraisal of the rightness or wrongness of an action must take into account the motive from which it is done. Philosophers who hold this position contend that moral actions are those for which an agent can be held responsible. But to say this is to imply, of course, that they are actions which the agent intended to do. It is thus not behavior per se which is capable of being right or wrong, but behavior which results from one's intentions and conscious motives. This explains why we do not morally condemn a physician who inadvertently kills a patient during an operation. According to these critics, it is thus clear that no moral action can be evaluated as right or wrong apart from some consideration of the agent's intention in performing it. But this is precisely what the utilitarian attempts to do. He attempts to distinguish between the action and the motive from which it is done, and he then applies his doctrine to the former factor. But in separating the motive from the action, the utilitarian rests his theory upon a misleading contrast—for what is *meant* by "moral action" is behavior which results from someone's intention. Subtract the motive and the action does not fall within the scope of morality at all.

Finally, it has been suggested that by neglecting the motives from which actions stem, utilitarianism has implications as a philosophy of life that no man of common sense can accept. One consequence of the theory, for example, is that a world in which everybody acted from evil motives would be a desirable world if such actions resulted in a balance of pleasure over pain. But the thought of living in such a world would be repugnant to ordinary men who feel that the kind of character people have, and the motives from which they act, are at least as important as the effects which their behavior will produce. Thus, utilitarianism, if pushed to the extreme, would seem to have implications that men of common sense would not accept.

The philosopher, above all others, who has stressed that the moral worth of an action depends on the motive from which it is done is Immanuel Kant. Let us turn to his theory now in order to gauge the force of his arguments in favor of this position.

THE MORAL THEORY
OF KANT

Of all the views we have considered in this chapter, Kant's is unquestionably the most difficult to expound in a brief compass. Not only is his moral philosophy tied to intricate epistemological and metaphysical speculations, but it is expressed in a compact, highly technical vocabulary, used with consummate skill to draw the finest distinctions. Accordingly, we cannot hope to trace all the ramifications of the doctrine—its concern with human freedom, God, and immortality—important though these may be in any complete exposition of it. We can at least bring out its essential features, especially if we center our discussion around Kant's efforts to provide answers to the questions "What is the good life for man?" and "How can we tell whether our actions are morally right or not?"

But the way into these central bastions is anything but straightforward; any attempt to approach them head on is likely to leave the reader more perplexed than enlightened. Therefore, let us begin with a question which may seem peripheral, but which, as we shall show, will quickly take us into the heart of the theory. This is the query, "When does a person have moral worth?" or to give it an alternative formulation, "What distinguishes a person of virtue from a person who is not virtuous?"

Kant's answer, in brief, is that what determines a person to be morally worthy is not what he does, but why he does it. A man who repays debts out of the fear of imprisonment is not a virtuous person, according to Kant, even though he does what he ought to; nor is a man morally worthy who repays a debt because he is inclined to do so. Kant describes the former person as acting from "prudential considerations" and the latter as acting "in accord with duty," not "from duty." Insofar as a person acts from such considerations, he is not virtuous. An agent has moral worth only when he recognizes that he ought to act in a certain way because it is his duty to do so. One who takes care of his children properly, because he understands that he is under an obligation to do so and is motivated by this consideration, is a person of virtue.

Thus, looked at superficially, Kant's view may not seem dissimilar to that of the utilitarians. Like Bentham and Mill, he distinguishes the rightness and wrongness of actions from the moral worth of the agent who performs them. The utilitarians held, it will be recalled, that a person who acts from evil motives (from the desire to cheat others, for instance) is not a morally virtuous person—although they conceded that sometimes individuals acting from such motives will perform actions that are morally right (i.e., productive of the greatest happiness for the greatest number). Kant also discriminates between the worth of the agent and the worth of his actions; but as we shall see, he differs sharply from the utilitarians in his account of what makes actions right or wrong and agents virtuous.

For Kant, the rightness or wrongness of an action has nothing to do with its consequences. The question of whether an act is right or wrong arises only if there is some obligation on the part of the agent to do it; that is, if in relevant circumstances, one could properly say to the agent, "It is your duty to do so and so." Therefore, an action is right if it ought to be done in those circumstances, and wrong, given those circumstances, if it ought not to be done. Thus, if I have promised to do something but fail to keep my promise, my action is wrong. It would be a right act only if, having promised, I carry out my promise. Even if fulfilling one's promise were to produce a balance of pain over pleasure, it would be morally right to keep the promise and wrong not to do so. This is why, for Kant, it is never right to lie, even from altruistic motives. Even if we could be sure that by lying we could contribute to the greatest happiness of the greatest number, it would always be morally wrong to do so.

Besides disagreeing with the utilitarians as to what makes an action right or wrong, Kant rejects the utilitarian account of what makes a person morally worthwhile. He does not think that an agent can be regarded as virtuous if he acts from prudential considerations, from inclination, or from benevolence. Both Bentham and Mill feel that an agent who is *inclined* to do good, or who wants to do good, is a morally worthwhile person, even if the actions which result from his intentions do not lead to the greatest happiness of the greatest number. But Kant rejects this claim. An agent has moral worth only if he acts from duty—from the recognition that he has incurred an obligation and must fulfill it. But insofar as he acts from inclination he is never morally virtuous.

Kant's view can therefore be summarized as maintaining that a morally good person is a person of "good will"—a man who acts "out of reverence for duty." To act in this way is always to act in a morally justifiable manner, for as Kant says: "Nothing can possibly be conceived in the world, or even out of it, which can be called good without qualification, except a Good Will."

With these initial remarks, we are at the heart of the theory and in a position to answer the first of Kant's fundamental questions, "What is the good life for man?"

At a first glance, Kant's answer to the question seems hardly original; in fact, one might suspect that the theory he offers is nothing but a composite of the views of Aristotle and Spinoza. For the highest good, as he conceives it (and which he alternatively calls the *summum bonum* or "the Kingdom of God") is a product of the two elements: personal happiness and the possession of a virtuous character.

Some of Kant's comments about happiness tend to reinforce this suspicion; indeed, they sound like remarks which Aristotle himself could well have made. Like Aristotle, Kant maintains that all men aim at achieving their *own* happiness ("it is the essence of men to do so"); moreover, like Aristotle, he holds that happiness is not an entity, thing, or object; nor is it to be identified with pleasure. Insofar as he is willing to characterize it at all, he seems to concede that happiness consists in a sense of well-being given this measure of agreement, his theory in other respects represents a radical departure from that of his Hellenic predecessor.

For one thing, since all men are in fact inclined to seek their *own* happiness, it follows for Kant, in the light of the distinction between "inclination" and "duty," that it can never be anyone's duty to promote his own happiness. But since happiness is part of the ultimate good and should be pursued, Kant concludes that it is the duty of men to promote the happiness of others (this is why, as we shall indicate later, he holds that "every man must be treated as an end in himself"). Secondly, Kant does not maintain that the purpose of being moral (that is, the purpose of acting from duty) is to attain happiness. The essence of morality consists in our fulfilling certain obligations which are binding on us as rational beings. In this respect, the theory is diametrically opposed to those of Aristotle and Mill, who regard the doctrine of the mean and the principle of utility (their criteria for morally correct behavior) as procedures to be followed for attaining happiness. As Kant says:

> Now it follows from this that *morality* should never be treated as a *doctrine of happiness,* that is, an instruction how to become happy; for it has to do simply with the rational condition (*conditio sine qua non*) of happiness, not with the means of attaining it.

Or again:

> Hence morality is not properly the doctrine how we should make ourselves happy, but how we should become *worthy* of happiness.[17]

Furthermore, when we look into the supposed resemblance between Kant's theory and Spinoza's, we find that the similarity is more verbal than factual. For although Kant agrees that the highest good for man, in part, consists in his having a virtuous character, he does not mean by "virtuous character" what Spinoza intends by this expression. For Spinoza, "virtuous character" denotes the possession of a state of mind which is immune to the exigencies of personal fortune. But the virtuous character of which Kant speaks is not like this at all. One has a virtuous character when he acts from duty, that is, when he acts in accordance with the good will. For Spinoza, one who possesses a virtuous character will be

---

[17] *Kant Selections,* ed. by T. M. Greene (Scribner's, New York, 1929), p. 365.

happy as a result of possessing it. But for Kant, one who possesses a virtuous character will not necessarily be happy because he possesses it, for acting morally is not necessarily a means for achieving happiness. In sum, the Kantian view can be stated as maintaining that the highest good which man can attain will consist (1) in the achievement of personal happiness, and (2) in the development of a character which makes him "worthy of happiness."

This brings us to the second part of the theory, Kant's attempt to provide an answer to the question, "How can we tell whether our actions are morally right or not?" His answer makes use of the concept of "the categorical imperative." This concept plays a basic role in helping Kant explain how a person can determine, in a given situation, whether he is acting rightly or not. For although everyone might agree that it is always a man's duty to act rightly, the practical question "How can one ascertain in a given case that one is acting rightly?" still remains to be answered.

Kant's reply to this query can be summarized in a sentence: *An action is morally right if one can will that it become a universal law which all should follow; otherwise it is wrong.* That is, the *test* of the moral rightness of an action lies in whether one could rationally allow that the action set an example which everyone should follow. If one cannot "will" this, then the action is wrong. This is why lying, even if expedient on a given occasion, cannot be accepted as morally right under any circumstances; for we cannot will that lying become a universal practice which everyone ought to adopt.

The concept of the *categorical imperative* was developed by Kant in order to state this point precisely and unambiguously; the effort to achieve clarity in this context leads him to the use of a technical vocabulary, involving such notions as "hypothetical," "categorical," and "imperative." We cannot explore all the avenues into which this excursus takes him, but let us try, at least roughly, to indicate what he means by the phrases "hypothetical imperative" and "categorical imperative."

Kant thinks the function of imperative sentences is to express commands; thus the categorical imperative will be a type of command, and this is true, as well, of hypothetical imperatives. What then is the difference between a hypothetical command and a categorical one? A hypothetical imperative, according to Kant, is always stated by means of a conditional sentence (a sentence containing the words "If . . . , then . . . ."). Because this is so, it functions as a directive to the effect that *if* one wants to achieve certain ends, one must act in certain specific ways. Hypothetical imperatives are thus always concerned with prudential considerations—the most effective means for obtaining given ends. For example, if one wishes to drive from Vancouver to San Francisco by the shortest route, instructions for doing this can be given by means of a hypothetical imperative, "If you wish to drive to San Francisco by the shortest route, then take Interstate 5 all the way."

On the other hand, a categorical imperative is a statement which commands one to act in a given way without laying down any conditions whatsoever. It states that one *must* do such and such, and it states this without any qualifications. It thus lays down an injunction which must be obeyed categorically, if it is to be obeyed at all.

Now Kant feels that one's duty in a given situation imposes an obligation which is not subject to any qualifications or conditions. Thus, the ascertainment of one's duty must always be arrived at through a categorical, not a hypothetical, imperative.

In the light of these considerations, Kant formulates the categorical imperative in various ways. His initial formulation states that:

> There is, therefore, but one categorical imperative, namely this: Act only on that maxim whereby thou canst at the same time will that it should become a universal law.[18]

As we have indicated, Kant means by this statement that a man should always act as if every action were to become a universal law or regulation. Thus, no man should lie, since no one can will that lying become a universal practice, or a universal law, which all should follow. Similarly with regard to stealing and the keeping of promises. In fine, the test of what one should do in a given situation consists in asking oneself: Can I will that the action I am about to do should become a universal moral principle which everyone ought to follow? If an act can pass the test of being universalized in this way, it will qualify as a morally right action, an action which ought to be done.

A second and equally well-known formulation of the categorical imperative is the following:

> So act as to treat humanity, whether in thine own person or in that of any other, in every case as an end withal, never as a means only.[19]

This formulation of the categorical imperative results from the Kantian view that it is the duty of everyone to seek happiness—but not his own happiness. Therefore it is the duty of everyone to seek the happiness of others; this entails treating each individual as an end in himself, not as a means to one's own happiness.

This second formulation of the categorical imperative represents Kant's interpretation of moral principles which are familiar to everyone in

[18] Kant, *op. cit.*, p. 302.
[19] *Ibid.*, p. 309.

other contexts. For instance, it is another way of stating the golden rule, "Do unto others as you would have them do unto you." In political theory, the injunction to treat every man as an end in himself appears as the maxim that "all men are created equal," where this is interpreted to mean that the law should treat each man equally and not discriminate against anyone on grounds of race, religion, or creed.

With these expository remarks concluded, let us now turn to a critical evaluation of the Kantian viewpoint.

Criticism of Kant

As might be expected with a theory of such scope and containing so many controversial theses, the range of critical remarks about the Kantian ethic is extremely large. Given this fact, then, let us exercise some selectivity and consider merely three (but important) criticisms which have sometimes been directed against the view.

As we pointed out in the introduction to this chapter, Kant's theory does not adequately handle cases where we have a conflict of duties. Such cases are not only difficult for the moral theorist to deal with, but even for the ordinary man who is caught in a moral dilemma. Suppose, for example, I promise to keep a secret, and then, while in court and under oath to disclose truthfully all matters under discussion, I am asked a direct question about it. I cannot both tell the truth and keep my promise—yet according to the Kantian doctrine I should do both. In such a situation, I cannot, logically, universalize my behavior. If I tell the truth, I will break my promise to keep the secret; if I keep my promise, I will not tell the truth. For some theorists this criticism alone is sufficient to destroy the moral advice contained in the categorical imperative.

A second criticism, closely connected with the former, is this: Kant insists that we should never tell lies, break promises, fail to repay debts, and so on. According to more moderate versions of ethical objectivism, no claim as strong as this need be made. Moral rules, according to philosophers who hold this position, should be treated as generalizations rather than as categorical propositions, holding without exception. In general we should tell the truth, in general we should keep our promises, and so on, but there may occur situations where we would feel morally obliged to break these rules. A physician would hardly be regarded as immoral if he failed to keep a promise in order to relieve a human being in great physical distress. Telling the truth, keeping promises, and so forth are obligations that one should keep, provided that no other overriding obligations are present. Kant's mistake, according to those who hold this position, is that he failed to see the difference between our "prima-facie" obligations and our "actual" obligations. Telling the truth, keeping promises, and repaying debts are prima-facie obligations. That is, one is obliged to fulfill such obligations, provided that all other things are equal. If a person has made a promise and is under no other obligation, then his prima-facie duty becomes his actual duty. But there may be cases where a given prima-facie duty will not become one's actual duty, since there may be overriding considerations against carrying it out (as in the case of the physician who relieves distress). The theory has difficulties in its own right (for example: How do we tell what our actual duty is, where prima-facie duties seem equally obligatory? Is there a hierarchy of actual duties, and how do we determine what it is?), but at least it enables one to circumvent certain objections which can be proposed to the Kantian doctrine.

Finally, utilitarians point out that although Kant tries to prove that the moral worth of an action depends only upon the motive from which it is done, in fact he surreptitiously introduces considerations of consequences into the determination of its rightness or wrongness. These theorists argue that Kant is tacitly showing that the *effect* of not behaving in accordance with the categorical imperative would be to make human life as we now know it impossible. But to say this is to refer to the consequences of our actions. Consider this quotation from Kant as an illustration of the point. Kant says:

> Then I presently become aware that while I can will the lie, I can by no means will that lying should be a universal law. For with such a law there would be no promises at all, since it would be in vain to allege my intention in regard to my future actions to those who would not believe this allegation, or if they overhastily did so, would pay me back in my own coin.[20]

In mentioning that if everyone lied it would be "in vain" to promise, and further, that if he always lied, he would be paid back in his own coin, Kant is obviously referring to the consequences of lying; but if so, the details of the doctrine run counter to its theory.

With this brief discussion of Kant, we come to the end of the second part of this chapter, that dealing with modern ethical theories. Let us turn now for a brief look at the picture in contemporary ethical theory.

THE STRESS ON META-ETHICS

At the beginning of the chapter, we referred to the terms "hortatory" and "meta-ethical" in order to help the reader discriminate between two different sorts of philosophical speculation about moral matters. Horta-

---

[20] Kant, *op. cit.*, p. 282.

tory speculation tends generally to issue in theories which recommend, appraise, and justify the selection of certain goals or certain courses of conduct as being morally worthwhile. Meta-ethics is concerned with understanding or explaining the *meaning* of the key terms which appear in such recommendations, appraisals, and evaluations.

Philosophers who put forth hortatory theories can thus properly be thought of as moralists—as individuals offering advice for living. But insofar as a philosopher engages in meta-ethical speculation, he is not a moralist in this sense at all. Insofar as he restricts himself to this activity, he offers no advice and makes no recommendations. His task is of a different order; it consists in clarifying the advice contained in hortatory theories so that this advice will be better understood.

Of course, most philosophers do not stop at this point. In general, their purpose in clarifying the meaning of the crucial terms and statements which make up "philosophies for living" is to put themselves in a better position to decide which of them they ought to adopt. Thus, "meta-ethics" should not be regarded as being incompatible with "hortatory" ethics; instead, it should be thought of as a supplement to such speculation, or perhaps, as a preliminary to it.

Both types of speculation are exhibited in the traditional theories we have considered. Aristotle's writings, for example, contain hortatory elements (for example, the advice that men should seek happiness, and that they should do so by following the doctrine of the mean), but they also contain meta-ethical ingredients as well (for instance, his analysis of the concept of responsibility). What is characteristic of such traditional theories, however, is that it is the hortatory elements which are given most stress by their authors; insofar as meta-ethical speculation occurs at all, it is assigned a relatively minor role.

In contemporary moral theorizing, this balance has been reversed, with the stress being placed upon meta-ethical or "analytical" speculation. The reasons for this change are complex; in part, they have to do with certain historical developments within ethics itself (to be discussed in a moment); in part they have to do with the emphasis which has been put on language generally by contemporary philosophers (see the discussion of philosophical analysis, pages 394 ff.); and in part they have to do with the noticing of particular ambiguities in the formulation of traditional theories. We might illustrate this latter point briefly by considering some of the difficulties which traditional formulations of the principle of utility give rise to.

According to Bentham and Mill, an action is right if it leads to the greatest happiness of the greatest number. But what precisely do they mean in saying this? Consider the phrase "the greatest happiness" for example. Does the sentence which contains this phrase mean that an action will be regarded as right if it produces *more* happiness than any other action one can perform in certain circumstances?

This may seem like a proper interpretation of the meaning of the statement, but a little reflection will show that Bentham and Mill must have meant something else. For suppose that the action produces more happiness than any other action one could do in those circumstances, but also that it produces more unhappiness than happiness. Would the utilitarians wish to say that it was the right action to do in those circumstances? Clearly not! This means, then, that in order to grasp their intent, we shall have to interpret the principle in some other way.

Suppose, then, that the principle is interpreted to mean that out of a set of actions, any one of which we can do, a right action is that which produces more pleasure than pain. Will this formulation do? Once again, we can see that it will not. Two or more actions may have this consequence. Is it right to do either? Suppose, further, that the actions differ in the amount of pleasure and pain they produce. Which of them is right in such a case? This latter situation raises all sorts of difficulties for the utilitarian. For suppose that one can do either of two actions, the first of which produces much pain and much pleasure, the second of which produces less pleasure than the first but no pain at all. Which ought to be done in such a situation? Some utilitarians might say that one should do the action which produces some pleasure but *no* pain, while others might say that if the former of these actions produces the *greater balance* of pleasure over pain, this is the action which ought to be done. As these remarks indicate, before one can accept the advice contained in an apparently lucid theory like utilitarianism, some explication of the advice is required.

Subjected to intensive analysis, the traditional hortatory doctrines we have considered can all be seen to be replete with vagueness, ambiguity, and some degree of inconsistency. The contemporary stress on meta-ethical speculation to a great extent results from the efforts of thinkers to rid these theories of such defects.

G. E. MOORE AND *PRINCIPIA ETHICA*

The work which, beyond all others, was responsible for this shift in emphasis is *Principia Ethica*, published in 1903 by G. E. Moore (1873–1958). Moore began *Principia* with an attempt to define the subject matter of ethics. In the process of doing this, he was quickly led into meta-ethical speculation about the meaning of the word "good." Like many moral theorists, Moore assumed that ethics was a discipline whose subject matter was conduct; indeed, that it was a discipline in which principles were to be developed for distinguishing between good and bad conduct. But, as Moore pointed out, although the concept of "conduct" seemed clear enough to be used in any definition of "ethics," this was not true of "good." He inferred from this that before a moral theorist could develop a set of principles for distinguishing between good and bad conduct, it was requisite that he understand clearly what was meant by "good." Since the passages in which Moore was led to these meta-ethical considerations are of some historic importance, we shall quote from them at length here. He writes:

> Ethics is undoubtedly concerned with the question what good conduct is; but, being concerned with this, it obviously does not start at the beginning, unless it is prepared to tell us what is good as well as what is conduct. For "good conduct" is a complex notion: all conduct is not good; for some is certainly bad, and some may be indifferent. And on the other hand, other things, beside conduct, may be good; and if they are so, then "good" denotes some property that is common to them and conduct; and if we examine good conduct alone of all good things, then we shall be in danger of mistaking for this property, some property which is not shared by those other things: and thus we shall have made a mistake about Ethics even in this limited sense; for we shall not know what good conduct really is. This is a mistake which many writers have actually made, from limiting their enquiry to conduct. And hence I shall try to avoid it by considering first what good is in general; hoping that if we can arrive at any certainty about this; it will be much easier to settle the question of good conduct; for we all know pretty well what "conduct" is. This, then, is our first question: What is good? and What is bad? and to the discussion of this question (or these questions) I give the name of Ethics, since that science must at all events, include it. . . . But our question, "What is good" may have still another meaning. We may, in the third place, mean to ask, not what thing or things are good, but how "good" is to be defined. This is an enquiry which belongs only to Ethics. . . .
>
> It is an enquiry to which most special attention should be directed; since this question, how "good" is to be defined, is the most fundamental question in all Ethics. That which is meant by "good" is, in fact, except its converse "bad," the *only* simple object of thought which is peculiar to Ethics. Its definition is, therefore, the most essential point in the definition of Ethics; and moreover, a mistake with regard to it entails a far larger number of erroneous ethical judgments than any other. Unless this first question be fully understood, and its true answer clearly recognized, the rest of Ethics is as good as useless from the point of view of systematic knowledge.[21]

[21] George Edward Moore, *Principia Ethica* (Cambridge, New York, 1959), p. 2.

But, as Moore recognizes, before one can even attempt to define "good," it is necessary to specify what will be meant by "define," since this is a term which is itself ambiguous and hence subject to various interpretations. For in some sense of "define," everyone is able to define "good." For instance, one might try to settle the question by consulting a dictionary, or one might translate the word into French and say that "good" means the same as *bon* in French. Moore is not looking for a definition of "good" in either of these senses. What he demands is a definition which will reveal the nature of the object which words like "good" and *bon* are normally used to stand for. As he says:

> Definitions of the kind that I was asking for, definitions which describe the real nature of the object or notion denoted by a word, and which do not merely tell us what the word is used to mean, are only possible when the object or notion in question is something complex. You can give a definition of a horse, because a horse has many different properties and qualities, all of which you can enumerate. But when you have enumerated them all, when you have reduced a horse to his simplest terms, then you can no longer define those terms.[22]

In short, the kind of definition which Moore requires will be identical with what some contemporary philosophers call a "correct analysis," or with what Plato called a "real definition"—that is, a definition that will reveal those conditions which are both necessary and sufficient for the correct application of that term.

The word "brother" in one of its standard uses has such a definition; this word stands for the complex idea of "being male and being a sibling." Each of the properties denoted by these words represents a necessary condition for anyone's being a brother, and taken in conjunction, they represent a sufficient condition for anyone's being a brother (anyone who is male and a sibling will be a brother). Thus what Moore is looking for, in effect, is a definition of "good" which is analogous to the sort of definition we have given of "brother."

But then the question arises, Is "good" a complex term which has a definition of this sort? Moore's answer, startling though it may seem, is no. For "good," he holds, is a term which denotes a simple quality, and because this is so, it is indefinable—that is, unanalyzable. It thus denotes a characteristic of things which is not further reducible to, or explainable in terms of, any other feature of the world. In this respect, "good" is like "yellow," which also denotes a simple, unanalyzable characteristic. As Moore says:

[22] Moore, *op. cit.*, p. 7.

My point is that "good" is a simple notion, just as "yellow" is a simple notion; that, just as you cannot, by any manner of means, explain to anyone who does not already know it, what yellow is, so you cannot explain what good is.[23]

There is, to be sure, a difference between the quality yellow and the quality good. The former, he points out, is a *naturalistic* quality; it can be grasped by an act of direct observation. But good is *nonnaturalistic*; it can only be apprehended by an act of intuition, never through the use of the senses.

At this point, the reader might ask, "What makes Moore think that good is a simple, unanalyzable quality?" The answer is that Moore is led to this position by a powerful semantical argument which might be stated as follows: There is a difference, he insists, between saying "Pleasure is pleasure" and saying "Pleasure is good." The former statement is a mere triviality, which communicates no information, while the latter is a meaningful, informative judgment. But if the judgment is informative, then "good" must mean something different from "pleasure," or indeed, from any other term which can be substituted for "pleasure." But if this is so, then "good" cannot be defined as being synonymous with "pleasure" *or with any other naturalistic term*; and if this is so, then "good" cannot be defined at all. But since, by hypothesis, the sentence "Pleasure is good" is meaningful, then the word "good" must mean (or denote) something; hence "good" denotes an indefinable, or unanalyzable, characteristic which exists just as certainly as yellow exists.

In the light of this argument, Moore classified any attempt to define "good" by means of *naturalistic* terms ("pleasure," "happiness," "desire," "approval," and so forth) as a fallacy. It thus appeared, if Moore were correct, that most traditional moral theories were mistaken in their estimate of what constituted the good life. For any theory which argued that the good life was identical with happiness, or with virtue, or with knowledge, or with pleasure, was guilty of the *naturalistic fallacy*. The impetus which this important result gave to further meta-ethical speculation in contemporary philosophy was, as the reader can well imagine, tremendous.

Criticisms of Moore

Let us select from the staggering volume of philosophical argument which this theory has engendered two powerful objections which contemporary philosophers have advanced against the view.

[23] *Ibid.*

One such was produced by William K. Frankena in a paper called "The Naturalistic Fallacy," which appeared in a 1939 issue of the periodical *Mind* (then edited by Moore). According to Professor Frankena, Moore's argument, if accepted, would rule out not only any definition of "good" but any definition of any other term as well. For one can hold, by a parity of reasoning, that any correct definition is, in a certain sense, "informative." Consider a definition like "All brothers are male siblings." Such a sentence differs from "All brothers are brothers" in being informative; yet at the same time, it does not follow that the sentence in question is not a definition, or that the terms "brother" and "male sibling" denote different objects or properties.

Moore's mistake was a technical error. He was led to infer that, because a sentence like "Pleasure is the sole good," is informative in a way in which a sentence like "Pleasure is pleasure" is not, the sentence in question cannot be a definition. Moore thought instead that the sentence must be *synthetic*, one in which the words "the sole good" and "pleasure" denote two different objects or properties. If such a sentence were synthetic and not a definition, then this inference would have been plausible; and Moore would have been correct in saying that the naturalist commits the fallacy of attempting to equate as one things which are radically different from each other, pleasure and goodness.

But, according to Frankena, this is not a mistake which the naturalist commits. What the naturalist is trying to say is not that two different objects are really one but that the two *words* "pleasure" and "good" stand for the same object; and as we have seen in the case of "brother" and "male sibling," no fallacy arises from one's desire to say this. In effect, then, the naturalist is offering a definition of "good" when he utters a sentence like "Pleasure is the sole good," and hence his statement is not to be regarded as synthetic but as analytic. Moore's refutation of the propriety of any naturalistic definition of "good" must therefore be rejected as being incorrect.

A second criticism of Moore's view that "good" denotes a unique, unanalyzable quality comes from an entirely different quarter. Moore assumes, as we have indicated, that moral judgments like "Pleasure is the sole good" are meaningful statements (that they are not mere nonsense). Since they are meaningful, the word "good," he argues, must therefore denote some actually existing property or characteristic which certain things possess. But what reason does Moore have for thinking that moral judgments are meaningful? If one rejects this assumption, one is not committed to the view that "good" denotes anything at all. This is the line of attack directed against Moore by adherents of "the emotive theory of ethics," as it has been called. Let us turn to this view now; in doing so, we shall bring out the power of its attack on Moore, as well as outlining its own positive analysis of moral judgments—an analysis which has, in its own right, exercised a great influence on contemporary theorizing.

THE EMOTIVE THEORY OF ETHICS: A. J. AYER AND C. L. STEVENSON

Let us begin our examination of this doctrine on a note of caution. Although we have spoken and will continue to speak about *the* emotive theory of ethics, the doctrine in fact takes two forms which are strikingly different from each other. The more radical version of the theory, as advocated by A. J. Ayer in *Language, Truth, and Logic* (1936), maintains that *all* moral judgments, in their typically ethical use, are "purely emotive" and hence cognitively meaningless; the more moderate form of the theory, as developed by C. L. Stevenson in *Ethics and Language* (1944), holds merely that *some* moral judgments are purely emotive. But both theorists, as we have indicated, reject Moore's thesis that "good" denotes a unique, unanalyzable property. Since we are primarily concerned here with the criticisms which these philosophers have directed against Moore rather than with the differences which exist between them, we shall confine our remarks to Ayer's version of the theory. The key to this formulation of the doctrine is contained in the following quotation from *Language, Truth and Logic*, where Ayer writes:

> But in every case in which one would commonly be said to be making an ethical judgment, the function of the relevant ethical word is purely "emotive." It is used to express feeling about certain objects, but not to make any assertion about them. . . .
>
> We can now see why it is impossible to find a criterion for determining the validity of ethical judgments. It is not because they have an "absolute" validity which is mysteriously independent of ordinary sense-experience, but because they have no objective validity whatsoever. If a sentence makes no statement at all, there is obviously no sense in asking whether what it says is true or false. And we have seen that sentences which simply express moral judgments do not say anything. They are pure expressions of feeling and as such do not come under the category of truth and falsehood. They are unverifiable for the same reason as a cry of pain, or a word of command is unverifiable—because they do not express genuine propositions.[24]

Ayer's attack on Moore rests upon two assumptions: (1) that the grammatical form of a sentence must be distinguished from the use to

---

[24] Alfred J. Ayer, *Language, Truth and Logic*, 2d ed. (Gollancz, London, 1948), p. 108.

which the sentence is put and (2) that there is a difference between the *assertive* use of language and its *expressive* use. Let us explain the second assumption first. Consider the difference between a person who says "I am sad" and a person who says "Alas!" The former person is *asserting* that he is sad, and his judgment will be true if he is sad and false otherwise. But the person who says "Alas!" is not making any assertion at all. The word "alas" expresses his sadness, or evinces it, just as the word "ouch!" indicates (but does not assert) that the person who uses it is in pain.

What Ayer wishes to suggest against Moore, first of all, is that moral judgments are generally used to express the feelings and sentiments of those who employ them and to arouse the feelings and emotions of those who hear them (this is why the theory is called "the *emotive* theory of ethics"). When a person says, "Stealing is wrong!", he is not making any assertion about stealing; rather, he is expressing an attitude of disapproval toward stealing and attempting in the process to arouse similar attitudes in the minds of those who hear the statement.

If this is so, then moral judgments, Ayer argues, are neither true nor false—just as a cry of pain is neither true nor false. But if such judgments are not capable of being either true or false, then they do not refer to any features of the world—and in particular, do not refer to any unique, unanalyzable feature of it called "goodness."

Ayer diagnoses Moore's mistake in the light of the first assumption we mentioned, the distinction between the grammatical form of a sentence and the use to which it is put. According to Ayer, Moore's mistake lay in his thinking that because moral judgments like "Stealing is bad" are normally expressed by sentences which are in the indicative mood, they must therefore be genuine assertions about reality; assertions in which a quality, "badness," is being attributed to an act called "stealing." What Moore failed to see, Ayer argues, is that the grammatical form which moral judgments have is misleading; that they in fact function like commands or cries of pain—to arouse and express feelings, not to make assertions about them.

Like Moore's own meta-ethical investigations, those of Ayer and the other emotive theorists have important repercussions for traditional moral philosophy. If Ayer is right, moral standards, moral principles, and moral recommendations are always the expressions of attitudes and emotions, having no objective validity whatsoever. The theory thus defends, in a sophisticated linguistic form, a skeptical attitude toward conventional morality. It is, accordingly, in much the same tradition as the views of Protagoras, Aristippus, and Epicurus, although, at the same time, differing in various respects from these philosophies. Since this is the point of view which Socrates, in a different context, was concerned to refute, we have—after a debate lasting more than two millenia—in effect come full circle.

The issues posed by the ancient Greeks are still with us. As we have indicated in the introductory remarks to this volume, it is characteristic of philosophical issues that the same questions should arise again and again, though often taking different forms. It is because of this pervasive feature of philosophical activity that philosophical problems, at their deepest level, are often spoken of as "perennial" problems, recurring in a set of different guises. But, in the end, they raise the same kinds of issues and are responded to in ways not dissimilar to the answers provided by Socrates, Plato, Aristotle, and their opponents.

Since our object in presenting this brief account of the emotive theory is to present a second criticism of Moore's doctrine rather than to discuss the theory itself, and because the emotive theory has lost much of its appeal for philosophers writing in the decade of the 1970s, we shall not discuss it critically at length here. Suffice it to say that three general types of criticism have been leveled at it:

1) The basic concept that the notions of truth or falsity do not apply to moral statements has been widely rejected by contemporary philosophers. It is true that statements comprising factual, mathematical and moral discourse must be distinguished from one another, but it does not follow that statements made about moral matters cannot be said, in certain circumstances, to be true or false. Just as mathematical language gives rise to statements that are nonempirical, but nevertheless may be true, so moral discourse may give rise to statements that are true or false. To say that genocide is evil, that racism is unjustified, or that benevolence expressed toward benefactors is desirable, seems to be true, in a sense that does not radically change the meaning of the term "true." The basic difficulty with the emotivist position is now diagnosed as stemming from a model of speech acts which restricts the application of the terms "true" and "false" to statements which in principle belong to the language of science. In arguing that moral discourse is not scientific discourse, the emotivists have therefore inferred that it is not capable of being true or false. But this is to assimilate the uses of "true" or "false" to those employed primarily in the domain of science. In fact, in ordinary speech—including the use of language to speak about moral matters—we do apply such terms as "true" or "false" to what is said. It is thus concluded by many contemporary writers that there is no need to adopt the emotivist analysis.

2) It is also felt that the language or morality is not wholly subjective in the way described by the emotivists, and especially by Ayer. One who says passionately, "Racism is evil," or "Abortion is never justified," may indeed be venting his or her emotions. From this observation, it does not follow that this is *merely* what such a person is doing, and, accordingly, that moral discourse is not merely a case of expressing one's feelings in a wholly subjective way. The point is made in this connection that a scientist who shouts with joy at discovering a new phenomenon in the laboratory

may both be expressing his feelings and making a statement that is true or false. There is no reason why moral language may not be used in much the same way.

The point may be put in an alternative way. Emotivists speak as if the language of morality is subjective, in the sense that no good reasons can be given in support of statements that persons make in such contexts. But persons who are arguing about the merits of a proposed course of action—such as genocide, or the need for a pure environment, or about the justification of euthanasia—often put forth reasons in support of these positions. In one important sense of "rational," their discourse is "rational" —that is, what they say can be supported or rejected in terms of the reasons given. According to critics of the emotive theory, the confusion identified here is parallel to that mentioned in (1) above. The emotivists hold that unless a body of discourse belongs in principle to the sciences (or to mathematics or logic) and is therefore in principle verifiable by experience, it cannot be said to be rational (or objective). But many contemporary philosophers reject this argument. They aver that it rests upon a "persuasive definition" of what counts as rational (or objective), a definition which subtly alters the ordinary meaning of these terms to coincide with the position the emotivists wish to defend. In opposition to this definition, they insist that in our ordinary employment of such words as "rational," "objective," and "reasonable," the language of moral discourse is such. They thus infer that there is no special reason to accept such a narrow and biased definition as proposed by the emotive theorists.

3) The third criticism leveled at the emotivists is more wide-ranging. It includes the entire emphasis which has been put upon meta-ethics since the turn of the century, rejecting this as being the sole legitimate function which philosophy can serve. In this respect, it argues that though the clarification of moral language is indeed useful, and is often a necessary prelude to talking sensibly about moral problems, it is not an end in itself. At best, it is contended, it is a first step, not a last step. Ethics is and ought to be about matters that are substantive in nature, and cannot end with linguistic analysis. The classical questions about the nature of the good life, and what counts as a right course of action for human beings, or for society in general, still remain fundamental issues for most human beings; and these cannot be dismissed as merely nonsense or as stemming from conceptual confusion. There has thus in the past decade been a strong swing away from meta-ethical philosophy to hortatory or substantive philosophy. The most notable example of work of this sort is contained in a remarkable book, *A Theory of Justice* (1971), published by John Rawls, professor of philosophy at Harvard University. Rawls' work harkens back to the premeta-ethical discussions of moral and political issues raised by the classical utilitarians, Bentham, the two Mills, and Henry Sidgwick in his *Methods of Ethics* (1974).

JOHN RAWLS: A THEORY
OF JUSTICE

Because of this emphasis upon substantive issues in morality and politics, Rawls' book has achieved enormous critical acclaim in philosophy itself, but also in related academic disciplines such as political theory, economics, sociology, anthropology, and indeed among the general public. It has been widely reviewed in such periodicals as the *New York Review of Books, The New York Times Book Review, The Economist, Nation, New Republic, The Listener, The Observer, The New Statesman,* and *The Washington Post.* The extensive interest shown in this work is to a great extent explained by its return to the older tradition of moral philosophy, and by the sharp contrast in which it stands to the work of the logical positivists and to the analytical school of philosophy in general. It is a work whose synoptic character not only concerns pressing issues in moral philosophy, but also in economics, political theory, legal theory, and sociology. Unlike the meta-ethicists, Rawls takes firm stands upon these substantive issues.

In its broadest sense, Rawls' book may be taken as providing a new defense of what is traditionally called "the liberal tradition." Liberalism in this sense must be distinguished from what is now called *libertarianism.* The two theories are often confused with one another. Libertarianism is the doctrine that government *per se* is evil, and that ideally there should be as little government as possible. Libertarianism is normally given its strongest defense in the economic sphere, where its proponents recommend an absence of intervention by the government in economic matters—the so-called doctrine of *laissez-faire* being the strongest expression of this position. On this view, the government should allow the marketplace to determine economic policy. Its emphasis should be merely to see that free economic factors are allowed full play. The opposite of libertarianism in this sense would be socialism or other forms of welfare economics, where it is held that the government should intervene to eliminate the exploitation of the poor by the rich, and in general, to fully use the coercive power of the state to bring about equality and minimally decent standards of living for all. A modern, powerful expression of the libertarian philosophy is to be found in Robert Nozick's book, *Anarchy, State and Utopia* (1974). Nozick there states:

> Our main conclusions about the state are that a minimal state, limited to the narrow functions of protection against force, theft, fraud, enforcement of contracts, and so on is justified; that any more extensive state will violate persons' rights not to be forced to do certain things, and is unjustified; and that the minimal state is inspiring as well as right. Two noteworthy implications are that the state may not use its coercive apparatus for the purpose of getting some citizens to aid others, or in

order to prohibit activities to people for their *own* good or protection (p. ix).

The confusion of libertarianism with liberalism in part stems from the fact that certain famous liberals, such as J.S. Mill, have argued that the state is never justified in intervening in the *private* affairs of its citizenry, even if it is for their own good, provided that their activities do not result in harming others. Thus, Mill would argue that the state is not justified in preventing people from smoking cigarettes, provided that their doing so does not harm others. To intervene in this private sphere, he contends, is an unjustified extension of the power of the majority, or the power of the state, over the rights of individuals to engage in idiosyncratic action which does not harm others, even if it can be shown to be harmful to the individual himself (see chapter on political philosophy, pp. 215 ff.).

But as we have seen in discussing Mill's views (see p. 216), Mill does not hold that the proper state is a minimal state in Nozick's sense. Like Marx, he felt that democracy in some real sense could not be achieved unless political democracy could be extended to the economic realm. Without economic equality, political democracy would be a meaningless formality. Mill's problem was how the *legitimate* (and indeed legitimately coercive) power of the state could be used to bring about economic, as well as political, democracy for its citizenry. The state must recognize the liberties of its citizens, but it must also take positive actions to make sure that each individual has the opportunity to realize these liberties in a practical way.

In *Utilitarianism*, Mill argues that these liberties could be obtained by developing political policies in accordance with the principle of utility. As we have explained earlier in this chapter, such policies would be initiated by the state with the aim of maximizing the balance of pleasure over pain for the greatest number of its citizens. Mill's liberalism is thus not identical with Nozick's libertarianism, but assumes that the state will intervene vigorously in certain dimensions of social life in order to maximize pleasure for the majority of its citizens.

Rawls' book is in the liberal tradition of Mill and Locke—he takes his stand with those who wish to extend the liberties of persons in society against the authority of the government. Like Mill, he believes that this can be achieved only if there is good government and if governmental policy is in principle fair to its citizens. He is thus opposed in principle to all forms of libertarianism in the sense depicted. But he also differs from Mill in that he is not a utilitarian. Rawls states that utilitarianism has been the dominant theory developed in the Western tradition in defense of liberalism; but he feels that as a foundation for this tradition it is seriously deficient. His aim is thus to provide a different justification for a defense of liberty, one not stemming from a utilitarian foundation.

Rawls' rejection of utilitarianism rests upon moral grounds. He feels that social policies carried out in strict conformity to the principle of utility would have consequences which are "unfair" or "unjust," and in this sense would violate the "intuitions" which ordinary men have about the nature of justice. Thus, a society which distributed its goods (money, power, offices, and so on) inequitably, so that some persons received larger shares of such goods than others, might be justified in following such policies on utilitarian grounds. Such policies might lead to a maximization of the greatest amount of pleasure or good for the greatest number, while allowing many persons to live in abject poverty. Or to take a still more striking case, a society might justify on utilitarian grounds the punishment of the innocent if this could be shown to have a deterrent effect against crime in general. By adopting such a policy, society might thus maximize the pleasure of most persons by punishing those who had committed no crime. For Rawls, any such policy would be a mockery of what is just. His own contention, then, is that public policies must rest upon principles of justice that are inherently fair. The basic thrust of his book is to develop a moral philosophy which is Kantian in nature rather than utilitarian; the fundamental question which he poses is: "What principles should a society adopt, as the fundamental bases for action, that would be just or fair in this Kantian sense?"

His answer is complex and takes up nearly one-third (about 200 pages) of his lengthy book. Rawls finds that the solution to this difficulty lies in social contract theory. We have seen in Plato's *Republic* (in the discussion with Glaucon) that already the outlines of a contract theory exist. It appears again in Hobbes, Locke, and Rousseau. The idea is that men, as free agents living in a pre-civil society—the so-called "state of nature"—find that for various reasons it is better to develop a set of rules (laws) that will apply to all and that all, as rational beings, would be willing to follow. As Rousseau poses the question:

> Is a method of associating discoverable which will defend and protect, with all the collective might, the person and property of each associate, and in virtue of which each associate, though he becomes a member of the group, nevertheless obeys only himself, and remains as free as before? (*Social Contract*, p. 130)

As Rawls poses the question, it becomes: "What rules or principles would men adopt if they were rational and given a free choice?" But Rawls recognizes that this question can be answered only hypothetically; for if it were asked of men as they *now are*, some of them having positions in society that give them advantages over others, they might choose to perpetuate the advantages they have. The question could arise only if men as they now are were subject to certain constraints on their knowledge and motivation. Thus men in what Rawls calls "the original position" must choose such principles of fairness or justice behind what Rawls calls a "veil of ignorance."

The veil of ignorance is not complete. Men in the original position are not primitives or aborigines, having only a minimal culture. Indeed, they are conceived to be people not much different from today's average man. They have their own interests at heart, they are concerned with obtaining for themselves (or for their immediate families) such "primary" social goods as wealth, income, power, authority, self-respect, and liberty. The mere existence of such "primary" goods means that men in the original position are already far removed from the most primitive forms of the state of nature, where there are no institutions, laws, forms of commerce, and so on. And indeed, for Rawls, men in the original position know all there is to know about the general laws of economics and social theory. The veil of ignorance operates only with respect to what they know about their natural capacities and characteristics, their present position in society, or the historical period they are born into. Not knowing these factors, they will then choose a set of principles which will allow everybody to be treated fairly; operating behind the veil of ignorance each person would arrive at the same rational calculation about how the primary goods of society should be allocated or distributed. They would arrive at the conclusion that any set of principles that allowed for some persons to receive a larger share of the primary goods than others would be unfair; indeed, each person would be aware that he might be the individual who suffers from such an inequitable distribution of goods. Not knowing in advance that he would not be such a person, he will therefore settle on a set of principles that would lead to a fair distribution of such goods. He would see, at the moment of choice, that in the long run it would be better for him to settle for equality of distribution than to take the chance that he might be deprived of his proper share of these primary social goods.

Rawls believes that the outcome of this choice will be two principles which are basic principles of procedural fairness in the distribution of primary social goods. The first principle requires the greatest equal liberty to be compatible with a like liberty for all. The second principle (which he calls "the difference principle") permits only those inequalities in the distribution of primary goods that benefit everyone, in particular the worst off. The first of these principles, the guarantee of liberty, is more basic than the second. It cannot be sacrificed for economic and social advantages unless they are so scarce or unequal as to prevent the meaningful exercise of equal liberty until material conditions have improved. Thus Rawls might hold that in severely disadvantaged Third World countries the principle of liberty might be suspended temporarily until economic conditions rose to a certain minimal level; but it is clear that no such suspension would be justified in most advanced industrial nations that now exist in the world. It is because of this basic emphasis upon liberty that Rawls can be characterized as belonging to the liberal tradition of Locke and Mill. He regards the possession of liberty of choice or action as fundamental, and prior to, all other social practices. Societies not having freedom in this sense—freedom to choose their own institutions by regular democratic procedures—cannot be just societies. All other arrangements would entail that the people were being governed, rather than being the governers. In sum, Rawls is defending self-government as a necessary condition for a society's being just.

The second principle—the difference principle—allows for some inequality in the distribution of goods, but only if such an inequality benefits in an absolute way the worst-off members of society. This principle, in effect, requires that those with various natural abilities and capacities must accept limitations on how much their natural aptitudes will benefit them. These talents can be exercised only if they lead to benefiting the worst-off members of society. Thus any gain made by the most talented or best-off members of society can be acceptable only if it has the consequence indicated.

To summarize, Rawls' theory is opposed to those forms of liberalism which simply argue that everybody should be given equality of opportunity. According to Rawls, such a system would ultimately allow for real inequities in the distribution of social goods. It also rules out counting a society's advanced cultural or intellectual achievements among the gains which can make sacrifice of the more primary goods just. Instead, Rawls insists that everyone must be provided with the basic conditions for the realization of his own aims, regardless of the absolute level of achievement that may represent.

The doctrine is thus a form of egalitarian liberalism, opposed to forms of perfectionism or meritocracy. The justice of social institutions is measured not by their tendency to maximize the sum or average of certain advantages—it is thus anti-Utilitarian—but by their disposition to counteract the natural inequalities deriving from birth, talent, and circumstance, pooling those resources in the service of the common good. The common good is measured in terms of certain basic benefits to individuals: personal and political liberty, economic and social advantages, and self-respect.

Criticism of Rawls

We here mention only two major criticisms of Rawls, considerations of space limiting further discussion. The first states that the mere fact that persons would agree in the original position to a set of principles is not itself a reason for saying those principles are just. It could be that men in that situation, and operating under the veil of ignorance, would in fact choose to gamble on their futures (there is a simpler notion expressed in the Myth of Er at the end of Plato's *Republic*, where each soul, blindly as it were, chooses a future life). What Rawls has done, some critics argue, is to build into the conditions of choice principles that are (or that he considers) just. But if that is so, then the original contract is not a *source* of procedural fairness or justice but *presupposes* such a conception. The criticism thus holds that Rawls has subtly introduced into the very notion of the original position the principles that that position presumably will give rise to. More generally, this criticism holds that from the conception of the original position as a kind of betting model about what counts as a rational choice one cannot *per se* abstract a moral position; for it is possible what may be rational to the person betting is that he should take a gamble that he is basically different and superior to others.

The second criticism is one that harkens back to a Platonic conception. It holds that men by nature are different from one another, do in fact have different aptitudes and abilities, and accordingly make different contributions to society. This view argues that merit is the basis of justice; in its modern form it is sometimes called "the entitlement theory." It holds that persons who make more important and valuable contributions to society should be rewarded differentially; that indeed they are entitled to a greater share of society's primary goods, whether or not their receiving such a share would benefit those who are worst off. This claim is clearly not an internal criticism of Rawls book, but rather poses a different conception of justice against his own egalitarian theory.

SOME APPLICATIONS: MEDICAL ETHICS, BUSINESS ETHICS—CODES OF CONDUCT

In concluding this chapter, we wish to emphasize that even prior to the appearance of Rawls' book, developments have been occurring in ethical theory of an applied sort, where the stress has been upon substantive practical problems which raise moral dilemmas. Philosophers have increasingly involved themselves in these matters, attempting to formulate coherent and systematic sets of principles which will allow for the appraisal as to the right or wrong, or the justification, of certain courses of action that persons follow or wish to follow in ordinary life. Let us describe, briefly, three examples of the sorts of issues that raise moral questions.

1. In medicine:

Physicians are bound by a code of conduct called the Hippocratic oath. This code attempts to define in a rough-and-ready way certain principles that guide a physician in his treatment of patients—for example, he must treat a patient whether or not the patient can afford to pay for his services. The Hippocratic oath presupposes that the patient is in a particularly vulnerable position. He is not only ill, but he stands in a dependency relation to a medical practitioner who is qualified by training to assist him in regaining his health. Under such conditions, it is easy for the physician to take advantage of the patient: he can exploit him financially by prescribing medication which the patient does not really need, requiring him to return for office visits and examinations which are not medically justified, and may refuse to treat him if the patient cannot pay. In some of these situations, the morally correct course of conduct is obvious, and a physician who does not live up to the code is clearly guilty of moral impropriety. For many of these situations, the Hippocratic oath provides the only sorts of general guidelines which a physician who wishes to engage in morally responsible conduct need follow. But there are cases that arise frequently nowadays, especially with the emergence of new techniques for keeping patients alive, that raise issues of a different order. It is here that philosophical principles which go beyond the guidelines of the Hippocratic oath become relevant. Suppose a patient is terminally ill; suppose there is no question about the accuracy of the diagnosis; and suppose further that the patient wishes to die. He knows that there is an enormous financial burden imposed on his family by keeping him alive; or worse, he may be in a physical and mental condition where he is little more than a vegetable, and yet through modern technology he can be kept alive in some minimally physical sense of that term. The Hippocratic oath requires that the doctor do everything within his power to keep the patient alive; yet is this, under these circumstances, a responsible thing to do? There is no prospect of the patient's recovering; the burden upon all is very great. What is the purpose or point in protracting his life? On utilitarian grounds, one might argue that the physician in these circumstances has the *duty*, let alone the right, to terminate the person's life. He can do this not by any positive action, let us say, by injecting a drug; but simply by not taking certain courses of action—for instance, by refusing to recommend that the patient be hooked up to expensive machinery that will keep him breathing, or keep his heart functioning. The dilemma here is that this course of action gives the physician a certain sort of power that could be abused. The physician may decide that it is merely inconvenient to keep the patient alive, that it is expensive and wasteful, so why bother; and he may decide to exercise this power even when the patient wishes to remain alive. Is such a power something that the state or society should grant to a physician? Or conversely, if the patient wishes despite the best medical advice, to die quickly, does the conscientious physician have the right to interpose his will and do what he can to extend the patient's life? Does the patient have a right to die which overrides society's wish or the physician's injunction, operating as he does under the Hippocratic oath, to keep him alive? The issue is a profound one and is now the subject of intensive investigation by philosophers.

2. Professional conduct:

In recent years, and in a variety of fields, the activities of various kinds of professional persons—lawyers, professors, legislators—have been subject to criticism by members of the public and by other members of their own professions. As the Watergate episode showed, the criticism stems from the recognition that professionals, including government office holders, have moral obligations stemming from the offices they hold. A congressman who, while representing the public in his capacity as a legislator, nevertheless has certain financial connections with companies doing business with the government is legitimately subject to scrutiny for having such connections. What sets of principles could be formulated which would allow him to function properly as a congressman, exercising his best judgment about matters of public policy, while at the same time constraining the range of his "outside" activities? Similar questions arise with respect to professors who are not only paid, say, by the state to perform a certain kind of service on a 100 percent basis, yet also engage in outside consultation that provides them with remuneration. Is such an arrangement legitimate? It has been argued that it is; that professors (say engineers) must engage in practical, consultative activities in order to stay abreast of developments in their profession. It has also been argued that such consultation *for pay* is illegitimate, and may involve a conflict of interests, in which students and the university are being short-changed in terms of a professor's time spent there while he receives private benefits for consulting. Again, philosophers have been intrigued by such practical questions, and have attempted to formulate principles that would distinguish between permissible and impermissible consultative arrangements.

3. Business ethics:

It is sometimes held that like love and war, everything is "fair" in business. Since the aim of business in a capitalist society is to maximize the profit of the businessman, the question arises: "Are there any circumstances in which the effort to maximize profits can be considered illegitimate?" In general, social critics have answered "Yes." They point out that every businessman must be limited in certain ways; clearly he cannot engage in outright fraud or deception. There are thus legitimate and illegitimate forms of advertising, for instance. But where does one draw the line? Can a businessman exaggerate the efficacy of a product, even if the claims he makes are not positively fraudulent? Who is to monitor such claims—the state? But if so, then the free enterprise system is at stake. How can restrictions be put upon entrepreneurs that will allow them the latitude to maximize their profits, while at the same time restraining the range of their activities? This problem, like those we have discussed, involves the application of general principles emanating from moral philosophy to particular detailed cases, and in general will issue in various codes of conduct, spelling out in a detailed way what would constitute legitimate behavior for the persons involved. As such, they constitute a particularly fruitful development in contemporary moral philosophy.

BIBLIOGRAPHY
History of Ethics
Broad, C. D. *Five Types of Ethical Theory* (Littlefield, New York, 1965). An excellent, analytical account of the moral theories of Spinoza, Butler, Hume, Kant, and Henry Sidgwick.

Dewey, John, and Tufts, James. *Ethics*, rev. ed. (Holt, Rinehart and Winston, New York, 1932). One of the best general introductions to the subject.

Sidgwick, Henry. *Outlines of the History of Ethics* (Humanities Press, New York, 1967). Probably the best short history of the subject in English, but it suffers from a dull writing style, and does not treat the contemporary period.

Warnock, Mary. *Ethics Since 1900* (Oxford, New York, 1974).

Classical Works
Aristotle. *Nicomachean Ethics*. Reprinted in *Introduction to Aristotle*, edited by R. McKeon (Modern Library, New York, 1965).

Augustine. *The Basic Works of St. Augustine* (Random House, New York, 1944). Contains the moral views of one of the seminal thinkers in the Christian tradition.

Butler, Joseph. *Fifteen Sermons on Human Nature* (Allenson Press, Naperville, Ill., 1970). Volume II of Butler's Works. Five sermons have appeared in the Library of Liberal Arts, 1950.

Hume, David. *An Enquiry concerning the Principles of Morals* (Bobbs-Merrill Library of Liberal Arts, Indianapolis, 1957).

Kant, Immanuel. *Fundamental Principles of the Metaphysics of Morals*, translated by T. K. Abbott (Bobbs-Merrill Library of Liberal Arts, Indianapolis, 1967).

Plato. *Protagoras, Gorgias, Republic, Philebus, Euthyphro*. Many editions of these works are readily available.

Price, Richard. *A Review of the Principal Questions in Morals* (Oxford, New York, 1975).

Modern Works

Ayer, A. J. *Language, Truth and Logic*, 2d ed. (Gollancz, London, 1948). An early version of the emotive theory is to be found in Chapter VI of this book.

Carritt, E. F. *The Theory of Morals* (Greenwood, Westport, Conn., 1973).

Dewey, John. *Human Nature and Conduct* (Modern Library, New York, 1930). An exposition of naturalism in ethics.

Ewing, A. C. *The Definition of Good* (Macmillan, New York, 1947). A defense of nonnaturalism.

———. *Ethics* (McKay, New York, 1975).

Hare, R. M. *The Language of Morals,* 2d ed. (Oxford, New York, 1961).

Moore, G. E. *Principia Ethica* (Cambridge, New York, 1959).

Nowell-Smith, P. *Ethics* (Philosophical Library, New York, 1958)

Nozick, Robert. *Anarchy, State and Utopia* (Basic Books, New York, 1974).

Prior, A. N. *Logic and the Basis of Ethics* (Oxford, New York, 1949).

Rawls, John. *A Theory of Justice* (Belknap Press, Cambridge, Mass., 1971).

Ross, Sir William David. *The Right and the Good* (Clarendon Press, Oxford, 1938).

Schlick, Moritiz. *The Problems of Ethics*, translated by David Rynin (Greenwood Press, Westport, Conn., 1964). The moral views of one of the leading logical positivists.

Stevenson, C. L. *Ethics and Language* (AMS, New York, 1976). The most complete exposition of the emotive theory to date.

Stroll, Avrum. *The Emotive Theory of Ethics* (University of California Press, Berkeley, Calif., 1954). A critical appraisal of the emotive theory.

Toulmin, S. *Reason in Ethics* (Cambridge, New York, 1960).

chapter 5

Above, clockwise from top left: Friedrich Nietzsche (1844–1900); birthplace—Germany; William James (1842–1910); birthplace—United States; Martin Buber (1878–1965); birthplace —Austria (Israeli); Dietrich Bonhoeffer (1906– 1945); birthplace—Germany

PHILOSOPHY
OF RELIGION

INTRODUCTION

Generally speaking, the characteristic problems of the philosophy of religion arise from an intensive, intellectual scrutiny of the beliefs and practices embodied in actual, "living" religions. Most religions can be looked at as the embodiment, whether explicit or implicit, of beliefs about the nature and limits of human knowledge, about the ingredients composing the world, and about the sorts of behavior which men, as moral beings, ought to follow. In the Old Testament, for example, we find views to the effect that the world is controlled by an all-powerful, all-wise, benevolent being called "God," that a special kind of knowledge about man's relations to God is obtainable, and that in the light of such knowledge, human beings ought to obey the moral precepts expressed in the Ten Commandments and in the Mosaic Law. The characteristic activities of philosophers of religion arise from the attempts to vindicate, reject, or even neutrally analyze, such claims. In particular in this area, the philosophical task revolves around the efforts to determine whether there is a special kind of knowledge to be called "religious"; if so, how it is gained; and if it is gained, what its implications will be for human conduct.

The activities of the philosopher thus at once resemble, and yet differ from, those of the historian of religion or the comparative religionist. Those engaged in these latter pursuits attempt to trace the origin and development of religions, and to compare the various features of different religions with one another. Material derived from these activities often is, and often ought to be, relevant to the inquiries of the philosopher. But

337

characteristically enough, his activities do not cease at this point. More typically, he is interested in analyzing and weighing such information with the dual aims of discovering what it means and whether it is true. And, as one might expect, philosophers have traditionally evaluated such information in radically different ways.

Voltaire and Hume are cases in point. They contend that when the conditions under which the great religions began and flourished are revealed, it would be unreasonable to accept the claims of religion as being valid. For them, the reasonable attitude is a skeptical attitude, as the following quotation from Hume's famous essay "Of Miracles" indicates. In speaking of the first five books of the Old Testament, Hume writes:

> Here, then, we are first to consider a book presented to us by a barbarous and ignorant people, written in an age when they were still more barbarous, and, in all probability, long after the facts which it relates, corroborated by no concurring testimony, and resembling those fabulous accounts which every nation gives of its origins. Upon reading this book we find it full of prodigies and miracles. It gives an account of a state of the world and of human nature entirely different from the present: of our fall from that state; of the age of man extended to near a thousand years; of the destruction of the world by a deluge; of the arbitrary choice of one people as the favorites of heaven, and that people the countrymen of the author; of their deliverance from bondage by prodigies the most astonishing imaginable—I desire anyone to lay his hand upon his heart, and, after a serious consideration, declare whether he thinks that the falsehood of such a book, supported by such a testimony, would be more extraordinary and miraculous than all the miracles it relates.[1]

Although Hume, Voltaire, and others utilized information of a historical or a comparative sort to disparage the claims of traditional religions, other scholars have taken a different view. In the seventeenth century, Bishop Pierre-Daniel Huet of France, in his *Demonstratio Evangelica*, made an immense comparative study. He maintained that the presence of so many similar elements in all of the religions of the world was an all-important indication of the truth of their common view of reality and morality. In this century, some of the important Biblical archeologists, among them W. F. Albright and G. Ernest Wright, have made significant discoveries about the course of history in the ancient Near East, especially in Palestine. They have then hypothesized that this information, which casts new light on the historical context of Biblical events, also strengthens the plausibility of the message of the Bible. In the last decade, with the discovery and unraveling of the Dead Sea Scrolls, more

---

[1] David Hume, *An Enquiry concerning Human Understanding*, Selby-Bigge ed. (Oxford, New York, 1963), p. 130.

factual data have come to light about the state of affairs in Palestine at the time of Jesus. Some scholars have insisted that this information makes Christianity more plausible, while others, on the basis of the same new data, have maintained exactly the opposite.

For the philosopher of religion, the historical facts are not sufficient in themselves to allow for an evaluation of the epistemological, metaphysical, and ethical contentions of various religions. The philosopher is concerned to examine the kinds of evidence that have been, or could be, offered to support these contentions, and then, in this light, to assess the status of the assertions made by religions. No matter what the historical circumstances are in which religions begin and develop, there may be a special type of evidence which provides the warrant for the claims of religions, or these claims may be based upon evidence that can be examined and scrutinized at any time. The philosopher, then, is concerned with the examination of the nature of these knowledge-claims, and with the assessment of the principles upon which religious knowledge and beliefs appear to rest.

The task of the philosopher of religion is also different from that of the theologian. Theological disputes sometimes involve philosophical issues, sometimes historical or textual ones. Insofar as the problems involved concern the general nature of religious knowledge, the theologian and the philosopher are interested in the same matters. But insofar as the disputes are about what happened at a particular time, as some of the disputes about the decisions of church councils seem to be, or about the proper reading of certain passages in the Bible, the philosopher of religion is not concerned with the same issues as is the theologian. For example, one of the basic disputes between the Calvinists and the Roman Catholic Church is over the proper interpretation of Jesus' words at the Last Supper: "This is my body." To the extent that this is a question of whether a particular interpretation of these words does or does not accord with the decisions arrived at by the early Council of the Catholic Church at Nicaea in A.D. 325, or the later one at Trent in 1545–1547, 1551–1552 and 1562–1563 during the Reformation; it does not really concern the philosopher as such. But to the extent that the dispute involves two radically different theories about the source and nature of religious knowledge, and the standards for judging such knowledge, the philosopher of religion is genuinely concerned. By and large, the philosopher is interested in critically evaluating the general assertions of religions about the nature of the real world and about morality, rather than the detailed contentions of certain churches or sects.

In assessing religious views, philosophers have been concerned with determining whether various religious beliefs are true, and with examining the evidence that can be adduced in favor of these beliefs. This chapter will concentrate primarily on the problem of religious knowledge: "What knowledge can be gained about the nature and existence of God?" We will deal with two kinds of issues, one the kinds of information that link historical documents with purported religious knowledge, and the other the rational and empirical claims to establishing knowledge of the existence and nature of God.

Generally speaking, every religion makes some claims about what can be, or is, known about the world, and how man should behave in his lifetime. Some of these purport to be historical facts, some metaphysical or moral conclusions. But what are these contentions based on? Many of the major religions state their basic contentions in documents, some of great antiquity. These contentions are supported by what various people have said over the ages, by what various institutions stand for, and by the arguments and information compiled by theologians. In addition, believers in these religions have insisted that certain experiences in their own lives confirm, or attest to, the truth of these contentions. Basic to the assertions of most major religions is the claim that some, if not all, of the knowledge offered is the result of man's relationship to a Divine Being, and that the warrant for the assertions is our knowledge of, or contact with, the Divine Being. Religious propositions are not accepted just because some other human being asserted them in the past. The believer is convinced that the propositions are ultimately based upon some knowledge about God. Hence the philosophers of religion have been concerned for at least two and a half millennia with examining the question of what we can know historically, scientifically and logically about the existence and nature of God. And, on the basis of answers to these fundamental questions, they have tried to show what we can justifiably say about the metaphysical and ethical contentions of various religions.

The evidence that has been offered to support religious knowledge-claims can be divided into two categories—natural and revealed. Revealed theology has appealed to supernatural evidence to support the truth of religious assertions. Information gained from revelation, from allegedly divinely inspired authorities, from miraculous events, from special documents, such as the Bible, has been offered, as well as appeals to faith. On the other hand, natural theology has attempted to support claims to knowledge about God's Existence and Nature by means of evidence that is not supernatural at all. Historical facts, scientific findings, and rational arguments have been utilized as *natural* evidences of the truth of certain religious beliefs. The contentions of natural theology and those of revealed theology are not necessarily in opposition. Many theologians have maintained that the two complement or supplement each other. They have said that natural means, such as those employed in scientific research, can provide sufficient information to justify certain religious beliefs, whereas supernatural evidence may be needed to establish others. In this chapter, we shall begin considering the problem of religious knowledge in terms of views about revealed information, and then turn to discussions about the nature and value of natural evidence that might be used to prove assertions about the Nature and Existence of God.

In beginning this task, we should stress that the distinction between "natural" and "supernatural" evidence is not to be identified with the distinction between *a priori* and *a posteriori* arguments. As the term "natural" is traditionally employed, arguments of both types purport to provide natural evidence for the existence of God. Rather the distinction, as we have said, is between evidence based upon revelation, and that based upon scientific, historical and logical inquiries.

In this chapter, we shall therefore consider a number of classic versions of philosophical arguments purporting to provide natural evidence in favor of the existence of God, among them St. Anselm's Ontological Argument, St. Thomas' five proofs, Hume's version of the Argument from Design, and so on.

THE DEVELOPMENT OF
THE PROBLEM OF
RELIGIOUS KNOWLEDGE

In the Western world, the problem of religious knowledge first arose in connection with Greek mythology. The Greek philosophers examined, and often questioned, purported facts of the Greek religious tradition. Socrates pointed out many inconsistencies in Greek mythology, and in his trial was accused of disbelieving the religion of the Athenians. Other Greek philosophers, such as the Epicureans and the Stoics, sought to show that many of the accepted popular beliefs of Greek religion were not only questionable but incompatible with other knowledge that had been gained about the world. Many of the basic theories of the nature of knowledge about God were first presented in the context of discussions about Greek religion.

However, for the last two thousand years practically all the philosophical examinations of the question of religious knowledge in the Western world have taken place in relation to the Judaeo-Christian and Islamic religions. From the time of the meeting of the Hebrew and Greek traditions in the Hellenistic Age, philosophers of religion have concerned themselves with analyzing the knowledge-claims contained in the Old and New Testaments.

In the Old Testament itself there is little concern about philosophical problems. A picture of the world is presented in which it is taken for granted that God exists, that He controls the universe which He has created, and that He has revealed certain fundamental information to man. A history of the world is related in which various people at different times receive additional communications from God. There is almost no discussion about the basis or warrant for the authenticity of the information presented. No philosophical proofs of the existence of God are offered, nor is any argument set forth to establish that God is actually of the nature described. The Book of Job, the most philosophical part of the Old Testament, discusses the problem of reconciling what is accepted as true about God with the facts of human experience. The human world is not precisely what one would expect it to be if it is controlled by a Just and All-Powerful God. Job's sufferings do not seem to be justified in a Divine Order. The book then explores several possible explanations of the problem of evil, always assuming that a Just and Omnipotent God exists, and concluding that God's ways are mysterious to men.

The contact between the Greek and the Hebrew worlds created a new problem, that of explaining and justifying the Hebraic religious view, and later the Christian outlook, in terms that would make sense to those who did not accept either the Old or New Testament picture of the world. As St. Paul discovered, the message of Christianity sounded like nonsense to the Greek philosophers. When he spoke to them at Athens, they ridiculed him. Jewish and Christian thinkers began to try to state their religious beliefs in terms that would be reasonable to someone schooled in Greek philosophy. They attempted to show that the assertions of their religion were justified on the standards employed by the Greek philosophers. Philo Judaeus, of the first century A.D., and the early Church Fathers Clement of Alexandria (A.D. 150?–220?) and Origen (A.D. 185?–254?) argued that the religion of the Bible was compatible with Platonic philosophy. They contended that philosophical reasons could be given for accepting certain religious views, and that various religious contentions could be interpreted as ways of stating philosophical theses. Over the next several centuries, many theories from the writings of the Greek philosophers were employed by theologians to clarify or justify their religious convictions. Proofs of the existence of God, and theories about His Nature were set forth to provide a rational justification for the religious knowledge-claims of the Judaeo-Christian tradition, and of the Mohammedan religion.

St. Augustine (354–430), Bishop of Hippo in Africa, developed the framework for a "Christian philosophy," drawing heavily upon ideas from Platonic and Neo-Platonic writers. Arabic and Jewish theologians in the Middle Ages, principally in Moorish Spain, used Aristotelian and Neo-Platonic views to work out arguments for, and interpretations of, their religious beliefs. In Europe, during medieval times, the great philosophers and theologians of the universities such as Paris and Oxford devoted themselves to explaining and justifying their faith. One way in which they did this was by attempting to construct satisfactory proofs of the existence of God, thereby showing that natural reasons alone sufficed to establish that there is a Divine Being. From the period of the Reformation and the Renaissance in the sixteenth century, problems about the real meaning and authenticity of the revealed information in the Bible came to the fore. These led philosophers of religion to develop theories of Bible interpretation so that the claims about religious knowledge could be understood or justified in the light of new historical and scientific evidence. We shall treat first some of the theories developed in this latter tradition, and then turn to the arguments offered to prove the existence of God.

BIBLE CRITICISM

From ancient times people within the Jewish and Christian traditions noticed discrepancies in the Biblical text. Early rabbis and Church Fathers sought ways of explaining these problems by interpreting various passages in the Scriptures allegorically, metaphorically or mystically. The Jews and early Christians were also in constant contact with Greek, Roman and Near Eastern groups that did not accept the Bible. Hence the Jews and early Christians had to develop bases for contending that the Bible contained genuine religious knowledge, whereas Greek, Roman and other pagan religious documents were merely mythological. The problem of the special status of the Bible was raised anew by the religious and scholarly crises of the sixteenth century. Scholars like Erasmus of Rotterdam (1467–1536), searching through the available ancient manuscripts of the Bible, found that the oldest texts varied from the accepted version of the Catholic Church. Reformation leaders insisted that one had to go back to the original Hebrew text of the Old Testament and the Greek text of the New Testament instead of accepting the Latin translation (done by St. Jerome at the end of the fourth century) authorized by the Catholic Church. As scholars examined the manuscripts then available, they found the oldest Hebrew text, the Massoretic text of the eighth or ninth century A.D., differed in many points from the oldest Greek text, the Septuagint, which is known to have existed as early as 270 B.C. Both texts differed from the Latin text and from other ancient texts in Armenian, Syriac, Ethiopic, and so on. Then, how does one tell which is the accurate text of the infomation God revealed to man? The Catholic Church insisted that God inspired St. Jerome in his translation, and that it is the right copy. Some argued that the Jews had altered the Hebrew text to avoid having to become Christians. But as Renaissance scholars explored the problem of the variants between the different texts, the problem became more perplexing. Could one find the actual words God uttered, or was one restricted to the various human versions of the words that have come down to us in different traditions?

The problem became more difficult to resolve in the seventeenth century when a revolutionary hypothesis was advanced which started what is now called the Higher Criticism of the Bible. A French courtier, scientist, and theologian, probably of Jewish descent, Isaac La Peyrère (1596–1676), wrote what was perhaps the most heretical book of the seventeenth century, a work called *Men before Adam* (1655). In order to defend his individualistic interpretation of the Bible, he argued that there were men before Adam; that Adam was only the first Jew, not the first man; that the Flood was only a local event in Palestine, not a universal catastrophe; that Moses did not write the first five books of the Bible, the Pentateuch; that what has come down to us is "a heap of copy of copy" full of errors and contradictions. Using anthropological data, materials from ancient pagan history, and analyses of apparently conflicting passages in the Bible, La Peyrère set forth his case. He himself was not trying to deny that the Bible contained special and unique religious information, but rather that Scripture ought to be interpreted in a certain way.

Some of La Peyrère's evidence was taken up by Hobbes and Spinoza. Hobbes, in *The Leviathan*, argued that Moses did not write all of the Pentateuch, but only those sections specifically attributed to him. Spinoza went further in his *Tractatus Politico-Theologicus*, denying that the Bible contained any revelatory or supernatural information. Instead, he insisted that the work just represented what the early Hebrews thought the world was like.

As a result of these early critics of the Bible, scholars began studying the Bible as a historical document that came into its present form as the result of human developments. Seeing it in this way, one could raise questions about when it was written, and who actually wrote it. If one accepted the view that Moses could not have written all of the Pentateuch (since it includes a description of his death and funeral), then who was or were the author or authors? The revelatory status of the information in the Bible had been linked to Moses having received The Message directly from God. If what we possess is not by Moses, is there any guarantee that the Bible does in fact contain revealed knowledge about God?

Starting with the great Bible scholar Father Richard Simon (1638–1712), who wrote *The Critical History of the Old Testament* (1678), and *The Critical History of the New Testament* (1689), people began examining Scripture in terms of historical, anthropological, and philological information in order to assess when the document could have been written, and what it meant in such a context. Father Simon, who was the greatest expert of his time in ancient Near Eastern languages, documents, history and customs, was trying to separate the human development of the Bible from the original revealed information. The more he found out about the human side of the existing Biblical text, the more the revealed side receded beyond recovery. The existing texts of both the Old and New Testaments, Father Simon concluded, were all human products to be explained in terms of human developments. The present text of the Old Testament he saw as the product of about 800 years of development, the New Testament as written a century or so after the death of Jesus. The problem of recapturing the actual revelatory information, before it became admixed with human factors, became more and more difficult the more one knew about ancient human developments. After Father Simon, Jean Astruc (1684–1766) offered the theory that one could account for the difficulties in the present Biblical text by recognizing that there were at least two original authors. Astruc separated them according to the passages where the word for God is "Elohim" and where it is "Yahve." Astruc's theory opened the way for the highly developed scholarship of the nineteenth century which separated out various strands and layers of the Biblical text, and dated them at various periods in ancient Jewish history.

Another kind of problem about interpreting the Bible arose from La Peyrère's Pre-Adamite theory. La Peyrère had claimed that the world had been going on for an indefinite period before God created Adam. In contrast to the orthodox view of the world's chronology set forth by Archbishop Ussher in the mid-seventeenth century that the world was created in 4004 B.C., La Peyrère appealed to evidence in ancient pagan history, Chinese history, Mexican calendars, and so on, to contend that the world was much older than the Bible indicated. The findings and interpretations of fossils, prehistoric remains, and geological evidences led many scientists by the end of the eighteenth century to argue that the physical and biological universe was hundreds of thousands of years older than 4004 B.C. Some theologians began to reinterpret *Genesis* as saying the world was created in six ages, rather than six days, and that only human history began in 4004 B.C.

In the nineteenth century, with the development of archeology, comparative linguistics, and anthropology, and with the intimate contact with the civilizations of India and China, the scientific estimates of the span of human experience on the earth began to expand rapidly to tens of thousands of years, to hundreds of thousands, until in our time estimates are given beyond a million years. The discoveries of ancient bones by L. S. B. Leakey in Central Africa indicate that human creatures were there at least one and a half million years ago. The anthropological studies of human types over the last hundred and fifty years have indicated that there are different races of mankind probably having separate origins in the dim, distant past. With the development of carbon-14 dating and other techniques, scientists are able to determine the age of various remains found on the earth and the moon. They now speak, on the basis of scientific tests, of our universe being 4,600,000,000 years old.

Throughout the nineteenth century, theories in geology, biology and anthropology were seen as conflicting with the Bible. Serious and strenuous debates went on between some of the theologians and some of the scientists. How were the claims made by the scientists to be reconciled with the account of the beginning of the world in Genesis? Some, those called Fundamentalists, insisted on the literal truth of the Bible. The scientific findings, they contended, could not take precedence over God's Revelation. And, they often argued, the scientific claims were tentative, and might be wrong. One writer, Edmund Gosse, asserted that God created the world as reported in *Genesis* in 4004 B.C. with all of the fossil and prehistoric remains in it. This would test man's faith as to whether he believed the Bible or his own limited scientific studies.

Others, usually called Liberals, contended that the scientific evidence required a reinterpretation of the Bible, that Scripture was not a textbook in geology or prehistory, but a work dealing with the nature and destiny of man. Thinkers in this camp joined with the Bible critics in assessing at least some of Scripture as an ancient presentation of beliefs then held about the world. The value of the Bible lay not in its account of ancient Hebrew cosmology, but in its view of human nature.

A dramatic and major clash between fundamentalism and liberalism occurred in the famous Scopes trial in Tennessee in 1925. Scopes, a high school teacher, was arrested for teaching Darwin's theory of evolution. A state law in Tennessee, which has only recently been repealed, banned the teaching of Darwinian evolution as contrary to *Genesis*. In the trial, two of the leading figures in America, William Jennings Bryan, the silver-tongued orator who had been a Presidential candidate, and the great lawyer Clarence Darrow, clashed and battled over the merits of the scientific evidence and the literal interpretation of the Bible. Though Scopes was convicted, for many people the trial became a turning point in which they could no longer accept the Bible as either literally true, or even as possessing special revealed information.

The effect of Biblical criticism from La Peyrère down to the present, and of the development of scientific findings that conflict with a literal interpretation of the Bible, has been to raise the question whether it is possible to locate any specific revealed information in Scripture. Some have concluded that the Bible is, as Spinoza claimed, just a compilation of ancient Jewish and early Christian writings, expressing how various people in these groups saw the world from around 1000 B.C. up to the second century A.D. Such accounts could be compared and contrasted with other ancient views of the world, without yielding any special information. Others, partly on the basis of archeological findings which have corroborated parts of the historical narrative in the Bible, have suggested that portions of the text have a factual basis, such as the story of Joshua's capture of

Jericho, and that the rest, if properly interpreted, has significant and special information for mankind.

Without going into the manifold possibilities involved in the second position, let us just concentrate on one major philosophical question that is central as the result of Bible scholarship and the growth of modern science, namely whether historical and scientific evidence can establish whether any information has been revealed to mankind. As we indicated at the outset of this section, this question is central for the Judaeo-Christian and Islamic traditions, since they center on certain documents, monuments, and institutions. The Bible critics have shown that when these items are treated as parts of human history, one can find out the best estimates of their dates, origins, original meanings and uses, and so on. But what does all of this establish in terms of the religious significance of these entities? A crucial matter that one would want to know is whether the documents, no matter what their history, do or do not convey special knowledge that God has imparted to man. Whether the documents are older or younger than people used to think does not settle this. But would any historical information accomplish a resolution of the question?

Let us consider some hypothetical cases. First, let us suppose that someone discovered a very ancient copy of the Pentateuch. Let us further suppose that by carbon-14 dating this manuscript could be dated around 1200–1300 B.C. Let us finally suppose that sufficient evidence could be found to lead historians to conclude that it was in the handwriting of Moses himself. Does that show that what Moses reported really happened, or only that the historical Moses reported that it happened? If other corroborating evidence were found, the broken tablets with the Ten Commandments written on them, an account by Aaron of what his brother told him, a journal by a disinterested bystander present during the period at Mount Sinai, would this settle the matter? Again the question would be, do these human artifacts show that God spoke to Moses, or again merely that Moses *said* that He did? The crucial feature of the situation is not in the documents, but in whether there is a relationship between God and human history. The documents are human historical ones. Their revelatory status depends upon knowing not just that the documents report an alleged revelation, but rather that a revelation took place. Can any historical information tell us this?

David Friedrich Strauss (1808–1874), who wrote *The Life of Jesus* from 1835–1836, was persecuted throughout his life for arguing that all the stories in the New Testament that spoke of supernatural events were really mythological accounts. This applied to Jesus' teachings and actions. A contemporary of Strauss', Bruno Bauer (1809–1882) wrote what Schweitzer called "a skeptical life of Jesus." He showed that all of the accounts of Jesus' activities contradicted one another, and that there was no objective basis for choosing one over others. Bauer went so far as to suggest that in view of all of these contradictions, perhaps Jesus of Nazareth did not in fact exist as a historical personage. (The only one who apparently preceded him in so drastic a conclusion was Napoleon Bonaparte. At St. Helena, Napoleon told some friends he had found out Jesus did not exist because he was not mentioned in a manuscript copy of Josephus' *Wars of the Jews* that Napoleon had "liberated" from the Vatican.)

Albert Schweitzer, writing in the early twentieth century, contended that the way most nineteenth-century scholars had approached the problem of searching for the historical Jesus, they would only uncover a nineteenth-century version of him. This version would make Jesus look like a good German pastor of that time. Schweitzer's own examination of the problem of uncovering the historical Jesus led him to conclude, "The Jesus of Nazareth who came forth publicly as the Messiah, who preached the ethic of the Kingdom of God, who founded the Kingdom of Heaven upon earth and died to give His work its final consecration, never had any existence" [Schweitzer, *The Quest of the Historical Jesus* (New York, 1960), p. 398]. Schweitzer did not deny the existence of Jesus *per se*, he was only denying that any accurate picture of the life and mission of Jesus could be constructed from the Gospel and other Scriptural materials. For Schweitzer, the historical research about people in time and space would never find a supernatural Jesus. And the historical Jesus who saw himself in some role in Jewish eschatology would also escape detection, since this would have been inside the historical figure, not in his public personality. What is valuable in the contribution of the historical Jesus is his message, rather than the historical aspects, which are all open to question.

The problem of who the historical Jesus was has been reopened by some of the findings of the Dead Sea Scrolls. Much more ink has been spilled on the question.

But what could all this research ever establish? It might settle some interesting historical questions, such as was there a historical figure named Jesus of Nazareth; what actually happened to him during his lifetime; what doctrines did he actually teach; were these doctrines original with him? But would any answers to these questions establish whether Jesus is or was God? At best they would tell us that Jesus said he was God, that he acted accordingly, and that some people believed him. But could any information gleaned from human history tell us if Jesus actually was God?

Let us assume that a crucial document is found, the diary of Jesus of Nazareth. Let us suppose it can be authenticated. This certainly would then be a more interesting document for finding out the message of Christianity than the accounts of Matthew, Mark, Luke, John, and Paul. But no matter what claims appear in the diary, they will not establish that

Jesus is or was God, but only that he wrote certain claims. The historical information will not confirm or deny what is essentially not visible in human history. One can find the historical data that may or may not be the results of Divine affairs, but to know that it is or is not related to God is more than the data can tell us.

The Bible critics have shown the extraordinary amount of information one can gain about a text by employing all sorts of scientific and historical analyses. But in so doing, they have raised the problem of whether one can find the Bible's revelatory content by means of historical and scientific study. In this century, a leading German Bible scholar, Rudolph Bultmann, has offered a new approach, called demythologizing the Bible. The method of demythologizing had been employed successfully to some of the ancient mythologies. The method was to remove from these accounts those elements that were clearly mythological. What remained, when critically analyzed, would be a picture of man's relation to his world, and a picture of what sort of a world people thought they lived in. Their encounter with this world through mythology provided a major basis for their outlook and behavior.

Bultmann applied this method of demythologizing to the Bible, especially the New Testament. This consists of divesting the Bible of those elements that scholars would generally now agree are the results of various strands of the Jewish, Greek, early Christian, and Near Eastern mythologies of the period. Bultmann has claimed that when this is done, the Message of the New Testament becomes clear. The Message is not some revealed information, but a genuine contact between man and God. In the debates that have raged over Bultmann's theory, some have argued that if he carried on his demythologizing program to its limits, nothing would be left to constitute a Message.

Not all of the Biblical scholars have come to such negative or skeptical conclusions. One present-day scholar, John Warwick Montgomery (see *Where is History Going?*, 1969), has tried to combat the results issuing from the Bible critics. Montgomery bases his counterattack on taking the Bible at face value, and insisting there are no good reasons to doubt the claims, and to doubt the eyewitness accounts. In the case of Jesus, one has several independent accounts of the same events. There is no reason to believe that all of the Biblical writers would lie. (Montgomery points out that it is standards like this which lead us to accept any historical account, religious or secular.) Regarding an event like Jesus' death, there were hundreds of eyewitnesses (according to the Bible). Similarly, the miracles of feeding the flocks with a few loaves of bread was witnessed by multitudes. So if these miracles were seen by reliable witnesses, Montgomery and the English theologian and science fiction writer, C.S. Lewis, claim, we then have direct factual knowledge of the supernatural events recorded in the Bible.

Another contemporary theologian, Edward John Carnell, has re-vived the fundamentalist position by combining the finding of modern philosophers about the nature of knowledge and some of Kierkegaard's views. He maintains that he has shown that "the claims of Christ are continuous with truth," and are acceptable to a modern person.

Biblical criticism has raised a fundamental problem for the philoso-phy of religion. If the Bible is examined as a historical document, then the central question arises whether one can ascertain what, if anything, in the Bible contains revealed religious knowledge. Some have concluded that since the Bible is a historical document, it cannot also have a privileged status of containing information that goes beyond human history. One result of this view has been to denigrate the Bible to being just a compila-tion of documents of the early Hebrews and early Christians, having no particular import about the nature of God. Others have rejected the results of Biblical criticism, either denying the claims of Bible scholars, or insist-ing that the historical interpretation does not deny that there is another dimension to Biblical material; namely its revelatory content. As Bible scholars have accumulated more and more information about the histori-cal context of the Biblical documents, the question of delineating what is the revealed information has become a central issue within philosophy of religion, and has led to a wide variety of interpretations of Judaism and Christianity, ranging from a denial that either of them contains any special religious knowledge, to modern presentations re-evaluating these religions in terms of modern scholarship, to fundamental rejections of the findings of the Bible critics. Another view was offered by the Danish philosopher of religion Søren Kierkegaard (1813–1855). He concluded that the basis for religion could never be found in history, but could only come from faith. If one had faith, then certain historical materials would have reli-gious significance.

The development of Bible criticism and the findings and theories of modern science have thus raised grave difficulties for philosophers of religion. A different approach has been to examine whether religious knowledge can be attained through arguments and proofs, using natural and rational evidence. Philosophers and theologians have claimed that proofs or demonstrations can be offered to show that God exists, and that certain things can be known about His Nature. Let us turn to a considera-tion of such proofs now.

ST. ANSELM'S ONTOLOGICAL PROOF
OF THE EXISTENCE OF GOD

One of the most important medieval proofs is called the Ontological Argument. Although there are various versions of this argument, some proposed even by contemporary thinkers, the classical formulation of the argument is due to St. Anselm. Anselm, who was born in 1033 and who died in 1109, was first a monk in Normandy, and then became the Archbishop of Canterbury. His famous argument appeared in his *Proslogium*. This proof was intended to show that one could establish by natural means that which was already known by faith.

The argument contends that anyone who understands the meaning of the term "God" will realize that such a Being must necessarily exist. Even the "fool" who denies that God exists has to understand what it is that he is denying. Once this fool examines the definition of "God," he will see that his denial is ridiculous, because it logically follows from God's definition that He must exist.

By definition, God is that being than which none greater can be conceived. According to Anselm, anyone who understands this definition has a conception of God in his understanding. God therefore exists at least in his understanding. But it is possible for him to conceive of a being who exists not only in the understanding but in reality as well. This being, who resembles God in all other respects, would thus be greater than the being who exists only in the understanding. But by definition, it is impossible to conceive of a being greater than God. God must therefore exist not only in the understanding but in reality as well. Thus, according to St. Anselm, from God's very definition, it follows that His nonexistence in reality is impossible, and therefore, that He must exist.

St. Anselm had tried to show that God's Existence could be established solely from our knowledge of the concept "God." No other evidence is needed. The definition of the concept is such that the proposition "God does not exist" must assert a logical contradiction. Descartes, several centuries later, used St. Anselm's reasoning in one of his own proofs of the existence of God. He insisted that God's Existence followed logically from His definition in the same way that mathematical theorems follow from the definitions of mathematical concepts:

> . . . I find that existence can no more be separated from the essence of God than the essence of a rectilinear triangle can be separated from the equality of its three angles to two right angles, or indeed, if you please, from the idea of a mountain the idea of a valley. Thus, there would be no less contradiction in conceiving of a God—that is, a supremely perfect being, to whom existence was wanting, that is to say, to whom there was wanting any perfection—than in conceiving of a mountain which had no valley.[2]

Hence, if one comprehends what a mountain is, one cannot think of a mountain without a valley. Similarly, Descartes maintained, once one knows what "God" means, one cannot conceive of God's nonexistence, since existence is part of the very meaning of the concept.

---

[2] René Descartes, *Meditations on First Philosophy*, Med. V.

Perhaps the most succinct version of the Ontological Argument is that stated by Spinoza. In his *Ethics,* he offered "geometrical" demonstrations of propositions. The eleventh proposition asserts: "God, or substance, consisting of infinite attributes, of which each expresses eternal and infinite essentiality, necessarily exists." Spinoza's proof of this proposition is that if one denies it, then "conceive, if possible, that God does not exist: then His Essence does not involve existence. But this is absurd (since it is contrary to the definition of God). Therefore, God necessarily exists."

In each of these versions of the Ontological Argument, the basic contention is that the definition of God is such that His Existence is part of His Nature or Essence. Hence it is a logical consequence of the definition that God exists. For St. Anselm, Descartes, and Spinoza, what differentiated the concept of God from all others was that His was the only one which necessarily entailed existence. The definition of any other entity allows for the possibility that the entity may or may not exist. Only God's Essence logically implies His Existence. Hence only God's Existence can be established *a priori*, from the concept alone, without any reference at all to any facts about the world.

Criticisms of the Ontological Argument were advanced as soon as it was made public. From that time up to the present day, philosophers have been analyzing the argument, attempting to show what is wrong with St. Anselm's reasoning. The earliest critique was written by a contemporary, Gaunilon, a monk of Marmoutier. He wrote a defense of the "fool," who, St. Anselm had said, could not really deny God's Existence once he realized what the term "God" meant. Gaunilon's defenses consisted chiefly in arguing that if the Ontological Argument were valid, many strange conclusions would follow. Using the same type of reasoning, he contended, one could also show that an amazing variety of unreal or imaginary objects necessarily exist. For instance, let us imagine a perfect island, an island than which none greater can be conceived of. Although no explorer has yet found this island, it must exist according to St. Anselm's Argument. If it does not exist, then it is not perfect (since it lacks the perfection, existence). And it is not that island than which none greater can be conceived of (since one can conceive of such an island as existing, a conception of a greater island than a nonexistent one). Since, by definition, the island is perfect, and it is that island than which none greater can be conceived of, its nonexistence is logically impossible. Hence from the concept alone, Gaunilon argued, it can be shown that a perfect island must necessarily exist in reality.

Gaunilon also sought to show that St. Anselm's Ontological Argument was absurd, in that, if valid, it would lead to ridiculous conclusions. It would, he argued, establish that a perfect island must exist, a perfect horse, et cetera. St. Anselm replied that these absurd conclusions would not follow, since the Ontological Argument could be applied *only* to the definition of God. No other concept is that of a Perfect Being. Hence, St. Anselm insisted, there could be no other Being than God whose Essence entails His Existence.

Another type of criticism of the Ontological Argument was advanced by the famous medieval philosopher and theologian St. Thomas Aquinas. His objections form a fundamental part of his own theory of religious knowledge. We shall turn now to an examination of his views.

ST. THOMAS AQUINAS' THEORY
OF RELIGIOUS KNOWLEDGE

St. Thomas (1225–1274) was born near Aquino, Italy. He studied at the monastery of Monte Cassino in central Italy and at the universities of Naples, Paris, and Cologne. Later he became a member of the Dominican Order, and taught at the University of Paris and in various schools in Italy. He was relieved of his teaching duties in 1272, as the result of attacks on his views by the followers of St. Augustine's theology. Two years later he died. He was canonized in 1323, was pronounced the *Angelic Doctor* in 1567, and was named the Patron of Catholic Schools in 1880.

St. Thomas lived during the era of the great impact of Aristotle's teachings on the theologians and philosophers of the Christian medieval universities. The rediscovery in Christian Europe of the works of Aristotle, as well as the influence of the Aristotelian and Neo-Platonic theories of Mohammedan and Jewish theologians of Spain and the Near East, created a crisis in the Christian schools. This crisis involved reconciling the teachings of Christianity with the best available information about the nature of the world, the views of Aristotle, and their interpretation by thinkers such as the Arabic philosopher Averroës (1126–1198) and the Jewish philosopher Maimonides (1135–1204). Battles raged in the great European universities over the merits of Aristotle's views and the relationship of these theories to those of the Church. Aristotle's theories and the theories of some of his proponents were banned for a while. Even the great University of Paris was closed for a brief time to prevent the dissemination of Aristotle's philosophy. Because of the efforts of St. Thomas Aquinas and his teacher, Albertus Magnus, a synthesis of some of Aristotle's theories and those of the Christian religion was worked out. St. Thomas formulated the basis for this synthesis in his two monumental works, the *Summa Contra Gentiles* (a summation of philosophical and theological knowledge against those who were outside the Judaeo-Christian tradition, that is those who had no revealed religious knowledge) and the unfinished *Summa Theologica*, both regarded by many as the highest achievements of medieval thought. Gradually, the views of St. Thomas were accepted by the Roman Catholic Church and in the course of time were proclaimed its official philosophy.

St. Thomas contended that it is possible to gain knowledge about the nature and existence of God, but that this could not be accomplished by purely *a priori* reasoning. Hence he argued that St. Anselm's approach and his results were invalid. In Question 2 of the *Summa Theologica*, St. Thomas examined the problem of the nature and the source of the knowledge that men, by means of their natural capacities alone, could attain about the existence of God.

First, he denied that it is possible to develop completely *a priori* demonstrations that God exists, based solely on a definition of God. Such demonstrations as St. Anselm's Ontological Argument for the existence of God presuppose that one knows the Essence of God, in order to define Him. From the definition, it is shown that it logically follows that God must exist. But, St. Thomas insisted, we do not possess the requisite knowledge to establish such demonstrations. Our natural knowledge is derived from sense experience, and cannot attain directly to an awareness of the Divine Nature Itself. Hence we cannot know naturally the Essence or definition of God. We can know only that if we had such knowledge, we could establish His Existence from His definition. The ultimate knowledge that we seek is the definition of God. Hence, St. Thomas contended, we can only state the truth involved in the Ontological Argument when we reach the summit of human wisdom and understanding. Until then, we can only note that St. Anselm's argument seems to be a hypothesis to the effect that *if* God is a Perfect Being, *then* He necessarily exists. If and when we are privileged to become directly aware of God's Nature, then we can tell if the hypothesis is true.

If we seek to know about God from the information available to us, we must begin, St. Thomas insisted, with the facts gained from sense experience. All of our natural (as opposed to "revealed") knowledge is derived, he said, from examinations of information gained through use of the senses. Hence, if it is possible to establish that God exists, there must be some data that furnish the starting point for such proofs. St. Thomas presented five proofs of the existence of God, each commencing from an observed fact. Then, in each case, he argued that this fact could be true only if there is a Divine Being.

The first and, according to St. Thomas, the most manifest proof is that from the fact of motion. It is certain and evident on the basis of sense experience that some things are in motion. Nothing moves unless it is acted upon by something else, that is, unless its potentiality is actualized by some entity already in a state of actuality. Nothing can move itself, since it would have to be actual and potential in the same respect at the same time. In the example St. Thomas used, something such as wood is moved to become hot only by something that is already hot, such as fire. An object cannot make itself hot, for it then would have to be hot and not hot simultaneously. Thus whatever is moved must be moved by something other than itself. The mover must also, by the same reasoning, be moved by some other mover, and so on. The sequence of movers and motions cannot go back infinitely, because if there is no first mover, there can be no second, no third, and so on. Hence there could be no present motion, which is contrary to our experience. "Therefore it is necessary to arrive at a first mover, moved by no other; and this everyone understands to be God." In this first proof, St. Thomas argued that by analyzing an obvious fact—that something moves—we see that this fact can be true only if there is also a First Mover, God. The argument proceeds by accepting Aristotle's theory of motion, and showing that according to this theory, any observable motion can be explained ultimately only by the existence of a First or Unmoved Mover.

The first of St. Thomas' proofs does not show, nor is it intended to show, that the sequence of motions taking place must have a beginning in time, and that the first motion must be the creation of the world. For the purposes of the argument, it does not matter whether the world had a beginning in time, and hence motion had a beginning, or whether the world and the motions in it constitute an eternal sequence with no beginning (as Aristotle believed). The first proof contends that the present fact of motion requires a First or Prime Mover, as the basis of any explanation of the present state of affairs. Thus at any point in the world's history, this would be true. If something moved, there must be a First Mover; otherwise there would be no way of accounting for the motion. Aristotle had offered a similar argument for the existence of an Unmoved Mover, even though he did not accept the belief that there was a first motion in point of view of time. For St. Thomas, the evidence that there has been a first temporal motion, a moment of Creation, is based on the Revelation presented in the Book of Genesis, and not on rational arguments.

The second proof argues for the existence of God from the observed fact that there are efficient causes of things (agents or agencies that make things happen), and that no action or effect can be the agent or agencies causing itself, since an efficient cause must be prior to its effect. In the chain of efficient causes, there must be a first cause. If there were not, the chain would have no beginning to cause the next step, to cause the succeeding, and so on, up to the present. Hence there would be no present effect, which is obviously false, since we perceive the present state of affairs. "Therefore it is necessary to admit a first efficient cause, to which everyone gives the name of God."

The third proof is a little more complex. It proceeds from the fact that we find in the natural world that it is possible for objects to be or not to be. The fact that objects are generated and that they degenerate shows that it is possible for them to exist and also to be nonexistent. The fact that they come into existence shows that it is possible for them to be and for them not to have been. It is not possible for objects that can exist or not exist to remain in existence forever, or to have been existing forever. St. Thomas argued, "That which can not-be at some time is not." (His point is that the nonexistence of an object is not a genuine possibility if it never happens, or if it never has happened.) Now, if *all* objects in the world could be nonexistent, then at some time each would be, or was, nonexistent. Then, St. Thomas announced, "If everything can not-be, then at one time there was nothing in existence." Assuming that the world has been going on for an indefinite length of time, there must have been a time before each object came into being, and hence a time when it was not. If each object is only possible, then there must have been a time when *none* of the objects existed. If this state of affairs had ever occurred, there would now be nothing in the world, because the things in the world would have had to be brought into existence by something else. If there really was nothing in the world at some time, no things could be produced thereafter. Since it is obvious that there is, in fact, something in the world, it could never have been the case that all things were once nonexistent, nor, therefore, that all the things in the world are only possible. Thus something in the world must have a necessary and not just a possible existence (otherwise everything would have been nonexistent at some point in time). Its necessity must in turn be caused by something else that also exists necessarily. For the same reason that there cannot be an infinite regress of efficient causes, there cannot be an infinite regress of necessary causes of the necessary existence of certain things. Therefore, we have to admit that there must be some being which is the cause of its own necessary existence, and which causes the necessary existence of other beings. "This all men speak of as God."

St. Thomas' fourth proof is based on the fact that a graduation is found among things; some things are better than others, some truer, and so on. In order to grade objects according to whether they exhibit more or less of a particular property, we must grade them according to a standard of what is the best. In terms of knowing what is best, we can then determine that some things are better or worse than others. St. Thomas then cited Aristotle's maxim that the maximum in any genus—in this case, the best—is the cause of the properties of all the objects in the genus. Hence every good thing is the result of what is best, insofar as what is best provides the basis for assessing the goodness of everything else. Therefore there must be something that is best, which is the cause of the existence, goodness, and other perfections of things, "and this we call God."

The last of St. Thomas' five proofs is a brief version of what is called "the argument from design." We see that it is a fact that everything in the world acts and moves purposefully, acting to achieve certain ends. This is true of both intelligent beings and also those that lack knowledge, such as stones and trees. It is obvious that these objects achieve their goals not by chance but by design. Since most natural objects lack knowledge, the design must come from outside them and direct their activities intelligently. "Therefore some intelligent being exists by whom all natural things are directed to their end; and this being we call God."

Each of these proofs, St. Thomas contended, starts from an obvious and indisputable fact of human experience. The examination and understanding of the facts, in terms of Aristotle's philosophy, leads by five different paths to the conclusion that a certain kind of being exists, whom men call "God." We gain the knowledge that God exists by natural and rational means, seeking to find the necessary and sufficient reason for certain facts. This is knowledge *that* God is. Next, we have to seek for knowledge of *what* God is, what His Essence or Nature consists in.

Unfortunately, according to the Thomistic theory, the Divine Essence is not a direct object of human knowledge, since the objects that we can know directly are those that can be sensed or intuited. We are able to gain natural knowledge of God's Nature only indirectly, and negatively, by discovering what God is not. We can establish certain negative truths about God from the five proofs.

From the first proof, we can ascertain that since God is not an object that moves, He is, therefore, not changeable. If He is not changeable, God then has no beginning or end. This in turn implies that God is not potential in any respect (in that He has no capacity for change). This negative conclusion, according to Aristotle's metaphysical theory, shows that God is not material, nor corporeal, and not made up of parts. The end result of this examination of what God is not, based on the five proofs, is the conclusion that because He is not made up of parts He does not fall in any classification. If He did, He would be composed of at least two distinct features, His Existence and His Essence. The summit of our negative knowledge of God's Nature is the realization that His Essence, that which constitutes His Being, is identical with His Existence. This, in turn, means that God's Nature cannot be defined, since any definition would involve placing God in some classification, which would in turn involve distinguishing His Essence from His Existence. If God's Nature is indefinable, it is then obvious that His Existence cannot be established by any *a priori* demonstration (such as the Ontological Argument) from God's Nature. Instead, our sole knowledge of God's Existence comes, as the proofs have shown, from the effects of God's Nature in the world of experience.

Thus, according to the Thomistic theory, the knowledge that can be gained about the existence and nature of God by natural means is restricted to the proofs of the existence of God, plus the negative conclusions concerning what God is not that can be drawn from these. The ultimate unknowability of the positive Nature of God is summarized in the assertion that God's Essence is the same as His Existence, thus indicating the radical difference between God and any knowable object, and indicating the absolute limit of knowledge of the Divine Nature by means of human reason.

Prior to St. Thomas, the Jewish philosopher Maimonides had contended that any attempt to gain further rational knowledge about God beyond the fact that He exists, and that His Essence is identical with His Existence, would lead to contradictory results. Reason could both prove and disprove that God created the world. This showed, according to Maimonides, that reason was an inadequate guide to any positive information about the Nature of God. Hence, as both he and St. Thomas insisted, the positive quest for knowledge about God must be carried on by faith and not by reason.

Faith, in the Thomistic theory, is not in opposition to reason, but instead carries us beyond the limits of reason. As human beings, if we rely solely on our rational capacities we are not able to obtain any genuine knowledge of objects that cannot be sensed or intuited. But, by faith, we can attain such knowledge. Faith carries us onward to the specific positive religious knowledge-claims of the Judaeo-Christian tradition. Reason is sufficient to convince one that there is a God. But only faith can lead one to realize that the God who exists is the God believed in by Christians. Hence the complexity of St. Thomas Aquinas' answer to the question of how knowledge about the existence and nature of God can be obtained. It can be attained by faith alone (as happens in the lives of most nonintellectual believers). Or it can be attained by reason, that is, by establishing that there is a God, and establishing what He is not, and then supplying the positive content of religious knowledge by faith.

The Thomistic theory maintains that human beings can gain at least the basis for religious knowledge by natural and rational means. Hence there is (to some degree) a genuine rational basis for religious belief. This view has been adopted by the Roman Catholic Church as its official theory. And because of this status, the Thomistic philosophy of religion has continued to have an important influence in discussions of religious knowledge down to the present day.

Beginning in the thirteenth century, however, criticisms were raised against St. Thomas' combining of Aristotelianism and Christian thought, and against his theory of the relationship of knowledge gained by faith and knowledge gained by reason. Some late medieval thinkers questioned whether reason could actually gain as much knowledge concerning the Existence and Nature of God as St. Thomas had maintained. In the course of the late thirteenth and fourteenth centuries, philosophers and theologians argued that man's natural capacity to gain religious knowledge was very limited. They insisted that practically all religious knowledge could be gained only by faith, and that reason could play little or no role in obtaining any positive knowledge *either* about God's Existence *or* His Nature.

After the medieval period, St. Thomas' views were sharply criticized, especially by non-Catholic thinkers. On both religious and scientific grounds, they seriously questioned whether the factual information that lay at the basis for St. Thomas' proofs had to be interpreted and analyzed in the Thomistic way. As Aristotelian philosophy fell into disrepute in the period from the Renaissance to the seventeenth century, many philosophers refused to accept the theories about motion and its causes that were employed by St. Thomas in developing his proofs.

The strongest and most influential criticisms of proofs of the existence of God based on either causal arguments or the argument from design were advanced in the eighteenth century by David Hume and Immanuel Kant. Hume devoted his intellectual energies to dissecting and demolishing the argument from design, and to showing the inadequacy of causal reasoning for reaching any religious conclusions. Kant, following immediately after Hume, carried these lines of criticism further. He sought to show, in terms of his theory of knowledge, that human beings have no means for reasoning successfully about the nature or existence of God. Hence, he contended, *all* proofs of the existence of God, whether Thomistic or based on St. Anselm's argument, are inconclusive. Let us now turn to the criticisms presented by Hume and Kant.

HUME'S THEORY OF
RELIGIOUS KNOWLEDGE

David Hume (1711–1776) was known in his own day as "the great Infidel" because of his continuous attacks on traditional religion and theology. Hume was raised as a Scottish Calvinist, but soon lost whatever orthodox convictions he may have had. Throughout his entire life he argued against the evidence offered for religion, and against the effects of institutional religion in the social and moral order. Just before his death, Hume wrote to the economist Adam Smith that he hoped his own writings would have the effect of eliminating that strange superstition, everywhere accepted, the Christian religion. Hume enjoyed debating with the liberal Calvinist ministers from Scotland, and all through his life he tried to poke holes in their arguments and beliefs.

Hume's main critique of religious knowledge was directed against the natural, rather than the revealed, evidence for religion, though, as we shall see, his analysis of miracles attempted to expose the complete improbability of even the revealed evidence for miraculous events. Those who contend that there is natural evidence for religious belief insist that there are certain historical events, or observable facts, or obvious truths, from which it is possible to infer definite conclusions about the existence and nature of God. According to these theologians, no supernatural or especially revealed information is required.

Hume examined the contentions of these "natural" theologians in terms of his findings about the nature and limits of human knowledge. In the chapters on "The Theory of Knowledge" and "Metaphysics" we have seen that Hume maintained that our information about the world is restricted to impressions and ideas gained from sense experience, and to the probable inferences made from these on the basis of the constant conjunctions of observed events. This led Hume to a completely skeptical view concerning the possibility of gaining information that transcended the limits of human experience, and hence to a rejection of all metaphysical theories about the nature of reality. In terms of his empirical theory of knowledge Hume analyzed the arguments purporting to establish religious knowledge. His principle target was the argument from design (briefly stated in St. Thomas' fifth proof), since this argument attempted to prove conclusions about the existence and nature of God from factual data.

Hume's *Dialogues concerning Natural Religion*

Hume's attack is advanced in the two works, *Dialogues concerning Natural Religion* and *The Natural History of Religion*. The former is regarded as a classic statement of what is wrong with the argument from design. It was written over a period of about twenty-five years, from 1751 to 1776, and was finally completed just prior to the author's death. Hume's friends had urged him not to publish the work because it was too seditious and irreligious, and recommended instead that he destroy the manuscript. As a result of this advice, Hume kept revising the *Dialogues*, setting it aside and reworking it. When he knew that he was dying, he finally completed the work and tried to make sure that it would be published immediately after his death. Neither his friend Adam Smith nor his publisher was willing to take the responsibility. It was not until three years later, in 1779, that a nephew of Hume's brought the book out anonymously. Ever since, the *Dialogues* has been considered one of the most important writings in the philosophy of religion, presenting one of the most challenging critiques of the contention that it is possible to gain knowledge about the nature and existence of God by natural means.

Most of the discussion in the *Dialogues concerning Natural Religion* centers on analyzing a form of the argument from design, which purports to establish knowledge about God on the basis of the scientific information about the physical and biological world. Over and over again, throughout the history of science, philosophers and theologians have maintained that the latest scientific findings lead to the conclusion that there must be an intelligent Being who is responsible for order that is found everywhere in Nature. In the eighteenth century, as a result of the scientific achievements of Isaac Newton, the results of Newtonian physics were commonly used as the basis for a proof of the existence of God, and as a means for establishing certain claims about His Nature. Newton himself had given new prestige to the argument from design by stating it as one of the important general results of his work. It is to this Newtonian version of the argument that Hume addressed himself in the *Dialogues*.

The following passage from the *Dialogues* states the argument and the conclusions drawn from it:

> Look around the world: Contemplate the whole and every part of it: You will find it to be nothing but one great machine, subdivided into an infinite number of lesser machines, which again admit of subdivisions, to a degree beyond what human senses and faculties can trace and explain. All these various machines and even their most minute parts are adjusted to each other with an accuracy, which ravishes into admiration all men, who have ever contemplated them. The curious adapting of means to ends, throughout all nature, resembles exactly, though it much exceeds, the productions of human contrivance; of human design, thought, wisdom, and intelligence. Since therefore the effects resemble each other, we are led to infer, by all the rules of analogy, that the causes also resemble and that the Author of Nature is somewhat similar to the mind of man; though possessed of much larger faculties, proportioned to the grandeur of the work, which he has executed. By this argument *a posteriori*, and by this argument alone, we do prove at once the existence of a Deity, and his similarity to human mind and intelligence.[3]

The basic contention of the argument from design is that investigations of nature show that there is order in the physical, chemical, and biological world. Scientific findings indicate that the various parts of nature are all related to one another in one vast, intricate, over-all natural system. The order in nature bears close resemblance to that which is found in human artifacts, as, for instance, in houses, ships or watches, where the various parts of the object are so adjusted to each other that they all function together harmoniously to achieve some end. In view of the similarity of the effects of human planning and the effects found in the natural world, we can infer that there are similar causes of the order in each case. The effects of human planning are due to thought and intelligence. The order and design in nature, therefore, must also be due to an

[3] From *Dialogues concerning Natural Religion*, Kemp Smith ed. (Thomas Nelson & Sons, Edinburgh, 1947), p. 143.

intelligent Being. And, since the order of the natural world is so much greater than that of any human achievement, the Designer of Nature must also exceed the human designer in intelligence.

Although Hume was always willing to admit that no rational man could avoid being impressed by the evidence of order in nature, he insisted that the argument from design was not logically compelling. The analogy between the universe and man-made objects is not a good one, since they are not actually very similar. Further, we are able to judge what causes result, for example, in the existence of houses or watches only from our experience—seeing houses being built or watches being manufactured. We have not, however, ever been present when a universe was being produced, so we cannot tell if similar causes operate in universe-construction as do in human productions. In our experience, we have observed causal processes other than human design, processes such as growth and attraction as the causes of effects in nature. For all that we can ever determine from our experience, any of these other processes might be the cause of the natural world and of the order in it. Until we actually experience the origin of worlds, and have the opportunity to peruse the entire process of development, we are not in a position to ascertain whether world-creation and development is or is not analogous to human productions, and, hence, whether the argument from design is valid or not.

Even if one accepted the basic premises of the argument—that there is a genuine resemblance between nature and the works of man, and that like effects have like causes—one would not, Hume contended, attain the sort of knowledge about the nature and existence of God that the proponents of the argument desire. The better the analogy, the more one would have to conclude that the Author of Nature is like a human being, with all of his limitations and defects. Man, who can make watches, houses, and ships, is still an imperfect creature, subject to all sorts of changes, passions, and errors. If we judge the Universe-Maker by what we know about man, we will come to many conclusions that are at complete variance with traditional religion: that God is finite, imperfect, subject to error, and so on. We find that even the best of human contrivances can be made by foolish, stupid people, capable of a great deal of bungling, and yet also able, at times, to create an intricate watch. Hence if we attempted to ascertain God's Nature by analogy to man's, strange and undesirable results would ensue.

On the other hand, Hume went on, if we tried to judge God's Nature from the effect, the created world, we would find ourselves at a complete loss. Since we possess no standard of comparison, we cannot tell if the observable universe is a good, a mediocre, or even a poor achievement in terms of possible universe-constructions. We cannot tell if the result is due to one or to many deities. Even if we agreed that the universe is the effect of something like intelligent design, we are not able, by scrutinizing the effect, to determine anything at all about the nature and character of the designer or designers, and each man is at liberty

> to fix every point of his theology, by the utmost licence of fancy and hypothesis. This world, for aught he knows, is very faulty and imperfect, compared to a superior standard; and was only the first rude essay of some infant Deity, who afterwards abandoned it, ashamed of his lame performance; it is the work only of some dependent, inferior Deity; and is the object of derision to his superiors: it is the production of old age and dotage in some superannuated Deity; and ever since his death has run on at adventures, from the first impulse and active force, which it received from him . . .[4]

These, plus many, many other hypotheses are all possible explanations of the order in the universe, once the argument from design is accepted.

Having revealed all these defects in the argument, Hume then proceeded to raise a still more devastating criticism. Given what the world looks like, there are other explanations besides intelligent design that can account for the order that is found everywhere, and these other explanations are at least as probable as the design hypothesis. Hume considered two possibilities: the order in the world is the result of generative or growth processes; and the order in the world is only the chance result of material particles coming together. Very frequently we observe order developing in the course of biological growth. Seeds are planted in the ground and develop into organized vegetation. No designer is observed placing the order in the plants. If we judge the source of order solely from what we perceive, one serious possibility is that the order is the unconscious effect of the generative process. Perhaps the world generates its own order just by growing, and requires no outside designer to place order in it. It appears, on the basis of our experience, that it is equally probable that the cause of the observed order is some inner developmental process in nature as to suppose that it is some intelligent designer of Nature.

Even Epicurus' hypothesis—that natural order is the result of "the fortuitous concourse of atoms"—is adequate to explain the world that we experience. The minute section of the cosmos that we can inspect has order. For all that we can tell, this order could have come about by the chance collisions of particles of matter, without requiring any outside director. If a large number of particles of iron were tossed into the air, they would fall in some pattern, simply by accident or chance. We cannot be sure that the observable universe is not the result of a chance or random distribution of particles, forming the ordered cosmos that we see.

[4] *Hume, op. cit.,* p. 169.

Hence a theory such as Epicurean materialism suffices to account for the observable order, without requiring that we suppose that there is an intelligent agency which caused the order.

Hume maintained that all these criticisms showed that if religious knowledge is to be gained solely from experience by empirical means, then there is no genuine basis for accepting one hypothesis concerning the source or cause of the observable order in the world over the other possible theories. The world as we know it can be accounted for in a large variety of ways. An almost unlimited number of religious and irreligious systems can be constructed offering explanations of the cosmic order that the scientists have discovered. But nothing in our experience justifies our preferring one of these systems over any other. .

After having exposed the weaknesses of the argument from design, Hume turned briefly, in the *Dialogues*, to a consideration of some of the other kinds of arguments that have been developed to prove the existence of God, such as causal arguments like those employed in St. Thomas' first and second proofs. The particular argument that Hume discussed is the cosmological or First Cause Argument, which contends that whatever exists must have a cause, or a reason for its existence. Either the chain of causes can be traced back infinitely, or there must be a first cause. The first possibility is ruled out by reasoning that if each effect is produced by the cause that immediately preceded it, there then must be a cause of the entire chain or succession of causes, or there would be no cause or reason for this particular succession occurring instead of some other. Unless, finally, there is some necessarily existent being, who is the First Cause of the causal sequence that takes place in this world, there will be no explanation ultimately for any happenings whatsoever. Therefore, if one accepts the premise that events must have causes, then, the argument contends, there must be a First Cause, which is God. This argument purports to establish the existence of God solely from the premise, which all rational people supposedly accept as self-evident, that every event must have a cause.

In terms of his empirical theory of knowledge, Hume rejected both this argument plus any other reasoning which claimed to establish that any specific matter of fact must be the case. In general, Hume contended, "nothing is demonstrable, unless the contrary implies a contradiction. Nothing, that is distinctly conceivable, implies a contradiction. Whatever we conceive as existent, we can also conceive as non-existent. There is no Being, therefore, whose non-existence implies a contradiction. Consequently there is no Being whose existence is demonstrable." Since it is always possible for us to conceive (in the sense of "think of" or "imagine") that any object that we can describe either exists in a particular place at a specific time or does not so exist, there can be no demonstration that such an object has to exist (since its nonexistence is conceivable). Applying this to demonstrations of the existence of God, Hume argued that in view of the fact that God's nonexistence is conceivable or imaginable, the purported demonstrations cannot be decisive arguments establishing that He must exist.

The causal argument, in particular, is criticized both in terms of the premise on which it rests and in terms of the conclusion drawn from it. In his theory of knowledge and his critique of metaphysics, Hume had challenged the accepted maxim that every event must have a cause, and he had shown that the maxim is neither self-evident nor demonstrable. We cannot tell whether events have to have causes. We can discover that we look at the world causally only because of our psychological constitutions. This means that we see the world in terms of sequences of constantly conjoined events, and we expect that these constant conjunctions will continue to occur in the future. But Hume emphatically denied that we have any reason to conclude that there must be a beginning to the sequence of regularly conjoined events, or that, as far as we can tell, there must be some ultimate reason or cause for the whole sequence. Hence, according to Hume's analysis of causal reasoning, there is no way of connecting our experienced information about causes and effects, and our feelings about what we experience, with any conclusive argument concerning the necessary existence of a First Cause. The experienced chain of conjoined events requires no explanation, and we have no basis for providing an explanation of it. As experienced, the chain can simply be accepted as a brute fact—the world as we know it is ordered rather than chaotic. But we have no way of ascertaining why this is the case.

Further, Hume contended, even if the cosmological or First Cause Argument were valid, it would not suffice to establish the conclusion that theologians have drawn from it. If a First Cause must exist, why could not this Cause be the material world itself, instead of a Deity? If the theologians insist that there must be a cause of the world and the properties it has, Hume answered that the same is the case with a Deity. Why does He exist, and why does He have the Nature He does? If the theologians are willing to accept the view that the Deity can be the cause of Himself, why could not this also be true of the material world? Hence if the cosmological argument were valid, it could as well establish a theory like Spinoza's as that of traditional religions.

Having indicated why he believed that the arguments offered to establish the existence of God were unsatisfactory, Hume then turned to the problem of ascertaining what information could actually be gained by natural means about the Nature of God. If we attempt to infer God's Nature from the world that we experience, have we any basis, Hume asked, for concluding that the Author of Nature must possess any moral attributes, that He must be just, good, or benevolent, as traditional religions have asserted? The world we live in contains many unpleasant and unsatisfactory features, such as floods, storms, droughts, wars, pains, and so on. On the basis of the miserable aspects of human life, and the disasters in the natural world, what conclusions could we possibly draw about the characteristics of the Creator and Designer of such a universe? If the world as we know it is the sum total of our natural information on the subject, it would be extremely difficult to conclude that the Designer must be either all-wise or good. There may be many plausible explanations of the evils found in this world, but they all suppose that, in addition to our natural information, we also know independently that the world is run by a good and wise Deity. But, Hume insisted, our natural information is entirely drawn from our observations of the product, the world, and cannot be based upon hypotheses that may or not be true. In terms of what we can know by natural means, we have to ask ourselves, "Is the world considered in general, and as it appears to us in this life, different from what a man or such a limited being would, *beforehand*, expect from a very powerful, wise, and benevolent Deity? It must be a strange prejudice to assert the contrary. And from thence I conclude, that however consistent the world may be, allowing certain suppositions and conjectures, with the idea of such a Deity, it can never afford us an inference concerning his existence."

The world, in fact, does not even provide the basis for concluding that there is a limited, finite, good Deity. If our knowledge about the cause or causes of the order and disorder in the universe is constructed by induction and inference from our experience, it is possible that the world is the result of the actions and plans of a good Deity, or a bad one, or of both, or of neither. All these theories are compatible with the facts. The mixture of good and bad events may lead us to conclude that a theory of mixed causes or neutral causes is more probable, but, just the same, we cannot determine from the natural facts at our disposal which of these theories is actually true.

Hume's answer to the question "What knowledge can be gained about the nature and existence of God?" is, in theory, an agnostic one. We simply cannot know what the Author of Nature is like, nor what sort of attributes He may have. We cannot know whether, in terms of His actual attributes, any explanations can be given for the features of the world of experience. If all our conclusions are based solely on the empirical facts at our disposal, then we are not justified in coming to any definitive views about either the existence or the nature of a Deity or deities. We are not justified in arriving at atheistical conclusions, denying that there is a God, nor in arriving at theistic conclusions, asserting that there is a God, and that He has any particular characteristics.

However, when Hume assessed the results of his examinations, especially of the argument from design, he was willing to be a little more positive than the evidence actually allowed for. The argument from design, he insisted, was an invalid argument, based on a very poor analogy. If it were valid, it would lead to a series of strange theological conclusions, based on a comparison of God to man, and judging the attributes of the Deity from the characteristics of the observable world. But, having said all this, in the *Dialogues* and elsewhere, Hume still admitted that the evidence of design in the natural world was overwhelming, and that one could not help being impressed by the ever-increasing amount of evidence of order in nature.

The fact of design or order, however, really established no definite conclusions about its cause. Both the theist and the atheist, Hume contended, actually agreed, but stated their respective views so that they appeared to be in disagreement. They both start from the fact of order, and agree that the cause of the order is probably due to some type of intelligent agency. The atheist insists that we cannot determine the degree of resemblance of the cause of cosmic order to human intelligence, and the theist admits that the Cosmic Designer, if He is an intelligent Being, is very different from a human being. Hence, instead of disputing, the two parties should recognize that the evidence of cosmic order that we find everywhere leads rational men to conclude that "the whole of natural theology . . . resolves itself into one simple, though somewhat ambiguous, at least undefined proposition, *that the cause or causes of order in the universe probably bear some remote analogy to human intelligence.*" This proposition, however, admits of no further qualification or extension. We cannot ascertain the degree of resemblance of the cause or causes of order to human intelligence. We cannot discover what other possible characteristics the cause or causes may possess. Thus, by natural means, we are able to arrive at only an extremely vague and limited amount of probable information about the nature and existence of God.

Hume's Essay, "Of Miracles"

In his notorious essay, "Of Miracles," published as a chapter in the *Enquiry concerning Human Understanding,* Hume offered some reasons for rejecting revealed information about religious matters. Specifically, he considered the kind of evidence that is often presented to justify belief in miracles. In one of his letters, he indicated that he felt that if he were correct regarding miracles, his argument would equally well apply to *all* of the evidence offered to establish the truth of the Christian religion (or any other supernatural religion as well).

A miracle is a violation of the laws of nature. Since the laws of nature are based on "firm and unalterable experience," Hume argued that the course of our experience is a complete and adequate reason for disbelieving that violations of the laws of nature have occurred or will occur. We base our conclusions about what is taking place in the world on the sequence of events in our experience. We arrive at our knowledge of the laws of nature from the constancy of experience. A reported violation of the course of nature would go against all that we know from our experience. Hence we could not accept the claim that such a violation had occurred.

The evidence adduced to show that miracles have occurred, Hume asserted, consists of the testimony of various people. This testimony, like anything else, is to be judged by the information and the standards we possess. We judge the testimony of historians and others by whether the events they describe are probable in the light of our experience. If they are not, then we have to decide which is more likely—that the testimony is false, or that the improbable events described actually took place. The fact that the miracles are ascribed to a Divine Being does not affect the case, since our judgment still has to be based upon *our* observations of the course of nature, and *our* information about the reliability of the witnesses who report the occurrence of miracles. In our experience, according to Hume, nature has always operated uniformly. Therefore any reported miracle would be considered improbable in the light of our observations, *unless* the testimony for the miracles was "of such a kind that its false-hood would be more miraculous than the fact which it endeavours to establish." In view of what we know about human nature, about various reports of miracles, and about the conditions under which these reports usually arise, Hume insisted that a reasonable man would always have to conclude that it was more probable that the reporter of a miracle lied than that the event actually took place. The same argument could be applied to revealed religious information in general, insofar as such information is at variance with the ordinary course of our experience. The "reasonable" man would have to judge concerning each reported revelation, whether, in terms of his own observations about nature, it was more probable that the revelation was true than that the reporter of it was in error. And since the probabilities would, in each case, be based on one's observations of the uniformity of nature, and the nonsupernatural character of daily events, one would, Hume asserted, always conclude that the truth of the revelation was less probable than the falsity of the testimony for it. Hence Hume stated in his famous conclusion to the essay "Of Miracles":

> So that, upon the whole, we may conclude that the Christian religion not only was at first attended with miracles, but even at this day cannot be believed by any reasonable person without one. Mere reason is insufficient to convince us of its veracity. And whoever is moved by *faith* to assent to it is conscious of a continued miracle in his own person

which subverts all the principles of his understanding and gives him a determination to believe what is most contrary to custom and experience.

Thus Hume contended that there was inadequate evidence to support any but the vaguest conclusions about the nature and existence of God. He rejected the revealed evidence as contrary to our natural information and to the "reasonable" ways that we judge such information. Hence the reasonable man would remain an agnostic about almost all the religious knowledge-claims made by theologians. He would accept the fact that the order in the world was sufficient to convince a rational man that there was probably some sort of intelligent cause of the design in nature, but feel that such information was insufficient to allow one to come to any further conclusion about the characteristics of this cause or causes.

Hume's critique of the arguments and the evidence employed to establish claims about God's Nature and Existence had an immediate and a continuing impact on the intellectual world. One of the first to be influenced was Immanuel Kant, whose views on this subject will be discussed shortly. He developed his own criticisms of all the proofs of the existence of God from points raised in Hume's *Dialogues*. (The latter work appeared for the first time shortly before Kant completed his *Critique of Pure Reason*.) On the other hand, various theologians immediately attacked Hume's arguments, seeking to show that he had not actually revealed any serious or basic faults in the standard proofs of the existence of God, and that his reasoning concerning the evidence that miracles have occurred was itself faulty.

In the course of the two centuries since Hume published his views on religious knowledge, philosophers of religion have continued to argue about what Hume actually did prove. Some have contended that he destroyed the basis for any rational knowledge of the existence and nature of God, while others have maintained that he only showed that one particular formulation of one particular argument, that from design, was unsound. But they have said that even Hume had to admit that the faulty formulation was convincing even if it did not constitute a sound argument.

Criticisms of Hume

Some of Hume's critics, such as the Danish theologian and philosopher Søren Kierkegaard (1813–1855), have pointed out that Hume actually established only what many theologians have also maintained: that empirical evidence and reasoning cannot establish any religious conclusions. Kierkegaard announced that the statement quoted above from the end of the essay "Of Miracles," is the "voice of orthodoxy," since religious knowledge can be based only on faith, and not on natural information. Hence anyone who believes in miracles or revealed information does so, according to Kierkegaard, because of his faith, and not for any reasons whatsoever. The warrant for his faith is not any public information, but only his own personal religious experience. Hence Hume may have shown, in a masterful way, that the attempt to base religious knowledge on evidence or reason cannot succeed. However, he has not thereby undermined religious knowledge based on faith or personal religious experience.

Others, including the contemporary English writer C. S. Lewis, have tried to show that Hume had come to unjustified negative conclusions on the basis of the evidence and standards that he employed. Lewis contended that in his analysis of miracles Hume had begged the question of whether we possess religious knowledge. Lewis pointed out that the question at issue is whether miraculous events should be counted as part of the observed information that we have about the world. Hume merely used the nonmiraculous information, and then employed it to judge the probability of miracles. But if miracles are actually part of the observed sequence, Hume's argument is not decisive.

Another criticism closely related to that suggested by Lewis might be stated as follows: The question is whether Hume defines the term "law of nature" in such a way as to make it impossible, by definition, for miracles to occur. For on his definition, if a highly unusual event did occur, it must be in accord with some law of nature and hence could not be a miracle. Therefore, by definition, all those events called "miraculous" by traditional religions either could not really have occurred, or if they did, were not genuinely miraculous.

There are still others who, despite Hume's devastating criticisms, contend that the argument from design is valid or, at least, that it is very convincing. Some recent thinkers have argued that scientific findings since Hume's time point to the conclusion that the known natural order must be the result of an Intelligent Designer. A recent arguer for this view is the great French biologist Le Conte de Nouy. In his book *Human Destiny* he contended that the intricate order discovered in the realm of living organisms and the course of evolutionary development could not be the result of pure chance. He offered a computation of the infinitesimal probability, based on present information, that inanimate molecules would ever combine by chance to form a protein molecule or a living organism. Since the probability of such events happening fortuitously is so slight, he argued that the world of living things has to be the result of design. And, hence, there must be a Designer. Even more recently, the French scientist and Jesuit anthropologist Teilhard de Chardin, in his monumental treatise *The Phenomenon of Man*, has tried to show that a consideration of the evolutionary process resulting in the human being leads to the conclusion that it must be directed by an intelligent purpose, and must be heading toward an intelligent, divine goal. The reasoning of both Le Conte de

Nouy and Teilhard de Chardin involves using present information about the natural world to infer certain conclusions about the religious character and the cause of the world in which we live.

KANT'S THEORY OF
RELIGIOUS KNOWLEDGE

Although new versions of the argument from design are still being developed, Hume's critique has been accepted by many as a decisive attack on this kind of attempt to gain knowledge about the existence and nature of God. As a result of Hume's arguments, many philosophers of religion have concluded that it is not possible to attain any religious knowledge at all by means of our sense information or of our reasoning ability. One such philosopher, Immanuel Kant (1724–1804), offered some theoretical reasons to explain why this is the case.

As we have seen in Chapter 3, "Metaphysics," Kant contended that we possess no means for gaining knowledge about entities outside the realm of possible experience. His analysis of our knowledge revealed that we can gain only a very limited amount of necessary knowledge, contained in synthetic *a priori* judgments, dealing only with the forms of all possible experience or with the nature of the judgments that can be made about the world of experience.

We can gain reliable and certain information by applying to possible experience the forms of intuition, the logical functions of judgments, and the categories. But, Kant insisted, any attempt to employ these principles beyond their warranted fields results in arguments and proofs whose legitimacy and validity cannot be determined. When reasoning goes beyond the limits of all possible experience, it produces paradoxes, that is, contradictory or self-contradictory claims, or antinomies, that is, equally valid arguments proving directly opposite conclusions. This shows that there is something peculiar about attempts to gain knowledge in areas where we possess no methods or standards for forming true judgments. We should realize, and accept the fact, that reasonings which transcend the limits of possible experience are fruitless and entirely speculative. Since we have no basis for judging in these areas, there is nothing here of which we can ever be certain.

When this analysis of the limitations on human knowledge was applied to proofs of the existence of God, Kant declared, it would be evident that these arguments are either fallacious or inconclusive. For example, Kant pointed out that the cosmological or causal argument assumes that we can infer from the contingent events (that is, events that depend upon something else for their occurrence, and events which do not necessarily have to occur) in our experience that there must be a necessary cause which produces or accounts for experienced events. Since every event must have a cause, contingent events must have a cause, a cause which must be noncontingent, or necessary. But, Kant argued, as far as we can ever ascertain, the principle of causality is only a necessary principle about experienced events. We have no way of telling if we are justified in extending the principle beyond all possible experience to a realm which might possibly explain the character of what we experience. Further, we have no reason to conclude that there must be a First Cause, since our causal principles, as far as we know, apply only to the way we must think about the unending sequence of phenomenal events. We are able to examine the course of events forward and backward in the temporal sequence, but we have no principles for judging what is beyond this sequence.

In general, Kant declared, we are unable to reason from any factual data, or any necessary features of experience, to conclusions about what *must* cause, or account for, experience. Any proof of the existence of God is thus an attempt to accomplish the impossible. Therefore, Kant, like Hume, contended that no knowledge can be gained from sense information, or by reasoning, about either the existence or the nature of God.

Hume and Kant have presented all-important critiques of the attempts by philosophers and theologians to base claims to religious knowledge on natural rather than revealed evidence. If all our knowledge is restricted to sense information or reasoning that is valid only within the limits of possible experience, Hume and Kant appear to have shown that we possess no means whatsoever for gaining any religious knowledge. Many of those who disagree with the agnostic conclusions of Hume and Kant have insisted that there is another means of attaining information about God: by means of faith, and faith alone. In what follows, we shall deal with some alternative approaches offered from the seventeenth century to the present.

OTHER APPROACHES: PASCAL'S THEORY OF RELIGIOUS KNOWLEDGE

A classic statement of the view that religion is based on faith, and faith alone, is that of Blaise Pascal, writing a century before Hume and Kant. Pascal was one of the scientific geniuses of the seventeenth century. He was born in 1623 in Clermont in southern France. His father, who knew many of the important scientists of the period, gave his son an intensive training in the "new science" and in philosophy. With no instruction whatsoever in the field, young Pascal worked out the principles of mathematics. By the time he was sixteen he had written a treatise on conic sections. In his early twenties he developed a theory about the nature of the vacuum, which he attempted to verify in 1648 by an experiment in which he carried a barometer up the mountain at the Puy de Dôme, in southwestern France, near Clermont-Ferrand. His writings on physics were followed by important studies in mathematics, some of which prepared the ground for the development of the calculus by Newton and Leibniz later in the century; others laid the foundation for the probability theory.

Pascal's interest in religious questions stemmed from his involvement in the movement of the extreme Catholic reformers, the Jansenists. The Jansenists, deriving their name from their leader, Cornelis Jansen (1585–1638), a professor at Louvain in Belgium, and later a bishop, advocated a return to St. Augustine's views, especially the need for God's Grace to save men. They were very strict moralists, opposed to what they regarded as the lax personal and institutional practices of the time. Pascal joined the Jansenists in 1648, during the period of their greatest influence in French religious life. After his father's death in 1650, he drifted into libertine life, until, in 1654, while he was crossing one of the bridges near Paris a sudden religious experience converted him once and for all to religion. It was an event which led Pascal to abandon the secular world, and to retire to the Jansenist religious society at Port-Royal. There he wrote his famous *Provincial Letters*, a polemic attack on the Jesuits, because of the Jesuit moral teachings, which Pascal and others regarded as much too liberal and tolerant of human sins. The book was also a powerful defense of the Jansenist cause (which was under constant attack in France until it was finally condemned and the Jansenists were driven out of France later in the century). Pascal remained at Port-Royal, living a monastic life until his death in 1662. His most famous theological work, the *Pensées* (*Thoughts*), was published posthumously from fragments that he had written during the last years of his life. The work has been regarded ever since as one of the great classics of the French language.

The *Pensées* consists of a series of aphorisms and short essays dealing with the nature of man, man's knowledge of God, and the evidences that can be offered concerning the truth of the Christian religion. The early portions stress the "misery of man without God," the meaninglessness of ordinary human life, and the futility of man's attempts to understand, by natural means, his world and his condition in it. Then Pascal portrays man's desperate need of and desire for knowledge of God. In brilliant vignettes and fiercely cutting observations, Pascal tries to force man to realize "the human predicament." We are unable to know rationally what is actually taking place. However, we have the greatest need to fathom what is happening so that we will know what to do and what to believe. Most people manage, in spite of their situations, to waste their lives in diversions. They refuse to recognize that man's life is empty and meaningless if there is no God. They ignore the apparently insuperable difficulties that stand in the way of obtaining any knowledge about God's Existence. Once men realize the frightening possibilities in their situation, they will see that there may be something crucial that must be believed and done so that their brief lives will not be wasted. Men can no longer refuse to face their plight. They must devote themselves completely to the all-important attempt to answer the question "Is it possible to gain knowledge about the existence and nature of God?"

Once aware of the importance of this question, men also see that scientific and rational information is of no help in ascertaining whether there is a God, and if so, what sort of a Being He might be. One can ignore the question only at one's own peril. However, there does not seem to be any way of answering it. In this situation, Pascal asserted, the first thing that man can do is to investigate the alternatives open to him in terms of beliefs, and to try to determine whether it is more plausible and more desirable to believe that God exists than that He does not.

Pascal's famous argument of the Wager seeks to show that any reasonable man, looking at the "odds," will see that it is better and wiser to "bet" that God exists than that He does not, even if he lacks any adequate information for choosing between the alternatives.

> Let us now speak according to natural lights. If there is a God, He is infinitely incomprehensible, since, having neither parts nor limits, He has no affinity to us. We are then incapable of knowing either what He is or if He is. This being so, who will dare to undertake the decision of the question?
>
> . . . Let us then examine this point, and say, "God is, or He is not." But to which side shall we incline? Reason can decide nothing here. There is an infinite chaos which separated us. A game is being played at the extremity of this infinite distance where heads or tails will turn up. What will you wager? According to reason you can do neither the one thing nor the other; according to reason, you can defend neither of the propositions.
>
> Do not then reprove for error those who have made a choice, for you know nothing about it. "No, but I blame them for having made, not this choice, but a choice; for again both he who chooses heads and he who chooses tails are equally at fault, they are both in the wrong. The true course is not to wager at all."
>
> Yes; but you must wager. It is not optional. You are embarked. Which will you choose then? Let us see. Since you must choose, let us see which interests you least. You have two things to lose, the true and the good; and two things to stake, your reason and your will, your knowledge and your happiness; and your nature has two things to shun, error and misery. Your reason is no more shocked in choosing one rather than

the other, since you must of necessity choose. This is one point settled. But your happiness? Let us weigh the gain and the loss in wagering that God is. Let us estimate these two chances. If you gain, you gain all; if you lose, you lose nothing. Wager, then, without hesitation that He is.[5]

Pascal's Wager contends that there are just two possibilities concerning the existence of God, He is or He is not, and there are two views we can adopt, we believe He exists, or we believe He doesn't. If He does not exist, then it makes very little difference whether we have bet that He does or that He does not. But, if He does exist, it can make all the difference in the world whether we have bet on His existence or not. Hence, in terms of the possible outcomes, any reasonable gambler should see that the potential stakes are so weighted that he should gamble on the one alternative from which he has everything to gain and nothing to lose: that God exists.

The Wager was not intended as a "proof" that God exists, but rather as a way of showing that, in the absence of any decisive evidence, it is more reasonable to bet on the religious hypothesis than to bet against it. Both atheism, the denial that there is a God, and agnosticism, the contention that one cannot tell whether or not there is a God, Pascal wanted to show, are more unreasonable than theism in the face of what is at stake, if God does, in fact, exist. And Pascal also wanted to point out that nobody could actually avoid choosing an alternative to bet on, since even indifference represents a decision not to believe.

Critics have argued that Pascal has "covered up" the real complexities of the situation in his presentation of the Wager. One does not bet for or against God's existence, but for or against the existence of the God believed in by Catholicism, Calvinism, Mohammedanism, Judaism, and so on. The number of possibilities to choose between is not two, the critics contend, but an unlimited number. Hence, they say, given the possibilities, and the infinite stakes involved in each choice, if it is the right or wrong one, the "reasonable" gambler really cannot make a decision, and can only realize how desperate the problem of choice actually is. Pascal's answer seems to be that the Wager is only supposed to make one see the possible advantages of believing in the religious hypothesis—that God exists. The content of such a belief is not yet at issue, since the content can be supplied only by revelation from God.

The exploration of the problem of gaining knowledge about the existence and nature of God, and knowledge about the nature of the world, reveals, according to Pascal, the heart of the human predicament. We

[5] From Blaise Pascal, *Pensées* (Dutton Everyman, New York, 1958), pp. 66–67.

cannot attain certitude by rational means, nor can we even be certain that nothing can be known. The central portion of the *Pensées* builds up this theme, showing the many roads that lead to skepticism about the possibility of gaining knowledge, and the inability of man to accept complete doubt as the answer to his search for true knowledge. The climactic presentation of man's paradoxical situation occurs in the famous lengthy passage where the bases for complete skepticism are examined. Such an examination indicated, Pascal contended, that faith alone could supply the knowledge that man desires.

> The chief arguments of the sceptics . . . are that we have no certainty of the truth of these principles apart from faith and revelation, except in so far as we naturally perceive them in ourselves. Now this natural intuition is not a convincing proof of their truth; since, having no certainty apart from faith, whether man was created by a good God, or by a wicked demon, or by chance, it is doubtful whether these principles given to us are true, or false, or uncertain, according to our origin. Again, no person is certain, apart from faith, whether he is awake or sleeps. . . .
>
> What then shall man do in this state? Shall he doubt everything? Shall he doubt whether he is awake, whether he is being pinched, or whether he is being burned? Shall he doubt whether he doubts? Shall he doubt whether he exists? We cannot go so far as that; and I lay it down as a fact that there never has been a real complete sceptic. Nature sustains our feeble reason, and prevents it raving to this extent.
>
> Shall he then say, on the contrary, that he certainly possesses truth —he who, when pressed ever so little, can show no title to it, and is forced to let go his hold
>
> What a chimera then is man! What a novelty! What a monster, what a chaos, what a contradiction, what a prodigy! Judge of all things, imbecile worm of the earth; depositary of truth, a sink of uncertainty and error; the pride and refuse of the universe!
>
> Who will unravel this tangle? Nature confutes the sceptics, and reason confutes the dogmatists. What then will you become, O men! who try to find out by your natural reason what is your true condition? You cannot avoid one of these sects, nor adhere to one of them.
>
> Know then, proud man, what a paradox you are to yourself. Humble yourself, weak reason; be silent, foolish nature; learn that man infinitely transcends man, and learn from your master your true condition, of which you are ignorant. Hear God.[6]

---

[6] Pascal, *op. cit.*, pp. 119–121.

For Pascal, any investigation of our faculties for gaining knowledge concerning natural or religious objects only reveals how uncertain all our views actually are. We find that we cannot be sure of the reliability of our faculties, and hence of any "truths" that we may discover by using them. As our doubts increase, we are led to complete skepticism. Then we find that we are not even able to suspend judgment, because nature compels us to believe various things. We are thus torn between realizing our total incapacity for possessing and recognizing any truths, and our natural compulsion to believe. The more we reason, the more skeptical we become. But nevertheless, we remain creatures of nature, unable to accept the doubts to which reason leads us. The only way out of this impasse, according to Pascal, is through faith. Only through Divine Revelation can we ever reach any truth (including truths about mathematics and science, since these depend on our faculties, whose reliability can be established only by faith or Revelation).

Revelation, given to us by the Grace of God, is the sole source of knowledge about the existence and nature of God. After one has received or accepted the faith, it is then possible to find proofs and evidences for religious knowledge, which show that what one believes, or knows through Revelation, is in keeping with other information.

The prophecies, miracles, and proofs that have been traditionally offered in support of Pascal's religion, Christianity, are, he insisted, "not of such a nature that they can be said to be absolutely convincing." It is still possible to doubt of the truth of the Christian religion in spite of the evidence available. But, Pascal contended, it is not unreasonable to believe on the basis of this information. The evidence available indicates that it is at least as plausible that the religious knowledge-claims of the Judaeo-Christian religion are true as that they are false. Therefore, it is not on rational standards that we decide whether we accept or reject this religious view. The believer accepts the knowledge-claims because of his religious experience. The disbeliever rejects them because of his attitude, and his personal prejudices: ". . . there is sufficient evidence to condemn, and insufficient to convince; so that it appears in those who follow it [the Christian religion], that it is grace, and not reason, which makes them follow it; and in those who shun it, that it is lust, not reason, which makes them shun it."

A large part of the *Pensées* is devoted to presenting "proofs of the Christian religion." These "proofs," drawn from the history of Christianity, the fulfillment of the prophecies in the Old Testament, and so on, do not purport to establish, independent of all one's beliefs and attitudes, that Christianity is true. Only Revelation can provide an adequate basis for assessing the "proofs" and for seeing that they constitute satisfactory evidence of certain religious knowledge-claims. Without any revelatory foundation, Pascal was willing to admit, one could always refuse to conclude from the "proofs" that Christianity was true, or one could refuse to admit that the evidence offered actually constituted "proofs." But, Pascal reiterated, disbelievers really had no evidence in their favor either, so that if they persisted in disbelieving, it was only because of their attitudes, and not because of any particular information at their disposal.

Thus, Pascal contended, much knowledge can be gained about the existence and nature of God. However, all of this knowledge depends, basically, on faith and on God's revelation of information to believers. Pascal did not accept the Thomistic view that it was possible by rational means to attain positive knowledge that God exists, and negative knowledge about what God is not like. No knowledge in any field whatsoever could actually be gained by rational means alone, since, for Pascal, only Revelation could eliminate the grounds for skeptical doubts about our faculties and their reliability.

On the other hand, Pascal's view is in accord with Hume's on many basic points. They agree on the insufficiency and inadequacy of the proofs of the existence of God based on fact and reason, and they agree that, ultimately, the religious knowledge-claims of the Judaeo-Christian tradition can be accepted only if one has faith. For Hume this conclusion appeared to be a decisive factor that would prevent "reasonable" men from adhering to a revealed religion, whereas for Pascal it only indicated man's desperate need for God's aid. At the end of the *Dialogues* Hume had asserted, probably ironically, that "to be a philosophical sceptic is, in a man of letters, the first and most essential step towards being a sound, believing Christian." Hume took only the first step. He saw that skeptical reasoning would undermine the arguments and the evidence that had been offered to show, by rational means, that certain religious views were true. He saw also that one could only accept these views in the absence of adequate rational evidence. On the basis of this examination, he remained skeptical, and accepted only the minimal religious conclusion that the cause or causes of the order in the world probably resemble human intelligence. Pascal, however, saw skepticism as the means of humbling man, and the way to make him aware of his own inability to find any truths. Once aware, man's own needs and his inability to accept complete doubt should drive him on to seek faith, and to receive the Revelation openly and gladly.

Hume and Pascal were both "theological" skeptics. They doubted that any necessary and sufficient reasons could be given to support any particular views about the existence and nature of God. Then each adopted opposite and similarly unprovable conclusions from this skepticism. Hume advocated a type of "religious" skepticism as well, doubting various religious beliefs because they could not be supported by evidence adequate to convince a "reasonable" man; on the other hand, Pascal advocated a type of blind faith, accepting the Revelation without question, and then seeking supporting "proofs" for what was already taken on faith.

Critics of Pascal's views about religious knowledge have pointed out that his "theological" skepticism seems to eliminate any standards for assessing what is actually true. Once it is admitted that our faculties may be unreliable, how then can we ascertain when we are actually receiving true revealed information? In the lengthy passage from the *Pensées* quoted above, Pascal proclaimed that the ultimate way to knowledge was to "Hear God." But how do we judge when we are really hearing Him, and when we only think that we are hearing Him? There are wide differences among the revelations that people say they have received. If we judge which is true in terms of what we have heard, are we not begging the question of what is the true Revelation? If there is no rational basis for religious knowledge, nor any rational criteria for judging it, is not any religious claim to knowledge transformed into an entirely subjective assertion about what a single individual feels has been revealed to him? Some theologians, such as Søren Kierkegaard, have been willing to accept this completely subjective conclusion of their skepticism about rational theology. Others have sought to establish some kind of adequate standards to defend their own revelatory information. Still others, including John Calvin and perhaps Pascal himself, have insisted that the experience of the Revelation includes within it a guarantee of its authenticity. Anyone, they contend, who "hears God" knows that this has happened, and knows that he is not being deceived. The religious experience, the basis for any religious knowledge, is self-validating. These theologians assert that if one has had such an experience, he cannot be in any doubt about God's Existence or His Nature. One cannot confuse this experience, they contend, with a personal hallucination. The critics, however, continue to point out that the fact that there are so many differing and conflicting reports of revelatory information, each claiming to be self-authenticating, suggests that some rational standards are still required to judge when genuine revelatory information has been received. These critics insist that as long as one accepts the irrational and skeptical views about the bases of religious knowledge of a thinker such as Pascal, one will not be able to demonstrate that any knowledge gained by faith and Revelation is absolutely true, no matter how much one is convinced of it. The believer, on the other hand, insists that his conviction is so great, after the revelatory experience, that the absence of rational standards presents no difficulties. In this state, he finds ample "proof" of the truth of his religious knowledge, even if his evidence is open to some question by others.

SØREN KIERKEGAARD'S THEORY OF RELIGIOUS KNOWLEDGE

Another important version of faith as the basis of religious knowledge is that of the great Danish philosopher, Søren Kierkegaard (1813–1855). He was schooled in the liberal and critical Bible scholarship of the day and in Hegelian philosophy. He rebelled against his upbringing and wrote a strange and somewhat baffling collection of works. They range from books such as *Either/Or*, which are works of fiction, to his *Edifying Discourses*, which are religious rhapsodies, to philosophical and psychological studies, such as the famous *Philosophical Fragments*, and its sequel, *The Concluding Unscientific Postscript*, as well as *Fear and Trembling* and *The Sickness Unto Death*, to polemical theological works such as *Training in Christianity*, to, finally, bitter tirades such as his last work, *The Assault on Christianity*. On the title pages the books are attributed to a series of different authors with such odd names as Johannes Climacus, Johannes de Silentio, Virgilius Hofnienis, Anti-Climacus, and Søren Kierkegaard. These different authors adhere to different positions. They argue with one another. In one work they all get together, and discuss their views. Throughout this entire collection of writings, Kierkegaard insisted his point and his message could be developed and presented only in this strange manner. Kierkegaard felt that only through what he termed "indirect discourse" could he communicate his ideas and arouse the reader to the realization of the importance of certain problems, and then of the need to solve them.

According to Kierkegaard, the crucial questions that have to be asked and answered are, "What should man do, and what should he believe?" Most people live their lives without ever asking themselves why they live as they do, and whether they ought to live as they do. Hence Kierkegaard felt that his first task was to disturb people, so that they would begin to look at themselves and at the way they lived. Once people had been made sufficiently uncomfortable, they might then commence the quest for a meaningful basis for human existence.

Therefore, the first stage of Kierkegaard's "indirect discourse" is that of making people interested in themselves. When people look at their own lives, they will see how barren, trivial, absurd, and unhappy these lives actually are. They will also realize that their emptiness and their anguish are due to the fact that they have been unwilling to recognize the human situations, nor have they sought to direct their lives in terms of serious goals. Kierkegaard first attempted to portray what he called the "aesthetic" level of human existence. This is the sensuous one in which we function in our daily lives. Kierkegaard's picture of ordinary existence, like Pascal's portrait, is supposed to make us aware of what we are—pleasure-seeking creatures, living absurd and meaningless lives. When we see ourselves in this way, we will, presumably, first become uneasy, then unhappy, and finally desperate. In our despair, we will frantically seek an answer to the question "What should we do?"

When we have reached this state, then Kierkegaard's philosophical authors can assist us in intellectually analyzing our plight. Each of us lives at a particular time in history. What we seek and what we need is a meaning and a purpose for our historical existence. What we want to know is whether there is any reason for living one type of life rather than another. We are searching for guidance on which we can rely completely and absolutely. This quest for an intellectual basis for the goals which should direct our lives leads us to a consideration of certain basic and traditional philosophical problems.

Kierkegaard developed the philosophical side of his "indirect discourse" in his *Philosophical Fragments*, allegedly written by Johannes Climacus. The work deals with the question of whether man can gain absolutely certain knowledge about the meaning and goal of human existence. In order to find an answer to the question "What should we do?" Climacus contended that we first must discover whether we are capable of gaining any eternal knowledge that can guide us in our historical lives. The argument of *The Fragments* purports to show that we cannot gain such knowledge rationally, but that we can and must receive it by another means, that of faith.

In order to develop his theory, Johannes Climacus begins by posing Plato's puzzle about knowledge from the dialogue *Meno*. Socrates had argued, in that work, that it is not possible to learn what one does not already know, since one would have no means of recognizing such knowledge when one learned it. If one does not know the product of 9856 and 3.447, how can one tell the right answer from the wrong one? If one could recognize the right answer when one was taught it, then, Socrates contended, one must have already known the product. If one actually did not possess this knowledge, in some sense, then how could one possibly ascertain that a given proposed answer was or was not true? Socrates concluded, from this line of reasoning, that learning is impossible, since one cannot acquire knowledge that one does not already possess. One cannot learn what one does not know, since one cannot recognize the truth of such knowledge. And, if one learns what one already knows, then no actual learning is taking place. To account for the apparent process of learning, Socrates offered Plato's Recollection Theory. Learning is actually recollecting what one knows, but has temporarily forgotten. Since one cannot acquire any new knowledge, one must already possess all possible knowledge within oneself, without being aware of it.

Kierkegaard's spokesman, Johannes Climacus, agreed that Plato had raised a serious problem, but Climacus proposed that a totally different hypothesis could be offered to explain how learning is possible. The Kierkegaardian hypothesis starts with the assumption that a learner does *not* already possess any knowledge. He then has no way of recognizing the truth of any knowledge that he might acquire. If such a person learns anything, a strange and radical transformation must occur to make the learner capable of ascertaining that what he learns is true. According to the initial assumption, and to the Socratic argument, the learner cannot learn. He is completely ignorant. If he then does learn, it is only because he must have been changed from one who could not recognize a truth to one who could. Hence, at the moment when learning becomes possible, this hypothetical learner must be transformed so that he now has knowledge, and also has the ability to recognize such knowledge as true. Thus, instead of explaining learning as recollection, the Kierkegaardian hypothesis contends that learning is miraculous, resulting from an inexplicable change in the learner that constitutes a decisive moment in his life. After this moment of enlightenment has occurred, what the learner knows is absolutely certain (since he can recognize that it is true).

The learner is not able to bring about his own enlightenment. Prior to its occurrence, he was completely ignorant. Even after it has taken place, he is not able to understand what has happened to him, or how it has happened. Thus, Climacus argues, on this hypothesis, the cause of the miraculous transformation that makes learning and knowledge possible must be something other than the learner himself. Kierkegaard called this cause "God," whatever He or It may be. In order to produce this total change in the learner, God must enter into the historical sequence of events in the learner's life.

In developing his hypothesis, Kierkegaard maintained that there is a further major respect in which his theory differs from that of Socrates and Plato. According to the Recollection Theory, the actual moment of recollection is not important, for the learner has always possessed all the knowledge that he can recall. However, according to the Kierkegaardian hypothesis, the moment of enlightenment is a decisive one for the learner. At that moment he becomes completely transformed from one who was completely ignorant to one who possesses certain knowledge. This moment, then, is the turning point in the learner's life. Although the radical change is a miraculous event from the learner's point of view, it is decisive for him only insofar as he is able to see it as a vital, dramatic culmination of developments in *his* own life. The transformation must, then, be seen by the learner as the fulfillment of his own desire, even though he could not tell what it was he desired prior to the moment of enlightenment. Before that moment he did not know what his new state might be like, nor how it could be brought about. But if the complete change is to be significant and decisive in the learner's life, it must constitute the full realization of what he wanted even in his state of total ignorance.

Johannes Climacus illustrated this Kierkegaardian point in terms of the tale of the mighty king (God), who wanted to marry a humble maiden (the human learner). He only wants to marry her, however, if she loves him for himself, and not for his power or his wealth. If she sees how powerful and rich he is, she may then consent to marry him, but for the wrong reasons. If he compels her to marry him, he cannot be sure that she does it for love of him. Hence the king can only by concealing his actual status succeed in gaining the maiden for the right reason, her love of him for himself. In this way, the maiden cannot choose to marry him for the wrong reasons, since she will not be aware of them. In the same way, God must conceal the benefits of enlightenment from the learner, lest he desire it for the wrong reasons. And, if God compels the learner to become enlightened, without the learner desiring the transformation, there will be no reason on the part of the learner, and the event will be neither significant nor decisive in his life. Thus, if the moment of enlightenment is to be desired by the learner for the right reason—as a culmination of what *he* wants for its own sake—then he must not be compelled or enticed into wishing for it.

Kierkegaard's hypothesis may be stated more prosaically as a type of skepticism. Human beings are unable to know anything with certitude by means of their own capacities. They can gain true knowledge only as the result of a miraculous transformation of themselves. The miracle that produces knowledge is decisive or significant in the life of a person only if he wishes for the event before he is able to judge whether it will be advantageous or disadvantageous for him.

In several of his philosophical works, Kierkegaard argued for a type of skepticism, contending men are incapable of gaining any knowledge by their own means. If man is completely ignorant, then, Kierkegaard argued, he can overcome his sad state only by first recognizing it for what it is, and then by blindly and irrationally seeking for a solution by faith. He must believe that there can be direct contact between God and himself in his own life, though he cannot tell whether it is either possible or probable.

In our state of ignorance, the only information that we possess is factual, historical data about what we have experienced, or information that we have derived logically from certain concepts. We are not able to ascertain if this information is actually true (since we do not possess any true knowledge), nor if it is about any genuine features of the world. Before we are enlightened, we cannot even determine if there is a God. (In fact, Kierkegaard contended, our ignorance is so blinding that we find that it is more probable, given the information that we possess in this state, that He does not exist than that He does.)

To justify his skepticism about our factual and historical information, Kierkegaard argued that these data are always based on sense experience. Our experience is continually changing. We are unable to ascertain if any of the information that we gain from it is, or must be, true. We could be certain of this information only if we could establish that it could not possibly ever be false. This cannot be established since our sense experience is of objects that are constantly changing. Any information gained through the senses may have to be revised as the qualities we experience are altered. Our senses do not inform us of any necessary conditions about the changing world. We can observe only the temporary arrangement of qualities that appears in historical events. But we cannot be sure that the objects that we experience *must* possess the properties we perceive, or that they cannot have different ones. (Kierkegaard's point is similar to Hume's contention that we cannot gain certain knowledge concerning matters of fact.)

The information that we gain in disciplines such as mathematics seems to be certain. Kierkegaard, however, maintained that all we can know in these areas is that, *if* concepts are defined in a certain way, *then* certain consequences must follow. In this manner, we may gain knowledge concerning the logical relationships of a group of concepts. But we are still unable to ascertain whether any of the objects we experience possess the properties of these concepts, or whether experienced objects are related in the same way as certain concepts. The axioms and definitions of Euclidean geometry, for example, enable one to deduce theorems about "triangles" and "circles." But geometrical knowledge is not sufficient to enable one to determine if there are objects we experience to which the theorems apply. Euclidean geometry provides a body of certain and necessary truths, regardless of whether triangles and circles actually exist in our world. But these truths are only about concepts, and are not necessarily about anything that we may experience. Our only information about whether Euclidean geometry applies to observed objects comes from sense experience, and this information is never completely certain.

Johannes Climacus summed up these skeptical views in the *Postscript* by proclaiming that a logical system of knowledge is possible, but an existential one is not. A logical system consists of a body of necessary truths derived logically from an initial set of concepts or definitions. An existential system, on the other hand, would be a body of necessary truths about the changing world of experience. Such a system cannot be discovered or constructed because we cannot know any necessary truths about factual or historical events. Kierkegaard's thesis about logical and existential systems is similar to the view of the logical positivists. The latter contend that all our information consists either of propositions which are logically true, but which have no factual content, or of factual propositions which cannot be deduced by logical procedures.

Kierkegaard next argued that one cannot prove the existence of a God who acts in history. Because of the severe limitations on what men can know, only conceptual proofs of God's existence are possible. If the term "God" is defined theologically as "a Being who is Eternal, Immutable, and Perfect," it may be possible to derive the proposition "God necessarily exists" from this and other carefully contrived definitions. Such a proof would not, however, establish that such a Being exists or acts in the historical world. It might establish that the definition and the conclusion are logically related, but not that the conclusion applies to the world in which we live. If we attempt to discover from our factual information whether God exists, we are then confronted with a serious difficulty. None of the objects we perceive by our senses is God, since He, by definition, is eternal and immutable, and all sense objects are constantly changing. Some of the objects we experience may be effects of God's actions. But we could only infer from the effects to their cause, if we were already sure that the Cause exists. Hence factual information cannot provide the basis for a proof of God's existence.

If one analyzed the theological definition of "God," Kierkegaard contended, one would realize that it would be logically impossible for such a God to take part in historical events. If God is an eternal and immutable Being, then He cannot have historical or temporal properties. Hence the theological conception of God would rule out the possibility that there is a God who acts in history. Anyone who believes in the existence of a historical God, a God who acts in the temporal world, believes then in a genuine logical absurdity.

With this much of the Kierkegaardian argument, as presented by Johannes Climacus, we can now turn to the positive side of Kierkegaard's philosophy, his answer to the initial question, "What should man do?" Human beings are in a state of complete ignorance. The examination of our condition makes us into skeptics, for we become aware of our own inability to discover necessary truths about the world in which we live. When we reflect on our predicament, we realize that we are trapped in an apparently hopeless situation. We possess no certain knowledge. We must have such knowledge in order to determine what we ought to do, and what we should believe. We cannot avoid the quest for certain knowledge if we are concerned to discover the meaning and purpose of human existence. Unfortunately, because of our total ignorance we have no means of our own for gaining the knowledge that we seek. We can gain such knowledge only if the miracle of enlightenment takes place. In our state of ignorance, we cannot even ascertain if there is a God who could cause such a miracle to occur.

We can find no guidance whatsoever. We have no means for determining what we should do. We cannot discover how we might become enlightened. Hence we can either remain in ignorance forever as complete skeptics, or we can make "the leap into absurdity," choosing to believe for no reason whatsoever that there is a God who can and does act historically, and who will enlighten us if we want Him to. If believing is our only solution to our predicament, can we tell what to believe? No! Before deciding to believe, there is no way of ascertaining what would constitute *the* right decision. In this state of ignorance, we cannot tell if enlightenment is actually possible, or how it could be produced. We can decide to believe all sorts of views; but, can we tell which may be *the* right one? Hence the risk in making "the leap into absurdity" is enormous. We can never know beforehand whether it is better to "leap" or not, nor where to "leap" to. But nonetheless we must choose. By an act of will, and not of reason, we must decide whether to be doubters or believers.

Kierkegaard's own choice was to believe in Christianity, interpreted in the light of his own theory of knowledge. Knowledge is only acquired miraculously. The miracle, in Kierkegaard's faith, is the Incarnation of Jesus Christ. God has appeared in human history and enlightens those who believe in Him. If, apart from faith, we attempt to ascertain if the Incarnation has occurred, and when and where it might have taken place, we quickly discover there is no evidence at all that might help us in reaching a judgment on these questions. Like the king in Climacus' tale, God has completely hidden Himself. Human beings have to choose to believe in His Existence solely because they want to, by faith alone.

Historical information is of no assistance in determining if God was Incarnate in Jesus. Those who were acquainted with Jesus of Nazareth in the first century A.D. knew Him only as a human being. They could also deduce that it is logically impossible for a man to be God. Historical data gathered since the first century tell us only about the human existence of Jesus and his followers. Theological reasoning proves to us that the central "fact" of Christianity, that Jesus is God, is absurd. The Bible provides us with no information on the subject unless we already believe that the New Testament contains the life of God on earth. The book itself does not establish this. Only faith can.

Hence Kierkegaard insisted that there is *no* evidence that Christianity is true. There is evidence, however, that it is a logical contradiction for God to have had a life or a history. The man of faith believes despite the absence of positive evidence, and despite the negative evidence. He follows Tertullian's dictum, "I believe that which is absurd." It may be implausible, or even ridiculous to believe that Jesus of Nazareth, a historical human being, is God. The believer can only say, as the German philosopher J. G. Hamann declared, "Lies, fables and romances must needs be probable, but not the foundation of our faith."

The view that man's problems can only be resolved by pure, blind faith was further analyzed by Kierkegaard in his famous work *Fear and Trembling.* Here he chose Abraham, as portrayed in the Old Testament, as the prime example of a "knight of faith." Such a believer is one who believes and acts "in virtue of the absurd." The test of a knight of faith's beliefs is whether he can actually hold to them in spite of overwhelming evidence that they are false or absurd. Abraham consented to sacrifice his one and only child, Isaac, when he was promised by God that if he did so, he would become the Father of the Faithful. The sacrificial act was absurd, in that if it were completed it would appear to have logically precluded the possibility of God's fulfillment of His promise. The act would make no sense by human standards. Yet, Kierkegaard pointed out, Abraham did not debate whether to sacrifice his son. As a knight of faith, he attempted to act in accordance with his beliefs, no matter how irrational (or immoral) they might be.

The solution that Kierkegaard offered to his original questions—"What should man do?" and "What should he believe?"—is a totally irrational one. Man can find true answers only through his own leap into faith. Hence no man is in a position to enlighten another. Each can discover true knowledge only by a miracle, provided that his own decision to believe is accompanied by God's producing the miracle. Hence Kierkegaard obviously could not teach anyone else what is true. Therefore, he insisted, he could only communicate obliquely with his fellow men, through "indirect discourse." He could pose questions and problems, but the reader would have to find his own answers in his own way. The various pseudonymous authors, Johannes Climacus and the others, could raise questions and suggest answers. The reader, however, would have to seek for his own enlightenment. His only assurance that what he found, or believed, was actually true would be his own subjective convictions. The discovery and the recognition of truth would forever remain an inner, personal event. One can neither learn the truth nor teach the truth. One can only believe.

Kierkegaard's view, which is a kind of fideism, is a type of "rationale" for religion which has become popular among many twentieth-century theologians, who have developed what they call Neo-Orthodoxy. Karl Barth and Paul Tillich were two of the principal advocates of this kind of defense of Christianity by faith alone.

FRIEDRICH NIETZSCHE'S THEORY OF RELIGIOUS KNOWLEDGE

An opposite but equally influential theory of religion and religious knowledge was set forth by the German thinker, Friedrich Nietzsche (1844–1900), who has had an enormous influence on twentieth-century existentialist thought. The son of a Protestant pastor of Polish origins, Nietzsche was raised in Prussia, and first studied in a military academy. He then went on to study classics, theology, philology, and philosophy at the Universities of Bonn and Leipzig. He was much influenced by the thought of Schopenhauer and by the grandiose musical compositions of Richard Wagner. After a brief period in the army during which he was seriously injured, he became professor of classical philology at the University of Basel, Switzerland, in 1869. He began publishing his views in 1872 with *The Birth of Tragedy*. By 1878 he had begun to attack his two former heroes, Schopenhauer and Wagner. A year later Nietzsche retired from teaching because of poor health. In retirement, mainly in Italy, he wrote many polemical and aphoristic works, culminating in his best known book, *Thus Spake Zarathustra*, (1883). Nietzsche, who was not a modest fellow, called it the most profound book in world literature. (In his autobiography, *Ecce Homo*, Nietzsche entitled some of the chapters, "Why I am so wise," "Why I am so clever," and "Why I write such excellent books.") One of his last works, before he went completely mad in the beginning of 1889, was *The Antichrist*. For the last eleven years of Nietzsche's life, he was totally insane.

Though a most brilliant, biting, satirical, and poetic writer, many considered Nietzsche a madman all his life, who ranted and raved against the world because of his inability to cope with it. Because of the interest shown by leading Nazis, including Hitler, in some of his ideas, he has often been condemned as a malignant source of some of the worst tendencies of twentieth-century thought. Leaving aside his personality and personal frustrations, and some of the political uses to which part of his ideas have been put, one can see in Nietzsche's work an incisive criticism of the meaninglessness of human life in the world in which he lived.

Like Kierkegaard, of whose works Nietzsche knew nothing, Nietzsche saw the intellectual, cultural, and spiritual life of the people around him as empty and bankrupt. Starting from Schopenhauer's analysis of will as the basic feature that shapes human existence, Nietzsche saw a positive rather than a pessimistic message in the situation. Life is meaningless only if one fails to make it meaningful. Schopenhauer, in seeing that there was no Absolute, or genuine purpose, in the world, lost his nerve, and tried to retreat into a quieting or denial of the will. Nietzsche, instead, urged people to give honest, forceful expression to their wills and creative energies, and to make up their own purposes. He saw the two major forces of nineteenth-century thought, Christianity and democracy, as snivelling attempts to protect the weak from their own and other's volitions. Christianity was a slave morality for weaklings. It was "pity nailed to the Cross." Democracy was the morality of the herd, afraid of the strong-willed creative people, a way of protecting the herd from them.

Unlike Kierkegaard's, Nietzsche's crucial message that must be understood before one can create a meaningful world is the message his spokesman, Zarathustra, proclaims: "God is dead!" There is no salvation for mankind beyond man. The concept of a Supreme Being who directs human affairs and makes them meaningful is no longer operative for modern intellectuals. The results of nineteenth-century biology and psychology show man for what he is, a willful animal striving for power. Instead of resisting this through Christianity, democracy, or Schopenhauer's pessimism, one should revel in it and base the solution to the human predicament on what man is actually like.

Stressing the warlike animal, and especially the creative drives of mankind, Nietzsche attacked those who feared or tried to contain them. Christian morality, especially as set forth by St. Paul; democratic theory, as exposited by John Stuart Mill; the pessimism expressed by Schopenhauer, were all denials of man's deepest urges. What people *really* felt to be good had been labeled bad by the cowards and protectors of the weak. One should, Nietzsche had Zarathustra proclaim, say, "Yea to Reality," that is, accept the real human situation, and not try to suppress it. What is needed, he said, is a "trans-valuation of values," a recognition that what has been called bad is good, and vice versa. Such an affirmation would lead to genuine creativity, to the construction of a meaningful world for man.

Most people were too fearful to take the risk of honestly acting on their urges, desires, and will to power. *Thus Spake Zarathustra*, Nietzsche asserted, is "a book for all and none." All needed it, but maybe none were ready to accept it. If one agreed that there were no absolute or divine standards, that man, without any extra human guidance, had to determine his life, then what should one do? Nietzsche boldly advocated doing what one really wanted to. This, he insisted, could lead to a man greater than man, a superman, the powerful realization of the creative possibilities within the bravest and the best men. (The Nazis made the superman concept a basis for the stormtroopers.) Nietzsche felt that the superman would not be just a military brute overpowering everybody, but a marvelously creative and free individual. He originally thought of the composer Richard Wagner as such an individual; but when Wagner sent Nietzsche a copy of his religious opera, *Parsifal*, Nietzsche saw that his hero had clay feet. He had succumbed to the ideology of the weak Christians, and hence was no superman.

For all of his bombast, Nietzsche was no romantic optimist. He also saw the ultimate futility of the heroic creative gesture he was advocating. It would not save the world, or conquer human frailty. Even the superman had to realize that, given what human nature was like, people would return to their cringing, empty, defensive lives. There would be an eternal return, an ever-repeating cycle of creative heroism and human weakness.

Although Nietzsche was not a systematic philosopher and wrote mainly in aphorisms and parables, rather than arguments, his picture of the human scene has had a great effect on twentieth-century thought. Instead of searching for an irrational basis for faith, he sought for an irrational basis for humanism, a human morality based solely on human drives. With the realization that God was dead, man would have to find himself and his values by himself. We will see shortly both the impact of Nietzsche's views on the so-called "Death of God" theologians, and on twentieth-century existentialists.

MARXISM AND FREUDIANISM

Two other theories, one approximately contemporary with Nietzsche's and the other developed shortly after him, presented atheistical accounts of religion, and sought to explain on sociological or psychological grounds how people could believe religious views when they were obviously false. These critiques of religious belief, Marxism and Freudianism, were concerned not so much with the evidence offered for religion, but rather with the causes or reasons for any sane man or woman believing in a religious view.

Karl Marx, in the *Communist Manifesto*, had declared that "religion was the opiate of the masses." According to this theory, religion was a means used by the dominant class (a) to keep the dominated group from realizing their true condition, and (b) to make them insensitive to their suffering. Marxists have also held that the religious authorities have tried to hold back progressive forces that would alleviate the condition of the masses. The religious beliefs and practices have been foisted upon the masses as one of the chief ways of keeping people from realizing their suffering, and as a way of drugging people so that they will accept the suffering (for example, by making them believe their suffering will be rewarded in an afterworld—"There will be pie in the sky when you die.") Detailed analyses have been offered by various Marxist scholars about how religions develop, and how they are used by the dominant group as a way of enforcing its will. Many Communist countries have taken over a large number of churches, and have turned some into museums of atheism, depicting the horrors of religion before the coming of communism. Nonetheless, sixty years after the Communist Revolution in Russia, there still seems to be an underlayer in the society of adherence to some religion, be it Russian Orthodox Catholicism, Judaism, the Moslem faith, or any other one. This would seem to indicate that more is involved in the reason that people adhere to a religion than an economic or sociological analysis can explain.

A further interpretation offering a purely psychological theory was that of another atheist, the father of psychoanalysis, Sigmund Freud. Freud, a Jew by birth, never practiced any religion, and from early in his career diagnosed the belief in, and the practice of any religion as the result of primitive and infantile psychological drives and desires. In an early work, *Totem and Taboo*, Freud analyzed the origin and development of religion in terms of how primitive people functioned, setting up a system of a totem and taboos to regulate and enforce sexual relations within the group. A major feature of such a system was to control the basic Oedipus complex (the desire to kill one's father and marry one's mother). The totem was a substitute for the primal father. Early on in human history, Freud claimed, an animal was used as the totem. Later on the totem grew to cosmic dimensions where the father became God. Freud's analysis enabled him to show how the symbolism and the practice of various present-day religions, especially Christianity, could be understood as developments of the primitive religious motifs.

In a later book, *The Future of An Illusion* (1927), Freud analyzed religious belief as projections of infantile experiences and interpretations of them. Man, from childhood onward, is surrounded by natural forces he cannot control. He also is dominated by his parents, especially his father. He personifies nature into powerful beings like his father and makes this personified nature into a system of all powerful father-gods. The function of these gods is to remove the terrors of nature, to reconcile the individual to the cruelty of fate and the inevitability of death, and to reward people for their natural and cultural privations. As Freud said, "I have tried to show that religious ideas have sprung from the same need as all other achievements of culture; from the necessity for defending itself against the crushing supremacy of nature."

Thus, according to Freud, the religious illusion arises out of the original experience of people as children, and then gets projected into nature and into symbolic systems as a way of warding off the "crushing supremacy of nature," and as a way of rewarding people for their perseverance (in an imagined afterlife or something of that order). People who have matured and realized that nature can be understood in scientific terms will no longer have need for the illusion. The illusion is natural, in that it develops with the maturation of a person. But it is still something that should and could be overcome in the rational adult.

Freud further claimed that outside the human belief system there is no independent evidence of the truth of any religious views. They are not subject to empirical verification and examination. Therefore, one can only deal with religions in terms of their diagnostic status in the human psyche. Like Nietzsche, Freud saw the religious "illusion" as basically a self-defense mechanism for those who are unable to accept nature as it really is.

WILLIAM JAMES'
THEORY OF
RELIGIOUS KNOWLEDGE

The next theory of religious knowledge to be considered in this chapter represents another possible line of development from the "theological" skepticism of Hume and Pascal; this theory attempts to answer the question, "What knowledge can be gained about the nature and existence of God?" in psychological rather than philosophical terms or psychoanalytic terms. In so doing, a less negative theory than Freud's was developed, without claiming that people could actually know if a Divine Being existed. William James (1842–1910), the founder of the philosophical theory called "Pragmatism" (which will be discussed in Chapter 6, "Contemporary Philosophy"), was the son of a minor New England transcendentalist who was a leading advocate of the Swedenborgian religious view, a movement based on the religious visions, special revelations, and Biblical interpretations of the Swedish theologian Emmanuel Swedenborg (1688–1772). The younger James was never able to accept his father's religious theories, but at the same time, he was also unwilling to join the many scientifically minded people of his time in condemning religious beliefs as foolish and valueless. In his writings about religion, especially in his famous essay "The Will to Believe," and in his *The Varieties of Religious Experience*, James attempted to evaluate views about the existence and nature of God not in terms of whether they were objectively true, but in terms of the consequences for the believers of accepting these beliefs. The basic question of religious knowledge became, for James, not what knowledge could actually be gained in this area, but rather, what difference it would make to a person if he believed certain things about the existence and nature of God.

"The Will to Believe" sets out to justify religious belief, despite the fact that there does not seem to be adequate logical or rational evidence to make one believe. Religious belief in the existence of a God is a hypothesis. Since there is insufficient evidence to enable us to decide whether to accept or reject the hypothesis, we have an "option," a choice, to decide what to do. The type of option at issue, however, James contended, is a living, forced, and momentous one. A living option is a hypothesis which represents a real possibility to the person to whom it is proposed. A forced option is one where a choice between two possibilities has to be made and cannot be avoided. And a momentous option is one where the choice involved could have important consequences in the future course of one's life.

In most cases where we do not have sufficient evidence to decide between hypotheses, the option involved is neither a living, forced, nor momentous one. If we are asked whether we think that Greek mythology is true, we do not see it as a real issue, nor are we forced to take a stand. We can avoid the question by suspending judgment in the absence of adequate information. Further, the question does not seem to be momentous, because it does not appear that it would make very much difference in our lives whether we believe or do not believe any given answer to the question.

The scientifically minded person usually does not want to believe or to commit himself until he has enough evidence. But in almost all of the cases where he exercises this caution, the questions at issue do not demand immediate commitment. He feels that he can postpone any decision until more data become available. This attitude, according to James, indicates that the questions he is considering do not pose forced or momentous options for him, and in many cases that the questions do not raise "live" possibilities.

The questions that are taken seriously will, obviously, differ from person to person, varying according to a person's interests, attitudes, and concerns. Hence what is a live issue for one may be completely dead for another. The religious hypothesis for some people, whom James called "tough-minded," is not a live issue. They cannot conceive, even in the remotest sense, that it could be true. In this case, James was not concerned to convince these "tough-minded" people, but only to show them that their attitude is no more justified by the facts available than is the believer's view. Their rejection is as much a "passional" act as is believing. In either case, one's attitude and one's feelings when faced with the option lead to one's actions in the matter. The "tough-minded" person who ignores the option, or sneers at it, is taking a stand based on his feelings. He can only show that a particular belief is unjustified on intellectual grounds. He cannot show, therefore, that he *ought* to disbelieve, or that he *ought* to ignore the question. If he feels like disbelieving or ignoring, this is an indication of his temperament. His reaction is not warranted by any rational conclusions.

For the rest of mankind, many of whom fall into James' classification of "tender-minded" individuals, the religious hypothesis represents a live issue, that is, they could conceive of its being true. But many intellectuals who will admit this much, then insist, for reasons similar to those offered by Hume, Pascal, Kierkegaard and the Bible critics, that because of the inadequacy of the evidence available, no one can ascertain what is objectively true in this area. Therefore, these people suggest we still should not take a stand even though this is a live issue, because in the absence of more information, we could very easily come to the wrong conclusion. James wanted to show that once one recognized that the religious hypothesis represented a live option, one should also realize that one was *forced* to take a stand. Then in terms of the momentous consequences involved, he argued that a stand in favor of the religious hypothesis was "justified."

Considerations similar to those presented in Pascal's discussion of the Wager indicate what is at issue. If the religious hypothesis is a live issue, it is also a momentous one. Pascal had appealed to the eternal and infinite stakes involved, an afterlife of salvation and bliss, or of condemnation and misery. But, James pointed out, even if the issue of the afterlife is not a live or momentous one nowadays, the religious hypothesis also contends that the believer gains something during his present life in terms of certain values and goods, and the disbeliever loses something. Hence the consequences of belief or disbelief should make a discernible and important difference during our lifetimes. The religious hypothesis, in its most general form, makes two contentions. First, it asserts "that the best things are the more eternal things," and, second, it maintains "that we are better off even now if we believe her [the religious hypothesis] to be true." From the present moment in our lives, we can then see that if the religious hypothesis is true the consequences could be very great for us. Hence, the religious hypothesis is obviously a momentous one.

If one objects, saying that all sorts of fictitious hypotheses could be shown to be momentous by this reasoning, James counters by pointing out that these would not be live options, and hence would not represent genuinely momentous ones as well. The hypothesis, for example, that if I wrote down one special sequence of one hundred numbers between 1 and 1000 in the next half hour, I would receive a reward of one million dollars, looks momentous. If the hypothesis is true, a radical change could take place in my life, leading to many other significant changes. Therefore, should I act as if it were true? James could point out that it is only for a very small number of people, who are usually classed as mentally ill, that such a hypothesis is a live issue. Most of us simply do not feel that it could be true. Hence, unlike the religious hypothesis, we cannot take it seriously. It then cannot constitute a momentous option for us, even though it might make a stupendous difference in our lives if it were true.

The religious hypothesis, because it is a live option for many people, and a momentous one for those for whom it is live, is also, James maintained, a forced option. In view of the good that is involved, the analysis that Pascal applied to the Wager situation applies here: "We cannot escape the issue by remaining skeptical and waiting for more light, because, although we do avoid error in that way *if religion be untrue*, we lose the good, *if it be true*, just as certainly as if we positively chose to disbelieve." As Pascal had earlier argued, the agnostic view toward religion is as much of a negative choice as the atheistical view. It amounts, according to James, to accepting the view that yielding to the fear of being in error is wiser and better than yielding to the hope that the religious hypothesis may be true. We are forced either to hope or to fear, if we once recognize the religious hypothesis as a genuine live option. Neither attitude is justified by the evidence available. But James, following in the spirit of Pascal's Wager, announced: "If religion be true and the evidence for it be still insufficient, I do not wish . . . to forfeit my sole chance in life of getting upon the winning side—that chance depending, of course, on my willingness to run the risk of acting as if my passional need of taking the world religiously might be prophetic and right."

In terms of how we are actually affected by the various options that confront us, James insisted that we have the right to believe, at our own peril, any hypothesis that is live enough to tempt us. There is no particular reason why we should reject a hypothesis that we want to believe, or a hypothesis that would make a momentous difference for us to believe, merely because sufficient evidence is wanting. This view is not the same as advocating that we go around believing in fairy tales, or any other views that might give us pleasure, because, James insisted, it is the living quality of genuine options that makes all the difference. We cannot believe, when we wish, that we have a million dollars in the bank, though this might make us very happy, and it might, if true, have very momentous consequences. The proposed hypothesis is, unfortunately, completely dead as a real possibility, for we know it is false. The Pascal Wager and the theory of live, forced, and momentous options are entirely restricted to those hypotheses which we really feel *could* be true, and whose truth is of genuine concern to us. In terms of such hypotheses, James maintained, the caution of the scientifically minded man was no more justified than the credulity of the believer, and, in terms of the function of believing, the credulous person might be more "justified" than the skeptic.

This much of James' theory of religious knowledge does not really seem to answer the question "What knowledge can be gained about the existence and nature of God?" but, rather, it deals with what *should be* believed about God's existence and nature. James always accepted the view that one could not gain any objective or certain knowledge on this subject. However, he felt that one could throw some light on the value of religious-knowledge claims by assessing their "cash-value," their consequences for the believer. The essay "The Will to Believe" attempted to provide a "justification" for belief in terms of its possible consequences. *The Varieties of Religious Experience* attempted a much more careful examination of the effect of religious belief on various people. James studied the world of the believers from a psychological point of view, looking at what they believed and how these beliefs affected their lives. His conclusion, as an "objective" observer, was that for many people, a religious outlook positively affected their feeling of well-being in the world in which they lived. It made them feel more at home and happier; it gave them goals to pursue; and so on. Their lives were far more satisfactory because they had certain attitudes and certain feelings toward life. The religious question, in this sense, "is primarily a question of life, of living or not living in the higher union which opens itself to us as a gift." The value of religious belief can be measured in terms of the subjective effects of believing, which, James contended, are very satisfactory for some persons.

The so-called objective content, or religious knowledge-claims, is in addition to the actual living psychological effects of belief. These fall in the classification of "over-beliefs," which are often involved in the spiritual excitement and feelings a person may have in his religious outlook. The over-beliefs may even be essential to the having of religious experience, and a religious life, but they are not the same as the psychological benefits of a religious attitude. The common core to religious experience James tried to examine as a scientific psychologist. There are a great variety of over-beliefs that are important to the people who hold them. Religious experience does not establish the over-beliefs; instead, the over-beliefs are ways of interpreting the experience. The over-beliefs, the specific knowledge-claims of various religions, can be examined, described, but not really validated or invalidated. James' own vague and general over-beliefs can be compared and contrasted with the more usual ones of the Judaeo-Christian tradition, but none of them can actually be argued for from any facts or reasons.

In terms of this psychological evaluation of religion, James did not actually show how religious knowledge can be gained or what it would consist in; rather, he examined the effect that a religious attitude and the acceptance of certain over-beliefs would have on people. We may be able to ascertain what beliefs it might be beneficial to adhere to, but we cannot determine whether these beliefs actually describe an objective state of affairs. As we shall see in the discussion on pragmatism, it was James' contention that a belief "becomes" true in terms of whether it works or has satisfactory consequences. To this extent, in his theory, a generalized religious view—that there is some sort of larger force with which we are in contact—is true for religious people in that it works for them. More specific over-beliefs work for particular individuals or groups of people and, hence, are true for them.

Critics of James' theory pointed out that his philosophy of religion did not indicate whether or not God exists or has a specific Nature. His theory showed only that certain people gain definite psychological benefits from believing in a Divine Being and that in terms of their psychological states, they may be "justified" in this belief, and in other over-beliefs they may add to this to explain their view and their feelings about God's Nature. (Nietzsche would claim these people are the weaklings who are unwilling to face reality.) James has not shown or tried to show that there is any religious knowledge in the sense of completely certain knowledge that cannot be false. His "justification" of religious beliefs is actually an entirely subjective matter, based on each individual's psychological make-up. What is a good or even a "true" belief for one person can be a bad or "false" belief for someone else. Some critics have contended that the outcome of the theory presented in "The Will to Believe" and *The Varieties of Religious Experience* was that one should believe whatever makes one happy or makes one's life more enjoyable, even though the belief may be false.

James argued that since all that one could, in fact, discover about the truth-value of the religious hypothesis was its "cash-value," that is, what difference religious belief made in the lives of people, his theory explained what religious knowledge actually amounted to. And since James' theory based its evaluation of this knowledge on the genuine psychological factors involved in religious belief, its author maintained that it was both more true to the situation than many theological or atheistical accounts, and more indicative of the reasons why certain beliefs were, in fact held, and others were not. The very conditions of actual belief would, James maintained, exclude the possibility of silly beliefs being taken seriously, or of a person's believing something that he knew to be false (since his knowledge of its falsehood would impede his ability to believe it).

James has been criticized by many orthodox religious thinkers who assert that he has "missed the point" of what it is that concerns truly religious people. As the contemporary French theologian Étienne Gilson has asserted, "It is psychologically interesting to know that it does one good to *believe* there is a God; but that is not all that a believer believes; what he actually believes is, that there *is* a God." James, these critics insist, has dealt only with side effects of religious knowledge, but not with its content, and has acted as if the evaluation of the side effects consisted of all that could be said on the subject. As a result, the religious knowledge-claims of the Judaeo-Christian tradition became of little importance to James as compared with psychological studies of believers, regardless of the nature of their over-beliefs.

Because of the emphasis on the effects of belief rather than on its content, James' views have mainly influenced the most liberal theologians and the most liberal religious movements, rather than the more conservative or orthodox ones. But from the time of the original presentation of his views down to the present day, agnostic and atheistic critics have chided him for not moving from a recognition of the fact that there really is no way of gaining religious knowledge about the existence and nature of God to the conclusion that no beliefs in this area are really justified. The introduction of psychological standards, these critics insist, changes the evaluation at issue from an epistemological one to one dealing with the beneficial effects of beliefs regardless of their truth content. Such a shift would make the psychologist and the psychiatrist arbiters of what is worth believing about religion, rather than the philosopher or theologian, who would want to judge the beliefs at issue on the basis of the evidence available for them.

James has actually advanced a theory which falls between two stools. He accepted some of the skeptical views of Hume and Pascal about the merits of the available evidence to establish religious knowledge. Next he proposed a "scientific," psychological means for judging religious beliefs. Some have found that this theory is not sufficiently objective in that it does not restrict its evaluations solely to the evidence available. Others have found that the theory does not do "justice" to the content of religious beliefs, since such content has played, and continues to play, a most important role in religious discussions. On the other hand, James' views have been most influential in encouraging researches in the field of religious psychology, and in leading some thinkers to attempt to develop religious views based on the findings of such studies.

OTTO'S AND BUBER'S THEORIES
OF RELIGIOUS KNOWLEDGE

An interesting and influential theory of religion of a semi-psychological kind is that of Rudolf Otto (1869–1937), in his famous work, *The Idea of the Holy* (1917). Otto insisted that the crucial element in religious knowledge is neither rational nor irrational. One first becomes aware of it as something numinous, comprising the idea of the holy. When one exhausts the cognitive ingredients of this concept, "the holy," there is over and above the idea that which is numinous. This is first encountered as a subjective feeling. If the feeling was all that existed, Otto's theory would be an analysis like that of William James. In addition, Otto insisted, "The numinous is thus felt as objective and outside the self." This transition, no matter how achieved, gives some aspect of objectivity to Otto's theory. He contended that by examining that aspect of the idea of the holy that transcended the self, one gained as much religious knowledge as possible, yet still not enough to comprehend God as He really is. After quoting a German poet to the effect that "A God comprehended is no God," Otto argued that God is the "Wholly Other." Through examination of both our objective and subjective idea of holy, we are able to approximate religious truth. One might criticize Otto in that he is really not able to get beyond James' psychology of religious experience. We are still aware of the so-called objective element of the idea of the holy only through our personal experience.

One of the most important figures in twentieth-century theorizing about religion is the Jewish thinker, Martin Buber (1878–1965). He was born in Vienna, but was raised in Lemberg (in what is now Poland), in both the German and Hebraic traditions. One of the most influential forces in his youth was the Jewish mystical movement of the Hasidim, from which he later drew an inspiring picture of what a living religious community is like. When he was eighteen, Buber went to the University of Vienna, where he, like many others there at the time, came under the influence of both Kierkegaard and Nietzsche. He also joined the embryonic Zionist movement, and played an important role in developing a Renaissance of Jewish culture along with the political Renaissance that Zionism represented. For several years he studied the Bible intensively, as well as the epics and religious documents of such disparate groups as the Hasidim, the Finns, and the Chinese. In 1905, he published the beginnings of the *Tales from the Hasidim*, based on rediscovery of the manuscript sources of this powerful mystical movement within Judaism, which was most active and creative in the eighteenth and early nineteenth centuries. In 1909, Buber published an important article on Taoism, and two years later his first important work on Judaism. He edited a Jewish newspaper and helped found schools for Judaic studies in Germany after World War I. His most important work for the philosophy of religion, *I and Thou*, appeared in 1922. The next year, Buber became both a professor at the Free Institute for Jewish Adult Education in Frankfort, and professor of religious studies at the university there. He then began what was to be a life-long project, the translation of the Bible into German. He and another important Jewish philosopher of religion, Franz Rosenzweig (author of the *Star of Redemption*) undertook this task. Rosenzweig died in 1929, leaving Buber to work on it up to 1961.

When the Nazis came to power, Buber, like most Jewish professors, lost their academic positions. Buber stayed on in Germany, under the Nazi dictatorship, until 1938. He helped and advised many Jews as to what to do under the terrible circumstances. Finally, in 1938, as conditions deteriorated, Buber moved to Palestine, where he became professor of social philosophy at the Hebrew University. After the founding of the state of Israel, he became director of a school for training newcomers to the new state. He was also one of the founders and very active members of the Arab–Israeli Friendship Society, devoted to trying to bring about peaceful and communal relations between Jews and Arabs.

Fundamental to Buber's intellectual position is pointing out that we are surrounded by objects and beings. We relate to various parts of our experience in different ways. Some we treat as pure objects, and our relationship, if it can be called that, is between I and it. It is hardly a real relationship, since the it cannot relate to me. The type of relationship where communication exists between an entity and myself (it can be another person, an animal, or a plant) is an I–Thou relationship. (Buber's most significant presentation of his views is in the book *I and Thou.*) This relationship involves speaking and being spoken to. It involves a continuous dialogue. The dialogue between man and man establishes the human community. And man only fully realizes his potentialities when he has the widest range of I–Thou relationships.

Beyond each I–Thou relationship, there is an indication of an Eternal Thou who speaks to us. This Eternal Thou cannot be described, because then it would be an It and not a Thou. ". . . [B]y its nature it cannot be established in measure and bounds, not even in the measure of the immeasurable, or the bounds of boundless being." Buber offered no proof that the Eternal Thou, God, exists. He just insisted that God is wholly present, and always present. Man, however, is not always open to the I–Thou relationship with God.

Buber contended that man's primary concern is with other men. But it is through this concern that man comes to God, and turns back anew to the world. God cannot be sought, but is encountered.

This emphasis on the I–Thou relationship between man and God and on the inability to codify the Eternal Thou, or prove that He, She, or It really exists, led Buber to criticize organized religions. They turn from religious experience to doctrine, and in so doing make God an object, an It. Organized religions, using Pascal's phrase, speak of the God of the Philosophers, not the God of Abraham, Isaac, and Jacob (who spoke to the Patriarchs). The religions replaced God by an idea. In contrast, the genuinely religious person's faith is rooted in his encounter with God. The only kind of knowledge of God that can actually be achieved is relational: I and the Eternal Thou.

Buber's mistrust of organized religion was so great that he suggested it be attacked by critical atheism, denying the traditional goals. Critical atheism would show up and discredit all the so-called rational approaches to God as an object, an It, and all of the images man has constructed of Him as an object. Atheism, in attacking the foundations offered by the philosophers and theologians, has the virtue of turning men away from religion. Buber saw Nietzsche as making a great contribution in announcing, "God is dead." The God of traditional philosophy, theology, and institutional religion has always been dead.

Buber found a much more important approach to religion in the Jewish mystical group, the Hasidim, than in the theological tradition. The Hasidim saw everything in the world as sacred, and found an ongoing joy in encountering God in any of life's byways. The Hasidim were originally opposed and hounded by the organized religious forces.

With this outlook, Buber turned away from the religious traditions functioning around him, and urged individual approaches to I–Thou relationships and what might be fathomed beyond them. Buber has become very popular for his personal and nonevidential theory of religion, and for portraying, in his *Tales from the Hasidim*, what a living religion can be like. Buber's influence so far has been much greater among Christians than among Jews. He has played a basic role in the secularization of religion. (In fact, one of his Jesuit admirers has called him the "Prophet of Religious Secularism.") He has also influenced most of those in the "Death of God" theological movement. Before turning to them, it should be noted that Buber made no effort to answer the critiques of religion of thinkers like Hume and Kant. He would accept their attacks of philosophical religion as well justified, and say instead that the issue of whether there can be religious knowledge is answered by an encounter with the Eternal Thou.

THE "DEATH OF GOD" THEOLOGY: BONHOEFFER AND OTHERS

The man who is reputed to be the founder of the "Death of God" theology is the German thinker, Dietrich Bonhoeffer (1906–1945), who was a young theologian before Hitler came to power. Bonhoeffer, who was vitally concerned with the social role of the churches, endeavoured as much as he could to keep them from accepting the morality of the Nazis. He came more and more in conflict with the Nazi authorities, and took a job in America in mid-1939. He decided he was needed more in Germany and returned a few weeks later. He was very involved in the underground movement seeking to overthrow Hitler, and was arrested in April 1943. His most important theological writing was his *Letters and Papers from Prison*, which he wrote during his eighteen months in Tegel Prison. He was executed a month before World War II ended, for being closely involved with those who tried to kill Hitler on July 20, 1944.

In the *Letters and Papers from Prison*, unlike his earlier, quite orthodox Christian writings, Bonhoeffer spoke of developing a religionless Christianity, and of developing a theology without the God-hypothesis. He said, "So our coming of age leads us to a true recognition of our situation before God. God would have us know that we must live as men who manage our lives without him. The God who is with us is the God who forsakes us (Mark 15:34). The God who lets us live in the world without the working hypothesis of God is the God before whom we stand continually. Before God and with God we live without God. God lets himself be pushed out of the world onto the cross." These paradoxical remarks may reflect the despair of a thoroughly moral person living, and being imprisoned, in Nazi Germany, where the traditional God and the traditional religions seemed to be helpless and even pointless in helping mankind. Bonhoeffer further wrote, "We are moving towards a completely religionless time; people as they are now simply cannot be religious any-more." He called for a religious Christianity.

Besides these proclamations about the uselessness of God and re-ligion, another side of Bonhoeffer's analysis was quite close to Buber's. One does not meet God or Jesus through a church, or through reasoning and evidence, but only through direct encounter in one's personal experience. Bonhoeffer seemed to be pointing towards a world beyond organized re-ligion in which each man would be responsible for himself. This would be a form of maturity that had outgrown the normal religious world.

The more radical of Bonhoeffer's views and slogans were taken over by the Anglican Bishop John A.T. Robinson in his work, *Honest to God* (1963), and then advanced by a group of American theologians as the "Death of God" theory. Nietzsche had talked of God's being dead, and was apparently referring to the death of the traditional God-figure of Western thought as a significant being affecting anyone's life. Buber had spoken of the "eclipse of God," in which the secular world took precedence over the religious. Buber had also stressed the need to secularize religion by disconnecting it from organized religion.

The group of theologians that has appeared on the American scene [Gabriel Vahanian, author of *The Death of God* (1961); Harvey Cox, *The Secular City* (1965); Thomas Altizer, author of *The Gospel of Christian Atheism* (1966); William Hamilton, *The New Essence of Christianity* (1961); and Paul M. Van Buren, author of *The Secular Meaning of the Gospel* (1963)] has raised the problem, in various ways, of whether the God of Western man is dead or passé.

Some of them (probably including Bonhoeffer) are bemoaning the fact that religion is not taken seriously by many people any more, and that organized religions have little to offer people as advice and counsel in the present mechanized age. Since these theologians are all Christians, they feel that Christianity as a living, vital force in modern society has evaporated. The state of man that one has to deal with is that of the human group's having lost contact with Christianity or pushed Christianity aside for secular concerns. (For Buber, "the eclipse of God" is that man has let Him be eclipsed by secular interests.) The most moderate of the so-called "Death of God" theologians, Altizer and Hamilton, both describe the bleak godless scene that humanity now encounters, and seek for ways in which God might be brought back into a significant role in human affairs. They (as well as Buber, and apparently Bonhoeffer too) saw hope in individual human efforts to be in contact with the Divine.

Others in the "Death of God" group paint a much grimmer picture. The Divine-oriented world that would protect and reward the good people and punish the bad ones is gone for good, if it ever existed at all. The personal God with whom one could commune, and from whom one could draw strength, is no more, if He, She, or It ever was. We live in what

Harvey Cox has called the Secular City, and the human race will be living this way until the end of its existence. The Secular City is much like the world of the atheistic existentialists, Jean-Paul Sartre and Albert Camus, that we will discuss in the next chapter. Man must find his values in the postreligious world. The "Death of God" theologians see this task not so much as one of creativity as one of refurbishing or revitalizing those elements of the previous religious traditions, especially the social and moral elements of Christianity. (Buber, through his *Tales of the Hasidim,* tried to show how a vital religious activity could exist and be taken seriously by people even in the secular age of the twentieth century.)

One of these "Death of God" theologians, Paul Van Buren, has developed his position out of another view we will deal with in the next chapter, that developed by Ludwig Wittgenstein, in his *Tractatus Logico-Philosophus* (1922). Van Buren has contended that the language of religious discussion is meaningless since there are no criteria for telling if the assertions made about religious affairs are true or false. Hence, there cannot be any truly significant religious discourse. If that is so, our world has to be purged of all the nonsensical mumbo-jumbo that has been uttered about religion.

All the variations on the theme of why "God is dead" point to the modern world as having spawned conditions under which a previously vital and potent religious tradition, that of Judeo-Christianity, no longer has anything to offer modern man. If anything remains living in the religious tradition, it is its social and moral message, not its supernatural one. This critical view grows also in part from the on-going Biblical criticism which eroded so much conviction in claims made in the Bible. Rationalist criticisms growing out of Hume and Kant also spawned strong doubts about the knowledge claims of religion as scientific rational claims. The irrationalism of Kierkegaard (in part taken over by Buber) has put the quest for religious meaning on a personal subjective basis rather than an objective scientific one. The "Death of God" theologians, taking Nietzsche's slogan, reflect one of the surviving attitudes. Some of them recognize that serious religious belief is disappearing and hope to do something about it. Others see the situation as having advanced beyond traditional religion, and then realize the problem of providing a meaningful set of values in such a new world.

CONCLUSION

As a result of the development of Bible criticism, modern scientific knowledge about man and the cosmos, and the philosophical criticisms of the arguments offered to establish knowledge of the existence and nature of God, many modern thinkers have concluded that there is no adequate historical, scientific, or rational evidence on which to base claims concerning religious knowledge. Some, as a result, have decided to abandon all traditional religious beliefs, and to contend that all of our information about the world can be accounted for independent of any religious knowledge claims. Others have followed William James' path, and evaluated religious claims in terms of their effects, stressing not only their psychological effects, but also their social ones. They have seen religions as expressions of man's needs, desires, and aspirations. The question of whether there is a God has, for them, become irrelevant. What is important is the human dimension, man as a religiously oriented being. The movement using the slogan, taken from Nietzsche, that "God is dead," has stressed the social value and the social message of religion, and has tried to reconstruct this in modern secular terms. It is not important if there is a God. The issue is not meaningful for contemporary man. He must find his values and his aspirations in a twentieth-century secular version of what traditional religion used to supply as a psychological and social prop and attitude.

On the other hand, many philosophers of religion have followed out the nonrational approach of men such as Pascal and Kierkegaard. Some, such as the antirationalist Russian Orthodox theologian Shestov, have proclaimed that the negative results of much of contemporary philosophy show what is wrong with the rational approach to religious questions, as well as showing the need for pure, blind faith. The great Protestant theologian Karl Barth has also stressed the primacy of faith. Others have tried to bring out what is still meaningful to a twentieth-century man in the religious traditions, and have tried to show that whether one still believes the historical claims of Judaism or Christianity or not, one can find religious (rather than just social or psychological) insight and value in these traditions. And it has been claimed that this insight or value can form the basis for a meaningful life, a life based on religious experience, in which aspects of traditional religion can play a major role. The impact, for instance, of the great Jewish philosopher and theologian Martin Buber's *Tales from the Hasidim* shows how the religious power of a mystical movement of a couple of centuries ago can illuminate the religious quest, and the religious attitudes of modern man, regardless of historical, scientific, or philosophical doubts.

In view of the developments in psychology and psychiatry in this century, the Jamesian evaluation of religious beliefs with respect to their effects, rather than their objective truth-value, has also seemed a promising and rewarding approach to the questions at issue. Many psychiatric investigators have tried to discover more precisely what religious belief does for or to the believer. Then, in terms of Freudian and post-Freudian standards, they have tried to assess the merits of various types of religious commitments from Zen Buddhism to Orthodox Judaism and Catholicism.

Over the many centuries in which philosophers have examined the problem of religious knowledge they have been no more able to come to an agreement about what is true in this area than they have with regard to the questions we have considered in other chapters. Some philosophers have concluded that atheism or agnosticism is the most reasonable view to hold, after all the evidence has been weighed. Others have found deism (the belief in an impersonal divine force) the most plausible view; still others have found that a careful scrutiny of the question has confirmed them in their belief in a personal God.

It is hoped that the serious student, after considering the views discussed in this chapter, will be more conscious of the beliefs that he himself holds and of the reasons why he holds them. He is then likely to understand better what it is that he believes, and why he believes it.

BIBLIOGRAPHY

Albright, W. F. *From the Stone Age to Christianity*, 2d ed. (Johns Hopkins University Press, Baltimore, 1967).

Altizer, Thomas. *Radical Theology and the Death of God* (Bobbs-Merrill, Indianapolis, 1966).

Saint Anselm. *Proslogium*, edited by Sidney Deane (Open Court, LaSalle, Ill., 1974).

Saint Thomas Aquinas. *Introduction to Saint Thomas Aquinas*, edited by Anton Pegis (Modern Library, New York, 1948). Selections from St. Thomas' major works.

Bartley, W. F. *The Retreat to Commitment* (Knopf, New York, 1962).

Bonhoeffer, Dietrich. *Letters and Papers from Prison* (Macmillan, New York, 1972).

Buber, Martin. *I and Thou*, translated by Walter Kaufman (Scribner's, New York, 1970).

————. *Tales from the Hasidim*, 2 vols. (Schocken Books, New York, 1961).

Carnell, Edward John. *Christian Commitment: An Apologetic* (Macmillan, New York, 1957).

Collins, James. *God in Modern Philosophy* (Regnery, Chicago, 1967). A study of theories about the nature of God that have been advanced by thinkers since the Renaissance.

Freemantle, Anne. *The Age of Belief* (New American Library, New York, 1954). Selections from various medieval theologians.

Freud, Sigmund. *Totem and Taboo* (Random House, New York, 1960).

————. *The Future of an Illusion* (Norton, New York, 1976).

Fromm, Erich. *Psychoanalysis and Religion* (Yale University Press, New Haven, 1950).

————. and Suzuki, D. T. *Zen Buddhism & Psychoanalysis* (Harper and Row, New York, 1970).

Gillespie, Charles C. *Genesis and Geology* (Harvard University Press, Cambridge, 1951).

Gilson, Etienne. *Reason and Revelation in the Middle Ages* (Scribner's, New York, 1938).

Hume, David. *Dialogues concerning Natural Religion* (Hafner, New York, 1953).

————. *An Enquiry concerning Human Understanding*, edited by L. Selby-Bigge (Oxford, New York, 1963). Contains the essay "Of Miracles."

James, William. *Essays in Pragmatism* (Hafner, New York, 1952). Includes the essay "The Will to Believe."

————. *The Varieties of Religious Experience* (Macmillan, New York, 1961).

Kant, Immanuel. *Selections*, edited by T. M. Greene (Scribner's, New York, 1929). Contains Kant's writings on the philosophy of religion.

Kierkegaard, Soren. *A Kierkegaard Anthology* (Modern Library, New York, 1959).

————. *Fear and Trembling* (Princeton University Press, Princeton, 1970).

Marx, Karl. *The Communist Manifesto* (Monthly Review Press, New York, 1969).

Montgomery, John Warwick. *Where is History Going?* (Bethany Fellowship, Minneapolis, 1972).

Nietzsche, Friedrich. *The Portable Nietzsche*, edited by Walter Kaufman (Viking, New York, 1959).

Otto, Rudolph. *The Idea of the Holy*, 2nd ed. (Oxford University Press, New York, 1950).

Pascal, Blaise. *Pensées*, translated by A. J. Krailsheimer (Penguin, Baltimore, 1966).

Popkin, Richard H. "Hume and Kierkegaard," *Journal of Religion*, Vol. XXXI, October 1951.

————. "Spinoza and La Peyrère," *Southwestern Journal of Philosophy*, Vol. VIII, No. 3, December 1977.

————. "Theological and Religious Scepticism," *Christian Scholar*, June 1956.

Robinson, John T. *Honest to God* (Westminster Press, Philadelphia, 1963).

Russell, Bertrand. "A Free Man's Worship," in *Selected Papers of Bertrand Russell* (Modern Library, New York, n.d.). A modern statement of the agnostic point of view.

Schweitzer, Albert. *The Quest of the Historical Jesus* (Macmillan, New York, 1968).

Shestov, Lev. *In Job's Balances* (Ohio University Press, Miami, Ohio, 1975). A modern statement of a completely antirational fideism by a leading Russian Orthodox theologian. Shestov's works are currently being published by Ohio University Press.

Smith, Homer W. *Man and His Gods* (Little, Brown, Boston, 1955).

Strauss, Leo. *Spinoza's Critique of Religion* (Schocken Books New York, 1965).

Teilhard de Chardin, Pierre. *The Phenomenon of Man* (Harper, New York, 1960). A recent attempt to establish religious knowledge from modern scientific findings.

Thompson, Josiah, ed. *Kierkegaard: A Collection of Articles* (Anchor, Garden City, N.Y., 1972).

Vahanian, Gabriel. *The Death of God* (Brazillier, New York, 1961).

chapter 6

John Dewey (1859–1952); birthplace—United States (below)
Edmund Husserl (1859–1938); birthplace—Germany (right)

Martin Heidegger (1889–   ); birthplace—Germany (center row left)
Jean-Paul Sartre (1905–   ); birthplace—France (center row center)
Alfred North Whitehead (1861–1947); birthplace—England (center row right)
Bertrand Russell (1872–1970); birthplace—England (above left)
Ludwig Wittgenstein (1889–1951); birthplace—Austria (British) (above right)

CONTEMPORARY PHILOSOPHY

INTRODUCTION

Alfred North Whitehead once remarked that "the safest general characterization of the European philosophical tradition is that it consists of a series of footnotes to Plato." (He would doubtless have conceded, in the cases of Locke and Hume, that the footnotes were sometimes critical.) This comment of Whitehead's, paradoxical though it obviously is, involves more than special pleading or an unlettered view of the history of the subject. Indeed, it only too aptly summarizes at least one knowledgeable appraisal of the present state of philosophy: namely, that it is an activity whose creative phases all occurred somewhere in the distant past.

It is easy to see what gives rise to this opinion. Issues raised by Plato and Aristotle are still as vigorously debated today as they were then. Not only does it seem that the same old problems are being posed, but apparently the same old answers to them are being suggested. Admittedly they may vary in detail, or they may involve the finer splitting of hairs, but the essential ideas they express remain at bottom identical with those advanced by the ancients. Do not contemporary philosophers as often as not refer to themselves as Platonists or Aristotelians, or perhaps more elaborately as Neo-Somethings-or-Other, such as Neo-Kantians, Neo-Thomists, or Neo-Hegelians? Much of what is called philosophy today is composed of the still-wearable remnants of these and similar traditions.

But this is not the only reason for suspecting there is nothing new under the philosophical sun. An even more formidable consideration is the feeling that philosophy nowadays has collapsed into a new scholasticism;

409

that it has fallen more and more into the hands of professional teachers, supposedly noncreative individuals paid to expound the original work of somebody else. But was it not otherwise in the olden days? In the seventeenth and eighteenth centuries, for example, who were the great philosophers? Not the academic hacks, but the gifted amateurs. Locke was a physician, Spinoza a lens maker, Berkeley a bishop, Leibniz a diplomat, and Hume a writer. In our time, the first-rate philosophers, even in some narrow sense of that term, all seem connected with institutions of higher learning. Dewey taught at Columbia; Russell, Whitehead, and Moore at Cambridge; Santayana, Whitehead, and James at Harvard; Husserl at Göttingen and Freiburg; Heidegger at Marburg and Freiburg—and so on down the roster to the present gallery of "greats."

So surely there is some plausibility in Whitehead's witticism; but plausible though it is, it is almost certainly incorrect. It is true that philosophy nowadays is intimately associated with the academic cloister—but then, to some extent, it always was (the names of Plato, Aristotle, Kant, Schopenhauer, and Hegel immediately come to mind). In any case, the greatness of a philosophical doctrine is to be determined not by investigating the profession of its author but by examining the doctrine itself. And if we do this with contemporary views, the evidence against Whitehead's position seems overwhelming. Even if we confine ourselves to developments which have taken place only in the Western world and only within the first half of this century, it is clear that there are movements extant today which constitute genuine advances over anything which occurred in the distant past.

Some of these, to be sure, have already had their moments of glory, and original and important though they were, have begun to fade from the philosophical scene. The most famous such *nova* is pragmatism, a hardheaded philosophy supposedly characteristic of the pioneering American temper, which dominated philosophy in this country up to the beginning of World War II. Because of its intrinsic interest and still-pervasive influence, we shall discuss its main ideas in this chapter. On the other hand, other philosophies, some of them with equally long histories, show no signs of weakening at all.

At the present time, two strikingly different philosophical movements dominate the stage. Both are essentially products of this century, although the roots for some of their characteristic doctrines reach back into the past. The first of these originated in England, spread to Austria, and then to the United States, Canada, and Australia. In one form or another, it is the prevailing philosophy in these nations, with the possible exception of Austria. The second strain is almost exclusively a product of the Continent (especially of France and Germany), although recently its influence has spread to the English-speaking world as well. The first of these two developments we shall call *philosophical analysis* or *analytic philosophy*; the second, *phenomenology* and *existentialism*. We shall consider these ideas in this order:

> Pragmatism
> Existentialism and Phenomenology
> Philosophical Analysis

PRAGMATISM

HISTORICAL BACKGROUND

Although the history of pragmatism can doubtless be traced back, through scattered hints, to the earliest beginnings of philosophical activity in Western Europe, the explicit formulations of the doctrine are generally associated with writers living in the late nineteenth and early part of the twentieth centuries. During this period, pragmatism arose as a reaction to the types of philosophy being taught in American colleges and universities —philosophies which generally reflected a Hegelian metaphysical bias. The pragmatists opposed to such metaphysical speculations a scientifically oriented program which they believed would prove not only useful in clarifying and resolving traditional intellectual difficulties, but of practical value in ameliorating the everyday conditions of human life.

Up to the time of the Civil War, philosophical activity in the United States was carried on in the European tradition, and in a very limited way at that. The French writer De Tocqueville, in his account of *Democracy in America* (written in the nineteenth century), asserted that there was no country in the civilized world in which philosophy was taken less seriously. To be sure, with much of the country still frontier, practical concerns occupied the center of interest and left little time for speculation of a philosophical sort. However, even from the time of the Colonial period, philosophical activity was never entirely absent from the intellectual scene. Philosophical studies were part of the academic curricula in the newly established eastern colleges; and the theories of various English thinkers and of the writers of the French Enlightenment played a vital part in the intellectual atmosphere out of which the new nation arose.

When we trace the intellectual antecedents of pragmatism in the United States, we find the following picture. In the early nineteenth century, the American philosophical scene was at first dominated by doctrines derived from the Scottish "common-sense" realists—doctrines which they had developed in order to combat the supposedly dangerous skeptical theories of David Hume. The stronghold of this philosophy lay in the scattered centers of academic learning—in the colleges of the nation. But at the same time that Scottish realism was almost the official philosophy taught in the colleges, new European influences were making a strong impact throughout the land. Immigrants from Germany brought with them an interest in the theories of Hegel, and soon a flourishing movement, centered in St. Louis, began making contributions to the American intellectual scene.

The St. Louis Hegelians, as they were called, were led by a German immigrant, H. C. Brokmeyer (1826–1906), who became first the Lieutenant Governor and then the Acting Governor of Missouri; and by W. T. Harris (1835–1909), who became United States Commissioner of Education. These men worked assiduously to raise the philosophical tone of the nation. They wished to lead Americans to the point where they could do original work of their own, and they thought they could do this by first acquainting them with contemporary European thought. To accomplish these aims, they founded, shortly after the Civil War, the first American philosophical journal—the *Journal of Speculative Philosophy*. This periodical contained translations of the writings of such German philosophers as Fichte, Schelling, and Hegel; but more than that, it provided a forum for American thinkers, including many of the early pragmatists and their opponents.

Apart from the activities of the St. Louis group in creating a general interest in philosophical speculation, new scientific ideas played an important role in setting the stage for the emergence of pragmatism. In particular, the evolutionary theory of Charles Darwin, with its implications for religion and society, caused intense intellectual activity throughout the country. Darwin's views were widely disseminated shortly after the publication of his major writings. In part this was due to a series of lectures given in the period after the Civil War by the three leading English spokesmen for Darwinism—Tyndall, Huxley, and Herbert Spencer. But in part it was also due to the significance which this doctrine had for the widely held religious views of the period. Some religiously minded American thinkers tried to find a way of reconciling the Darwinian conception of a world evolving through the struggle for survival, and through the survival of the fittest, with a theological view of the universe. Others, especially some of the early pragmatists, found in Darwin's method and in the theory of evolution the basis for a new approach to the understanding of the universe in which we live.

C. S. PEIRCE AND THE
BEGINNINGS OF PRAGMATISM

In the intellectual ferment which developed after the Civil War, a group of Harvard students and teachers met to form what they called the

"Metaphysical Club." The members of the club discussed various problems and attempted to work out new solutions to them. Three of the leading figures in this group are usually credited with being the cofounders of pragmatism: Chauncy Wright (1830–1875), Charles Sanders Peirce (1839–1914), and William James (1842–1910). Wright, who was in correspondence with Darwin, was a lecturer in psychology and in physics. He was one of the first Americans to argue that, through the use of scientific and practical methods, metaphysical questions could finally be resolved.

Peirce, who invented the name "pragmatism" (which he took from the Greek word *pragma*, "a thing done," "a business"), was a highly original thinker. He was the son of Benjamin Peirce, a professor of mathematics at Harvard. Peirce taught briefly at Harvard and Johns Hopkins, but spent most of his life working for various bureaus of the United States government. He also did a considerable amount of free-lance writing, which included reviews of philosophical works for *The Nation* and the *North American Review*, and articles for magazines such as *Popular Science Monthly*. It was in this last publication that his famous essay, "How to Make Our Ideas Clear," first appeared.

At a time when studies in the history of philosophy were rare in America, Peirce was amazingly well versed in medieval thought, especially in the theories of the great Scholastic metaphysician Duns Scotus, and in the original works of some of the founders of modern science, such as Kepler and Galileo. Peirce devoured the learning available in the library at Harvard; he also wrote voluminously on scientific, mathematical, logical, and philosophical subjects. Much of this material has appeared only since his death, in the collection of his papers that is still in the process of being edited and published. These writings reveal that Peirce made contributions of fundamental importance to many subjects, especially to modern mathematics and to logic, and that he was, perhaps, the most original and creative metaphysical mind this country has yet seen. His contribution to pragmatism, apart from naming it, was to outline its method. For Peirce, the method was primarily one for rendering our ideas clear, so that philosophy could be transformed into a positive science. He was dismayed when James used the method to construct a new philosophy, much at variance with his own metaphysical views. From then on, Peirce called himself a "pragmaticist" to differentiate his position from that of James, John Dewey, and others.

WILLIAM JAMES

It was William James who made the most complete formulation of the new philosophy and who was to be its leading advocate. James was the son of a philosopher and theologian who, though immensely erudite, played a minor role in the transcendentalist movement in New England. The young James was also the elder brother of Henry James, Jr., one of America's most important novelists. William James' initial intellectual training was mainly in the sciences. He studied and was tutored in Europe, and then attended the Lawrence Scientific School and the Harvard Medical School, where he received his degree as a physician. He traveled widely, and even took part in an expedition to the Amazon in Brazil. In 1873 he was appointed instructor in anatomy and physiology at Harvard. Later he was made a professor of psychology, and, finally, of philosophy. The discussions at the Metaphysical Club, as well as his scientific interests, led James to the theory he labeled—using Peirce's term—"pragmatism."

Pragmatism is, first of all, a method to be employed for solving intellectual problems, and for evaluating them. Second, it is a theory about the various types of knowledge that can be acquired. And third, it is a metaphysical view about what the universe may be like in regard to what can be known about it.

THE PRAGMATIC METHOD

The pragmatic method, developed from Peirce's article "How to Make Our Ideas Clear," attempts to explain the meanings of concepts and theories in terms of their practical effects and consequences. Instead of treating theories and concepts as abstractions, the pragmatic view regards them as proposals for doing something within the realm of actual experience. Ideas are to be considered meaningful only if it is possible to conceive of consequences that would affect our experience if the ideas were either true or false. The examination of ideas and theories in terms of their possible practical consequences reveals what James called "the cash-value" of ideas.

Thus the pragmatic method is a way of examining ideas and theories with respect to their function in, and application to, experience. For example, the concept "canals on Mars" is meaningful only in terms of possible practical ways it can enter into and affect our experience. What we mean by such canals is, according to the pragmatic theory, what we would do if we believed that canals existed on Mars as contrasted with what we would do if we believed they did not exist, and how each belief would affect our expectations of our future experiences. If there were no difference at all between the possible consequences of believing or not believing that the canals exist, then apparently there is something peculiar about the concept "canals on Mars": it is meaningless in practice, or it has no cash-value. However, in this case, the concept is meaningful since we can state a series of consequences indicating what we would expect to see if we took a rocket ship to Mars, what we would expect to see if a rocket photographed Mars, and what we would expect to happen if an attempt were made to land on Mars. Each of these expectations would be different if we believed that there were canals or if we believed that there were none.

By stating the meanings of ideas in terms of possible consequences, the pragmatists believed that they were employing the method used by scientists and ordinary, practical men. The scientist can define terms like "hot" and "cold" in terms of measurements that can be performed under specifiable conditions with instruments, such as thermometers. The cash-value of these terms enables the scientist to avoid confusion and ambiguity, so that he knows what to do in order to answer the question, "Is this water hot?"

Unfortunately, the pragmatists contended, many intellectual problems and discussions involve concepts that are not clear, and have no definite or discoverable cash-value. Application of the pragmatic method will reveal this and should then lead to the exposure of the empty nature of the ideas and problems at issue. Both Peirce and James appealed to Bishop Berkeley's analysis of the concept "matter" as a case in point. Philosophers traditionally had disputed about the existence and nature of matter. But Berkeley, the pragmatists said, showed that it would make no practical difference whether matter existed or not, since all of one's possible experience could be exactly the same whether a material world "really" existed or did not. Therefore, the concept "matter" has no cash-value.

According to the pragmatists, Berkeley exposed the emptiness of materialist theory that differs from the way one would act if one did not result from the concept "matter." There is, in fact, no way of acting on the materialist theory that differs from the way one would act if one did not accept the theory. This indicates not only that the theory is meaningless, but also that the philosophers who have argued about the existence and nature of the material world in a metaphysical sense have wasted their time, since there is nothing practical to discuss on this subject.

The pragmatic method, then, is supposed to clarify concepts, to reveal which ones are meaningful, and which ones are no more than "metaphysical rubbish." Once this hard-headed, practical means of evaluating concepts has been adopted, this method can then be further employed to evaluate theories. Theories, James maintained, are instruments for dealing with problems that arise in experience. They are ways of employing concepts in order to direct activities to bring about certain envisaged results. Hence theories can be judged in terms of their cash-values, the anticipated consequences, and in terms of whether these consequences do, in fact, occur. A theory is meaningful only if its terms are meaningful, and if it proposes different consequences if the theory were true rather than false. And a theory is true insofar as its anticipated or predicted consequences happen, or insofar as it works in actual experience.

Thus, for the pragmatists, theoretical activity arises in the attempt to deal with actual practical difficulties that we may confront. Such activity tries to use ideas to bring about a desired result or to overcome an undesirable situation. Theories are plans of action for dealing with the situation, and they are to be evaluated in terms of whether or not they fulfill their function. They obviously cannot do so if the terms involved mean nothing, or have no relation to activities that could be performed or no consequences that could be related to the context in which the problem arose.

For example, if a person were lost in a forest, he might develop a number of theories as instruments to help him out of his predicament. Each would then be judged by whether or not it worked. Certain metaphysical theories about the nature of reality would have no relevance whatsoever. For one would still be lost in the forest if one acted on the theory that the world is made of atoms, or on the theory that it is made up of ideas. These metaphysical theories would have no cash-value in the situation. Certain other theories would prove unworkable. A theory asserting that if the number of visible stars was odd, then one would immediately be rescued, would, in all probability, fail when put into practice. But other theories, predicting future successful results on the basis of geographical factors, remembered data, and astronomical observations, might prove workable. These theories could be judged by whether or not the predicted successful results did or did not occur when one acted in certain ways, and whether or not the initial problem was solved.

THE PRAGMATIC
THEORY OF TRUTH

The pragmatists, then, advanced a theory about the nature of truth in terms of the method proposed for clarifying and testing ideas and theories. Theories are true if they work. Theories have their meanings in terms of their practical consequences in actual experience. They are instruments for doing something *with* and *in* experience in order to achieve certain desired results. Hence they can be said to be true when they work satisfactorily to achieve these goals. Theories are verified in experience by testing and applying them to actual situations. Where they are found workable they are said to be true. Thus the very processes that are employed in practice to determine that any proposition is true are the ones that define what is meant by calling it "true." A theory predicts that certain features will occur in a future experience. The process by which the prediction is verified establishes whether the theory "works," and hence whether the theory is true.

The pragmatists, in advancing this conception of truth, were also attacking the view that "truth" is a static, fixed property which belongs to some theories and ideas and not to others. James announced, "The truth of an idea is not a stagnant property inherent in it. Truth *happens* to an idea. It *becomes* true, is *made* true by events. Its verity *is* in fact an event, a process; the process namely of its verifying itself, its veri-*fication*. Its validity is the process of its valid-*ation*." The only way we are ever able to ascertain if a proposition is true is by some verification procedure that involves using the proposition and seeing what results follow. Hence, James insisted, those who believe that "truth" is a static property of propositions still have to employ the pragmatic criterion of truth if they wish to establish that a given proposition is, in fact, true. Therefore, other truth-criteria have no actual cash-value, since the pragmatic procedure is the sole means of assessing the truth or falsity of a theory or idea.

The view that truth is something that happens to any idea has disturbed many of the critics of pragmatism. They have contended that this seems to make the notion of truth too flexible, subjective, and personal. It would appear that the same proposition can be true and false at different times, depending upon its efficacy, or that the same proposition could be true for one person and false for another. The notion of "working satisfactorily" would seem to eliminate all objective standards in that each person might have different desires and expectations, so that a belief which failed to work for one person could be true for someone else because it worked for him. James in *The Meaning of Truth* (1909) tried to answer his early critics by showing why he held that, on the pragmatic theory, truth was objective in some sense. The sorts of difficulties raised by his opponents, James argued, were not found in the actual verification procedures used by human beings.

The use of ideas and theories always occurs, James contended, in a specific context in which there is direct, immediate awareness of certain "brute-facts." Ideas and theories are employed to deal with these brute-facts. Ideas and theories become true, and are accepted as true, if, and only if, they work satisfactorily in the context of immediate experience. Hence beliefs such as "Snow is green" or "Arsenic is edible" simply will not work. Employing such beliefs in the context of actual experience will lead to unsatisfactory results. " '*The true,' to put it very briefly, is only the expedient in the way of our thinking, just as 'the right' is only the expedient in the way of our behaving.*" It would not turn out to be expedient to attempt to believe ideas and theories which did not fit in, or were not compatible with the content of immediate experience. Hence James and many of the pragmatists have contended that there is an objective or "real" limitation on what can be "true," supplied by the actual content and order of experience.

It can be, and often is, the case that a belief can be accepted as working at one time and rejected as not working at another. Such a change in belief occurred after the voyages of Columbus and Magellan. Before their explorations, it was possible to believe that there was no large land mass between Europe and Asia. After their findings, such a belief had become false and its denial had become true. But, James insisted, this did not indicate that truth was flexible, since in terms of the content of experience at a given time, only one possible view would work. As experience itself expands and grows, the beliefs that will work with it can also expand and grow. However, what is true will still be limited by the brute-facts, and what is now true will be accepted as always having been true in the light of present experience.

James maintained further that certain facts about the basic conditions of human nature show that truths do not vary from person to person, and that one cannot believe whatever one wants. It may be that the concept "working satisfactorily" is vague. However, this concept does not simply mean that an individual is enjoying happy or pleasant feelings about the way his thoughts relate to his experiences. It also involves the notion of an over-all satisfaction that is attained only when one's conceptual and immediately experienced worlds form a consistent and harmonious whole. Our human nature and the basic psychological conditions under which we operate prevent us from being satisfied if what we believe conflicts with our experience, or with beliefs that have worked for us in the past, or if what we believe is at variance with what most other people believe. What James called "our sentiment of rationality" makes us demand a consistent and coherent intellectual life that is in harmony with our experience (which includes our experience of what the rest of the world believes). Hence, James insisted, beliefs would not work for a person if others produced evidence against them. There could be no satisfactory "working" of a belief unless it fitted in harmoniously with all that we knew or accepted about the world, in view of our basic demand for a rational order to our beliefs.

Following James' lead, several of the early pragmatists, especially C. S. Schiller, maintained that our acceptance of the rules of logic could be explained psychologically, and could be validated in terms of the successful working of logical principles in solving problems that arise in experience. The principles of logic are not, they asserted, independent formal principles that must be true. Instead, they are principles for relating our beliefs to our experiences. They satisfy a basic psychological need for order and coherence in our thinking and living. The success of logical thinking, as compared with illogical thinking, in overcoming difficulties that occur in our lives indicates, according to the pragmatic theory, that the logical principles work, and hence are true.

The pragmatic theory of truth, its advocates contended, is actually that employed by the natural sciences, and accounts for their immense success in solving problems and in making genuine progress in expanding the limits of human knowledge. The scientists consider a theory true only when they can test it, and when they can determine that it works, either in a laboratory situation or in the prediction of facts that can later be verified. As long as a theory works, in this sense, the scientists consider it to be true, although they always do (or should) recognize the possibility that there may be future situations in which the predictions of the theory will not be verified and in which the theory will no longer work. Scientists, by accepting the relative and growing nature of "true knowledge," do not find themselves bound, as philosophers do, to a rigid, absolute structure of truths that cannot possibly be changed or revised. This "open-minded" attitude is, James insisted, a crucial part of the pragmatic view. It allows for the occurrence at any time of new data and new ways of dealing with them. The willingness to test and retest one's beliefs, and to evaluate them in terms of how they work, has enabled the scientist to progress by finding better (and hence "truer") theories, and by seeking for a greater range of experiences with which to verify his beliefs.

In contrast, the philosophers, especially the metaphysicians, have made little or no progress. They have advanced grandiose theories which supposedly contain the complete and absolute truth about the cosmos. They have supported these theories by appealing to arguments and not to facts found in experience. As a result, these theories turn out to be "dead," having no cash-value and no relevance to human situations. Metaphysical theories do not work. They do not have consequences testable by concrete experience. Idealists and materialists can find fault with each other's philosophies, but they cannot test their views as scientists test theirs. By employing the pragmatic criteria of meaning and truth, one would find that the characteristic theses of traditional philosophy, especially in the area of metaphysics, have no actual meaning, and therefore cannot be determined to be either true or false. Philosophy, according to the pragmatists, will begin to make significant progress only if it adopts some of the "hard-headed" attitude of the sciences, and restricts itself to pragmatically meaningful questions.

The pragmatic theory not only indicates what has been wrong with traditional philosophy, and what constructive role modern philosophy can play; it also provides new ways of interpreting the traditional problems in various areas in philosophy. In Chapter 5, "Philosophy of Religion," we have seen how James interprets the question "Does God exist?" as being decidable by assessing the cash-value of believing in "the religious hypothesis." The everyday role that religious belief plays and the effects of religious organizations and institutions upon human affairs indicate whether or not the religious hypothesis works in solving certain human problems. James, and John Dewey after him, contended that from a psychological standpoint religious belief played a constructive role in making the lives of many people more satisfactory. However, they argued that much of the theological and institutional superstructure of religion could be dispensed with since it did not succeed in resolving human difficulties. James advocated, as a personal conviction, a type of theistic belief, whereas Dewey and his followers rejected this proposal. They suggested that in man's potentialities for beneficial activity, based upon his increasing scientific knowledge, lay the way to the solution of human problems.

With regard to the traditional issues in ethics, the pragmatists have asserted that there is a close connection between their notion of "truth," and the notions of "good" and "right," so that pragmatic solutions can be discovered for moral problems. We have seen in James' remark that the true is equated with the expedient way of thinking, while the good is equated with the expedient way of behaving. We establish what theories are true by whether they work when they are applied as conceptual guides to action. Similarly, we ascertain what actions are good in terms of whether they satisfactorily resolve difficulties which confront us. In James' writings, the good is identified with that which leads to satisfactory and harmonious living; in Dewey's views, it is identified with that which leads to the well-being of a biological organism or of a community of organisms. In these terms, moral statements of the form, "It is right to do X," or "X is good," or "One ought to do X," can be examined pragmatically by interpreting them as proposals for dealing with specific situations in order to bring about certain results. Moral principles can then be tested "scientifically," instead of being accepted or rejected on the basis of arguments, theological views, or philosophical theories. Thus, the pragmatists maintained, morality would cease to be an arid list of pronouncements about what one should or should not do, and would become an all-important intellectual activity aimed at achieving human betterment through the constant evaluation and re-evaluation of proposals for solving man's problems. This would lead not to a fixed moral and ethical system, but to a constantly growing body of knowledge about man and society. James saw ethical inquiry as essentially melioristic, and aimed at the improvement of man's individual situation in life. Dewey, and the more recent pragmatists, have seen ethical study as a basic guide for social reforms. Through studies of man and society, more and more can be learned about what to do to overcome difficulties that confront human communities, and thereby to achieve a "good" world. Throughout much of the twentieth century, Dewey and his followers have been in the fore-front, inspiring various social reform movements in the United States and relating to the solution of moral problems the latest findings in sociology, social psychology, and economics. Ethical activity has become, for them, the way to guide social scientific research toward the achievement of desired ends in terms of human betterment and well-being. And moral activity, like any other human intellectual enterprise, is seen as constantly evolving and developing with the growth and change of human experience.

The pragmatic theory not only leads to certain "constructive" interpretations of the role of philosophy in the areas of religion, ethics, and social thought; it also sets forth a metaphysical view about the universe. In his theory of the "pluralistic universe," James contended that experience is not a fixed object to be examined (as it was for the British Empirical thinkers from Locke to J. S. Mill). Instead, immediate experience, James asserted, is a "humming-buzzing" confusion. It consists of qualities, such as noises and smells, and it consists of relations between them. An ordered, coherent picture of the world begins to emerge only when we differentiate and distinguish some of these qualities and relations from others. Then one such group may be isolated and identified as a table; another, as a particular person, John Jones. We make these differentiations and distinctions because of problems that occur in our lives. We try to overcome difficulties by "carving out" identifiable portions of experience and using them. Our interests and our needs lead us to shape and organize the confusion and profusion of qualities. The ordered world that emerges is then utilized by us. When we can no longer solve our problems, we have to reorganize the elements at our disposal. Thus we continually select and order portions of experience in terms of our needs and interests.

This picture of experience and the way in which it becomes differentiated leads to the view that there is no fixed universe that will be discovered through the analysis of experience. Instead, various universes will be found in the unending quest for successful solutions to problems. Most metaphysicians have thought in terms of a "block universe," one that had fixed and immutable characteristics. Our knowledge about the world, however, James maintained, does not reveal such a cosmos, nor does it indicate that there is any one picture of the world that is adequate to encompass the many ways we have ordered and will order the features that we differentiate in experience. Instead, as our knowledge of the world develops and expands, our conception of the nature of reality also grows. In pragmatic terms, a meaningful theory of the universe is always one that is in keeping with what we can do with the world we experience. As novel ways of selecting and organizing portions of our experience are developed, new aspects of the universe emerge and are identified. Both what we know and the cosmos to which we attribute our knowledge are conceived of as possessing an evolutionary characteristic, both growing and developing in terms of new situations, problems, and needs. The "pluralistic universe" possesses many different and divergent characteristics and possibilities that cannot be examined and understood entirely at any given time. The universe has to be studied as it emerges, develops, and unfolds. Each stage of comprehending it is to be considered as tentative, and as subject to correction in terms of its future growth and development.

James' version of the pragmatic theory, with its emphasis on ascertaining the cash-value of ideas, testing their truth by how they work, and applying the pragmatic outlook to ethical, religious, and metaphysical issues primarily in terms of *individual* experiences, problems, and solutions, was in large measure superseded by the views of John Dewey (1859–1952), who was perhaps the most influential American philosopher in the first half of the twentieth century. Most of his academic career was spent in teaching philosophy at Columbia University in New York City. Beginning in the late nineteenth century, he developed a form of pragmatism which is often called "instrumentalism," a view that stressed the biological and psychological aspects of thought as well as the social nature of problems and their solutions.

JOHN DEWEY'S
INSTRUMENTALISM

Dewey maintained that "brute" experience already involves the interaction between a biological organism and its environment. Experience is not something that impinges upon a passive spectator. Instead, it involves action and activity on the part of an organism reacting and living in its world. The intellectual experience we call "thinking" occurs in certain types of organisms as a way of meeting situations in which action is blocked. Intelligent behavior arises as a means of overcoming such situations through developing hypotheses as guides to further action. Intellectual activity is then evaluated in terms of the pragmatic criterion of whether the organism is able to function satisfactorily again or not. Thinking is thus instrumental, serving as a means to problem solving. Problems arising in the actual context of biological activity lead to a sequence of mental activities aimed at finding means by which the organism can continue to function by overcoming its immediate difficulties. Theories become the instruments by which higher organisms succeed in dealing with the complex variety of situations in which they find themselves. The sciences, as highly developed sets of theories, are the most successful result of intelligence developed in the face of experiential difficulties—most successful in that they lead to a wide range of instrumental applications to situations, which enable people to function more successfully within the context of human experience.

If intellectual activity is, and ought to be, instrumental in solving problems, then, Dewey argued, most of the philosophies developed in the course of human history are deplorable examples of the misuse of intelligence. Theoretical activity has unfortunately become divorced from practical concerns. Philosophers have been seeking solutions to purely theoretical questions without relating these questions to the biological and psychological situations from which they arose. The problems treated abstractly, and *in vacuo,* have led to a series of rigid abstract theories that philosophers insist on imposing on all thought and activity without reference to their applicability. The result is that philosophy, like theology, according to Dewey, has become almost completely useless in meeting human needs, and is often a genuine hindrance to constructive intellectual activity. Dewey advocated a "reconstruction in philosophy" that would bring philosophy back to its initial role as the guide of all intellectual activity directed toward solving human problems. Philosophy would cease to be an abstruse and abstract subject dealing with problems of no genuine importance; instead, it would become a basic directing force, aimed at encouraging the development of new means and techniques for assisting human beings to cope successfully with their environment, so that there could be continual progress in resolving the problems that confront us.

Since human beings are essentially social in nature, their problems arise primarily in social contexts. Hence philosophy, if it is to serve a constructive purpose, should take the lead in directing studies of man and society in order to develop better instruments for dealing with the difficulties that beset mankind. Thus, according to Dewey, philosophy should serve as the guiding light in developing research in the social sciences, and in seeing that the work in this area is applied toward solving human problems. Philosophy is to direct human intellectual activity toward achieving social reform and betterment.

In the course of the first half of the twentieth century, the instrumentalism of John Dewey was highly influential in the rapid development of the social sciences, especially sociology and social psychology. Dewey's outlook has also been of great importance in influencing workers in these fields to apply their findings, and not merely to rest content with descriptions of what is taking place. The aim of philosophy, to use a phrase introduced by Karl Marx, is not simply to understand the world but to change it.

In particular, Dewey's philosophy has had far-reaching effects in the United States upon education. Dewey and his followers have introduced a new view about the purpose of education and the way in which it ought to be achieved. This view has greatly altered the entire character of the American educational system during the last fifty years. Education,

Dewey maintained, should be directed toward developing methods of problem solving so that young people will be trained to meet the situations that will actually confront them in life. Previous systems of education have tried to make students learn a mass of factual information and "dead" subjects, instead of training students in the creative use of their intelligences. The progressive education movement, growing out of Dewey's views, recommended that children be trained by learning to deal with problem-situations instead of being trained in the mastery of various disciplines. In this way the child would find out how to "adjust" satisfactorily to his environment, and would learn techniques and attitudes that he could carry over into the larger social world in which he would have to function.

Dewey and his followers believed that this type of training would prepare people for living and acting in a democratic society. Such a society, they contended, is more flexible than others in that it does not have rigid or fixed standards and rules. It is an "open" society willing to explore various approaches in the attempt to solve problems. The student who has been prepared to meet problem-situations can take an active part in a democratic society by applying his techniques for resolving difficulties to the problems that exist, in cooperation with others in the society. In this way, progressive education and democracy will presumably foster the cooperative efforts of the people to meet the problems that confront mankind, and to resolve them in the most satisfactory way.

As a result of Dewey's theories, curricula have been altered throughout the educational systems in this country. Some critics, especially in recent decades, have argued that this has led to a watering down of the educational programs in America. The formal subjects, they have contended, such as languages and mathematics, have been neglected to the extent that many students are ready to live happy, well-adjusted lives but are not prepared to work on serious intellectual problems. Some of Dewey's followers have insisted that the present state of American education is not what Dewey preached, but rather represents a misrendering and oversimplification of his theory, since the purpose in his proposed educational reforms was to make students able to cope with the actual problems confronting society. Hence, if the intensive study of foreign languages, mathematics, and science is needed to deal with the problem-situations of today and tomorrow, the educational process ought to include these subjects as part of its preparation of the student for his role in society.

CRITICISMS OF PRAGMATISM

The pragmatic movement made a deep impression on the philosophical world, especially in the United States. It has led many people to reject the outlooks of traditional philosophies. It has also inspired the view that philosophy should deal with more practical and immediate questions, which can best be treated by methods and techniques like those used in the sciences. Pragmatism has been seen by some as the expression of the American dream, with its emphasis on practical affairs and its quest for success through innovation. In the same way that American industrial techniques have revolutionized man's relations to his environment, the pragmatic theory has been portrayed as a way of revolutionizing the relationship between the intellectual world and man's problems.

However, in spite of such enthusiastic attitudes toward pragmatism, there have also been serious criticisms of the view. The effect of these criticisms has been to increase interest in other contemporary philosophical approaches. As a result, pragmatism is no longer as powerful a philosophical force as it was in the earlier part of the century. Analytic philosophy in its various forms, such as logical positivism and ordinary-language analysis, existentialism and phenomenology, and other movements appear to be making greater and greater inroads on the American philosophical scene.

Critics have challenged the basic pragmatic contention—its theory of truth. They have questioned whether one can or should evaluate ideas and beliefs in terms of whether or not they work. Some have contended that "working" is too vague a concept, and, as a result, that it is difficult, if not impossible, to determine whether an idea or a belief has "worked." If ideas and beliefs are to be evaluated in terms of whether their consequences "work" out satisfactorily in experience, how does one delimit the possible consequences in order to test ideas and beliefs? The possible consequences that ought to enter into any evaluation of whether any idea or belief has "worked" seem to be potentially infinite or, at least, indefinite. The consequences, for instance, of believing that today is Thursday involve beliefs and actions about every future date for the rest of history, as well as every dated event. If today is Thursday, tomorrow should be Friday, and the day after should be Saturday, and so on. Then, the critics ask, at what point can one be said to have tested the consequences if they go on forever? One may be able to ascertain that a belief has worked up to a certain point, but not that it will continue to work in the indefinite future.

Other critics have argued that in order to employ the pragmatic theory of truth, one would also have to accept a different conception of truth. How, they ask, does one ascertain if theory X works? Does one test this pragmatically? If so, one then tests a theory Y, which asserts, "Theory X works." Is theory Y true? Pragmatically, theory Y is true if it works. To determine if theory Y works, one would then test a theory Z, which asserts "Theory Y (the theory that theory X works) works," and so on. In fact, these critics insist, one does not ascertain that a theory works by testing another theory, and yet another. One sees if the assertion made by the proposition "Theory X works" corresponds to the facts. This then indicates that a different truth-theory, the correspondence theory, is, or has to be, employed in order to apply the pragmatic theory. (James, in his reply to Bertrand Russell on this point, insisted that one would actually have to use pragmatic tests in order to ascertain if a theory were true according to the correspondence criterion.)

Beside raising these questions, some opponents have also maintained that the pragmatic theory cannot adequately deal with mathematical and logical truth. Can a mathematical proposition be verified in a scientific or practical way? What is the cash-value of such a proposition? Is it applicable to experiential situations? If so, what about those branches of mathematics that do not, as yet, have any practical applications? Also, the critics point out that mathematicians and logicians do not, in fact, offer experiential tests as evidence for their theorems. They present only logical reasonings. Hence many philosophers have insisted that logical and mathematical truth cannot be properly analyzed in pragmatic terms. Under the influence of these criticisms, several contemporary pragmatists, such as C. I. Lewis and Ernest Nagel, and logicians with pragmatist leanings such as W. V. O. Quine, have attempted to reconcile the traditional interpretation of logic and mathematics with a pragmatic philosophy.

Other critics have sought to defend speculative philosophical investigation from the pragmatist's attacks. They have contended that such investigations are of such a different nature from scientific or practical ones that they ought not to be judged by the same standards. The speculative philosopher is concerned with the consistency and coherence of his views rather than with their practical consequences. Hence though the pragmatist may discover that these speculations have no cash-value in his terms, this may not be a proper judgment of the worth of these views.

The pragmatists have replied to such objections by contending that there is, in fact, no means of investigating the truth or falsehood of ideas and beliefs, except by examining pragmatically how they affect human beings. They have insisted that this criterion applies to mathematical, logical, and speculative views as well as to any others. The critics are appealing, the pragmatists say, to abstruse standards that are meaningless in the context of actual human problems, and the critics have raised problems that do not, in fact, cause genuine difficulties in anybody's attempts to ascertain if a belief or an idea is true.

Today the once heated arguments between the pragmatists and their critics are dying down. Under the impact of criticism, the pragmatic position has been modified in some respects. And, although the view continues to play a significant role in contemporary intellectual life, it no longer holds as dominant a position. Pragmatism has greatly influenced developments in many fields, especially in the social sciences. However, many thinkers have felt that this view is not adequate to deal with the wide and complex range of current problems. Hence, in recent years, interest in other theories has grown. We shall now turn to a consideration of some of these theories.

EXISTENTIALISM AND PHENOMENOLOGY

The second set of contemporary theories that we will consider are those of existentialism and phenomenology. Although these theories differ in many essential respects, we shall consider some aspects of them that have come to dominate contemporary continental European thought, as well as much of Latin American thinking. It is only recently that these views have begun to influence thinkers in the English-speaking world. The existentialist theory, though relatively new, actually developed from certain nineteenth-century philosophies, primarily that of Kierkegaard, so we will turn to his views first.

SØREN KIERKEGAARD'S THEORY

The "official" founder of existentialism is the Danish philosopher and theologian Søren Kierkegaard (1813–1855). Although he died over a century ago, he is a contemporary philosopher in a real sense, for his views were practically unknown in the nineteenth century. Only in recent times have they been studied and taken seriously. Kierkegaard spent most of his life in Copenhagen, leaving Denmark but once, when he briefly studied philosophy at the University of Berlin. In the 1840s he published a series of strange, cryptic writings attacking the current philosophical and theological views. His contemporaries in Denmark regarded him as a slightly mad crank. The Danish Church, which he attacked furiously up to the moment of his death, saw him as a dangerous nuisance. Outside Denmark, his polemics against rational philosophy and institutional Christianity were almost unknown. Histories of philosophy written in the nineteenth and early twentieth centuries hardly mention him. However, in the last sixty years Kierkegaard and his work have been rediscovered. His writings have been translated into many languages. A century after his death, Kierkegaard has come back to life. His ideas are now, for the first time, having an important influence. Books and articles about his views and their repercussions on the contemporary scene appear frequently nowadays. (For a review of Kierkegaard's philosophy, see pages 380ff.)

For those for whom Kierkegaard's leap into religious faith was no longer a live option. Nietzsche's blatant atheism, plus his insistence on the creative expression of man's will, have played an important role. Thinkers who have accepted Kierkegaard's analysis of man's inability to find out what to do by rational or scientific means, plus Nietzsche's contention that "God is dead," have shaped a form of atheistical or humanistic existentialism. Before coming to this theory, we will turn to one of the other views that has helped shape contemporary existentialism, the theory of phenomenology.

EDMUND HUSSERL

The philosophical movement called "phenomenology" is mainly the result of the writings and teaching of Edmund Husserl (1859–1938). Husserl was originally a mathematician, and then turned to philosophy, which he taught at Halle, Göttingen, and Freiburg in Germany. During the last years of his life he was victimized by the Nazis because of his Jewish ancestry (and even his protégé and successor, Martin Heidegger, mistreated him). During his life he published few books, but he left 45,000 pages of manuscript in shorthand, which were smuggled out of Nazi Germany, and are gradually being published and translated.

Unlike the irrationalist thinkers Kierkegaard and Nietzsche, Husserl was convinced that philosophy could be an exact and certain science. Husserl started his philosophical career publishing a volume, *Philosophie der Arithmetik* (1891). The work was an attempt at analyzing the psychological bases of certain logical and mathematical concepts—that is, examining the psychological processes that seemed to lie behind our awareness of these concepts. The book was severely criticized by the mathematician-philosopher, Gottlob Frege, who argued that the psychological acts involved in doing mathematics were different from the mathematical concepts themselves. Frege accused Husserl of mixing up psychology and logic. Husserl accepted the criticism and in his next work, *Logische Untersuchungen* (*Logical Investigations*) (1900–1901), he insisted that mathematics and logic must be based on a priori, rational concepts and necessary truths, rather than on the psychological thought processes through which they are worked out. Husserl moved on, especially in his next major work, *Ideas—General Introduction to Pure Phenomenology* (1913), to insisting that one should try to make philosophy into a rigorous science.

The kind of science Husserl had in mind was neither that of the natural world (physics, chemistry or biology) nor that of logic and mathematics. Both of these kinds of sciences depended on presuppositions—the natural sciences on the laws of nature, and the logical-mathematical ones on the laws of logic. What Husserl sought for philosophy was a kind of absolutely certain formulation that rested on *no* presuppositions or assumptions. That such a presuppositionless foundation was possible, Husserl sought to show from the starting point of Descartes' quest for certainty. The *cogito* examined in and by itself is absolutely certain. Its certainty is not known through any sort of demonstration, or any sort of evidence. It is rather directly intuited as certain. When we examine our conscious awareness of the *cogito*, we "see" that it is completely certain, just from the examination.

Husserl rejected following Descartes beyond this point (and even here his view is somewhat different than Descartes, in that the latter justified the certainty of the *cogito* on the grounds that not even the skeptics would challenge it). Husserl was not interested in what propositions might be claimed to follow logically from the *cogito*. He was instead concerned with the exploration of human consciousness to find if our intuitively certain truths could be found. To accomplish this, the philosopher should try to develop a view of exactly how things appear in his conscious experience. They are to be considered strictly as objects of consciousness, as they appear to us, rather than in terms of something really hidden from us, or something that is part of a world apart from us (Kant's world of things-in-themselves.)

Husserl was definitely not proposing another version of traditional phenomenalism—identifying what is known with items in sense experience. Rather, he was insisting that we should examine what is true in our immediate experience and why it is true. Needing no presuppositions, we can just tell intuitively what is true. We do not accomplish this by psychological examination, as John Locke or David Hume proposed. Such examination may be illuminating, but unfortunately it does not reveal what is actually involved in knowledge through experience. The psychological process that goes on does not show what is true and why. The intuitive process in consciousness does accomplish this. By employing what he called the "phenomenological reduction," Husserl contended that what was uncovered as the object of consciousness via intuition was not a fact or an image, but rather an essence which comprises the factors of necessity and universal validity. The essences are invariant features that make experience what it is. They are also the features that give experience meaning.

This phenomenological method, which Husserl claimed revealed such a world of essences, is a descriptive procedure, rather than a deductive one. What differentiates Husserl's efforts from those of other philosophers who have sought certainty in philosophy is that Husserl was not proceeding from prior assumptions, but instead was examining the world of conscious experience and finding out what it is like. Husserl's insistence that his method was descriptive was part of his basic contention that he was philosophizing without presupposition. The process of applying the method was extremely laborious. But the fruits of it are that objects are brought to "self-givenness" in intuition, their essential natures become the objects of consciousness. They, the objects, are stripped of all that is unneeded in their appearance. And at this point in the phenomenological reduction, essences can be found. Everyday experiences must be transformed by extracting their phenomenological components. Then these components are examined by consciousness. If some aspect is found that is as certain as the *cogito*, an essence has been discovered.

Husserl's method is not a hit-and-miss affair. From his laborious employment of his method, he came to the conclusion that the essences that emerged in the consciousness revealed a formal and invariant structure in the objects of experience. This structure is intuited through cognitive acts—that is, intentions. We are conscious of something (this is our intentional cognition) and there is something we are conscious of. Through the phenomenological method, the knowing act is not reduced to what is known, but the formal characteristics of each are revealed. We come to realize exactly what is known, what its essential characteristics are, and what cannot be doubted about it. This does not involve making traditional metaphysical assumptions about the knower and what is known, rather it delineates what is certain in the knowing experience, in terms of the object of knowledge and the knower. One uncovers the essences present in pure consciousness, as well as pure consciousness itself, by reducing experience to its invariant and certain elements rather than to its psychological and transitory features. One also suspends judgment as to whether what is experienced is a reality independent of the experience. Husserl himself, in the mature presentations of his view, developed a kind of idealism, seeing the ego, the pure self that has experience, as the ultimate certainty. This is often described in Husserl's writings as the transcendental ego, taking over Kant's term for the ego that Kant thought could not be known. The writings in which Husserl stressed the transcendental ego as the ultimate reality gave his phenomenalistic theory a strong idealistic bent. On the basis of these writings, he could be interpreted as holding that only the mental world existed, the transcendental ego and its cognitive intentions and the essences as mentally grasped. Later on, in his final lectures and writings, he saw that there was a community of egos that experienced, and that this commonality could be described and analyzed. In his *Die Krisis der europäischem Wissenschaften und die transcendentale Phänomenologie (The Crisis of European Knowledge and the Transcendental Phenomenology)* (1954), which was written two or three years before his death, the transcendental ego was no longer the absolute center of knowledge. It was now correlative to the world. But of greater significance was the fact that Husserl now recognized that the world was not just what it appeared to be for a given transcendental individual. It was the intersubjective community of individual egos that determined what is. The phenomenological method, unlike empirical, psychological, or metaphysical ones, could describe and point out just what in knowing and in the content of knowing involved certain and indubitable information. By reducing the knowing experience to its indubitable core, Husserl believed he had gotten beyond the traditional metaphysical debates and assumptions, and beyond the reduction of philosophy to psychology. He had found a science of knowledge.

Of course, many dispute that he really discovered anything more than another form of psychological certainty. Aside from that, skeptical opponents would argue that Husserl was interpreting his essences, intentional cognition, and transcendental ego in a manner that went far beyond the descriptive data.

Husserl's theory is extremely complex. Much of it still remains unpublished; if it were published in its entirety, the new material would probably throw light on the works that have appeared. Husserl's students and other philosophers have developed various aspects and tendencies within it. In various forms it has become a major form of contemporary philosophy, especially in continental Europe. Since several of Husserl's leading disciples came to America as refugees from Hitler, his views have gradually become better known and appreciated here as well.

For the existentialist movement, it is more Husserl's method than his theory that has played a major role. The method of examining consciousness has been used to bring out other basic aspects. One of Husserl's students, Martin Heidegger, combined the phenomenological method with the insights of Kierkegaard and Nietzsche to develop modern existentialism. Later the French philosopher, Jean-Paul Sartre, set forth another version of the combined views.

MARTIN HEIDEGGER

Martin Heidegger (1889–1976) was born of peasant stock in Messkirch, Germany, where his father was a sexton. Young Heidegger was originally trained to be a Jesuit. He began his academic work as a theological student at the University of Freiburg. At this university he was first influenced by Husserl's writings and then by Husserl himself. Heidegger's doctoral thesis, *The Theory of Judgment in Psychologism* (1914), shows the impact of phenomenology on him, as does his later dissertation on the medieval philosopher, Duns Scotus. From 1917–1922

Heidegger and Husserl worked together, Heidegger being the leader of Husserl's seminar at Freiburg. In 1923, Heidegger was appointed professor at the University of Marburg, and five years later professor at Freiburg when Husserl retired. Heidegger's major work, *Sein und Zeit (Being and Time),* was published in 1927, originally in Husserl's yearbook of phenomenological writings, where it was dedicated to Husserl. Later it appeared as a separate book. From 1929 until the early 1940s, Heidegger published nothing. When he started publishing once more, it appeared that he had seriously changed his views (and commentators have been arguing ever since as to whether his earlier views can be reconciled with his later ones). When, after World War II, the French existentialists claimed Heidegger as one of their chief intellectual heirs because of what he wrote in *Sein und Zeit,* he wrote a long letter entitled *Letter on Humanism* (1947), attacking them.

One of the darkest episodes in Heidegger's career was his association with the Nazis at the beginning of the Hitler period. In 1933, Heidegger was made rector of the University of Freiburg. He was at the time a National Socialist (Nazi), and delivered a lecture on "The Role of the University in the New Reich." Also at this time, he publicly dissociated himself from Husserl (who was Jewish), and allowed the university to ban Husserl from using any of the facilities of the institution, including the library. Heidegger later withdrew from the Nazi party, but remained an ardent nationalist throughout the rest of his life. Heidegger's early relations with the Nazis has led to a continuing discussion of his war guilt. He was investigated in 1945, and there was a dispute as to whether he should be allowed to stay in the university. This dispute only terminated with Heidegger's retirement in 1959.

Setting aside politics and the Nazi problem in order to deal just with Heidegger's major early contribution to philosophy, his important work, *Sein und Zeit,* first appeared, as we have mentioned above, in Husserl's phenomenological yearbook in 1927, and it is dedicated to Husserl. To some extent it builds on the methodology of Husserl's phenomenology, but on the whole it departs radically from it. Heidegger's book is one of the most complicated ever written in philosophy. It is developed in terms of analyses and constructions of German concepts and words which have proven extremely difficult to translate into English without sounding like either gibberish or a totally opaque language. We shall not attempt to describe his whole theory, but shall only try to explain certain key portions of his views, not necessarily in the sequential order in which they occur in *Sein und Zeit.*

For Heidegger, the fundamental problem of philosophy is to find out the nature of Being. Heidegger felt that all of philosophy from Plato to Heidegger had failed in this search because they had abstracted and categorized Being, but not discerned it in itself. Being was removed from its actual setting, and was described not as it is, but in terms of abstract classifications which do not really fit the nature of Being. The phenomenological method allows one to seek for Being without any presuppositions. Thus, it can be found in consciousness without any conceptual apparatus, and its nature is not distorted by any conceptual scheme of things.

The key aspect of Being, or kind of Being, that Heidegger is concerned with analyzing in *Sein und Zeit* is *Dasein*, or human being (not an individual human being, but rather the kind of existence that humanity has). Only mankind, or human being, tries to find Being. Hence, analyzing *Dasein* is an important preliminary to the search for Being itself.

Dasein is a particular kind of being. Its German meaning indicates its special character; *Dasein* equals "being there." Human being is always in a world which is already constituted in various ways. Man's ordinary existence in this situation is inauthentic. It is inauthentic because the world in which *Dasein* finds itself is not its own creation. It is there and is what human being has to work with, whether it wants to or not. Human beings make the world their own by anticipating what their world will be like. In this sense, they are not strangers in a foreign and hostile world, but rather they fit in by participating in their world. This participation basically takes the form of expecting certain developments to occur. Through this process one gets to understand one's world. One also gets seduced into caring about particular beings instead of the relation of *Dasein* and *Sein*. The individuals matter, the anonymous public beings, rather than oneself and one's relation to Being.

For Heidegger, all of this indicates that man is determined by the character of the world, and is also free, as a being that can constitute its world. Yet in spite of this freedom, man is also enslaved by his actual relations to human being in general and to the world in which he exists. This describes some of the basic aspects of ordinary or inauthentic existence. Then what would authentic existence be like?

It would first require that human being turn away from the distractions of everyday life, and turn back to itself. The self must be willing to face itself with complete Kierkegaardian honesty, and must be willing to find itself as a totality, and not as a fragmented function of the many aspects of ordinary life. The self would be seen by itself as a whole, and not as a self involved in everyday living. This is accomplished by examining the *moods*—that is, the states of mind—that signify human condition at various moments. Among the moods, one of them leads *Dasein* back to itself. This mood is dread. The other moods relate to features of the world. Dread (*Angst*) has no object as such. Instead, it is a feeling of the loss of objects, a feeling of nothingness with regard to being in the world.

One's complete life, which is what one's world amounts to, is seen also as having a terminus—death. Dread is an attitude toward life as a whole. Life as a whole is pointing toward death. Dread is that mood which brings us back to the knowledge that we are being-to-death—that is, our existence extends until our demise. Dread also makes us aware of our freedom and our authenticity. My death is authentically mine. It belongs to nobody else, and as death, only affects me. (This is not to deny it can affect the other moods, sorrow, compassion, and so on, of others.) In seeing myself as a being-to-death, I regain my freedom from the aspects of the world that seems to determine me, or occupy me. *Angst*, or anxiety, is related to conscience. It is one's conscience that is asked to face and accept the responsibility for one's individual being, and that is one's freedom. And it is *Angst* that reveals to one's conscience that one is a finite being, whose finitude is revealed in death. This finitude reveals a boundary of one's own existence, and a significance to it. Put in another way, if there was no awareness of death, and one envisaged one's future as stretching out indefinitely, then there would be no serious sense of urgency or responsibility in life. And such an attitude would yield an inauthentic view of life.

The central function of the realization of one's own death in establishing one's freedom and one's authenticity indicates part of the debt Heidegger owes to Kierkegaard and Nietzsche. From the former he has taken over the need for the individual to establish a meaningful life without any guideposts, other than that it is the individual's life, because it includes his death. Heidegger has taken over Kierkegaard's picture of the completely free individual. From Nietzsche he has adopted a kind of nihilistic element—that there are no values beyond humanly created ones. *Dasein* as such has no purpose of going anywhere except to be in a temporal sense. An individual member of humanity has as goals those that he or she sets for himself or herself. Nietzsche's message that God is dead is perhaps stronger than Heidegger's picture of *Dasein* and *Sein*'s existing without any real purpose. (And as Heidegger later claimed, the central issue of philosophy is, why *is* there something instead of nothing? This question turns out not to be really answerable though Heidegger regarded its consideration as all-important). And no Kierkegaardian God is going to be discovered by the "leap into faith."

This being the case, how does one find one's place in history? First of all, the realization of what one is like, a being-unto-death, makes temporality and destiny basic features of one's world. Time becomes not a standard measure, but the measure of *my* being, the measure of my lifetime. Existential time is also pointed to the future. In fact, it is the measure of the future that reflects back to the present. And this existential time is finite—that is, my time will terminate at some point. Yet my time also had a beginning. So that in terms of my time, I have a history. I may not be responsible for its having the characteristics it has. However, when I see it as *my* history, I become responsible for it.

Dasein, in one sense is time. When this is realized, conscience is that which calls *Dasein* to its freedom, to act in finite time, to construct its own life in the face of death. With this freedom goes guilt, in that there is also a discrepancy between what has been, and what an individual could and should have created in its freedom. When one lives in the awareness of death, with a feeling of guilt, an aware conscience, and a sense of freedom and of finitude, then one is a historical being with a destiny. There is, of course, no objective historical destiny for any and all members of the human race, but only that which mankind makes for itself through this process of becoming free and historical.

The picture Heidegger gives in *Sein und Zeit* of the human predicament is quite gloomy. Only by facing a pointless death ahead of us do we gropingly arrive at our individuality, at our freedom, and at our ability to be historical actors. We are torn continuously by guilt for not having been able to control our past, present, and future. And though we are free to create our future, there is no particular character it should have in any objective sense. Nonetheless, we are responsible for the free choice we make. (We will see some of these claims again soon in our discussion of the philosophy of Jean-Paul Sartre.)

Heidegger's Later Works

Heidegger's influence, especially on existentialist thought, stems from his analysis of the human situation as it appears in *Sein und Zeit*. In his many writings thereafter, he stressed that he saw himself as a metaphysician, concerned with one central matter, the quest for Being. *Sein und Zeit* enabled him to clear space so that the infinite question of the nature of Being could be faced by finite man. Heidegger found that when people try to look directly at Being, they are unable to say anything. When we distinguish Being from any particular thing, it is just about nothing. And this, Heidegger contended, is the doing of mankind. Being has just about become like nothing because we have fallen out of Being. We have lost the nearness and shelter of Being. We have pursued particular things and goals, and forgotten our real goal, to seek Being itself. This state of affairs and its consequences Heidegger described as "the darkening of the world." This unfortunate situation began with the Greek philosophers after Plato, and continues with the scientists of today who look into separate problems, but not into Being itself. Heidegger saw more hope for getting a glimpse of Being through poetry. Much of his later work deals with poetry and with language analysis. What carried over from *Sein und Zeit* was man's realization of nothingness through dread and through the awareness of his own imminent nonbeing. Through further examination of nothingness, one might find some clues as to what Being was like as the opposite of nothingness. (In Heidegger's *What is Metaphysics*, he had said, "The nothing nots," to explain what it does. The Logical Positivists, whom we will discuss shortly, have used this as a prime illustration of metaphysical nonsense.) Through the examination of nothingness, we can make room for Being and possibly come in contact with it.

Heidegger's later works are very complex, often mystical with nationalist overtones. There have been a great variety of interpretations. Heidegger himself was reediting and reevaluating his works up to his death in 1976. He apparently hoped to leave a clearer indication of what he had been driving at in his later years. As yet there is no consensus as to what his final message was. As we have said, he dissociated himself in his "Letter concerning Humanism" (1949) from French existentialism. We will turn now to that movement and consider the views of one of its leaders, Jean-Paul Sartre.

CONTEMPORARY EXISTENTIALISM: JEAN-PAUL SARTRE AND OTHERS

The contemporary existentialist movement has developed and generalized some of the views of Kierkegaard, Nietzsche, and Heidegger. Starting from their description of the human predicament, many of the present-day existentialists have sought for a different solution to man's problems. Some of these thinkers, such as the important French author Jean-Paul Sartre (1905–), reject Kierkegaard's irrational Christianity because they deny that there is a God. They have accepted Nietzsche's announcement that "God is dead." Others like the late Albert Camus (1913–1960) have expressed the wish "that there was a God" but find themselves psychologically unable to believe that God exists. For all these thinkers, therefore, any solution to the human predicament cannot depend upon the miraculous assistance of a Deity. It must come from man himself.

The existentialist theory is probably stated in its best-known form by Jean-Paul Sartre. Sartre, born in 1905, studied philosophy at the École Normale Supérieure. He received his degree in 1929, and then taught philosophy in high schools around France. In the period from 1932–1934, he studied in Germany, at Berlin and Freiburg. At the latter institution, he studied Husserl's phenomenology and Heidegger's development of it. In 1937, he was assigned to teach philosophy at a high school in Paris and stayed there until 1939, when he was drafted into the army. Sartre, along with much of the French army, was captured in 1940. He was a prisoner for a year, and then returned to teaching. He also joined the Resistance to the Nazis. He gave up teaching at the end of World War II and has since devoted himself to his literary and intellectual pursuits, including founding and directing the magazine, *Les Temps Modernes*. In recent years he has been trying to harmonize his views with certain currents in contemporary Marxism. A few years ago, he was offered, but refused, the Nobel Prize in Literature.

He developed his theory during the 1930s. One of the first presentations of it was in his first major novel, *Nausea*. The presentation of his views in the form of a philosophical treatise appears in *L'être et le néant (Being and Nothingness)* (1943), which was heavily influenced by the views of Husserl and Heidegger.

According to Sartre, we find ourselves "trapped into existence." Whether we like it or not, we are here—here in a world that basically makes no sense (or as Camus contended, that was absurd). We differentiate this world into what is *pour soi* (for the self) and *en soi* (in itself). The latter, the objective characteristics of objects, is not what concerns us. However, the former, how we are affected by objects, is crucial to us. There are no justifiable principles for determining how objects should affect us. But just the same, we have to adopt some principles in order to comprehend events and to deal with this world. We find ourselves forced to find some meaning or purpose in it. When we examine the world we are confronted with, the world *pour soi*, we discover only that it is completely arbitrary. There is no explanation we can uncover for its existence and its nature. We realize that the world we are confronted with is unintelligible to us. Nonetheless, we are trapped in it; that is, we cannot escape being in the world. We search desperately for some way of making the world intelligible. It is at this point that we become dizzy, overwhelmed by the "nausea of existence." Everything in and about the world we live in is totally arbitrary. There is no reason why it should be one way rather than another. And there is no reason why we should live one kind of life rather than another kind in this world. There is no reason why we should accept one set of beliefs or values instead of any other.

When we reflect upon our situation, we become aware that we are confronted by a "dreadful freedom." We are completely free to choose our own outlook. We are completely free to decide how we wish to live in this meaningless world. And since we are completely free, we are unable to find any guidance to assist us in making our basic choice, which will determine the others. Nonetheless, we *must* make a choice if we are to live in a meaningful world. If no choice is ever made, one remains forever in the "nausea of existence," and all one's actions make no sense—they merely occur in the meaningless incoherent jumble of events. If our lives are to be "authentically" our own, they must be based upon, and must be seen in terms of, our own choices. The realization of our freedom provides us both with the opportunity to become "authentic" individuals, and with the dreadful responsibility for our own individuality. We become individuals only through our own willingness to decide what kind of life we want to live, and how we want to interpret the world we live in. When we make such a fundamental decision, we then become responsible to ourselves and others for the life to which we have committed ourselves. The commitment determines what we value, what we take seriously, and what we disregard. This, then, affects all our future actions, and all our relations with the rest of the world. We are totally free to determine where we stand in our outlook on the universe, but then we must bear the heavy burden of responsibility for our decision.

The concept of "dread" is as important for Sartre as it is for Heidegger, but it has a different role. In Heidegger's thought, dread is the realization of our being-unto-death. And from this realization of our finitude we realize our authenticity and our freedom. For Sartre, dread is the effect of the realization of our freedom. We can do what we want, live as we want, but we are responsible for our choice, not only for how it affects us but how it affects others as well. The dread is of the enormously heavy burden of choosing a way of life. In the light of this difference, Sartre stressed, much more than Heidegger, the intersubjective character of human action. (Some critics have claimed that neither of these two philosophers has any basis for moving from a solipsistic analysis of the human situation to a world peopled with persons.) Sartre insisted, especially in his essay, "Existentialism is a Humanism," that it is the social effect of one's choice that causes the anxiety or dread about making a choice. One is choosing not just for one individual, but, in a sense, for the whole human race. Sartre's more social version of existentialism may be the result of his wartime experience. This version leads to a much more ethical picture of what the human predicament is, and how men should behave. We may not be able to capture what reality or being is, but we can delineate man as he functions in the world.

Perhaps a clearer picture of Sartre's philosophy occurs in his earlier novel, *Nausea*. Most of the novel is devoted to picturing man's plight in terms of the miserable life of the hero. He has been living according to an outlook that he has never questioned. However, his dissatisfaction with the course of his own life finally forces him to question everything he has always accepted. He then begins to search for some justification or rationale for his way of life. As soon as he does this, his whole world begins to crumble. Once he realizes that his previously accepted outlook was completely arbitrary, he becomes nauseated. The world that he used to see, and live in, vanishes, and all that remains is complete confusion from which

(handwritten margin note: P.157 Egoism)

the hero cannot escape. He realizes that the world he experiences has neither coherence nor order at all. He becomes completely dizzy trying to find his place in the world.

At this point he realizes that he can organize his experience and his life only if he himself is willing to decide what it all means, without any assistance from any other source. The magnitude of what he must do totally overwhelms him. He cannot avoid choosing. He cannot escape his freedom. But, until he is able to make the fundamental decision, the basic commitment that gives an order and a sense to his life, he will not be able to perform a meaningful action. His life is paralyzed until he exercises his freedom and becomes an "authentic" person, directing his own life in terms of his own decision.

Sartre's hero is terrified by the frightening consequences of what he must do. Once he chooses, he, and he alone, will be responsible for all the results of his decision. He must bear this burden by himself, since there is ño God to help him. Kierkegaard's solution, that the knight of faith can put his trust in God, is ruled out in Sartre's picture of man's plight. There is, in Sartre's existentialist view, no objective way of ascertaining what the *right* decision might be, either before or after the choice is made. Man must make the commitment by himself, and he alone is to be held responsible for it. At the very end of Sartre's story, his hero, having suffered through all the miseries of his situation and the realization of what he must do to solve them, finally makes his commitment, and then is, at last, able to act.

The existentialists are concerned primarily with the questions Kierkegaard has posed: "What should man do?" and "What should he believe?" If our world is irrational and meaningless, how can we find answers to them? In posing the basic problems in these terms, the existentialists have treated as of secondary importance the kinds of issues that concern analytic philosophers. "Technical" philosophical problems enter into some of the writings and arguments of existentialist thinkers. But such problems are only tangential to their work: wrestling with man's tragic predicament.

In posing answers to what they regard as the fundamental questions, some existentialist philosophers insist that the solution lies in the acceptance of a religious faith. In the tradition of Kierkegaard, and of some of the more recent Russian Orthodox theologians, such as Berdaeyev and Shestov, many contemporary existentialist writers have advocated a modern "leap into faith." On the contemporary scene, there are adherents of different religious traditions, Judaism, Catholicism, and Protestantism, and Zen Buddhism—all proposing their faiths as the choice that will resolve man's difficulties.

On the other hand, there are many existentialist thinkers and writers who agree with Sartre's outlook. Starting from an atheistic denial that there is any supernatural Being who could supply or justify the acceptance of a solution to man's plight, these philosophers insist that we seek for a "humanistic" faith. Such a faith would consist in a basic commitment to the importance of certain human values. If one decided to base one's life and one's actions on such a commitment, all of one's experiences could then be organized in terms of this choice. No Divine Being would provide the sanction for the choice, so that one would never have any absolute assurance that the choice was correct. But the atheistic existentialists insist, if there actually is no God, man can do no more than make his own decisions and live by them.

The existentialist view, in both its theistic and atheistic forms, has flourished in Continental Europe since the end of World War II. The terribly destructive events of the war period, especially the horrible effects of the Nazi dictatorship in Germany and in the occupied territories, left many people with a feeling that their original outlook on life no longer made any sense, and no longer had any relevance. What had happened, and now what may happen in the era of atomic and nuclear weapons, seems to be incapable of rational explanation and comprehension. Why has all this happened? Does it make any sense at all? Is there anything that one should do, or should believe in such a chaotic, meaningless world? To many people, living in the shattered remnants of what was once an organized and intelligible world, the acceptance of arbitrary beliefs appeared to be the only way to find a new basis for living in an absurd universe. The existentialist picture of the human situation seems to many to portray modern man. The earlier hopes and ideals have been destroyed. The fabric of the human world seems to have disintegrated. In the face of the cataclysmic events that have dominated this century, what *can* one still believe, and what can one hope for? The existentialists have sought to show man where he is, and to show him that only he can answer to questions for himself. Seen in this light, existentialism appears to express the mood of the European intellectual world in the postwar years.

CRITICISMS OF EXISTENTIALISM

By and large, there has been comparatively little interchange between the existentialists and the analytic philosophers during the last fifteen years. Each side has regarded the other as having abandoned the task of philosophy. Only in the last few years are there signs that each group of thinkers is making any real effort to comprehend what the other is doing, and to appreciate the merits of the other's contribution.

The existentialists have been criticized for abandoning the quest for a rational examination and understanding of the world of human experience. Critics have contended that the existentialists have refused to use the tools of analysis developed by modern philosophy as means of studying problems. Such tools might clarify the nature of the problems at issue, and the types of solutions, if any, that men might find. Instead, critics have said, existentialists are offering moral exhortations. These exhortations may be inspiring, perhaps depressing, but they do not lead to a clearer understanding of issues. Hence, some critics have asserted that the existentialist writers are actually poets and novelists, expressing their feelings about the contemporary world, rather than careful, serious philosophers, trying to analyze present-day issues.

The existentialists, on the other hand, have regarded other philosophers as thinkers who are wasting their time, who are "fiddling while Rome burns." Some philosophers they see as frittering away their intellectual energies in constructing defenses of intellectual systems that can no longer be believed. Such systems have no genuine foundation. They cannot be proved, and they cannot be accepted. The analytic philosophers they see as refusing to face the "real" issues of our time. The problems that these thinkers deal with concerning logic and language have little or nothing to do with modern man's predicament. Hence the existentialists have reproached the analytic philosophers for ignoring the questions that vitally concern man, while using their talents on intricate, technical problems that are irrelevant to his plight. Let us turn now for a look at analytic philosophy to see if these claims can be substantiated.

PHILOSOPHICAL ANALYSIS

WHAT IS PHILOSOPHICAL ANALYSIS?

As we shall indicate in what follows, the term *philosophical analysis* refers to a set of philosophical activities or doctrines, some of which differ so markedly from each other that one might well wonder whether the same term can properly be applied to all of them. But in some significant sense the answer is surely "yes." For in spite of many divergences, a common outlook runs through all of these views—an outlook which might briefly be described as follows: it is the belief that philosophy when properly performed consists, at least in part, in an activity called "analysis." What is meant by this term is, again, a matter of dispute, but even here there is a core of agreement. It is accepted (1) that philosophical problems are mainly the products of conceptual confusion, (2) that such confusion is due, at least in part, to misuses of language, and (3) that a process of linguistic clarification is therefore, at some stage, requisite to the ultimate solution of these problems. "Analysis" is the name commonly assigned to the various forms which the process of clarification may take.

Thus, in spite of the many and often subtle differences which exist within this movement, the main tendencies in analytical philosophy are not beyond description. Patterns are gradually emerging—patterns which suggest that this movement today splits into two broad streams. Both of these owe their origin to a common source, mainly to the work of Alfred North Whitehead and Bertrand Russell in mathematical logic. One of these streams is directly in the tradition of this work; for purposes of convenience, we shall designate it as the "formalist point of view." Its leading exponents, whose views we shall take up in a few moments, are first of all Russell himself; then Ludwig Wittgenstein (during his *Tractatus* period); Moritz Schlick, the founder of logical positivism; and certain contemporary logicians, among them Rudolf Carnap, W. V. O. Quine, and Alfred Tarski. The other stream begins, as we have said, from this common source, but its characteristic methods are, if anything, diametrically opposed to the formalist point of view. In what follows, we shall call it the "ordinary-language point of view." Its major exponents are G. E. Moore, Wittgenstein (during the period which followed his rejection of the *Tractatus*), and certain contemporary British philosophers, among them John T. Wisdom, Gilbert Ryle, and J. L. Austin.

Since it is wisest in explaining these matters to begin at the beginning, let us look first at the common source itself—the work of Whitehead and Russell in mathematical logic.

THE WORK OF WHITEHEAD
AND RUSSELL IN LOGIC

As one might suspect, the history of the development of mathematical logic is a lengthy study.[1] To attempt to relate it in any detail would take us too far from the path we intend to follow in tracing the influence of this

---

[1] For those readers who may wish to explore the history of logic more fully, we recommend that they study *The Development of Logic* by William and Martha Kneale, Oxford University Press, 1962. In particular, we suggest that they study Chapters 7 and 8 of this book, which deal with the contributions of Gottlob Frege. W. Kneale states that the deductive system or calculus which Frege elaborated "is the greatest single achievement in the history of the subject." During his own lifetime, Frege's works were largely ignored by scholars. It was only after World War II that his reputation began to grow; for a discussion of this development see "The First Flowering of Frege's Reputation," by Avrum Stroll, in the *Journal of the History of Philosophy*, Vol. IV, No. 1, January 1966.

subject upon contemporary analytic philosophy. But a few remarks about its history may not be out of place. Not only will they allow us to illustrate how mathematical (or "symbolic") logic differs from Aristotelian logic, but they will also support our earlier contention that the history of philosophy is not merely a series of footnotes to Plato. Mathematical logic and much of the philosophy which has emerged from it are essentially creations of the past hundred years.

Recent research reveals, curiously enough, that mathematical logic might have been invented earlier than it was. Certain Stoic logicians were working on lines similar to those which were to be explored more fully some two thousand years later by Boole, Frege, Peano, Russell, and Whitehead. Unfortunately, though, the results of these investigations were never to pass into the main traditions of philosophy. For one thing, mathematics itself had not developed to the point where these logical inquiries could be seen to be relevant to it, and for another, with the growth of Christianity and the subsequent emphasis put upon Aristotle's writings, his sytem of logic chased all others from the field. Aristotelian logic came to be thought of as "the" logical system—indeed, so much so that Kant writing in 1787 (in the *Critique of Pure Reason*) felt justified in stating that logic, as developed by Aristotle, was to be regarded as the only complete and perfect branch of philosophy.

Less than 100 years later—in 1879 with the publication of his *Begriffschrift*—Gottlob Frege (1848–1925) showed conclusively that Kant's comment was, to put it mildly, premature. In this great work, which attempted to establish the identity of logic and mathematics, Frege produced a new type of logic which far exceeded the classical system in scope, power of analysis, and rigor. Though writing later, and more or less independently of Frege, Russell and Whitehead attempted to show that all of mathematics could be derived from logic. These advances were so great as to totally eclipse their Aristotelian counterpart. Indeed, as Professor Benson Mates has remarked, "the present-day student of logic is likely to find Aristotle mentioned only in the historical footnotes of his textbook."

Because of its complicated symbolism, and perhaps because it was so far in advance of its time, Frege's work had little direct influence in general philosophical circles. But it made a profound impact upon Russell, and then later Wittgenstein and Carnap. The era of modern logic thus begins, according to most critics, with the publication of the *Begriffschrift* in 1879, though it was only some thirty years later, with the publication of Volume I of *Principia Mathematica* by Whitehead and Russell in 1910, that the fundamental importance of mathematical logic for philosophical inquiry began to be appreciated generally. Since it was the later system of Russell and Whitehead, with its simpler notation, which took the philosophical world by storm, let us trace the influence of their work on contemporary philosophy.

Alfred North Whitehead (1861–1947) and Bertrand Arthur Russell (1872–1970) collaborated for more than ten years in the research which culminated in the publication of *Principia Mathematica*. After this period, their paths diverged. Whitehead moved to London, where he taught for a decade before accepting a professorship in 1924 at Harvard. Though his subsequent work continued to be important, its direct impact upon the development of contemporary analytical philosophy diminished considerably; rather it was as a speculative metaphysician, elaborating systems of great complexity, that he influenced modern philosophy. But Russell continued to deal with logical problems, and closely associated epistemological considerations, until the late 1940s; though the political and social concerns which came to dominate his later years were always closely at hand as well. To a great extent, contemporary analytic philosophy thus emerges from the work of Russell, beginning with his early writings, such as *The Principles of Mathematics* (1903), and culminating in *Principia Mathematica* (1910–1913)—"one of the great intellectual monuments of all time" as W. V. O. Quine called it.

Whitehead and Russell were led to construct the system in *Principia Mathematica* through an effort to solve certain difficulties which had appeared in a branch of mathematics now known as set theory. It turned out that the rules of set theory gave rise to contradictions (or logical paradoxes) which, unless resolvable, would indicate this fundamental branch of the subject to be defective. More than that, since set theory was a higher logical development from the more elementary parts of mathematics, it seemed that the occurrence of such contradictions showed mathematics itself to be unsound. Whitehead and Russell thus set out to investigate the foundations of mathematics, hoping to reconstruct these out of logically impeccable elements and in this way to demonstrate that the main results of classical mathematics could be accepted as correct. The attempt to carry out this program is contained in their monumental study, *Principia Mathematica*.

This work contains a deductive system, which begins with elements that are known intuitively, and which, using these elements as a foundation, constructs a more and more massive system upon them, each link in the developing chain being proved to follow rigorously from the ingredients that precede it (Euclid's *Elements* is a system of this sort, but of lesser generality and, perhaps, rigor). *Principia*, for instance, begins with a set of axioms, and gradually, by a process of deduction (which includes the additional axioms of infinity and the multiplicative axiom) expands them—deriving as a consequence a set of propositions known as "Peano's postulates." These postulates, which were first formulated by the Italian mathematician G. Peano, contains laws from which all the fundamental theorems of arithmetic can be deduced. By showing that Peano's postulates themselves rigorously follow from the axioms of *Principia*, Russell and Whitehead were, in effect, showing that classical mathematics is, to a great extent, a subdivision of logic and accordingly, that it embodies the exactness and rigor of that most precise of all disciplines. In this way, they defended the accuracy of the main achievements of classical mathematics.

This result could never have been accomplished by the use of Aristotelian logic. Aristotelian logic restricts itself to four types of sentences ("All men are mortal," "Some men are mortal," "No men are mortal," and "Some men are not mortal"). Each of these sentence types expresses a relationship which holds between a pair of classes. For example, the sentence "All men are mortal" states that the entire class of men is included in the class of mortals. But many characteristic statements of mathematics are not of this form. They may be expressed, for instance, as identities ("$2 + 2 = 4$") or as conditionals ("If we assume a and b and c . . . then d . . ."). Aristotelian logic did not apply to arguments containing such statements and hence its use in mathematical contexts was almost nil.

The logical system in *Principia* starts from a different base entirely. It contains machinery for constructing all sorts of assertive sentences, from those which are very simple ("John is mortal") to those which are much more complex ("The head of a horse is the head of an animal," "Scott is the author of Waverley," "Phillips and Lloyd were acquainted with each other," "If it rains tomorrow, then the streets will be wet," and so forth). The four types of standard sentences dealt with in classical logic thus appear in *Principia* as parts of a much larger array. Even the statements of mathematics do not begin to exhaust its inventive possibilities.

THE INFLUENCE OF
MATHEMATICAL LOGIC

The impact of *Principia* upon mathematics was understandably great; upon philosophy it was equally so. Its main effect was to give rise to the belief that *Principia Mathematica* contained an ideal language—a language which, with suitable additions, could be used to make any assertion which everyday languages, like French, German, and English, could, but which had an immense advantage over these languages: namely, that it was much more precise. Ambiguities, equivocations, and other forms of misrepresentation could not occur in its symbolism. Of course, the "language" contained in *Principia* was not, strictly speaking, a language at all. It was a symbolism, a bare logical skeleton, which nobody could learn to speak or learn to use for his everyday activities. Rather, it was the very model of a perfect language—a symbolism in which, in principle, every true statement could be expressed without vagueness or ambiguity. To those philosophers who really understood it, *Principia* thus seemed to contain a magnificent instrument—mathematical logic—which could be used, with absolute accuracy, for analyzing various kinds of statements and thus, in the end, for solving philosophical problems which otherwise had seemed intractable.

THE FORMALIST POINT OF VIEW

In the light of this brief account of the nature of mathematical logic, we are now in a position to begin to describe the two great divisions within contemporary analytical philosophy, the formalist point of view and the ordinary-language point of view. Roughly speaking, those who accept the formalist position claim the use of mathematical logic to be indispensable in solving traditional philosophical problems. Naturally there is a spectrum of differing outlooks within this movement. Some philosophers hold that a combination of logic and ordinary discourse can be used for this purpose, while others maintain that exact solutions can be arrived at only within an ideal language. Ordinary-language philosophers, on the other hand, deprecate the use of mathematical logic for philosophical purposes. They argue that typical philosophical problems arise from a misuse of ordinary discourse and accordingly, that the solutions to these problems can be obtained, so to speak, from within ordinary discourse itself. In what follows, we shall begin by considering three variations on the formalist point of view: (1) logical atomism, (2) the picture theory, and (3) logical positivism. After concluding our discussion of these, we shall turn to an examination of the ordinary-language viewpoint.

LOGICAL ATOMISM

Although it is clear that logical atomism is a philosophy directly influenced by Russell's work in mathematical logic, there is some doubt whether the credit for founding it should go to Russell himself or to the late Ludwig Wittgenstein. Russell, as a matter of fact, has added to the confusion on this point. In the preface to a published version of a group of lectures he gave in 1918, entitled "Logical Atomism," Russell remarked that the lectures are "largely concerned with explaining certain ideas which I learnt from my friend and former pupil, Ludwig Wittgenstein."[2] But in the text itself, he asserts that "the things I am going to say in these lectures are mainly my own personal opinions and I do not claim that they are more than that." In any case, since the earliest formulation of this

[2] Bertrand Russell, "The Philosophy of Logical Atomism." Reprinted in *Logic and Knowledge*, ed. by R. C. Marsh (Allen and Unwin, London, 1956), p. 177.

philosophy is to be found in these lectures of 1918, we shall begin by discussing the view contained in them first and then turn, afterward, to the not dissimilar doctrine developed by Wittgenstein in the *Tractatus Logico-Philosophicus* (1922) and sometimes called "the picture theory."

Russell opens the lectures on logical atomism by saying:

> As I have attempted to prove in *The Principles of Mathematics*, when we analyze mathematics we bring it all back to logic. It all comes back to logic in the strictest and most formal sense. In the present lectures, I shall try to set forth in a sort of outline, rather briefly and rather unsatisfactorily, a kind of logical doctrine which seems to me to result from the philosophy of mathematics—not exactly logically, but what emerges as one reflects: a certain kind of logical doctrine, and on the basis of this a certain kind of metaphysic.[3]

What was this logical doctrine—and what was the metaphysic which Russell based on it? In answering these questions, we can bring out the fundamental characteristics of logical atomism; but in order to do so, let us look again at *Principia Mathematica*, this time in a little more detail.

The Logical Doctrine

As we mentioned earlier, *Principia* contains machinery for generating compound statements out of simple ones. Russell called the most simple statements of his system "atomic propositions," and these he distinguished from more complex statements which he called "molecular propositions." Roughly speaking the difference is this: an atomic statement has no parts which are themselves statements, whereas a molecular proposition is itself composed of statements. The following examples may serve to illustrate the distinction. "Mary is blonde" is an atomic proposition, since its parts are individual words, not sentences. On the other hand, a statement like "Either the party will nominate Smith or the party will nominate Jones" is molecular. Upon examination, it can be seen to be composed of two statements: (1) "The party will nominate Smith" and (2) "The party will nominate Jones." These two statements are combined into one compound utterance by the use of the words "either . . . or."

Now it should be noticed that the statements making up this molecular proposition are both atomic in nature ("The party will nominate Jones" has no parts which are sentences). In effect, the first part of Russell's logical doctrine consisted in showing that molecular propositions are, in all cases, nothing but atomic propositions combined in various ways by the use of a small set of connecting words, such as "or," "if . . . then," "and," and "not."

---

[3] Russell, *op. cit.*, p. 178.

This part of the logical doctrine proved of great value in simplifying certain problems of philosophical analysis. Molecular sentences now seemed to present no special difficulties, since they could always be analyzed into their constituent atomic sentences, plus a residue consisting of the logical connectives (which possessed no independent meaning but were merely syntactic, that is, grammatical devices for forming compound statements out of simple ones). In a sense, then, problems about the meaning of molecular sentences had been solved—for in every case they reduced to problems about the meaning of their constituent atomic sentences. Of course, this still left unanswered the question of how one analyzes atomic sentences—but here Russell invoked the second part of the logical doctrine by way of reply.

Russell claimed that atomic sentences are always of a certain logical structure. His exact characterization of this structure is too involved to be discussed in full here, but roughly speaking, he thought that an atomic sentence must not contain more than one occurrence of a verb (it must not have parts which are themselves sentences); further that it must contain at least one proper name that functions as the subject term of that sentence; and finally that it must contain either a predicate term or a term standing for a relation. Thus, "John is tall" is an example of the first type of atomic sentence, while "John is to the right of James" is an example of the second type. But more than that, Russell believed that the meaning of the terms in an atomic sentence (exclusive of the verbs, of course) is always the "items" which these terms denote. Thus the meaning of "John" is the person, John; the meaning of "tall" is the characteristic or property of being tall; the meaning of "to the right of" is the relation, being to the right of, and so forth. Through this doctrine of denoting (or naming) Russell was led by natural steps into the metaphysical view which he subsequently called "logical atomism." Let us examine this view now.

The Metaphysic

The connection between Russell's logical doctrine and his metaphysic is a close one. Russell assumes that through the use of mathematical logic, one can discover the basic ingredients of which the world is constructed. Indeed, he means by "logical analysis" the process which, in principle, culminates in this kind of discernment. Such analysis shows us that there must be two kinds of "basic things." These Russell calls "simples" and "facts," respectively. Simples turn out to be, in accordance with the doctrine of naming, the entities denoted by the ingredients of atomic sentences—those things named by proper nouns, predicates, and relational terms. These simples have a reality not possessed by anything else. They are the ultimate constituents of "facts," so that, in a sense, they are more basic than facts themselves.

What role, then, do facts play? Facts, according to Russell, are what make some statements true and some false. For instance, the fact that John is hungry makes the statement "John is hungry" true and the statement "John is not hungry" false. There is a sense, then, in which facts are also part of the ultimate furniture of the world. For if one wanted to give a complete and true description of the world, one would have to do more than list all the simples in it. One would also have to describe all the facts there are. Indeed, the world can be thought of as being the totality of all the facts there are.

Unlike facts, simples, considered in themselves, cannot be described but only denoted or named. Thus, John, apart from the qualities he possesses or the relations in which he stands to other things, can only be denoted, not described. To describe him would be to state a fact about him (for example, John is human). Thus if one listed all the simples there are, such a list would not count as a description of the world. It would merely contain a set of otherwise unrelated names. In order to arrive at a complete description of the world, then, one would have to do more than prepare such a list. One would have to assert each member of the entire class of true atomic sentences. Each of these sentences would describe a fact. Each fact described, like the sentences about them, would be atomic, since, as Russell shows, there are no special kinds of facts corresponding to molecular statements. The totality of the true atomic sentences would constitute a complete description of reality.

Of course, since there is an indefinite number of atomic facts, it would be impossible, in practice, for anyone to describe them all. But at least in an ideal language like *Principia*, one would have an instrument for performing such a task *in principle* (every true atomic sentence could be accommodated within such a language). And thus, in principle, a complete description of the world could be arrived at within a logical language. This is why Russell describes his work in logic as culminating in an "excursus into metaphysics" or into "what there is."

Be this as it may, in order fully to understand Russell's metaphysical outlook, one should not only know his work in logic but also something about the prevailing tendencies in the philosophizing of the day—tendencies which Russell reacted against. Around the turn of the century, the main philosophical systems were types of monism, of a complicated idealistic sort. The sources of such views lay in the writings of the nineteenth-century German idealists who followed Kant, notably Fichte and Hegel. British philosophy of this period was almost entirely dominated by this type of idealism. Its main exponents were McTaggart, Bosanquet, and Bradley, all of whom were older contemporaries of Russell. These philosophers were "monists" in the sense that they claimed that reality consisted of one fundamental "stuff," and they were "idealists" in holding that this basic "stuff" was mental. The world seemed to them one vast substance all of whose parts were indissolubly linked to all others. Reality, they asserted, was accordingly not composed of discrete, separate things but was a homogeneous totality, an absolute "mind."

Russell, as we have said, reacted strongly to this doctrine. In his opinion it ran counter to the common-sense view that there are many individual, real things in the world, some of which, at least, are surely nonmental. In mathematical logic, he seemed to find strong support for his belief. Logic, he felt, showed the world to be made up of a multiplicity of things or "simples" which were not logically tied to one another in a single homogeneous totality. There was thus not *one* fundamental "stuff" but many discrete, particular things which formed the basic material of the world. Moreover, such "simples" were not "mental" as the idealists had asserted. Being simple, they possessed no characteristics in themselves whatsoever. They merely existed. Of course, they could occur in the sorts of complexes Russell called "facts," and some of these facts could be labeled as "physical" and some as "mental." But the simples composing such facts were neither physical nor mental—they were just what they were and nothing more could be said about them.

As can be seen from this account, these ultimate entities or simples play much the same role in Russell's philosophy that atoms do in the metaphysical systems of the ancient Greek thinkers Democritus and Epicurus. Recognizing this, Russell described his theory as a form of atomism. But since he had arrived at his "atoms" through logical analysis, he labeled his system "logical atomism" to distinguish it from the earlier doctrines.

The Theory of Descriptions

In concluding our account of Russell's version of logical atomism, it may be useful to explain, in more detail, why he is to be classified (1) as an analytic philosopher and (2) as a formalist. As we have pointed out, it is characteristic of analysts that they look upon (at least) some philosophical problems as being the products of linguistically grounded conceptual confusion. "Formalists" form a subgroup of analysts who claim that such confusion can be dispelled via the media of ideal languages, like the language contained in *Principia Mathematica*. That Russell is both an "analyst" and a "formalist," as we use these terms, can be shown by even a summary account of one of his most famous doctrines, *the theory of descriptions*, one of the main bulwarks of logical atomism.

From the time of Plato onward, philosophers had wondered how it is possible to make significant, and sometimes even true, statements about fictitious objects, unless these objects existed in some sense. For instance, if it is true to say "Hamlet murdered Polonius" or "The Fountain of

Youth does not exist," then are we not, in some sense or other, talking about the entities, Hamlet, Polonius, and the Fountain of Youth? But if we can speak significantly about these things, then do they not exist?

Russell's answer was a firm "no." His attempt to explain how such remarks can be meaningful—and sometimes even true—without thereby implying that such entities exist is the main burden of his theory of descriptions. The theory itself is complex; without attempting to explain it in detail, let us discuss its main features.

Russell makes a sharp distinction between what he calls a "description" and what he calls a "proper name." By a description, he means a linguistic expression having a certain logical form—it must be a phrase and it must be either of the form "the so and so" or of the form "a so and so." Examples of such phrases are expressions like "the queen of England" and "a queen of England." Phrases of the former sort he calls "definite descriptions," since they connote uniqueness (they suggest we are speaking about one person or thing only), while phrases of the latter sort he calls "indefinite descriptions," since they are not subject to the uniqueness limitation.

By a proper name, on the other hand, Russell means a symbol which names only a particular person or thing and whose sole meaning is the particular person or thing which it names. "Richard Nixon" is such a symbol. The meaning of this expression is literally Mr. Nixon himself. Nothing can be a proper name, in Russell's sense, unless there is actually something which it denotes (that is, unless the thing exists); thus nothing can be both a proper name and meaningless. This is why, if we know that an expression is a proper name, we can also know that what it names must exist.

Both proper names and descriptions play important roles in the use of language. But their roles are very different. Through the medium of proper names, we connect up language with reality. The existence of such names assures us that language speaks about the world and the things in it. The connection is made through the act of naming or denoting, since the very meaning of such words is the items to which they refer. But descriptions have a radically different use. They enable us to speak about objects with which we are not (and perhaps could not be) acquainted.

I can speak meaningfully about Julius Caesar, for example; but I have never been acquainted with him. Yet I have a tremendous amount of information about him—the date of his birth, to whom he was married, and when and where he died. How is all this possible? Russell's answer is that whatever knowledge I possess about Caesar I possess by description. I come to understand true sentences containing definite descriptive phrases about Caesar. What I am directly acquainted with, therefore, are certain linguistic expressions—words in books or words uttered by my teachers. But my knowledge is not based upon direct acquaintance with Caesar himself.

Now it is characteristic of sentences containing descriptions that they can occur in meaningful statements even when such statements are false. In such a case, the descriptions refer to nothing at all. For example, if I say "The Roman general who invented the airplane was clever," this statement is perfectly meaningful—but it is false, for the description "The Roman general who invented the airplane" refers to no one. This shows that descriptive phrases, unlike proper names, can occur in significant statements without necessarily referring to anything.

The situation is, of course, more complicated than we have made out so far. Sometimes symbols seem to be proper names, but are not. Thus, a word like "Hamlet" seems more like a proper name such as "Richard Nixon" than it does like the description "The Roman general who invented the airplane." But "Hamlet" is not a proper name, since proper names must name something and there is nothing which "Hamlet" names. All that I know about Hamlet, therefore, I come to know through the media of statements containing descriptive phrases—namely that "Hamlet was the prince of Denmark who spurned Ophelia" or "Hamlet was the prince of Denmark who killed Laertes," and so on. The word "Hamlet" is thus, for Russell, a disguised description—or more accurately, an abbreviation for a descriptive phrase like "the prince of Denmark"—and not a genuine proper name.

In the light of the distinction between descriptions and proper names, Russell diagnoses the confusion which has led certain thinkers to believe that such entities as "the Fountain of Youth," "Hamlet," "Medusa," and "the round square" exist. The confusion has developed because these authors have assumed such words to be proper names and then inferred from this that they denote items of the world whenever they occur in significant statements. Russell's point is that they are not proper names and hence the inference is unwarranted.

Mathematical logic plays an important role in this theory. The appeal to the ideal language contained in *Principia* enables Russell to state in detail how sentences containing descriptions differ from those containing proper names, and therefore why they do not necessarily denote anything. In the ideal language, it will be recalled, all statements that directly denote facts are atomic statements. This is so because all facts are atomic, never molecular. But when we translate sentences containing definite descriptions into such a language, the resulting statements are never atomic. For example, if we render "The queen of England is wise" into the symbolism of *Principia*, this statement turns out to be a molecular statement, composed of three *general* statements, namely: (1) someone is monarch of England and female, (2) not more than one person is monarch of England and female, and (3) whoever is monarch of England and female is wise.

These three sentences which, taken together, give us the "analysis" or "real meaning" of the original statement, do not contain the phrase "*the* queen of England" or any other expression functioning as a subject term, which could be thought to be a proper name. Since in this translation we have unpacked the meaning contained in the original statement, it must never have contained a genuine proper name at all—it merely seemed to.

Once this is realized, the problem of explaining how sentences containing supposed proper names can be significant without necessarily denoting anything vanishes. The problem arose only because it was believed that such sentences were atomic sentences containing proper names. The error giving rise to the resulting conceptual confusion was thus, at bottom, linguistic, produced by a misconception of the role which descriptions play in language. In finding the remedy for such confusion in an ideal language which clearly differentiates between proper names and descriptions, Russell shows himself to be within the formalist wing of the analytic movement.[4]

LOGICAL ATOMISM AND THE PICTURE THEORY

In 1922, Wittgenstein published the *Tractatus Logico-Philosophicus*, one of the most remarkable and highly influential works written in philosophy in this century. It is remarkable not only for the profundity of its ideas and for the influence which it has exercised upon the subsequent course of analytical philosophy but also' for its style. It is written in a cryptic, terse, aphoristic manner. Each aphorism summarizes a long chain of implicit argumentation, sometimes so succinctly as to be barely intelligible, even to the initiated. Because of this mode of presentation, the book has lent itself to various interpretations. But almost all authorities agree that in it Wittgenstein is at least propounding a version of logical atomism not fundamentally different from that of Russell but much more intensively developed. Wittgenstein's version is often called "the picture theory," since one of its main theses suggests that significant utterance is possible because language "pictures" or "mirrors" reality.

The sense in which language "pictures" reality is analogous to the sense in which a map "pictures" the terrain to which it refers. What is

---

[4] It should be mentioned that many contemporary philosophers who construct formalized languages to solve philosophical problems do not subscribe to Russell's definition of "logically proper name," or even to his theory of descriptions.

characteristic of a map, Wittgenstein points out, is that for every point of the map, there is a correspondence between the elements of the map and the elements on the ground. This, or at least a similar, correspondence relation holds between language and reality. When we utter a true atomic statement, there is a one-to-one correspondence (an "isomorphism") between the elements in the statement and the things it speaks about. Thus, for every proper name there is a corresponding entity, for every predicate expression there is a corresponding property or quality, for every relational term a corresponding relation. When a statement is false, however, this correspondence breaks down. In such a case there is some incongruity between the elements in the statement and the things it speaks about.

Obviously, the concept of an ideal language is suggested by this view. Wittgenstein does not suppose that actual, spoken languages (like English) accurately picture the facts they purport to describe. Indeed, like Russell, he supposes that much conceptual confusion arises from the capacity of natural languages to give misleading pictures of reality. It is only in an ideal, purified language that we find statements which mirror the facts they purport to represent. In holding to this view, Wittgenstein— at this period—was clearly a formalist; but, as we shall see in a moment, this was a view he later abandoned.

THE *TRACTATUS* AND
LOGICAL POSITIVISM

The *Tractatus* contained not only a fully worked-out statement of the views which Russell had suggested in his lectures on logical atomism but also the seeds of a very different sort of philosophy, one which, as things turned out, proved highly antagonistic to logical atomism. This was *logical positivism* (or *logical empiricism*, as it was also known) which swept over the philosophical world during the 1920s and 1930s. The logical positivists utilized Russell's technical work in logic as part of a program designed to show that *any* sort of metaphysical doctrine was nonsense; and since logical atomism was admittedly metaphysics in the most obvious sense of that term, it was rejected by them along with most of the traditional philosophical systems. Of course, Russell's work in pure logic was exempted from this proscription, and only the metaphysical ramifications which he thought his work implied were condemned.

The full story of the role which the *Tractatus* played in the development of logical positivism is exceedingly complex. In tracing its influence, we are bound to distort the historical picture somewhat. But the following account contains the essentials of a correct explanation, even if it is somewhat shy in detail.

In discussing, in the *Tractatus*, the conditions under which language can significantly refer to the real world, Wittgenstein was led to the following view. Every *meaningful* statement, he argued, falls into one or the other of two categories. It is either "logically determinate" or "factually determinate."[5] He also maintained that no statement could belong to both categories at the same time. By a logically determinate statement, he meant one whose truth or falsity can be determined or arrived at by purely logical methods. A statement like "$2 + 2 = 4$" is an example of such a statement. If we analyze it, it can be seen to reduce to a law of logic, in this case to a statement having the logical form "$a = a$." Thus upon replacing the numbers 2 and 4 by their definitions, we arrive at the following statement, namely, $1 + 1 + 1 + 1 = 1 + 1 + 1 + 1$. The two expressions which flank the "$=$" sign are obviously identical with each other; the sentence in question is thus a special case of the law of identity, one of the basic logical laws. Such statements as "All bachelors are unmarried" or "No spinsters are married" are logically determinate in this sense. In order to show that they are true, we do not have to conduct any actual investigation into the marital status of bachelors or spinsters; we merely have to understand what the statements mean. Once we understand them, we can see that they mean, respectively, "All unmarried males are unmarried" and "No unmarried females are married." These statements are again thus reducible to special cases of the law of identity.

Now Wittgenstein argued that *all* the truths of mathematics and logic (as well as certain statements in ordinary discourse) are logically determinate in this sense, namely, that they can be ascertained to be true by an examination of their logical form and independently of any matter of fact. Or putting it otherwise, but equivalently, he argued that these statements are true "by definition," meaning in this case that they can be determined to be true by virtue of the meanings of the words which compose them.

From this analysis, Wittgenstein drew a very impressive consequence. He argued that if the statements of mathematics and logic have this characteristic, they cannot tell us anything about the real world. His contention, in effect, was that from the truth of a statement which is logically determinate nothing follows about what does or does not exist. This can be seen from an example like the following. It is true that all giants are tall; but from the truth of this statement, it does not follow that there are giants. Wittgenstein inferred from this and similar examples that no logically determinate statement has any "existential" import.

He thus argued that if any statement is to give us information about the world, it must be factually determinate—decidable only by an appeal

---

[5] This is Rudolf Carnap's terminology rather than Wittgenstein's. We have adopted it, rather than Wittgenstein's own usage, because it lends itself more readily to simple exposition.

to matters of fact. Even though we understand all the words in the sentence "Russell's typewriter is black," we cannot determine, without some sort of factual inquiry, whether this sentence is true or not. But if such a statement is true, it follows immediately that at least one typewriter exists.

Wittgenstein utilized the distinction between logically and factually determinate statements in a way which greatly influenced the logical positivists. For he went on to contend that every statement which is factually determinate belongs to one or another of the empirical sciences. Thus, a statement like "All bodies fall at 32 feet per sec" belongs to physics; a statement like "All men are motivated by self-interest" belongs to psychology, and so forth. He was thus led to the view that every meaningful statement belongs either to logic (in the sense in which logic includes mathematics as a subcase) or to one of the empirical sciences.

Since philosophy was neither logic, in this sense, nor an experimental science, Wittgenstein concluded that the statements of philosophy, including his own in the *Tractatus*, were all literally nonsensical.

LOGICAL POSITIVISM AND THE
PRINCIPLE OF VERIFICATION

Wittgenstein's views in the *Tractatus* have often been described as a form of *scientism*—the doctrine that science alone can give us information about matters of fact. This, at least, was the interpretation given to the *Tractatus* by the members of the Vienna Circle, as it was called, a group of thinkers who met informally in Vienna during the middle 1920s to discuss philosophy. Most of the members of the circle had scientific backgrounds, and hence the doctrines contained in the *Tractatus* were very congenial to them (Moritz Schlick, the leader of the group, had a Ph.D. in physics; Hans Hahn was a mathematician; Rudolf Carnap, a mathematician and logician; Otto Neurath, a social scientist; and so on). The views they propounded, in part as a result of reading the *Tractatus*, came to be known as *logical positivism* or *logical empiricism*.

These philosophers agreed with Wittgenstein that the class of meaningful statements was divided into those which were logically determinate and those which were factually determinate. But at this point, they were faced with a problem: how did one tell whether a given statement was significant—how could one decide upon reading or hearing a group of words that they belonged to one or the other of the two classes mentioned above.

Statements which belonged to the class of logically determinate utterances seemed to them to present no special difficulty. They assumed that the logical techniques developed by Russell and Whitehead could enable anyone to decide (at least in most cases) whether a given statement was logically determinate or not. The more serious difficulty arose with those statements which purported to describe reality, or matters of fact, but which seemed to belong to none of the usual sciences. Utterances such as "God has infinitely many attributes" or "Reality is mental" fell into this category. How did one decide whether utterances such as these were factually meaningful or not (it was, of course, clear that they were not logically determinate).

Their answer consisted in laying down a principle which would enable one to decide such questions. This principle is usually called the *principle of verification*. Although it can be—indeed has been—formulated in many different ways, the essential idea behind it maintains that a statement has factual meaning if, and only if, it is empirically verifiable. This, of course, shifts the issue to what is meant by "empirical verifiability"—and here the answer is somewhat more complex.

A typical answer to this question is that given by A. J. Ayer in his book *Language, Truth and Logic*, published in 1936. According to Professor Ayer:

> A statement is factually significant to a given person if and only if he knows how to verify the proposition which it purports to express; that is, if he knows what observations would lead him under certain conditions to accept the proposition as being true, or reject it as being false.[6]

The key term in this statement of the principle is the word "observation." The point of the principle is that it must be possible to describe the sorts of observations one would have to make in order to determine whether a sentence is true or false. If observations could be described which would count toward determining the truth or the falsity of a given utterance, then the utterance is to be counted as meaningful; if not, then as meaningless in the factual sense.

Even this explanation is not complete, though. At least one further distinction must be made before the full meaning of "empirically verifiable" can be understood. This is the distinction between the *technical* possibility of verifying a statement and the possibility of verifying it *in principle*.

If this distinction is invoked, then certain obvious difficulties in the application of the principle are immediately eliminated. For instance, it is clear that a statement like "There are canals on Uranus" is meaningful. But in one sense of the term this statement is not verifiable. Given present-

---

[6] A. J. Ayer, *Language, Truth and Logic*, 2d ed. (Gollancz, London, 1948), p. 35.

day astronomical equipment and present-day limitations upon the possibility of travel in outer space, there is nothing anyone can do either to confirm or disconfirm this statement. But no positivist would therefore say that it is factually meaningless. For *in principle*, they point out, it is empirically verifiable. One can state what kind of observations would count for or against its truth. These might be observations one could make by improving existing telescopes, or observations one could make if one could actually travel to Uranus. We know *now* what sorts of observations would prove relevant for deciding the question, and this is why the statement is meaningful. But to say, on the other hand, that a statement is unverifiable *in principle* is to say that no observations one could make under any conditions would serve to prove it true or serve to prove it false.

To illustrate what is meant by saying that a statement is unverifiable *in principle*, Moritz Schlick produced a striking example of such an utterance. Suppose, he said, somebody were to assert that the whole universe was shrinking uniformly. Suppose, further, that by the phrase "uniformly" this person intended to imply that everything in the universe was shrinking proportionately to everything else. This would include of course all the apparatus we use for making measurements, including such things as tapes and yardsticks. Now if everything were to shrink uniformly in this way, Schlick went on to say, then there would be no measurable or discernible difference in the world after the supposed shrinkage had taken place. For if we were to measure a room after it had shrunk, the results of our measurement would be the same as they would have been before the shrinkage took place, since our measuring sticks would have shrunk proportionately, too. There is thus no conceivable observation we could make which would either deny or confirm the statement that the universe is shrinking uniformly—and if not, then the statement has no factual meaning whatsoever. *In principle*, it is empirically unverifiable.

Like Wittgenstein, the positivists assumed that most of the traditional statements of philosophy were factually meaningless in this sense. No observation could verify, even in principle, such statements as "Reality is mental," "Only I exist," "There are no physical objects," and so forth. But, unlike Wittgenstein, they did not therefore assert that all philosophical statements were necessarily nonsensical or metaphysical. They felt that philosophy had a positive function, that it could be used for purposes of clarification, for the resolution of conceptual difficulties of one sort or another. Philosophy when properly pursued, they argued, was thus identical with logical analysis.

By "logical analysis," though, they did not mean an activity of the sort which Russell had described, an activity resulting in the discovery of the ultimate constituents of reality. In accordance with Wittgenstein's views in the *Tractatus*, they felt that only science could tell us anything about the basic features of the world. Nor did they mean by "analysis" an activity in which statements in ordinary discourse are translated into statements which exhibit their *real* meaning. This conception of "analysis" was suggested by Russell's work in the theory of descriptions and was made explicit by Wittgenstein in working out the picture theory. Any conception which involved an appeal to "real" meanings or to a notion of "logical form" which mirrored reality was regarded by them as metaphysical.

Instead they thought of logical analysis as a branch of science, a branch which was a combination of mathematics and physics. The purpose of this branch of science was to explicate, or make clear, some of the main concepts of science and ordinary life, such as "law," "cause," "motive," "drive," "demand," and so forth. The explicating sentences themselves were not nonsensical, as Wittgenstein had maintained. Instead they were logically determinate statements of a well-formed (mathematical) language, which were about statements and terms occurring in the language of science or even everyday language. Philosophers who adopted this point of view were thus "formalists" who refused to concede any metaphysical status to the language of mathematics.

Rudolf Carnap (1891–1970) was perhaps the outstanding exponent of this point of view. The following passage from his book *The Logical Syntax of Language*, published in 1934, lucidly summarizes this outlook:

> The fact that Wittgenstein does not believe in the possibility of the exact formulation of the sentences of the logic of science has as its consequence that he does not demand any scientific exactitude in his own formulations, and that he draws no sharp line of demarcation between the formulations of the logic of science and those of metaphysics. In the following discussion we shall see that translatability into the formal mode of speech—that is, into syntactical sentences—is the criterion which separates the proper sentences of the logic of science from the other philosophical sentences—we may call them metaphysical.
>
> In spite of this difference of opinion, I agree with Wittgenstein that there are no special sentences of the logic of science (or philosophy). The sentences of the logic of science are formulated as syntactical sentences about the language of science; but no new domain in addition to that of science itself is thereby created. The sentences of syntax are in part sentences of arithmetic, and in part sentences of physics, and they are only called syntactical because they are concerned with linguistic constructions, or, more specifically, with their formal structure. Syntax, pure and descriptive, is nothing more than the mathematics and physics of language.[7]

[7] Rudolf Carnap, *Logical Syntax of Language* (Routledge & Kegan Paul, London, 1949), p. 284.

It should be mentioned, in passing, that not all philosophers who called themselves "logical positivists" accepted this extreme conception of analysis. Some held a more moderate position, arguing that the function of analysis is to take any problem, to show which questions in it are capable of being answered by mathematical reasoning or which questions are capable of being answered by some sort of empirical investigation. These philosophers claimed that it is not the function of the philosopher, as such, to answer these questions: it is merely his function to clarify the meaning of the questions so that one will know what sort of questions they are and how to proceed to answer them.

In particular, philosophical problems of the traditional sort, they asserted, are very complex. They are a composite of a whole host of queries, puzzles, and questions, some of which are answerable only by empirical investigation and some of which require mathematical techniques for their solution. Some questions are the products of emotion and bias; some are simply senseless for one reason or another. Philosophical analysis is thus conceived by these writers as a process which is preliminary to any sort of answer to a question. But the analyst himself suggests no answers. His activities merely are directed toward making sensible answers possible. Philosophy, as thus conceived, makes no claims about the world, as Russell had maintained.

THE ORDINARY-LANGUAGE POINT OF VIEW

G. E. Moore

The writings of G. E. Moore (1873–1958) greatly affected the development of the second main wing of the analytical movement, the *ordinary-language point of view*, as we have called it.[8] Moore differed in certain important respects from the philosophers who were to become identified with this point of view, but at least in two ways his work influenced them. For one thing, Moore thought of himself primarily as a defender of common sense. The ordinary-language philosophers, like the logical positivists who preceded them, were antimetaphysical in their outlook—and they interpreted Moore's defense of common sense as having this implication. Strictly speaking, this was a mistake. For Moore, under the influence of Russell, was deeply involved throughout his career in

---

[8] Moore's academic career began as a student at Cambridge, and continued, first, as a university lecturer there (from 1911 until 1925) and then as professor, until his retirement in 1937, when his chair was occupied by Wittgenstein. He received the Order of Merit in 1951.

traditional metaphysical speculations, both in ethics and in the theory of knowledge. Indeed, he looked upon his defense of common sense as supporting a form of traditional realism which stood in opposition to the idealist tendencies which had dominated British philosophy during the last part of the nineteenth century.

In any case, it was the second aspect of Moore's work which had the most impact upon these writers. This was the method or technique which Moore constantly used in defending his common-sense outlook. This technique importantly involved an appeal to the ordinary, common, everyday use of language. It was thus not *what* Moore was defending that impressed them so much as *how* he conducted the defense. Moore himself never became singularly self-conscious about his philosophical method; he utilized it because he regarded it as an effective weapon in the battle against his opponents. It was the ordinary-language philosophers who, looking back at Moore's work, saw there the ingredients of a powerful technique which had philosophical implications in its own right. They were to work out these implications in ways which Moore, at that time, could never have suspected and doubtless would not have approved of had he foreseen them. What, then, was the method that so greatly impressed them?

As a supporter of the common-sense outlook, Moore was led to reject any philosophical explanation which ran counter to certain statements that, as a man of common sense, he knew to be true. For instance, if as the result of a complicated argument, a philosopher (like Berkeley) accepted the "paradoxical" view that no physical objects exist, Moore assumed there must be something wrong with the argument—since, as a man of common sense, he knew, with absolute certainty, that physical objects do exist. If it was then contended by the philosopher that nobody could "know" anything with absolute certainty, Moore rejected this further claim by pointing out that in the ordinary, common, everyday sense of "know" this is not true. If the philosopher who says that we cannot "know" anything means this statement in the ordinary sense of those words, then he is palpably mistaken and the statement is to be rejected out of hand. If he means them in some other sense, then they do not attack the common-sense position at all—and, in fact, are irrelevant to it.

Moore's constant appeal to ordinary discourse, to the familiar, normal employment of words as a means of showing that the philosopher's use of them is often wildly paradoxical, or even nonsensical, was one of the two major influences in the development of the ordinary-language movement. The other, which was even more important, was connected with a radical change in Wittgenstein's philosophical outlook, a change which took place in the early 1930s. These two sources produced the new movement as we now know it.

Wittgenstein in His Later Period

Wittgenstein's *Tractatus* ends with the following propositions:

> 6.53   The right method of philosophy would be this. To say nothing
> except what can be said, i.e., the propositions of natural science,
> i.e., something that has nothing to do with philosophy: and then
> always, when someone else wished to say something metaphysical,
> to demonstrate to him that he had given no meaning to certain
> signs in his propositions. This method would be unsatisfying to the
> other—he would not have the feeling that we were teaching him
> philosophy—but it would be the only strictly correct method.[9]

> 6.54   My propositions are elucidatory in this way: he who understands
> me finally recognizes them as senseless, when he has climbed out
> through them, on them, over them. (He must so to speak throw
> away the ladder, after he has climbed up on it.) He must surmount
> these propositions; then he sees the world rightly.[10]

> 7.   Whereof one cannot speak, thereof one must remain silent.[11]

Thinking that in this work he had solved all philosophical problems,
Wittgenstein followed the advice contained in these final comments of the
Tractatus. After World War I, he gave up philosophy, worked for a time
as a school teacher in Lower Austria, and then occupied himself with
building a house for his sister in Vienna.[12] During this period, he was not
entirely cut off from philosophical contact, forming personal friendships
with some of the members of the Vienna Circle, among them Moritz
Schlick, Friedrich Waismann and Herbert Feigl. But, according to some
reports, it was a lecture given in Vienna in 1928 by the famous intuitionist
Dutch mathematician L. J. Brouwer which stimulated him to take up
philosophy again. Shortly after this lecture, he decided to return to Cambridge. It was decided there that he could present the *Tractatus*, published
some eight years earlier and already a famous book, as a doctoral dis-

---

[9] Ludwig Wittgenstein, *Tractatus Logico-Philosophicus*, ed. by C. K. Ogdon
(Routledge & Kegan Paul, London, 1922), p. 187.

[10] *Ibid.*, p. 189.

[11] *Ibid.*, p. 189.

[12] Wittgenstein was born in Vienna in 1889 and died in England in 1951. He
first came to England as a research student in the department of engineering at the
University of Manchester in 1911. At the advice of Frege, he went to Cambridge
in 1912 to study with Russell. While there he kept a series of notebooks (now published as the *Notebooks* of 1913–1914) from which the doctrines of the *Tractatus*
were ultimately to grow. When World War I broke out, Wittgenstein entered the
Austrian army. He was taken prisoner by the Italians in 1918, and spent some
months in captivity. When captured he had with him the manuscript of the *Tractatus*
which he had completed while on leave in Vienna in 1918. While in captivity he
sent a copy of this work to Russell, and through Russell's efforts it was published
in 1921.

sertation. With Moore and Russell as members of his "thesis" committee, he was awarded the Ph.D. in June 1929. In 1930, he was made a fellow at Trinity College, and in 1937 succeeded G. E. Moore as professor at Cambridge.

Whether his return to Cambridge stimulated him to rethink the doctrines propounded in the *Tractatus* or whether he had already begun to revise these views is not clear. But as early as 1930 he completed a lengthy manuscript (first published posthumously in 1964 under the title *Philosophische Bemerkungen*) which is a transition document; though some of the main ideas of the *Tractatus* are retained, it already heralds new developments in his thought. In 1933–1934, he gave a series of lectures which were preserved by his students in the form of mimeographed notes, and circulated by them without Wittgenstein's permission. These notes came to be known as the *Blue Book*, a title deriving from the cover of the notebook. In 1935, a similar set of notes appeared, this time in a brown notebook and was therefore called the *Brown Book*. Though never authorized by Wittgenstein, these works created a sensation among those who read them. They revealed a powerful mind, grappling in a new and profound way with philosophical problems. In these monographs, the break with the philosophy of the *Tractatus* becomes complete.

During the next two decades, Wittgenstein worked feverishly at philosophy. But the full impact of his research was not felt until after his death in 1951, for he published nothing during this period. In 1949 he completed a lengthy manuscript, originally begun in 1936, which was published posthumously under the title *Philosophical Investigations*. This is the chief work of his later period; in it the questions raised in the *Blue Book* and the *Brown Book* are explored in further depth; new issues are brought out and treated expansively. Since that time, additional writings have been edited and made available for publication by his literary executors, Miss G. E. M. Anscombe and G. H. von Wright. Among the most important of these are *Zettel* (*Snippings*, 1967) and *Uber Gewissheit* (*On Certainty*, 1969). According to Professor Norman Malcolm much additional material still remains to be edited; the total corpus of Wittgenstein's writings when available will thus run to many volumes.

Wittgenstein's "New" Philosophy

Because Wittgenstein's later philosophy is not presented in a neat or systematic form, it is difficult to summarize, especially in a brief compass. Not only are the main themes developed with great subtlety, but they merge into one another so that it is often difficult to determine where a given line of inquiry begins or ends. Wittgenstein himself recognized the difficulty, but thought it was unavoidable, being necessary to the nature of the investigation. There is probably no better simple description of the style of the *Investigations* than he himself gives in the Preface:

> The thoughts which I publish in what follows are the precipitate of philosophical investigations which have occupied me for the last sixteen years. They concern many subjects: the concepts of meaning, of understanding, of a proposition, of logic, the foundations of mathematics, states of consciousness, and other things. I have written down all these thoughts as *remarks*, short paragraphs, of which there is sometimes a fairly long chain about the same subject, while I sometimes make a sudden change, jumping from one topic to another. It was my intention at first to bring all this together in a book whose form I pictured differently at different times. But the essential thing was that the thoughts should proceed from one subject to another in a natural order and without breaks.
>
> After several unsuccessful attempts to weld my results together into such a whole, I realized that I should never succeed. The best that I could write would never be more than philosophical remarks; my thoughts were soon crippled if I tried to force them on in any single direction against their natural inclination. And this was, of course, connected with the very nature of the investigation. For this compels us to travel over a wide field of thought criss-cross in every direction. The philosophical remarks in this book are, as it were, a number of sketches of landscapes which were made in the course of these long and involved journeyings.[13]

These comments apply to the *Blue Book* and the *Brown Book*, which are also composed of similar "sketches of landscapes." The initial impression upon even a sophisticated reader is that each of these works is fragmented and kaleidoscopic; yet a deeper study indicates that certain fundamental themes run through all of them. Each of these works in fact contains a similar pattern of development, beginning with questions concerning meaning and naming, questions that tie his later work directly into the main subjects of the *Tractatus*. These questions merge into questions about the nature of language itself, how it is learned and taught, and what the relation of meaning and naming are to these processes. This leads to the development of a notion called "language games" in terms of which the teaching and use of language are explained. But language games in turn work according to certain rules, and this subject leads Wittgenstein to ask "What is a rule?" and "What is it to follow a rule?" In the *Blue Book*, for instance, these issues are posed in terms of brilliant questions: "If you are whistling a tune and are interrupted, how do you know how to go on?" From these considerations, Wittgenstein moves on to remarks about the nature of philosophy; what sort of a discipline it is and what its results can hope to achieve, and in particular why philosophy tends to give rise to

[13] Ludwig Wittgenstein, *Philosophical Investigations*, trans. by G. E. M. Anscombe (Basil Blackwell, Oxford, 1958), p. ix^e.

paradoxical views about the nature of language. This discussion is closely connected with an attack upon the search for essences—for the essence of language—and that in turn leads to a new theory which attempts to explain "common characteristics" in terms of family resemblances rather than essences. From these considerations, the argument moves on to discuss the question of whether there can be a *Private Language*, that is, a language which only one person can speak. This raises issues about whether a language which reports "pains" would be such a language, and this then in turn gives way to a discussion of the nature of the mind. The *Blue Book*, for instance, which opens with the question "What is the meaning of a word?" ends with a remark about the nature of the mind, "The kernel of our proposition that that which has pains or sees or thinks is of a mental nature is only that the word 'I' in 'I have pains' does not denote a particular body, for we can't substitute for 'I' a description of a body." The *Investigations* has a similar pattern of development. It opens with a theory of meaning and naming which Wittgenstein himself held in the *Tractatus*—the Picture Theory as we called it earlier—and ends with such comments as "Remembering has no experiential content . . . I get the *idea* of a memory-content only because I assimilate psychological concepts. It is like assimilating two *games*. (Football has *goals*, tennis does not.)" The pattern of development in each of these important works runs from questions concerning logic and language to questions of philosophical psychology. In the end, the wheel comes full circle, since the issues of naming and meaning are seen to be directly connected with issues about the nature of the human mind.

It is, of course, in the theory of meaning and its relation to language that the great break with the doctrines of the *Tractatus* takes place. Wittgenstein begins the *Investigations* by quoting from St. Augustine on the nature of language. The doctrine which he finds in this quotation he describes as follows:

> These words, it seems to me, give us a particular picture of the essence of human language. It is this: the individual words in language name objects—sentences are combinations of such names.—In this picture of language we find the roots of the following idea: Every word has a meaning. This meaning is correlated with the word. It is the object for which the word stands.
>
> Augustine does not speak of there being any difference between kinds of words. If you describe the learning of language in this way you are, I believe, thinking primarily of nouns like "table," "chair," "bread," and of people's names, and only secondarily of the names of certain actions and properties; and of the remaining kinds of words as something that will take care of itself.[14]

14 Wittgenstein, *Investigations*, p. 2ᵉ.

But though the quotation is from St. Augustine, Wittgenstein is really talking about himself, about the view he advanced in the *Tractatus*—the so-called Picture Theory, which in turn was connected with the doctrine of logical atomism. According to the Picture Theory, significant discourse is possible about the world because the elementary sentences of such discourse mirror the world; and this is due to the fact that their elements— conceived of as logical atoms—stand in a one to one correspondence with the individual elements of the world. As we remarked earlier, the resulting picture of language is that it has a simple essence: namely, its basic propositions can be significant because they stand in an isomorphic mapping relation to the world.

It is this whole conception of what language is, and how it works, that Wittgenstein now rejects. The new view shows that language has no simple essence; that it is an enormously complicated activity, learned in a variety of ways and used in ways too numerous to count. All this is explained in terms of language games which, in the *Investigations*, are simple, complete languages in which various uses of language and various learning processes are represented. Such a simple procedure, Wittgenstein describes in the following way:

> I send someone shopping. I give him a slip marked "five red apples." He takes the slip to the shopkeeper, who opens the drawer marked "apples"; then he looks up the word "red" in a table and finds a colour sample opposite it; then he says the series of cardinal numbers— I assume that he knows them by heart—up to the word "five" and for each number he takes an apple of the same colour as the sample out of the drawer. It is in this and similar ways that one operates with words. "But how does he know where and how he is to look up the word 'red' and what he is to do with the word 'five' "—Well, I assume that he *acts* as I have described. Explanations come to an end somewhere. But what is the meaning of the word "five"? No such thing was in question here, only how the word "five" is used.[15]

In everyday language, which is a very complicated kind of "language game," the procedures are still more diverse. And there is nothing in common between these languages, no "essence" they all have. Instead, they exhibit family resemblances, a "complicated network of similarities overlapping and criss-crossing: sometimes overall similarities, sometimes similarities of detail."

It is the search for an essence, the search for the "real" meaning behind the everyday flow of experience, which characterizes the activity of the philosopher. He is driven by the impulse to find a simple picture, a simple model which will fit all phenomena and in terms of which he can

---

[15] Wittgenstein, *Investigations*, p. 3ᵉ.

understand them. The theory of meaning thus gives way to a theory about the nature of philosophical activity, and it is to this subject that we now turn, attempting to connect it up with the foregoing remarks.

For Wittgenstein, typical philosophical "problems" have the peculiarity that they cannot be solved either by mathematical or empirical procedures (in part, this is why any attempt to solve them by means of an ideal language will prove abortive). The reason for this is that they involve "perplexities" that arise from the attempt of a reflective person to give a theoretically satisfactory picture of facts which are known to him. In giving such a picture, the person in question is not attempting to discover new facts (to make a scientific contribution). Instead, he is trying to order these facts in a way which makes them seem significant to him. He is, in short, trying to give a general explanation of the world. But the results of this activity often issue in statements that are unverifiable and run counter to common sense. As Wittgenstein says in a remarkable passage: "Language is a labyrinth of paths. You approach from one side and know your way about; you approach the same place from another side and no longer know your way about." Thus, the man who says "Everybody is basically selfish" is aware of the fact that some people are motivated to act only in their own interest, and that some people are motivated to act so as to further the interests of others—yet he is inclined to describe both sets of people as "selfish." In doing this, something has gone wrong with his way of characterizing or describing these facts. The result is perplexity, because he is inclined to say both that such people are selfish and yet, in view of the obviously contrary facts, that they are not selfish. In the end, he does not know what to say.

How, then, is such perplexity to be resolved? Not by an appeal to the facts, since the man suffering from such perplexity knows the facts as well as anyone. His problem is that he does not know how to describe them. The solution to this problem, accordingly, does not consist in giving him new information, but (as Wittgenstein puts it) "by arranging what we have always known." We must convince him that the *ordinary* way of describing these facts is the correct way. "What we do," Wittgenstein says, "is to bring words back from their metaphysical to their everyday use."

What has caused our reflective man to fall into this kind of intellectual confusion are certain subtle misuses of ordinary language. In one way or another, he has gradually extended the ordinary uses of words in ways which importantly change their meaning. He may, as a consequence, begin to doubt that his normal, unhesitating application of these words is in fact correct. When this occurs, he is in the state of perplexity described above. The way to resolve such perplexity, therefore, is to exhibit the ordinary, correct use of the key terms in his discourse in order to show how, in subtly misusing them, his activities give rise to such conceptual bewilderment.

The aim that lies behind Wittgenstein's writings is thus mainly thera-peutic. It is to rid philosophy of conceptual confusion by diagnosing its causes. In the *Investigations* all sorts of procedures for achieving this result are adopted. The main one is the technique we have described earlier—the use of "language games." This technique assumes that every-day language is learned analogously to the way in which certain games are learned. The rules which we learn for the proper employment of certain terms have much the same function as the rules we learn in order, say, to play chess. To illustrate, then, how the philosopher misuses ordinary ex-pressions, Wittgenstein shows, through developing various language games, what the actual rules for the use of these expressions are: what they will and will not allow us to do with these expressions. In the light of this sort of description (which replaces explanation), he is able to pin-point those deviations from actual use which lead to conceptual confusion —those confusions which arise, as he puts it, "when language goes on a holiday."

The therapeutic impulse in the *Investigations* is thus not dissimilar to that we have found in the *Tractatus*. In the *Tractatus*, the claim was that philosophical pronouncements were literally senseless; and some such no-tion pervades the *Investigations* as well. As Wittgenstein says (Paragraph 109):

> And we may not advance any kind of theory. There must not be anything hypothetical in our considerations. We must do away with all *explanation* and description alone must take its place. And this description gets its light, that is to say its purpose, from the philosophical problems. These are, of course, not empirical problems; they are solved, rather, by looking into the workings of our language, and that in such a way as to make us recognize those workings: *in despite of* an urge to misunder-stand them. The problems are solved, not by giving new information, but by arranging what we have always known. Philosophy is a battle against the bewitchment of our intelligence by means of language.[16]

And in Paragraph 124 he adds:

> Philosophy may in no way interfere with the actual use of language; it can in the end only describe it. For it cannot give it any foundation either. It leaves everything as it is.[17]

Yet, in spite of this seemingly common therapeutic outlook between the *Tractatus* and the *Investigations*, both contain positive and construc-tive features which offset this negative thrust. In the *Tractatus*, this con-sisted in a philosophical endeavor to discover the "real" meaning of certain terms ("the form of the proposition") through "analysis" in the

---

[16] Wittgenstein, *Investigations*, p. 47ᵉ.
[17] *Ibid.*, p. 49ᵉ.

Russellian sense. In the *Investigations*, it consists in the attempt to *describe* the workings of our actual language (this is the meaning of the advice to replace explanation by description). In effect, this led Wittgenstein to develop a positive philosophy which attempts to indicate what a term means by describing the rules which govern its actual use in ordinary contexts. As he puts it, "The question, 'What is a word really?' is analogous to 'What is a piece in chess?' " Wittgenstein's negative and positive contributions in his new philosophy may thus be summarized in a now famous epigram, "Don't ask for the meaning—ask for the use."

Gilbert Ryle and
The Concept of Mind

A conception of philosophy similar to that of Wittgenstein, though much different in tone and literary style, is to be found in the writings of Gilbert Ryle (1900–), the editor of *Mind* and now professor emeritus at Oxford. Ryle's remark in his book *Dilemmas* (1954) that "a live (philosophical) issue is a piece of country in which no one knows which way to go. As there are no paths, there are no paths to share," is reminiscent of Wittgenstein's comment in the *Investigations*, "Language is a labyrinth of paths. You approach from one side and know your way about; you approach the same place from another side and no longer know your way about." Like Wittgenstein, Ryle sees philosophical issues as arising from conceptual confusions which have their genesis in language. Like Wittgenstein, he sees his own task as that of "clearing the undergrowth" which prevents one from finding one's way about. But like Wittgenstein, this negative, therapeutic task is intimately connected with constructive philosophical efforts of great originality and power, which at once reject simplistic solutions in favor of detailed and piecemeal analyses of the matters under consideration. His over-all positive views do not, accordingly, lend themselves to easy summary.

Ryle's own analyses of the sources of philosophical confusion, though frequently traced to the influence of language, have altered during the course of his career. In his earliest important work, a paper entitled "Systematically Misleading Expressions," his diagnosis was strongly influenced by Russell's work on the Theory of Descriptions. In this paper, published in 1933, he argued that philosophers were disposed to accept the clues given them by the grammatical form of utterances as invariable indices of their logical form, and that this gave rise to serious mistakes. In this article he distinguished three main types of such linguistic expressions, which he termed "quasi-ontological statements," "quasi-Platonic statements," and "quasi-descriptions." As an example of a quasi-ontological statement consider the statement "God exists." This statement is thought to contain a proper name "God" which names a certain entity, and a predicate "exists" which denotes a certain property possessed by this entity. Grammar sanctions such an analysis, but if one rests with the clues thus provided by English syntax, one quickly runs into trouble. For in the negation of this statement, "God does not exist" (which might be asserted by an atheist), one seems to be saying that a certain named entity, "God," does not exist. But if "God" is a proper name, then there must be something it names; how can one then sensibly deny that such an entity exists? Atheism, on this analysis, would appear to be self-contradictory—that is, in at once asserting and denying the existence of God.

Following Russell's lead, Ryle contends that "God" is not a proper name in the *logical* sense and that "exists" is not a predicate in the logical sense either. Indeed, logically "God" is shorthand for a description and is thus equivalent to a complex logical predicate (in this case to the expressions "being omniscient," "being omnipotent," "being benevolent") while "exists" functions logically as a quantifier or indefinite pronoun. When the sentence "God does not exist" is rewritten to exhibit its logical form it states that "It is false that something is omnipotent, omniscient, and benevolent." Such a rewriting does not give rise to the presupposition that anything exists, and thus reduces the disposition of philosophers to assume that if language is significant there must be something to which its grammatical names correspond. Ryle's point is that English grammar and logical grammar do not always coincide, and that this can be seen for the above classes of expressions. They are thus "systematically misleading" in the sense that they are always improper to the facts they purport to describe.

In *Dilemmas*, the philosophical thrust is similar, though the diagnosis no longer depends on the distinction between grammatical form and logical form, which Ryle in this later stage of his work regarded as itself being misleading in certain respects. In *Dilemmas*, he maintains that typical philosophical problems present themselves in the form of perplexities. One finds oneself maintaining two or more theses which turn out to be incompatible with one another; for example, that we have free will and also that all of our behavior is controlled by antecedent forces so that we cannot act differently from the way we do act. Such dilemmas are to be resolved, not by arguing for one or the other of the two theses, but by showing that the conflict is spurious and arises from various types of conceptual confusions—for example, those involving the ordinary uses of "voluntary" and "involuntary." The resolution of such difficulties is equivalent as he puts it to "freeing conceptual traffic jams," and involves the clarification of the ordinary use of certain key notions—words—which lay out the conceptual geography of everyday speech. Confusion arises from a failure to see what ordinary language tells us about the use or uses of these words, and what kinds of distinctions they mark out.

Ryle's most important work is *The Concept of Mind*, published in 1949. This is clearly one of the most influential philosophical books in recent years in Anglo-American philosophy. In this treatise Ryle sets out to dispose of a certain untenable, but powerful, conception of the human mind—a view arising from a special kind of linguistic error. Ryle terms this error a "category" mistake; in effect, it consists in assuming that things of a different category, like a team and the individual football players composing it, have the same properties or function in the same way. The particular items he is concerned with are Mind and Matter. Philosophers treat these as items belonging to the same category, but then puzzles arise over their relation. If mind is a mysterious, inward, invisible, massless sort of entity how can it relate to, influence, and affect something that is outward, obvious, visible, has mass, and so on. Ryle is thus out to attack an error which is memorialized in the philosophy of Descartes (he calls it "the Cartesian Myth") that mind and matter are two distinct and wholly different kinds of substances which belong to the same category in the sense that together they make up what we call a "human being." This erroneous doctrine arises in part at least from certain misunderstandings of the logic of the language that we normally use to describe mental phenomena, the logic of such words as "knowing," "believing," "inferring," and so forth. Ryle terms the doctrine under attack, "the ghost in the machine."

By these words, he is referring to the belief that there exists within the body a certain mysterious entity called "the mind." This entity is invisible and undetectable (and hence like a ghost) but nonetheless it is active. It thinks, feels, deliberates, believes, supposes, doubts, and knows. These operations, like the mind itself, are also supposedly internal and secret. They are not publicly observable in the way in which bodily operations such as jumping, walking, and running are. Presumably only the person who is doing the thinking, believing, knowing, or doubting has access to them.

Those who adhere to some form of this doctrine are thus led to suppose that mind and body are both "entities"—only entities of a radically different kind. The usual formulation, for example in Descartes, is to say that each is a substance: the body is a material substance, while the mind is a mental substance.

According to Ryle this picture of the nature of the mind and of its relation to the body is seriously mistaken. The mistake is a subtle one and hard to expose. The simplest way of describing the error is to say that although the body can be regarded as a thing, the mind is not a thing at all. "The mind" thus does not belong to the same logical category as "The body," and to think otherwise is the source of the error. This can be seen if we analyze the use of those words that normally refer to operations of the mind, such as "know," "believe," "doubt," "suppose," and so forth. A study of the normal employment of such words reveals that they do not refer to the hidden operations of a secret entity, but to the observable exercise of various human capacities. Putting it somewhat succinctly, we may say that the study of the use of these words indicates that they refer to "dispositions" rather than to things. The mind can thus be regarded as a set of dispositions rather than as an entity or thing.

What, then, does Ryle mean by a "disposition"? In order to illustrate his analysis, let us take "solubility" as an example, since the word "soluble" is a dispositional term of the sort Ryle has in mind. To say that sugar is soluble is to say that if we put sugar in water, under normal conditions, it will dissolve. Solubility is thus not a thing or an entity. Rather it is the disposition or tendency which sugar has to dissolve when put into water. Now knowing, believing, doubting, and so forth, according to Ryle, are dispositions in exactly this sense. For to say that a man "knows" something is to say, in effect, that under certain conditions (as on a test) he is able to give a performance of a certain kind. This performance is observable (as when we grade an examination paper); thus knowing is not a secret operation of a hidden entity, but the observable exercise of a capacity. Accordingly, the view that the mind is some internal, mysterious, ghostlike *thing* is as implausible as holding that "solubility" is a mysterious, ghostlike thing possessed by sugar. The correct view is that mental words describe capacities or dispositions whose exercise is just as observable as such bodily operations as walking or running.

Ryle has sometimes been charged with presenting a form of philosophical behaviorism in *The Concept of Mind*; but he has denied this charge. In its strongest form, behaviorism would deny the existence of any hidden or latent characteristics at all. This is clearly not Ryle's view. He does believe that there are "twinges," "aches," "throbs," "flutters," and so on, which can be felt or had only by a specific individual. But his point is that one cannot identify "mental" activity with these sorts of "internal" episodes. More generally, he is arguing that the human mind must be viewed as a complex set of episodes, dispositions, and activities, and accordingly, that none of these can be taken as privileged in any definition of the mind. But at the same time, in making this point, he is not denying behaviorism either. For him, this is primarily a factual thesis; and what he is doing is not to supply new information or new facts about the mind, but to change our perspective or view of what it is. As he says in the Preface:

> This book offers what may with reservations be described as a theory of the mind. But it does not give new information about minds. We possess a wealth of information about minds, information which is neither derived from, nor upset by, the arguments of philosophers. The philosophical arguments which constitute this book are intended not to

increase what we know about minds, but to rectify the logical geography of the knowledge we already· possess. . . .

To determine the logical geography of concepts is to reveal the logic of the propositions in which they are wielded, that is to say, to show with what other propositions they are consistent and inconsistent, what propositions follow from them and from what propositions they follow. The key arguments employed in this book are therefore intended to show why certain sorts of operations with the concepts of mental powers and processes are breaches of logical rules.[18]

This way of looking at problems has deeply affected contemporary philosophical theory. Unlike the logical positivists who felt that philosophy's sole function was to clarify the various questions involved in a problem so that they could more profitably be answered by some other discipline, Ryle believes that philosophy can itself solve certain problems, and that, in a sense, its activities can give one knowledge of the world. This is not knowledge of new facts, but knowledge nevertheless. One might say that it is knowledge of the use of certain concepts in everyday life— concepts such as "mind," "knowledge," "belief," "responsibility" and "pleasure," to mention but a few. By "charting the logical geography" of such concepts (to use Ryle's felicitous phrase), we become clearer about the nature of the mind, even if what we learn in so doing are neither facts of neurophysiology nor psychology. Ryle's work thus has an important positive thrust which reaffirms the value of philosophical activity as a way of coming to understand the world.

Though both Ryle and Wittgenstein constantly appeal to ordinary speech and contrast it with the language of the philosopher, their own work is mostly programmatic in dealing with the details of ordinary language. There are places in Ryle's work—as distinct from Wittgenstein's— where close analyses of ordinary speech are to be found; however, the major part of his writing does not focus upon the use of language *per se*. As distinct from these two writers, John Langshaw Austin (1911–1960) is the meticulous ordinary-language philosopher *par excellence*. No writer of the contemporary era has pursued with such vigor the nuances of everyday speech, and has made such original and striking contributions to philosophy as a result of such inquiries. It is with his attention to such detail that ordinary-language philosophy reaches its zenith. In concluding this chapter, therefore, let us turn to Austin.

The Philosophy of J. L. Austin

As in the case of Wittgenstein, the bulk of Austin's work was published only after his death, much of it being reconstructed by editors from

---

[18] Gilbert Ryle, *The Concept of Mind* (Hutchinson's University Library, London, 1949), p. 43.

lecture notes and unfinished manuscript materials. During his lifetime, and excluding his translation of Frege's *Foundations of Arithmetic*, his published writings consisted of seven papers. These seven articles, plus three others, were published as a book in 1961 under the title *Philosophical Papers*. In the following year, two other books appeared, *Sense and Sensibilia* and *How To Do Things with Words*, both of which are reconstructed from lecture notes. In 1966, a paper which he had prepared for publication shortly before his death in 1960, was published by the *Philosophical Review*, entitled "Three Ways of Spilling Ink." The total corpus of his writings is thus small; yet its influence has been great.

This influence is not only a function of his highly original approach to philosophical issues, but is also a function of a lucid, exciting, and witty literary style. In this respect, he resembles Hume, Hobbes, and Russell. Here are some typical remarks:

At the end of his paper, "The Meaning of a Word," he says:

> To summarize the contentions of this paper then. Firstly, the phrase "the meaning of a word" is a spurious phrase. Secondly, and consequently, a re-examination is needed of phrases like the two which I discuss, "being part of the meaning of" and "having the same meaning." On these matters, dogmatists require prodding: although history indeed suggests that it may sometimes be better to let sleeping dogmatists lie.[19]

The opening paragraph of his paper, "Other Minds," contains the following sentences:

> I feel ruefully sure, also, that one must be at least one sort of fool to rush in over ground so well trodden by the angels. At best I can hope only to make a contribution to one part of the problem, where it seems that a little more industry might still be of service. I could only wish it was a more central part. In fact, however, I did find myself unable to approach the centre while still bogged down on the periphery. And Mr. Wisdom himself may perhaps be sympathetic towards a policy of splitting hairs to save starting them.[20]

In the initial sentences of "Truth" Austin writes:

> "What is truth" said jesting Pilate, and would not stay for an answer. Pilate was in advance of his time. For "truth" itself is an abstract noun, a camel, that is, of a logical construction which cannot get past the eye even of a grammarian. We approach it cap and categories in hand: we ask ourselves whether Truth is a substance (the Truth, the Body of Knowledge) or a quality (something like the colour red, inhering in truths) or a relation ("correspondence"). But philosophers should take something more nearly their own size to strain at. What needs

[19] J. L. Austin, *Philosophical Papers* (Clarendon Press, Oxford, 1961), p. 43.
[20] *Ibid.*, p. 44.

discussing rather is the use, or certain uses, of the word "true." *In vino,* possibly, *"veritas,"* but in a sober symposium *"verum."*[21]

Austin's comment that what needs discussion is ". . . the use, or certain uses . . ." is perhaps the main key to his work. No other writer has so painstakingly explored the uses of various key words with such a sensitive ear. That he gloried in this is obvious not only from the results he obtained, but from what he himself says. In "A Plea for Excuses," he states:

> Much, of course, of the amusement and of the instruction, comes in drawing the coverts of the microglot, in hounding down the minutiae, and to this I can do no more than incite you. But I owe it to the subject to say, that it has long afforded me what philosophy is so often thought, and made, barren of—the fun of discovery, the pleasures of co-operation, and the satisfaction of reaching agreement.[22]

The preceding passage supplies us with a good, if incomplete, description of Austin's approach to philosophical issues. Mainly his technique rests upon three assumptions: (1) That everyday speech is built up over a long period of time, and accordingly that the different words and other types of expressions it contains are not merely accidental occurrences in the language, but are there to serve specific purposes. It is thus part of his creed to assume that different words tend to be subject to different uses, and that these in turn mark out different logical distinctions. One of the main purposes of philosophy is to explore such distinctions, and then to see how they bear upon traditional philosophical issues. A good example of his technique is to be found in "Three Ways of Spilling Ink," where he shows that the words "deliberately," "purposely," and "intentionally," which are often thought to mean the same thing, have different uses. Thus a man who wishes to play the ponies may dip into the till for the money to do so. He may have intended all the time to pay it back as soon as he had collected his winnings. That was his *intention.* His *purpose* in taking the money was not to pay it back, but to play the ponies. And whether he did this *deliberately* or not will depend on whether or not he reflected beforehand about whether or not to do his action. One who steals money *impulsively* is not acting deliberately. Thus a child could spill ink in three different ways: deliberately (after thinking about it carefully), intentionally (this is what he wished to do) and purposely (his purpose was to attract attention). The notions are all different, as these examples show.

(2) Austin's second assumption is that philosophers tend to approach a philosophical problem before they are clear about the facts of a

21 *Ibid.*, p. 85.
22 Austin, *op. cit.*, p. 123.

case, especially the linguistic facts. To a great extent his objection to the long tradition in epistemology which holds that we never see or *directly* perceive physical objects, but only sense-data (or our own ideas), is that this is a typically scholastic view which is attributable, as he puts it:

> ... first, to an obsession with a few particular words, the uses of which are over-simplified, not really understood or carefully studied or correctly described; and second, to an obsession with a few (and nearly always the same) half-studied "facts." (I say "scholastic," but I might just as well have said "philosophical"; over-simplification, schematization, and constant obsessive repetition of the same small range of jejune "examples" are not only peculiar to this case, but far too common to be dismissed as an occasional weakness of philosophers.) The fact is, as I shall try to make clear, that our ordinary words are much subtler in their uses, and mark many more distinctions, than philosophers have realized; and that the facts of perception, as discovered by, for instance, psychologists but also as noted by common mortals, are much more diverse and complicated than has been allowed for. It is essential here, as elsewhere, to abandon old habits of *Gleichschaltung*, the deeply ingrained worship of tidy-looking dichotomies.[23]

In his book *Sense and Sensibilia*, which is primarily an attack upon doctrines advanced by H. H. Price and A. J. Ayer, Austin works out the implications of the above views. He points out that the so-called argument from illusion, which is designed to show that some of our perceptions are delusive, assumes (a) that all cases cited in the argument are cases of *illusion* and (b) that cases of illusion and delusion are cases of the same thing. But both of these assumptions, he asserts, are quite wrong.

He points out that the kinds of cases cited by Ayer—for example a stick which normally "appears straight" but "looks bent" when seen in water, or a reflection in a mirror where "my body *appears to be* some distance behind the glass"—are not cases of illusions at all. Some genuine examples of illusion would be such things as optical illusions—say where two lines of equal length are arranged in such a way that one is made to look longer than the other, or the sorts of illusions produced by magicians, who make a woman on a stage appear to be headless; or a wheel which is rotating rapidly enough in one direction to look as if it is rotating quite slowly in the opposite direction. Delusions, on the other hand, are quite different. Typical cases would be delusions of persecution and delusions of grandeur. According to Austin, these are primarily matters of grossly disordered beliefs and may have nothing to do with perception at all. A patient who sees pink rats suffers from delusions if he is not aware that his pink rats are not real rats.

[23] J. L. Austin, *Sense and Sensibilia* (Clarendon Press, Oxford, 1962), p. 3.

These distinctions seriously affect the cogency of Ayer's argument. They not only show that illusions are not typically cases of seeing things that are "unreal," but, further that the supposed illusions Ayer mentions are not cases of illusions at all. For seeing things in mirrors is a perfectly normal occurrence, completely familiar and with nothing "conjured up"; moreover one is not seeing something "unreal," but oneself; and there is usually no question of anyone's being taken in. "No doubt," he says, "if you're an infant, or an aborigine and have never come across a mirror before, you may be pretty baffled, and even visibly perturbed when you do. But is that a reason why the rest of us should speak of illusion here?" And similar considerations apply to other visual phenomena. The bent stick in water is too familiar a case to be properly called a case of illusion. We may perhaps be prepared to agree that the stick looks bent; but we can also see that it is submerged in water, so that is exactly how we should expect it to look. "It is important," he adds, "to realize here how familiarity, so to speak, takes the edge off illusion. Is the cinema a case of illusion?"

But the term "delusion" on the other hand does suggest something totally unreal, not really there at all. As he puts it:

> For this reason, delusions are a much more serious matter—something is really wrong, and what's more wrong *with* the person who has them. But when I see an optical illusion, however well it comes off, there is nothing wrong with me personally, the illusion is not a little (or a large) peculiarity of my own; it is quite public, anyone can see it, and in many cases standard procedures can be laid down for producing it. Furthermore, if we are not actually to be taken in, we need to be *on our guard*: but it is no use to tell the sufferer from delusions to be on his guard. He needs to be cured.[24]

It thus does not follow that cases of illusions are always "delusive" nor does it follow, as Ayer and Price believe, that one who is seeing an illusion is thus not seeing a "material object"—as the cases of the rotating wheels and of the headless woman illustrate.

(3) Finally, Austin believed that the study of words and their bearing on philosophical issues could profitably be pursued as a cooperative endeavor—he speaks in a passage we have cited above of the "pleasures of cooperation." He thought that a group of people, experimenting with words in various contexts, interchanging them, seeing what other words naturally go with them and then applying them to particular cases to see if they "fit" could lead investigators to new discoveries. These were discoveries of logical and linguistic distinctions, and their import and significance could be agreed upon objectively by such a community of

[24] Austin, *Sense and Sensibilia*, p. 23.

investigators, working together cooperatively. Indeed, at times he intimated that most philosophical problems could be disposed of by making fifty or sixty important distinctions, which amounted to true descriptions of use and usage, and which profitably could be brought to bear upon specific philosophical issues.

Because of this stress upon language, Austin has sometimes been accused of being a mere "lexicographer" and not a philosopher at all. Yet his work to a great extent centers about his efforts to deal with three classical problems: the Other Minds Problem, the Problem of Truth, and the Free Will Problem. In dealing with each of these, his outlook was commonsensical, and supported by considerations based upon careful linguistic distinctions and factual evidence. For instance, his analysis of the Other Minds Problem leads him to say:

> It seems fair to say that "being angry" is in many respects like "having mumps." It is a description of a whole pattern of events, including occasion, symptoms, feeling and manifestation, and possibly other factors besides. It is as silly to ask "What, really, is the anger *itself*?" as to attempt to fine down "the disease" to some one chosen item ("the functional disorder").

And his solution to the problem ends with these words:

1. *Of course, I don't* introspect Tom's feelings (we should be in a pretty predicament if I did).
2. *Of course, I do* sometimes know Tom is angry.

Hence,

3. To suppose that the question, "How do I know that Tom is angry?" is meant to mean "How do I introspect Tom's feelings?" (because, as we know, that's the sort of thing knowing is or ought to be) is simply barking our way up the wrong gum tree.

Austin's interest in the Other Minds Problem led him to diagnose, as one of the sources giving rise to the problem, what he called "the descriptive fallacy," that is, the mistake of thinking that all locutions of a certain class describe the mind and its activities. He argues that locutions such as "I promise" are not generally used to describe anything, but are employed as ways of *doing* something: thus to say, in appropriate circumstances, the words "I promise" is a way of promising, not a way of describing one's mental set. Such locutions he called *performatives* or *performatory utterances*. The distinction between performatives and statements came in fact to dominate his later work and in *How To Do Things with Words* led him to construct an ingenious theory of "speech acts" which amounts to a new system of logic. In this system, various types of acts are distinguished from one another—locutionary, illocutionary, and perlocutionary—and then under each of these, subcases are delineated and their uses described. The theory advocated in this work is exceedingly inventive and one of the main achievements of twentieth-century philosophy.

One other feature of Austin's work which is highly original and not sufficiently recognized in the literature is his disposition to look at the other side of issues. Thus, instead of studying statements and assertions straight on, he examines things which are not statements, for example, "performatives." Instead of looking directly at responsibility, he looks at those situations in which we refuse to accept responsibility (for example, "excuses"). It is this ability to see traditional issues from a radically different perspective which has led to some of his most important insights and results.

CONCLUSION

Because of space limitations, we have not dealt in this section of Contemporary Philosophy with criticisms of the foregoing philosophers. Such an endeavor would involve too much detail and matters which are often highly technical. Moreover, because of the comparatively recent development of analytical philosophy in either of its modes—formal and informal treatment of philosophical issues—it is difficult at the present time to foresee its future or to generalize about its achievements. But at least the following two comments may be made: (1) Ordinary-language philosophy now seems, of the two contemporary forms of analysis, to be the more widely accepted, and (2) unlike the procedures adopted by formalists, its analytical techniques seem more adaptable to diverse domains of human intellectual endeavor such as history, theology, and the social and physical sciences. But whether it will achieve notable results in these areas is a question which only the future can answer.

POSTSCRIPT

As we explained in the Introduction, we have attempted to present a picture of philosophy within these covers. The picture does not purport to be complete, or to deal deeply with the issues that it does discuss. But it does deal with many of the fundamental problems of the discipline, and with most, if not all, of the major thinkers in the Western tradition who have endeavored to grapple with them.

We hope that our book has not only been of some assistance to the reader who finds himself beset by similar problems, but in addition that it can and does point out avenues for pursuing these matters more fully. With the broader picture we have painted as a backdrop, the reader may now wish to narrow his focus and come to grips with the issues in a more intensive and detailed way. In this exciting adventure, we wish him well.

BIBLIOGRAPHY
Pragmatism

Cohen, Morris R. *Studies in Philosophy and Science* (F. Ungar, New York, 1959). This work contains a critical examination of the pragmatic theory.

Dewey, John. *Intelligence in the Modern World*, edited by Joseph Ratner (Modern Library, New York, 1939). Selections from many of Dewey's works.

————. *Reconstruction in Philosophy* (Beacon Press, Boston, 1957).

James, William. *Essays in Pragmatism* (Hafner, New York, 1948).·

————. *The Meaning of Truth* (University of Michigan Press, Ann Arbor, 1972) James' answer to his early critics.

————. *Pragmatism* (New American Library, New York, 1965).

Nagel, Ernest. *Sovereign Reason* (Free Press, Glencoe, Ill., 1954). A recent statement of pragmatism by one of its foremost contemporary spokesmen.

Russell, Bertrand. *A History of Western Philosophy* (Simon and Schuster, New York, 1945). The chapter on John Dewy presents a severe criticism of his view.

Schneider, Herbert W. *A History of American Philosophy* (Columbia University Press, New York, 1963).

Thayer, H. Standish. *Meaning and Action: A Critical History of Pragmatism* (Bobbs-Merrill, Indianapolis, 1973).

Wiener, Philip P. *Evolution and the Founders of Pragmatism* (Harvard University Press, Cambridge, 1949). A study of the origins of pragmatism.

Existentialism and Phenomenology

Barrett, William. *Irrational Man: A Study in Existential Philosophy* (Doubleday, New York, 1958).

Berdyaev, Nikolai. *The Divine and the Human* (G. Bles, London, 1949). One of the major works by an important Russian Orthodox existentialist.

Collins, James. *The Existentialists* (Regnery, Chicago, 1959).

Grene, Marjorie. *The Dreadful Freedom* (University of Chicago Press, Chicago, 1948).

————. *Introduction to Existentialism* (University of Chicago Press, Chicago, 1959.

Heidegger, Martin. *Being and Time* (Harper & Row, New York, 1962).

Husserl, Edmund. *Cartesian Meditations* (Humanities Press, New York, 1960).

————. *The Crisis of European Knowledge* (Northwestern Press, Evanston, Ill., 1970).

————. *Ideas: General Introduction to Phenomenology* (Humanities Press, New York, 1931).

Jaspers, Karl. *The Perennial Scope of Philosophy* (The Shoe String Press, Hamden, Conn., 1971). An exposition of existentialism by one of the leading supporters of this view.

————. *Reason and Anti-Reason in Our Time* (The Shoe String Press, Hamden, Conn., 1971).

Kockelmans, Joseph. *A First Introduction to Husserl's Phenomenology* (Duquesne University Press, Pittsburgh, 1967).

————. *Martin Heidegger: A First Introduction to His Philosophy* (Duquesne University Press, Pittsburgh, 1965).

Sartre, Jean-Paul. *Being and Nothingness* (Citadel Press, New York, 1965).

————. *Essays in Existentialism* (Citadel Press, New York, 1965).

————. *Nausea* (New Directions, Norfolk, Conn., 1959).

Schmitt, Richard. *Martin Heidegger on Being Human: An Introduction to Sein und Zeit* (Random House, New York 1969).

Spiegelberg, Herbert. *The Phenomenological Movement: A Historical Introduction* (Nijhoff, The Hague, 1965).

Wahl, Jean. *Philosophies of Existence: An Introduction to the Basic Thought of Kierkegaard, Heidegger, K. Jaspers, Marcel, and Sartre* (Schocken Books, New York, 1969).

————. *A Short History of Existentialism* (Greenwood Press, Westport, Conn., 1972). A brief survey of the existentialist movement by one of its leading French members.

Philosophical Analysis

LOGICAL ATOMISM

Pears, D. F. *The Nature of Metaphysics* (St. Martin's, New York, 1957).

Russell, Bertrand. *Logic and Knowledge: Essays 1901–1950*, edited by R. C. Marsh (Putnam, New York, 1971).

Urmson, J. O. *Philosophical Analysis* (Oxford, New York, 1967).

Wittgenstein, Ludwig. *The Tractatus Logico-Philosophicus* (Humanities Press, New York, 1974).

LOGICAL POSITIVISM

Ayer, A. J. *Language, Truth, and Logic*, 2d ed. (Dover, New York, 1936).

Linsky, Leonard, ed. *Semantics and the Philosophy of Language* (University of Illinois Press, Urbana, 1970).

Pap, Arthur. *The Elements of Analytical Philosophy* (Hafner, New York, 1972).

————. *Semantics and Necessary Truth: An Inquiry into the Foundations of Analytic Philosophy* (Yale University Press, New Haven, 1958).

Rynin, David, ed. *A Treatise on Language by Alexander Bryan Johnson* (Dover, New York, 1969).

ORDINARY-LANGUAGE PHILOSOPHY

Austin, J. L. *Philosophical Papers* (Oxford University Press, New York, 1970).

————. *Sense and Sensabilia* (Oxford University Press, New York, 1962).

Passmore, John. *One Hundred Years of Philosophy* (Pelican–Penguin, Baltimore, 1968).

Ryle, Gilbert. *The Concept of Mind* (Barnes & Nobel, New York, 1962).

————. *Dilemmas* (Cambridge University Press, New York, 1954).

Schilpp, Paul, ed. *The Philosophy of G. E. Moore* (Open Court Press, La Salle, Ill., 1942).

Warnock, G. J. *English Philosophy Since 1900*, 2d ed. (Oxford University Press, New York, 1969).

Wisdom, John T. *Logical Constructions* (Philadelphia Book Co., Philadelphia, 1969).

————. *Other Minds* (University of California Press, Berkeley, Calif., 1968).

————. *Philosophy and Psychoanalysis* (University of California Press, Berkeley, Calif., 1969).

Wittgenstein, Ludwig. *On Certainty* (Harper & Row, New York, 1969).

————. *Philosophical Investigations* (Macmillan, New York, 1973).

————. *Zettel* (University of California Press, Berkeley, Calif., 1967).

NAME INDEX

Abbott, T. K., 332
Abraham, 386-7
Achilles, 102, 116-117
Acton, Lord, 200
Adorno, Theodor, 247
Aeschylus, 25
Albertus Magnus, 353
Albright, W. F., 338, 405
Alexander the Great, 25, 110, 284
Allen, Reginald E., 184
Altizer, Thomas, 402, 405
Anaxagoras, 104
Anaximander, 99
Anaximenes, 99
Andronicus of Rhodes, 97
Anselm, St., 341, 350-353, 405
Anti-Climacus (Kierkegaard), 380
Antisthenes of Athens, 262, 285, 285n
Aquinas, St. Thomas, 119, 341, 353-359, 364, 405
Arcesilaus, 278n
Archimedes, 123
Aristippus of Cyrene, 262, 269, 277-280, 299, 343
Aristophanes, 25, 28, 262
Aristotle, 41, 97, 104, 110-119, 122, 124, 125, 126, 184, 255, 263, 270-277, 279, 295, 308, 309, 312, 332, 353, 355, 357, 358, 409, 410, 443
Arnauld, Antoine, 128, 146
Astruc, Jean, 345
Augustine, St., 109, 126, 332, 342
Aurelius, Marcus, 285
Austin, J. L., 442, 473-479, 481
Averroes, 118, 353
Ayer, A. J., 318-320, 333, 457, 457n, 474, 481

Bacon, Francis, 66, 124, 184
Bakunin, Mikhail, 212
Barrett, William, 480
Barth, Karl, 404
Bartley, W. F., 405
Bauer, Bruno, 229, 347

Bauer, Edgar, 229
Bayle, Pierre, 63, 84, 147, 173
Beardsley, Monroe C., 184
Beethoven, Ludwig von, 298
Bentham, Jeremy, 280, 299-307, 312
Berdaeyev, Nikolai, 439, 481
Bergson, Henri, 164, 167-168, 184
Berkeley, George, 75-84, 93, 146, 155-157, 163, 173, 184, 410
Blackmary, Harry A., 11
Blanshard, Brand, 184
Bonhoeffer, Dietrich, 401-402, 405
Boole, George, 443
Bosanquet, Bernard, 449
Bourdin, Pierre, 60
Boyle, Robert, 65, 66
Bradley, F. H., 166-167, 449
Bretall, Robert, 481
Broad, C. D., 333
Brokmeyer, H. C., 412
Brower, L. J., 462
Bryan, William Jennings, 346
Buber, Martin, 398-401, 402, 403, 404, 405
Bultmann, Rudolph, 349
Burtt, Edwin A., 184, 213, 255
Butler, Joseph, 281, 333

Calvin, John, 379
Camus, Albert, 436
Carnap, Rudolf, 442, 455n, 456, 459
Carnell, Edward J., 350, 405
Carritt, E. F., 333
Castro, Fidel, 242
Cephalus, 232
Chappell, Vere C., 93
Charles I, 202, 203
Charles II, 202, 205, 208
Chillingworth, William, 66
Chomsky, Noam, 53
Christina, Queen of Sweden, 42
Clement of Alexandria, 109, 342
Climacus, Johannes (Kierkegaard), 380, 381-387

483

Thales, 99, 183
Theodorus, 37
Thucydides, 25
Tito, Premier, 240n
Toulmin, Stephen, 334
Trotsky, Leon, 235
Truman, Harry, 215
Tufts, James, 333
Turbayne, C. M., 94
Tyndall, John, 412

Urmson, J. O., 481

Vahanian, Gabriel, 402, 406
Van Buren, Paul M., 402, 403
Van Meergeren, 23
Vermeer, Jan, 22–23
Voltaire, F. M. A., 152, 280, 338

Wahl, Jean, 481
Waismann, Friedrich, 462

Warnock, G. J., 482
Warnock, Mary, 333
Watson, John, 132
Weldon, T. D., 256
Whitehead, Alfred North, 164, 168–170,
    185, 291, 409, 410, 442–445, 456
Weiner, Philip, P., 480
Wild, John, 297
William of Orange, 67, 208
Wisdom, J. T., 442, 482
Wittgenstein, Ludwig, 442, 443, 446–447,
    454–456, 458–459, 460n, 462–469,
    482
Wright, Chauncy, 413
Wright, G. Ernest, 338

Xenophon, 28, 262

Zamiatin, E., 240n
Zeno of Citium, 285
Zeno of Elea, 101–103, 104, 116–118

SUBJECT INDEX